Tales of the Old Indian Territory

John Milton Oskison

TALES *of the* OLD INDIAN TERRITORY *and* ESSAYS *on the* INDIAN CONDITION

EDITED & WITH AN INTRODUCTION *by* LIONEL LARRÉ

UNIVERSITY *of* NEBRASKA PRESS / LINCOLN & LONDON

Acknowledgments for the use of copyrighted material appear on pages 457–59, which constitute an extension of the copyright page.

Library of Congress Cataloging-in-Publication Data
Oskison, John M. (John Milton), b. 1874
Tales of the old Indian Territory and essays on the Indian condition / John Milton Oskison; edited and with an introduction by Lionel Larré.
p. cm. — (American Indian lives)
Includes bibliographical references.
ISBN 978-0-8032-3792-6
(pbk.: alk. paper)
1. Oskison, John M. (John Milton), b. 1874 2. Cherokee Indians — Biography. 3. Indian authors — Biography. 4. Cherokee Indians — Fiction. 5. Indian Territory — History — Fiction. I. Larré, Lionel. II. Title.
E99.C5.O75 2012
976.6004'97557 — dc23
2011051136

Set in Garamond Premier by Bob Reitz.
Designed by Nathan Putens.

Frontispiece: John Milton Oskison. Courtesy of Western History Collections, University of Oklahoma Libraries, Dalquest 15.

Contents

Acknowledgments

Because I live and work in France, I would not have been able to do the research necessary to complete this volume if I had not been able to stay for six months in Oklahoma, researching at Oklahoma University. Millie Audas, then director of Education Abroad and International Student Services, and Jack Hobson, then assistant director for Program Development at Oklahoma University and now director of Study Abroad at Loyola Marymount University, as well as Pr. Joe Watkins, made my stay at Oklahoma University possible.

When I was away, Nassima Baamara Mutis found and scanned documents for me.

During my desk work, Wanda and David Stevens and Michèle and Christian Larré were the most available grandparents to my young daughter.

Melinda Smith Mullikin helped me solve a few riddles about Oskison; Randy Lewis provided secondary sources from the University of Texas at Austin; James Parins, A. LaVonne Brown Ruoff, and Gretchen Ronnow helped me locate a few texts.

Martin Olstad and Carolyn Somer allowed me to publish their grandfather's texts.

I took as much advantage as I could from the kindness and helpfulness of the personnel at the Western History Collections in Norman, the Oklahoma History Center in Oklahoma City, as well as the staff in the Interlibrary Loan service of Bizzell Library. The autobiography of Oskison is published courtesy of the Western History Collections, where the original typescript is located. "The Apples of Hesperides, Kansas," "'The Quality of Mercy': A Story of the Indian Territory," "The Biologist's Quest," "Young Henry and the Old Man," "When the Grass Grew Long," "The Man Who Interfered," "The Problem of Old Harjo," and "Friends of the Indian" are published online by the University of Virginia Library, which authorized me to reprint them in this volume. James Parins and Daniel Littlefield allowed me to reprint "Tookh Steh's Mistake," "'Only the Master Shall Praise,'" "When the Grass Grew Long," and "The Problem of Old Harjo," all included in their *Native American Writing in the Southeast: An Anthology, 1875–1935*.

LaVonne Brown Ruoff, Bernadette Rigal-Cellard, Matt Bokovoy, Wanda and David Stevens, Aaron Carr, and LeAnn Stevens-Larré closely and carefully read parts or the whole of the manuscript.

Alyénor Stevens-Larré, Wyatt Reeves, Scarlett Reeves, and LeAnn Stevens-Larré allowed John Milton Oskison to share a huge part of my life for two years.

For all these reasons, I owe all these people great gratitude.

Thank y'all!

Merci.

Tales of the Old Indian Territory

Introduction

LIONEL LARRÉ

> Suppose I were able to write these stories? I might make a book of them, and call it "Tales of the Old I.T." I would let the world know about Indian Territory! Much later, some of the tales were written, and published in good magazines, but I never collected them into a book. My title, which I still think is a good one, has never been used.
>
> JOHN MILTON OSKISON, "A Tale of the Old I.T."

Rediscovering John Milton Oskison

REFERRING TO his father, John Oskison, John Milton Oskison wrote in the first paragraph of his autobiography, "I could not tell my own story without first sketching his nomadic life, although I have little material, and no documentation whatever. I have known no one else as reticent about himself in talk as father; and he never learned to write, except to scrawl his signature." This opening paragraph could perfectly fit with what is to be expected from a Native American autobiography. The yet uninformed reader, whose knowledge of the Indians is shaped by popular culture, imagines indeed the nomadic life of the noble hunter roaming the endless plains in a pre-Columbian style. That reader may picture the stoic chief, talking little but always wisely, who learned to write only enough to sign the treacherous treaties of the white man. It can therefore be a surprise when the reader is called back to reality by the second paragraph: "On a tenant farm somewhere in England, he was born in 1835" ("A Tale of the Old I.T.").

Anyone expecting to read a Native American autobiography à la *Indian Boyhood*, by Sioux writer Charles Alexander Eastman, Oskison's contemporary, is in for a disappointment. Eastman wrote of the Indian boy he was as of "a prince of the wilderness" (53). In Oskison's autobiography there is none of the idyllic descriptions, reminiscent of the European invention of the noble savage, that can be found in Eastman's life story.

In an article titled "An Oklahoma Indian's Long Road to Literary Success," published on 2 July 1911 in the *Oklahoma City Times*, Oklahoma journalist and naturalist Frederick Barde[1] summed up John Milton Oskison's life: "From the back of a cow pony to an assistant editor's mahogany chair in the editorial office of *Collier's Weekly* in a few years is the trail that has been traveled by a Cherokee Indian citizen, John M. Oskison, whose father was one of the pioneer cattlemen of Indian Territory." Oskison had a long career in New York journalism. He worked first as a reporter for the *New York Evening Post* from 1903 to 1906. He then worked as a financial editor for *Collier's Magazine* from 1909 to 1914. In his weekly articles he did not exclusively address Indian issues, and in a series of papers he wrote for *Collier's* in 1913 he actually encouraged city men to go and buy land in the West and undertake farming.

A rather well known author and journalist in his lifetime, Oskison (1 Sept. 1874–25 Feb. 1947) became somewhat forgotten. Since the posthumous publication of *The Singing Bird* in 2007, he has started to attract scholarly attention again.[2] In the foreword to *The Singing Bird*, Jace Weaver wrote: "Why has Oskison been largely ignored while his peers have been revived? In the end, he is simply not the writer that McNickle, Mathews, or Riggs is" (xiii). Weaver quotes Daniel Justice, who wrote that Oskison's "characters and plots leave much to be desired," with "forced drama and didacticism" (Justice 115). Arnie Strickland wrote that generally, "his works are quite melodramatic and sentimental, are filled with digressions . . . and too often reveal even main characters that are stock and stereotyped" (126). A. LaVonne Brown Ruoff noted that in his *Brothers Three*, Oskison himself "perceptively evaluates these two novels [*Wild Harvest* and *Black Jack Davy*] when Henry Odell, the fictional version of the author, describes his first novel as 'a mess, misty, sentimental, badly knit, with impossible situations and caricatures of human beings' and the second as 'amateurish' but containing 'the people and the country I knew'" (*Brothers Three* 343–44, qtd. in Ruoff 71).[3] Charles Larson wrote the most damning review: "Regrettably, *Wild Harvest* and *Black Jack Davy* are unconvincing both in plot and character. Events in both novels border on the ludicrous, the unbelievable, the cliché, and I suspect that few readers today would have the patience to struggle through either work" (51). He found *Brothers Three* "a more rewarding novel" (51), although not "without flaws: it is too long (the longest novel written by a Native American); at times overly sentimental; and in spite of the author's attempts at writing a kind of regional epic, read today the story is dated if not simply boring in places" (52).

Although I do not share Larson's harshness, the purpose of this introduction should not be to try to prove him wrong. As far as the quality of Oskison's writings is concerned, I encourage readers to form their own opinion. Although judging the quality of a literary work does not necessarily have to be what Weaver calls a "Eurocentric trap," I agree with him when he writes that this trap "has led, albeit by inadvertence and with honorable intentions, to a denial of Native personhood and damage to Native subjectivity" (*That the People* x). What I find worthy to discuss in Larson's critique, though, is that at least part of his negative review seems to result from his opinion that Oskison's "three novels have very little to do with American Indian life" (36), an opinion he repeats insistently throughout his book. In his fiction as well as in his journalism and editorials, Oskison often dealt with non-Indian subjects, and he has been reproached because of this by scholars who probably expect more "Indian" writings from Indian writers. Along with Larson and several others, Gretchen Bataille argued that Oskison's novels "have little to do with Indian experience" (61), and Paula Gunn Allen claimed that Oskison's three novels — scholars have been aware of *The Singing Bird*, the fourth novel, only recently — had "little or nothing to say about Indian life" (*Sacred Hoop* 76). She concedes, however, in the same paragraph, that although "Oskison's three novels do not treat identifiably Indian themes . . . they are each set in Indian Territory and include Indians as minor characters. In his last novel, *Brothers Three*, Indians (breeds like himself) appear as major characters and the futile struggle to function in the white world is that book's major theme" (76–77).

One way to understand who Oskison was as a writer, and more specifically as an Indian autobiographer, is to invoke Eastman again. Because they were both born in the second half of the nineteenth century, because both of their lives were tremendously determined by their fathers, and because both ended up advocating similar ideals in the Society of American Indians, the comparison might be a good starting point. They both wrote about their childhood and education, Eastman in *Indian Boyhood* (1902) and in parts of *From the Deep Woods to Civilization* (1916), Oskison in the autobiography presented in this volume, which he entitled "A Tale of the Old I.T." When the former was raised as a hunter and a warrior supposed to avenge his father's death, the latter was raised, by his father mainly, as a farmer and a cattle driver. One learned to read the signs of nature: "We were close students of nature. We studied the habits of animals as you study your books" (*Indian Boyhood* 3); the other approached literature in the dime novels that had already started to mythologize the Wild West. One tells of his games as "the practice of a few simple arts in warfare and the chase" (*Indian Boyhood* 53); the other writes of parties with childhood girlfriend Clara, with whom he would play "such games as spin the plate, going to Jerusalem, and one where we marched to the accompaniment of a song that began, 'King William was King James' son, and from the royal race he sprung'" ("Old I.T."). Eastman tells the story of how he was named Ohiyesa (The Winner) after a traditional game of lacrosse; Oskison — whose only other name seems to have been Jinks — admits unsuccessfully trying "for the freshman football team" at college and being more successful at tennis, quintessentially British. In the light of what seems to be a typical Indian boyhood, Oskison indeed does not look very "Indian," and the scholars' reservations mentioned above might appear logical.

Yet the reading of the present volume will reveal that there is more to "Indian experience" than meets the eye. Oskison's writings, notably the texts presented here, offer an unusual and different insight into Indian — especially Cherokee — life and concerns as they were taking shape in Indian Territory at the turn of the twentieth century. To put it differently, as a regionalist, Oskison did not write of Indians for Indians' sake, but he wrote of American life in a little-known part of the West — a part that suffered from a bad reputation, as we will discuss later — as Indian and non-Indian neighbors experienced it in his day.[4]

Oskison was still writing his autobiography when he died in February 1947 in Tulsa, Oklahoma. Friend and writer LaVere Anderson wrote in an obituary in the *Tulsa Daily World*: "It was significant that John Oskison, despite his wide travels in this country and abroad, never left — in spirit — the old I.T. His stories and books dealt with Oklahoma, and the southwest generally. He came home to Vinita to write his best books. Finally he came, for the last time, to do his autobiography." Oskison did not have time to finish his autobiography, "but the opening chapters, those that went back to his boyhood in the Territory . . . were carefully, lovingly finished. They were letter perfect," according to Anderson. In the first part of this volume I present what Anderson called the opening chapters (chapters 1 to 4) and the middle section. In these pages, as in the other texts collected in this volume, my editing consists of mere corrections of rare typos and slight grammatical adjustments (such as regards the use of *which* and *that*). No change was made that altered the style or the meaning of the author. I also keyed the corrections that Oskison himself had added by handwriting on the typescript of his autobiography. To my knowledge, the rest of the autobiography, which according to Anderson was "only summarized," is lost.

Arguably, the finalized chapters of the autobiography are some of the best of Oskison's writings. If what remains of the autobiography does not allow us to understand Oskison as a complete human being — complete autobiographies hardly ever do that anyway — it is very useful to understand Oskison as a writer and to have an insight into how a human being — whether he or she is a writer or not — relates to his or her environment. It also portrays a geographical area that is not well known to a general audience.

Oskison's father, the main subject of the first chapter of his autobiography, was an English immigrant. According to Oskison, his father was the quintessential pioneer. He took part in almost everything history would remember as adventurous parts of the myth of the West. In 1852 he crossed the continent to go to California, where he unsuccessfully searched for gold. He arrived at Indian Territory at the beginning of the 1870s. He married Rachel Crittenden, a one-quarter Cherokee widow, and thus became a Cherokee citizen, which entitled him to the right to farm a tract of communally held land. In the 1880s he became a cattle rancher in a transitional Indian Territory. Oskison writes very little of his one-quarter Cherokee mother, since she died when he was four.

The scholarly comments quoted previously about the supposedly "non-Indianness" of his writings suggest that Oskison was not, in historian

W. David Baird's phrasing, a "'real' Indian." Baird has aptly demonstrated that if we infer that accommodating cultural changes or having white ancestors make individuals "any less real as Indians," we confront at least two difficulties. First, "we deny the vitality of Native American society and its ability to adapt dynamically to change [and] we assume instead that culture is static, and that once it is altered, regardless of extent, the real Indians disappear." Second, we "deny them the right of self-definition" (16–17). John Milton Oskison defined himself as a Cherokee. In a groundbreaking essay in an ongoing debate among Native American scholars, Simon J. Ortiz explained that his uncle Steve was no less Acqumeh because he called out Spanish names in celebration of Catholic saints. "Obviously, there is an overtone that this is a Catholic Christian ritual celebration because of the significance of the saints' names and days on the Catholic calendar," Ortiz wrote. "But just as obviously, when the celebration is held within the Acqumeh community, it is an Acqumeh ceremony" (7–8). Ortiz added that "this is so because this celebration speaks of the creative ability of Indian people to gather in many forms of the socio-political colonizing force which beset them and to make these forms meaningful in their own terms" (8). Oskison spent his childhood and teenage years in the Cherokee Nation, and he came back to it often throughout his life. The texts presented in this volume are testimony of how he used his status of journalist and writer to "bring about meaning and meaningfulness" (Ortiz 9) out of his region and mixed origins. The fact that he did not have the same upbringing as Eastman's makes him all the more interesting and no less Indian. In reference to Paula Gunn Allen's comments quoted above, Craig Womack speaks for me when he explains her confusion about how much Oskison's novels are dealing—or not—with Indian matters by the fact that these texts "do not present the kind of Indians she is looking for" (30). I would argue that this statement also applies to the other scholars who cannot find enough "Indian stuff" in Oskison's work, such as Priscilla Oaks when she claimed that "there are no special Indian characteristics attributed to anyone in the families of Roger, Timmy and Henry" in *Brothers Three* (63) or that "Oskison's people are devoid of the specific Indian culture" (64). These statements are difficult to take seriously without impossible definitions of "Indian characteristics" and "Indian culture." In defending the "Indianness" of *Brothers Three*, Womack aptly states that the novel "relentlessly interrogates the meaning of land, and since the land is within Cherokee jurisdiction and is discussed in relation to its Cherokee inhabitants, it does not take much of a leap to call this a Cherokee discussion" (29).

What is striking in such judgments of Oskison's writing is that in the very same breath, scholars have asserted the very Cherokeeness of it at the same time as its non-Indianness. After stating that "the attitude expressed toward the land in *Brothers Three* is the one truly Indian aspect of the novel" (53) and after acknowledging that the three main characters are part-Cherokee, Larson concludes that "other than this attitude toward the land (and the fact that the three Odell sons are one-sixteenth Cherokee), Oskison makes few references . . . to his Indian heritage" (54). It seems to me that a novel whose main characters are Cherokee and whose main theme is Cherokee attitude to the land is pretty much a Cherokee novel!

It is true, however, as is the case in the texts published in the present volume, that Oskison does not necessarily represent the Indians in a way that fits the preconceived ideas that the readers might have. If the reproaches of "non-Indianness" are the reasons why Oskison has been so widely neglected by Native American studies, I insist that attention to his work is long overdue and that the current questioning of the notion of "Indianness" undertaken by such scholars as Ortiz, Womack, and others is relevant to a better understanding of Oskison, because Oskison himself very early questioned the preconceived notion of "Indianness." To paraphrase Vine Deloria Jr. in *Custer Died for Your Sins*, "[non-]Indianness never existed except in the mind of the beholder" (265). While Larson wrote that if Oskison's texts "are read for what they reveal about the Cherokees in Oklahoma, the reader will be disappointed" (15), I argue that if they are read for that very reason, the reader will see his or her preconceived notions of what it means to be an Indian shattered and learn a lot about what it was to be a Cherokee, or an Indian in general, in Indian Territory and in the United States at the turn of the twentieth century. As for Oskison's quality as a writer, it is now for a wider readership to judge.[5]

Discovering a "New Indian"

In the very first lines of his essay "Making an Individual of the Indian" (1907), Oskison wrote: "A new series of Indian portraits is needed. The 'noble red man' of Fenimore Cooper and of Catlin, the fierce figure in war-paint and feathers, lost his romantic interest when he was confined to a reservation and fed on rations. He became of no more interest than any other stall-fed creature. Admiration of the untamed savage gave way to contempt for the dirty beggar in the streets and under the car windows." In his short stories and in his autobiography, Oskison did exactly what he called for as an activist in his essays: he portrayed what he called a "new Indian." Although it has a significant place in the history of representations of the Indian, the Indian figure Oskison invented has been so far widely neglected. Before Oskison's Indian, there was William Bradford's and most seventeenth-century authors' Ignoble Savage, Occom's or Apess's Christian Indian, Winnemucca's Indian Mediator, and Catlin's or Curtis's Noble Savage — an old European invention reappropriated by Eastman. After Oskison's Indian came Mathews's, McNickle's, Momaday's, or Silko's struggling Indian and Vizenor's mixed-blood trickster, both trying more or less successfully to come to terms with the antagonistic worlds that shaped their identities. Oskison's Indian was different from all those. To elaborate on Lucy Maddox's notion of "performances *by* Indians" (4; her emphasis), in his performance as an Indian intellectual, Oskison positioned himself and his representations of the Indian on the "stages of American public life" (5). In chapter 8 of his autobiography he told the story of a Parisian woman who fell in love with an Indian performer of Buffalo Bill's Wild West show. When she found him again on his reservation, she did not recognize her former lover in the man "in a ragged undershirt and dirty overalls, his long hair tangled and filthy." The world needed to know more than the Indian represented by Wild West shows. Oskison invented the Indian Farmer, or more interestingly, the Indian Cowboy. This type of Indian, whom Oskison and his friend Will Rogers embodied and who was part of Oskison's everyday life in his childhood, is epitomized by Hanner the Runt in "Only the Master Shall Praise" (1900) or by Roger in *Brothers Three*, and is the archetypal Indian Oskison advanced in his essays.

So far, literary scholars have failed to see that Oskison and his Indian characters were actually quite typical of the Cherokee culture and society of his time. Historians, however, have shown how the Cherokees — and the Five Civilized Tribes in general — had expertise in ranching, among other economic practices. When the Indians known as the Five Civilized Tribes moved or were removed westward during the 1830s, they brought with them an old tradition of cattle raising. Norman Arthur Graebner explains that "these Indians had begun raising livestock with the early infiltration of the Spanish and French into their original homeland. At the time of their migration they had achieved a highly developed pastoral economy with large herds of cattle and hogs. Quite naturally they resumed this culture in the West" (300). In one of his very first texts, "Cherokee Migration" (1902), Oskison himself had emphasized how flourishing the Cherokee cattle industry had been in the Southeast.

When some scholars claim that the ranching industry "began on a gigantic scale soon after the Civil War and had its inception in the great State of Texas" (Dale, "Cherokee Strip" 61), others demonstrate that as early as the antebellum period, open-range herding "became the central feature of the Indian economy" in Indian Territory (Doran 49). By 1860 the Indians, using a natural environment propitious to cattle herding, "were as heavily involved in cattle export to the East as were their American neighbors in Texas" (49). George Butler, a Cherokee agent, reported in 1859 that cattle raising had become the "leading occupation with some of the largest farmers" (*Annual Report 1859* 172). Butler estimated that Cherokee herds contained about a quarter million head. A cattleman was reported to have judged Indian cowboys "the best in the world," adding that if he "had a million head of cattle, [he] would place them all under Pawnee herders" (Hine and Faragher 312), a statement that contradicted one made by Samuel C. Armstrong in a report he wrote for the Indian Rights Association in 1884, in which he remarked that "white men do not, as a rule, employ Indian herders; even the Indian cattle owners of the Territory, so far as I observed, hire white men as herders. Indian employees are fickle, uncertain, and, while highly adapted to herding cattle, need looking after" (21).

Considering this history, Barde's calling Oskison's father "one of the pioneer cattlemen" in Indian Territory can only be described as an exaggeration. Even if the Civil War had devastated the Cherokee cattle industry, no Englishman arriving in the Cherokee Nation in the 1870s can be considered a *pioneer* cattleman. Doran writes that the great herds of the Territory were indeed "destroyed by marauders from both North and South" (49). Graebner explains that because of the difficulties enforcing the law during this period, "cattle stealing became after 1862 a wide-spread frontier industry, practiced by civilians and troops alike" (302). Immediately after the war, the Indians became overwhelmed with Texas cattle crossing their territories. Oskison writes in his autobiography that his father saw how the Texas owners of longhorn steers "had devised a way to utilize the Nation's rich grazing land," which gave him the idea to come back to Indian Territory as a cattleman. Three major cattle trails — the Western Trail, the Chisholm Trail, and the Shawnee Trail — were going through present-day Oklahoma from Texas to Kansas cattle towns such as Abilene or Dodge City, located on the eastward railroads. The Chisholm Trail was blazed by Jesse Chisholm, a Cherokee who had come west with the Old Settlers. The Shawnee Trail was going through the Cherokee Nation itself. The communal ownership of the land, which had benefited Cherokee cattle raising because of the open and extensive range it allowed, also benefited the Texas cattlemen intruding upon a land that no individual owned, thus probably making the intrusion easier, notably in the Cherokee Outlet.[6] "As a result, tens of thousands of Texas cattle crossed Indian Territory and grazed on Cherokee lands, consuming the pasturage of the Indians and exposing their cattle to Texas fever" (Graebner 304), a tick-borne parasitic disease carried by longhorns that had no effect on the Texas breed but was deadly for other cattle.[7] In "Tookh Steh's Mistake," Oskison placed Tookh's decision in the context of the intrusion of white stockmen's cattle and wrote that "stockmen began to realize what a mine of wealth lay in the luxuriant grass growing waist high on the hills and prairies, and soon long trains of cattle were turned loose to get fat and make profits for their owners." Yet even if in the post–Civil War period, "when the heyday of the trail drives began, the Indian country was no longer equal to Texas as a concentration area of cattle . . . the Indians began to build up their herds once again, and by 1884 their animals . . . numbered roughly 700,000" according to the commissioner of Indian Affairs (*Annual Report 1884* 308–9).

What has been called the renaissance of Native American literature in the United States, and the development of Native American studies, have coincided with an era of civil rights movements and Native political awareness and resistance against the crimes of the federal government.[8] If Oskison has been forgotten for a long time, it might not be so much because he was a poor writer, as some scholars implied, but because his Indian figure lacked the dimension that appealed to readers and scholars of Indian literature in the second half of the twentieth century. The Indian Cowboy did not appear to be a resisting Indian. He seemed to be on the wrong side of the conquest of the West; indeed, he was too much cowboy, not enough Indian. Yet that is the Indian Oskison knew. That was the Indian he was for part of his life, and the one he wrote about. More importantly, the Indian Cowboy was the Indian that proved the notion of the "vanishing" Indian wrong. One of the questions Robert Warrior asks in his introduction to *Tribal Secrets* is, "what impact can the increasing awareness of and engagement with American Indian writers of earlier periods have upon the way Native intellectuals develop Indian critical studies?" (xiii). I argue that the figure of adjustment that Oskison's Indian Cowboy embodies can appeal to many scholars who endeavor to produce an alternative narrative to the essentialist critical discourse that dominated the field for years. Oskison will interest scholars who, like Warrior, deplore a critical discourse that is "more interested, for instance, in the Charles Eastman . . . who grew up in a traditional Sioux home than in the Charles Eastman who attended Mark Twain's seventieth birthday party or who read a paper at the First Universal Races Congress with W. E. B. Du Bois and others in 1911" (xix–xx). Oskison will also be of interest to readers who appreciate authors who "push the boundaries of creativity by bringing European vampires to Navajo country," as Warrior puts it, thinking of Aaron Carr's *Eye Killers* as an example (xx). Like Deloria and Mathews for Warrior, Oskison might "provide ideal subjects for working against the grain of contemporary discourse" (xx). From this point of view, Oskison's Cherokee cowboys and Carr's Navajo vampires might have more in common than meets the eye!

Was Oskison an Assimilationist?

Partly because of his adjusting Indian figures, Oskison has been called an assimilationist. Weaver wrote: "Oskison's politics were, though complicated, fundamentally assimilationist. This can be seen in his involvement in the Society of American Indians," an "aggressively assimilationist" organization (xi). Weaver admits, though, that Oskison's stance regarding assimilationism is complicated. He quotes Gretchen Ronnow, who considers the assimilationist interpretation of Oskison a "naïve reading" ("John Milton Oskison" 272). In his original and self-declared "activist" study of the Cherokee literary traditions, Daniel Justice also acknowledges the tension in some of Oskison's works between the acceptance of what Justice calls "the 'Beloved Path' of accommodation and cooperation" (16) and the certainty of "the inevitability of U.S. treachery and greed" (119), thus implicitly questioning the assimilationist interpretation of his work.

So far, scholars have drawn conclusions based on too little of Oskison's work. Oskison is the author of numerous essays on the condition of the Indian that must be read in order to understand better what their author's positions were on such key issues as assimilation. As Justice writes, "Cherokee realities are far more complicated than [the] simplistic and simple-minded stereotypes" of the "civilized savage" and the "Cherokee Princess" (6). He adds: "Our long history of intermarriage, adaptation, and innovative accommodation has brought a wide range of physical features, cultural practices, languages, and ideas into our varied understandings of what it is to be Cherokee, and we thrive as a result" (6). In his staunch activism against stereotypes and bigotry, Justice also claims: "We're not a doomed race that sacrificed Indigenousness for White civilization; such antiquated progressivism has impoverished outsider perceptions for centuries" (8). Sean Teuton wrote of Robert Warrior that he "recognizes that Indian traditions necessarily change in order to persist" (159). This is also Justice's point, and a close reading of Oskison's prolific work will reveal that it already was his at the turn of the century. Consequently, labeling Oskison as an assimilationist does not allow the necessary scholarly scrutiny of the complex positions he expressed in numerous texts.

Although this introduction is not the place for an exhaustive and definitive analysis of Oskison's positions on the Indian condition, it might be the place for laying groundwork. I would like to attempt a movement beyond the very sensitive dichotomies — traditional/progressive, resistance/acceptance, opposition/submission — often implied by the assimilationist label. I want to privilege a vantage point that is, at least temporarily, above these dichotomies and the colonized/colonizer one and from which I will conduct an examination of a large body of Oskison's writings, of his essays in particular, the most significant of which are gathered in the following pages. I believe that this examination should allow us to move beyond controversial and simplistic labels. At stake is a better knowledge and recognition of a Cherokee writer well worth rediscovering.

In a very useful "Note on Terminology" at the beginning of his study, Justice defines the terms *assimilation* and *acculturation*, as well as several other notions essential to understand any study of Native American history and literature: "*Assimilation* here is the wholesale rejection of Indigenous values and their replacement with Eurowestern values, either through choice, coercion, or violence. *Acculturation* is both more proactive and amenable to Cherokee continuity, being the adaptation of certain western ways into a larger Cherokee context, thus changing some cultural expressions while maintaining the centrality of Cherokee identity and values" (xvi). As I will try to show, a close reading of Oskison's essays suggests an oscillation between — in Justice's terms — the "choice" of the *partial*, not wholesale, "rejection" of *some* "Indigenous values" and a position that was "proactive and amenable to Cherokee continuity." Oskison's assimilationist stance is indeed complicated. In a few texts he even uses a word Justice does not mention: *amalgamation*. As a matter of fact, in the more than forty following texts, Oskison never uses the terms *assimilation* and *acculturation*. He uses only once the verb *assimilate*, when referring to Georgia's pre-removal claim of its "utter inability ever to assimilate a body of Indians" ("Cherokee Migration").

Etymologically, to assimilate is to make similar, to transform into the same. Thus, the process of assimilation implies the vanishing, the annihilation, of what is culturally Indian. Literally, an amalgamating process is more likely to preserve the distinguishing values and virtues of the Indians than an assimilation process. Amalgamation does not make mercury and the other metal it is amalgamated with similar. First, it transforms both into something different from what each was before. Second, it enables a separation of precious metals from their gangue of undesirable matter in order to enhance their intrinsic value. Assimilation implies that the Indian be transformed into a European American to become part of the European American society. In "The President and the Indian: Rich Opportunity for the Red Man" (1902), Oskison wrote that "graduates of the great government schools, and mixed-bloods who have penetrated to the universities are taking their place as leaders in the movement toward amalgamation." In

"The Outlook for the Indian" (1903), he wrote that the idea of "an ultimate amalgamation of the two [races] . . . is worth considering." He adds that "the sooner all the foolish talk about the impossibility of uniting the two people ceases, the better." Ultimately, Oskison wants to put the Indian side by side with the European American so that the former resorts to his intrinsic qualities, enhanced by a proper education, to compete with the latter. The metallurgic process of amalgamation seemed like an appropriate metaphor.

Finally, the political definition of assimilation can hardly be dismissed, since assimilation policies were contemporary to Oskison's lifetime. Politically speaking, assimilation refers to the Indian policy that officially began in the 1870s with President Ulysses Grant's "Peace Policy." In the 1930s, Commissioner of Indian Affairs John Collier endeavored to put an end to it in order to move official policies toward self-determination.[9] It needs to be noted that I am referring here to the *official* beginning of overtly assimilationist policies. In fact, Grant's policy only prolonged and institutionalized the work that missionaries had been doing for a very long time, and assimilation had always been a purpose, if only tacit, of federal policies before. Scholars such as Lawrence C. Kelly and Henry E. Fritz described what such assimilation policies consisted of: teaching "the agricultural arts," "subsidiz[ing]" missionary societies "to bring them the benefits of Christianity and formal education," "weaken[ing] . . . tribal autonomy and the authority of native leaders" along with "enlarging the powers of Indian agents" — something Oskison denounced in "The New Indian Leadership" — emphasizing "individual ownership of property and personal responsibility" (Kelly 148). In a nutshell, the aim of Grant's "Peace Policy" was "to prepare Indians for life in the white man's society" by "teaching [them] to support themselves as well as . . . supplying sufficient rations while they were learning the agricultural, pastoral, and industrial arts" (Fritz 135).

Fritz also explains that these policies failed because Congress was reluctant to appropriate the money necessary to meet its objectives. Congressmen from the West "fought lobbying philanthropists inch by inch with the result that supplies usually arrived too little and too late. From nearly every quarter of the West came complaints that the Indians were starving, that agricultural equipment was insufficient or worn out," and that schools cruelly lacked the means to provide the children with a proper education (135).

Before I explain in what terms Oskison criticized such policies, and which aspects of them he endorsed, it is significant to note that Grant's "Peace Policy" had been popular among some Indians. After Grant's death in 1885, the principal chief of the Cherokees, Dennis Wolf Bushyhead, gave a proclamation in which he declared that "the Cherokees and other Indians have special cause for sorrow in the fact that General Grant was at all times, and especially when their rights were in peril, their firm and constant protector and friend." In the same proclamation he summed up what, according to him, was the purpose of the "Peace Policy": "It was General Grant who initiated what is known as the Indian peace policy, a policy which had for its main feature the treatment of the red man as a man, entitled to a man's natural rights and privileges, and subject to control by the same means and influences as other men" ("Proclamation").

At the beginning of the twentieth century, many Indians lived in miserable and demoralizing conditions. In a short preface to his *Indian Boyhood* in 1902, Eastman wrote that "the Indian no longer exists as a natural and free man. Those remnants which now dwell upon the reservations present only a sort of tableau — a fictitious copy of the past." To Oskison, the same Indian was a "stall-fed creature" ("Making an Individual"). His whole work signifies that the only struggle worth fighting was the struggle against the ultimate dehumanization that the paternalistic reservation system tended to accomplish. The only way for the Indians to preserve some of their threatened dignity was not to try to go back to a pre-Columbian time but to fit into modern times, on an equal footing with the white man, without necessarily forgetting who they were and where they were coming from. Oskison offered the world representations of such successful Indians. When he was told that most Indians who go through Carlisle Indian school went "back to the blanket," he would respond: "You're wrong. . . . They go back to useful, serviceable lives. They plow and trade, become soldiers and mechanics, enter the professions" ("The Indian in the Professions"). It was convenient for the European American to believe the Indian useless because it could justify the paternalistic manipulations he was subjected to. These counter-representations of Indian modernity were the acts of resistance that Oskison, Eastman, and other Indian intellectuals of the time accomplished in their writings. Oskison's ultimate purpose was not to transform the Indian into a European

American but to re-humanize a human being that had been transformed into a "stall-fed creature," or a reservation Indian "fed on rations" ("Making an Individual") that he also called "pauperizing rations" ("Remaining Causes").

To Kill the Indian or Save the Indian American?

As is often the case with labels, the very term *assimilation* is too limited, with pejorative associations, to encompass the sociohistorical reality of Native people's lives. Moreover, it is often used too loosely to signify anything specific. Oskison's positions and opinions need to be analyzed in the light of a clear definition of assimilation and the real experiences of ordinary Indian lives.

Assimilation as it is often used refers to a spectrum more than to an unequivocal government policy. It can simultaneously convey Richard Henry Pratt's proverbial statement that the Indian needs to be killed to save the man and Francis Paul Prucha's phrasing that "the federal government determined upon an all-out effort to turn the American Indians into Indian Americans" (ix). Socially speaking, these two expressions refer to fundamentally similar results. The governmental effort, says Prucha, was "to destroy the tribal communities and to absorb the Indians as individuals into the mainstream of American society" (ix). I would like to strip these two phrases — "kill the Indian to save the man" and "turn the American Indians into Indian Americans" — of whatever deep original meaning with which their utterers endowed them. I use them literally and consider them as the limits of the spectrum of assimilationism. Read superficially, the first expression conveys the annihilation of whatever is culturally Indian in people in order to redeem and incorporate them into society before they get lost as "civilization" advances. The second expression evokes the identities of indigenous people as intrinsically defined as Indian and qualified as American: they are indigenous to a continent called America. The phrase conveys that these people should be transformed into individuals who would be identified primarily as Americans, because they would belong to the society colonizing America, although their identities might be qualified by what remains culturally Indian in them. In the first instance, the aim is to see the Indians culturally vanish indeed, as they are literally *assimilated* — etymologically, transformed into the same, *made like* European Americans. In the second instance, the Indians are *integrated* or *incorporated* in the American society as Indians; they are made to participate in society without relinquishing their Indianness. Oskison's position on this spectrum needs to be understood to avoid any simplistic definition of his writings.

Assimilation policies as they are described by Kelly and Fritz above seemed to aim at "killing the Indian to save the man" rather than turning the American Indian into an Indian American. They did not seem to aim at the conservation of an Indian component in the future American society after the absorption of the Indians. Besides, and this is the key issue for understanding Oskison, a ration system was part of assimilation policies, and only lip service was paid to the personal responsibility that the Indians themselves should be given in the social evolution they were asked to undergo. In his first inaugural address, on 4 March 1869, President Ulysses S. Grant declared about "the proper treatment of the original occupants of this land" that he would "favor any course toward them which tends to their civilization and ultimate citizenship." Under Grant's presidency, though, the Native Americans officially became wards of the state after Congress decided to no longer recognize the tribes as legitimate powers. This ended the negotiation of treaties, that is to say, the very documents that legally made nations of Indian tribes. From then on, the Native Americans would be managed as the U.S. government would see fit. There lay the rub as far as Oskison was concerned.

The Creed of the Society of American Indians

Oskison was a founding member of the Society of American Indians (SAI). At its first annual conference he gave a talk on "The Indian in the Professions." In subsequent years he published several articles in the *Quarterly Journal* of the society. In 1917 he was its vice-president, and the annual conference of the society had to be canceled because he and Arthur C. Parker, its president, joined the army (*The Oklahoman* 3 Oct. 1917). Since Oskison was so closely associated with the SAI, a brief analysis of this organization's creed is necessary before examining Oskison's positions regarding assimilation policies.[10]

At the first annual conference of the SAI, Oskison was a member of the committee to draw up a constitution (SAI, *Report of the Executive Council* 22, 67). He was also a contributing editor of the society's *Quarterly Journal* for a few years. Some of the objectives stipulated in the SAI's constitution were "to promote and co-operate with all efforts looking to the advancement of the Indian in enlightenment which leaves him free as a man to develop according to the natural laws of social evolution"; "to present in a just light the true history of the race, to preserve its records, and emulate its distinguishing virtues"; and "to promote citizenship and to obtain the rights thereof" ("Constitution and Laws" 324). The natural laws of social evolution of the SAI creed could refer to what Claude Lévi-Strauss would later call "cultural collaboration." This expression refers to all the instances of exchange and hybridization that naturally result from the encounter between two human groups whose cultural core values are a priori different. From the moment of the encounter onward, these instances of hybridization make the characteristic features of each group evolve, with a tendency to level the differences. Spectacular and well-known examples of this kind of collaboration are numerous in the case of the encounter between Native Americans and Europeans. The horse, the firearm, and the metal containers, for example, coming from Europe, changed Native lifestyles radically. Cultural collaboration, though, is a two-way process, and it is also well known how the Europeans greatly benefited from Native American contributions, especially in agriculture.

This kind of cultural collaboration is part of a social evolution that was not so much called for by the SAI as it is an inevitable process that can be observed objectively. Besides, social evolution is not necessarily social Darwinism as distorted by the Spencerian notion of "the survival of the fittest," a concept used at the time to justify scientific racialism. Cultural collaboration need not imply the disappearance of one of the two cultures. The SAI was calling for the emulation of Indian "distinguishing virtues" at the same time it was calling for citizenship, while the common belief was that both were mutually exclusive. Yet Maddox demonstrated in *Citizen Indians* that for the SAI intellectuals, "citizenship and assimilation were not at all the same thing" (129). What the SAI activists wanted was an incorporation of their identities in the white civilization in order to participate in their own way to the betterment of what consequently should be called "American civilization" rather than "white civilization." The SAI wanted "to bring about a condition whereby the white race and all races may have a better and broader knowledge of the red race . . . and its ability to contribute materially and spiritually to modern civilization" (SAI, *Report of the Executive Council* 14). As Andrew Wiget argued, the SAI "promoted a pan-Indian perspective and opposed the paternalism of the Bureau of Indian Affairs (BIA), advocating instead a self-help policy" (70). A careful reading of Oskison's texts will reveal that this is indeed more fitting with his views.

Far from promoting the end of resistance, the SAI also advocated the establishment of "a legal department to investigate Indian problems, and to suggest and to obtain remedies" and "to exercise the right to oppose any movement that may be detrimental to the race" (*Quarterly Journal of the SAI* inside cover). These positions hardly seem compatible with the promotion of an assimilation that would be as submissive as the term, and the official policies thus called, imply.

A Paradigm Shift to Go beyond Simplistic Dichotomies

A more comprehensive, albeit hardly exhaustive, analysis of Oskison's work will shed more light on the controversial assimilationist interpretation of it. In "Making an Individual of the Indian" Oskison wrote of "efficient workers" and mentioned a photographer whose "most telling pictures show the Crow Indians in Montana and the Apaches in Arizona handling scrapers, driving teams, and working in the concrete mixing beds." He quoted an engineer in charge of the building of an irrigation system for the Zunis who "reports that a considerable number of this tribe have become fairly skilful drillers, quarrymen, and derrickmen." He wrote that "missionary workers say that Indian women make lace quite as beautiful as any made in Italy." He was clearly happy about these and many other examples of adjustment to European American ways that he listed because they proved his point in this essay and others: the Indians were able to support themselves, notably financially, and were capable of "active individual competition with white men." Oskison even applauded the federal government in the role it played to achieve that end: "Plainly, so far as providing employment is concerned, the government has fulfilled its obligation to fit the Reuben Quick Bear type of Indian to compete with his white neighbor as an individual. The schools that Indian children attend are also, as a rule, *admirably* fitted for the work that they must do" ("Making an Individual"; my emphasis).

It appears from even a superficial reading of his essays that Oskison advocated personal responsibility. What does this tell us about Oskison as an assimilationist? When the SAI promoted "the advancement of the Indian in enlightenment which leaves him free as a man to develop according to the natural laws of social evolution," what kind of assimilation was it calling for?

Trying to determine whether Oskison was an assimilationist or not is to place oneself in a paradigm that does not operate anymore and which did not even operate in Oskison's time. It suggests that, no matter what, a return to a pre-Columbian lifestyle was in any case a possible alternative to the European lifestyle and that both were mutually exclusive. This paradigm had been defined by centuries of conflicts and Indian armed resistance against the invasion of the colonizers, but since the end of the nineteenth century it has diverted our reflection onto abandoned paths that used to lead somewhere but which became dead ends at the closing of the frontier. So far scholars have often been on either side of this inoperative paradigmatic division. The spectrum on which they move the indicator of Oskison's assimilationism goes between a wish to return to a mythic Golden Age and an urge to become a white man. Yet this was not the choice faced by the Indians in Oskison's days. As Fritz puts it, "the alternatives to adjustment were cruel and undesirable: either death or parasitical existence upon a reservation" (19).

In Oskison's day, the buffalo hunter embodying a mythical Golden Age was what he called "the Old Indian" or "the old type of Indian" ("The Closing Chapter: Passing of the Old Indian"). In the same text he wrote that that Indian "has gone." The Indian Oskison was writing about and for which he is said to have wanted assimilation was not that "Old Indian" but what he called the reservation Indian. To Oskison, there was nothing noble or to be nostalgic about in the life of the reservation Indian. In the reservations, the Indian was vanishing. Oskison's writing and activism in and out of the SAI were fighting the idea of the "vanishing Indian."

Thus, I would like to suggest a paradigm shift in the way we approach the issue of assimilation, a theoretical shift that might be useful to understand not only Oskison but also many other Indian writers. In his day, some kind of acceptance of the European American ways was inevitable. What is important to understand is what kind of acceptance of European American ways Oskison advocated and, maybe more crucially, at what cost. Oskison himself suggested the paradigm move to which I am referring: "We are far enough away from the crunching of cavalry hoofs and the rallying yell of warriors to see that there are two sides to the question. Only the most rabid and ignorant enemies of the Indian still maintain that unfortunate, cynical doctrine that 'the only good Indian is a dead Indian.' And only the most obstinate of our Indians still rail against the domination of the white race" ("The Outlook for the Indian"). At the turn of the century, many Indian leaders—and the most vocal Native intellectuals such as Oskison, Eastman, Arthur Parker, or Carlos Montezuma—believed that a return to pre-Columbian times was neither possible nor even desirable. Even the Keetoowah society, a Cherokee group of traditionalist full-bloods who resisted white encroachments the most, did not hope for that much. Traditionalist groups within the tribes of Indian Territory mostly opposed allotment and defended tribal governments. Wovoka's prophecy, which gave birth to the Ghost Dance, had been the last spiritual belief with a significant following that advocated for the (nonviolent) disappearance of the white men from the American continent to allow the Indians to return to a mythical time of perfection. To argue that Oskison was an assimilationist is in a way to argue in a theoretical context where such a mythical return is an option people could believe in. Arguably, this return was not even the purpose of the many movements of armed resistance of the nineteenth century. Most of the time, Indians were not at war against the American society because they wanted to eradicate it and retain pre-Columbian lifestyles; rather, they fought because they wanted the white men out of the territory secured by the last treaty with the federal government, or they did not want to be removed to barren lands. The latter kind of resistance is actually the subject of "An Apache Problem," in which Oskison unquestionably shows great respect and sympathy for Apache resisting leaders Chief Victorio and Geronimo. After the closing of the frontier, and more specifically after the land runs in Oklahoma (from 1889 to 1895), the Indians resisted neither against the advent of white civilization nor against removals that had already taken place. When they resisted, it was against the white American citizens' prejudice and the paternalistic attitude of their Great Father in Washington. This is exactly the kind of resistance that Oskison exerts.

An Indictment of the White Man

To understand Oskison's complex stance regarding the relationship between the Indian and American society on the one hand and the Indian and the federal government on the other, his awareness and recognition of "U.S. treachery and greed" (Justice 119) needs to be reasserted. In some of his essays, Oskison clearly denounced American violence against Indians. In spite of his conviction that the Indians must be proactively part of the American society, Oskison was far from being subservient to white men and their government. In several articles and essays his rhetoric is close to the discourse of resistance of Indian spokespersons such as Apess and Winnemucca, who preceded him. Oskison never refrained from stating that "the usurer and the trickster [were] familiar pests in the white man's West" and that they had "succeeded the conscienceless old traders." All had one common purpose: "to strip the ignorant Indian of everything that can be obtained" ("Remaining Causes"). In his novel *Brothers Three* he has the narrator draw a very negative picture of "the invaders of this Indian land" at the end of the 1880s. After describing how poorly their farms were set up and maintained, he depicts the racism of a

> shiftless, drifting class, given to windy talk and indiscriminate "borrying." Loafing on the main street of Avra, they laughed inanely, spattered the sidewalk with tobacco juice. They were contemptuous of the Indians, and promised to hasten the movement for making the Indian Territory into a "white man's state." They carried on, in grotesque caricature, the tradition that the "savage red man" must, because of his incompetence, give way to the white. Their dirtiest tow-headed moron child of fifteen was taught to feel superior to such boys as Timmy — to any child however slightly "tainted" by Indian blood. (54–55)

In "Cherokee Migration," published in 1902 in the *Tahlequah Arrow*, Oskison had recalled how unfairly the Cherokees had been treated by the federal government at the time of their removal. In this article, Oskison gave a detailed list of the accomplishments of the very "advanced" Cherokee Nation, describing a flourishing agriculture and economy, an increasingly educated and industrious population living in a land of plenty that "General Scott was sent in 1838 to destroy." The federal government had authorized the use of violence against a nation that had very successfully and enthusiastically adopted the European American ways. Yet the Cherokees' white neighbors, hungry for more land, denied their progress, and Georgia's profession of its "utter inability ever to assimilate a body of Indians" precipitated the removal of peaceful and "advanced" Indians. As General Scott made clear in an address he sent the Indians after he had stationed his powerful army, "the destruction of the Cherokees" was the only alternative to peaceful removal ("Cherokee Migration").

Oskison wrote "An Apache Problem" (1913) more than ten years after the publication of "Cherokee Migration," a couple of years after Apache leader Geronimo died a prisoner of war at Fort Sill, Oklahoma, and after the authorities announced that the remaining Apache POWs were to be set free after twenty-six years of forced exile. In that text he condoned the armed resistance of Apache leaders Victorio and Geronimo; he denounced the treachery of the government, which attempted to remove the Apaches to a reservation they found "a rocky, desert waste"; he lamented the inhuman circumstances of their captivity, during which many of them died of tuberculosis; and finally, he accused the military authorities of cheating the Fort Sill Indian neighbors out of their lands.

Yet the conclusion of "An Apache Problem" is that "the modern Apaches have nothing to do with hunting." They must "learn trades," send their children to school, and "learn just as fast as they can how to live like the white people around them." Oskison did not attack the government for preventing the Indians from keeping their old lifestyles but for not allowing them to succeed in their adoption of the European American lifestyle. In "Arizona and Forty Thousand Indians" (1914), Oskison accused the big cattle companies of lobbying the political authorities to make sure the Navajos were contained in their reservations instead of being allowed to drive their herds on public lands to seek pasture. He shed light on the incoherence of the authorities, which claimed they wanted to "civilize" the Indians but made sure that their "advancement" did not get in the way of the white men's interests.

Careful to avoid antagonizing any person of goodwill who might read him in Washington, at times he would sound soft on the authorities, writing, for example, in "The Little Mother of the Pueblos" (1913) that the Indian Bureau "does what it can." Yet in terms quite harsh indeed, he did bring home in the same paragraph a very accusatory message and a call for change in Indian affairs: "often, however, it stands helpless, moves too slowly, blunders sadly, obstructs justice through no motive of malice. Patiently, silently, the Pueblos have endured the Bureau's intrusion — the introduction of schools badly taught, the replacement of their orderly self-government by the unfamiliar civil law of New Mexico, stupid interference with religious ceremonials and family practises" ("Little Mother").[11]

The change he wanted so badly, though, was not the abolition of the Indian Bureau — contrary to other SAI members such as Carlos Montezuma (Maddox 113) — but a more efficient bureau in helping the Indians "to pass from medieval to modern America." Indeed, even his most damning texts end up calling for an integration of the Indians into American society. In reparation for all the injustices and the sufferings caused by the federal government, Oskison did not ask for the independence of Native tribes from the United States but for the citizenship of their members.

The "Old Indian" Is Dead! Long Live the Indian Citizen!

Certainly, Oskison's discourse can sometimes sound rather radical. In "The Closing Chapter: Passing of the Old Indian" he approved of the fact that "in two generations the Indian as a distinctive person will be all but a memory" and of "what a century of close association with whites has done to destroy the Indian identity of the Five Civilized Tribes." Yet the very purpose of the same essay is to pay unconditional tribute to the "old type of Indian," to past leaders such as Metacom, Red Jacket, Tecumseh. About the last he also wrote a whole book. These leaders and other figures such as Sitting Bull, Cochise, and Geronimo, among others, he praised and immensely respected as "great statesmen" ("Closing Chapter"). Nevertheless, he considered their era over, although the new leaders should live up to the "wonderful standard of leadership" ("Closing Chapter") left by the old ones. The power should then be transferred to the Indian citizen.

Oskison's discourse can seem to fit into the racialist rhetoric of his time. In a commencement address given at Carlisle in 1912, in which he started by reminding his audience, "My friends, I am an Indian," he called the Indians "lazy"; "You have got to spur us on," he continued, in a comparison of the

Indians to Jack, the mule of his cowboy years ("Enduring Qualities of the Indian").

The distinction between full-bloods and mixed-bloods seemed to be fundamental to his thoughts. Daniel Justice shows well that the use of these words as absolute terms, equating full-bloods to traditional Indians and mixed-bloods to assimilated Indians, is "rarely accurate" (xv). Yet that is how Oskison often seems to use them. He did consider the full-bloods as the "real 'problem,'" although his use of quotation marks seems to indicate that he used the term reluctantly. In "In Governing the Indian, Use the Indian!" he wrote: "Here live our real 'problems;' the pure-strain Indians who do not talk English, whose education is hardly started, who are still vague about the meaning of white civilization." However, the hierarchy he drew between the full-bloods and the mixed-bloods was a cultural one only, not a biological or moral one. He simply thought that because the full-bloods were not directly, genealogically connected to the European American culture, they were slower to adjust, partly because of white resistance to their adjustment. He claimed, however, that the full-bloods were capable of adjustment if they were simply given the opportunity. Reuben Quick Bear, in "Making an Individual of the Indian," is an example of a successful full-blood Indian. When he called the Indians "lazy" in his address at Carlisle, it was only to emphasize the point he wanted to make in that speech: "But we are dependable. . . . The more I go about among the Indians, the more firmly convinced I am that you can depend on them. They are there. They deliver the goods in the end" ("Enduring Qualities").

Although he never mentioned that one "race" was superior to the other, he did mention the "domination of the white race" and believed worthy of consideration the idea that "the next inevitable step is the complete absorption of the Indian into the white race, which will result in an ultimate amalgamation of the two." As I remarked before, he insisted that "the sooner all the foolish talk about the impossibility of uniting the two people ceases, the better" ("The Outlook for the Indian"). He had written, in "Cherokee Migration," of the consequences that such foolish talk had had on the Cherokees in the 1830s. Although he did not overtly promote miscegenation, he seemed to look favorably to the fact that, in the Indian Territory, "many of the girls [were] to become the wives of white men" after they came out of school ("The Outlook"). He indeed often cited the Indian Territory as an example of successful amalgamation. The conclusion of "The Outlook for the Indian" is that "the Indian problem, so far as the tribes of the [Indian] Territory were concerned, was being solved by extinguishing the Indian as a distinctive individual and merging him with his white neighbors and competitors" ("The Outlook").

The conclusion of "The Outlook" seems to echo Pratt's doctrine of killing the Indian to save the man. However, the very term *amalgamation*, which Oskison used instead of such alternatives as *assimilation* or *acculturation*, rather conveys Prucha's transformation of the American Indian into an Indian American. The seemingly radical tone of the early texts became a bit more nuanced in subsequent essays in which he made his call for Indian citizenship clearer. In modern terms, what Oskison awkwardly called amalgamation would be something closer to Will Kymlicka's notion of minority rights in a multicultural society.

What does remain consistent from "The Outlook" to the later essays is Oskison's insistence on education and his criticism of how the assimilation policies were implemented. Oskison was not advocating for the integration into mainstream America of the "old Indian" — who had been long gone — but for a better integration of the Indian who had been reduced to a "stall-fed creature" in the reservations.

From Reservation Indian to Enlightened Indian American Citizen

As he makes clear in his autobiography, Oskison inherited from his father a sense of how extremely valuable education was. This emphasis on education should not be taken for granted in the pioneer world of his childhood. Anytime he could, John Oskison Sr. sent his children to school and made sure he secured enough money to finance their education. This paternal influence is enormous on Oskison's work. In his writings about the Indian condition, Oskison emphasized how essential education was for Indians in particular, and he believed that these children should "be educated, wherever possible, in the same schools with white boys and girls" ("Remaining Causes"). Although he would criticize it in later essays, in "The Outlook" Oskison appears to approve some form of the proverbial government paternalism toward the Indians: "They must be taught how to work. It is not yet enough to say, 'Here are lands well protected and productive: take them and develop their resources.' The Indians do not know how to do it, and they must learn." He argued that at least for some time, the Indians needed to be guided by the "Great Father": "Think of them how we will, we cannot close our eyes to the fact that they are still children, with all of the child's ignorance of modern life, with the child's helplessness in practical affairs. For a little longer the 'Great Father' at Washington must direct them" ("The Outlook"). The Indians needed to be helped, but only for a little longer. They also needed to be given the means, via education, to take care of themselves at some point. He believed the Indians had the intellectual means to take their future into their own hands.

Paternalism aside, it is essential to understand that Oskison did not think Indians should be educated to become farmers only. Recurrently, and more specifically in "The Indian in the Professions" (1912), he expressed his conviction that the Indians could do and be anything they wanted, provided they benefited from a proper education: "The Indian who fits himself for the company of those at the top will go up. He will go as swiftly and as surely as his white brother. There is no easy, short road up. . . . Conscientious, thorough training, character, hard work — the formula for success in the professions, is simple. I believe the average Indian would rather work his brain than his hands."

Repeatedly, and in keeping with the creed of the SAI, Oskison promoted the enlightenment of the Indians and praised the industriousness of educated Indians, whether they were full-bloods or mixed-bloods. In "The Outlook" he praised the Sherman Institute in California, where the Indians learned about irrigation methods that they would be able to take back to their tribes. Fourteen years later, in "In Governing the Indian," he rejoiced at the fact that "education has gone forward, — through many mission schools, through government reservation schools and such outside institutions as Carlisle, Haskell, Hampton, and Sherman Institute." For this, and however critical he could be of other aspects of governmental assimilation policies, Oskison was thankful to the government. No indictment of the disastrous effects of boarding schools on Indian children and Indian cultures can be found in Oskison's work, which can be felt as a disconcerting lack considering how many Indian children, including Cherokees, suffered from this system and even died in the boarding schools.[12]

Although he deplored the "absolute failure" of assimilation in spite of the huge sums spent "in subduing and attempting to educate the Indians" ("The Outlook") as early as 1903, his critique of assimilation policies became more and more precise over the years until he pinpointed the exact problem. The Indian needed to be involved in these policies, much more involved than the agency system allowed him to be. The paternalistic government tended to believe the Indians incapable of leading the way to progress. Oskison, on the contrary, was convinced throughout his career that the educated Indians were "eager to help forward any movement that tends to advance their people toward economic independence" ("The President and the Indian").

In 1917, Oskison published two essential essays, "In Governing the Indian, Use the Indian!" and "The New Indian Leadership," in which he regretted that in 1883 the missionary control of the agencies that Grant had ensured "was abandoned in favor of the spoils system," because "under the guidance of church workers, the reservation Indian was encouraged, not merely to become a religious leader, but also a leader in the industrial education of his people" ("In Governing"). According to him, under the spoils system, the Indian agent was problematic in two respects. First, he was not motivated by a personal urge to help Indians: "The political agent has seldom been in sympathy with the Indians. Unlike the agent working under the stimulus of missionary zeal, he has regarded his exile to the reservation as a real hardship" ("In Governing"), which encouraged him to cheat Indians for his own profit. Such agents had been denounced long before Oskison, notably by Sarah Winnemucca. Second, the political agent, who did not know anything of a tribal government, tried to impose on the Indians under their authority the same system of regulations that a white community would need. These agents did not try to remedy their ignorance of Indian government methods by consulting with their so-called protégés. This became a cornerstone of Oskison's viewpoint on federal policies regarding Indian affairs. As the title of his essay expressed clearly, the federal government could not successfully govern the Indian without using the Indian. When he wrote that "the real Indians are disappearing" ("Closing Chapter"), he was talking about the old lifestyle, impossible to maintain in the reservations. However, the

Indian figures he praised in the same essay for their wisdom, their courage, their leadership, and their statesmanship hardly needed to be treated like children. They needed to be involved in the changes that the government required of their people. Unfortunately, "old-time leadership and wisdom fell under the ban along with long hair and the shoulder blanket," Oskison despondently stated ("In Governing"). Instead of being asked to help reform their way of life, the old leaders were "neglected, debauched and broken by the Government ("The New Indian Leadership").

In almost all his essays about the Indian condition, Oskison emphasized the need for personal responsibility. Although he thought the federal government was doing a relatively good job as far as providing education was concerned, he apparently believed the authorities were only paying lip service to the need of Indian personal involvement in their future. As it became clearer to him, such a notion was not compatible with the paternalistic attitude of a government that treated the Indians as wards of the nation. That is why he disapproved of the weakening of the authority of Native leaders. Without going as far as openly defending Indian sovereignty, he explained in his two 1917 essays that the agents needed to consult with the tribal leaders in order to understand the system of governance needed by the Indians.

"Mistaken Philanthropy" versus Proactive Resistance

The nefarious effects of philanthropy on the Indians are now well documented, notably regarding the allotment policy.[13] Interestingly enough, Oskison was also critical of what he called the "mistaken philanthropy" of groups such as the Friends of the Indian, whose "ignorant sympathy" could make them too prone to failing paternalistic attitudes as well ("The Outlook"). In "Friends of the Indian" Oskison criticized such organizations, whose conference at Lake Mohonk he was yet a member at least from 1904 to 1909 (see "Essays" n. 15), for being "merely well-meaning" but not living up to their words. Sometimes this ill-used sympathy turned out to be destructive. Oskison warned the philanthropists against wanting the assimilation of the Indians without defending their rights, notably their rights to be in control of the natural resources found on their lands.

While the philanthropists sometimes encouraged the Indians to go to court, "the Indian," however, "'not taxed, not voting,' has . . . no real standing in the courts organized by and for the American people" ("Friends of the Indian"). When such a "silver-tongued," well-meaning member of a philanthropic organization convinces the Indians they have a good case in court to defend their rights, it usually ends in a trial dragging on for years before being concluded by a failure to reach a protecting decree.

In order to resist legally, the Indians needed to know the white man's legal system well enough to take care of themselves; even better, they needed to be part of the legislative system: "In Congress, the final court where the cause of a dependent people is decided, the white invader has representation, and the Indian has none." He reproached the Friends of the Indian for overlooking such "elementary considerations." They had understood that the Indians were "human beings whose rights are co-extensive with those of the whites," but they needed to go further by understanding these human beings would not be "persons" until they got involved in the representative body of government. In 1914 he wrote about the Arizona Indians for whom the lack of representation was the fundamental issue. To him, "the matter [was] simple": "Grazing land is precious in Arizona, and the white stockmen are unanimous in the belief that they can make use of it all. White men are voters and pay taxes; the three men who represent Arizona in Congress have been sent there by the whites. They prefer to see the wealth-creating resources of the state in the hands of white voters and taxpayers" ("Arizona and Forty Thousand Indians"). At the core of the issue was the non-involvement of the Indian. It did not matter how friendly some European Americans were to the Indians if they were condescending enough to know what was best for them without consulting them.

Oskison did not urge the Indians to take up arms or even to remain separated from the whites in order to retain their traditional lifestyles. However, he did believe that some kind of resistance was possible in court, as long as the Indians — as citizens — were properly and truly represented there. For decades, the Cherokees had famously resisted white injustice in the white judicial system. To resist is to inhabit the present, to apprehend the current state of affairs and gauge where the forces are that you want to resist in order to confront them. The Cherokees had understood this for a long time. To resist, they needed to fight with the same weapons. Symbolically,

Sequoyah — the Cherokee hero who put the Cherokee language into writing — had accomplished such effective resistance. According to Justice, the syllabary "became an incredibly effective tool for resisting Removal; it subsequently helped to rebuild educational and cultural institutions after the Trail of Tears" (6). Thanks to Sequoyah, the Cherokees could face the powerful written sign of the white man with an equally powerful weapon. By developing their education system, their press, and their law expertise, they had taken further steps into this resisting stance.

It was of prime importance to Oskison that the Indians understood how to solve their problems without waiting for the federal government to solve them in their stead. In his autobiography he mentioned one very influential Cherokee lawyer, Bill Hastings, from Tahlequah, Indian Territory.[14] In "In Governing the Indian" he wrote of Hastings, "one of my fellow tribesmen, now a member of Congress from Oklahoma," that he had "helped me to form my ideas of the ability of the Indian to understand his own problems, and to fight effectively for their right solution." Hastings had been one of the seven Cherokees to represent their nation in the negotiations with the Jerome Commission (1889–93) — also called Cherokee Commission — that would secure the purchase of 15 million acres of land from Oklahoma tribes, including the 6-million-acre Cherokee Outlet. Hastings had warned his people that "unless the Five Tribes are cautious, diplomatic and vigilant, and unless they act in concert a change of conditions is likely to be forced upon us" (Gittinger 201).[15] In the same essay, Oskison deplored the fact that Indian students who returned to the reservation in the employ of the Indian Service were mere "subjects of the white man put there by the government to administer Indian affairs," that they were left on the sidelines without any possibility to participate, without even being consulted in any way, shape or form: "They had no standing, no voice, no influence" ("In Governing"). In "Friends of the Indian," Oskison quoted a commissioner of Indian Affairs who had claimed that "no man has a place or a fair chance to exist under the Government of the United States who has no part in it." Repeatedly, Oskison would speak and write in order to get the Indian more involved in solving his own problems. He would call for more representation in Congress. He would call for citizenship. Without representation, all decisions regarding the Indians were taken by representatives of the settlers, in the interests of the settlers. It is, of course, highly ironic that this cry for representation should echo one of the cries that had crystallized so much of the spirit of the American Revolution.

Rehumanizing the Indian

Oskison's language about the Indians was not as radically derogatory as the one of the Indian Rights Association in a statement in 1884: "The Indian as a savage member of a tribal organization cannot survive, ought not to survive, the aggressions of civilization, but his individual redemption from heathenism and ignorance, his transformation from the condition of a savage nomad to that of an industrious American citizen, is abundantly possible" (qtd. in Prucha x). Nevertheless, he did believe the improvement of the Indian condition was possible and vital. Yet he would probably not have disagreed with Prucha's conclusion of what the assimilation policies of the 1880s resulted in: they "broke down the Indians' heritage and cultural pride without substituting anything in its place, until many Indians became demoralized, lost between their historic identity and the white American culture they could not totally accept" (xi). Oskison had essentially said the same in "The New Indian Leadership" when he wrote that the old leaders "had been neglected, debauched and broken by the Government." That was the "absolute failure" of a policy Oskison dismissed as a "ration system." This failure is why Oskison advocated for better education and for policies that would not ignore the Indians' cultural pride and would not treat the Indians as irresponsible or incompetent. The remedy to such demoralization was involvement of the Indians in the policies that would advance their enlightenment and their freedom.

If Oskison applauded the "advancement" of the Indians, it was because he fought a kind of representation of the Indians that stopped them from achieving a better life: "the 'middle-period' idea of the reservation Indian as an overfed loafer is a persistent one" ("Making an Individual"). In the same essay, Oskison listed successful Indian workers to undermine the theories of people in the Reclamation Service that "the red workmen employed by the government and by contractors on various reclamation projects are fitted only for 'pick-and-shovel work,'" that they "can't manage teams," and that "complicated tools 'stump' them." At a time when Indians were still widely considered as inferior human beings by European Americans, Oskison wanted to argue that they were as capable as the white men and that they did not need to be considered wards under the protection of a paternalistic federal government. At a time when white people were "crowding on every side," Oskison believed the Indians had no choice but to show off their abilities in order to undermine "frontier white prejudice," which still prevented reservation kids from "attend[ing] the district schools of the states" ("Making an Individual").

If Oskison was positively a progressive Indian, he was an integrationist rather than an assimilationist. Remaining who they were intrinsically, "in blood and in traditions" ("Making an Individual"), the Indians must be fully part of American society. Within this society, it must be possible for the Indians to compete with the European Americans without forgetting who they were. After all, within their own tribes, whatever the tribe, the Indians were often individualistic competitors and farmers. His rhetoric sometimes reflects the pervading racialism of the time, notably when he appeared to correlate the lack of "advancement" of the Indians to the percentage of full-bloods in the reservation ("In Governing"). He also approved of President Roosevelt's claiming that "the mixture of blood has gone at the same time with progress in wealth and education" ("The President and the Indian"). Oskison, however, never wrote that the Indians somehow lacked competitive spirit and individualism and that they must forcefully be transformed into something they never were, competitive individuals. Oskison and other Indian writers were put in a situation that one might call the predicament of the colonized. They had to prove and demonstrate the humanity of their people. Simply because the dominant, colonizing narrative argued that Indian individualities were subdued and submitted to the group, Indian writers such as Occom, Apess, Winnemucca, Mourning Dove, Eastman, or Oskison, among many others, were forced to explain that the Indians could be individualistic, as their everyday practices proved. They also have had to justify farming skills that should have been taken for granted. In "Making an Individual of the Indian," Oskison wrote: "The point is that the modern Indian must be thought of as an individual, not merely as a unit in certain tribal groups." Oskison perceptively wrote that the Indian should not be *thought of* as a unit in the tribe. He referred to all the misrepresentations, all the inventions of the Indian, that the white men have imposed thanks to their historical narrative. When colonized Indians were drowned in imposed definitions that depicted them as mere units in a group and mere hunters or gatherers, they ended up being stripped of their real identities. From the very beginning of European colonization of the American continent, treating the Indians as mere indistinguishable members of groups has been the most effective way to dehumanize them and consequently to justify oppressing or "civilizing" them. These classic dehumanizing techniques — used by all colonizing powers all around the world — became the powers against which the Indians had to resist by trying to insert in the master narrative their own definitions of themselves — that is, they have always been farmers, are very competitive individuals, and are responsible adults.

Often taking the Cherokees as an example, Oskison explained that the Indians had not necessarily waited for the white men to teach them how to solve their problems but that they had acted on them of their own volition. He mentioned the first laws prohibiting the selling of liquor passed by the Cherokee legislature as early as 1819, "a quarter of a century before any such laws were enacted by the whites" ("In Governing").

Thus, when Oskison wanted the Indian to be an individualist in the white world, he pleaded not for the transformation of the Indian but rather for the already individualistic Indian to be given the right and opportunity to be himself in the new world that was being imposed upon him, to become an Indian American rather than a vanishing American Indian in a reservation. When obstacles to the integration of the Indian remained, they were not necessarily due to the Indian's unwillingness to fit in. They were often due to insufficient means offered by the government, and most of the time to white prejudices and dishonesty.

Quite paradoxically, the biggest obstacle to the "civilizing" of the Indian was very often the European American. So Oskison wrote for all reservation Indians to be allowed to be as responsible as the Cherokees had been for their own life. A careful reading of his essays is a key to understanding that Oskison was not a supporter of governmental assimilation policies. And he was not resigned either, accepting the fate of the vanishing Indian and hoping for the best. "This is not written merely as a lament over lost opportunities," he wrote before addressing how, according to him, Indian affairs should be dealt with ("In Governing").

On the contrary, Oskison called for more involvement of Indians in the dealing of Indian affairs. He encouraged federal agents to meet with the elders in order to understand better what the Indian needed: "If you want to know about the government of the vital affairs of the Navajos, go back into the mountains of Arizona and New Mexico, not to the office of the superintendent!" ("In Governing"). He believed and argued that there were on the reservations some Indians capable of taking the responsibility bestowed on agents who did not want it and did not know what to do with it. Oskison could be extremely harsh with Bureau of Indian Affairs employees, as when he evokes the superintendent whom he called "a skilled shirker of moral duties" ("Little Mother"). When the village teacher contained an epidemic of diphtheria, he blamed her for doing the work he should have done had he not been too "afraid to enter the village."

Everywhere he went, Oskison saw "opportunity for some Indian who could see clearly, who could talk sanely and moderately, to take a place of leadership; to take from the shoulders of the agent and superintendent at lot of work which he was not equipped to do" ("Acquiring a Standard of Value"). At stake were notably all the natural resources belonging to the Indians. If they did not want to see them escape their control, the Indians needed to be able to lead their own people to "civilization" and not let themselves be led by white agents who might use the Indian resources in a way that would not benefit their true owners. To that end, the Indians should be entrusted with the money that was kept for them by the government, a point that he stresses in several essays.

Oskison and Allotment

Just like his position on assimilation, Oskison's stance regarding allotment, a policy that was so devastating and disastrous for all Indian nations in Indian Territory, is not easy to assess in clear-cut, simplistic terms. What can be ascertained more clearly is that Oskison wanted the end of the reservation system, which, he wrote in "The New Indian Leadership" (1917), "amounted to imprisonment." Oskison favored allotment inasmuch as it put an end to the reservation and enabled Indian individuals to compete with their white neighbors.[16]

Many people, including Indians, supported allotment in severalty for very different reasons. As William T. Hagan puts it in *Taking Indian Lands*, "greed and humanitarianism rarely coalesced so beautifully in support of a policy" (6): land-hungry white settlers wanted "surplus" Indian land, and reformers wanted to make (in Oskison's terms) individuals of the Indians, which, they believed, could not be done as long as the land would be held communally. Sometimes, though, people who first supported the idea of allotment realized later that it was implemented unfairly or not rationally enough and asked for it to be improved. The Lake Mohonk Conference, for example — where Henry Dawes had come to advocate allotment in oft-quoted, strangely illogical terms in October 1885[17] — in the words of its president Charles J. Bonaparte in 1904, called the work of the Dawes Commission in the allotment of lands belonging to the Five Civilized Tribes an "injustice," quoting a report to the secretary of the interior he had signed:

> The principle of "first come, first served," adopted by the Commission in permitting the selection of lands . . . was and is essentially unjust as applied to Indians, the priority thus gained inuring usually to the advantage, not of those most deserving among the Indians, but of white speculators and corporations. The latter, for their own profit, induce Indians — usually the most shiftless and improvident of their race — to file at the earliest possible moment so as to obtain choice lands, to be subsequently enjoyed by the speculators themselves. (Bonaparte 12)

When he mentioned allotment in his essays, Oskison did so rather matter-of-factly but never expressed a wholehearted endorsement or condemnation. In a relatively noncommittal way, he reported that "the Cherokees and Creeks finally agreed to give up tribal existence as soon as the details of allotment and rearrangement could be completed" ("The President and the Indian"). He wrote that land allotment was "bitterly opposed by the tribes" in 1887 but "became a popular measure with the progressive Indians who were ambitious to distinguish themselves as individuals" ("Remaining Causes"). He also described the improvements individuals had achieved on their lots ("Making an Individual"). Before becoming an activist, Oskison was a journalist, and it is as such that he was writing these texts. This dispassionate tone can also be explained, of course, by the fact that when he started writing, the Dawes Commission had already started its work, and nothing much could be done to prevent or support it. His first known text, "A Trip to Yosemite Valley," was published in 1895, a few months after the Dawes Commission had started the mission it had been sent to accomplish in Indian Territory. Oskison was twenty-one at the time. During the first years of the commission's work in his "Old I.T.," Oskison was away at Stanford. When the first surveyors came to Indian Territory "to lay out the Cherokee country into square mile sections" (*Brothers Three* 27), he was just a child. *Brothers Three* has a rendition of their visit and the warm welcome they were given by Francis and Janet Odell, the characters inspired by Oskison's parents. Personally, Oskison applied for Cherokee citizenship to the Dawes Commission, but as we will see, this experience appeared to be quite unpleasant.

Beyond Oskison's journalistic phrasing, a closer analysis reveals that as far as allotment put an end to reservations and granted citizenship to the Indians, he thought it was a good idea, although it needed to be improved. Moreover, Oskison was acquainted with many Cherokee citizens, many of them by intermarriage, who monopolized huge tracts of communal land for the benefit of their very prosperous cattle business. These wealthy citizens offered an argument much used in the pro-allotment propaganda. In 1884 Armstrong claimed in his report for the Indian Rights Association that these citizens were increasing and gaining more and more control (23).[18] These "white Indians" (Holm 120) became the targets of many of the Friends of the Indian, who accused them of opposing allotment to protect their greedy interests. Bushyhead then invited the Senate Committee on Indian Affairs to Tahlequah in order to counteract these accusations. Henry Dawes was one of the delegates who visited Indian Territory in 1885. Holm writes that "despite testimony to the contrary," their report supported Armstrong's views (120). Although complete credit cannot be given such propaganda, there was some truth to it that the proponents of allotment did not miss to use and exaggerate. Wealthy ranchers like Bill Halsell, J. O. Hall, and others, whom Oskison mentioned in his autobiography as part of his childhood social environment, enjoyed access to large tracts of free land, causing many Cherokees to see in allotment a fairer and more equitable share of the territory

(Miner 130). Whatever the reasons that pushed Oskison, as well as many others, not to oppose allotment, the fact of the matter is that at the beginning of his writing career he did not see — or he overlooked — the nefarious effects such policies would have on the Indians, although some, including in the Cherokee Nation, had warned against them. In 1907, calling for a self-sufficient Indian, Oskison even asked for "that other prop, the tribal fund, [to] be removed" because he believed that the individual who "could convince the Government that he is qualified to use it" would "bestir himself" if allowed to receive his share of the Trust Fund ("Remaining Causes").

Several years later, though, he might have become aware of the wrongs allotment had caused to the Indians. In the second chapter of his autobiography, which he probably wrote in the 1940s, Oskison wrote of how he witnessed the opening of Indian Territory to settlement: "Pressure on Washington to open Indian lands to purchase and lease by whites had borne fruit. The Nation had been surveyed, the land graded and assessed, and allotted as individual holdings to Cherokee citizens" ("Old I.T."). He also told an anecdote that highlights the Indian dependence on the federal government. After receiving payment of $274 per citizen in "one big tent roped off and protected by rifle-armed guards . . . , payees passed from the main tent to another . . . in which merchants of Vinita, Nowata, Chelsea, Claremore, Miami, and other trading centers sat with lists of debts owed by Indians to whom they had extended credit. They paid unquestioningly the amounts demanded, some emerging with pockets turned inside out." These impressions, both the positive and the negative, would urge him in the essays presented in this volume to promote for the Indians self-help rather than assimilation.

For Oskison, the key to making individuals of the Indians — individuals who could participate fully in the American society with their distinguishing virtues, values, and identities — was self-reliance, self-respect, and self-support "in the sense that they are provided by the government with neither work nor rations" ("Making an Individual"). In that sense, the rhetoric of "Making an Individual" was very much in keeping with the values Oskison promoted in his essays on non-Indian subjects in which he praised famous industrialists or, in the words of Ronnow, sometimes "gave self-assured Puritanical, work-ethic advice, especially to women" and warned against the "sharks" ("Cherokee Journalist" 3).[19] These values and the related concepts of self-reliance, self-respect, and self-support were at the core of Oskison's thought for the improvement of the Indian condition. He probably believed that allotment could be a means to achieve these goals. Not considering the destructive effects this policy would have in terms of land loss, he thought this controversial policy could help turn the Indians into competitive individuals. When he wrote his autobiography years later, after these effects were visible, he seemed to regret the circumstances in which the authorities had implemented allotment: "Great changes had come to Indian Territory in the twenty-four years since Father arrived at Tahlequah. By now there were many more whites than Indians in the Cherokee Nation, in the towns and on farms and ranches. Pressure on Washington to open Indian lands to purchase and lease by whites had borne fruit" ("Old I.T."). At the end of his life, these fruit somehow seemed to have a bitter taste. Support of allotment seems to have been a dilemma. Although he brought attention to health hazards triggered by "the change from tepee to cabin" ("Remaining Causes"), he also expressed satisfaction that the Dawes Land Allotment Act of 1887 had put "every tribesman into his own house, on his own land, and at work for himself. The effort has begun to tell" ("Making an Individual"). In the very first lines of "Remaining Causes of Indian Discontent" he referred to the White River Utes, who protested against allotment as "a vanishing type of discontented Indian." For Oskison, "the progressive Indians" understood that allotment would enable them "to distinguish themselves as individuals." Holding the land in common "made the Indians feel as if they were heirs to an estate in chancery" and did not encourage personal improvement. The only issue that remained to be settled in order to further the transformation of the Indian into fully fledged individuals, in an economic sense of the word, was "the distribution of Indian Trust and Treaty Funds."

He developed this point the most extensively in "Remaining Causes of Indian Discontent." He trusted that the Indians did not need the "prop" that discouraged them from endeavoring to provide for their own needs, and he clearly claimed it "should be removed" from under them. As an example, he took the Osages, who had become rich almost overnight after the discovery of oil under their lands: "So long as a member of the Osage tribe knows that he is one of 2,000 heirs to a fund of $8,360,000, and that his proportionate share of interest at 5 percent on this tribal fund will be paid to him regularly, he feels no spur to become a producing member of his community." If each member of the tribe received his money only after he proved his competence, that individual "would bestir himself." Oskison was satisfied that "few Indians now live on the direct bounty of Congress," that "nine out of ten 'reservation' Indians are self-supporting," and he thought that the Trust Funds were leaving "the way back to idleness and dependence" open.

At the turn of the century, Oskison felt that the Indian should be portrayed as the Indian farmer or the Indian lawyer, an Indian relying on self-help to have the same chances of success as any American citizen. Oskison called for a "new Indian," "the new man, Indian only in blood and traditions, who is stepping up to take his place in the life of the West" ("Making an Individual") in order to insert his own identity into the fabric of American society.

Oskison thought it was necessary to learn how to live in the English-speaking world that America had become, and some of his statements can be rather ambiguous. However, nowhere in his writings does he express any kind of disdain or condescension toward Indian cultures and systems. Nowhere does he write that white civilization is better, in any way, than Indian civilizations. On the contrary, he recurrently points out how some white men, whether they were liquor sellers, usurers, or tricksters, "familiar pests in the white man's West" ("Remaining Causes"), exploited the Indians, and he urged the government to protect the latter from the former. Oskison simply believed that in the future there was no other solution for the Indians than to adjust if they wanted to make a place for themselves in American society. An old chief whom he quoted in "In Governing the Indian" summed it up for him: "We must all go the white man's way. There is no other way now. The buffalo are gone. There is no game." The key to understanding Oskison's advocacy is his recognition that the world in which the Indian had to make a place for himself was the American society, and more particularly the American West. In the historiography of the West, Oskison wanted a place for the Indian that was different from the place of the victim. From a reservation Indian, he had to become an Indian American citizen. If the Indian were assimilated, he would disappear. This is not the disappearing act Oskison desired. He called for the Indian to vanish from the reservation but to reappear as an equal in the white society.

From Essays to Fiction

A brief analysis of "Tookh Steh's Mistake" might be an appropriate bridge to link the examination of Oskison's positions as expressed in his essays and an understanding of how he fictionalized them. "Tookh Steh's Mistake" is one of the very first stories written by Oskison, and probably the most political. It was published a few years after the Dawes Commission had arrived at Tahlequah to force the Cherokees into allotment. In "Tookh Steh's Mistake," the "commission" — an unnamed fictional version of the Dawes Commission — played a key role in Tookh's life. "Tookh Steh was a full-blood, and his convictions concerning things were very strong." This is the first sentence of the story, and this characterization of the eponymous protagonist is almost identically repeated at the very end. According to the narrator, Tookh Steh's mistake is to escape, by fleeing to Mexico, the allotment policy that the white man attempts to impose upon the Cherokees.[20] A simplistic conclusion would be that Oskison supported allotment and that he believed that opposing it was "foolish," a term used three times to describe Tookh. However, a closer look at the story tends to show that Oskison's support of allotment was not blind and unconditional. Tookh is not said to be "foolish" because he opposed allotment. Tookh's mistake was to think "he could change the course of what men call destiny." His opposition itself was not foolish; after all, "he had a principle to back him," he had strong convictions, and he "had something of right on his side, when he made the one foolish move of his life." In a way, Tookh is a simpler, more visceral and instinctive, less intellectual version of Hastings, the lawyer who helped Oskison realize "the ability of the Indian to understand his own problems, and to fight effectively for their right solution" ("In Governing"). Oskison did not admire Hastings for his opinions but for his conviction that the Indians could take care of themselves. He had a similar kind of admiration for Tecumseh. Although he thought the Indian leader "was the dreamer of a hopeless dream," Oskison admired the fact that "he followed it straightforwardly and courageously to the inevitable end," when he died "while battling for the right of his red brothers to live in freedom according to their own conceptions" (*Tecumseh* vii). Tookh, who "was not blind to reason," trusted his white friend and neighbor, Mr. Verte, when he explained the good intentions of the commission: "Verte believed what he said. He was not largely experienced in the politics of the world. Tookh believed what Verte said, because he had learned to trust the words of the white man." However, when the commissioner told the Indians that "they had no choice in the matter," that the "instructions were to make the change" and that the "treaties were good so long as they did not stand in the way of progress," then Tookh resolved that "he would not live in a country where his old freedom would be restricted." What Tookh reacted to was not a policy but the *imposition* of a policy. According to the narrator, that is why "Tookh had something of right on his side."

"But out of the corrupt soil of the reservation system has grown a new type of Indian — the one who intermarries with white neighbors, who goes to school, raises cattle and horses, opens up and cultivates farms, learns a white man's trade and works at it" ("Closing Chapter"). For Oskison, the "new type of Indian" was self-reliant. If not for the slight issue of his having two wives — an issue only for the dogmatic religious authorities which thus deny his eager desire to integrate — Old Harjo is the perfect embodiment of the self-supporting Indian that Oskison called for in his essays: "Materially, Harjo was solvent; and if the Government had ever come to his aid he could not recall the date" ("The Problem of Old Harjo").

As Littlefield and Parins noted, "Oskison's fiction was a response to the historic changes that were occurring in his native land" ("Short Fiction" 32). Oskison's essays on the historic events of his time shed much light on how and why he wrote fiction. The "new type of Indian" he conveys in his essays is precisely the Indian Oskison knew and wrote about in his autobiography, his short stories, and his novels. His family was a result of Cherokee and European American intermarriage. He went to school with other kids with the same background. Oskison was raised as a cattle driver and a farmer. The Indians he knew during his childhood and whom he described in his autobiography and his fiction all fit this definition of the "new Indian," best embodied in the figure of the Indian Cowboy.

The Outlaw, the Indian Cowboy, and the Singing Bird

The "new Indians" peopled the Indian Territory that Oskison knew and described. The Cherokees of the time "were not all like the nomadic hunters" his father had seen on the Plains during his crossing from Illinois to California. "They were farmers, stockmen, merchants; they ran gristmills and sawmills and saltworks" ("Old I.T."). There were also lawyers whom Oskison's father admired so much that he pushed his son to study law. And there were Indian cowboys. Oskison was one before he went to college, and he would probably have remained one if his father had not made sure his son could get a college education. His lifelong friend, humorist and social commentator Will Rogers, was another one. Many Indian cowboys give regionalist color to Oskison's short stories. They are simple, sometimes poignant characters as exemplified by Hanner the Runt in "Only the Master Shall Praise."

Oskison's stories are stories of outlawry and posses, roping contests, prairie fires, and romantic escapades, but the figure of the Indian Cowboy can be a useful type to understand Oskison's representations of the Indians. Of course, not all Oskison's Indians are cowboys, and not all his cowboys are Indians. However, this figure, embodied by Hanner the Runt, the "half-breed Cherokee cowboy," typifies the protagonists of Oskison's short stories. Whatever their ancestry and their actual occupation, they are all from Indian country, and most often from Cherokee territory, a land most characterized by the intermingling of Indian life and cowboy occupation. To Oskison, the type of the Indian Cowboy is the embodiment of life in the "Old I.T." The Indian Cowboy is a symbol of the possibility for the Indians to have any occupation they want, even those perceived in the mainstream, eastern society of the beginning of the twentieth century as reserved to European Americans. In the real world, and in Oskison's essays, the profession of the metaphorical "Indian Cowboy" could be "teaching, nursing, the law," and so forth ("The Indian in the Professions").

Interestingly, Oskison's characters are not systematically identified by ethnicity. The Indian ancestry of his characters is secondary, so much so that sometimes it is not even mentioned, which probably led some readers to believe that Oskison did not write about Indians. As Ronnow aptly put it, "it should be remembered in reading Oskison's stories that *any* given character — farmer, merchant, or lawyer — could easily and probably be Cherokee, and not just the obviously 'Indian' types" (*John Milton Oskison* 10–11). I would add that the obviously "Indian" type — as performed by the Wild West Show Indian Oskison mentions in his autobiography — is utterly absent from his fiction, as it was absent from the Indian Territory. When they are identified as Indians, it is to emphasize features that Oskison — or literary tradition — considered typically Indian. Hanner, for example, "combined with the stoicism of the Indian something of the physical energy and mental weakness of his white father." When they are white, they are in their element in Cherokee Territory. Billy, the protagonist of "When the Grass Grew Long" (1901), whose disfigured body echoes Hanner's and whose teenage history recalls Oskison's father's, is ethnically unidentified. He is likely to be a white man, since his boss tells him that "there's some half-breed girls, an' full-bloods too, that ain't so bad comp'ny as you'd think." Yet we learn he fits into the Cherokee world and speaks some Cherokee. At the end of the day, "in the context of ranching in Indian Territory, the distinction [between Indians and non-Indians] was usually irrelevant" (Ronnow, *John Milton Oskison* 12).

Oskison's protagonists are characterized by their acts. Indians are not better than whites, nor are whites better than Indians. The Indian is not typically always the hero or the victim. If the protagonists are mixed-bloods, they do not seem to suffer from their mixed ancestry in the way Momaday's Abel or Silko's Tayo do. Jim Freeman, the hero of two stories, could be Cherokee, white, or mixed-blood. So could Thomas Henry or his old man, Chris Farrell, JIC-Bert or the other ropers.

Oskison's characters therefore do not tell us much about what it means to be an Indian or an encroaching European American. They all tell us what it means to live in multicultural or "multiracial" Indian country.[21] There, with the notable exception of Jim Blind-Wolfe and his Keetoowah companions in "The Singing Bird" — who resent European American intrusion — they seem to live without undue interference from their neighbors, whether they are Indians or white settlers. Ironically, the only character, named "Wolf" in "The Man Who Interfered," who is an "enraged brute" with "primitive passions" and a "primitive soul" — a language that had traditionally been used to characterize the "savage" Indian — is a white man, whose Indian wife is called "the white girl" by her family because she "went away to school among the whites and married a white man." This kind of reversal of the common cliché is recurrent in Oskison's writing. Another one is Hanner the Runt, a sober Indian who tries to prevent his presumably white companion from drinking.

What many of Oskison's characters have in common is their trust — however naive sometimes — in the others' humanity, although they live in a world where that humanity can sometimes be driven into a corner and tested. Whether they are Indians or European Americans, they are humans in a somehow inhuman world. In the Wild West of train robbers and posses, in this world where "the effect of a lynching . . . is felt to be good" no matter the former standing of a man ("Only the Master"), Oskison finds gems of human innocence. Sometimes, when the justice rendered by the posses is too blind, these gems get lost and crushed. Hanner's "innocent trust in humanity" will be his doom. Walla Tenaka — a true character in a fictional rendition of his tragic story — the father of a two-week old, will be executed for his drunken crime. Other times — as when Billy is saved by the sacrifice of Jinny Jake — these gems are possible ways of redemption.

Other than neighborly relationships, the reader also sees Oskison's characters loving and/or struggling with their Indian or European American spouse. In his autobiography he tells the story of a friend of his, Ken Stillman, who had fallen hopelessly in love with Ida, a streetwalker. In a subsequent passage, Oskison ponders his own literary weaknesses. According to him, one of them was that he "mistook form for substance. For example, it did not occur to me to write the dramatic story of Stillman and Ida, and Maugham beat me to it!" in *Of Human Bondage*. Nevertheless, Ida's recklessness and Ken's blind infatuation seem to have inspired Oskison with many characters and with the story of "Yvonne the Terrible" (1927; see "Autobiography" n. 147). Again, whether they are Indian (in "The Singing Bird") or European American (in *The Singing Bird*) is irrelevant to the fact that Oskison's female characters are sometimes "singing birds" — according to a Cherokee legend, wives who are leaving the nest and who sing "with notes to lure others than [their] mate" ("The Singing Bird"). Consequently, many of his male characters are "cock redbirds [who] fight among themselves" (*Singing Bird* 2).

The outlaw is another type that can be found in Oskison's writings. Because Cherokee courts did not have jurisdiction on criminal matters involving a non-Indian, many outlaws found refuge in the Indian Territory after committing their crimes in the neighboring states. Isaac C. Parker, United States district judge for the Western District of Arkansas from 1875 to 1896, who had jurisdiction over the Indian Territory, and about whom Oskison wrote

"A Border Judge and His Court" (1903), was reported saying that most of the trouble coming from the Indian Territory did not come from Indians but from intruders: "It has been the custom for all these years that when a man committed a crime in an older state, or in any state, and he could get away from the officers, he would run into the Indian country," Parker declared, before adding that the area contained many men "who are stained with crime, whose tendencies are corrupted by the crimes that they have committed elsewhere, and it is with this corrupt element assembled from all the States of this Union that this court and the juries of this court have to contend with" (in Stolberg 19–20 and Shirley, *Law West* 263).

According to Conley, this situation became very convenient for the American authorities: they could claim that "the Indian governments were incapable of maintaining law and order, and therefore, the United States must do it for them" and intervene in Cherokee affairs (*Cherokee Nation* 186).[22] The situation was so convenient, in fact, that the reputation of Indian Territory as an outlaw's paradise might have been exaggerated. Littlefield and Parins suggest that the "unflattering descriptions of the Indian Territory" published on a regular basis by magazines at the end of the century contributed significantly to the popular support of the movement to statehood ("Short Fiction" 36). One good illustration of such propaganda is the rhetoric used by someone like William M. Fishback, governor of the neighboring state of Arkansas (1893–95), which had jurisdiction over Indian Territory in all cases where white men were involved. Fishback wrote that, as a result of the dual jurisdiction in the Indian Territory, "the Indians indulge[d] very freely in murder among themselves," while they would do nothing to prevent white men from committing crimes, watching as spectators robberies being performed, seeming "to enjoy the robbery as a joke" (96). Because he saw the Territory as a "safe harbor for criminals," a situation that was "a temptation to crime in all the adjacent states," including his, Fishback had a vested interest in depicting Indian Territory as a lawless haven, "a school of crime to the young Indians" (97), "a national pest-house," "a disgrace to our country," "a disgrace to civilization," "a disgrace to humanity" (98). He made his agenda clear: "I do have a very decided conviction that this *imperium in imperio* — this amorphous government — should be abolished, and some sort of civilized system adopted, and at once" (97). In the pre-statehood years, such propaganda was common, including the old savagery versus civilization rhetoric. In December 1892, Senator George G. Vest of Missouri, also a neighboring state, introduced a resolution "to Appoint a Commission to Treat with the Five Civilized Tribes With a View of Making Agreements to Induce Them to Take Homesteads in Severalty" arguing that Indian Territory was "a menace to civilization" and a place where "crime is rampant and corruption is rife" (Carter 2). Three years earlier, in the debate the senators had over the Springer Bill, which aimed at acquiring the Cherokee Outlet, Vest had already described the territory as "a refuge for criminals, a Botany Bay with no law, a blank, unoccupied piece of territory, so far as civilization is concerned" (Hagan, *Taking* 13). In support of white settlers, the *Washington Post* wrote in an editorial that the time had come to "supplant barbarism and lawlessness with civilization, law, tilled fields, and all the . . . blessings of thriving industry" (qtd. in Hagan, *Taking* 16). The commission called forth by Vest in 1892 would be the Dawes Commission, whose first report to the secretary of the interior, in November 1894, argued that "violence, robbery, and murder are almost of daily occurrence," that "a reign of terror exists, and barbarous outrages, almost impossible of belief, are enacted" (Carter 8). In 1895, scholar Henry Gannett would write of Indian Territory as "a large tract of country which is practically unexplored, is without organization or government except such as is afforded by the tribes which own it, and in which most of the elements of civilization are extremely primitive," all the more an incongruity as it is "in the heart of a region thoroughly well known, densely peopled and well organized" (272). Since then, historians, Native and non-Native, have nuanced these descriptions. At the time, the tribal authorities had accused the authors of such reports of lying and exaggerating, but of course, there were stronger ulterior motives against which they could do little.

Although Oskison does not tell of any close encounter with outlaws in his autobiography, he does evoke such figures as Jesse James, the Dalton brothers, the Younger gang, and Cherokee outlaw Tom Starr in fictional stories based on true material like "To 'Youngers' Bend'" or "Working for Fame," as well as in his assessment of Judge Parker, all published in *Frank Leslie's Popular Monthly* in 1903. Posses are also recurrent features in his short and long fiction. Yet Oskison's work did not contribute in a large way to the bad reputation of the Indian Territory. If the outlaws' adventures had a dramatic appeal to him, his entire work is far from describing the Gomorrah that popular media had a tendency to see in the Indian Territory. His story titled "The Greater Appeal," with Belle Starr as a protagonist, starts as a classic outlaw story with the famous "bandit queen" being chased by deputy marshal Jim Marks but ends as a humanistic tale of redemption through motherhood.

Indian Territory Identities

Oskison was born just before the decade — 1875 to 1885 — that historian V. A. Travis called "the 'Golden Age' of the Cherokee Nation." According to Travis, "it was about this time that reconstruction ended and a period of development began which culminated in the best conditions reached under tribal government" (16). The Cherokees seem to have had several "golden ages." Michael Wallis remarks that some historians will consider the period between the removal and the Civil War as the Cherokees' "Golden Age." For Wallis, "this was, in spite of the removal, a time of prosperity, marked by the development of businesses, schools, and a flourishing culture" (Mankiller and Wallis xxi–xxii). Robert Conley describes the period Wallis refers to in a chapter titled "The Golden Age," although he points out the Eurocentric irony that that period "became known as the Cherokee Golden Age purely and simply because during that time the Cherokees adopted more and more of white culture, and the Cherokee Nation became more like the United States." He describes that era as one "of relative peace and prosperity" during which "the federal government was not coming around demanding new treaties and more land cessions" and when "tremendous strides [were] made by the Cherokees . . . toward becoming a so-called modern nation." Of course, he also concedes that "some might very well feel that the real Golden Age of the Cherokees was before the arrival of Europeans on the North American continent" (*Cherokee Nation* 167).[23]

The definition of a "golden" age, then, is only relative, and the dates chosen by Travis to define one are arbitrary. Nevertheless, the period during which Oskison grew up was a prosperous one — one when the Cherokees had once again recovered from some previous tragic events and many hardships. After they had been forcefully removed from their eastern territories and taken on the infamous Trail of Tears, sometimes violent internal clashes hurt the Nation. Factions appeared or strengthened between what is commonly called the Treaty Party and the John Ross Party—that is, between the Cherokees who signed the Treaty of New Echota in 1835 and moved to join the Western Cherokees, or Old Settlers, and the people who resisted removal but were forced out on "the trail where they cried."[24] When the Civil War broke out, Chief John Ross wanted to keep the Cherokee Nation neutral. However, Stand Watie and his followers sided with the Confederates. In reaction, full-blood Cherokees formed the Nighthawk Keetoowahs.[25] After the war, the whole Nation suffered the consequences of defeat. Conley calls the Cherokee Nation at the end of the war "a wasteland" (*Cherokee Nation* 179). James Mooney wrote that it had been "ravaged," that "all the prosperous accumulations of twenty years of industry [had been] swept off in this guerrilla warfare" (149). Yet after the Civil War, the Cherokees prospered again. In the words of Wilma Mankiller, "after every major upheaval, we have been able to gather together as a people and rebuild a community and a government. Individually and collectively, Cherokee people possess an extraordinary ability to face down adversity and continue moving forward. We are able to do that because our culture . . . has sustained us since time immemorial" (Mankiller and Wallis xxi). Oskison wrote that his father, at the beginning of the 1870s, "saw the Nation as a land of plenty and promise" ("Old I.T."). The historians' debate about what period in the history of the Cherokees is their Golden Age points to the fact that every time they came close to being destroyed, the Cherokees managed to adapt to their new environment, recover, and flourish with a resilience against overwhelming hardships that almost defy imagination. As Daniel Justice suggests, it was indeed appropriate to associate the word *Cherokee* and the name of the mythical phoenix to give its title to the first Cherokee newspaper.

Since pre-removal times, the Cherokees had been successful farmers and businessmen, as Oskison himself explained in "Cherokee Migration." In an 1826 letter to statesman and intellectual Albert Gallatin, a prominent Cherokee of the time, John Ridge, took "pleasure to state . . . that there is not to my knowledge a solitary Cherokee to be found that depends upon the chase for subsistence and every head of a family has his house & farm" (Ridge

36). They had been living under a government system defined by a written constitution. Their language had been developed into a written syllabary by Sequoyah in 1821. Since then, newspapers had been published—first the *Cherokee Phoenix*, then the *Cherokee Advocate*. They had fought for their sovereignty in the U.S. Supreme Court, which ultimately defined them, along with all other Indian tribes, as "domestic dependent nations" (*Cherokee Nation v. Georgia*, in 1831). In Indian Territory, the Cherokees had founded Tahlequah. The Nation's capital had a good education system with elementary schools and seminaries; the Male Seminary and the Female Seminary, where "young and lovely Fanny Bly," young Oskison's teacher at the Pawpaw school and the first person that put books into his avid hands, had been trained ("Old I.T.").[26]

Oskison's multicultural family was rather typical of Indian Territory at the end of the nineteenth century. At the time, European Americans were more and more present on Cherokee territory. Some of them were welcome and became Cherokee citizens when they married Cherokee women. Although the Final Rolls of Citizens and Freedmen of the Five Civilized Tribes in Indian Territory, established in 1907, were divided in categories such as "Cherokee by Blood," "Cherokee by Intermarriage," or "Cherokee Freedmen," living in the Cherokee Nation and not staying away from it for too long seem to have been more determining criteria than blood quantum, as illustrated by the application for enrollment of John M. Oskison himself.

On 16 March 1901, Oskison, who had applied to the Commission to the Five Civilized Tribes (better known in the Nation as the Dawes Commission) for enrollment as a Cherokee citizen, was submitted to harsh interrogation from Commissioner T. B. Needles and J. L. Baugh, "representative of the Cherokee Nation." After he was asked several times where he was born, where he resided, and how long he had been away from the Cherokee Nation, although Commissioner Needles certified that "the name of John Oskison is found upon the authenticated roll of 1880 as well as the census roll of 1896," the Cherokee Nation representative "protest[ed] against the listing for enrollment of the said John Oskison as a Cherokee citizen by blood, because of the fact of non-residence." The problem for Baugh seems to have been that Oskison spent too many of his twenty-six years away from Indian Territory. Since being a Cherokee by blood did not appear to be enough, Oskison insisted on his links to the place where he was born and that he had made his home. To the question "Did you always consider the Cherokee Nation your home?" Oskison answered "Yes sir." In a final statement he gave Needles and Baugh after they had pressed him to repeat that he had been away notably when he arrived at his majority, Oskison insisted that "all interests I have are in the Indian Territory, Cherokee Nation, and that I have never regarded any other place as my permanent residence. I have been away for educational purposes."

On that day, "final judgment as to the enrollment of said John Oskison [was] suspended" and his name placed on "a doubtful card." Citing the Cherokee Constitution, Oskison's attorneys argued that "the conditions upon which a citizen may lose or forfeit his rights, privileges and immunities as a Cherokee citizen are: 1st. He must remove from the limits of the Cherokee Nation; 2nd. He must take with him his effects; 3rd. He must become a citizen of some other government." They reasserted that their client had never "left the Cherokee Nation with the intention of becoming a citizen of some other government. He never took any of his effects, except what was necessary for school purposes. And he never at any time declared by word or act that he was or desired to be a citizen of some other government." Finally, on 11 September 1903 — that is to say, two and a half years after he applied — Oskison was granted citizenship by the commission, which stated that "the evidence . . . shows that the said John Oskison has resided in the Cherokee Nation all his life, excepting from 1894 to 1898, during which time he was attending college." Oskison had convinced them that he truly belonged to his Old I.T.

This anecdote is interesting in different ways. At a time when people often defined themselves by the blood flowing in their veins, Oskison's Cherokee lineage was acknowledged but his Cherokee citizenship was challenged on the grounds that he spent a few years outside the Cherokee Nation. In the words of Rennard Strickland, "tribal identification was so strong that an eighth-blood Cherokee, John Ross, led the full-blood faction while a full-blood, Major Ridge, led the mixed bloods" (15). Daniel Justice concurs when he writes that the "degree of blood quantum should not be read as a measure of commitment to Cherokee nationhood or identification *as* Cherokee" (xv). Baird wrote that "historically, 'being Indian' for [the Five Tribes] was a cultural rather than biological process" (17).[27] In *Blood Politics*, Circe Sturm demonstrates how the place of blood in the definition of Cherokee identity evolved over time. In Oskison's day, when the Cherokee Nation received money for the sale of the Cherokee Outlet and when political divisions appeared over whether or not the Cherokee freedmen should share in the benefits, "the Cherokee state was using blood not only as a basis for racial, cultural, and national identification but also as a mechanism for controlling access to economic resources" (76–77). Sturm adds that "this policy alienated most of the non-Cherokee citizens of the tribe and contributed to a general sense of unrest in the nation" (77).

Beyond showing how much Oskison felt his identities to be grounded in Indian Territory, the anecdote of his application to citizenship testifies to the testiness of the Cherokee authorities at a time when an increasingly diverse population in the Nation contributed to threatening their sovereignty, already partly confiscated by the Dawes Commission. This diversity is largely reflected in Oskison's fiction, where people live together for better or worse and where they struggle engaging one another, although some people — Cherokee citizens of African descent — are left largely unmentioned by Oskison (see "Autobiography" n. 66 and "Essays" n. 129).

Much more than an ethnic writer, Oskison was a regionalist, or what could be called a "territorial writer." His autobiography and short stories reflect the life of the Cherokees in the Indian Territory in this transitional period before statehood in 1907. As testified by the people who questioned his Cherokee citizenship, he was not an individual defined by any blood quantum but a writer first and foremost of and from a specific geographical part of the American countryside. His identities as a writer were also defined by his connections to the Indian Territory, which he affectionately called "the Old I.T." His citizenship apart, Oskison can be defined as a Cherokee writer because he was deeply rooted in the Cherokee territory and he wrote of the territory to which the Cherokee Nation was removed. However, it is important to note that the identities of the Cherokee people that he represents are not the identities of a removed, uprooted people. Oskison's themes are the exact opposite of "the estrangement from the land" Larson sees in his writing as well as in Pokagon's and Mathews's (34). Apart from the article in which Oskison describes the "Cherokee Migration," all his tales and their protagonists give life to and embody the Indian Territory as Cherokee land. Nowhere in his writings does he show some nostalgia for his tribe's former lands in the East. Oskison even emphasizes how fast the Cherokee took root in the I.T. In the part of the Indian Territory where he was raised, people were farmers or stockmen, whether they were European American or Cherokee. So Oskison's identities were defined by farming and ranching. When *Wild Harvest* was published he declared that he "wanted everything that had impressed me during the time I grew up in the old Indian Territory to go into the story. I had done every variety of farm work; I had become a fairly good cowboy, considering that I started on that work riding a gray mule bareback" (*The Oklahoman* 13 Jan. 1929). For a large part, his career as a journalist and editorialist was also determined by his growing up as a farmer. He wrote numerous articles on the farming economy for *Collier's Weekly*, notably a series entitled "$1,000 on the Farm." It just so happens that, contrary to clichés that Native writers and scholars still try to undermine, many Indians were farmers or cattle raisers, and the Cherokees were very successful in that business.

To some extent, the mirror held by Oskison reflects a rosy image of the transition his region had to go through. A generation after the beginning of Oskison's writing career, another Oklahoman, John Joseph Mathews (Osage, c. 1894–1979), represented in darker shades the transition the Indians of Oklahoma had to endure. In Oskison's fiction, factionalism serves only as an occasional backdrop; outlaws aside, the European Americans are guests or spouses of Cherokee people rather than profiteers and intruders, and the politicians are relatively absent. There is violence, but it is hardly gratuitous. His characters often accept their death, which has a sacrificial or redemptive value. It is not a white anti-Indian violence. There are tragedies, of course, but they are mostly personal or intimate tragedies of unrequited love. With the notable exception of Tookh Steh's story, the tragedies Oskison represents have very little to do with the very negative political and social transformations endured by the Cherokees.

In later works, starting with "The Singing Bird" (1925) and continuing in the three novels he published in his lifetime, the plight of the Indians, the greediness of the white men, and the tension between the different factions in the Cherokee Nation occupied more and more of his narrative space. His writing became more political. He expressed a more sympathetic view of the traditionalist Cherokees. In "The Singing Bird" the villain is actually a "half-breed," a pejorative term that refers to people Oskison originally equated to progressive Indians. As for the white men, Oskison's tone became harsher. In *Black Jack Davy* (1926), the thoughts of Ned Warrior reveal that "there were many honest whites, good friends of the Indians and good neighbors. ... But they appeared, sometimes, to be a helpless minority. They seemed to count for so little compared with the horde of lawless invaders, the whiskey peddlars, cattle thieves, store thieves, train robbers, greed crazed land grabbers like Jerry Boyd" (272).

In the same novel, a highly accusatory speech by tribal chief Ross Murray is one more opportunity for Oskison to appeal to the energy and intelligence of his fellow Cherokees to change their destiny: "It is said that the history of a nation is the history of its wars, but in our case it is the history of forced cessions of land. That process is now ended, we can cede no more, and the course of our history must change. We must become builders. Put the money you get into the development of good farms. Avoid the pitfalls set by the gamblers, let drink alone. Your own future, and that of your families, demands it" (169–70).

Occasionally, his fictitious characters served as illustrations for the positive Indian figures Oskison simultaneously portrayed in the political discourse of his essays. In 1912 he had admitted a degree of indulgent optimism: "The greatest handicap I have is my enthusiasm. I know a lot of Indians who are making good. When I try to write about them I lose my critical sense" ("The Indian in the Professions"). The role Indians play and the place they occupy in Oskison's writings might have been surprising to the general audience of his time, but they powerfully reflect the role they played and the place they occupied in his life. He adamantly expressed his refusal to contribute to the propagation of imposed definitions of the Indian: "I will not repeat the old lies about the Indian for any editor that ever paid on acceptance!" Impressions of Indian cowboys or "young half-breed rioters drunk on bootleg whiskey" ("Old I.T."), devoted Cherokee women or dedicated teachers, even members of the Cherokee gentry—all would find their place in his tales. The corrupt agents and superintendents, the prejudiced pioneers, and all forms of violence directed at Indians would remain ingredients of his essays.

In his autobiography, an amused and self-deprecating Oskison remembers how bad his attempt at writing a sea story had been: "I submitted to the [*Post*'s] Supplement editor some of the short stories the magazines had rejected, and found him receptive until some unaccountable impulse led me to write a sea story. He printed it, and was forthwith overwhelmed by letters from readers pointing out that I had made every mistake it was possible to make" ("Old I.T."). Oskison was reputable and poetic, however, when he wrote of the land he knew. In an article about Oskison after he returned to Oklahoma to write *The Singing Bird*, LaVere Anderson wrote of her friend: Oskison "believes that a man can't do a good story unless he knows, from grass roots up, the flavor and appearance of a country, its people, its character" (*Tulsa Daily World* 29 Jan. 1939). John Joseph Mathews felt the same way when he decided to isolate himself in the blackjacks of northeastern Oklahoma because he "wanted to become a part of the flow in so far as I was able; to learn something of the moods of the little corner of the earth which had given me being" (*Talking to the Moon* 2). In *The Way to Rainy Mountain*, N. Scott Momaday echoed this notion when he wrote that "once in his life a man ought to concentrate his mind upon the remembered earth. . . . He ought to give himself up to a particular landscape in his experience, to look at it from as many angles as he can, to wonder about it, to dwell upon it" (83). This is what Oskison did when he wrote. Every Old I.T. story is an exploration of an aspect, a dimension of the Indian Territory.

John Milton Oskison did for the Indian Territory what all regionalist writers did for their part of the world. He contributed to giving it a literary dimension. He declared that his ambition was "to bring out of the vivid Oklahoma range-cattle period a character as appealing as Owen Wister's 'The Virginian'" and that he hoped "to write a book that will reflect the spirit of those far-off frontier days" (*The Oklahoman* 7 July 1935). If Oskison first encountered literature via masters such as Stevenson and Kipling, it was riding his mule in Indian Territory that truly convinced him that he would be a writer and that truly gave him his own style and inspiration:

> On those daylong rides, especially in the afternoons when hunger stimulated the imagination, I began recalling some of the characters in the fiction I had read, and the sort of detail used by the writers I liked

> best. Gradually it dawned on me that many of the characters in my favorite stories were remarkably like real people. From that thought, I progressed to another, Why wouldn't the folks of our neighborhood make interesting characters in stories? Why couldn't such scenes and incidents as fast-running prairie fires, roundups, night rides of quietly gathered posses to nab cattle thieves, spectacular fights between deputy United States marshals and train robbers, the violent rebellion against father's hard discipline of brother Will, be used in stories? ("Old I.T.")

Oskison showed it was possible to find inspiration in the Indian Territory. He proved that this land, often described as a godforsaken and lawless country by people who could benefit from such descriptions, had a lot of potential to be grasped by the artist's imagination. Oskison clearly shaped the writer he would become as he was roaming the wilderness of the last frontier that the Indian Territory was. His autobiography, however incomplete, gives us much of what we need to know to understand where he found the inspiration for his stories and novels. On the other hand, Oskison also believed that regional writers had a responsibility to make their homelands known better for what they were. He was reported saying that "Oklahoma is fast becoming recognized as a civilized state as Oklahoma writers identify themselves with eastern editors in increasing numbers" (*The Oklahoman* 10 Dec. 1930). This supports the point Littlefield and Parins made about the "historical accuracy" of the local color Oskison used in his stories. The verisimilitude it creates actually does much more for the Indian Territory: Oskison wrote "at a time when the public image of the Indian Territory was at perhaps its lowest point. During the last two decades of the nineteenth century . . . the popular magazines published unflattering descriptions of the Indian Territory as a place where whiskey flowed freely, lawlessness and violence were the rule, tribal officials were incapable of ruling and enriched themselves with tribal funds and white inhabitants (though there illegally) were virtually without protection of the law" ("Short Fiction" 36).

The necessity to change the reputation of the I.T. is tackled in *Wild Harvest*, where Harvey convinces Nan to "help . . . get up a Friday evenin' 'Literary' to sort of bring the folks together. Looks like if we intend to change the reputation of Thunder Creek from an outlaw hang-out, it's time we done somethin' like that" (191). Another character of the same novel expresses the ignorance Oskison wanted to fight. After learning that Cherokees had courts, Gabe Horner laughed: "You don't say! . . . I'd always thought of Indians, before I looked into the situation up here, about the way a fellow back in New York would. I'd thought they was all more or less like old Geronimo, still oncivilized [*sic*] an' hell bent for the warpath if they got half a chance . . . But up here . . . well, they ain't that way at all" (255).[28] In *Brothers Three*, Janice, a lady from New York, cannot believe that the cowboys she meets do not correspond at all to the cowboys she read about in romance novels. What about chivalry toward women? she asks Henry, her husband. "Western chivalry?" he answers. "That's phooey. There's no more of it in the west than anywhere else, except in the imagination of the wild west school of romancers" (205). In "The Fall of King Chris" (1903), a story that contains several autobiographical elements, notably the character JIC-Bert (see "Fiction" n. 67), there is a character who can be assumed to reflect Oskison's New York persona and opinion about the literary potential of Indian Territory: "Been writin' some about the Territory in that New York newspaper?" protagonist Chris Farrell asked the newspaperman. "'This kind of thing interestin'?' . . . It had much action and color, the scribe thought."

Yet Oskison can be seen as somewhat of a paradox in his geographical identities. However deeply rooted in the Indian Territory his writings are, his autobiography is the history of a cosmopolitan Oklahoman. The traveling bug seems to have bit him when he was two, traveling with his family to Oregon and California in a prairie schooner. While the first chapters tell us about life on the prairie of the Old I.T., the following ones also relate some of the author's numerous and extended journeys. In 1930 he gave a talk at the Oklahoma Hospitality Club titled "Confessions of a Wandering Writer," in which he stated that to him, "globe wandering is a stimulation to the mind and imagination, is broadening, and offers wide opportunities for comparisons" (*The Oklahoman* 20 Dec. 1930). In an interview with Joseph A. Brandt published in the *Daily Oklahoman* in 1936, he declared: "I suppose I've inherited my restless feet from my father. He was nomadic in spirit, although a builder, too." Oskison was a nomad who traveled around the world, and he lived most of his adult life in New York. Brandt described him as "a genuine cosmopolitan. He has been to Europe seven times and during the last 12 years, when he has been devoting himself exclusively to the novel, he has spent winters in Hawaii, California and Arizona, summers in France and Switzerland and in Santa Fe, and, of course, summers and winters in Oklahoma" (*Daily Oklahoman* 1 Mar. 1936). If anything, his traveling wide and large across the world and his uprootedness in New York only reinforced his sense of belonging. He always came back to Oklahoma, and Oklahoma kept emerging again in his writing. In 1941 he coedited with Angie Debo *Oklahoma: A Guide to the Sooner State*, compiled by the Work Projects Administration in the state. In the preface, he and Debo expressed their feeling that the guide might be "the most comprehensive history of Oklahoma thus far published" and pointed out that the staff "kept in mind the need to make clear the complicated and significant story of the close human and political contacts between the Indians and the whites in the century and a quarter since the two races first met in Oklahoma" (vii).[29] The stories contained in the present volume—autobiographical, fictional, and nonfictional—represent the territorial identities of a nomadic man who often came back to the Old I.T., where he died before finishing his last "Tale of the Old I.T."

As he had come back to Oklahoma in search of possible material for his novels, he returned in 1946 to Vinita to write his autobiography. Then, the local press reported that the "noted author" "feels his home town will provide the proper atmosphere in which to write the story of his life" (*Tulsa Tribune* 25 Mar. 1946). Even if half of the autobiography presented here deals with his numerous travels and life outside the Indian Territory, in many respects Oskison wrote of his landscapes in order to tell about himself.

Besides the primordial emergence of a people, according to Momaday, identities are shaped by the people's interactions with the land. Momaday argues that "the events of one's life take place, *take place*," by which he means that one's life literally takes bits of places which then become inseparable from one's self: "Events do indeed take place; they have meaning in relation to the things around them. And a part of my life happened to take place at Jemez. I existed in that landscape, and then my existence was indivisible with it. I placed my shadow there in the hills, my voice in the wind that ran there. . . . It may be that the old people there watch for me in the streets; it may be so" (*The Names* 142).

In the same way, the Old Indian Territory determined John Milton Oskison. He also left his shadow and his voice there, and he wrote of the places he took in order to write about himself. If we go back to the comparison we made earlier between Eastman's and Oskison's childhood as each told about it, we should add that the landscapes in which their life took place — or the places their life took — were radically different and were bound to shape completely different childhoods. Eastman was raised in the yet untamed wilderness of his ancestors; Oskison grew up in a wilderness the taming of which was already under way, albeit under the plow of the Cherokees if not of the European American pioneers. In Oskison's literature, the taming of the wilderness, at the core of so much American literature, is reenacted by the noble figure of the roper struggling with the runaway steer or the wild brute at a rodeo.

Tales of the Old I.T.

In many respects, Oskison depicted the Indian Territory as the melting pot that the United States was supposed to be for European immigrants. For example, he wrote in "Why Am I an American?" that the children of immigrants in Oklahoma "will sit in the schools with the children of parents from Kansas, from Ohio, from Missouri, and with the dark-skinned mixed-blood children whose mothers and fathers let in the whites upon the Indian reservations and welcomed them into their families" (212). This region, more precisely the northeast corner of what is now Oklahoma — the territory of the Cherokee Nation — could be the place where the "New Indian" could be shaped. His tribe, the Cherokee Nation, was one of the Five Civilized Tribes, so called because they had adopted the European American ways, or — in a less assimilationist phrasing — they had adjusted to the European American ways. Most of Oskison's ancestry was of English stock; he was raised as a farmer and cattle driver; he went to Stanford and Harvard before moving to New York to work as a journalist and financial editor. He was never raised in any traditional Indian way unless one considers — and one probably should — that at the end of the nineteenth century, cattle raising had become a traditional Cherokee way. His mother, from whom he got his Indian ancestry, died when he was very young. My point is that Oskison was no Jacob Eastman. Charles Eastman's father, a warrior made prisoner by the American army, came back to his son, convinced of the superiority of the white man's civilization, to persuade him to reject the Sioux traditional ways. Oskison, however, never was in a situation to repudiate traditions and a lifestyle deemed inferior to the white man's ways. Oskison was raised as a Cherokee multicultural citizen by an English father. Oskison was not an assimilated Indian; he was the result of what he called amalgamation. The Indians he described and fictionalized were very much the same.

The Indian Territory that Oskison depicted in his autobiography and in his Old I.T. stories was a farming and ranching territory, a conquered West whose particularity was that it was conquered by the Cherokees after they were forced to settle there. He was not painting a romantic picture of Indian life in the wilderness. He was depicting a struggling life on a kind of frontier where the people struggling were the Cherokees rather than the white pioneers. Piute activist Sarah Winnemucca and Sioux writer Charles Eastman had known the wilderness and had witnessed white encroachments. Oskison, in some ways, was the result of white encroachment. People like Eastman, Winnemucca, or Mourning Dove are sometimes called transitional Indians because their lives were transformed by a colonizing process. The most striking example is probably Eastman, who was raised as a warrior whose mission would be to avenge his father's supposed death, and who ended up being a physician on the Pine Ridge Reservation. Oskison was not such a transitional Indian, but he lived on a transitional territory and was the product of this territory. This is the transition that his autobiography and his tales reflect.

To my mind, Oskison deserves to be rediscovered because some of his writings are very much worth reading, specifically for the point his *Brothers Three*'s Henry Odell persona made: he wrote about the people and the country he knew. As it happens, what he knew of the country and the people at the center of his fiction writing can be very useful to understand a part of the history of the United States and more specifically a part of Native American history. Ronnow uses George Lukacs's rhetoric to portray Oskison as an "important social spokesm[a]n": "He deserves attention as an important realist writer in the Lukacsian sense. He attempted to be 'articulate in the national voice,' and his words 'arose from a history which is visibly in the making' — a criterion which George Lukacs says identifies important social spokesmen" ("Cherokee Journalist" 2).

His incomplete autobiography and the short stories and essays included in the present book are valuable because they are about a time that was a turning point for a place that still remains widely unknown, at least from a point of view different than the Sooner's: the Indian Territory during its transition to becoming the state of Oklahoma. Moreover, the Indian Territory, a land on which the Cherokees, among others, had learned to escape the condition of the reservation Indian to become successful Indian American farmers, lawyers, journalists, and statesmen, was the ideal setting for the "new Indian" he called for. In that respect, I think that Oskison is the author of western tales that put the Indian — so blatantly overlooked or misrepresented by other writers of the West — back into the picture of the conquest of the West in another way than as a victim or an obstacle to European American conquest. His writings are essential to complete the history of the representations of the Indian.

Before being a financial editor, journalist John Milton Oskison had become, in his own terms, "an acknowledged editorial authority on the West" ("Old I.T.") for the *New York Evening Post*. The short stories he wrote about his western experience also gained him some deserved fame. However, he never got around to publishing a collection of these stories that — he tells us in his autobiography — he would have entitled *Tales of the Old I.T.* You have now such a collection in your hands.

« PART ONE »

Autobiography

A Tale of the Old I.T.

AN AUTOBIOGRAPHY
BY JOHN MILTON OSKISON

Chapter 1

I HAVE thought of myself sometimes as a replica in temperament of my restless, nervous, short-tempered father. I could not tell my own story without first sketching his nomadic life, although I have little material, and no documentation whatever. I have known no one else as reticent about himself in talk as Father; and he never learned to write, except to scrawl his signature.

On a tenant farm somewhere in England, he was born in 1835. When two years old, his parents having died, he was brought to America as an unwanted orphan by an uncle who settled on a farm in Illinois so near St. Louis that an oxteam could haul produce to that market in the hours between supper and dawn. When he was not yet ten years old he was set to driving one of two wagons that made frequent trips between the farm and St. Louis. He remembered with bitterness winter nights on the road, and the agony of staying awake as he trudged along beside the oxen, thinly clothed and badly shod.

There was a neighborhood school, but he was never sent to it, although he recalled being taken to a Sunday school by a cousin. I think of him in his infancy and teens as a waif whose portrait only Dickens could have drawn adequately in words. The one time he talked with me about his boyhood he described himself as sickly, scrawny, half crazy with hatred of his tyrannical uncle. "That sonofabitch," he said, "expected me to die before I grew up, and wanted to get all the work he could out of me while I was alive."

In 1852 California-bound wagon trains were still being formed. One was organized by a neighbor; Father stole away at night to beg to be taken along. The man listened to his plea, looked him over, and said, "I doubt you'd last the trip, son, but — oh, damn it, it'd be no worse than leavin' you to die here, an' you *can* drive oxen." At the start, Father was hidden in a covered wagon, and stayed there until danger of pursuit by his uncle had passed. He was seventeen, and weighed less than sixty pounds, "just skin and bones," he said.[1]

The wagon train boss had a heart. Father said, "He used to come around every day to see that I got plenty to eat, and made me climb into the wagon when I got tired walking and driving the oxen. Toward the end of the trip, after I'd plumped out and felt as spry as a young rooster, he'd come around and laugh and say, 'Well, son, you're goin' to see Californy after all!' He was the finest man I ever knew, and all my life I've felt grateful to him."

On a farm somewhere between Oakland and San Jose, California, Father found work as a hired hand, saved his wages, and planned to attend school. He was nineteen, however, five feet ten, and weighed 170 pounds, before he decided he could afford to knock off work and start his education. The teacher asked about his previous schooling and, when Father said he had not had any, put him in the first grade with boys and girls of six. That was intolerable, and as the teacher insisted he must sit with the first graders he walked out of the schoolhouse and never went back.

Two years in the gold diggings along the American river failed to enrich or satisfy him, and he returned to farmwork in the neighborhood he knew. In speaking of the next eleven years, he said little more than, "If I'd taken the advice of the man I worked for and bought a farm I could have paid for in two or three years, it would be worth a hundred thousand dollars today. But I wasn't of a mind to settle down then."

After fifteen years in California, with his savings, in gold, in a broad money belt, he set out to see New York. He had, meanwhile, taught himself to read and was curious about the metropolis of America. From San Francisco he sailed to Panama, crossed the Isthmus on horseback, and took ship again for New York. About how long he tarried there or how the city impressed him I know little.

From New York he returned to the Illinois farm of unhappy memories. His uncle had died, and the rest of the family received him cordially. Why he decided to go to the Indian Territory I do not know.[2] I can guess that the name attracted, that he sought an opportunity to get acquainted with a people he had hardly more than glimpsed on the way to California. By way of the Texas Road,[3] he reached Tahlequah, the Cherokee Nation tribal capital in 1870.

The Indians he came to know in Indian Territory were not all like the nomadic hunters he had seen on the plains. They were farmers, stockmen, merchants; they ran gristmills and sawmills and saltworks. They had good neighborhood schools and, at Tahlequah, two high schools — the Male and Female Seminaries — staffed by competent teachers from New England.[4] They had a complete system of government under a constitution modeled on that of the United States, district courts and a supreme court, and law enforcement officers. Their chief was a well-educated man, a graduate of Princeton.[5] Among the tribal judges, senators, and councilmen were other graduates of eastern colleges, Dartmouth and Princeton. They published *The Cherokee Advocate*, a weekly newspaper printed half in English and half in the Cherokee characters devised more than forty years before by Sequoyah.[6]

Securing the permit to live and work in the Cherokee Nation that was required of white men, Father found the Cherokees hospitable, friendly, and saw the Nation as a land of plenty and promise. Soon he met my mother, Rachel, dark, soft-spoken, and sweet-faced daughter of parents whose Cherokee name, in English, was Buzzard. Her Indian blood had been mixed with white until she was only a quarter Cherokee. The widow of a white man named Crittenden, she had a four-year-old daughter named Sarah.[7]

When Rachel and Father married, he became by Cherokee law an adopted citizen of the Nation, with all the rights and privileges of any full-blood.

He used his savings to build, not far from Tahlequah, a double log house, with a breezeway between kitchen and living quarters, buy teams, plows, and other needed implements, break sod for and fence farmland, and start a herd. He was thirty-five years old, strong and wiry, eager to make a home and "raise a family." There was, he felt, no limit to the amount of work he could do. He plowed, harrowed, sowed, planted, cultivated and husked corn, cradled oats and wheat at harvest time, and in the hours when he should have rested, rode out after his cattle, bringing in the ailing to doctor and the young to brand, earmark, and castrate (in the case of bull calves). Help was all but impossible to hire. Indians seldom worked for wages. Living simply, they did not need them to supplement the produce of their little farms and the work of their women — spinning, weaving, quilting, soap making, preserving and drying wild and orchard fruits. And aid they gave was freely tendered as a neighborly gesture.[8]

My eldest brother, William, was born in 1872; two years later, I came into the world. My mother was not well, and excessive physical labor had brought Father to the verge of a nervous breakdown. When he realized that the farm and stock enterprise had grown beyond his power to handle alone his action was decisive, and characteristic. He found a buyer for his cattle, horses, mules, the house, and other farm improvements (he could not sell the land, for all land in the Cherokee Nation was communal tribal property). Out of all his possessions he retained only two teams and wagons.[9]

The proceeds of the sale banked with a Tahlequah merchant, he went to Illinois to fetch the cousin, now widowed, who had taken him to Sunday school and been kind to him. With her came her three children, one a boy old enough to drive a team.

That wagon train trip to California in 1852 had saved Father's life. Now in the spring of 1876, he started on another long trip, this time to Oregon, driving slowly, staying as long as he pleased in camps he liked. As mother's time neared, he stopped to call a doctor and she was delivered of a son they named Richard.

They reached the mild Pacific Coast climate before winter set in, explored the Willamette Valley, then returned to the growing town of Portland. There his cousin met and married a man of middle age, and there she and her children stayed. Father gave them one team and wagon, and something besides, to help establish a home, before driving with the rest of us to the California neighborhood in which he had worked. It was in his mind to settle there, but he found no land cheap enough for him to buy.

The trip had restored Father's health, but Mother was still ailing and longing to return to the Cherokees, saying that it would not be good to die in a strange land. So Father went back, on a railroad train, and she died as she had wished to do at her old family home. By now, my stepsister Sarah could, in a fashion, fill the role of housekeeper.

Father did not care to settle again in the Tahlequah neighborhood, but bought the improvements on a Pryor Creek farm some forty miles to the north. He was not satisfied, however, and moved to a raw prairie location four miles west of Vinita. A half mile from Cabin Creek, he built a story-and-a-half frame house: sitting room with fireplace, a bedroom and attached kitchen downstairs, and two bedrooms upstairs. A dug well, barn, and horselot came next. The house he painted white; the barn, with stalls for eight horses and mules, a hayloft and attached corncrib and granary, was, of course, painted red. He set out an orchard of apple, peach, and plum trees, and maples for shade in the yard, which he enclosed with pickets.[10]

Between the house and creek he fenced and turned the sod on eighty acres of level cropland. West of the house and orchard, he made a twenty-acre pasture for horses and milch cows.

This was the first home I can remember. The first clear memory I have of life there is of Father, on a hot summer day, smelling not unpleasantly of sweat, his bearded face split by a rare grin, prying me loose from the sloping stake of the stake-and-rider rail fence surrounding our vegetable garden and sending me staggering to the house. His mild astonishment at finding me there asleep, and his words, live in my mind, "Jinks, dogged if I don't believe you could go to sleep standin' up!"

I was not only a sleepyhead but also a worrisome forgetter. Often, tagging along behind Father in the field or on a fence building job, I would be sent to the barn for a needed tool or a pocketful of wire staples. On the way, such an insignificant diversion as a meadowlark rising from the grass or a half-grown rabbit hopping into view took my mind completely off my mission. Where the lark nested, how far it could fly, how it made the song I tried to imitate; how a baby rabbit was fed — did it suck its mother's teats, like a calf, or just begin nibbling grass or garden lettuce as soon as it was born? — these were matters of absorbing interest.

At times, I arrived at the barn before realizing that I had been sent to fetch something. But what? I could not remember! Trembling with fear of Father's anger, I must go back to him and ask. After my first wool-gathering excursion of this kind, my incredible forgetfulness ceased to amuse him, and I received a lusty swat that sent me off again sniffling and muttering, "Dam little ol' rabbit!"

Other distractions were mice in the corncrib that fouled the good-smelling ears whose shucks they nibbled through to get at the grain. I liked it when Tobey, the big-headed, ragged-eared old barn cat, sat alertly at my side, hopeful that the next ear of corn I moved would uncover a mouse. Forgetting how many ears I had been told to shuck for the four mules and Father's saddle horse, I would go on and on, pretending that the cat and I were fellow mousers, until Father's shout, "Jinks, come in to supper!" sent me scrambling backwards out of the crib to drag the bushel basket through the alley between the stalls and pile corn hastily into the animals' feedboxes. In my hurry, I gave some of the animals less than their proper ration, and some more than they could eat — a waste that angered Father when he discovered partly eaten ears mixed with the slobbery-wet cobs. Counting the cobs, he would roar, "Great Jehosephat, fifteen ears for that ornery Jack mule!"

Our nearest neighbor, a red-haired peppery white man named Jess Thomas, who had married into the Cherokee tribe as Father had done, lived half a mile away. Will and I made friends with his son Hoot, went fishing for perch in Cabin Creek with him, but Father was too like quick-tempered Jess to get along with him. Our next nearest neighbor, a mile west, "Old Man Fritz," worked a small farm. A bandy-legged man not quite five feet tall, with a gray billygoat beard, he was dwarfed by his enormously fat Cherokee wife; when they drove past our house on the way to Vinita, I wondered why the spring seat of the wagon, sagging as far as it could at her end, did not collapse.

We all liked old Fritz, were fascinated by his funny German dialect, and by his antics in haying time when he came to build our stacks. The men who pitched the hay up to him often threatened to bury him, but never did. Sometimes they scared him by tossing up snakes that had been dragged in by the bullrakes. His son Joe became the favorite butt for brother Will's rough teasing and his slavish admirer.[11]

The Shanahans lived a mile to the southwest, near the point where the Frisco railroad crosses Pawpaw Creek.[12] Father's friendship with Pat was real, but qualified by an English-born man's instinctive suspicion of professional Irishism. I have heard him rail, "The damned old flannel-mouth don't know he's living in America; he reads nothing but the *Irish World*!" The weekly *Globe-Democrat* of St. Louis supplied Father with news and shaped his politics.[13] I used to read in it the sermons of Rev. T. Dewitt Talmadge,[14] and wonder what they were all about. The Shanahan boys, Ned and Tim, were older than Will, and we saw little of them. Their sister Jennie, however, became a good friend of Sarah's. Before we came into the neighborhood, surveyors for the Frisco railroad had proposed to stake a right-of-way across Pat's productive fields. He said no, and for weeks (so the local legend ran) held them off with a shotgun.

Three miles west of us, on Pawpaw Creek, was what we called the full-blood settlement, including a relative of my mother whom we knew as Aunt Betsy, and her two grown-up daughters Liza and Jennie.[15] Twice, at Aunt Betsy's urging, Father sent me to stay a week with them. I could not speak Cherokee, and they knew no English, yet we got on together perfectly. I reveled in their loving care, and thought their homegrown fare better than anything I had ever tasted.[16]

Center of the full-blood settlement was the one-room log schoolhouse, warmed by a smoky wood-burning fireplace, that also served as a church. Bear Timson,[17] beloved by everyone, preached there in the Cherokee language on Sundays and worked a fertile creek-bottom farm on weekdays. His nearest neighbors were Jake Longtail and Jimmy Horsefly,[18] the one thrifty and prosperous, the other scatterbrained and experimental. Once Father was both amused and chagrined when, after lending Jimmy twenty dollars and the date of the promised repayment having passed, he began traveling a road to Vinita that did not pass our house. "Jinks," Father said to me, "if you want to lose a friend lend him money. I like Jimmy, and feel sorry for him. He ought to know I don't care if he never pays back that twenty."

I was nearly six years old when young and lovely Fanny Bly, lately graduated from the Cherokee Female Seminary, came to teach the Pawpaw school, boarding with us and driving to school in our buggy with Will and me.[19] After supper, which she helped Sarah to prepare, Miss Fanny guided us through our homework. Will had no enthusiasm for book learning, but for me books opened a new and fascinating world. I plunged into it avidly. That pleased Miss Fanny, who pushed me along as fast as I could go. More pleased was Father; he wanted me, as he wanted all his children, to achieve the education that had been denied him. He could not, however, overcome Sarah's stubborn resistance to schooling.

Those first months at the Pawpaw school seem now like fragments out of an incredibly remote past, yet on the very day I set down these recollections of Miss Fanny (May 7, 1946) she attended the one hundredth anniversary of the opening of the Cherokee Female Seminary,[20] representing the class of 1879. From time to time since Miss Fanny gave me my first schooling I have encountered her and been embarrassed by her praise of me as her star pupil. Perhaps I have embarrassed her, also, by swearing to her in the presence of friends that I fell in love with her at sight and never recovered. Her career as a teacher ended when she married a deputy United States marshal who had much to do with curbing the depredations of white outlaws when Indian Territory, where the tribal courts lacked jurisdiction over them, became a favorite refuge.[21]

Before school opened the next year, Father married again, and Miss Fanny did not return to teach the Pawpaw school. My stepmother, a widowed white woman, brought to our home a son and daughter both older than brother Will, and an uncertain temper. It was not a harmonious household. Will, Dick, and I resented our stepmother, brother, and sister. Sarah quarreled with our other stepsister, and sulked at giving over housekeeping responsibilities.[22]

Within a year, twin sons were born to my stepmother. Alfred died two days after birth; Albert, frail, with great staring blue eyes and an infectious smile, became Father's best-beloved son and special care.[23]

Discord in the home, and the hard work of developing the Cabin Creek farm, threatened to wreck Father's nerves for the second time. Again his thoughts turned to California as a cure and a haven. Again he sold all stock and farm equipment, rented the house and farmland, and put us all into an emigrant car routed to Sacramento by way of the Katy, Texas and Pacific, and Southern Pacific railroads.[24] Three memories only of that trip have stuck in my mind: the board seats that became beds by night, made up with our own bedclothes; a cookstove at the end of our car, where our meals were prepared; and the man who shot at antelope with a Winchester rifle through an open window.

From Sacramento Father took us to a farm, near the small town of Elmira,[25] that had been recommended by Tom Melbourne, brother of our Indian Territory neighbor. Melbourne's own three hundred acres, on a gently sloping hillside a mile away, comprised a big vineyard, orchards of apricot and almond trees, and wheat and barley fields. Childless, he and his wife occupied a big two-story house in a grove of tall eucalyptus trees. To balance a barn ample to care for a score of stout teams was a winery which he had been stocking for years. To Will, Dick, and me, whom Melbourne made welcome, it seemed a truly magnificent establishment.

Our school, a sun-bleached box-like building a half mile from home, I remember for only two reasons. First, a boy taught me at recess time to lasso lizards with loops made in the end of wild-oat straws, to be released surreptitiously under the girls' desks after school took up. Second, in a pole-and-gunnysack shelter for horses ridden by some of the students, I first saw human sexual intercourse demonstrated by a shameless boy of fifteen and a girl a year younger. That shocked me terribly. I thought that people ought not to act like the animals I had seen being bred on the farm!

Two thirds of our 120 acres was wheatland, and the rest sheep pasture. Our small farmhouse was set in a grove of trees, eucalyptus, apricots, and figs. Nothing I had ever tasted before, or have eaten since, seemed as delicious as the dead ripe black figs from our trees.

In winter, when the young wheat was two or three inches high, myriads of low-flying ducks and geese from the marshes below Suisun swarmed in to feed on it. The flights began coming over after dark, and we stood in the yard to listen to the swish and whistle of wings and the blasts of shotguns fired at the sounds by our neighbors. Birds thus knocked down might or might not be found at daybreak. Father would not do night shooting, saying that he didn't want the thought of a crippled and suffering bird on his conscience.

During our second summer, an epidemic hit our small flock of sheep and all but wiped it out. I remember going with Father and Will to help skin the dead animals, so bloated and sun-ripened that their stench was sickening. The pelts could be sold for the wool and for tanning, and Father was not one to allow anything of value to go to waste. Vultures by day and snarling dogs at night worried the carcasses; their obscene squawkings and growlings invaded my dreams, along with the menace of the monsters I had read about in a gruesome book for children called "Jack the Giant Killer."[26] Sometimes I woke screaming, wet all over with perspiration, my heart thumping violently. Will and I slept together, and when I roused him by my screams I could count on painful jabs from his elbows — never the yearned-for comfort of my stepmother's arms, her soothing voice and quieting kiss.

To escape the friction of the household, both my new stepsister and stepbrother left, she to go into service in a home in Napa Valley and he to do chores and light farmwork at the same place. They wrote that they were well pleased, and then, as though she had fought off the creeping menace of tuberculosis only to stand by her children, my stepmother succumbed to invalidism. She begged Father to take her away, said that the hot Sacramento Valley was stifling her. He agreed, and soon found a buyer for the farm who paid twice what it had cost. Before we could start for Texas, however, where Tom Melbourne's brother had found a farm for Father, my stepmother died.

Her children chose to remain in California when we took the train for Fort Worth.

On Bird creek,[27] six miles from Fort Worth, our 160-acre farm was half good upland pasture and half rich bottom farmland that had been badly cultivated and was overrun with weeds and crabgrass. Father stocked the pasture with milch cows and work teams, and undertook to grow cotton, corn, and a small patch of wheat on the rich black gumbo soil ordering the creek.

Excessive rainfall, the first spring, made plowing almost impossible after crops were planted, and Father, Will, Dick, and I cultivated the corn and cotton with hoes; and where hoes could not be used without risk of chopping down young cornstalks and cotton plants, we pulled out weeds and crabgrass by hand. Then came the thinning of the cotton plants. For two months and more, we each carried a coarse file for sharpening hoe blades. Father and Will wore out two hoes apiece; my second was well worn; and Dick's first was down to a two-inch blade before we finished hoeing. It was hard, back-tiring work, but we kept the crops free of weeds, and they flourished.

Our ten acres of wheat, cut with a reaper, bound into bundles by wisps of wheat stalks, shocked and threshed in an afternoon by a steam threshing machine that served the neighborhood, supplied a welcome diversion in our labors, and filled to overflowing the two-hundred-bushel granary Father had built. Then came a short respite from hard work, during which Father was persuaded by a young man to send me to a class at the Birdville schoolhouse where he taught me and fourteen girls Spencerian penmanship. Our teacher could draw a wonderful bird with a pen, but he had little control over the sex-conscious girls of fifteen and sixteen who "deviled" him and me unmercifully.

Harvest meant daylight-to-dark work with wagons and teams for cornhusking and cribbing, cotton picking, hauling and marketing, with chores and milking to be done by lantern light before dawn and after dark. How spent we boys were before cleaning and folding away the long canvas bags we had dragged between the rows of heavily burdened cotton plants at picking time!

But we had our reward. Father estimated that the fields had produced fifty bushels of corn to the acre, and almost two bales of cotton. The farm, stock, and machinery was paid for, there was money in the bank, and after the crops were hauled to market at Fort Worth over the sticky black road, there were only fences to mend and the daily chores to do, except go to school at Birdville.

Will and I walked to school, I to become absorbed in books, he to get all the fun he could out of noon and recess periods. At home, I read Dickens, Scott, and Reade; Will favored "Old Cap Collier," and dreamed of becoming a hard-riding, straight-shooting hombre in a wild west that was already hardly more than a tradition.[28] One Saturday, while Father was away for a week, having gone to look over the place in Indian Territory he had rented to a tenant, Will proposed that we haul a load of corn to Fort Worth, sell it, say nothing to Father, and spend the proceeds as we pleased. I protested, but was persuaded. I don't remember how much the corn fetched, but it was enough to pay for a nickel-plated .32-caliber pistol Will wanted, a box of cartridges, and to buy beer in a saloon we entered with Simon and Bummer Melbourne. I gagged at the taste of beer, and went home quaking with fear lest Father find out about our adventure.

One Saturday in the late fall as Will and I and a neighbor boy were fishing for perch in Bird creek, Bob Hardy said a thing that upset me violently. He had overheard his father say that my father had been seen entering a whorehouse in the Fort Worth district known as "Hell's Half Acre." Bob's explanatory gestures as he added, "You know what he went in there for," recalled the scene in the California schoolyard, and I flew at him in fury, crying, "That's a dirty lie; Pa wouldn't do such a thing!" I tried to beat his brains out, and Will had all he could do to pull me off. Whether or not Father did seek release from the tension of a strongly sexed and seasonally idle worker in the arms of a prostitute, I didn't, of course, know, but Bob Hardy's manner made the thought intolerably ugly.

To the Hardys, whiskey drinking was also an evil practice. Father kept a jug under his bed, and mixed his before-supper toddy untroubled by his children's presence. When we first found it, Will and I, of course, had to sample its contents. Father came in on us as I was sputtering, laughed, and said, "Jinks, I reckon you're too young yet for that!"

The short visit to our Indian Territory farm gave Father an idea that he translated into action two years later. He saw the beginning of the cattle business on a large scale in the Cherokee Nation. Texas owners of herds of longhorn steers had devised a way to utilize the Nation's rich grazing land by making real or fake sales of cattle to Cherokee citizens, shipping up in the spring trainloads of three- and four-year-olds, along with their own cowboys to look after them, until they fattened on good bluestem grass and were sent in late fall to market at St. Louis or Chicago.[29]

Our second and third crops, made with less backbreaking work than the first, added materially to Father's bank account; he saw his way to becoming a bona fide cattleman in the Territory. Instead of buying longhorns, however, he proposed to put yearling steers on our Big Cabin range. He found that he could buy them from Tarrant Country farmers at from five to seven dollars a head. He would send them up by train, hold them until they were three or four years old, and, he believed, make more money than he could by buying mature steers and grazing them only one summer.

One third crop sold, Father found a buyer for the farm; and again our work in reconditioning proved profitable, for the price he received was almost twice what he had paid. The teams and two saddle horses he kept;

and with two wagonloads of household goods we drove north to reoccupy our Cabin Creek home.

With the family settled and spring nearing, Father said, "Jinks, you and I will go back now and pick up the yearlings." He chose me to accompany him because I was as good at figures as I was at reading and writing. I could draw checks for the young cattle, check feed bills and freight charges, and keep a tally of the calves he bought. Working out of Fort Worth, where Father rented a room and two saddle horses, we combed scores of farms, picked the good milklot calves he wanted, and had them driven to a Fort Worth feedlot. When he had bought the four hundred he figured he could afford to hold to maturity, they were loaded into cattle cars consigned to Big Cabin switch. We went with them, riding the train caboose.

It was early March, too early for new grass to sustain them, when we unloaded the yearlings. Father had foreseen the necessity for feeding, and had bought hay from his friend, J. O. Hall, a farmer-turned-cattleman who had gone in for summer-grazed longhorns.[30]

According to instructions, Will and Henry Falling,[31] a hired Cherokee cowboy, met us at Big Cabin switch with a team and wagon, a tent, provisions for camping, and saddle horses for Father and Henry. Sleet was driving into their faces as we turned the dogies out of the stockyard and headed them east toward the feedlot Mr. Hall had put at our disposal. As we penned them at noon, he came out to ask us in to dinner and offer Father the use of a wagon fitted with a hayrack. Before the first afternoon feeding got under way, Will and I made friends with the young Hall children, Clint, Ludie, and Janie, and were warmed by Mrs. Hall's gracious hospitality.[32]

Will returned to our Cabin Creek home, leaving Father, Henry, and me to pitch the tent, cook supper, and take a final look at the fed and rested yearlings.

As long as it was necessary to feed, Father turned the yearlings out in the daytime, and drove them in to the hay at night. With the coming of grass the little steers ranged far and fast in search of greener pasturage, and I, whose duties had been to stay at camp and prepare meals of Dutch oven bread, beans, bacon, canned stuff, and coffee, was now drafted to help keep them from trying too far and corral them at night. My mount was a stout gray mule. I rode Jack bareback, and what with my sore buttocks and thighs and the mule's inbred stubbornness, I suffered such pain and humiliation as I have never felt since. Trying to force Jack into a run in order to head a fractious yearling, kicking his ribs with my boot-heels and laying on with a hickory stick, I called up every cuss word I had ever heard to damn that gray beast for his reluctant stiff-legged travesty of a gallop. For Father and Henry, the mule and I were a comedy team that never failed to amuse.[33]

The evening came when the yearlings refused hay. Next day, Mr. Hall and his hired man helped us brand and earmark them. Recalling the great trotting stallion Jay Eye See he had read about, Father had the letters JIC welded on his branding iron, to be burned on the left hip; his earmarks were a swallow fork in the left and underbit in the right.[34] Later, in the *Indian Chieftain*, Vinita's weekly newspaper, there appeared the black silhouette of a steer so branded and earmarked, together with the notice that the brand and earmarks identified cattle belonging to "John Oskison, range four miles west of Vinita." Some forty other men in the Cherokee Nation also advertised their brands in the two or three columns of space sold to them for the purpose by the *Chieftain*.[35]

We drove four hundred little steers, minus five that had died in spite of special feeding, to our Cabin Creek horselot, held them overnight, and turned them out next morning to range as they would. Thereafter, it was Henry Falling's job to keep them within a reasonable distance of home, and drive in for doctoring any that had become infected by screw worms in brand sores or gashes made by the horns of bullying longhorn steers. Days we were not occupied with farmwork, Father, Will, or I rode out to help Henry.

Father bought a saddle for me, but Jack remained my only "cow hoss." I became accustomed to his stiff gait and hard mouth, and learned how to control his erratic bursts of speed when I roweled him with the spurs for which I had traded. I thought, with some pride, I bet I'm the only mule-mounted cowboy in the world!

Fall roundups meant for us that Henry joined one big outfit that worked the eastern half of the Cherokee ranges from Arkansas river north to the Kansas line, and that Father (later Will) rode with another that covered the western half. Practically all longhorns rounded up and cut out to their owners were driven to shipping points and sent off to market. Our JIC dogies were returned to our Cabin Creek range for winter feeding.

With grain harvested and corn laid by, summer became a long haying season. In the five or six weeks before frost, Father figured to cut and stack a ton of hay for each animal. To be on the safe side, we would stack five hundred tons of the abundant wild meadow grass nearest our farm. My first job in haying was to hitch Jack to a sulky rake and, when the mowed grass had dried exactly right for stacking, roll it up in long windrows for sledding to stack sites by "go devil" bull rakes. Often, this meant missing the noon meal in order to rake the early morning cutting; both Jack and I resented Father's command at such times, "Keep going!"

Goaded by Father, I worked out from my arithmetic book an approximately accurate formula for measuring the tonnage of a haystack; we had half of a stack left over, plus a full haymow when April brought ample grass for the steers.

Two seasons of the sulky rake brought me promotion to the mowing machine. Dick fell heir to Jack and the sulky rake, and greatly expanded his profane vocabulary, while I sat behind a span of big black mules, Kate and Bess, that stepped along without urge of whip, goad, or shouts. My only grief as I cut down the meadows of wild sweetgrass came from forcing myself to stay awake as I listened to the soporific hum of the sickle, or control my own and the team's panic when we stirred up a hornet's nest and the hornets swarmed out to sting the mules and me impartially. In the hour of nooning, too, while longing to nap with the other workers in the shade, I must find someone to turn the grindstone while I sharpened the seemingly innumerable sections of the seven-foot sickle.

Sundays in haying time meant going with Father to bathe in the deepest pool we could find in Cabin Creek, putting off smelly sweat-soaked shirts and drawers, getting into clean garments. I recall my first sight of Father nude, and trying to connect his spare frame and gray hair and beard with some patriarchal picture I had seen; it may have been a Doré illustration of the Bible or Dante.[36] Then the noon meal, long hours of sleep in the shade, and finally evening chores to which I went reluctantly.

For three years there was no schooling. Winter mornings meant for Will and me hauling hay from the fenced stacks (sometimes on windy days loads blew over) to spread on a dry feedground sheltered from the cold north wind, while Father and Henry saw to it that every steer was driven in to the hay and that the weak and ailing were put in the barnlot and given extra rations of shelled corn. Many afternoons Will and I spent cutting and hauling from Cabin Creek timber, wood for the kitchen stove and fireplace. Then milking, watering, feeding, and currying the teams. Then supper — often only big bowls of corn meal mush and milk — sometimes a dishpan full of popcorn afterwards, popped over the fireplace coals. Then the rush upstairs to bed in the cold, first removing boots, socks, and pants in front of the fire. Little Bert slept with Father in a bed he had put in the living room.

Riding the range with Henry Falling, as the only mule-mounted cowboy in captivity, I attracted the amused attention of the Texas and part-Indian punchers who worked with the longhorns. Out of that seasoned, fearless lot I came to know well such expert riders and ropers as John Franklin, Aud Ryder, Blake Gore, Jim Kell, and the professional bronco-buster Henry Woolman. I have forgotten the name of the educated Texas cowboy who once impressed me enormously by describing someone as an antediluvian hand-me-down. With Father, I visited the homes of longhorn owners Bill Halsell, J. O. Hall, Nat Skinner, Boog Little, and Judge Clark, heard cattle discussed as property, and hot debate concerning the policies of Grover Cleveland.[37]

Vivid pictures of those three school-less years have stuck in my mind: big herds of longhorns trotting, their horns striking together like clacking castanets; sudden rushes of infuriated steers at mounted cowboys, and agile evasions by their trained mounts; the swirl of ropes thrown expertly over horns and under hind feet, and the taming effect of tobacco juice squirted into a stretched-out outlaw steer's eyes; late fall fires sweeping for miles across the prairie, flames bursting high in tall ungrazed bluestem grass like colossal leaping dragons. Such running fires meant for us night-long fights, backfiring and whipping out flames with wetted gunny sacks, to save our stacks and the rank dead grass we valued as bedding for our cattle. Like the long days with hoe and dragging cotton sack in Texas, they were among the first of the prolonged physical strains that taxed my heart.

Stepsister Sarah married Sam Calvert,[38] who had come from an Indian farm and had worked for Father, and went to help her man, who, with Father's assistance, undertook to develop a prairie farm west of the Pawpaw Indian settlement. Then Will, Dick, and I took turns at cooking and keeping house until Dick proved best at indoor work, fighting flies and ants as he prepared the meals, and keeping little Bert out of mischief.

Looking back, I have thought of our life at that time as a bleak, pagan existence. It was unbroken by children's parties, Thanksgiving and Christmas celebrations, and churchgoing. One thing only dominated our minds, Father's iron determination to make our cattle venture succeed.

Dick and I understood better than Will that this would be a time of temporary hardship only. Will rebelled in sullen silence for months, then fought openly against Father's stern discipline. He left home at fourteen, drifted from neighbor to neighbor, working at various jobs, and finally headed for Colorado, where he fancied he would find the adventure he craved in a wild west he had dreamed about. I grieved in secret for Will; he had been an exciting if often harsh and overbearing companion. However, the comparative peace in the home that followed his departure was welcome.

After Will went, I discovered from the Donnelly boys[39] the Timber hill Sunday school, and Sunday after Sunday I rode there on my saddle mule. On the third Sunday, in the interval of dawdling about before going home, I found courage to speak to Clara LeForce, a girl of my own age whose natural shyness was enhanced by embarrassment due to her slightly crossed eyes. That defect mattered not at all to me, and I dared to ask if I might be her escort the following Sunday. She said yes, and like the little lady she was paid no attention to the gibes of boys who thought it screamingly funny to see me on a mule squiring a cross-eyed girl.

Through more than a year of early adolescence Clara was my steady girl. We liked the Sunday-evening picnic suppers with her family in Cabin Creek timber, and the play parties she asked me to attend. At these parties she steered me through the unfamiliar routines of such games as spin the plate, going to Jerusalem, and one where we marched to the accompaniment of a song that began, "King William was King James' son, and from the royal race he sprung." We became close friends.[40]

Clara, too, liked books, and told me of the pirated cheap-paper reprints one could get from an Augusta, Maine, publisher by sending a dime for each one.

Among the pamphlet stories she and I acquired with dimes our fathers gave to encourage our appetite for reading were many packed with sentimental trash, but also some that stuck in my mind a long time because of a literary quality I could only vaguely sense. It was from these limp reprints that I first came to know Stevenson's *Treasure Island* and Kipling's *Plain Tales from the Hills* and *Soldiers Three*.[41]

Chapter 2

Our first shipment of fat steers went off in the late fall after they had been fed through two winters and grazed three summers. Father selected 200 sleek, prime animals out of the 340 we were able to round up, consigned them to a commission man at the Chicago stockyards, and rode the caboose of the train that hauled them.

As we drove the cattle to Vinita, Father said, "I wouldn't be surprised if they bring five cents a pound."

"What do you reckon they'll weigh?" I asked.

"Eleven hundred; maybe a little more," he guessed.

When I met him with a saddle horse on his return, he showed me the check he had received before depositing it in the Vinita bank. It was something over eleven thousand. You guessed mighty close, Pa!" I said, and asked, grinning, "What are you going to do with all that money?"

"For one thing, Jinks," he answered with deep satisfaction, "you can go to school again, you and Dick, as long as you want to. Bert'll be old enough to go too, before we know it." He did not refer to him, but I thought Will was in his mind, and that perhaps he hoped his errant son might come back, submit to the pattern of life as we lived it, and continue his schooling.

Of course I expected to ride Jack to and from Vinita each day of school after Father decided upon Willie Halsell College, rather than Worcester Academy.[42] However, he surprised me by saying, "Jinks, you'll get along faster if you live in town. You can board at Mrs. Cooper's, where Jim Mehlin's boy stays."

I would like that. I remembered Charlie Mehlin, a boy of my own age, driving a wagon in to our place at dusk one winter's days ahead of fifty fat hogs that his father was following on foot. They had come nearly fifteen miles since daybreak and, when they had rested overnight in our hoglot, would be driven on to Vinita next day. I remembered evenings, after supper, when Father and Jim Mehlin made talk that fascinated me about the world as they saw it.[43]

"Aunt Alice" Cooper's big house, known as The Annex, provided homes for some twenty boys who could not be accommodated in the living quarters of the three-story-and-basement brick building, set in the middle of a quarter section of pasture, that was Willie Halsell College. Aunt Alice, her two lively and hardworking daughters, Alice and Oneida, and a hired girl fed us and cared for our rooms. Because Charlie Mehlin was one of her favorites, and also because of the promptings of her big heart, Aunt Alice took pains to make me feel at home. One thing she did was to convert me, tactfully, from sleeping in my underwear to the use of nightshirts.[44]

The college was one in name only; students included boys and girls in all grades from the first to the ninth. It had been established by the Methodist Church, and completed with money given by W. E. (Bill) Halsell as a memorial to a deceased daughter. A patriarchal looking ex-preacher, appropriately named Bishop, served as president.[45] With his wife and a small grandson whom we called the Pest, he lived in the college, fed those who roomed there, and prayed fervently every morning to the assembled school. I cannot remember either the names or personalities of any of the other teachers employed to guide the 150 roomers and day students.

We used all of the 160 acres of school pasture as a playground, sharing it with a herd of cows and yearlings. Of the considerable number of boys who rode in on horseback from farm and ranch homes, two were good enough ropers to catch, during noon recess and after school, stout yearlings and challenge the rest of us to ride them. One who accepted the challenge eagerly we called Rabbit, the grinning, likable son of a Verdigris River cattleman named Clem Rogers.[46] The boy, of course, was Will Rogers, later to become as well known in America as Mark Twain—and for much the same reason.[47]

Vinita schooldays meant release from the hard physical labor (too varied to be called drudgery) of the farm, the consciousness that I had earned the release by helping Father to make money on the steers, and the certainty that he would make more. I tackled textbooks as avidly as any winter-gaunted old cow ever crowded up to a feed trough filled with corn. Games attracted me, too, one old cat, rounders, baseball, and the crude beginnings of football.[48]

As in the case of the schoolless years, incidents of that unconventional

Willie Halsell experience stand out in memory: my vicarious feeling of guilt when an opulent black sheep student from Georgia opened a bureau drawer to show me a hundred boxes of forbidden Sweet Caporal cigarettes, each containing the picture of an actress; an evening at Aunt Alice's when I helped to subdue a crazy drunk boy who had failed to realize the potency of the bootleg whiskey he had somehow obtained; another evening in the loft of a big barn in town when three of us joined the son of the barn's owner in passing around and drinking gingerly from a jug of liquor and wondering who the strange girl was who came up to drink with us.

One of my friends was Ewing Halsell, son of the school's benefactor.[49] He made flattering reports to his mother and father about me as a student, and I was asked to stay overnight in the big brick Halsell home. After supper, Mr. Halsell asked me to help him with certain accounts he wanted to check before going to Texas to buy cattle. We got through them an hour before the midnight train left; he kept me in his bedroom-study to talk about cattle, compliment Father on his small success, and inquire into my ambitions. I was thrilled when I saw him put into the little valise he packed for the trip a 45 Colt "hogleg" pistol, a reminder that all men did not agree with Father that you're more apt to get hurt if you carry a gun than if you don't.

J. Gore Jr., son of a cattleman, who lived at The Annex, loved to tell of the exploits of his cowboy brother, Blake. I recall one that ran like this: "Blake's ridin' along by the Katy tracks yon side of Bluejacket where it's uphill for trains goin' north when a slow freight comes puffin' up an' the engineer leans out of the cab an' yells, 'Hi, leather pants!' Blake lopes in close an' yells back, 'Hi, dirty face!' They keep on joshin' back an' forth till the engineer finally says, 'Aw, go skip yer rope!' So then Blake shakes out a loop an' says, 'If you'll lean out of that cab a leetle further, I'll rope you an' drag you out.' But the engineer just laughs an' draws back, so Blake says, 'I'll rope your damned ol' engine then!' He shore done her, too, spurred up an' slung his loop over the smokestack. Darned near busted the saddle horn the rope was tied to an' drug Blake's horse under the wheels before the rope broke. You shore can't faze ol' Blake!"

After the second year at Willie Halsell, I lived in the college building and studied under the guidance of W. E. Rowsey, a young Vanderbilt University graduate who had succeeded Grandpa Bishop as president. His younger brother J. E., whose small stature prompted us to call him, out of his hearing, Peanut, and a youth named Dugger were the males of the faculty.[50] Two young women, teachers of music and art, completed it. I studied under neither of the girls, but the memory of Miss Laura Croom, the art instructor, was kept alive for years by the "Yard of Roses" she copied and presented to me as a graduation gift.[51] Some of the boys explained the present by saying that Miss Croom had a crush on me.

I carried the Yard of Roses to college with me, and in a letter telling her how well it looked on the wall of my room, I recalled the ride Miss Croom and I took in a "borrowed" buggy the evening John Barrett, Rube Comstock, and I competed for the W. S. Dugger gold medal for oratory. I recalled her confident prediction that my performance would win the medal. On that moonlight evening drive, from which we returned only a minute before the buggy's owner came out to wonder why his team was sweating, it had not occurred to me to try guiding the horses with one hand. As for kissing the teacher![52]

Before the spring term of 1893 ended, we began to hear from those who had visited it alluring accounts of the World's Fair at Chicago. With three other boys eager to go, I plotted the strategy to be used in persuading our fathers to finance the trip. We decided to concentrate on the argument that Frank Walker, one of us four, was twenty years old and capable of managing the trip and looking after the others. We would assume that, of course, the cost meant nothing to such opulent ranchmen as Clem Rogers, Mr. Walker, and Father. It worked, and the day after school closed Frank and Jim Walker, Will Rogers, and I took the train for Chicago. Frank decided upon an overnight stop in St. Louis so that we might hit the fair next day fresh for a first evening's preliminary look around.

Spotting us for the country lads we were, the train news butcher undertook an intensive sales campaign, urging upon us apples, oranges, candy, Sweet Caporal cigarettes, and such magazines as *Harper's Weekly*, the *New York Ledger*, and *Leslie's Popular Monthly*. When we proved to be poor customers for these innocuous items, he dropped copies of the *Police Gazette* on our knees; and finally, with a wink and a whispered warning not to let it be seen by other passengers, he thrust at us a cheap-paper pamphlet entitled, "Only a Boy."

Illustrations made perfectly plain the gist of the story. We fell for it. Frank paid the fifty cents it cost, and jotted down the figure in the expense account he kept. Huddled close, we took turns riffling the pages and reading in loud whispers the hottest passages. I have been told that "Only a Boy" is a classic of American pornographic literature, comparable to the rare English item "Fanny Hill."[53]

In St. Louis, Frank led us to the Green Tree Hotel near the levee. We ate a late supper, then sat in the lobby trying to appear as men-of-the-worldly as the cigar-smoking regulars. The man who approached us with a cordial "Howdy, boys" was probably a racetrack tout. He spotted Will Rogers's small, trim physique and alert manner and suggested, "Bud, you look like you'd make a good jockey. Can you ride?"

"A little bit," Will admitted, grinning. Jim Walker added, "You ought to see him ride yearlings!"

"Say, do they race where you boys come from?"

"Yearling steers, he means," Will corrected, "and we sure don't race them dogies."

We went to bed, the four of us in two wide beds in one room, taunting Will: "Bud, I bet you'd make a rip-snortin' jock!" and "Say, Rabbit, why don't you learn to ride a horse, with a saddle and bridle, and go to the races?"

"Aw," Will sent us into spasms of laughter with the retort, "you fellows remember I'm 'only a boy.'"

Frank found for us two cubbyhole rooms in a barracks-like wooden building just outside the World's Fair grounds that cost only seventy-five cents a day for each of us. Will and I slept in one, and Frank and his brother in the other. Cots, tin pitchers and wash basins, nails on which to hang clothes, electric ceiling lights, and cloth curtains for the small square windows amply met our needs. We ate twenty-five-cent meals in fairground restaurants. We spent a wholly satisfying week scuttling from exhibit to exhibit, riding the Ferris wheel and the intramural railway, trying the shows on The Streets of Cairo that proved less exciting than the promises of their barkers, and testing other attractions of the Midway Plaisance. To us the discovery, in a western supply house exhibit, of a wonderful silver-decorated saddle and bridle priced at $250 was far more important than the Rembrandts and Corots in the Palace of Fine Arts. However, we did like Rosa Bonheur's "Horse Fair."

Will endorsed it heartily, "Them overgrown broncs wouldn't be any good to ride, but they'd sure make a he-man plow team!"[54]

Home from the fair, I spent the summer doing the usual farmwork, cutting hay, and riding after our cattle on a long-legged, fast-stepping horse named Rowdy (Jack had been honorably retired).

Days in the saddle began before sunrise and ended after dark. I rode out with Henry Falling, but usually separated from him soon after in order that we might cover as much territory as possible. On those daylong rides, especially in the afternoons when hunger stimulated the imagination, I began recalling some of the characters in the fiction I had read, and the sort of detail used by the writers I liked best. Gradually it dawned on me that many of the characters in my favorite stories were remarkably like real people. From that thought, I progressed to another, Why wouldn't the folks of our neighborhood make interesting characters in stories? Why couldn't such scenes and incidents as fast-running prairie fires, roundups, night rides of quietly gathered posses to nab cattle thieves, spectacular fights between deputy United States marshals and train robbers, the violent rebellion against Father's hard discipline of brother Will, be used in stories?[55]

I began to outline in my mind crude plots, and assign roles to Father, Henry Falling, Old Man Fritz, Pat Shanahan, Jim Mehlin, my Vinita pal John Barrett, Henry Woolman the bronco buster, the Big Creek outlaws that Jim Martin had cursed so heartily once when he stayed overnight with us because they had let his son "Wolf George" Martin astray. Tentatively, I tried also to fit girls into my plots: Sarah, Clara LeForce, Ludie Hall, Grace and Lucille Fortner, Jennie Shanahan, Mattie Donnelly, Miss Croom.

Suppose I were able to write these stories? I might make a book of them, and call it "Tales of the Old I. T." I would let the world know about Indian Territory! Much later, some of the tales were written, and published in good magazines, but I never collected them into a book. My title, which I still think is a good one, has never been used.

Graduating from Willie Halsell the next spring, in a class of three, I ranked second to Eva Patton, favorite of the school's head and soon to become his bride, who was chosen as valedictorian. Professor Dugger, with whom I was a favored student, let me know that he believed I should have been given that honor, and Father raged profanely because "that damn dude Rowsey put that girl ahead of you!"[56]

I can't recall the subject of Eva's essay, but as salutatorian (how we loved such titles!) I composed a memorized piece with the all-inclusive title "Progress!" and heard John Barrett say that it put Eva's in the shade. Father heartily agreed with him, and Dugger professed to see for me a fine future as a public speaker.

Next evening there was to be an entertainment, piano recitals, recitations, and one-act play. While the stage was being decorated, we rolled down the heavy wooden partition that served to divide the big assembly room into two classrooms. It was to be rolled up as the audience began to arrive, and I was assigned to raise it at the proper moment. I proposed to make my gesture dramatic, stooped, grasped the handholds at the bottom, and flung up the heavy partition with all my strength. It hit the top with force enough to snap the cords holding the counterweights, and descended faster than it had risen. Unfortunately, I was in the direct line of its descent, and its lower edge hit me across the face as I looked up. I fell, as they say, like a pole-axed ox, thinking in the instance before losing consciousness, This is the end of me!

I came to life lying in bed at John Barrett's home with a thick beefsteak bound to a greatly swollen eye and cheek. His mother had thought of that first aid measure, and Dr. Fortner,[57] called in to see me, could suggest no better treatment. John Barrett had driven out to tell Father of the accident. He rode in on his fast saddle horse Selim, looked at my steak plaster, saw me squirming lustily in pain, and laughed, "Jinks, you remind me of something they serve in a short-order restaurant!" then, "It was a close call, son; too damn close to suit me." That was as near to an emotional expression as I ever heard from him.

It was Father's idea that I should study law. To him, lawyers were the cream of the white-collar professional crop, with the possibility of earning most money. He admired such members of the bar in Vinita as gnome-like Kornegay of the drawling voice and trenchant wit, boomingly eloquent Jim Davenport, and the shrewd flat-bellied and successful Bill Hastings, a Cherokee Indian lawyer of Tahlequah.[58] Another lawyer friend in Vinita, F. M. Smith, pleased Father by telling him he had liked my commencement-day essay, and Father said, "I want John to study law, and the sooner he starts the better. F. M., do you reckon he could read in your office this summer? Maybe he could help you out someday to make it worth your while?"

Smith took me in. I accepted gratefully the invitation to stay at the Barretts, rooming with John and paying the little Mrs. Barrett thought my meals and laundry would cost. Chunky, affable, and not too enterprising, my mentor set me to reading Blackstone in a small second-story office crowded with a desk, chairs, shelves laden with books on contracts, torts, criminal practice, the Arkansas statutes, and rows of sheepskin-bound law reports. Both this room and Smith's private office got the full blast of the summer sun; in the afternoon the suite was an inferno, hotter than the hinges of hell, as Father said when he came up to see me one day in July.[59]

F. M. spent little time in his office, explaining, as he ruffled a thick red beard, "An attorney at law in a town like Vinita picks up his business on the street — in the coolest shade he can find, of course." But I could not lug the five-pound volume of Blackstone out to the sidewalk in front of the bank, so I sat and stewed, wiped sweat out of my eyes, and longed for the day when I could go off to college, for Father had readily agreed that a college course ought to precede law school. I had no yearning for the law; I read with Smith only to please Father.

Great changes had come to Indian Territory in the twenty-four years since Father arrived at Tahlequah. By now there were many more whites than Indians in the Cherokee Nation, in the towns and on farms and ranches. Pressure on Washington to open Indian lands to purchase and lease by whites had borne fruit. The Nation had been surveyed, the land graded and assessed, and allotted as individual holdings to Cherokee citizens. To satisfy other claims, the United States government would pay each citizen $274.[60]

For the Cherokees of our section the payment was made at Vinita, in a big tent roped off and protected by rifle-armed guards patrolling inside the ropes. One by one, Indians ducked under the ropes, identified themselves, and received from the tribal treasurer the cash to which he and his family were entitled. Lawyer Bill Hastings was there to consult with the treasurer when necessary, and advise with full-bloods who could not speak English or who had difficulty in identifying themselves. Hastings seemed to know every full-blood family in the Nation.

Names checked off on the roll of citizens made by the allotting authorities, bills and silver in their pockets, payees passed from the main tent to another, long and narrow, in which merchants of Vinita, Nowata, Chelsea, Claremore, Miami, and other trading centers sat with lists of debts owed them by Indians to whom they had extended credit. They paid unquestioningly the amounts demanded, some emerging with pockets turned inside out, and grinning, after creditors had taken all. Only a few came out with the whole amount they had been paid. Dick and I were among these, handing our money to Father to be put into his account at the bank and kept for us. Neither Father nor Bert received the payment; adopted citizens, it had been ruled, could not share, and Bert, the son of white parents, had no claim either to land or money.

The payment proceeded slowly, lasting a week. Each morning I watched from Smith's office clerks carrying chests of money from bank to pay-tent, surrounded by guards who had stood in front of the bank all night. At sunset, the chests were carried back to the bank.

When I decided that I had read as much of Blackstone as I could absorb for the day, I went down to make a tour of the attractions set up on vacant lots and the Frisco railroad right-of-way: shooting galleries; ring toss, spin the wheel, and fortune-telling booths; guess your weight and get your nickel back scales; ring the bell with a maul and get a good cigar pitch; pale imitations of Little Egypt and other shows "straight from the Midway at Chicago's Mammouth Fair"; the taffy-pulling hook where the sweating manipulator chanted, "It cleans your teeth, curls you hair, and gives you a smile that's fit to wear!" I remember the shy, soft laughter of Indians emerging from the dime traps, pistol shots in the night, and shrill whoops of young half-breed rioters drunk on bootleg whiskey, and the clatter of running horses' hooves along the dirt streets. These are among the impressions that were later incorporated into some of the stories I wrote.[61]

An actor from the cast of *East Lynne*, playing in a tent, had persuaded Mrs. Barrett to take him as a boarder. Mack Landrum, another boarder who had lately been graduated from Emory and Henry College in Virginia and had talked to me about the relative merits of small and large colleges, introduced me to the actor. Knowing nothing of the stage, I sat tongue tied, but Mack chatted glibly of Henry Irving and Joseph Jefferson and other titans who had "trod the boards," and pitied such strollers as the man who boarded at

Mrs. Barrett's for having to prostitute their talent by playing in *East Lynne* and Uncle Tom tent shows. However, Mack graciously accepted a pass and begged another for me.[62]

I watched the actors in *East Lynne*, and listened to their lines with the same avid absorption with which I had devoured the Mrs. E. D. N. Southworth mushy romances Clara LeForce and I had exchanged, but ten days later not a glimmer of its plot remained with me. No character of the melodrama walked firmly beside me as did Long John Silver, Mulvaney, and Mrs. Hauksbe.[63]

Chapter 3

In talks with Father I had narrowed my choice of colleges to Vanderbilt University, at Nashville, and Leland Stanford Junior University, at Palo Alto, California, about which I had read in a lavishly illustrated magazine article.

The western university was a new and different institution, made possible by the millions of Leland Stanford, once United States senator and richest of the group of pioneer California merchants, railroad builders, and mining nabobs. He had chosen a scientist, David Starr Jordan from the University of Indiana,[64] as president, and instructed him to make the school a worthy memorial to an only child, the young son who had died while he and Mrs. Stanford were on a tour of Italy. He promised that "the children of California shall be my children," and later consented to the admission of students from other states and countries. Instruction was to be free.[65]

Father made the decision for me. "Jinks, don't you reckon you'd better go to school in California?"

"Yes, maybe I'd better."

Eastward to Monett, Missouri, northwestward to Newton, Kansas, changing trains at each place before taking the Santa Fe to San Francisco, it was a devious and tiring trip. To save money, I did not take a sleeper.

At Newton, it was an all-day wait at a sun-baked station, with the little town set in the level prairie a quarter of a mile away. There was nothing to do except walk to town, return to ask the station agent if he had later information about the train, walk to town once more, eat a twenty-five-cent meal, return to the depot, watch the fiery late-August sun sink slowly toward the horizon.

Bleary-eyed and disheveled, I took a horse-drawn bus from the Southern Pacific station at Palo Alto to Encina Hall, the big men's dormitory where I was to live. "Old John," the driver, talked to us entering freshmen in his bus as though he were the most important member of the university staff, reciting impressively the facts I already knew. While the low quadrangle of buildings devoted to instruction was still only a distant mass, he pointed to a mausoleum-like structure at the right of the young-palm-lined drive and said, "Yonder's the Museum, built by Mrs. Stanford after the senator died to contain the relics of her boy. You can see in there the last breakfast served to little Leland. Not the real eggs and so forth, but rep — you know, copies in china."

I resolved to see that exhibit soon. I didn't think the idea ludicrous, and never understood the ridicule heaped on it by smarties. I still think of it only as the understandable, impulsive gesture of a loving mother.

Before turning off to Encina, the one-story quadrangle (now the "inner quad") designed in the Spanish mission style and built of brown stone and roofed with red tile, with an arcade all around an enclosed patio, came clearly into view. It was even more beautiful than I had imagined. I gazed with a country boy's reverence for a "great seat of learning."

My first letter was to be an effort to describe the quad with its circles of palm and pepper trees dotting the spacious patio, its cool arcade, ample classrooms and quiet library, the girls and boys, some on bicycles, crisscrossing as they thronged to the first classes of the semester, and my impressions of the two hundred or more young men who roomed at Encina and ate together in the great dining hall.

"One thing," I wrote, "will surprise you. The first group of roomers I saw in the lobby of Encina were seven seniors gathered around a *negro*, shaking hands with him, clapping him on the back and asking how he had spent the summer. The negro lives and eats in the Hall with the rest, only he has a room to himself. The fellows say he's a fine student, and intends to go to a San Francisco law school next year."[66]

In later letters I wrote of the "Farm," the nine-thousand-acre Stanford estate in the Santa Clara valley of which the university had, in the four years of its existence, become the center. Before Senator Stanford's mind turned to the university project, the Farm had been principally a racehorse-breeding establishment; its stables were still a magnet to draw farm-bred students like me. Pastureland, over which some horses still grazed, lay across the rolling hills above the quad and "faculty row." On the flatland between the hills and the railroad, flanked by an extensive arboretum, were big vineyards; their grapes yielded the wine stored in a capacious winery. At the edge of the vineyard area, set in a grove of soaring eucalyptus trees, the old-fashioned brick Stanford mansion made no such arrant boast of wealth as I had expected to see.

Entrance requirements were, to say the least, elastic, as I learned when I was received without question on my record at Willie Halsell, a school about which the registrar had never heard. The one test was the applicant's desire for education and his willingness to work for it. Dr. David Starr Jordan and the well-paid, brilliant, and cosmopolitan faculty he had recruited from many colleges tried with notable success to make us feel that we all belonged to one big family.

At that time, when evolution was a hotly debated theory, the Stanford teachers took it for granted. Many of the students, of course, had attended sectarian schools and fundamentalist churches, and to accept the man-from-monkey theory, however logical, seemed daring and exciting. I was not troubled; as I have said, my early environment had been literally pagan. But one of my close Stanford friends, from a pious Philadelphia family, was converted to Darwinism only after agonized soul-searching.[67]

The Stanford spirit was electric. Professors who conducted the courses I chose stimulated me immensely. In English, I quivered under the lash of black-bearded Lathrop's incisive comments as he mercilessly snuffed out my love of fine writing; I was soothed by the approval of an occasional paragraph I produced by the soft-spoken Newcomer; I took an actual physical delight in the swift-running, crystal-clear stream of apt words used by London-born Hudson; and though I had no classes with them, I crashed some of the lectures for advanced students given by the erudite Anderson and Pflugel, and heard for the first time of Chaucer and the Anglo-Saxon bards.[68]

Finding that a pre-law course under Professor Nathan Abbott would count toward an AB degree, I enrolled to please Father, and pursued it with enthusiasm because of my admiration for that fine teacher and gentleman.[69]

The university was elective in the fullest sense; the only requirement was that minimum of English which would guarantee a reasonable literacy at graduation. I ranged far in my selection of subjects. One was a course in shorthand offered by the assistant registrar! Another was the history of art, under the nervous Kriehn, who provoked an indignant, starry-eyed girl student to say (outside the classroom, of course) that he profaned the altars of medieval art with the muddy boots of his awkward fumbling for words — a classic of mixed metaphors.[70]

Yet another choice, recommended as a snap course, was ethics under Edward Howard Griggs, a young teacher who resented bitterly the tag fastened on him by an enthusiastic woman writer in a San Francisco Sunday newspaper of "the perfect man." Girl students were crazy about him, and with reason. He was more than handsome; he was beautiful, with abundant wavy black hair, mobile lips that seemed to invite kisses, alive soulful eyes, baby-soft white skin, and a voice that soothed the senses. In confidence, he once said to a roughneck friend of mine, "I wish all these silly damn girls could see me as I really am, a swearing, beer-drinking so-and-so!"[71]

A choice I never regretted was a course in economics under the tall, gangling Ross, whose pungent classroom comments on the sort of capitalism then running rampant alarmed Mrs. Stanford and a majority of the university trustees and led to his dismissal. We who sat under him admired his honesty, his plain speaking, and were as indignant as earnest Professor Howard of the history staff, who resigned in protest against this attack on academic freedom. I studied under Howard, too, with him lived through the growth, decline, and fall of the Roman Empire, and got more than a glimpse of the meaning to us of the long sweep of history.[72]

My elementary physiology course under Jenkins, a small, understanding teacher who seemed always about to break into laughter, explicit in lectures and laboratory instruction, led to an unexpected and satisfying development in my college career.[73]

One chore in lab, during the torpid afternoon hours, was to prepare, and study under the microscope, slides on which amoeba scuttled and divided. In an effort to enliven this period one day, I imagined a dialogue between two of the microscopic playboys, and jotted down their remarks instead of the notes we were supposed to make. Observing my unusual concentration, Jenkins came to lean over my shoulder, pick up and read what I had written.

But far from bawling me out for wasting time, as I feared he would do, he chuckled and said, "Good! You ought to send that in to the *Sequoia*."[74]

I knew Dane Coolidge,[75] editor of that college weekly, and gave him a liberal thousand words of dialogue to read. I watched as he read, stroking his treasured thick mustache, grinning, then laughing aloud. "Sure, Johnny, I'll use this. Do something else for me." Following my "Two on a Slide," the *Sequoia* printed a number of my observations on life at Stanford, some meant to be humorous and some heavily critical. One was a blast at the fraternity system "by a Barb" (short for barbarian, a non-fraternity student). I had carried to Stanford a letter written by Mack Landrum recommending me to his fraternity brothers, but had not presented it because I found that the barbs inhabiting Encina, whose leading spirit was a senior student of geology, an anti-frat man and a successful campus politician named Herbert Hoover,[76] more interesting and companionable than the fraternity members I had met.

My piece brought Charley Field, an enthusiastic fraternity brother, to my room to protest against what he thought was unfair criticism. I had admired Charley's light verse, and found him a delightful person. While at his first mention of my blast I was inclined to be combative, his sweetly reasonable defense of fraternities made me regret that I had attacked them. After he left, I thought, Maybe I'm not cut out for a reformer; maybe I'd better try something else. Coolidge, a rabid barb, tried without success to stir me to writing a rebuttal of Charley Field's arguments.[77]

My next offering for the *Sequoia* was one of the short stories I had outlined vaguely in my mind as I rode the range, and had fitted into the imagined series of "Tales of the Old I.T." In fewer than fifteen hundred words, I attempted to picture our Cabin Creek neighborhood, and develop a plot that involved Old Fritz, his fat wife, their son Joe, and a neighbor who schemed to run them off and grab their improvements. Under another name, of course, I used my father as the strong man who foiled the villain.

Coolidge was doubtful about the yarn, it seemed so different from the usual college literary magazine piece, but used it to please me. He was cheered when one of the professors praised it as containing fresh and authentic detail. Encouraged, I labored over other vignettes of range and farm life, and was rewarded by being named as associate editor of the *Sequoia*.

In my second year, I began playing tennis, and uncovered a savage competitive spirit that had lurked, unsuspected, in my rather sluggish, heavy-footed body that, nourished by the abundant good food at Encina, had increased in weight from 160 to 190 pounds. From the first, I sought more experienced players to face across the net on the asphalt courts. Going into battle under sizzling afternoon sunshine, knowing I was overmatched, I ran for lobs and expertly placed drives to the corners, plunged to intercept volleys, and put everything I had into serves with which I hoped to ace my opponent. Three sets wore me to exhaustion, and sometimes brought on headaches that sickened me.

Until I learned a tricky forehand chop and a backhand good enough to make the other fellow chase my soft placements, I was in a fair way to overstrain my heart, as the gym instructor warned. The new technique I worked out to save myself was wholly unorthodox, but it enabled me to overtake most of the players who had beaten me in my hard-charging days. In my senior year, I won a place on the intercollegiate team, and went down before an agile University of California opponent in straight sets. Tennis had "got into my blood," and I played with unabated energy for years after leaving college.

I tried for the freshman football team, but was too slow. The captain, Charley Fickert,[78] later to become captain and star guard of the varsity, did put me in at end for five minutes of the game against the sophomores when we had piled up a safe lead. I was swarmed over, thrust aside, pulled in, and humiliated before Fickert replaced me. I never got into a football suit again, but sat with other rabid fans to cheer the teams that Walter Camp coached expertly in the three autumn seasons he took off from his coaching at Yale.[79] The annual Thanksgiving Day game with University of California, played at a dilapidated old athletic field in San Francisco, marked the climax of our frenzy.

In my first two years at Stanford, the university was under a cloud; the federal government had brought suit against the Stanford estate to recover the millions given as an endowment. The suit dragged through the courts and finally reached the Supreme Court.[80] Its decision in favor of the university set off a wild, spontaneous celebration, led by two high-spirited students, Will Irwin and Chris Bradley, whose suggestion to capture Dr. Jordan and draw him in a carriage to the Stanford home and call on Mrs. Stanford to come out was acted upon by a thousand cheering girls and boys.[81]

The news had reached us after supper, and we made a torchlight procession first to Jordan's home and then to Mrs. Stanford's. As many as could lay hands on the long rope attached to a commandeered carriage trotted over the course, the rest of us dancing and yelling alongside.

Mrs. Stanford came out to welcome us, to climb into the carriage with Dr. Jordan, and bless us for thinking of her in that hour of happiness. There were tears in her eyes, and many of us wept unashamed. We were like a group of family heirs assured after a long will contest of our fine heritage.

Holidays were a problem until I found that I could write well enough to make the pages of the *Sequoia*. Then, instead of seeming dreary because I had nowhere to go, they became welcome intervals, especially the two weeks at Christmas, in which, alone in my room, to write and rewrite the stories that I wanted to tell.

My first long summer vacation I spent as a self-invited guest of Tom Melbourne and his wife.[82] That is, I wrote to ask if I might come for a few days, and stayed on at their urging trying to make myself useful on their big farm.

The second summer I spent at home, ran the mowing machine through haying, visited in Vinita, rode out with Father or Henry Falling or Bert — now a husky lad of sixteen — noted that the longhorns had disappeared from the now-limited free range, and went to see Aunt Betsy, Liza and Jennie, and other Indian friends on Pawpaw.

One day, as Henry and I rode back to the house at noon, a stranger galloped up, looked at Henry, and asked excitedly, "Are you the fellow that can cure a rattlesnake bite?"

"Yes. Why?" Henry answered.

"I've got a lead horse in the lot at Joe Harris's that's been bit. He told me about you. Will you come?"

"Yes." Henry mounted at once and loped away. I followed with the horse's owner. He told me that within a hundred yards of the Harris place his lead horse began limping, and when he dismounted to find out why discovered a rapidly swelling hock and knew that a rattlesnake had struck it.

We arrived at the lot as Henry was approaching the lamed horse, saw him kneel beside the greatly swollen leg, rub the swelling gently with his hands as his lips moved in what I supposed was some sort of incantation. This continued for perhaps five minutes. It seemed to me that the horse grew visibly quieter, relaxed, and began to put some weight on the snakebitten foot. It may have been imagination, however.

Henry came out to mount and ride home with me, waving aside the man's question, "What do I owe you?" and saying only, "You can lead your horse away in the morning."

Henry would say nothing in answer to my questions. From other Cherokees, however, I learned that his secret healing power had been passed down from a long line of snake doctors, and that it had always been passed on from a man to a woman then from the woman to another man. Whether or not the horse had actually been struck by a rattlesnake, whether or not Henry's treatment effected the cure, it is a fact that the horse was quite fit to be led away the next morning.

Early on the morning of the Fourth, Bert and I drove in the buggy to Bluejacket, a little town on the Katy ten miles away. Before starting, Bert said, "Jinks, you'd better take along that tennis racket of yours; there's a fellow up there thinks he can lick you." Bert was to compete in a rodeo, then called simply a roping, using one of the horses he drove and taking his saddle, bridle, and rope in the back of the buggy.[83]

I played a tennis match with a young Cherokee named Hicks,[84] expecting, of course, to beat him. Far from showing him up, however, I was licked in straight sets. Then he told me he had learned his hard, smooth-stroking game at Princeton. Meanwhile, in a cow pasture at the edge of town, Bert won first money by roping and hog-tying a steer in twenty-three seconds. We ate supper with Hicks and drove home in the cooling dusk. Bert wrapped the lines around the stock of the buggy whip, went to sleep leaving the team to go their own gait and find their own way back to our barn. I did not touch the lines, and the horses made no wrong turnings. Long before, I had learned that when I was overtaken by darkness and was uncertain of finding my way home I had only to drop the reins on the neck of my saddle horse and let him go as he pleased.

The third summer vacation I went north from Stanford, at Father's request, to look up our kinfolks. Some I found in Portland, Oregon. Another family lived at Pendleton, Oregon, still another at Walla Walla, Washington, and a fourth on a big wheat ranch near Walla Walla. The wheat grower's spacious, hospitable home lay under a mesa-like expanse of grain fields, beside a tree-shaded trout stream which I followed for miles in company with his expert fishermen sons — and caught just one fish in the two weeks I stayed.

Ten days before college instruction began, I returned to stay in San Francisco with Gail Nichols, a student friend who had spent his vacation as assistant to an interior decorator. With him, I went to art exhibits, seeing not such yards of roses as Miss Croom had been pleased to copy but a few Corots that I remembered from the World's Fair, some Cézannes and youthful Monets, two Italian primitives of the school that Kriehn had attempted fumblingly to characterize in the classroom. With Nichols, I attended a Sunday service at a little Swedenborgian church, set back from the street in the midst of a lush garden, with redwood beams overhead and rope-bottom chairs instead of pews. It was a place where one couldn't help feeling at home, and Mr. Worcester's talk (not at all like any sermon I had ever heard) seemed like a friendly chat. Beauty and serenity pervaded the setting.[85]

I guided Nichols on his first visits to quite other San Francisco scenes, the Barbary Coast[86] dives and honky-tonks, the cheap and good Italian restaurants where laughter, song, and clean ribaldry mingled to create genuine bohemianism. Too, I led the way to the Chinatown I had explored, and showed him the opium dens in which utterly indifferent Chinese lay on mats, cooked and smoked their tiny pills, then relaxed to dream of Paradise — so our guide had said.

In such vacation wanderings I felt that I was following, in some obscure fashion, a loose-footed pattern set for me by my restless father.

Not until my senior year did social activities attract me, and then only because I had fallen in love with Susan (she was the first girl I knew to bob her hair).[87] The Spanish-American War broke in my senior year; campus patriots drilled without rifles on the football field. My brother Will wrote that he had joined the army and would soon be sent to the Philippines.[88] I had a short visit with him before his regiment sailed, and heard from him that brother Dick had enlisted, along with other neighborhood and Vinita boys, in the

Rough Riders, and expected to see action in Cuba under Leonard Wood[89] and Theodore Roosevelt.[90]

Graduation seemed less thrilling than the war; I hated the effort to appear elated at receiving the oblong of parchment that proved I was now a Bachelor of Arts. I headed homeward heartbroken at parting from Susan.

Chapter 4

I spent the summer at home, doing the usual work of the farm, riding out with Bert to bring back far-straying JIC steers, then six weeks of haying. To the soothing clatter of the old McCormick mowing machine, I daydreamed of Susan and repeated to myself her half promise to wait for me. On sultry evenings, before going to sleep in the wide doorway of the hayloft, cooler than the upstairs rooms of the house, I almost forgot sweat-filmed wrists and palms as I wrote diary letters, picturing for her the farm, telling about Father, brother Bert, giving all the news I had of brother Will, in the Philippines, and Dick, in Cuba, and boasting of the work I was doing. Not as often, Susan wrote to me. Her replies were buoyant, sparkling, stimulating, but not the ardent love letters I hoped for.

My last chore of the late summer, before settling off for Harvard, was a trip to the tiny settlement of Gallina, New Mexico.[91] A German-born neighbor who had gone out there a year before had written urging Father to follow, describing the surrounding forested hills as good cattle range. The prospect pleased Father, still eager at the age of sixty-seven for new adventures in living. However, instead of taking the long and somewhat difficult trip himself to investigate Emil Strauch's remote cattleman's paradise, he sent me.

It was truly a roundabout journey, with the train changes at Monett and Newton which I had made four years before, another change for Pueblo, Colorado, a fourth change to the narrow-gauge Denver and Rio Grande, a fifth change at Alamosa, then a change to a mail stage at Chama for the little town of Tierra Amarilla. Before taking the stage, I slept almost around the clock in a Chama hotel; I felt that I had earned this opportunity to bathe and sleep after two days and nights of rocking, cinder-showered day coaches and waits between trains.

The mail stage driver told me there was no public transportation beyond

Tierra Amarilla, and gave me the name of a Mexican who might be hired to drive me on to Gallina, sixty miles farther. I found José Nutrias at Tierra Amarilla and made a bargain, ten dollars for the trip to Gallina and back. It was too late to start that day, and I accepted José's cordial invitation to spend the night at his one-room-and-lean-to home, where for a brief time I tried to sleep on a rolled-out mattress on the dirt floor, sandwiched between him and another of his numerous family, with the door and the room's one small window closed. When the smell of unwashed Mexicans became overpowering, however, I sneaked out to make a nest in the hay he had heaped in the wagon he was to drive next day. All night the team, which was tied to the light wagon, nudged me with their noses to get at the hay under me.

We reached Gallina before sunset the following day after ten hours of clattering over a dim, rutted, and stony road. The town (the latest Rand McNally atlas credits it with a population of eighty) was a huddle of flat-topped adobe huts on a slightly pine-and-cedar-forested mesa. One of the huts was Strauch's home, where he lived alone. The only Americano in the place, he made me welcome with exaggerated enthusiasm, waving his short arms like an amateur orchestra conductor, and scratching a scraggly beard. After five minutes he excused himself and went off with José, to return presently with a young goat draped across his wide shoulders. Hanging the bleating animal by its hind feet from a wooden peg at the corner of the hut, he cut its throat, skinned it, sliced strips from the carcass for our supper, and kept up a ceaseless flow of boasting about the wonderful opportunities for a cattleman Rio Arriba County offered.

I was ravenous and, trying to forget the rank smell of raw goat flesh, ate what Strauch forked onto my plate. Then, exhausted and torpid, I seemed to hear his words coming from a great distance. Eventually he became aware of my state, and rolled out a mattress for me.

Next day, on borrowed saddle horses, we rode out to inspect the "wonderful" range to which Strauch hoped Father would come with cattle. The whole setting—sun-baked huts, shy dark-skinned children, the inevitable strings of red peppers against whitewashed walls, ubiquitous goats, twisted cedars and scrub pines of the scantily grassed mesa—seemed like something out of the Old Testament, the end of nowhere, an ideal refuge for a refugee from civilization. I wondered, though I did not ask, why Strauch had come to Gallina.

More great meat for supper, more eager sales talk by Strauch until I could no longer stay awake, a night of sound sleep, then off with José in the early morning to begin the long trip back home. The last thing Strauch said, looking up at me rather forlornly after I had climbed into the wagon, was, "Mr. John, will you do something for me? Send me please an atlas. Sometimes I get lonesome, and want to take a trip; on the maps I find places in the world where I have been, and other places I want to see. Please!"

I sent back from Vinita the only atlas I could find, and told Father that Strauch was half cracked, dying of loneliness, and had hoped to lure him to Gallina by a purely imaginative description of its possibilities.

After convoying his fall shipment of 150 grass-fattened steers to Chicago and returning with a check for not quite ten thousand dollars, Father traveled with me to New York. We took time to explore the city, going on conducted tours to Chinatown, Grant's Tomb, Riverside Drive, Coney Island, and the Statue of Liberty. I kept for years a large photograph of a score of sightseers ranged in rows on one of those early day autobuses that resembled tilted haywagons, which showed Father in his broad black hat, boots, and white beard, relaxed as though saying, Bring on the elephant, I'm here to see everything. I was glad to be with him in this holiday mood, his habitual sternness put off and his high temper only a memory.

His comment on New York, when our touring ended, was, "It don't seem like the same place I saw in 1870. It's too noisy, smells bad, and you have to look around to find a horse car even; all these trolleys and cable cars and little old trains on stilts and autobuses move too fast for me." I hoped he would tell me more of the city he had glimpsed on the way from California to Indian Territory thirty years before, but he relapsed into the reticence about his experiences which I knew my questions could not break through.

On the morning of the day I was to go to Cambridge, meet Dane Coolidge, and enroll at Harvard, I saw Father to the train for Vinita. We shook hands, and he said, "Good luck, Jinks. Let me know when you need money." I carried three hundred dollars, which I hoped would see me through until Christmas.

Dane and I found a big, comfortable top-floor room in a house near the Yard, only a block from Memorial Hall, where we ate, and only two blocks from

President Eliot's home.[92] Squaring away to our first evening study period, after congratulating ourselves on finding such a quiet room, we were suddenly startled by the youth who lived across the narrow hallway bursting in upon us wild-eyed, chattering unintelligibly, and gesturing weirdly as he ran back to his room. We followed, to find two gas jets, from which he had removed the tips, flaring almost to the ceiling and books and clothing scattered pell-mell over the floor. I shut off the gas and attempted to calm our neighbor while Dane raced to fetch the landlord. The demented student could mumble only broken sentences when the landlord came, but followed him downstairs without protest. We guessed that he was either a dope addict or, as Dane suggested, a victim of an intolerable loneliness. We, too, had at first contact found Harvard cold, indifferent, seemingly hostile to such as us from the wide-open spaces. "These damn Willie boys," Dane said resentfully, "don't know we're here, and don't care!"

One of Dane's New England cousins lived in Lexington and, learning that Dane was at Harvard, asked him to tea on the second Sunday after our arrival. Coming back to our room at nine o'clock that evening, he had a tale to tell! "I got to my cousin's house," he said, "at three. We chinned a while, then his wife served tea. I got to talking—you know how I go on and on sometimes—they listened politely, and the first thing I knew it was supper time. I found that out when he excused himself and went to the kitchen; I could hear him rattling knives and forks and plates. Half an hour or so later, he came back to the living room, then she excused herself to go to the kitchen for her supper. Of course, when I realized what was going on I left, and had my supper at a restaurant in Harvard Square."

"But why," I demanded, "didn't they want you to eat with them?"

"I believe," Dane grinned, "they were ashamed to ask me to share the scanty fare they had provided for themselves. That's New England for you!"

By this time my interest was concentrated on English. The writing I had done for the *Sequoia* at Stanford had served to drive the law from my mind, and Father no longer insisted upon it as a career for me. Three courses in English, one in Spanish (which I flunked), and another in psychology were my choices in a Harvard almost as elective as Stanford.

I don't remember the name of the good counselor who suggested Barrett Wendell's popular course in English composition, but I have been deeply grateful to him ever since. So many students flocked to it that Wendell lectured in the big auditorium of the Fogg Art Museum. He was a compact, muscular, dynamic teacher of forty-five, with a cropped beard, who dressed in English tweeds, flavored his clipped sentences with a Boston-English accent, threw out casual damns and hells where they fitted, and strode back and forth on the platform like one condemned to waste his erudition on a congregation of simpletons. He was rich, a self-confessed snob, and belonged to a well-known Back Bay family. His "ers" and "ahs" as he looked down upon us "young gentlemen" suggested a medieval grandee struggling to find words the peasantry would understand. But he knew and loved forthright English, could tell us how good writers had used it. Many of us derided him for his mannerisms, but all respected and admired — and remembered — the essence of his teaching, his repeated insistence on clearness, force, and elegance. His flock of assistants, who read and graded our papers, were his worshipful imitators. I never had a comment from him, no individual contact, nor I believe did the other 250 students in the class; and I pictured him spending his vast leisure taking tea in Back Bay salons, adding to the high color of his cheekbones by drinking wine at dinner with the Cabots, Lowells, Saltonstalls, Adamses, and other Brahmans who, according to legend, walked and talked only with each other and, ultimately, with God.[93]

Another of my English teachers was venerable Asa Hill, whose textbook on rhetoric was standard. We caught from him, along with the reflection of a precious personality, something of the deep-rooted conviction of a teacher dedicated to the task of taking apart the language and showing us why it could ring bells in the mind, equip a Webster for an oratorical flourish or a Justice Marshall for a clear exposition of a point of law. He must have been past seventy. His white beard and bloodless frailty rather absurdly reminded me of Father, who had never spent a day in school and could barely write his name.[94]

George Lyman Kittridge, as I recall, taught us essay writing and was busy outside his teaching hours editing English classics, Anglo-Saxon poetry, Chaucer, old farmers almanacs, and books on witchcraft. He was in appearance the perfect scholar, middle-aged, tall, austere, precise in speech and in his short marches across the dais from which he lectured. I could not imagine a student under his compelling gray-blue eyes becoming restless and inattentive, or popping an irrelevant question. Some of the young men in his class did ask questions, astonishing and shaming me by revelations of literary backgrounds utterly unfamiliar to one who, at Stanford, had merely nodded at Addison, Lamb, and Emerson.[95]

The psychology course was conducted by Hugo Munsterberg, an enormous bear-like man, who suffered banishment from Harvard in the First World War for, I suppose, the same reason Wagner's music was banned from the Metropolitan Opera House — he was German.[96]

At the time, of course, Munsterberg was under no cloud. On the contrary, he was one of Harvard's really popular teachers. He added to the interest of the course I took by asking such colleagues as William James, George Herbert Palmer, and Josiah Royce to lecture in his stead.[97] An assistant who graded papers once praised a theme in which I confessed to a curiosity to see what would happen if I should bounce a pebble from a pea shooter off the bald head of our distinguished teacher.

The two lectures by red-bearded William James were periods of mild agony for me. He fought so hard for words that would make important psychological abstractions intelligible to us that I thought of Jacob wrestling with the angel. I wondered if obscurity of language was a family trait of the James boys, for it was in my year at Harvard that I began to read such short fiction by William's brother Henry as *What Maisie Knew* and *The Turn of the Screw*.

Josiah Royce's one lecture, on some elementary phase of philosophy, gave me a glimpse of what I think of as a whole man, learned and human. I could believe that it was indeed Royce who, discussing evolution, answered a student's query as to the ultimate effect of circumcision by quoting Shakespeare, "There's a divinity that shapes our ends rough hew them how we will." I felt sure that had Royce's lines fallen aptly he would have been a successful Texas cattleman.

Then, as a wonderful extracurricular stimulant, there was "Copey" in his prime — Charles Townsend Copeland, without whom for more than forty years Harvard would not have been so rewarding to many hundreds of students. A bachelor, he occupied rooms in one of the old dormitories in the Yard (Hollis, I believe). I was in none of his classes, but somehow contrived to join the flow of students that, two or three evenings a week, converged upon his quarters. The first time I ventured, timidly, inside his door he looked up at me — he was a little man — gravely and asked, "Who are you? If the name is not Smith or Jones, spell it for me." I did, and I can testify that over the span of seventeen years between the last time I saw him at Harvard and the week before I sailed for France, in March of 1917, he had not forgotten my name nor the year of my stay in Cambridge. He has been the only man of my acquaintance whose memory for names and personalities matched Theodore Roosevelt's.[98]

The evenings at Copey's were pure intellectual delight. His talk was of writers and writing he liked. He stirred us to talk, too, chuckled at occasional apt phrases, interrupted without apology the floundering and long-winded. He read to us anything from a sentence to a chapter that had lately caught his attention. It might be a bit of brilliant reporting from the *New York Sun*, a paragraph from one of that newspaper's weekly ten-thousand-word book reviews, a pregnant comment from an Edward Martin editorial in *Life*, an episode out of Charles Stewart's "The Fugitive Blacksmith" that was, he declared, as good as anything Mark Twain had ever done.[99] Kipling, then stirring young men by his robust extrovert prose and ballads, was one of his favorites. He read, I thought, perfectly, using no gestures, no dramatic tricks, just pouring out words which, if you closed your eyes, seemed like clean, clear type on a well-printed page.

There was coffee for any who cared to brew it, and gossip about writers, ancient or modern — and no shadow of discrimination by Copey between rich or poor, well dressed or shabby. You were one of his boys if you cared for what he loved in the vast range of printed words from *The Canterbury Tales* to *Mr. Dooley*.[100] (Does what I have written here seem a bit mushy and extravagant? Well, of the many who have written of Copey and his evenings I can't recall one who did not become more or less sentimental and lyrical.)

Of course, responding to such a stimulus as I found at Harvard — and able to laugh at the snobbery that troubled Coolidge — I wrote short stories in every spare hour. They were Indian Territory tales, more "Tales of the Old I.T." which I had projected in my mind as I rode the prairies before going to college.

Confident that I could broaden its fiction range, I sent one of the stories to the *Harvard Literary Magazine*. It was returned promptly with no comment. I sent another, and another, and a fourth and a fifth and a sixth before I was convinced that the *Lit* wanted nothing I had to offer. Then appeared an announcement from the *Century Magazine* of New York that prizes of $250 each would be paid for the best short story, the best essay, and the best poem submitted by college graduates within a year of graduation. It stirred me to action. I rewrote and somewhat expanded one of the tales the *Lit* had rejected and, with a Now, damn you, we'll see what real editors think of my stuff! mental gesture, mailed it in time to make the deadline.

A week before my year at Harvard ended, a telegram from the *Century* notified me that my story had won, and asked for credentials. I wrote that I would appear at the *Century* office within ten days, and triumphantly thumbed my nose at the *Lit*'s editors — and much they would have cared had they been aware of it! An added satisfaction to me was that friendly John Macey, who had sat beside me in Kittridge's class and had also been ignored by the *Lit*, won the essay prize.[101]

Writing to Father that I planned to come home soon with good news, I stopped at New York for a conference with the *Century*'s editor.

At the office of the *Century*, after I had established my identity, the three middle-aged men who conducted what was then the outstanding general magazine of America talked with me as we sat before a cannel-coal fire in Mr. Gilder's room of the editorial suite that overlooked Union Square. The three were the fine-featured Richard Watson Gilder, a poet of real distinction, who as editor in chief had successfully dramatized in the pages of the *Century* the critical clashes of the War between the States; his first assistant, Robert Underwood Johnson, essayist and poet, whose beard and bushy eyebrows suggested a friendly Scotty; and C. C. Buell, just a workhorse editor.[102]

I was shown the preliminary sketches of illustrations for my story which Frederic Remington,[103] at the peak of his career as painter and illustrator of western scenes, had been commissioned to supply. They liked my choice of title, "Only the Master Shall Praise," which I had taken from Kipling,[104] and approved my restrained handling of a melodramatic plot in which the principal character was easily recognizable as the Cherokee cowboy, Henry Falling, who had ridden for Father since the first shipment of yearlings had come to Indian Territory from Texas. In this conference with the Olympians, I was literally the tongue-tied country boy dazed by his almost incredible luck. Their talk, and Mr. Gilder's urging to submit more stories, sent me off walking on air.

At home, I thrust the *Century*'s check into Father's hand, and told him how I had come by it. He studied it for a moment, then broke out, "I'd rather hear you'd won that prize than have a thousand dollars handed to me!" No stronger endorsement could he have given to my determination to write; and he promptly duplicated the check.

Chapter 5[105]

I carried away from Harvard a varied assortment of other memories:

A word with, and a fleeting close-up look at President Charles William Eliot at a crowded afternoon reception. He was sixty-six, tall, straight, and unforgettable, aside from his intellectual integrity, because of a wide red birthmark splash on one cheek. Looking at him, one might mistake his seeming austerity for a narrow Puritanism. One might, that is, until one remembered the strong wind of liberalism he had caused to blow across the old Yard and through the lecture rooms, and had sat under individualistic teachers like Wendell whom he had drawn to Harvard and successfully supported through more than one such tempest of protest as had blown Ross and Howard out of Stanford.[106]

An evening at the big, dignified, and beautiful home of Charles Eliot Norton that was like moving back in time to the lush old days of Emerson, Lowell, and Holmes. Norton was of their caliber, a true intellectual; why I was asked to make one of those who flocked around him in his spacious drawing room and bent over the hand of his friendly, charming wife I don't know—"Just your damn fool luck," Dane said when I told him about the evening.[107]

A sermon by Samuel McChord Crothers in the small Unitarian church on Harvard Square that was the sanest talk about things of the spirit I had ever heard except for that well-remembered discourse by Mr. Worcester in the lovely little Swedenborgian church in San Francisco. Those two I thought of as spiritual brothers.[108]

Chapter 6

. . . Also, he promised whatever additional backing I should need.

Coolidge wrote that he had been commissioned by the Smithsonian

Institution to trap and prepare for its collection field mice in the Naples region of Italy, in Sicily, and in southern France. I should explain that for more than ten years, in school and college vacations, he had made himself known to the Smithsonian as an expert collector of wildlife.[109] He would sail from New York to Naples in two weeks, and urged me to go along. "I know you can't help on the job," he wrote, "but you could have a good time while I'm working, and when I'm through we could take in the Paris Exposition, maybe see other places, then come back together. It would be your 'wander-year,' at least a big part of one, and be good for you."

Father, ever sympathetic with the Odysseus urge, said, "I expect he's right; how much will you need for the jaunt?"

"I don't like to take anymore from you, Dad," I protested." You've spent so much already — "

"Hell, Jinks," he flared, "it's no more than I'd have spent on the rest of my boys if they'd wanted the schooling you've had — and it won't break me."

So I carried to New York another five hundred dollars, opened a bank account, and bought eight hundred dollars' worth of travelers' checks.

Dane and I took a small, low-fare freight ship of the Fabre Line that stopped for two days at Marseilles and another two days at Genoa before docking on the eighteenth day at Naples.[110] Only three other passengers were aboard, none of whom interested us, and throughout the long, smooth crossing under cloudless fall skies Dane and I sat for hours every day on a tiny sundeck and talked. That is, he talked; I prodded with occasional questions, and listened to incidents and chapters of the story of his life which he told extremely well. He was twenty-seven, a young man of course, but to me he seemed old, vastly experienced, and equipped with a mature philosophy — until he came to the subject of women. Specifically, to Susan, with whom, he confided, he had fallen in love before I had.

At the first intimation of his romantic interest in her, I felt a sharp stab of jealousy, and thought, This is bad; he's not just another erratic Wild Bill Newell to cope with, but a serious rival, her equal in intellect and social idealism.[111] I said nothing about my own passionate interest, however, and at the end of his confession breathed freely. He had asked my warmly responsive Susan to marry him in the formal words of a shy suitor of the 1840s! She had kissed his cheek and told him she would always admire him for his sterling character.

After finding a room in a well-kept Naples pension facing the curving Bay shore and distant Capri, I went with Dane to interview the English-speaking director of the biological station to whom the Smithsonian people had written. When he heard of Coolidge's plan to go out into the country to trap mice, he showed concern, and said, "My friend, I must warn you that what you propose is hazardous. Our peasants are ignorant and superstitious; they will not understand your purpose. To them it will appear that you are making strange black magic, and should a child die or some other misfortune befall the neighborhood while you're at your work they might very well attack, possibly kill you."

"Surely," Dane protested, "you're joking, or — " I thought I detected in his tone a suspicion that the man was trying to divert him from his mission out of a jealous desire to have the mice taken by his own staff.

"No, no, my friend," the director insisted, "I am quite serious. However — well, let me think it over; I will try to arrange something. Come back in two days." Two days later he laid a plan before Dane: "My good friend who is American consul at Sorrento has a small hunting lodge in the hills four miles away, and he will be pleased to have you use it. He will take you to the lodge, introduce you to the priest of the village nearby, tell him exactly what you are to do, and ask the priest to explain it if possible to the peasants — in any case to insist that they must not molest you or disturb your traps. However, I tell you frankly that it is a risk I should not take if I were you."

Coming back to the pension, Dane scoffed at the warning, and we moved across the Bay to Sorrento, he with his trapping and stuffing equipment to the lodge in the hills and I to an attractive cheap hotel, favored by German tourists, whose garden ran back to a cliff that overlooked the Mediterranean. For three weeks I loafed, swam, and walked with a young German guest and, every other day, went to talk with Dane, after he had made a morning round of his traps, and watch him skin and dissect mice. On my third visit I found him considerably perturbed, for in the night prowlers had thrown stones against the door, and he had heard angry mutterings outside. Before my arrival, he had gone to the priest, made him understand what had occurred, and the priest was on the way to consult the consul. In the afternoon, the consul arrived with the priest and assured Dane, "We shall do all possible to prevent other such happenings, but I hope you will soon be finished with your work!"

Coolidge stuck it out, in spite of a second night bombardment, until he had the specimens he needed, then he and I went to Capri for four days before he sailed for Sicily. The one outstanding memory of Capri was that I, yielding to Dane's scornful refusal to follow the ordinary tourist routine, did not enter the Blue Grotto in spite of the guides' frantic urging.[112]

Instead of sailing with Dane to Palermo, I set off to visit Rome, Florence, Venice, and Switzerland before meeting him in Paris. At Rome I had the good luck to meet young Charles Upson Clark, a postgraduate student of Latin preparing for a teaching job on the Yale University faculty, who spoke Italian and knew Italy well.[113] With him I walked Rome's old streets, saw the Colosseum by moonlight, visited two small churches seldom seen by tourists, and stood under the great dome of St. Peter's. The Vatican's chapel's Raphaels brought to mind the mock rapturous description I had heard Betty's mother read from her book.[114]

Clark's studies would keep him in Rome until the middle of July, and we arranged to meet in Venice shortly before the Feast of the Redemption[115] — a celebration which he said was well worth seeing — then make a short walking trip across the eastern spur of the Dolomite Alps from Belluno to Toblach. From Toblach, we would go on to Innsbruck, where our paths would diverge.[116]

No longer restrained by Coolidge's horror of following the usual tourist routine, at Florence I spent hours in the Uffizi and Pitti Palace galleries, even falling in behind conducted parties whose guides poured out, in broken English, much of the information about the Italian Primitives I vaguely remembered from Professor Kriehn's snap course at Stanford. I lingered on the Ponte Vecchio, gazed at Giotto's Tower and the tombs of the Medici, walked along the banks of the Arno, and made one foolhardy night prowl alone through narrow, dark medieval streets where furtive, gesturing women attempted to attract my attention and where, I imagined, assassins might be lying in wait.[117]

Early one sparkling bright morning, I took a tram to Fiesole,[118] and from that considerable elevation looked down upon the city and the winding river and understood why people spoke of "sunny Italy." On the return trip,

I stopped for the greater part of the afternoon at the villa of a rich New Englander who had lived for years on the hillside overlooking Florence. How I came to know him I cannot recall. (I have never succeeded for more than a week in keeping a diary, assuring myself that anything worth remembering would stick in the mind anyway.) It was my first close-up view of an expatriate American who had chosen to live a life of leisure and luxury in the midst of an old civilization. Both he and his charming wife seemed a bit restless, avid for talk with folks from home, overeager to show off their gardens, the wonderful mosaic floor of their great salon, and their authentic art treasures.

With Clark, I saw all of the well-known attractions of Venice, threaded the canals in gondolas, fed pigeons in St. Mark's Plaza, invaded the ancient Doge's Palace, and swam at the Lido, that lovely Adriatic beach not then overrun by tourists.[119]

Then came the July night fiesta, with its hundreds of flower-decked and lantern-lighted gondolas and barges on the broad Giudecca, a big band making sensuous music on a huge float, and spectacular fireworks going up from another float, the myriad family groups gliding slowly to the accompaniment of mandolin and guitar music and old songs, the feasting and wine drinking. Gay it all was, but I saw no rowdyism — not even when, at dawn, most of the revelers crossed to the Lido for the traditional sunrise purification plunge. Clark and I had engaged a gondola for the night, followed the crowd to the Lido, and came back to breakfast at our hotel dazed and tired, and assuring each other that life could bring no more satisfying indulgence of the senses.

I recall one surprising comment of his: "John, you know the average male tourist yearns for a girl on an occasion like this, but I don't think of it as a setting for lovemaking. Do you?"

"No," I agreed, and wondered that throughout the night I had hardly thought of Susan; and my letter to her from Venice was brief, with only a mention of the unforgettable Festa del Redentore.

Staying overnight at an inn at Belluno that hung over an Alpine torrent, where I strangled [*sic*] in downing my first tiny glass of the fiery white brandy called grappa, we checked our bags at a stage line office and set off on foot for the pass and such draughts of mountain air, such eyefuls of titanic bare rock peaks, glaciers, and snowfields as I had never dreamed of getting. Clark had turned out to be the rare traveling companion who doesn't feel obliged to call attention to every delight that meets the eye. Thinking of my good fortune in being with him, I recalled what Coolidge had once said of Betty after going with her to Faneuil Hall,[120] "Hell, she seemed to think I was blind the way she kept grabbing my arm, pointing, and exclaiming, 'Oh, Dane, just look at that!'"

At the summit of the pass, we peeked into a refuge hut provided with bunks, bedding, fuel, and food for stormbound hikers, ate snow, and where, facing south, I brought a decisive grin to Clark's lips by quoting "Beyond the Alps lies Italy!"[121]

Recovering our bags at Toblach, we pushed on for a pleasant two days at Innsbruck. Before leaving me, Clark told me that his father was an editorial writer on the *New York Evening Post* and that if I cared to try for a job on that paper he would write to him recommending me. Later, I learned that my friend's mother was the well-known feminist Kate Upson.[122] I regretted not going on to Munich because Clark said that there one found the best beer in the world, a brew, I learned later at the Hofbrau in New York, that made the California steam beer we Stanford hellions drank at the Little Vendôme in Mayfield on Saturday-night busts seem like hopped-up dishwater.[123]

At Lucerne, I waited until it was time to set off for my rendezvous in Paris with Coolidge, living inexpensively but luxuriously (for me), going out to look at Thorwaldsen's much-viewed *Lion*, venturing timidly into the Kursaal, climbing the Rigi and Pilatus along with other tourists who scorned the cog railways, and thinking that Lucerne would be an ideal refuge in my tottery old age. Two weeks of it was too much.[124]

I learned from an American, on the train to Paris, of a small Left Bank hotel near the Luxemburg Gardens and the Odeon which he said was in the heart of the city's Bohemia, a recommendation that meant nothing to me. However, when he said that it was cheap and clean, I wrote down the name and address; and took a horse-drawn cab from the Gare de Lyons to engage a big room for Dane and myself.[125] Next day, I met him at the railroad station, and listened to an evening-long account of his collecting adventures after leaving Sorrento.

If the Italian peasants were suspicious and resentful of his presence among them, those of Sicily were downright hostile, and he had been unable to devise a method for overcoming their superstitious opposition. He said, "If I had tried to trap in their fields, I'm sure one of them would have stuck a knife in my back. No one I talked with at Palermo could ensure even reasonable safety, so I had to give up and sail for Nice."

French farmers and vineyardists of the Basses Alpes region, however, welcomed him, were politely curious but seemed to understand his purpose, helped him to set his traps, and hospitably invited him into their homes. "Believe me," he chuckled, "I heaved one big sigh of relief when I started to work among them!"

Recollections of my week at the Chicago World's Fair, seven years before, took the edge off the Paris Exposition for me, but I trailed Dane through the grounds and buildings willingly, was lifted to the top of the Eiffel Tower, and met again the huge rearing Percherons [that] Rosa Bonheur had painted on eight-by-twelve-foot canvases and which had provoked Will Rogers to exclaim, "Them overgrown broncs'd sure make he-man plow teams!" In that same gallery, I made Dane sit down, while I rested my feet, directly in front of a small painting titled *Beethoven*. Vaguely, I knew that Beethoven had been a musician and composer; now, taken by the picture, I began to realize that his music could be magic. It was a shabby attic setting, with a pianist and violinist playing, their backs to me, and a group of listeners, relaxed and unselfconscious, lost in dreams evoked by the music, a painting of pure, unposed rapture. I wanted to know more about Beethoven, hear his music; and many times since I have felt that I was listening, at Carnegie Hall and other concert halls, to the concerto for piano and violin the musicians in the painting might have been playing.[126]

To a Londoner at our hotel we owed an evening at a café-concert we long remembered. It was a mellow, unpretentious place where we sat at a table for two hours, had all the drinks we wanted, and listened to a small orchestra made up of advanced music students, all for the equivalent of one dollar each. Our newly made friend told us that they played classical pieces; I knew only that I liked them better than anything I had heard since, in my freshman year at Stanford, Herbert Hoover promoted a concert at nearby San Jose and young Paderewski, with the shock of wild blond hair, kept a thousand or more of us student barbarians quiet through a long program. I thought of how, when Hoover confessed to Paderewski's booking agent that he had only twelve hundred dollars of the fifteen hundred that had been guaranteed, the great pianist had said, "Of course, I will play for whatever he has," and of the generous encores he gave us. On a number of later and longer stays in Paris, I never found another café-concert like that one on the Boulevard Saint Michel.[127]

We had planned to spend two weeks in London, but Dane ran out of francs, and we figured that my remaining travelers' checks would not cover the cost of that diversion and also pay for passage on a low-fare ship to New York. So we said au revoir to Paris — at any rate, I did, for I was determined to come again.[128] On docking at New York, I loaned Dane ten of the fifteen dollars I had in my pocket to pay his railroad fare to Washington and buy meals until he collected from the Smithsonian.

I tried in vain to convince him that the ten-dollar loan and the price of his steamship ticket were my contribution to science, in grateful remembrance of my thoroughly satisfying months abroad. Within a week came a money order for the amount he owed. As Susan had discovered, sterling was stamped all over him, and he spelled conscience, as Betty's mother spelled culture, with a big C.[129]

Chapter 7

It was time to get to work, to justify if I could Father's confidence, show some return on the money he had spent on my education. Time to combat a liking for idleness and a growing tendency to think of myself as a favorite of fortune. Specifically, I must find a job, and a place to live, in New York.[130]

On a visit to the *Century* office, where my naive proposal to write about my Italian and Parisian experiences for the magazine met a politely cool refusal, I met Isabel Hapgood, a handsome gray-haired woman who had won a deserved reputation as a translator of Russian classics. As we left the office together, she graciously accepted my invitation to lunch at Mouquin's, which I had heard was as good as many of the best-known restaurants of Paris, and better than the Duval chain [of] eating places Dane and I had patronized. Its second-story front window beside which Miss Hapgood and I sat looked out on the Sixth Avenue Elevated, over which dwarf steam engines pulled clattering trains up and down New York.[131]

She suggested the food and wine, talked French with the waiter, and in the two hours we lingered over lunch drew from me my vaguely formed ambitions. I liked her very much, and thought, Thirty years ago, she must have been a lot like Susan; and when she said she would speak about me to Mr. Garrison, literary editor of the *New York Evening Post* and editor of the *Post*'s weekly *Nation*, I felt flattered, and reassured.

The *Evening Post* was hardly a *news* paper at all judged by the standards of the *Sun*, *World*, and *Herald*. It was as little like the present-day *Post* as Mary's snow-white lamb after its visit to Pittsburgh. Its very limited circulation, some twenty-five thousand, however, was almost wholly among the most influential people of New York and the East, bankers, Wall Street brokers, anti-Tammany politicians (called "Goo-goos" by Richard Croker's derisive followers), professional men, publishers, and literary folks. Nationally, it was bracketed with the *Springfield (Mass.) Republican* which Samuel Bowles, father of the first OPA [Office of Price Administration] administrator, had made a potent political weapon. Its editorials were widely quoted, its book reviewers respected and feared, and its financial page, ably edited by Alexander Dana Noyes, was required reading among the sounder members of the financial community. Its music and drama critics, Henry T. Finck and J. Rankin Towse, ranked in influence with William Winter of the *Tribune* and W. J. Henderson of the *Sun*.[132]

Mr. Garrison, of the family of William Lloyd Garrison, gadfly abolitionist of slavery days, was a quiet, bearded man of sixty with a fine New England literary background. He was sufficiently appreciative of my *Century Magazine* achievement — my prize story had recently been published — and Miss Hapgood's endorsement, but obviously was not impressed by my western farm rearing and schooling. However, he took me in to talk with Rollo Ogden, lately made editor in chief in a succession of editors from William Cullen Bryant down through E. L. Godkin, his belligerent immediate predecessor. Mr. Ogden took me to Mr. Lynn, veteran managing editor, who passed me along to Franklin Clarkin, the young city editor, whose stabbing eyes and wry grin seemed to challenge my brashness.[133]

After a brief inquiry into my background, Clarkin showed me a desk in the small reporters' room I could use if I cared to go to work at space rates — five dollars a column.[134] Then I asked to see Mr. Clark, who asked me many questions about Charles, and our Italian experiences. I was glad to say that I had liked his son and had been impressed by his ability. While talking with Mr. Clark, young Oswald Garrison Villard came into his room and offered a soft-handed greeting when he was told that I would work for the paper. Villard, son of the prominent financier Henry Villard, who had once dominated the Northern Pacific Railroad and had acquired a controlling interest in the *Evening Post*, was living with his widowed mother in a vast, luxuriously furnished apartment on Fifty-ninth Street overlooking Central Park. He was eager to make himself a power on the paper's not-too-well-paid editorial staff.[135]

Alone in a boardinghouse room that evening, I began going over in my mind the names of former Stanford students I knew who had come to New York. I recalled that of my good friend Gail Nichols, assistant head worker at the University Settlement; and next day, after initiation into the job of reporter, I went to see him in his pleasant rooms on the top floor of the new and impressive six-story Settlement building at Eldridge and Rivington Streets, in the very heart of the Jewish quarter, then called the Ghetto.[136]

Nichols asked if I would like to be a resident worker for a year, help with clubs and other activities of the Settlement three or four evenings a week in exchange for a room and meals with the head worker, his wife, and the eleven other workers. Would I! I jumped at the offer, and thanked my lucky stars that I had found Nichols.

New York's big East Side Ghetto was an area of dirty, shabby old four-story tenement buildings, swarming with screaming children, shawled women, old men wearing black skullcaps, raucous-voiced pushcart peddlers, and permeated by myriad smells that seemed to culminate in the overpowering tang of sour pickles in barrels outside odorous delicatessen shops. The thousands upon thousands of Jewish families that for twenty years had been pouring in from Poland, Russia, Austria, and Hungary, unrestricted by immigration quotas, made it outwardly a bedlam. Our Settlement workers, however, found that the universal hunger for betterment that had caused their uprooting from Europe led them, here, to urge their children to seize avidly every opportunity to get ahead in this strange new world where no bars to their advancement existed.

Their eagerness was bound to stimulate us, as it did. The boys and girls, and some of their parents, who crowded the clubrooms and auditorium that made up the first four floors of the building were poorly dressed; they washed all over infrequently; they talked clamorously, pushed and milled all over the place once they got over their first shyness. But they were quick to absorb whatever we had to offer by way of precept and example; and each of us formed friendships among them that lasted long after we had given place to other workers and their families had moved out of the Ghetto. They were quick to note that we resident workers bathed daily, dressed neatly, spoke grammatically, did not shout to make ourselves heard, seemed to know how to behave correctly at parties, and were equipped to tell them a good deal about America's history and way of living.[137]

Both "Jimmie" Reynolds, our head worker, and Nichols were tactful and tireless pilots of this teeming hive of activity. Upon Reynolds and his charming, socially well connected wife rested the responsibility for finding the required financial support; Nichols was the practical house manager. Nearly every evening, at the long dining table of the Reynolds' suite, appeared guests from uptown and out of town whose interest had been, or might be, enlisted in our work. Some were merely rich men and women who found it both satisfying and fashionable to help the underprivileged. Some, like the wealthy Stokes family, contributed effective personal service as well as money; one of the resident workers was J. G. Phelps-Stokes, who married Rose Pastor, a Jewish girl "graduate" of the Settlement. Some, like the Hewitts, gave generously of money and practical job help for boys and girls who fitted themselves for the work they could offer, and stirred ambition by the well-known Hewitt family record of turning out distinguished scientists, inventors, merchants, and a mayor of New York City.[138]

One of our best-liked guests, who came from time to time, was Dr. Trudeau, director of the sanitarium for the tubercular at Saranac Lake in the Adirondacks, at which Robert Louis Stevenson had been a patient. His problem was also twofold—to find the funds for its support and to care for the many patients, rich or poor, who came to him. He was, in the best sense, a friend of man.[139]

I wondered why few rich Jews dined with us, or seemed to be interested in the Settlement. Later, I learned that they preferred to support and manage their own charities, hospitals, and uplift institutions. This tendency toward self-segregation in large centers of population had not added to the popularity of Jews in an America which, otherwise, has been a true melting pot of races.

However, as the youngsters with whom we worked grew up, made money, and became more or less important in the life of the city and state, they volunteered in considerable numbers as workers, and gave freely to support the Settlement.

Our workers were indeed an assorted crew, drawn to New York from various sections; among them were a talented, self-effacing editorial writer on the *Sun*, an official of the Charity Organization Society, an assistant librarian, an insurance man who had lived for a time at a London East End settlement, an English Fabian Socialist who knew Bernard Shaw and Sidney and Beatrice Webb, two young lawyers, Stokes, and — I could name them all if I had kept a diary![140]

Working in shifts as we did, we had half of our evenings free to spend as we pleased. Often, we went out in parties of three or four to so-called bohemian cafés, at one of which we could listen to gypsy music, and another, far over near the East River, where we liked the ebullient proprietor and his potent Hungarian wine — all you could drink for fifty cents, and God help you if you tried to make a pig of yourself! Two or three cafés on Second Avenue were favored by prostitutes, professional streetwalkers, and occasional prowlers. I came to know one of the second type when, going out with Ken Stillman, a fellow resident, I was asked to meet Ida. Going back to our rooms, he confessed that he was so deeply in love with her that he could not imagine living without her.

Somerset Maugham had not yet written *Of Human Bondage*, but he might well have used that predatory Second Avenue girl as his model for the tea shop waitress in his unforgettable novel.[141] She was perhaps twenty-five, thin, nervous, with a sharp and bawdy tongue and a conviction that the cards had been stacked against her. Yet there were moments, as she sat with us sprinkling salt on the foamy head of a freshly drawn stein of beer, then taking quick sips, when the spirit of a completely innocent, freckled-nose country-bred tomboy shone through. In those moments I saw flashes of the impish loveliness that had enraptured Stillman.

I believed him when he told me that Ida had tried honestly to live up to his conception of her as a reformed character, after a first easy stint as a gold digger. Yet that evening when he left us to go to the men's room, she broke out resentfully, "He's so damn dull! He won't dance, he can't drink without gettin' soft, and—I'm gettin' sick an' tired of him." I didn't take her words to mean an invitation to me; they were only the expression of an angry revolt against boredom.

The letter to me in which Stillman tried to explain his infatuation and express his despair was written less than a month later. Reading it, I was profoundly shocked, and frightened by its revelation of a soul tormented by a hopeless passion. I thought, God deliver me from a love like this! I tore the letter in small pieces and prayed to forget it before doing what he begged me to do.

Baldly, he wrote in the opening sentence that his body would be found in a room at the cheap Second Avenue hotel he named, then asked that his family be urged to permit his burial under the name he had assumed on registering there. He went on to say that he had at last realized the hopelessness of his struggle to lift Ida out of the mire when he went to her room to take her out to a café, knocked at the door, entered at her bidding, and found her in bed with a man. I shall never forget the words that followed, "John, she laughed at me as I opened the door and stepped in. She laughed and laughed and laughed—damn her to hell!"

Her laughter was for Stillman the trump of doom. The shaky lines he wrote to me were set down as soon as he was able to get the poison he required and go to the hotel room he rented. His final act, he wrote, would be to stamp and mail the letter.

On one free evening I went with Gerould, the assistant Columbia University librarian, to a meeting addressed by Theodore Roosevelt, who had lately been made governor of New York.[142] His speech ended, he came to the cloakroom as Gerould and I were recovering our hats and overcoats. On turning away from the counter, Roosevelt heard my name spoken as Gerould introduced me to a friend, beamed on me, and demanded, "Are you Dick Oskison's brother?"

I said, "Yes, I'm John Oskison." He shook hands vigorously, asked about Dick, told me that he had read and liked my *Century* story, and spent five minutes praising Dick's Rough Rider service and urging me to write the story of that picturesque regiment.

I was greatly flattered, but considering that I had not been within three thousand miles of San Juan Hill at the time of the battle, and that such a celebrated war correspondent as Richard Harding Davis went up the hill with the troops, I thought it best to forget T. R.'s generous offer to help me do the job.[143] After that meeting I saw Roosevelt occasionally through the years — during his presidency, before he went to Africa to shoot lions, and while he was an editorial contributor to the *Outlook*, the weekly magazine of opinion edited by the patriarchal ex-preacher and liberal Lyman Abbott[144] — and each time he recalled my name and asked about Dick. I'm sure he could have called thousands by name, and had for more thousands the sort of real personal friendship that made him a truly beloved American.

I found time to write short stories, sold another Indian Territory tale to the *Century*[145] and one to *McClure's*, leader in its field as a popular fiction and "muck raking" magazine,[146] then began collecting rejection slips. It was puzzling, for I did not realize that I was trying to market thin plots all but drowned in floods of description and characterizations. I had never studied the technic of fiction writing; my instruction had been in *writing*. Like so many amateurs, I loved such appealing phrases as Susan and I had hammered out together and which had pleased my instructors at Stanford and Harvard. In short, I mistook form for substance. For example, it did not occur to me to write the dramatic story of Stillman and Ida, and Maugham beat me to it![147]

On the *Post*, greedily anxious to lengthen my weekly "string" of published pieces, I fell for the temptation to squeeze all possible juice out of the assignments handed to me by Clarkin. Both he and Mr. Lynn approved my attempts to work in paragraphs of human interest, a trick that, on the *Sun*, reporters like Lindsay Denison and Samuel Hopkins Adams were doing superlatively well.[148] It was not long before my Saturday total of contributions, carefully measured by the office manager Byron Pink after I had clipped and pasted them together end to end, ran to more than six columns.

Then, for the *Post's* Saturday supplement, I began to write articles, usually on western topics. Next I submitted to the supplement editor some of the short stories the magazines had rejected, and found him receptive until some unaccountable impulse led me to write a sea story. He printed it, and was forthwith overwhelmed by letters from readers pointing out that I had made every mistake it was possible to make in describing details of boats and boat racing. If his face was red, on reading the experts' jeers, mine was flaming! It was months before he would even look at another story of mine.[149]

My self-confidence at length restored, I tackled the sacred editorial page, where contributed matter was paid for at the rate of eight dollars a column. My first two or three offerings, which ran to a third of a column each, brought friendly comment and advice as to rewriting from Mr. Odgen. Thereafter they were seldom turned back for rewriting, either being altered by the chief to conform to his ideas or thrown into his wastebasket with a word to me about why he rejected them.

Then came the great day when the *Post* went out with the first of my column-long editorials, under a headline, based on the antics of hatchet-wielding, saloon-wrecking Carry Nation in Oklahoma Territory;[150] and soon I became an unacknowledged editorial authority on the West, that region which to most *Post* readers was a vast proving ground for bizarre social and political experimenters.

Among the five reporters on the staff to whom I became strongly attracted was Norman Duncan, a reticent Scot, who discovered the Syrian quarter, not a rifle shot from Wall Street, and was inspired to write some of the tenderest, most heart-warming short stories about the café characters he came to know that have appeared in American magazines. Then there was Charley Selden, thin, solemn faced, nursing a sparse billygoat beard, and endowed with an authentic "dry wit," whom I shall always remember for his thumbnail word sketches of his New Jersey farm, where he crooned "Only a Pansy Blossom" over his wife's flowerbed and had named his two strutting roosters "Tom Jones" and "Joseph Andrews."[151]

Selden's roosters sent me to a leisurely rereading of Fielding's lusty yarns in which, according to Thackeray, an English novelist last dared to draw a *man*. Then I tackled Richardson's *Pamela* and *Clarissa Harlowe*, learned about women from that co-creator with Fielding of the novel, and wondered when such word portraits of amorous lovers and easily seduced ladies could be published in America. Next I tried and enjoyed the broad humor of Smollett's *Humphrey Clinker*, graduated to Sterne's *Sentimental Journey*, discovered the innocuous and inexplicably interesting long novels of English country life and political intrigue Anthony Trollope had turned out by the score, and sniffled over the sweetly sentimental masterpieces of Barrie.[152]

What a decline! I thought, If ever I try to write a novel I must remember that "Nice Nellie" has convinced fiction readers of this generation that the sex urge cannot possibly awaken until the marriage vows are said. I will stick to *The Virginian* model of the immaculate, romantic cowboy and his equally immaculate school-ma'am sweetheart. To be sure, that would bar from my yarn a goodly number of my Indian Territory cowboy friends and more than one interesting girl I had known whose lapses from the straight and narrow path had neither driven them to a life of prostitution nor barred them from the society of their community.[153]

Of course, there was another kind of realism, that of William Dean Howells's *Rise of Silas Lapham*, but I knew I could never reach such *Atlantic Monthly*–like heights. However, it might be possible to become a more or less worthy disciple of Hamlin Garland, whose *Main-Traveled Roads* seemed as authentic as John Steuart Curry's paintings of midwestern farm scenes did in 1938.[154]

Chapter 8

The goodwill of the *Century*'s editors, who hoped perhaps that I might become a dependable contributor, plus my connection with the *Post*, brought invitations to meetings of the Authors' Club and luncheons and dinners at the Century Club, both dominated by literary veterans; among them, I felt sure, I could find sponsors should I wish to join either or both.[155]

I could not convince myself, however, that I was fit for such exalted company as Edmund Clarence Stedman, William Dean Howells, Frank Stockton, Henry Van Dyke, Thomas Nelson Page, S. Wier Mitchell, Gilbert Parker (the American Winston Churchill), and Richard Watson Gilder. We youngsters revered these high gods, but I wondered if they were not already on the way out, if among them only Mark Twain would find a lasting place in the Pantheon. In fact, the Authors' Club ceased to exist not long after I settled in New York, to be followed into oblivion by the *Century Magazine*. The next generation of stars made the Players' Club, in the old Henry Irving house on Gramercy Square, their favorite rendezvous.[156]

I tried for a time to adapt myself to the climate of the oldsters and learn to speak their language, appreciate their Latin-flavored essays, their epic historical novels, their emasculated "modern" fiction, and laugh at the "gay blades" among them who recited "naughty" limericks at club smokers.

For one, Henry Holt the publisher, a handsome big man in his fifties, I took a strong liking. He asked me to lunch and urged me to do for his firm a western book, fact or fiction, in the manner of certain articles and short stories he had read in the *Post* under my name. My suggestion to write enough short stories in addition to those already published to make a book to be printed under the title I had thought of while riding the range, "Tales of the Old I.T.," did not appeal. "Books of short stories," he said, "don't sell unless they're by writers as well known as Kipling." I mentioned Hamlin Garland's "Main-Traveled Roads." Mr. Holt acknowledged that it had been successful but said it was one of the rare exceptions that proved the rule. He was too tactful to say that I was no Hamlin Garland.[157]

He wanted me to try a novel, with a stout framework of plot and peopled by Indian Territory characters, such as I had used, developed to more heroic proportions. There was, for instance, the shoulder-deformed Indian cowboy who, in my *Century Magazine* story, sacrificed his life to save that of the dashing, reckless white rider who was his ideal.[158] "A sympathetic principal character like him," Mr. Holt suggested, "dominating a full-length story would be new in western fiction, and could be exceptionally popular."

I told then, at some length, the story of Henry Falling's years of service with Father, and promised to think about making him the hero of a novel.

At later luncheon meetings, I felt that Mr. Holt talked to me as he might to his son Roland, who succeeded him as head of Henry Holt & Co. He urged me to be more deliberate in writing, warning against the "fatal facility" that had wrecked many promising careers. "Writing that comes hardest," he said, "is apt to be clearest and easiest to read; that which is done easily is usually hard to read." If I meant to make a business of writing, he advised, I must fashion my life to that end. I must be especially careful to avoid making a wrong marriage; a badly chosen wife could divert a sensitive writer, bedevil him intolerably, ruin him; the right wife could be a wonderful help. Like a good athlete, a successful writer must keep fit physically. "What you put down for readers to read," he insisted, "has to be manufactured out of brain and brawn, and few worthwhile products come from defective — overfat or undernourished — bodies and dissipation-sapped brains."

He liked my living at the Settlement. "The more close associations you have with people the better, provided you save time to convert your contacts into story material—as you've done thus far with you Indian Territory family and friends." I have thought since that if I had told him about Ken Stillman and Ida he might have stirred me to attempt the tale Maugham told so well in *Of Human Bondage*.

It was my misfortune to be practically immune to advice. To myself I said, Sure, Mr. Holt is right as far as he goes, but isn't there something more important to a writer? Inspiration! That was a fondly cherished word among us "talented" writers, confidently expecting the divine afflatus to descend upon us. Once inspired, we would write, no matter how difficult the circumstances of our living. Wasn't Morgan Robertson,[159] for instance, drink-raddled and half starving in a midtown tenement, swarmed over by a numerous family that cared nothing for his writing, using a cluttered kitchen table as desk, turning out wonderful sea stories under the whip of inspiration? So, reverting to one of Mr. Holt's axioms, if I should be inspired to write a novel with Henry Falling as hero, nobody and nothing could stop me! Lack of inspiration was a perfect alibi for a lazy writer.

Another widely circulated counsel to writers that boiled down to the one boldly capitalized word LIVE, I found, too often meant to us young bucks having an affair of the heart. If the affair was illicit and the woman a bitch who gave us plenty of misery, we could wring masterpieces out of our agony. That conception of living was probably far from his mind when Lincoln Steffens, newly installed as managing editor of *McClure's Magazine*, fixed his probing eyes on me and said that a story I had submitted showed that I had not *lived*, yet I felt it was what he meant.[160]

Instead of seeking out an Ida of the streets, as Stillman had done, and putting her into heart-searing fiction, I moved from the University Settlement when my year of residence ended to join four other sane-living extroverts in a big, shabby apartment on the fringe of Greenwich Village. Phillip Allen and Dwight Whitney were fellow reporters on the *Post*, and Emery Pottle assistant editor, under Albert White Vorse, of the *Criterion*, a thin weekly magazine of comment on life in New York City that ran its brief course long before the *New Yorker* came into existence. Ned Bill was our one non-writer; his was a selling job with the Fairbanks Scales Company, and he came in with us because Whitney was engaged to marry his sister.

Inevitably, our disorderly apartment became known as the boar's nest. The cantankerous middle-aged woman we engaged to care for it and cook breakfast and dinner took her obligations lightly. When she felt like it, Mrs. Sheridan cleaned, made the beds, and cooked; when she didn't, we made our own beds and breakfast, went out to dinner at inexpensive spaghetti-and-red-wine joints we liked, and thought, Oh, hell, what's the difference? Such is life in the Village!

At one or another of the half-dozen Italian restaurants within ten minutes' walk of our apartment whose proprietors became friends of their patrons and encouraged table-to-table visiting, we made a good many acquaintances among the Villagers. With a few who, like us, worked at writing jobs we held prolonged sessions, chewing over plots of stories we meant to write and discussing markets for them if and when we got around to putting them on paper. On the fringe of the group of real writing men and women who had settled in the Village because it was a cheap neighborhood in which to live, we met some of the long-haired "geniuses" who talked much and wrote little; also, one or two of the type that flocked in later — uptowners looking for "color" and thrills, sexual and other kinds, in New York's "Bohemia."

None of us of the boar's nest became involved with a predatory female who might have represented "life," and none of us drank more than enough good Chianti to loosen our tongues.

Pottle was our most successful collector of authentic Village notables, bringing to our table for occasional dinners Bliss Carman, his poetic collaborator Richard Hovey, and Richard LeGalliene — all three talented and delightful talkers. On these occasions, Pottle's employer and editor of the *Criterion*, Albert Vorse, and his vivacious wife, Mary Heaton Vorse, helped us to entertain. We were especially fond of Mrs. Vorse, who was just then beginning to write, doing book reviews for her husband. In the following decade she blossomed into a successful fiction and essay writer, and still later won a name as the most extreme radical of the Village's left-wingers.[161]

Pottle's social explorations, furthered by tall good looks, a mannered personality, and meticulous grooming, began to extend to upper Fifth Avenue and the dinner tables of Astors and Vanderbilts; and culminated eventually in an extended affair, in Italy, with a rich and highly connected contessa. Before that connection became established, however, he made liberal use of his uptown admirers as models in short stories for which he was well paid by the *Saturday Evening Post*. I believe he was the first New Yorker of the artistic group to discover the social value of the insult direct, a trick that was to be so well advertised by the Algonquin Hotel group, Dorothy Parker, Alec Woollcott, Art Samuels, Edna Ferber, Heywood Broun, Neysa McMein, F. P. A., Sally Farnham, and their satellites.[162]

For a short time, Pottle and I worked together in an abortive attempt to make a play from *The Cardinal's Snuff Box*, a popular romantic historical novel by Henry Harland, editor of the esoteric English *Yellow Book*.[163] Incidentally, we did not trouble to secure permission for our dramatization from Harland, thinking naively to present both to the author and a producer a fait accompli. We abandoned the project before finishing act two. Though Pottle, under the name Gilbert Emery, went on, much later, to make a considerable career as playwright and stage and screen actor, my close interest in the drama was thereafter confined to a long and somewhat hectic association with Sandra B——, an actress of talent.

Ned Bill became bored with us and went off to live with a business associate. Walter Arndt, a *Sun* reporter, came to take his place in our household. Now we were five writers together in search of markets for our after-hours output.[164]

Philip Allen, promoted by the *Post* to exchange editor, found in a Boston newspaper the announcement of a $250 prize offered by the *Black Cat* magazine for the best short story submitted within the next three months. "Let's all take a shot at it," he proposed. Pottle wasn't interested. The rest of us, however, bought copies of the *Black Cat* and studied its spine-tingling requirements. Four stories went out from our address, and a week after the contest closed the magazine's editor came surging down from Boston, had dinner at our apartment and, with a flourish, distributed checks to all of us. Mine was for the prize award, the others for $100 each; and, "Boys," he urged with editorial enthusiasm, "I want more stories from all of you!" The incredible outcome of our adventure in weird fiction was that none of us could ever sell another yarn to the *Black Cat*: we turned out to be just four one-shot-in-the-locker boys. I have only the haziest recollection of what my story was about.[165]

Besides Lincoln Steffens's earnest counsel, stories I submitted to *McClure's*

Magazine brought a brief contact with the erratic, highly charged S. S. McClure, then under the fictional spell of brilliant Willa Cather, and the prized friendship of Viola Roseboro, the magazine's story editor. She accepted one of the dozen or more tales I offered, and gave me expert and sympathetic criticism of the others. Better, she made me welcome to her apartment in a ramshackle old building shaken by trains of the Ninth Avenue El passing under her windows. Here she held court much in the same spirit as that of "Copey" of Harvard. A dowdy semi-invalid of fifty, she won the hearts of us young men who came to listen to her fascinating talk about the writer and writing that had been tied in with [her] own life. We brought flowers, fruit, and whatever other good things we thought would please her. She told us of the thrill she felt at reading the manuscript of the first Jack London story that came to *McClure's*. She lived for such thrills, and enjoyed many.[166]

Another editor friend I made in this phase of adventures in writing was Bob Davis, who bought stories for *Munsey's Magazine*. It could be said of him, as Will Rogers said of himself, that he never met a man — a writing man, at any rate — he didn't like. If a manuscript that came into his hands showed a gleam of talent, he asked the writer to come and talk with him; and at luncheon in the grill of the Fifth Avenue Hotel, across the street from the *Munsey* editorial rooms, gave shrewd criticism, suggestions for rewriting, and poured out details of plots and situations which he hoped his guest might be able to use.[167]

A story he told me because he knew I am part Cherokee Indian and might be especially interested has stuck in my mind and roused regret that I have not been able to make it over successfully into fiction. Its principal character was a lusty full-blood Plains Indian, Iron Head, who had been recruited from a western Nebraska reservation by "Buffalo Bill" Cody for his Wild West show.

After touring extensively with the show in the United States, Iron Head went along with it to England and the Continent. During its long stay in Paris, a French woman of good family and independent fortune became infatuated with him, pursued him with fanatic persistence, and made him her lover when he said he could not marry her.

Cody refused to allow her to follow the Indian when the show left Paris. Brokenhearted, she brooded over her lost lover for a year, then undertook to find him at his home on the reservation. All she had to guide her was a post office address. She sailed to New York, found out from the French consul how to get to Nebraska, and bought a train ticket to the station nearest the reservation post office. Then came three days and nights of travel, with the necessary changes and waits, and the final two hundred miles of bleak, seemingly boundless prairie, which, as it unrolled hour after hour, began to frighten and daunt her. But she stuck it out, and at last, bedraggled and exhausted, stepped down on the wooden platform of a sun-baked little depot, where the station agent told her that Iron Head lived with his people fifteen miles west. Asking no questions, he found for her a team and driver.

Then the last miles under a pitiless summer sun, with the drive ending at a wire gate twenty yards from Iron Head's shack. Sitting in the shade with his back to the wall, stripped of his show trappings, in a ragged undershirt and dirty overalls, his long hair tangled and filthy, and all but hidden by his staring Indian wife and their brood of children, Iron Head looked up indifferently.

Hysterically, she demanded of her driver, "You are sure it is he, that one?"

"Hell, yes," was the answer, "I've knowed that Indian since he was knee-high to a grasshopper."

"Then — then-" she gasped, "take me please to the train. Please!"

"But," the driver laughed, "don't you want to git out an' say howdy?"

"No, oh no! Please, I beg of you." Out of sight of Iron Head, she collapsed to a trembling, weeping heap on the bottom of the buckboard.

Bob Davis said of the story, "Of course, *Munsey's* couldn't print it, but there must be a market for a human drama like that." Later, when I talked with Frank Munsey about doing an article for his magazine, I understood Bob's point. Munsey was a straight-backed and strait-laced State of Maine man whose one aim was to print a magazine with the widest possible popular (and sexless) appeal. Ambitious to enter New York society, he had on his payroll Frank Crowninshield, a talented uptown socialite, who served as his secretary and guide to the Four Hundred. On quitting Munsey, when the publisher gave up his quest for a place in the *Social Register*, Crowninshield became editor of *Vanity Fair*, in the Condé Nast group of publications, including *Vogue*, that reflected the dress, manners, and distractions of the rich.[168]

I had swung wide indeed of my first New York literary associations, but

I was having fun capitalizing on my limited inspirations. At the same time, I was spending less than half of my earnings, and was beginning to wonder what to do with my savings. Father was pleased by my financial success, and it pleased me to believe that if his career had been that of a writer he would have experimented in the way I was doing.

My increasing facility in editorial writing—I had lashed out occasionally in column-long scoldings of corruption in local and national politics—led Mr. Ogden to recommend me as editor of *The Citizen*, a four-page daily newspaper of Ossining, thirty miles north of New York City. Its new owners meant to use it in a campaign to oust the ring of greedy politicians that was in control of the local government, and they briefed me at length on the situation and what I was expected to accomplish.[169]

A pleasant room, and meals, at a large military school in the center of Ossining made up the contribution to the cause by the school's proprietors, Mr. and Mrs. C. F. Brusie; and they and the teachers soon became good friends. In a way, the following year was a repetition of my twelve months at the University Settlement, although I missed the effort we settlement workers had made to satisfy the hunger for whatever we had to give the eager Jewish boys and girls of Rivington Street.

My writing staff were a good-natured, tireless veteran reporter named Sheldon, who knew all the local news sources, and a belligerent Irishman who had been a printer and still helped out when needed in setting type for display advertising. Walsh resented not having been made editor and attempted to show me up as an amateur gangbuster by turning in vitriolic attacks on the editor of our opposition weekly paper. Supported by *The Citizen*'s owners, I vetoed direct assaults on our opponents and undertook to make our editorial policy constructive, pointing out in detail what was lacking to make Ossining a good town for decent citizens.

The crux of the campaign was to put over at a forthcoming election a bond issue for badly needed improvements. The opposition fought it on the ground that the increased taxes necessary to meet interest and sinking fund charges would be a hardship on the workingmen and their families. Also, as we knew, if bonds were to be issued, the ruling clique wanted their "cut."

Ossining's ten thousand residents were made up in approximately equal parts of workers in three prosperous factories (one made a nationally known patent medicine) and well-to-do commuters to New York City offices — lawyers, brokers, jobbers, partners in wholesale businesses, publishers. Among our faction were two of the most effective workers in the anti-Tammany Citizens' Union of New York City, who knew how to organize a campaign and get out the voters. They became my close advisers.

As part of my work, I contributed to the *Post* occasional editorials on the local fight for good government, news items, and special articles.

One news story I suggested doing was of a daybreak electrocution in Sing Sing prison. Breakfastless, I took my place in the semicircle of newspapermen and official witnesses facing the Chair in the death chamber, and in an atmosphere of grim silence watched the iron door behind which the condemned man waited. It was not long before he appeared, but the wait seemed endless; and when the shoeless little man who was to be executed came out with a muttering priest at one side and a guard at the other, and darted frightened glances at us and the Chair, I wished with all my soul that I had not suggested writing the story of his extinction.

A sickening sensation in my stomach increased; I was afraid I would vomit before we could leave the death chamber. As the prison guards swiftly adjusted the stout leather straps that held the man's arms and legs in place, then crowned him with the helmet-like metal cap to which the lethal wires were attached, I thought, I can't write this!

The priest uttered the final word of extreme unction, made the sign of the cross, and stepped back from the metal plate on which the Chair was bolted. The prison warden, who had come in at the last moment, swept us in the semicircle with his eyes, queried the guards with a look, received their nods to indicate that all was ready, then stepped to a point from which he could signal the executioner behind the panel on which the required electrical contacts would be made.

There came a low hissing sound, and a sudden convulsive stiffening of the man's arms and legs, as though the current running through him was straining to break the straps that held him and lift him out of that ponderous Chair. The current was turned off momentarily; the unconscious man sagged; saliva ran down his chin; then his body stiffened as the current was turned on again. After the third shock, a guard opened the door at our back and said, "You can go now." Outside, someone asked, "Are we supposed to attend the autopsy?"

"Not unless you want to," the guard answered.

I certainly didn't want to! As fast as my trembling legs would take me, I hurried to my room and was sick. Cursing myself for a chicken-hearted sentimentalist, I balked at the thought of breakfast. At *The Citizen* office, I begged Sheldon to write the piece I had promised to wire the *Post*. He needed no details from me, for he had witnessed electrocutions, and was glad to have the small check that came in payment for his two hundred matter-of-fact words.

Our campaign to defeat the local political machine succeeded, although I doubted that my efforts had much to do with the outcome. After the election, I told the paper's owners that I could not continue to earn the liberal salary I had been getting. The prospect of laboring on in an effort to turn a money-losing into a profit-making little daily seemed bleak, and I asked to be taken back on the *Post*. Fortunately for me, Philip Allen had just been made assistant to Francis E. Leupp,[170] the paper's Washington correspondent, and I was given the exchange editor's desk. My pay would be thirty dollars a week, plus whatever I earned by space-rate contributions of editorials and articles.

A Trip to Yosemite Valley[171]

GRAPHIC PICTURE OF GRAND SCENERY
DRAWN BY A VINITA BOY

"HO FOR Yosemite!" and four of us college boys echoed the refrain while raking up blankets, old camping clothes, guns, snake medicine, and other necessary things for a four weeks' camping trip in the Sierra Nevada Mountains. On the first of June, a few days after Stanford University closed, our quartet started from San Francisco, going as far as Stockton up the San Joaquin River on the boat, and from there about thirty miles further on the train to the foot of the mountains. At the terminus of the railroad we secured two burros, or pack mules, on which to carry our provisions, blankets, and so forth, while we walked to the valley from this place and we tramped the distance in a week, taking our time, hunting wherever we could find game, and fishing when we reached some cold mountain stream where the fly is not often cast, resting when we were tired, and enjoying every change in landscape, mountains, and rivers. We entered the valley one bright morning and reached the camping grounds at noon. Our tent was pitched just on the bank of the Merced River, which flows through the valley, and under some sheltering pine trees. The first afternoon we had a delightful rest, and the next morning we started out to see the valley, or part of it. There is so much to see and say about the valley that one could not do it in a week, and so I will not try to do more than give a few impressions of what I saw.

I had heard of the valley being surrounded by great granite walls, but I was not prepared to appreciate the immensity of these walls, rising as they do from two thousand to five thousand feet above the valley floor, until I climbed to the summit of one of the highest peaks. Looking from this point down to the valley below it looked like a fairy garden, or the playground of a child, with its smooth, grass-covered floor, its rank mosses, ferns, and flowers, its wreath of pine, cypress, and live oak trees, with hotels, cottages, and Indian huts scattered picturesquely about; and flowing obediently down the middle of the valley, the clearest, coldest, and most beautiful river out of storybooks. In reality, however, this miniature valley is about seven miles long and from one to two miles wide, while the Merced River receives the water from some half-dozen large falls, and was, while we were there, full to the banks.

Everybody in the valley has a desire to climb and, of course, our first trip was up one of the hardest trails to the top of Clouds Rest, passing on our way Vernal and Nevada falls. It was a hard climb but the view from the top was grand enough to repay us for the exertion. Clouds Rest rises ten thousand feet above sea level and four thousand feet above the valley. Looking to the east we could see the summit of the Sierra, snowcapped and towering still higher, while between and below us and the summit stretched a vast field of snow, broken in places by small valleys and cañons. To the west could be seen range after range of lower mountains, and far away the broad San Joaquin valley stretched to the Coast Range, whose outlines were barely discernible in the distance. Over all a sort of blue haze hung, which softened the sharp outlines of the mountains and showed dark in the valleys.

We next visited Yosemite Falls, where the water plunges down in successive leaps, twenty-five hundred feet. The first leap is one of fifteen hundred feet, and there are two more of five hundred each. One cannot appreciate the height of these falls; he simply looks and wonders. You stand at the foot of the falls and watch the great cloud of spray rising with rainbows, arching themselves wherever the sun shines on it favorably; they appear and disappear, one is formed before your face and the spray is blown to one side and it is gone. Then you look at the falling water, watch it as it comes over the brink, slowly at first, but increasing in speed as it descends, until finally it plunges with terrific speed into the seething moss below. Rocket-like formations of water shoot far out from the top, plunge downward, and burst into millions of glittering, sparkling water drops that are instantly lost in the great mass of descending water. And the roar! It is loud as the thunder of Jove and as unceasing as the waters themselves. One listens to it and is fascinated; it is speaking of an awful power, it is telling a story. On the door of a deserted hotel near the foot of Nevada Falls I saw a few lines of very bad poetry, but very expressive thought. They are as I remember these:

Nevada, Vernal, and Bridal Veil
Are roaring a story, a wonderful tale,
Of nature's greatness
And human vagueness.

One feels these things but does not care to try to express them. The roar of the falls is in your ears for weeks.

Of course we visited Mirror Lake before sunrise and saw the still, mirror-like surface of the lake reflect trees, clouds, mountains, and rocks like so much polished steel. And when the sun rises it seems to come from behind a buried mountain, and become brighter and brighter until it bursts into a perfect blaze on the water. Step to one side so that the mountain is between you and the sun and see it rise again, and so repeat it until you have beheld a dozen gorgeous sunrises, and then say what you think of Yosemite.

One must see a sunset from the summit of some of these lofty mountains, or he will miss one of the grandest sights in the Sierras. It does not seem to set, it only drops behind a mountain, and long streaks of sunlight flash over the top of a low-lying mountain and color this side of a mountain farther back with the most splendid of sunset hues. You watch it as it changes from bright red to the paler crimson, fading gradually into a pale yellow, then to a light gray, and just then you see the shadow envelop the whole mountainside and very soon it is dark.

As everyone knows, the Italian skies are praised as being the most beautiful in the world, but if they are any bluer, or show any more delicate tints than the California skies in the Sierras, they must be wonderful indeed. At midday, when the sun is high and the atmosphere is as light and dry as it can possibly be, the blue of the sky is so light, the little cloud fleeces are so delicate, and airy and the sunlight that barely warms the blood makes you feel that it is good to live.

Not the least interesting part of the trip, to me, were the people I met on my way to the valley and also after I got there. Everybody visits the Yosemite Valley who can. There are two first-class hotels in the valley and, of course, there are any number of summer tourists there, but it is among the campers that you find variety. They comprise rich and poor, pleasure seekers and those who hope to gain health; married men who claim they are not married, and wives loath to admit that they are such. I witnessed a little farce-comedy one day when I had climbed alone to the top of Glacier Point. In coming down I joined a party who had ascended before I did. Mr. S. had started up with his wife and children, and when they were about halfway up the children gave out and the man went on up, leaving his family there to rest. In the party was a lady whose husband was too ill to climb, and Mr. S. naturally became interested in her. They came down together until they were almost in sight of the place where Mr. S. had left his wife when he told the lady to wait until he went on to see if his wife was where he had left her, explaining that his wife was very jealous of him, which, considering that she was some ten years his senior, was not strange. When he found that his family had gone down before they got back, he remarked sententiously, "She's been boss for fifteen years now, but I guess I'll do as I please 'till I get to the valley." Then there were the old Forty-niners who live only in the past, full of reminiscences of "the days of old, the days of gold." Some among them you will find who can discuss the "silver question" quite as intelligently as the average statesman; all of them are shrewd, honest, and inclined to "give the devil his dues." We were royally treated by some of them, and I shall always remember them kindly. The music of the violin at the camp above is hushed, the wind in the trees above sings a lullaby, and the roar of the falls makes sweet music. We sleep and dream of Yosemite.

A Letter to His Father

JOHN MILTON OSKISON WRITES OF HIS VISIT IN EUROPE[172]

Venice, Italy, July 16, 1900

Dear Father: — If I remember correctly, I have not written to you since I left Naples, about a month ago, and am beginning to think I would do well to send word that I am still alive and healthy. I left Naples on June 12th and went to Rome, where I stayed five days. There I met the son of the man who is now editor of the *Post* and who has been studying in Italy for about two years.[173] He was very nice to me there and went about with me to see everything. Rome, you know, is the head of the Catholic Church, the residence of the pope, and has the biggest church in the world, St. Peter's. About fifteen hundred years ago, the Romans were the most important and richest people in the world. At that time they built splendid palaces and temples and theaters which have since been torn down and fallen to ruins, and people go to Rome principally to see these ruins and the galleries of pictures and statues that are filled with ancient works. It is as interesting as anything I know of and worth a longer visit than I made.

From Rome I went up to Florence, further north in Italy. This is a city where great things were done about four hundred or five hundred years ago — great palaces built, pictures painted, and a great political center named. It is not politically important now, but the other things remain — the palaces and pictures. And the country around the city is beautiful. I stayed there three weeks, enjoying myself greatly, and then came on to Venice.

Venice is on the eastern coast of Italy, built on a number of little islands of the Adriatic Sea. Six hundred years ago it was a big power, reaching far east into Turkey and North Africa. Its big palaces date from that time, the greatest being the one occupied by the Doges, or ruling Dukes, of Venice. You know that nearly all of the streets of Venice are canals and have to be gone over in boats. A little way out there are sea baths where I have gone most every day since I came here six days ago. This is also a place where great pictures were painted and great statues made. The churches here — there are one hundred — are beautiful structures and have good pictures in them.

Young Clark, the son of the editor, came up from Rome soon after I did and is with me now here. He and I plan to go from here in three days up into the Alps, where the mountains cross the Tyrol. We will spend some days climbing mountains, and then he is going on to Germany. I will go to Switzerland instead and spend a week or so in the mountains. Then I will go across France to Paris, stay there a week or more, go to England, staying a week or so in London, to Oxford and Cambridge, and then perhaps to Scotland before I sail for New York.

Mr. Coolidge, the man I came over with, left me at Naples and went to Sicily. He is trapping rats and mice over here and can't go to the interesting places. He came up to Florence a few days before I left, and I expect to find him in Paris when I get there. We will then go to England together, and probably back to New York on the same ship.

I am learning a good deal of Italian and could speak the language pretty well if I stayed here a week or two longer. I expect to be able to get along pretty well in France with the French I know. The whole trip has been very satisfactory, not expensive, and I have lived well. I am in fine health, and when I return to New York will be thoroughly rested. I will write you later, when I have got further on my way. If you and Dick will write, I will get the letter addressed to me at 11 Rue Scribe, Paris, France, Care of the American Express Co. Yours affectionately.

John Oskison

An Autobiographical Letter to Journalist Frederick S. Barde[174]

416 W. 13 ST
NEW YORK

April 13

Dear Mr. Barde: Native modesty and I have had it out, and I've won:

I went away from Vinita in 1894 to find out what a college—a real college—was. In some magazine I'd read an illustrated article about Leland Stanford Junior University out in California and the romantic circumstances of its founding. That article turned my thoughts from Vanderbilt University, one of whose graduates had helped to steer me through the little preparatory institution founded at Vinita by Bill Halsell, the cattleman.

My father and I took up this matter of college education, and some differences of opinion developed. He was a good farmer and an honest cattleman, and I don't believe there was a man in Indian Territory who stood better among his fellow men. My father wanted me and my three brothers to follow in his business. Also, he was willing to go the limit in the matter of education. I said if I ever got to college the farm would never reclaim me. That was the rash statement of youth—does anybody know of a good farm that needs an editorial-office-trained manager? In my father's mind, the law represented about the most respectable and profitable business next to land and cattle. So, I said I'd be a lawyer when I got through college.

A great big diploma from Bill Halsell's college—the sort that, spread out, just fits a trunk tray—got me into Stanford University, after the registrar found out where Indian Territory was on the map, and that the diploma wouldn't tear when he held it up by one corner with the seal and ribbon and fixings hanging down.

I studied law, without enthusiasm, during my four years at Stanford, and in the last two years wrote some Indian Territory fiction—full of cowboys, square dances, whiskey peddlers, and train robbers—for the *Sequoyah*, the college magazine. I liked to do the stories. When I graduated, in 1898, I went home and said that the Harvard Law School was the best in the country. What I would have said if I'd been frank was that the English Department at Harvard was the best. Before the summer was over, however, I broke the news to Father—I wanted to be a writer. He proved conclusively that I was throwing away my only remaining chance for fortune and fame. I believe him now. Anyway, he was game, and financed my year at Harvard.

Living up in a cold, roomy, and healthy attic in Cambridge with a chum from Stanford who had to finance himself, I turned out in one college year a great bulk of written stuff. Some of it seemed to please the professors and their assistants, but I came near jumping into the Charles River because neither the *Advocate* nor the *Monthly* would print my tales. My roommate, Dane Coolidge, tried to console me by saying we were too crude for the effete East. Dane was full of ambition to be a writer, too—perhaps, you've read the novel of his, *Hidden Water*, published by McClurg a few months ago?[175]

One day we read that the *Century Magazine* was testing out the question Do the colleges teach their graduates how to write? by offering three prizes for the best short story, the best poem, and the best short essay submitted by graduates of American colleges who had been out of college one year or less. Each prize was $250. To the competition I sent one of my Indian Territory stories, artfully disguised in a title quoted from Kipling—"Only the Master Shall Praise." Maybe the Kipling title did it — it's hard to imagine now how popular Kipling was in the spring of 1899 — or maybe the chance to put Frederick Remington on to a new job of illustrating tempted the editors. Anyway, I got the $250 for the short story, and for a time I wondered just what I'd do next to show the editors of the *Harvard Advocate* and the *Monthly* what chumps they'd been to turn down my stuff.

Meanwhile, I'd gone down to New York to hunt a job. I fell among good, serious people, and in a month I was grabbing off space in the *New York Evening Post* as a reporter. The only comment I heard during the year I chased assignments that seemed worth remembering was the city editor's admission that at least my copy didn't need much editing.

After that $250 effort I sold another story to the *Century* — for $40. And then — a long, long blank. I think it was five years at least before I got into that magazine again. Others printed my tales — *McClure's*, *Leslie's Monthly*, *Ainslee's*, *Leslie's Weekly*, the Saturday supplement of the *Evening Post* among them. I went to Europe in 1900 and never looked inside a Baedeker during the five months over there — Dane Coolidge with a commission from the Smithsonian Institution to collect small mammals (that meant trap, skin, stuff, and prepare the skulls of rats and mice) from Italy and southern France. He did the work, I stuck around more or less closely, and neither of us felt the need of guidebooks. Once the superstitious peasants threw stones at Dane until the priest came along and assured them that this American was only a harmless magic maker.

Coming back to New York, I spent a winter writing a novel — an Indian Territory novel. In spots, it was so good that the rest of it seemed depressing. That's what the publishers said.[176] Then I began writing short stories again, so that I could spend more than four dollars a week for room and board and buy some clothes. Next came a sweatshop job with Dodd, Mead & Co. In a loft building on Washington Place, directly across Green Street from the Asch building, which furnished 145 victims to fire two weeks ago, Dodd, Mead & Co. were making the *International Encyclopaedia* and *Yearbook*. I wrote biographies for eight months, and can feel to this day the eyes of restless old Mr. Dodd boring into my neck. That job expired, and I went back to freelancing.[177]

Later — this was early in 1903 — two jobs sought me on the same day. (This is a true story!) The *Evening Post* wanted to start me on a political assignment — the muckraking (it wasn't called muckraking then) of Boss Brayton of Rhode Island. Lincoln Steffens did the story for *McClure's* later. The second offer came from a group of village reformers of Ossining, NY, who wanted me to run a new four-page daily newspaper that was established to clean house and stir up a sentiment in favor of good streets and a liberal bond issue for village improvements. The chief owner of the paper also owned a new bank, which wanted to handle the bond issue. See?[178]

I suppose getting married in the fall of 1903 was the only thing that could have pulled me away from the editorial chair at Ossining and a gradually diminishing salary. Very skillfully, the chief owner contrived this. For each five dollars cut from my liberal weekly pay the future was to return fifty dollars in dividends on stock that came to me in lieu of wages. But getting married meant earning real money. Back to the *Evening Post* as exchange editor I went, and from November 1, 1903, to July 1, 1906, I certainly did work. Day by day I dug through a huge pile of newspapers from all parts of the country, fed information to the writers of political editorials, wrote two columns a week of comment based on non-serious material culled from the *Atchison Globe*, the *Tombstone Epitaph*, the *Kansas City Star*, the *Yonkers Statesman*, and other papers that tolerated human writing, and began to get regular editorials printed in the regular brevier type.

Before leaving the *Evening Post*, I was a regular editorial writer, with an editorial writer's salary, cubbyhole of a room, and deskful of prejudices and favorite topics. Some editorials I wrote for *Collier's Weekly*, together with some special work, got me the chance to connect with the *National Weekly* in January 1907. From that time to this I have stuck to *Collier's*. I wrote two of the "Senate Undesirables" series for *Collier's* — Long of Kansas was one. I wrote a series of articles about the loan sharks that helped to start the Russell Sage Foundation on the job of driving them out of business with good loan agencies. I fired birdshot into the flock of get-rich-quick promoters that roost in New York, and as one result *Collier's* had established a department called "The Average Man's Money," and my present principal job is the writing and editing of that. I suppose

I start about one libel suit a month — possibly my average is a little better. My title is associate editor. Now and then I get time to write a short story that I sell.[179]

P.S. See *Who's Who in America* for a few personal details. Too much have I written — my native modesty rises up, too late, to cry stop!

I am enclosing a photograph taken in the office here, as well as one taken with a group of other Indians at a conference of Friends of the Indian at Lake Mohonk, NY, in October 1909. I've written a good deal about the Indians and am interested in the whole question of the Indian's forward progress.

Sincerely,
John M. Oskison

August 18, 1911

Dear Mr. Barde:

I appreciate your friendly note. I suppose the only way to get into the magazine is to keep trying. From my own experiences I know that the percentage of failures is mighty big; and the number of men who are actually making a living from magazine writing alone is so small that I believe they could be counted on the fingers of two hands. I think the magazine business will be reconstructed in time so that there will be a chance for one to find out rather definitely what there is in it for him. As yet, however, it is certainly a wicked gamble.

By all means let us have a look at whatever you turn out; it might fit our pages.

Very sincerely yours,
J. M. Oskison

« PART TWO »

Fiction

I Match You: You Match Me[1]

CONFORMANT TO the laws of natural selection, there are a number of students who leave college before their course is ended; and it is often a matter of speculation as to the probable cause, when a few of his friends notice such a student's absence and meet to discuss matters of common interest on a Saturday evening. I heard the story of such an elimination once, under conditions as foreign to the atmosphere of the recital as the man was at the time to his former college self.

Walter Knight was a thoroughly good fellow, generous and manly, with a man's appreciation of the worth of character. When he entered college he promised himself that his course should be a brilliant one if striving counted for aught. That he was capable of attaining the highest honors, all his friends at home were assured. He had been the bright particular star of his class in the high school, and his favorite teacher had talked seriously to him about the right use of great talent. His father had said to him: "My son, make the most of your opportunity, for it will be in your power to do a lot of good. I have money and considerable influence to start you with, and I expect great things of you."

On the big Colorado cattle ranch, "Wiry" Cooke—his real name was Williston Cooke—was known as the best rider of wild horses and the youngest ranch foreman in the country. Why he ever left a paying job and went to college was a mystery to all who knew him. And how he ever found time to acquire knowledge enough to pass the entrance examinations at the university was a matter about which they knew little and cared less. That the herders were sorry to lose so good a boss was demonstrated when, just before Cooke was to leave the ranch, "Shorty" White entered the dug-out shanty which served temporarily as a ranch house, followed by the other boys, and presented an elaborately made and silver-bitted bridle to "one old boss that ain't been afraid to mix with the boys, and that kin ride the wust hoss that ever wore hair." Replying to this sincere and characteristic speech of his favorite herder, the full extent of whose praise was appreciated, Cooke had told the boys that, though he might never need the bridle, he would regard it as one of his most valuable souvenirs, and that he would be pleased if the boys would come in and sample that little brown jug of "snake medicine" that belonged over there in the darkest corner.

It would be difficult to explain just how Walter Knight and Cooke came to be friends. Walter was sought after by the well-dressed popular fellows, and smiled on by the equally well-dressed and popular young ladies, from the day of his arrival, while the only introductory notice Cooke received was to have his name printed in the college paper along with three hundred other "new students," and a visit from the collector of student dues, who was no respecter of persons. However, that does not affect the story. Suffice it to say that they did become firm friends, and after Knight's initial popularity had waned a bit they went to live in the same house together.

"So you're going to become a civil engineer, are you, Cooke?" observed Knight, soon after the beginning of their acquaintance. "Great opportunities in your country, I suppose. Well, I don't mind telling you that I'm going in for politics! You see, I'll study law first, get a good practice worked up, and then, with my father's help, who has been superior judge for ten years, I believe I can get almost anything I want at home."

In this way they began their college life, each filled with a real desire to accomplish something; ambitious to leave behind him a record of leadership; and, more important, to start into life, after graduation, with ability to endure the success which was sure to follow. Each felt as he turned the pages of the '95 Annual that he would try to be like one of those old "pioneers"[2] — win half a field day by himself, or be a member of all the important committees and editorial boards. To be president of his class toward the end of his course would not be unpleasant.

In Knight's case, college life was only a continuation of his former work. He found that he could stand well in his classes without a very great effort of his really quick intellect. It was so easy for him to say that he knew he "had it on" a lot of the other fellows in his class, and he need not work so hard. He was a more regular attendant at football practices than at his classes, and it came about that not so very long after his brilliant entrée into the university his ideals were lowered and his striving relaxed.

But Cooke had a great deal more difficulty in the beginning of his course than Knight had encountered. Engineering, as he found, involved much more than the carrying of transits and picturesque field work. The mathematics courses necessary in his work did not have an absorbing interest for him, but, as they had to be mastered, he put the whole of his strong energy into the work, and succeeded, pleasing his professors immensely.

Cooke, with his stories of rough experience and his vivid, energetic descriptions, proved an entertaining sort of a fellow — one who carried the force of a strong personality with him — and he came to be sought after by the "good fellows" of the college, the Bohemians, who drink more beer, attend more dances, and are slapped on the back oftener than those men who think a student's life is a serious one. He spent more money than he could afford, and before he was aware of it the funds he had saved while on the ranch were greatly diminished. Cards had always exercised a strange fascination over him, and it had never been any trouble for him to win from the men he had played with. But he had never yielded to the influence to the extent of betting heavily. At college Cooke came to know certain young men with gaming instincts, who were willing to lose money for the excitement of play, and he unconsciously acquired the habit of spending a few evenings each week in their company. Moreover, he found that his winnings tided him over many a financial stringency that otherwise might have resulted in the loss of a certain amount of respect due to his fashionable dress, which he had learned to value more than he would have confessed.

Matching pennies furnished amusement for some of the boys at odd moments, while nickels and twenty-five-cent pieces were freely hazarded by others. Cooke began to match coins, more because others did it than from any desire to win or lose money. He often matched nickels with Knight, neither of them winning or losing enough to speak of. But one evening he was very unlucky, and had lost his coin on almost every turn.

"Let's make it a quarter a turn, for I want to win back what you've got from me, and then we'll quit," Cooke had said after losing several dollars. No better result attended this increase, and, becoming excited over his losses, he had quite forced Knight to raise the value of the coins to a dollar.

"I match you: You match me!" cried, alternately, one and then the other, as the coins were shaken in the hand and thumped down on the study-table between them. Over and over the phrases were sounded, "I match you: You match me!" Cooke's losses were becoming serious, and Knight had, for the time, not remembered that he was winning from his best friend, and he iterated as eagerly as Cooke, "I match you: You match me!" Knight turned "heads," and won; Cooke called "tails up," and lost; and so they kept on repeating, monotonously, "I match you: You match me!"

It was long after Cooke had exhausted all the money in his purse, and a formidable stack of IOUs had accumulated, that their neighbor from the next room asked if they were ever going to quit fooling and go to bed, as it was past midnight. The interruption broke the spell of the game for the two, and each rose and gazed stupidly at the other. At length Cooke turned and told the neighbor that they were just going to put out the light, and wished him good night.

"Did you ever read Kipling's story of 'The Madness of Private Ortheris'?" Cooke asked, running over the slips of paper that represented the amount he owed Knight. "Well, Private Ortheris was, as he said, only a 'bloomin' Tommy!' and he was saved from the madness of desertion in India by his friends. I'm not a Tommy Atkins, desperate with homesickness, but my madness has cost me the means of finishing my university course, which has come to be a reality to me. No, I couldn't take back the money you've won. My training is against such an act."

This was the story told me, not by Mr. Williston Cooke, but by "Wiry" Cooke, the "cow puncher," as he sat with his leg over the horn of the saddle, and tapped nervously on his boottop with his quirt. We were "on night herd" together, and I drew the details from him, not so fully as I have given them, but expressed with a greater depth of feeling, while the moon lighted up the tile roof of the adobe ranch house, and the regular breathing of the steers showed that they were at rest.

Tookh Steh's Mistake[3]

TOOKH STEH was a full-blood, and his convictions concerning things were very strong. But Tookh had something of right on his side, when he made the one foolish move of his life, as this story is written to show.

For forty years Tookh Steh had lived in the White Oak hills, a neighborhood not known outside the Indian Territory, or, one might safely say, the Cherokee Nation. During this time he had seen many changes come over his country. When he came to these hills with old Wana Steh, his father, he was not old enough to remember anything of his former home down in the Flint Hills, where the "hogbacks" of Arkansas and Indian Territory jostle each other, and throw up boulders into each other's arms. The White Oak hills were neither so high nor so rugged as those down in Illinois district, and it was only a few miles to the prairie in any direction. Tookh grew up half on the prairie and half in the rocky solitude of the timbered hills. The prairie was an inspiration to the boy. From its wide, rolling sweep he imbibed a love of freedom, the love that is not voiced by brazen lunged patriots, but the kind that the coyote pup sucks from its mother's breast, and which prevents you from ever taming the little vagrant. From the hills the boy got that secretiveness which tells you nothing of what a full-blood feels.[4]

Twenty years after the little log cabin was built and hidden away in a ravine far up under the edge of the sandy ridge that separated the waters of Pryor Creek from those of White Oak Creek, Mr. Verte came to live nearby. Verte was a white man, and a seeker after solitude. He lived, Indian like, within a mile of old Wana Steh's cabin, and did not come to know his neighbors for more than a year. This ensured a lasting friendship between young Tookh Steh and Mr. Verte when they met finally over the grave of the Indian's father. Because an Indian is difficult to know. No other white man came across the hills to settle for many years, and Verte found his full-blood friends, hunters as well as residents, excellent neighbors. They did not steal his stock, and minded their own business. Verte was a musician, fashioned in the school of Indiana "fiddle parties," or more politely, musicales. He played his violin in the doorway of his cabin when the shadows of the post oaks stretched away into the tangle of underbrush to the east, and Tookh came often to listen. Conversation between them was not extensive, and was carried on in a concessionary mixture of English and Cherokee. If Verte wished to buy a calf from old Acha Dilla, he made Tookh understand in a few words, and the bargain was struck by Verte's friend and interpreter. Verte could be trusted to treat the Indians as men, and they discredited the tales that floated about concerning some whites who had come to the territory and had driven away half of the cattle thrifty old Chief Ross had collected. The railroad came down from the north, in time, and flashed on into Texas, and the intruding whites followed its trail. Stockmen began to realize what a mine of wealth lay in the luxuriant grass growing waist high on the hills and prairies, and soon long trains of cattle were turned loose to get fat and make profits for their owners. The clean-limbed, long-horned Texas steers came up into the hills and nosed about the cabins at times, when some serious-faced Indian boy would come rushing out of the hut waving his arms, and bursting into fits of laughter when the curious beasts stampeded through the brush.

It did not happen that the United States wished to stamp out tribal government in the Cherokee Nation until Tookh had lived in his hill home for forty years. The rafters of the cabin were much worm-eaten then, but the old place fitted so well that neither Tookh nor his family, a pleasant-faced squaw and a ten-year-old boy, ever thought of building another. They might have put up a frame house now, for Coxton's sawmill was cutting up the splendid oaks not two miles away. The year the commission came to the territory was a year when the Indian elections were held, and orators from rival parties declaimed loudly and vaguely about the ancient, honorable and inviolable rights of treaty the commission had been sent to abrogate. They left the impression that the United States meant to rob the poor Indian outright. The delegation sent by the Senate of the United States was made up of half a dozen sensible, educated, and conscientious men. They were acting under instructions from the Senate, and tried to do justice in the work. But political ambition is the birthright of a Cherokee, and so those who talked ancient vows hindered the commission's work more than a stranger would imagine.[5]

Tookh Steh showed a lively interest in the negotiations entered into by the nation with the commission, because he desired the best possible results to come of the proceedings. He was not blind to reason, and when Mr. Verte tried to explain that the United States, far from contemplating any robbery, wished to effect an organization along firmer lines and institute a civil and educational reformation, he saw how good might come from a change. The change he had in mind would never disturb the serenity of his life. His small, rail-enclosed corn patch would not be taken away; each citizen would keep the home of his birth. The wild country to the west, where he shot deer and turkeys, would surely not be taken up; there were not enough people out of homes to occupy it. Mr. Verte told the trusting fellow that white men were real friends, and wished to do the best they knew by the Cherokees. These men knew that the Indian government was almost efficient, that their schools were ample in number, if poor in teachers, and that the Indians were working alone, a splendid solution of the Indian problem. But Verte said that many things could be better, the solution hastened and happiness consummated sooner, with the change. Verte believed what he said. He was not largely experienced in the politics of the world. Tookh believed what Verte said, because he had learned to trust the words of the white man.

When the commission sat in the town nearest to Tookh's home, he rode in one day to hear the proceedings. Mr. Verte told him that a number of full-bloods would meet the commission that day. It was not often that the Indian, Tookh, went to town. His long black hair, dark face, and feather-decked hat created no more favorable impression among the snobbish little store clerks than his dingy, mouse-colored pony, blind in one eye for ten years, and his old twine-mended saddle did among the bespurred and fully equipped cowboys. But Tookh did not care about such a simple matter as external appearance; he had the welfare of the country on his mind. He felt that he was partly responsible for the action of the nation, whatever it should be, in the issue at hand. No politician had yet explained to him what a difficult matter it is to look after the welfare of one's country, because it was not believed that silent old Tookh Steh had any "pull" with his people. So it came about that he went into the conference of the commission with a mind quite unprejudiced.

The meeting was called, the commissioners announced, to get the sentiment of the full-bloods on the question of the extinguishment of the tribal government, and the substitution of a territorial one, under the laws of the United States. Tookh listened eagerly while the full-blood spokesman set forth the views of his people. The old orator, speaking in his native tongue and very earnestly, said: "We do not want to change. We are satisfied with our own government. You would cut up our land into squares and make us stay on the little chunk we got in the cutting up. You would put down our courts, and drag us into your own docks where we could not understand your strange justice.[6] You made treaties with us. We have kept our part faithfully. You say you will not keep yours. Is the great head of your nation so poor that he must have our lands? Is he such a good father that he must destroy our government, and take us to his own breast, for fear that we cannot keep up our institutions? We are not of your race, we do not understand you, and we would rather be left alone. We are not ignorant, we are not savage; and the criminals that you tell us invade our country came from your land. You ought to catch them and hang them, as we do our own lawbreakers. You tell us that the man with many cattle grazing over our land, and with many miles of wire fences, is the one who is getting the good of our system. We tell you that this man is here because we let him stay. We can drive him out by law, and he will not use up our lands. You tell us we are ignorant. We tell you that we have our schools, our churches, and some of our sons are in the big colleges with your children. They will come back, and will keep up our institutions. They love their country and will make it great. Treat us fairly and we will respect you. Break your treaty and we will despise you."

One of the commissioners spoke next, and told the full-bloods that they had no choice in the matter. They had instructions, and those instructions were to make the change. They had already dealt with the tribes in the South and must deal now with the Cherokees. The United States was sorry that the change would work hardship on the Indians, but sentiment would not control. The Cherokees would no doubt be greatly benefited in the end, and so the change must come. Treaties were good so long as they did not stand in the way of progress, but they could not last forever. It would be better to make the change at once and get the best terms while there was yet opportunity for securing favorable conditions.

While he was listening to the speech of the commissioner, and with the full-blood's words fresh in his mind, Tookh Steh made a resolve. He would not live in a country where his old freedom would be restricted. They had said that thousands of eager home-seekers were waiting to file into the country to get homes. No more hunting; and even his dear, secluded hills would be peopled, the timber cut down, and his boy would have only the corn patch and the two ponies when the old man was gone. He would go to Mexico. He had heard that there one could find boundless freedom, amid mountains more rugged than any he had ever seen.

"You tell me the white man honest," Tookh said to Mr. Verte a few days later. "You tell me he not want my land. You do not know. He tell me all, we have to give up lands. We no more hunt deer, no shoot turkey. Land all gone. I go to Mexico where Great Father no take my land. I tell you, good-bye." Tookh shook hands with Mr. Verte, and a week later he left his old log house in the White Oak hills and started south. His poor old horses and tumble-down wagon furnished conveyance. The determined Indian did not know how many long moons he would be compelled to travel before he came to Mexico. He was filled with the idea that he must leave this place where, if he stayed, he would feel like a coyote shut in a box pining to get out.

One day in the middle of winter, a letter came to the officials of the town where Tookh had traded. An old Indian who called himself a seeker after freedom, and who babbled foolishly about Mexico and deer and turkeys, had died in a small Texas town. The old man had said he was dying because he could never reach the land he was going to; his horses were dead. But most of the people believed that he had starved to death, since the wife and boy were almost dead from lack of food. They would not beg, and they would not say they were hungry. The man had died, begging brokenly to be sent back to the White Oak hills. Did anyone know of this person? What should be done? The wife and child were in the poorhouse.

Yes, one knew. He was Tookh Steh's neighbor from the head of Pryor Creek, and he said shortly when he heard of his friend's death: "Big fool, Tookh Steh. Leave his home and go away. Leave his corn not gathered. He starve. Get mad 'cause he take away. Big fool, he!"

Perhaps Tookh was foolish to think that he could change the course of what men call destiny, simply because he had a principle to back him. But then, Tookh was a full-blood, and his convictions concerning things were very strong.

A Schoolmaster's Dissipation[7]

SCRUPP HIMSELF said that his story was not worth telling, but Scrupp was then a world-weary, hopeless, stooping old man. We knew that he had been tried, and were anxious to hear his story of the trying. I told my friend that I believed I could get Scrupp to tell me, because I made it a habit to sit on the old schoolmaster's doorstep on a Sunday evening, saying few words and listening unweariedly to the reading of *Enoch Arden*.[8] Then, darkness coming on, we would sit silent, each dreaming his own dreams; mine young and mostly unimportant, his, I came to know, old, sadly pleasant, despairing, absurd.

"You should have heard Professor Shadson's lecture on that poem," I began once, after the reading. "He made me feel the tragedy of it so keenly. There must be many things happen in real life like those set forth by the poet, don't you think so?"

"Many a one, young man, and you don't have to take a four years college course to know that either. I'll tell you something of what I know of the story of a man's life. I knew him very well." The old man looked at me curiously, and I gazed out over the prairie where the gloom was settling, and traced figures on the rough hewn, low doorstep with my pocketknife. He hitched his chair a little nearer the open door and continued: "I was the one. And since you want me to tell you, I'll make the worthless story short."

His recital was incoherent in places, and I give it in my own words:

Milton Scrupp, besides obtaining a second grade teacher's certificate in Kansas, had attended lectures for two months in St. Louis. This was in order to understand better the psychology of his profession, and especially to learn something of the nature of the little Indian children he was going to teach in the Indian Territory. He was to associate with the Reverend Scott, who had been an earnest worker there for years. He had assumed his duty with a rather exalted idea of its importance, and meant to do much good quietly.[9]

The school at the head of Thompson's Branch was small, and the salary was not large. Twenty-five dollars a month for two years, then thirty-five. The pupils were dull, as a rule, being made up of a dozen Cherokee boys and girls more or less pure-blooded, and half as many white children whose parents were renters in the Territory for numerous reasons. It was generally known that Anderson, who sent two children for several years, had been run out of his neighborhood in Arkansas because he persistently killed and peddled the beeves of his neighbors. Then there were tales told of the others, but it does not matter what they were.

Scrupp found, naturally enough, that he did not understand the children under his charge.

"The brats are not at all like ordinary children," he was wont to declare. "You can't scare 'em by whipping, and you can't get 'em out of the sulks by coaxing, and those little white kids have lived around here so long that they're just as bad as the others — probably worse."

The fact that he could not reach the hearts of these children of the prairie by any of the arts he had learned in the Cherryvale training school worried him a great deal at first.[10] He called on the fathers of the white children and talked to them of "the States" until they believed that he was a special detective sent to spy upon them. He ate hominy and wild onions at the log cabins of the Indians, patted the heads of the little fellows, and talked with crazy signs to the silent old fellows until they laughed in his face, and the little children hid their grimy selves in the bedclothes.

The life of a schoolteacher twenty years ago in the small settlements of the West was not a very cheerful one at best, and shut off from familiar intercourse with the people about him, Scrupp grew exceedingly lonely. If he had been anyone else, he would have left the place and entered civilization, but being poxey old Scrupp at thirty, and sensitive, he sat quite still in his little attic room at Jack Shorthair's and brooded over the fact that he was not properly appreciated. He dreamed of doing some fine thing one day that would astonish the world. None but the poets had ever felt as he did, and, half-ashamed, he began an epic that was to embody his great thoughts. But he found it extremely difficult to make his rhyme and thoughts agree, so he gave that up.

He saw a little pinched-faced boy die once, because the boy was not strong enough to stand the sanitary conditions of the Indian home, and he began to think about studying medicine in a small way, fancying that he might be able to save some lives. While he was in St. Louis he had seen a student use morphine to relieve insomnia. He remembered very distinctly seeing him bare his arm, insert the hypodermic syringe with a slight twinge of pain, and compose himself almost at once. He did not remember that the student was almost a wreck, and deathly pale. He reflected that the drug was powerful, and if he had known how to use it, he could have relieved Panting Bear's child when it cried with pain. He reasoned that it was a duty to do the best for his unsympathetic but human charges. Then he wondered if the pricking of the syringe was painful, and how long it would be after the injection before the drug acted. He felt the fleshy part of his own arm and asked himself how an injection there could possibly affect every nerve. He became curious to know how one felt who dreamed pleasant dreams under the influence of narcotics. He ended his speculation by having a quantity of the drug and a syringe sent to him along with full instructions, carefully skulled and crossboned, as to how to use it.

Scrupp had little of the modern scientific spirit, which investigates before it believes, and which sacrifices scores of animals to its investigations, but he deemed it wise to begin his experiments in the use of morphine with cats. He killed one before he learned to put it to sleep. After that he knew just how to send them, as he imagined, to a happy dreamland. Cats could not tell him how the experiment made them feel, and no other children sickened, so one evening Scrupp injected himself. The third time he did it he felt no desire to break away from the habit, and some of his pupils noticed that the schoolmaster was growing pale and restless, but said no word about it, for that is the Indian child's way.

He would have died prematurely from the effects of morphine if the now famous Dr. Maria Pless of Kansas City had not come to the Indian Territory to report on "the sanitary condition of the schools of the savages, and the inception of germ disease therein." Miss Pless had been one of the very first of the modern type of women to take up the study of medicine seriously, and she had struggled through unbelievable difficulties in her training to come out, applauded by her professors, to the end. She was young, vigorous, and enthusiastic when she came to visit Scrupp's school. It was not long before she changed her inquiries regarding the scholars to speculation concerning the condition of the teacher. A shrewd guess backed up by pretty eyes and a sudden direct question brought a confession from the schoolmaster's lips.

Yes. He had been using morphine until he couldn't leave off. It wouldn't be long anyway, and why did she interfere? Nobody understood him, nobody cared, and his relations were all gone — at least all whom he cared to remember. She cared? But did she, really? That would be such a new experience, to have someone care. Old George Boots, the full-blood, had chuckled when he noticed how pale he grew, and had grunted, "Him got fever and ager, eh!" No one else had remarked on the change.

Maria, MD, did care. She was young with a good share of impulsive, girlish pity about her yet, and she believed that it was a terrible thing for this strong man to yield to such a slave driver as morphine. She was to stay in the country for some time, and she resolved to help Scrupp get away from his habit. Here was simply a professional interest, she told herself, but it was necessary to interest the teacher intensely in something, and since there was nothing else in the half-savage land to attract a civilized person, she started in deliberately to make the disheartened schoolmaster fall in love with herself. She got him to go out with her on horseback, when they rode for miles over the wide expanse of prairie, and returned tired out. Then she would almost force him to smoke pipes of very strong tobacco, for that served in a measure as a substitute for the old drug. Above all she depended upon the influence of her bright eyes. The promise he gave her nightly as she left his lodging house, changed from "I'll not take more than three doses until

I see you again" to "Only one tonight, my dear friend." In two weeks more he said bravely as he bid her goodnight: "No more of that stuff until you say so," and his eyes were full of a blind devotion.

It was not an easy task that Maria Pless had to perform when she told Scrupp that she could never marry him; that she had a work in the world to accomplish; that she should always think of him as the one who had given her more aid than anyone else. She did not say "professional aid," for he would not have understood how good a "subject" he had been, and it was not necessary. She succeeded in leaving with the lonely fellow a hope that things might come right in the end. He had given up morphine, and had looked proudly on while the girl broke up his syringe, and scattered the drug to the winds. He felt no strong desire to return to its use, now that he could quit, and she had disapproved of it.

She went away to the railway station, twenty miles to the north, one morning, and Milton Scrupp rode beside her. His school term would end soon: the grass on the hills brushed the knees of the horses. She spoke to him in serious mood of one's duty to oneself. She made him see the perennial beauty of the old familiar hills which in wintertime were covered with a mass of dead grass, twisted and matted, until some sweeping prairie fire left them bare and black. These hills were a bright, waving green now, with gray, jagged projecting masses of limestone breaking the monotony of color. Away to the east was the long, wavering line of trees that marked the turns of Cabin Creek. The line seemed to twist and jostle the shoulders of the enclosing hills like a sentient being crawling fast to join the great bottoms and rock-broken torrents of the Grand River.[11] The blackjacks, far to the south, set in relief on the brow of the rise which bonded a broad level plateau of green, showed fresh and strong despite their stunted proportions. There were no high mountains, she told him, to elevate one's eyes to, but couldn't he fancy a rude fork, such as he used to cut for his old twice-mended "bean shooter," where Little Cabin joined the main creek and both went down through the prairie together? The small branch of the fork was not so thick with timber as the other, nor so large, but then it had to fret itself almost to death away up there in the limestone region, before it was able to start for the Gulf. Far beyond that log house on the creek, where a late breakfast was cooking for an indolent full-blood, he could see a number of small tents and a faint line of fresh, yellow earth. She told him that this railroad now building would be completed within a few years, and that he might travel from Texas, if he ever found himself there, up to Kansas City, her home, with only half a dozen stops for food. In short, she made him see the simple beauty of his life and surroundings where he had supposed all beauty was lacking. He saw, through the changing light of her eyes, sufficient motive for old Panting Bear's stopping on hill crests, when on an early morning chase, to invoke the rising sun. The silent old fellow knew how to worship nature while resting his pony, though he never spoke his devotion.

Scrupp missed the frequent talks he had been enjoying since the strange young physician had come down to gather material for a report, though he was bad enough company for her during those times. She had been a chance bit of life, blown out into the prairie to him from the outer world, and she carried back with her his whole heart; a burden light enough for her. The schoolmaster kept his school, and it grew larger year by year as more white men came to the Territory to reap the rewards of early settlement. The stoop in his shoulders grew more noticeable, and the old consuming love for the girl who had saved him grew into a settled melancholy. The few letters that drifted over the plains to him from the woman gave him small hope, but he clung to the fancy that everything would come right in the end. He said this over and over to himself as the years passed, losing no faith, but filling his mind with bright fancies of what might have been if—still he had the hills over which they had ridden, though industrious men were burrowing into their green sides, leaving small ground-squirrel holes out of which they were taking coal for their winter fires. The wide valley between the creeks now showed black, cultivated fields, and wire fences straggled out toward the blackjacks. Cowboys spoke to him at times as he went from his home to the school, and wondered among themselves "what made the old duck so blue." One of them, curious and diplomatic, had talked to old Scrupp about his own girl, and had drawn from him a passionate outbreak, which frightened the fellow, and ended with: "It's the staying here forever, the waiting for her till she rides in over the hills to make her next report, the feeling sometimes that maybe she won't come at all; the same old whittled benches in the old log schoolhouse; the hoping, hoping, the crazy notion you get at times to go away over there and tell her that everything is ready now. The pictures that will come of what a happy pair we would have been. Children — not these dirty, soulless, unfeeling ones that I teach — but bright-faced, clean children that you could take on your knees. It's that that keeps me from being cheerful always. But she will come after a while." The puncher had ridden away without a word, leaving the old lover to his hopes.

▾▾▾▾▾▾▾▾▾▾▾▾▾▾▾▾▾▾▾▾▾▾▾▾

It was just fifteen years after the young medical student had come to Scrupp's school to make her report, and twenty years since he had opened the school on the head of Thompson's Branch, that my friend and I rode over to "sit up" with the dying schoolmaster. He spoke of her in his last moments, telling us to watch for her as she rode up to the house from behind the hills, and say to her that he had not used a bit of the old drug since she went away.

While we jogged slowly home in the morning I told my friend the story I had learned a year before, and he whistled pensively, remarking, in the end: "That habit of his — wasn't it a terrible dissipation?"

"I think it was rather pleasant," I answered. But he was thinking of the morphine, while I thought of the schoolmaster's long indulgence in his dream of hope.

"Only the Master Shall Praise"[12]

ON THE cattle ranges of the Indian Territory ten years ago he was known as "the Runt," because he was several inches shorter than the average puncher. His other title of "Hanner" had been fastened upon him by a ludicrous incident in his youth. "Hanner the Runt" was a half-breed Cherokee cowboy who combined with the stoicism of the Indian something of the physical energy and mental weakness of his white father. One of his shoulders was knocked down a quarter of a foot lower than the other, two ribs had been "caved in" on his left side, and a scar high up on his cheekbone indicated a stormy life. It was a matter of speculation in the cow camps as to the number of times Hanner had been thrown from horses and discharged by his employers; he would have been called the football of fate had these cowboys been modern and college-bred.

No trick that was ever perpetrated upon him, no service that another imposed upon him, no jeer flung straight in his face, could destroy the innocent trust he felt in humanity. Bill Seymour had caused him to break his ribs by falling from a wild pony, and had then thrashed the puncher who laughed at the fall. In this way Hanner had become the slave of Seymour.

The two, Seymour and Hanner, now rode for Colonel Clarke, and were generally together. It was convenient for Seymour to have his "valet" to do his work, and it was the chief joy of Hanner's uncolored existence to do something for the man who had fought for him. The grotesque little figure never stopped to ask whether his friend was worthy of his devotion. Bill Seymour was a short, athletic fellow, and good to look upon, but he bore in his nature a too large share of the devil to be dependable. Silent, gruff, and capable when sober, he became a laughing, steel-hearted fury when drunk, and he got drunk as often as he could reach liquor. More than Hanner had felt the sting of his quirt as Bill reeled laughing and jesting on the streets, and had feared to show the anger that rose in their hearts. He made enemies when drunk, and gravely apologized to them in his sober days. One man, a traveling cattle buyer, braver than most, and not knowing his man, had drawn a small pistol and shot the puncher in the body. Bill, who was not hurt at all seriously, laughingly strode up to the shooter, seized the weapon, and pointing at his feet, said:

"Now dance for me, you impudent son of a mosquito! Dance till you drop! Tryin' to plug me with a toy like that — a cursed little thirty-two!" He flung the pistol noisily into the street, caught the man by one ear, and slapped his face.

There is one time in the year when the cowpuncher feels that he must get away from his work and indulge in a "good time." He does not know the significance of the Fourth of July except in a hazy way, but he does know that on that day he may have abundant whiskey for the buying, even though its sale be prohibited by law. He knows, too, that he will find at the big celebrations in the Territory all his friends and enemies worth meeting and fighting; and this meeting of friends and fighting of enemies gives the spice of variety to his life.

As the two companions rode to the largest town in the Territory on the morning of the Fourth, one could see that their outfits were typical of themselves. Bill Seymour rode the best and fastest horse on the ranch; his saddle was new and modern in make, his spurs rare and shanked long — only a leader of cowboy fashions had dared to wear them; his hat was a Stetson, and hardly discolored by the weather. Hanner might have fitted himself up from the ranch dump-heap. Two old, unmated spurs dangled from a pair of "run-over" bootheels, the patched corduroy trousers he wore had been traded to him long ago by his champion, and between the bottom of a dirty waistcoat and the top of his trousers there showed a greasy cartridge belt, with scattering cartridges stuck in it. A "floppy" black hat, which almost concealed his dark, pinched features, completed the queer figure. The pony he rode was called "Pignuts" and was knotty and scrubby and tough enough to deserve the title.

"Bill, ye ain't a-goin' to git drunk today, are ye? They say they's goin' to be a lot of extra marshals 'at ain't lettin' any drunk walk the streets today. I wish ye wouldn't drink too much, Bill!" Remembering other celebrations, Hanner wished to get through the day with as little trouble on Bill's account as possible.

"Oh, go to the devil, you old woman! Who said I was goin' to get drunk? Somethin' I never do. Come on; let's ride up," Bill replied shortly; and the two galloped into town through a cloud of dust raised by many incoming wagons.

"Hello, Lem! How's the Convict? Keepin' healthy now, Smear? What's the show and the price?" Bill greeted the punchers from the ranches in all parts of the country with a familiarity possible only to one who knows and does and dares as much as the best of them.

"Got the dangdest mule fer buckin' down here they's goin' to have rode today ye ever seen. Five dollars in it fer the man that rides it. Why don't ye try, Hanner?" The Convict winked at Bill, and insinuatingly confronted the Runt with the question.

"I don't hardly think this here saddle of mine 'u'd stand it," the Runt returned, after glancing at Seymour. "Think I'd better try it, Bill?"

"Get your bloomin' neck broke if you do, but I expect it 'u'd be good for you. Yes, go ahead and ride it, and I'll lend you this saddle."

Bill's words were spoken in jest, but Hanner meditated upon them seriously during the day, and when the vicious mule was led out for its first trial, Seymour noted with some anxiety that his own saddle was buckled upon it. He was careless with drink now, and grinned in anticipation of the sorry figure the Runt would present astride the mule. He made a foolish drunken wager that "Hanner'll stay with that there mule till its tongue sticks out and it can't hump its back anymore."

The bucking mule was the closing scene in the day's spectacle. The high-heeled, stiff-muscled cowboys had chased a greased pig over a fifty-acre field, and been sadly beaten by the street boys of the town; they had pitched rings at the heads of canes over the handles of cheap penknives, and wasted their efforts trying for a gilded watch pegged down with a large-handled awl; they had ridden in the tourney, flying past rings hung in the air, and picking them off with wooden spears, causing strangers to gaze with open-eyed wonder at their dash and recklessness; they had bucked the scores of games that gamblers had devised to part the fool and his money, and were gathered now to watch a game they could understand and appreciate.

Out of a knot of excited men Hanner went straight to the waiting, restless mule. With a mock air of bravado he struck the excited mule across the flank with his sombrero, after roughly seizing the reins. No one who has not learned by experience how to mount a plunging horse can understand how Hanner lifted himself out of the chaos of rearing mule and struggling attendants into the saddle before he signed to the men to turn the animal loose.

When the mule found itself free to act there was a momentary pause. Then began the short, nasty jumps straight into the air, with the animal's back bowed, its legs stiff, and its head lowered. It was the first powerful effort of the angered beast, made with devilish confidence. Hanner was scarcely shaken by these first straight jumps, but then began the twisting series, which is the second expedient of a bucking animal. A jump high into the air, with a seemingly impossible twist to the side, landed the mule with its head turned almost half round. Before the rider caught his breath another jump and another half turn were made. These are the motions that make a bronco buster's life shorter. Hanner was bleeding at the nose in half a minute. The twisting jumps were continued until the strength of the mule was almost exhausted, and as yet only the hat of the puncher had been dislodged. A short pause followed, during which the mule changed its tactics, and Hanner thwacked its sweaty neck with his open hand. The next motion was a sudden rearing by the mule. As it rose on its hind legs the rider yanked fiercely on the reins, and, slipping to the ground on one side, allowed the brute to fall on its back. The saddle horn buried itself in the earth, and the mule's hoofs beat the air a moment before it scrambled to its feet.

Hanner was cooler than the mule now, and swung himself back into the saddle with the first long leap of the desperate animal. This was the easy part of the trial for the rider, and the spectacular part for the world. The mule ran straight away for the opposite fence of the fairgrounds with long, lunging jumps, rising and pitching forward with the speed of a racing yacht. Hanner brought his craft about before it sailed into the fence, and beat it fore and aft with a flourishing hand. He was wild with triumph now, his hair blowing in the wind. He leaned forward as in a race, urging the thoroughly tired and conquered mule straight for the crowd. A particularly vicious dig with the spurs made the beast plunge into the scattering knot of spectators and rise to a four-barred gate. At the opposite side of the track no fence barred its way, and it ran, frightened and quivering, under the awning of a lemonade vender's stand, scattering glasses and confections to the winds, and wrecking the stand. Hanner slowly dismounted, stroked the sweaty flank of the subdued mule, then turning and picking up an unbroken bottle of soda, proposed a toast "to our gentle old family-buggy hoss!"

The punchers cheered Hanner with the heartiness of men who can appreciate the feat.

"Hanner, you're all right. I knowed you could do it." Bill's praise fell sweetly upon the Runt's ears. "Where's that wooley I made the bet with? Hanner, we'll drink; yes, sir, we'll liquor up now and have a good time. I won the bet and you won the five for ridin' the mule. We'll drink, Hanner." Seymour slapped Hanner's shoulder in a cruelly hearty fashion.

"No, Bill; let's not drink any more today," Hanner protested, though he had not drunk anything.

"Hanner, I don't understand you; blast me if I do." Bill was argumentative. "Here you are, just rode the buckinest mule in the Territory, and you won't take a drink with your best friend! Now, if anybody else 'u'd refuse to drink with Bill Seymour I think they'd have trouble. But you, Hanner, I reckon I'll just have to pour it down you." The drunken puncher tried to carry out his plan, but changed his mind at Hanner's appeal.

"Don't, Bill; fer God's sake, Bill, I'm too sick to drink! Let's go home, Bill. I'm shore sick. Won't ye come on home with me?"

"I believe the darn little skunk is sick," muttered Bill to himself. Then aloud: "If you want to go home with me you'll have to come along pretty quick. I'm tired of this show, and anyway, I've got to get over to the roundup on Big Creek tomorrow.[13] Get your horse and wait for me here; I'm goin' to see Smear before I go home."

Hanner knew that his companion went for another bottle of whiskey, but knew also the futility of protesting.

They rode out of the tired, dirty, and heated crowd, where the dance platforms were beginning to fill up, and where the owner of the two-headed calf, the five-legged mule, and the biggest steer in the world was beseeching everybody to come and view his collection. Bill rode at a gallop, with his companion spurring at his heels, until they passed quite out of sight of the revelers. Then he turned with an air of real concern to the Runt, and asked:

"You shore 'nough sick, Hanner? That mule shore put up a stiff article."

Hanner was not diplomatic, and spoke out truthfully: "Sick? No, I ain't sick. What 'u'd I want to see ye get drunk an' run in for? They'd 'a' run ye in tonight, Bill, I know. Did ye ever notice the color of the sky this time a day, Bill? Seems to me it ain't so darn purty as some people think." The sun was setting in a dull, coppery sky, the air was sultry, and the dust rose in thick clouds.

For a minute Bill did not reply, but looked at his companion with a half-puzzled expression. Then he broke out:

"Well, you're a nice one, ain't you? Do you know what I'm a mind to do to you for this dirty trick? You think I'm a darn kid to sneak like this to keep from gettin' run in? Oh, you baby! For a cent I'd make you walk all the way home, and lay this quirt over your shoulders every step of the way."

"Oh, no, Bill; ye wouldn't think o' doin' that. D'ye want to go back? I didn't know ye cared to stay so bad."

"Go back? You think I'm crazy? What 'u'd the punchers say? No, curse you; you've robbed me of my fun. That mule ought to 'a' killed you!"

Hanner had learned long before the value of silence, and rode beside his morose companion with now and then an anxious glance at him. Bill was meditative, and quite forgot the rider at his side. The pale light of a young moon deepened the shadows and illuminated the heavy, sluggish dust clouds that rose in the wake of the riders. Hungry calves, neglected at the ranches since early morning by the celebrating ranchmen, bawled in useless appeal; scurrying, skulking coyotes answered with their threatening cries the challenge of the ranch dogs. A mile away, and coming toward them with rhythmic hoofbeat and noisy rattle of hub on axle, the two riders heard a wagon and team.

"Who do ye reckon kin be goin' into town this time o' night, Bill?" asked Hanner.

"Hold on here, Hanner; we'll stop." Bill meditated a moment, then went on: "You know what that team is? It's the mail stage from Coffeyville[14] to Vinita. Darn old rattle-trap; it's a disgrace to the country. Ought to have a railroad through this godforsaken land. That driver's a fool, and you know what I'm goin' to do? Darn your skin, Hanner, you made me miss the fun at Vinita; now I'm goin' to have some fun of my own. We'll rob the stage! Ever hear about the road agents, the James boys and the Younger gang?[15] Well, they robbed overland stages and trains for swag; but we won't get anything here, only some fun, and scare the fool driver. Stage robbers always jump out and grab the horses' heads and poke a gun in the driver's face. We'll tie our horses over there in the gully and hide in the grass here by the road. You jump out and get the horses, and I'll fix the driver. See? Come on; tie up over here!"

"Ye don't mean that, do ye, Bill? Oh, come on and let's go home." Hanner detected a determined ring in the puncher's voice, and he dared not protest more.

"You don't have to get in on this unless you want to. I can do it myself." Bill considered the plan a good joke, being drunk enough to forget that robbing the mails is a very serious crime in the eyes of the law, and the most serious in the eyes of citizen posses, who sometimes take the law into their hands. He galloped down the rain-washed gully and tied his horse out of sight of travelers on the road. Hanner, expecting an end of the joke, rode with him; but when Bill turned to go back to the road on foot, the little puncher announced his intention of having nothing to do with it.

"Then give me that floppy old hat. I got to wear some kind of a mask. Let me have that old red handkerchief round your neck, too. Now I look like a shore-'nough stage robber — or like you, and that's worse. Well, ride out of the way if you ain't goin' to help." The amateur highwayman half stumbled, chuckling at the prospect of fun, to a place in the long grass at the roadside.

Hanner rode far down the dry wash and waited in anxious silence. He heard the scarcely understood command of Bill Seymour to the driver. The rattling of the wagon suddenly ceased. There was a brief moment of absolute silence, and a pistol cracked. Another shot from the same gun rang out. In a short moment an answering shot was heard. Hanner could have sworn that it was the bark of Bill's revolver. An angry shout from Bill was followed by a fusillade of shots. The rattling of harness indicated a struggle with the horses. Then a yell from the driver started the stage team at a gallop. The firing ceased, and trembling with fright, Hanner heard the noisy wagon pass on toward Vinita.

Thoroughly sobered now, Bill ran to his horse, mounted, and rode to meet his companion. The two galloped on their way for five minutes before Seymour trusted his voice to explain. After breaking into a string of furious oaths, he said:

"What a fool I was! Softy Sam wasn't drivin' the blanked wagon at all. When I got holt of the horses they shot at me. I yelled to 'em to stop, that I was only jokin', but the fools kept on pluggin' away at me. I got behind the horses and yelled again. Then I had to shoot. One of 'em fell back off the seat, and then the other one whipped up the horses. I let 'em go quick. That unshot fool plugged at me till he got out of sight. No, I didn't get hurt, but your hat got a hole in it all right."

"Ye didn't kill one of 'em, did ye, Bill? Ye don't think ye did? That wouldn't do, ye know, at all."

"Kill one? Hit one, all right; maybe killed him. The fool! Oh, that's just my luck. Curse you, Hanner, it was your fault, you cur, takin' me away from the fairgrounds with your old-granny tale about bein' sick. Say, what we goin' to do about it now, eh? We got to get out of this, or we'll get strung up, shore — I will, I mean. We'll ride for the Verdigris River[16] timber and hide there. Well, have you got anything better?"

"Bill, couldn't we explain, tell the marshals it was a mistake, and — "

"Get strung up to a limb before we got through tellin' that, you darn fool! But it ain't a question of 'we'; I'm the only one in this. You kept out of it, you cowardly skunk, and you're safe. You want to run away now, and keep your skin whole?" Bill grew incoherent, scarcely retaining sense enough to spur on toward his destination.

Meanwhile the stage had reached Vinita, with the wounded man at the point of dying, and the driver too much confused to do anything to help him. Quite by chance, a considerable sum of money had been sent through the mails that day, and the regular driver had been replaced by two well-known deputy sheriffs. After the driver had finished telling of the attack made by a short man wearing a big, floppy black hat, and with a dirty red handkerchief tied over his lower face, a posse was immediately formed to hunt the bandit down. No one could guess who the guilty one might be.

Dick Brewer, the leader of the party, questioned minutely: "Would you know the hat if you saw it?"

"Yes," the driver answered; "Tom Forbes put a hole through it before he got shot. I saw it nearly fall off his head — a great big, wide-brimmed floppy thing, with what looked like a piece of rope for a band."

"Somethin' like the hat that Hanner the Runt wore today, wasn't it, Smear?" the Convict commented. Then he asked: "Where *is* Bill Seymour and Hanner, anyway? You seen 'em last, didn't you, Smear?"

"They started home an hour ago. Bill said he had to get over to the Big Creek roundup tomorrow, an' he got a bottle of my whiskey before he went." Smear remembered the unusual incident of Bill's early departure; ordinarily, duty was not allowed to interfere with the puncher's pleasure.

To Smear, who made one of the pursuing party, the words "a big, floppy black hat and a dirty red handkerchief" kept repeating themselves in his mind. At each repetition he recalled with distinctness the appearance of the Runt as he had gone out to ride the wild mule. No other puncher in the country would wear that hat, and none would feel quite respectable with that dirty red rag about his neck at a Fourth of July celebration.

"But, shucks!" Smear muttered to himself, "it can't be him. But he's got nerve, the little devil, ridin' that mule the way he did! He ought to 'a' been with Bill Seymour, though; couldn't tear the cuss away from him. Well, we'll see."

Hanner and Bill rode at a steady gallop until, in the middle of the night, they plunged into the Verdigris River timber. No definite plan of action had been formed; they felt only a strong desire to get away out of sight. The horses must rest, and overcome by fatigue, Bill dropped asleep. The consciousness of a crime done did not disturb him; in his mind it was an accident, the unfortunate result of a joke. Hanner did not sleep. He stared up through the treetops into the starlit sky and pondered the significance of the deed.

The course he had suggested to Bill, that of confessing and explaining the matter, still seemed to be the wisest one to him. "Surely," he thought, "they would understand, for they all know Bill's nature. Didn't everybody know that he must indulge in a joke whenever he could?" A plan began to form in his mind.

"I kin sneak away before Bill wakes up, an' go explain to the marshals. They'll let Bill go, I know they will. I kin do this fer ye, Bill, an' ye'll be glad of it. I don't want to have ye scoutin' round the country; I want ye here, so we kin still ride together. I made ye come away from the fair, an' I got to git ye out of the trouble I got ye into." Hanner scarcely spoke his thoughts. He waited undecided for two or three hours. The dawn was just beginning to filter in to the hiding place as he stole forth quietly to his horse and rode to find the posse.

More than one gang of outlaws had made the river bottom their headquarters and been captured there. The pursuers of the lonely mail-robber inferred that he was one of a number, and that he was very likely to be heard of in the old haunts. So early morning found the posse scouring the country outside the timber, inquiring of ranchmen and the women of the houses for a trace of the man they sought. It would do little good to try to rout him out of the great forest of brush and swamp until some trace of his location had been found.

Dick Brewer and Smear were riding together near the road that plunges through the thickest of the timber when Hanner rode out. They stopped, attracted by his action. The little puncher looked anxiously about until he saw the waiting horsemen, then galloped toward them. Smear felt sick at heart on seeing the floppy hat and the dirty red handkerchief that he wore. Brewer saw them, too, and his hand flew to his revolver. He had not voiced his suspicions before, but now Smear exclaimed with excitement:

"If that there hat's got a hole in it, we've got the man!"

"It's the Runt!" Brewer had not heard the insinuations that were made before the posse started.

The appearance of the bullet hole in the crown of the old hat sufficed to make Brewer and Smear bring Hanner to a halt before their pointed pistols. At sight of their stern faces and threatening weapons, Hanner's power of speech was gone. He tried to say that he wanted to explain, and grew quite incoherent.

"Never mind; explain when you get up before all of us," the leader commanded.

Half an hour of scurrying about by Smear and vigorous blowing of signal calls brought the party together. Everything was extremely orderly and businesslike. A man who robbed mails and killed drivers had no claim on their consideration; the only question was, to be sure of the man. When they were sure of him, no matter what his former standing, he must be hanged straightway. The effect of a lynching they felt to be good. Dick Brewer called upon the driver of the mail wagon to step forth and declare truthfully whether or not he recognized the prisoner.

"Yes, sir; I can swear that that hat is the one the robber wore, and allowing for the difference between daylight and moonlight, I'd say that handkerchief was around the robber's face."

"Is he of the same size and build?" asked the leader.

"About the same; but I won't swear to anything but the hat. I know that."

It grew clear to the mind of the confused little puncher that if he told the story that he had planned to tell, Bill Seymour would be caught and hanged within the day. No excuse that he had perfected would stand for an instant against the plain fact that an attempt to rob the mails had been made and a man murdered. He saw, too, just as plainly, that if he did not tell the truth concerning Bill, he, as the owner of the hat, would suffer the penalty. He knew that very soon he would be asked to tell his story, to clear up the evidence against him. There was none of the great excitement present that nerves men to self-sacrifice. The day was young yet, and the air was chilling. The legs of the horses and the boots of the men were dew-splashed and dripping. It was not pleasant to die now, even though life had been hard and mean to him. He felt a shudder of repulsion when he thought of the mode of death.

On the other side he considered what he owed to Bill. Out of a host of cowboys he had known, Bill was the only one who had ever recognized the fierce desire for comradeship that had consumed him, the only one who had not passed him by in open ridicule.

"Bill fought fer me when I was down," Hanner whispered to himself. "He knowed I was human. An' I brought this on to him. He come away yesterday because he thought I was sick. He'd 'a' got away, maybe, if I hadn't left him asleep to explain. If he had to go I wouldn't have nobody to ride with, an' if

I take his place — if I go he'll know an' — " Hanner did not trust himself to go on, but turned to the leader and said:

"I reckon ye got the man all right."

Under the misshapen body and the half-foolish features there was a stoic in Hanner. To save the life of his friend, the man whom he worshiped and the other punchers respected, was the one great service he could render. He died there with a blind terror in his heart at the blackness of the unknown, and with the thought of Bill Seymour in his mind. The men who hanged him felt no exultation at having avenged a crime, but only a nameless pity for the poor fellow.

A day later Bill Seymour, while dodging about in the timber, learned from a chance-met friend of Hanner's fate. Looking this friend full in the face, he said:

"The poor little fool, to do a thing like that!"

When the Grass Grew Long[17]

TEN YEARS ago every cowboy in the northern part of the Indian Territory knew "Sermon Billy" Wilson, for he was such a slouchy, tireless, moody, and altogether strange figure that one did not forget his face after once seeing it. Everybody knew that one of Billy's hips was dislocated, and that he walked with a difficult side-swing of his right leg, but none knew or cared how the disfigurement had occurred.

It was when the puncher was seventeen years old that he came to the Territory, leaving a rather miserable Indiana home and the ridicule of an Indiana community behind him. His first job, after he reached the country of wide prairies and wider license, was as horse rustler for "Jimmy" Thompson, whose ranch skirted the edge of the Paw Paw Creek timber.[18] Jimmy paid ten dollars a month to his puncher, furnished a horse and saddle, and stood ready to act as schoolmaster to the young rustler.

"Look here, Billy," advised the ranchman one day, "this ranch is a long ways from any excitement, an' I know how it is with young bucks like you. Girls an' drink are the general things. I don't like to change punchers ever' month; an' I'd not care if you went down into the timber once in a while.

There's some half-breed girls, an' full-bloods too, that ain't so bad comp'ny as you'd think. Better consider it some."

Billy considered the words of his boss, placing more confidence in them each time he recalled them. He rode past the cabins of the Cherokees, stuck on narrow, fertile strips of open land under the shelter of rocky hills, and watched the girls plodding about their outdoor tasks. At first he could not understand how romance might be fostered here. The girls were rather heavy-bodied, with large, regular, and unresponsive faces. They would not talk to him when he called for a gourd of water or asked to be allowed to rest in the shade of a big live oak. They brought the water and went back to their work, or pointed silently to the tree.

But at "Cherokee Jake's" cabin, one day, he gained the daughter's favor by helping to pen a calf that had wormed its way through the milk-lot bars. When Billy, at the third attempt, swung the noose of his lasso over the calf's head, the Indian girl showed her teeth in a smile, and spoke her thanks:

"Much welcome. Awful nice rope. Bad little *oyah* [sheep]!" And Billy felt that he had made distinct progress.

The little puncher had occasion to ride that way often afterward, and, noting the growing cheerfulness of his rustler, Jimmy Thompson reflected: "If there was any white girls in sight that wasn't a darn sight worse than the Indians, I'd rather he'd take up with them; but the way it is, the Cherokees are the best. I reckon he'll marry her some of these days, settle down on his corn patch, an' raise shotes an' two calves ever' year."

It could scarcely be called a courting, this unconscious fluttering of the young puncher about the cabin; for old Jake, Jake's wife, and "Jinnie Jake," as the girl was called, apparently accepted him as only another piece of furniture to be given room, when necessary, in a crowded cabin. But Billy knew they were friendly, and his desire for female companionship was almost satisfied.

Before the great herds of cattle from Texas were turned loose on the prairies, the grass grew incredibly tall and thick every year, and in the late fall great fires raced across the country, leaving it black and bare. Ranchmen who were thus early settled in the country provided fire guards — strips of grass cut while green, left to dry, and burned — to protect their ranges from destruction. The Indians generally provided the same protection for themselves; but sometimes they would forget, and be forced to build again after the annual conflagration.

A year after Billy had hired himself to Jimmy Thompson, at the end of a remarkably dry and hot summer, the prairie fires began to break out earlier than usual. A black cloud of smoke rolling up from the west side of Paw Paw attracted Jimmy's attention one day. Calling to Billy to follow, he rode over to drive his cattle to a place of safety on his own range.

Reaching the open prairie, on the edge of which was Cherokee Jake's cabin, the ranchman took in the situation at once, and instructed Billy: "I can get the steers back all right by myself. You'd better go over to Jake's cabin an' see if they're all safe. If they ain't burnt a fire-guard, get 'em away to my side the creek—an' hurry!" The fire was sweeping across the open furiously.

In this strip of country, west of the creek, and lying east of a range of low, blackjack-covered hills, where few cattle ever grazed, the grass grew to the height of a rider's cinch buckle. The day was hot, and the air was dry; the long stems of the dried grass were like trains of cotton. From the south the wind carried the flames straight up the valley, forcing the wild prairie chickens and rabbits to scurry for safety to the timber on each side. Billy spurred his pony in front of the line of fire, beating it to Jake's cabin with a margin of only a few minutes.

As he rode near the cabin he saw Jake, Jake's wife, and the girl standing outside the cabin, apparently unconcerned and delighted with the spectacle. Billy decided that they must have burned a fire-guard about their home since he had been there two days before; but when he came up to the three he saw the mistake. Jake stood near the cabin with an old wet grain-sack in his hand, waiting to beat out the flames when they should come up to him. Jake had never before neglected a fire-guard, and he did not understand the resistlessness of a prairie fire. Jinnie Jake held another wet cloth, ready to help with the fighting, and the mother had carried two pails of water from the spring to keep the sacks wetted. There was an element of humor in the situation that appealed to Billy, and he muttered to himself: "Darnedest funniest bucket outfit I ever seen!" He had seen and applauded the drills of the Plainfield, Indiana, bucket brigade. He turned to Jake, and shouted: "Git out o' here, quick! This way," and he pointed toward the creek. Old Jake only grunted, gripped his sack firmly, and looked toward the roaring line of smoke, which rolled up in thick, black clouds, rose for an instant as the flames leaped out over the tops of the yet unburned grass, then closed down, and pressed forward with new speed. "Git out, git out, quick!" the puncher screamed above the roar.

But now the answer was a half-crazy, exultant light in the old Indian's eyes and a vigorous shake of the head.

"Here, you two, git on my horse an' ride for the timber!" Billy turned to the two women standing stolidly at one side.

"No," said the girl, shortly; "we stay, put out the fire. You help."

But the old woman weakened. Bits of charred grass-tops, carried up in the billows of flame, fell about them; the crackling of dry stems, snapped by flashes of outreaching fire, could be plainly heard. Billy noticed the woman's willingness and carried her bodily to his horse. Then he turned to the girl, and tried to place her behind the mother. Jinnie only pushed him away with powerful arms, and stood defiant at her father's side. The mother galloped away safely to the creek when she saw that Jinnie would not come. The young puncher was desperate.

"Don't be such awful fools! Are you crazy?" He shouted the words in Jake's ear, and seized the Indian's arm to drag him away. The fascination of the oncoming wall of destruction was upon the full-blood; he was mad with the impulse to save his home. He grabbed the little puncher as one might grab a furious, irritating terrier, and threw him against the corner of the log cabin with crushing force. A jutting log, left rough and sharp-edged at the corner, stopped Billy's fall, smashing his hip, and stunning him for a moment. When the girl saw her father fling Billy against the corner of the cabin, and heard the thud of the impact and the groan of pain that escaped him, she ran to the fallen form with a single comprehending cry: "Oh!" In the one exclamation she loosed all of that which we call love and tenderness, which had been so long and so carefully hidden. Billy regained his senses, tried to rise, and fell back limp with pain.

"Git to water — the well — the spring — quick!" he gasped, and the whirling smoke-clouds made breathing difficult.

The Indian girl picked him up in her arms and ran to the spring. She shouted over her shoulder for old Jake to follow. As well have shouted to the fluttering, frightened bird as it flew into the singeing heat to its late-built nest!

Jake put down his head with a fierce shake of his long black hair, seized the wet rag with both hands, and plunged into the consuming flames. The girl saw him disappear as she put Billy on the ground at the edge of the shallow, walled-in well. She dipped some water from the spring with her hands, and dashed it in the face of the young puncher, for she saw the faintness that was coming upon him. The flames leaped up the side of the cabin, and the smoke swallowed it up. Then the fire raced on toward the two at the spring.

"Maybe so, this way!" the girl half sobbed to herself as the heat singed her hair; then she plunged the body of the puncher into the spring. The water was not deep enough to cover the upright man, and she forced him to his knees on the bottom of the pool. She leaned over to see if he was completely covered and conscious, and when she rose, she whispered to herself: "Maybe so, save him, little fellow!" There was no chance for the girl to escape now. She knew that in the narrow spring there was not room for two, and, turning away, she disappeared in the crackling bed of flames. She went into the choking, blinding, cinder-laden smoke to find old Jake.

When Jimmy Thompson rode back with the frightened old Indian woman, he found some twisted bucket-hoops and two charred skeletons. The cabin was blazing furiously, and Jimmy wondered where he would find Billy's bones. While hunting for them, he discovered the little puncher, half drowned, struggling to get out of the spring. Jimmy pulled him free and allowed him to faint; but before he lost consciousness Billy broke out angrily:

"Fools!" Then questioningly: "What come o' the girl? Think she done somethin' for me, didn't she?"

"Maybe she did," agreed Jimmy, though Billy had fainted and did not hear the answer.

The Biologist's Quest[19]

LAKE WAS a collector of small mammal skins for the Smithsonian authorities in Washington and for the British Museum. His work had been done mainly in the mountains of southern California and on the big stretches of Arizona deserts. In the winter of 1895 there was a good deal of heated discussion between Professor McLean of the Pennsylvania Scientific Society and one of the scientists at Washington over the question of whether or not a certain species of short-tailed rat still existed in the Lower California Peninsula. The Smithsonian authority believed that it did, from reports sent in by Aldrich, who had collected in the Southwest until 1893, when he was killed by a superstitious Mexican. The rat, if it existed, was a curious survival, and the scientist who could secure and classify it would earn an enviable reputation. So Lake, in the early spring, received orders to go down into the Lower California region and make a thorough search, following Aldrich's lead.

The collector had a free hand in the matter of expense, and when the baggage man dumped his outfit onto the platform at the Yuma station it might have been mistaken for that of a prospector bound for the Yaqui

Mountains. There were two hundred traps, varying in size from the little, flat ones used for catching a very small brown field mouse to the yawning, iron-jawed kind that a boy must not play with. There were jars of formalin, vials of arsenic, cornmeal, cotton, dried raisins for bait, and a case of delicate, keen-edged skinning tools that Lake would have swallowed to protect. There was food enough to keep three men alive for six months.

At Yuma, Lake went to the keeper of the Sandbar Hotel and asked for reliable guides, Indian or Mexican, for the Lower Colorado River, for he intended to float down the river to the Gulf of Lower California and there rig sails to take him farther down the coast. The next day he engaged Kitti Quist, a nut-faced, broad-footed old Yuma Indian, and "Joe" Maria, a Mexican desert guide.

The boat which the three set out in was as broad and stable as a giant tub. They rigged for it a stubby mast, put in a kit of repair tools, thumped the bottom for possible imperfections, and bolted a watertight chest to the side in which Lake's precious tools, cotton, arsenic, and notebooks were stored. Then the Mexican, after pushing it out into the big, muddy river, stretched himself in the bottom with a cigarette and told the others that they were safe in the grip of the steady currents for three days. After that, he said, they must row and steer for a day to reach the open water of the Gulf. Joe had gone up and down in this way with traders who had ideas about the payment of duties that are countenanced by neither the Mexican nor the United States governments.

While the Mexican dozed in the shade of a propped square of blanket, Kitti Quist told the collector tales of the glory which had been Yuma's years before. He said he had been the most feared medicine man in the Southwest. He had laughed in those days at the timorous Yaquis who danced their snake dance with serpents that were young. He had done that dance with five big rattlesnakes twined on his arms and around his neck. But the Yumas grew poorer, less energetic, and careless of the fame of their great man. He had been compelled to go up to Yuma and do tricks for the tourists when the railroad came crawling in from the plains. Then he had guided prospectors to the mountains, and looked on with a smile when they came back half starved and cursing the day they were born. After that he had cured an Arizona Governor of the rheumatism by sucking the man's knee-joints and shoulder blades, and he had become a self-important white man's medicine doctor. But he neglected to advertise and business fell off. Now he was going to help the new doctor catch rats — for what he knew not. And next he would be? — well, he didn't know.

By night the boat was tied to the riverbank. The Mexican woke and made camp. Lake used the few minutes of daylight in beating the cactus patches for lizards, showing Kitti Quist how to noose them with a horse hair fixed to a slender pole. He tied tags to these lizards with curious markings on them, and soused them into a formalin jar. When Lake told the old Indian that, fixed in this way, the lizards would not decay if kept until the stars came out no more, he was deeply impressed. The collector caught a desert rat once and skinned it. Kitti Quist watched with astonishment the transformation from a limp corpse to a flabby, empty skin, then back again to a cotton-stuffed, perfectly shaped rat, pinned out in a scampering attitude.

"You have showed me strange medicine tricks with the rat and the lizards," said Kitti Quist once, as the two were exploring the riverbank. "Now I will show you what I can do as a Yuma medicine man." Immediately the Indian stepped to the side of a loose stone. He knelt at the side, pushed his hand carefully over the top, then made a quick lunge, and, without suspecting what he was about, Lake saw a four-foot, dull-striped rattler writhing in the grasp of the old man. For five minutes the snake writhed and fought, held firmly by the neck. It hissed the venomous battle note that comes after the warning rattle. Its rattles made an unceasing, deafening whir. The Indian remained calm, letting the snake draw its body through his free hand as it twisted and contracted. He put out his arm to serve as a support for the dangling body when the whippings grew less violent. He twined the snake, always keeping a tight grip of the neck, around his right arm, and pulled his fingers gently back and forth along the smooth sides. Then he relaxed the grip of the neck, gradually, and slid the fingers of that hand down slowly, imperceptibly. He spread out his hand in three minutes more and extended the snake's head to the fingertips. Now all motion had ceased; the rattler lay along his hand and arm, pliant and quiet as a huge cord; the unwinking eyes were still and the rattling had ceased. Kitti Quist raised the big reptile, shifted a part of its body to his head, then worked it down to the back of the neck, stretching its length along his shoulders until the tail dropped easily over the shoulder blade. The snake's head he transferred to an upraised elbow, then drew it back toward his face. Here it lay with its nose held close to the big veins of the old man's neck and moved its tail gently from side to side.

Lake stood as helpless and complaisant as the snake. He felt no surprise when he saw the Indian drop slowly to a sitting position and put his left hand to the sand. Soon the snake glided easily down the extended arm to the earth. Suddenly Kitti Quist sprang to his feet and pounced upon the snake again. But he did not touch it this time. He circled it with a swift moving hand while the snake's head followed in rhythmic movement. Soon it fell, quivering and inert. The Indian's eyes lost the stare that had grown into them. He picked up the body of the rattler with no more concern than he would show in handling a whip. Holding the tail, he whirled it about his head and brought it back with a jerk that separated the head and body, and flung the mutilated trunk away. And when he turned to go back to the camp Lake saw that the sweat was thick on the old man's painted forehead.

The voyage down the Colorado River was accomplished in the manner prophesied by the Mexican. The currents were steady and kept clear of dangerous rocks and cliffsides until near the outlet, where they are broken by spits of sand and whirled by tides and cross currents. Then Joe Maria threw away his cigarette and kept awake. He brought the boat out clear on the smooth waters of the Gulf, set the crude sail, and began to beat down the Lower California Coast.

Inland stretched a flat expanse of salt marsh, only a few feet above water level when the tide was in, and back of this a range of low, cactus-topped hills. These hills were about five miles from the shore and, when the boat had gone down the coast for a day, seemed to give promise of a rich trapping ground behind.

Early in the afternoon Lake decided to leave the boat, go inland to the hills to look the country over, and come back to the shore a few miles farther down. He told the Mexican and Kitti Quist to land where he expected to meet them and get the camp ready. He took a few traps, a pipe, and a small pewter flask of water. He set out for the hilltop, skirting a narrow lagoon of sea water that was ten and twenty feet deep as the tide swung in and out. The salt swamp grass was heavy and thick, and Lake was relieved to get out on the hill, though it was but a great sandbar piled and packed by the wind. He went on over the crest, looking for water courses, near which he was likely to find the mammals he wanted. The land was puzzling — where ordinarily a dip would show the trace of a surface stream, there was only an evenly rounded hollow of sand. Yet small brushwood grew in scattered groups along these depressions. The streams, Lake decided, were underground, and he started back toward the boat, intending to go down for another day before going inland again.

As the collector came back across the hill he saw the boat going down the coast and noticed that the wind had increased perceptibly. He decided to go down to the shore and walk along the beach to the camping place. But when he reached the shore a quarter of a mile farther down, he came on another of the canal-like inlets that he had skirted in going back to the plain. It was impassable, and he began to walk toward its head. This was three miles in-shore, and when he had rounded it and reached the shore again the afternoon was almost gone and he was tired.

Less than a quarter of a mile farther down another of the invisible saltwater canals met him, and for the first time Lake gave a thought to the formation of the long flat marsh. He reflected that tide streams would block his way as long as the flat country was before him. Then he looked at the boat that was, strangely enough, tacking far out in the Gulf and seemed to be in considerable difficulty. He knew that he must get out again to the sand hills and walk down on them until the boat had been brought to shore. He had not spared the half pint of water in the flask, and now, when it flashed upon him that he might spend the night onshore, he grew uncommonly thirsty. But he saved the little that remained, wondering as it splashed and tinkled in the metal if some of it might not be lost by the continual beating and shattering inside.

He was panting when he reached the sand hills again, for he had made nervous haste to get out of that tangle of long salt grass and treacherous tide ditches. He looked eagerly for the boat. What he saw was a scarcely distinguishable flat hull and a slender rectangle of sail which a fierce wind was bellying. Now Lake remembered that this Gulf was swept by little two-day hurricanes that danced in mad fury when they got away from the cactus and hampering sand hills. He was in the edge of the storm only, yet the flying sand stung his cheek, and his dried throat craved the little water that remained in this flask.

The boat would be driven miles out on the Gulf, the watcher knew, and if it survived the hurricane, would land far south of this point. So Lake set out to walk as far as he could toward the possible landing place. Farther down the coast, where the formation changed from the monotone of salt marsh, with its single low relief of yellow sand hills, it might be possible to find water. But here it would be risking too much to turn inland to seek it. While he was gone the boat might put in unexpectedly, and the two guides, not finding him, sail still farther south.

Unconsciously, Lake began to walk fast, and when the darkness closed down he was fairly running toward an invisible boat that sailed in the tail of his eye to an anchorage on the shore directly at his feet. Then he pulled himself up and walked slowly. Soon lagoons, gulf, and salt marsh were lost in the gloom, and only the jagged cactus clumps stood out like giant, distorted shadows on the horizon. Lake took counsel with himself and lay determinedly down to sleep through the night. He woke often to feel his jacket where the four spoonfuls of tepid water were. But he would not drink. The screaming wind showered sand on him, forcing him to draw the jacket over his head, giving small promise of an early landing for the boat, and questioning its mere survival. The collector got through to the daylight, sleeping a little and dreaming of the wonderful short-tailed rat, swimming forever from bank to bank of a sluggish salt pool that rose and fell as the tide crept in and out.

As the morning broke, Lake, who had been sitting in the sand for a long time, peering distractedly into the darkness, rose and looked over the Gulf. There was no sign of the boat. The wind, its force spent in the night, scarcely ruffled the water. The sun came out big and glowing, and the desert heat soon penetrated the temporary early-morning chill. The marooned man was seized with a bitter morning thirst, and raised the flask halfway to his lips before he remembered that the little fresh water must be saved for a more dire necessity. He drew off the coat that had begun to weigh him down. He was about to fling it aside when he felt the pewter flask strike against him. He drew it from the coat pocket in a genuine panic. He felt the pipe, a heavy briar, in another pocket, and the thought of smoking with a parched throat made him smile. He threw it with all his strength at a clump of cactus, then trembled at the prodigal waste of a failing energy. Jamming the flask into his shirt bosom, he laid the coat aside and stepped carefully on. For two hours he kept his head, then the swishing and tinkling of the water in the canteen became maddening. There was a too perfect harmony between its music and the rhythm of his steps. He broke this by making longer strides, then stopping suddenly.

Before noon he sat down in the shade of a cactus. He knew that sleep, when the scorching sun and want of water would drive men crazy, had often saved the sanity of desert travelers. But he could not sleep. He rose when the sun was two hours from the western horizon and tramped doggedly on. For an hour after setting out he tramped slowly, holding his hat clear of his head to protect it from the sun and to let the faint breeze blow in his hair. To hold it in this way, however, tired him, and soon the eternal rhythm recommenced. A lizard that flirted its tail and ran to cover entered the orchestra of his fevered imagination, its tail going up and down like the baton of a conductor. The music grew louder and clearer, and he forgot that the pewter flask held water that might cool the fever. It was the great drum whose beating kept the whole orchestra from turning to a riotous babble of individual performers. So the drum must not quit beating.

Unconsciously Lake increased his speed under the stimulus of the fever. To his mind the orchestra was in breathless chase of a melody that grew faster and faster in time and louder in volume. There would be one final crash, he knew, when the strange new symphony was ended, and he wondered if the drum would be equal to its part. The crash came as the collector, exhausted from a mad scamper down the side of the sand hills, pitched into the rank salt grass near the edge of a tide inlet.

Lake slept through most of the night from sheer exhaustion. He was conscious when he woke of a slap-slap of sound near. At first he thought it was the lapping of the water against the side of the boat, and wondered if the Mexican had yet cooked the breakfast. Then he rose to search the Gulf with his eyes for a sign of his companions.

He thought he was far south of where he had first landed, but in fact he had come only a few miles. He was sure that he had gone past the point where the boat would put in, and turned to tramp back up the coast. He went in, unthinking, to the water's edge, and had to tramp back to the sand hills again. He was at the former symphony rehearsal again by this time.

Calling up his straying faculties, Lake deliberately chose a low bit of ground and began to dig with his hands to find water. And he fainted on the edge of an unpromising hole before the sun was in mid-sky. All the while the idea remained fixed in the man's mind that he must not drink the water that he carried.

The shifting of the breeze so that it blew into his face revived Lake early in the afternoon. He sat up and looked at the horizon, where the Gulf met the sky, with an air of calm indifference. He thought only that it would be a novel sight to see a little, full-bodied tub of a boat drop out of the sky and bring a nut-faced old Indian and a Mexican with a cigarette up on the salt marsh. But it was a bore to watch anything so lacking in variety, and Lake, under the impression that he was only to finish an interrupted siesta, stretched himself on his back to die. The flask he placed at his side, determined to take a full drink when the Mexican roused him for supper.

All through the first night of Lake's absence, Kitti Quist and the Mexican had been driven by the storm out into the Gulf. They realized that it would be impossible to make land after the hurricane came upon them. They retained a tiny rectangle of sail on the stumpy mast to keep the craft's head square to the waves that drenched the boat from stern to bow, and the gale had driven them far out. And the next day they had sailed back toward the west without sighting the coastline.

In the middle of the second night the boat had jammed its nose into a mud bank, and the two had tied up and waited for the daylight. When the morning broke, neither could tell whether this flat marsh, bordered by low sand hills, was the same through which the new doctor had disappeared, or another, fifty miles down the coast. They decided to sail north on the chance of having passed the collector. All day they sailed, firing a heavily loaded rifle at intervals. Once the Indian had gone ashore to search the tall salt marsh. But he met the sullen tide streams and had to get back to the boat. The possibility that Lake might be without water had not occurred to them, and they thought only of relieving his anxiety about themselves and the boat.

Near sundown Kitti Quist pointed out a spit of sand upon which he said the white man had gone ashore. The Mexican doubted, and the boat was pulled in against the bank. The Indian was right — Lake's tracks led off toward the sand hills. He said that they would tie up the boat and follow the tracks. But Joe Maria was lazy and suggested that they set off a great blast of gunpowder. Lake, he declared, would hear it if he was within reach and come to them. Kitti Quist agreed; and when Lake was about to pass into the long sleep, which he thought, fretfully, he had been wanting for ages, the roar of the blast brought him to his knees.

What he saw was worth looking at — it provided variety. A big column of smoke was going up, and at one side were a nut-faced old Indian staring at him and a lazy Mexican waving his sombrero frantically. A little, full-bodied tub of a boat was there, trying to climb ashore. He would go and see if supper was ready. But his strength, nerve, voice, feelings were gone — he tottered headlong into the grass.

The Mexican had seen the collector rise from the grass like a specter, and yelled to Kitti Quist to look. They found Lake, his tongue swollen and protruding, his face scorched, holding a flask with four spoonsful of tepid water still in it. They wondered at that, but set it down to the new doctor's curious theories. They used the water to revive Lake, and carried him to the boat. The next day they sailed back for the mouth of the Colorado River. The two guides brought Lake's wandering mind back to the rational world, and restored his parched face and swollen tongue to a comparatively normal state by a wise use of broths and careful watchfulness. Two days before the awkward tub was pulled up at the Yuma landing Lake could talk, but with considerable difficulty, of his experiences.

"The doctor will go back for the rats when he is rested?" inquired Kitti Quist as he bustled about the boat. He accidentally kicked Lake's water flask into view.

"Go back!" the collector shouted hoarsely. "Kitti Quist," he went on quietly, "the white Medicine Man can no longer do strange medicine tricks with the rats. Not with the short-tailed rats," he added under his breath.

Lake gave his outfit, even the delicate, keen-edged skinning tools, to Kitti Quist and the Mexican guide. Then he took the train for San Francisco. Cooley, who went down to Yuma the next spring to catch chipmunks for the new zoological park in New York, bought the traps and cotton from the old Medicine Man. Professor McLean, of the Pennsylvania Scientific Society, published a pamphlet in the fall of 1897 to show that the short-tailed rat described by the Smithsonian authority never existed except in the imagination.

I Saw an Eagle Strike[20]

HIGH POISED, a spot of gray against the sky,
He sweeps a lazy wing; his eye seeks out
A desert rat, a timid bird exposed,
Or helpless, panting mite somewhere unhid.
But at his thin-drawn, plaintive, searching cry
No creature starts; the sand is echoless;
The sprinkled floor swept clean, save where a guest
Sends spirals whirling up to dance a space
Across the aching plain, then faint to earth,
Invites no prey.

A puff of salted air
Drifts in — a far-sent breath, impalpable,
And passing for a desert dream, except
That with it wings a gull — a tired thing,
Quite spent and crying plaintively to God.
A rush of rigid, whistling wings; a quick,

Exulting shriek; a fearful dart downshot;
A hopeless, troubled, almost human cry,
That lasts a tiny while, then is no more.
The great bald head rears up, the wings fold in,
The talons grip a shapeless thing.

Hot sand
Once more; the clean swept desert floor unrolls;
No salt whiff here; the plain in loneliness —
In God's great loneliness — is still again.

To "Youngers' Bend"[21]

> But, my lads, my lads, to-morrow morning, by four o'clock, early at Gadshill! There are pilgrims going to Canterbury with rich offerings, and traders riding to London with fat purses.
>
> — *King Henry IV*, act 1, scene 2

AROUND THE little station of Gad's Hill the shadows of the pines were lengthening, and the last day of January 1874 was drawing to a close. In the boxlike shanty that served as ticket office, baggage room, waiting room, and storehouse the single official of the Iron Mountain Railroad was polishing his switch lights and cursing the raw Missouri winter. The Little Rock Express was not due for half an hour, but the agent, taking up the two clean-burnished switch lamps, went out to the platform to stare away into the northeast where the train was coming from St. Louis.[22]

He drew his old army overcoat close about him, buttoned it where it could still be buttoned and, pulling his cap down to his ears, darted out to place the north switch light.

As the station agent stooped to arrange the light a tall man stepped from the shelter of a pine hard by and, gripping the other's shoulder, remarked:

"It ain't time to fix that lantern yet, my friend." The old watchman turned quickly. He saw a square of white cloth, with absurd round holes in place of eyes and mouth where he had expected to see a face. A scrap of dark moustache twitched humorously in the lower aperture, and through the eyeholes two blue eyes laughed at his sudden terror.

"Come, let's go up to the platform and get warm," said the voice behind the mask. "You might as well bring that light along," the voice added. The old man walked back obediently beside the tall man.

"Step up and join the band," laughed the captor, pointing to a group beside the station platform, guarded by four other tall men similarly masked. The watchman saw the whole population of Gad's Hill there, a dozen men and boys, including young Rock, the St. Louis doctor's son, who had stopped here to meet his father and go on with the express to Little Rock at 4:45.[23]

"Let's kindle a fire, boys," said the man who had brought the agent up to the group. "This is cold business for the gents here." He chuckled under his mask as he went out to gather an armful of pine sticks. These, with two or three planks ripped from the old platform, furnished fuel for a cheerful blaze which crackled invitingly in the cold wind.

The tall man stepped back from his employment. "Gather around the hearth, friends," he called out cheerily.

Half amused, half terrified, the company hugged the blaze, aware that the eyes behind those five masks were too watchful to make flight a safe or even possible course.

"They got $800 from him," said one of the huddled group, half whispering to his neighbor, and pointing toward Gad's Hill's leading citizen. The man indicated was a prosperous farmer, a grave man, now dejectedly hugging the blaze.

"They took his rifle, too," volunteered the man addressed.

"They smashed my old musket," said a third, his eye lighting somewhat as he joined in the mumbled comment.

Said Tom Kerrigan, the sawmill man, a note of humorous complaint in his voice: "They opened my closet without leave, took my ammunition all away, and throwed my gun in the well — what do you think of that!" He had raised his voice as he spoke.

"It's at the end of the well rope," interrupted one of the masked men, turning to Kerrigan. "You can pull it out easy."

"Thank you, sir," said the Irishman, his eyes searching the masked face of the tall man. "'Twas good of you, Mr. — ?"

"Colburn," the other volunteered with a laugh.

"I'm much obliged to you for your thoughtfulness, Mr. Colburn!" The group chuckled nervously.

Very deliberately, one of the five masked men walked to the north switch, unlocked it with the old agent's key, and threw it over savagely, leaving the bar bent and wedged. Down to the south switch he walked, opened it, then came up to ransack the station for a red flag. This he planted in the middle of the main track by the north switch, then retreated into the trees that crowded close to the railroad. Another of the tall men went down to guard the south switch.

The train was late. The pine shadows lengthened out to lose themselves in the dusk of the enclosing forest. Again and again the fire was replenished by the three watchful guards, and in the pine shadows the two outposts paced feverishly to keep out the numbing chill. But at 5:10, almost half an hour late, the whistle of the approaching engine was heard. The engineer saw the red flag, fluttering dimly in the failing light, whistled "down brakes," and, as his reversing lever went back, the train glided out on the side track.

The tall man at the south switch ran back to the engine, climbed aboard, jammed a large pistol into the engineer's face, and ordered him, with the fireman, down from the cab. He marched them to the group about the fire, now held passive by the drawn pistol of a single bandit.

As the conductor stepped from the forward end of the sleeper to the platform, the man who had set himself to guard the north switch seized him roughly by the collar and, presenting a formidable pistol, commanded roughly:

"Stand still, or I'll blow the top of your d——d head off!" There was no trace of levity in the tall man's tone as he spoke, and the conductor stood quite still until he was moved on to the group around the bonfire.[24]

Meanwhile, the two unoccupied tall men were shouting warnings to all curious persons who put their heads out of the car windows; one promised that if a shot was fired from the train the conductor would at once be killed by the robbers; another explained that those passengers who refused to take in their heads would lose them. This latter message was backed by a double-barreled shotgun and a determined voice.

The two who had guarded the switches now climbed into the combined baggage, mail, and express car and dragged out the baggage man and a frightened brakeman. These they added to the increasing group at the platform edge. Returning, they demanded of the mail agent all the registered letters and packages, and, when these had been rifled, they brought the mail agent to join the men under guard. The express messenger, waiting the pleasure of these methodical men, was next to receive a visit. As the leader of the two opened the door to the express compartment, he faced the messenger's revolver. In a flash the man in the rear had the express official covered and, with an oath, commanded him to lay his "gun" down gently.

The keys were given over, the safe opened, and the money packages taken out. A parcel marked "watch" was opened, but when the robbers found it to be a cheap silver timepiece it was dropped. Putting the treasure into bags, they turned to the baggage compartment. Some small boxes were broken into and their contents scattered about the floor. Before they left the car, one of the two asked for the express messenger's book. On the first blank line, where the receipt of goods is acknowledged, he wrote: "Robbed at Gad's Hill."

"There," he explained, "is our receipt for what you have so kindly delivered. I think I have had the honor of writing in this before," he added, turning the pages of the book, before giving it back. He bowed, showed the way out of the car, and escorted the messenger to the throng around the blaze.

Back to the coaches, where the passengers cowered in their seats, the two methodical robbers went, and none of the thirty was overlooked. Of each they asked name, business, and address, verifying each answer as far as possible by inspecting letters and papers. To chief engineer Morley, who protested against their thoroughness, they explained that they were looking for that "—— detective that's been sent down to hunt us out." A clergyman, who was exempted from robbery, offered to pray for the regeneration of the two outlaws. The offer was accepted, but it was courteously requested that the petition be postponed.

The passengers plucked, the two robbers came back to the little group of train men at the fire and cleaned out their pockets. The conductor was accompanied into the car where his bag was opened and his pistol taken. Then, calling for telegraph blanks, one of the tall men wrote a dispatch to a St. Louis newspaper that, he insisted, had misrepresented his men in accounts of previous robberies. He requested the conductor to telegraph his message as the true story of this affair. Headline and narrative, his version ran: —

THE MOST DARING ON RECORD!

> The south bound train on the Iron Mountain Railroad was robbed here this evening by five heavily armed men, and robbed of —— dollars. The robbers arrived at the station a few minutes before the arrival of the train, and arrested the station agent and put him under guard, then threw the train on the switch. The robbers were all large men, none of them under six feet tall. They were all masked, and started in a southerly direction after they had robbed the train. They were all mounted on fine blooded horses. There is a hell of an excitement in this part of the country. IRA A. MERRILL

In one particular the bandit's story of the Gad's Hill robbery was incomplete. The blank should have been filled with $11,000.

So this other Gad's Hill affair became history, and five of the most reckless train robbers of the Southwest added one more to their list of crimes. They were experienced hands that did the work — it was not difficult to guess the names of the perpetrators. Cole Younger was the leader, and with him were his brother Bob, Clell Miller, Arthur McCoy, and Jim Reed, picked members of the free-booting gang that survived Quantrill's guerrillas in the Civil War.[25]

When the looted express reached Piedmont, the next telegraph station, a full account of the robbery was wired to St. Louis, Little Rock, and the nearby towns. The posses that had disbanded from the chase of the Hot Springs, Arkansas, stage robbers scarcely a month before were collected again from Ironton and Piedmont, and sent off to take up the trail at Gad's Hill.[26]

Sixty miles to the southwest the pursuers found the breakfast camp of the five; they had, indeed, been well mounted. On the second day the posse found the outlaws' night camp, but soon after the trail vanished in a swamp, through which only the initiated could ride.

But the hunt was not abandoned, for the prizes were too rich to be given up without effort. Down through southwest Missouri and western Arkansas the five bandits were followed step by step. They rode fast and far, with an intimate knowledge of the country to aid them. At the end of February they were far south in Texas, where a confederate welcomed them. Here for a month they remained inactive, effacing themselves from notice as effectually as men of energy can.

Then the spirit of adventure called. The enforced lethargy was shaken off, and it was planned among them to rob the stage running between Austin and San Antonio. On April 7, as the dusk was closing down, twenty miles out of Austin, the five stepped from the bushes at one side to form a barricading line across the road. The stage came up, its four horses at a swinging trot. There was the grip on the leaders' reins, the command of "Hands up!" which the driver so well understood, and, with the characteristic courtesy of that band, the eleven passengers were requested to line up at the back of the stage. It was hands up here, too, with no time for parley. A bishop, a bank cashier, three ladies in a panic at sight of the big pistols, a fussy, sputtering little man, a good-natured, philosophical drummer, and four who moved like automatons — they were ranged in a row, their hands aloft, like an odd chorus in a comic opera.

One bandit guarded the driver, one stood at either end of the line, and two went down the row transferring everything of value from pockets to a wide-mouthed bag. The express box and the mailbag yielded their quota, and the five found themselves $3,000 richer.[27]

The robbery completed, the two lead horses were cut out of the stage team and the bandits rode away into the night. The stage reached San Antonio in the early morning, hours late. A sheriff's posse was sent out to take up the trail, eighteen hours old when it was found. This time the trail led north — the sheriff's posse followed it until it was discovered that the men had separated into two pairs and the fifth had taken up a fresh companion. A reward of $500 each for the criminals was offered, and the Texas official returned to forget the matter in his immediate work.[28]

It was to "Youngers' Bend," in the Indian Territory, at the southern edge of the Cherokee Nation, that the bandits turned, a long, five-hundred-mile run that should land them in the shelter of the Canadian River canebrakes at the ranch of old Tom Starr. Starr was a Cherokee Indian, a man of giant stature, cool, cautious, with a large appetite for crime. He had established his reputation as a terror among his people, and his house had become a refuge for the Missouri outlaws. His ranch was in a great bend of the Canadian River, between Briartown and Eufaula, shut in on the north by rugged, flinty mountains, impenetrable except to horsemen, and surrounded for five miles by rank canebrakes that closed round like big billows of prairie grass. Here the old man lived, defying law and rejoicing in the occasional visits of the Youngers and their friends. So deeply was this border chief impressed by the daring of these visitors that he gave to his retreat the name of "Youngers' Bend."[29]

On the ride north the Younger boys were together, Miller rode with McCoy, and Jim Reed took up a companion named Morris, who said that he was a fugitive from Texas officers. He won Reed's confidence and proved to be a diverting companion.

Some days after the band separated, Reed and Morris rode up to a farmhouse for dinner, and, at Morris' suggestion, their guns were left on their saddles. During the meal, Morris made an excuse to leave the table. He went to his horse, took his Winchester, and returned in time to meet Reed's defiant curse with a shot. At the first fire Reed grabbed the edges of the table and raised it in front of himself as a shield, scattering the dishes in a smashing wreck. Morris shot again, splintering the tabletop, and the bullet took effect in Reed's body. Releasing the table, the wounded man fell back, searching his pockets for a pistol to kill his assassin. Morris shouted to the farmer as he saw Reed fumble at his pocket:

"Kill him, he's a murderer! He's a murderer — there is a reward for him, dead or alive. I'm an officer!" And the farmer, coming forward, disarmed the dying man, helping to finish Morris's ghastly work.[30]

The tale of Reed's death reached the four who had come safely to Youngers' Bend. Morris had learned of the rendezvous on the Canadian River. A posse would be gathered and sent up there — they might be upon them at the moment, for it was rumor that brought the story to them, and determined officers could outride rumor. Old Tom Starr was called to a council.

Youngers' Bend was impregnable, said Starr. Its evil reputation protected it from invasion. In the years that had passed since he cut away the canebrake to plant his cornfield, no man had penetrated to that log stronghold without his knowledge and consent. A few men had come in who never went out — these had not been able to explain their presence to the satisfaction of Starr.

Even as the old man spoke, a Texas sheriff with a posse of ten men who had followed him the two hundred miles across the Indian country were riding on the trail through the canebrakes. Five miles from the log house they had waited, until the stars came out and the warm, early June air had given way to the cooler breezes of the timber. Then they took up the march, going forward, single file, silent as dead men. Over a trail that was nowhere broad, and often scarcely defined, they picked their way slowly. At the corner of Starr's field, a quarter of a mile from the cabin, the sheriff gave his final word of instruction. The house was to be surrounded, swiftly, silently. With a cordon drawn close about them, with a brilliant moonlit sky to show them if they ran, the Texas officer was confident of their capture. A hundred yards farther the horses were left, tied to the rail fence. The ten crept forward, spreading into two lines to surround the house.

The moonlight showed the big log cabin, set squat among a group of log outbuildings, the long, black shadow of a cottonwood cutting a sharp track across the bright clapboarded roof. A faint flicker of light showed from a window at one end, a note of angry red in the quiet yellow radiance of the moon. As the men came closer, dodging from tree trunks to woodpiles and chance-placed farming tools, the light in the house disappeared.

The council inside ended abruptly. The sensitive ear of the old Indian had caught the gentle rustlings as the pursuers shifted closer in. Starr had commanded the extinguishment of the lamp with a gesture, and as the thin, sharpcut features of a tall man were revealed for an instant sweeping down toward the light, the Texas sheriff came up to rap imperiously at the thick front door.

"Starr!" the sheriff called, "Oh, Starr! Come and open this door." At this command a lithe, tall figure rushed through the darkness of the room as if to break out upon the unfortunate officer. But the old Indian caught the man roughly by the shoulder, whispering a word of command in his ear. The word was whispered from one to the other, until the message was understood.

Grouped at the back door, across which the shadow of the tall cottonwood cut, the four outlaws waited with the old Indian, wondering at his actions.

"Now, follow me," Starr whispered, pulling back the door, "to the little smoke house." He sped across the twenty feet of shadowed space to a low, squat outbuilding, the sagging door of which gave way at a touch. "Catch hold of me, so!" he commanded, lifting an outlaw's hand to his shoulder and instructing the others to follow in the same way. Then he raised the cover to what was ostensibly a milk cellar, and plunged into the tomblike darkness. Two steps farther, and another door came open. "Stoop low," commanded the leader, plunging forward through a damp passage. On and on they followed, backs bent, and aching with the strain of the cramped posture.

Then they could stand up. Starr spoke out unrestrained, then laughed. In all the years that he had kept open house to these Missouri freebooters he had not revealed his cave in the hillside and the secret of the passageway. Now he had discovered it to them, with the theatrical effect that he loved. Lighting a candle, the old man showed them the furnishings of the place — straw and blankets, food, and a great pile of wood for cooking. Opening into the main room was a narrower room, where Starr promised [that] the outlaws' horses should be brought and stabled.

Back again at his cabin, the old Indian protested, with a gleam in his eye, that he had never heard of the Younger Boys, and that he could not guess why ten men should come to surround his poor house. But the ten men stayed, for they had seen the face of one man they wanted, and had heard something of that quick rush of escape. They stayed to guard the trail out through the canebrakes and to shadow old Tom Starr. One night the keeper of Youngers' Bend drew the guard from the trail and hustled the men in the cave away. They rode back to Missouri and to their old life there.

One by one the Younger gang was captured or killed — Tom McDaniels was shot at Pine Hill, Kentucky, in 1875; a year later Bruce Younger and Hobbs Kerry were taken at Granby, a little zinc town in southwestern Missouri; Charley Pitts was caught in Kansas early in 1876. Then, in the autumn of 1876, came the famous raid into Minnesota, the attempt to rob the Northfield bank, the killing of Bill Chadwell, Clell Miller, and Pitts, the pursuit and capture of the three Younger brothers, Coleman, Bob, and Jim. The time for laughing at the law passed — rewards mounted to extravagant figures, and public sympathy gave way to a better feeling for law and order.[31]

Over Youngers' Bend for some years fell a new and strange quiet. Tom Starr missed his former guests, and he was growing too old to form other connections that pleased him. The cave in the flinty mountain, just beyond the cabin, that had always been well stocked and defended, became littered with leaves and choked with chance-blown rubbish, echoing only to the growl of a stray coyote or the flutter of a bat's wings. The law had claimed its due; justice was a force mightier than wrong, and its workings were inexorable. For a long time a strong man could make his own law and break it as he listed, but the day of reckoning would arrive — that was as certain as death, Old Tom Starr fell into a half-blind dotage, and Youngers' Bend had a new history.

A Border Judge and His Court[32]

A MAN who sentenced 172 criminals to death, 88 of whom were hanged;[33] an upright judge, holding sway for twenty-one years over seventy-four thousand square miles of the most lawless territory in the United States; a stern, just judge whose name became a terror to evildoers; a very kindly, sympathetic gentleman and public-spirited citizen — few characters have been developed in our West who have played a more striking role than Isaac C. Parker, United States district judge for the Western District of Arkansas from May 1875 to September 1896.

He was born in Belmont County, Ohio, in 1838 and came to his post at the age of thirty-seven after serving two years as a circuit judge in Missouri and four years as a member of Congress from the same state — for one term as a member of the Committee on Territories.[34] The new judge found in his district a condition bordering on anarchy. In western Arkansas the fierce Brooks-Baxter feudal war was raging, the authorities admittedly helpless;[35] in the extensive Indian Territory crime was running rampant among the lawless whites who were flocking across its borders. The court at Fort Smith — whither it moved from Van Buren shortly before President Grant appointed young Parker to the bench — had been powerless to check crime or adequately to punish those brought to trial. Perjury was common; a feudal assassin laughed at the law with his clan behind him. Whiskey sellers rode unharried among the Indians in violation of the code and the treaties; horse thieves fled to safety in the Territory; and fugitive murderers intermarried among the tribes with impunity, sowing the seed for dark trouble in the future.

The opening of the first railroad through the Territory in the early seventies let in a horde of outcast and desperate men who set out to defy the law, often banding themselves together to carry terror into the homes of the natives. The Indian courts, adequate for tribal business, had no control over this "criminal intruder" class. Trained in crime, bold and fearless, their appetites whetted by adventure, these men made up a formidable element in the new country. Before Judge Parker came to the bench, the Fort Smith court had been practically ruled by them, so numerous and influential had they become.

When the Indian Territory was set aside for the various tribes in 1828, the United States promised the Indians protection from all intruding, criminal whites; but this promise was forgotten. As a matter of form, the court for the Western District of Arkansas was given jurisdiction over all the whites in the Territory — a judicial area absurdly large and difficult to govern. And until Judge Parker's time there was scarcely a pretense made of protecting the tribes. He saw crime running rampant over that country, and deliberately set himself the task of checking it. How sternly he pursued his appointed task and with what aid he succeeded in accomplishing it is shown by the simple record that, during his term of office, sixty-five of his deputies were killed in fights with lawbreakers.[36]

Before Judge Parker's time the court had been, not only incompetent, but grossly extravagant. The federal authorities were hesitating over an expenditure of $400,000 a year to support an ineffective institution. A resolute, dominant man, and one who understood conditions among the Indian tribes, was needed for judge. A nephew of General Benjamin F. Butler failed of confirmation by the Senate, after he had been nominated to the judgeship of western Arkansas, and Parker, recently appointed chief justice of Utah, was transferred to that post.

The new judge turned to his task with unusual energy, and set vigorously into motion the machinery which ran with scarcely a day's interruption until his jurisdiction over the Indian Territory was taken away by the Curtis Law twenty-one years later, only a few weeks before his death.

"Gradually, slowly, under Judge Parker's rule," wrote a biographer, "the opposition to the law's enforcement was weakened. Juries, strengthened by his splendid courage, upheld the law. The officers of the court, including the two hundred deputy United States marshals, were inspired to heroic efforts. The days of chivalry never produced a body of men more courageous and fearless than the deputies who executed the processes of the court of the Western District of Arkansas."

Eighteen murder cases came before Judge Parker at the June term, 1875, the first at which he presided, and fifteen convictions were secured.[37] At the November term of the same year, six men of the eleven arraigned were convicted of murder. Of the ninety-one criminal cases tried at that term there were forty-eight convictions for larceny (principally horse stealing), six for murder, six for assault, six for whiskey selling in violation of the law, and eleven for various other offenses, including one conviction for manslaughter. When it is remembered that *all* of these cases came from the Indian Territory, with a total population at that date of sixty thousand, including at least forty thousand Indians over whom the court had no jurisdiction except where one of the parties concerned was white, some conception of the prevalence of crime may be formed.

"Yet appalling as was this record," wrote a commentator, "it was asserted by good and reliable authority to show less than one-fourth of the murders and other crimes committed within the confines of the Indian Territory." And for twenty years this gruesome work continued. The Territory's population became more and more mixed, shifting, and unstable in character. One generation of lawbreakers, wiped out or frightened into semi-respectability by the Fort Smith court, gave way to a new and unafraid one.

In a single day, August 5, 1895, after the notorious "Cherokee Bill" had been arraigned for the murder of a jail guard,[38] eleven separate convictions were obtained and sentences passed. Twenty-five prisoners were brought in during that same week to the Fort Smith jail, including Mollie King and Barry Foreman for killing the woman's husband; Will Benton for shooting an engineer named Gibson; Tom Root, a negro, accused of being a train robber and all-round desperado;[39] Ben Howell, a trusty, who, it was said, furnished "Cherokee Bill" with the pistol to murder the jail guard; and Louis Girard, who had robbed the Eureka Springs (Arkansas) post office.

These records were not unusual — they were many times exceeded — for the grist of crime came to the mill of justice in lavish abundance, and the court never shirked its work.

Such statistics mean nothing if not that in Judge Parker the law had a stern, inflexible exponent who banished sentiment and sympathy from his courtroom. It was not an easy thing to do, but the necessary and inevitable thing if he would enforce the law as required by his oath. Personally he was a man of deep sympathies and wide interests. "Never will those who were in the courtroom," wrote one who had performed jury duty there, "forget the scene when Judge Parker pronounced his first death sentence. Eight men convicted of murder had been brought up for sentence. Daniel Evans was the first man up. Judge Parker spoke the fatal words with a clear voice and in measured tones, but as soon as he had finished he bowed his head and wept."[40] During the years he sat at Fort Smith the impression got abroad that he was too stern a judge, and some of those who defended criminals in his court began to say that he was heartless and bloodthirsty, and to picture him as a second terrible Jeffreys.[41] But in no case that came before him could it be said that "here he was too severe" or "there he was not fair." Two — indeed, three — maxims he kept before him throughout: "Do equal and exact justice; permit no innocent man to be punished, but let no guilty man escape"; and later, in the turmoil of state politics, he enunciated in no uncertain tone the rule, "No politics shall enter here."[42] Justice, calm and unwavering, was his guide, his divinity. He believed that no judge who is influenced by any other motive is fit for the bench.

To Judge Parker the law appeared as a terrible and sublime avenger, exacting a life for a life. Lawbreakers fought the law, so the law must fight back, using the weapons criminals understand. "I never hanged a man," he said as he lay on his deathbed; "it was not I. It was the law. The good ladies who carry flowers and jellies to criminals mean well. There is no doubt of that; but what mistaken goodness! Back of the sentimentality are the motives of sincere pity and charity, sadly misdirected. They see the convict alone, perhaps chained in his cell; they forget the crime he perpetrated and the family he made husbandless and fatherless by his murderous work."

Among the first cases tried before Judge Parker was that of Sam Fooy, a half-breed Indian who was charged with murdering and robbing the "Barefooted Schoolteacher," a young white man named Neff. Fooy shot him in the back, secured the money he had earned, $250, by teaching a small school near Tahlequah, and hid the body. It was a year later that the skeleton was found, and beneath was the flyleaf of a teacher's manual, which finally led to the identification of the victim and the apprehension of the murderer. Significant was this from Horace, written on that chance bit of paper:

"Pallida Mors aequo pulsat pede pauperum tabernas Regumque turres."[43]

It was too true — pale death was abroad in that land, seeking his victims impartially among paupers and princes.

At the end of the first year of the new regime an even dozen desperate characters had been hanged and the fame of the new judge got abroad. On the old trail running north and south through No Man's Land — a narrow strip of territory jutting out between the southwestern border of Kansas and the Texas Panhandle, at the crossing of the North Fork of the Canadian River, there stood for many years a stout signpost. This legend was painted on it:

FORT
SMITH
500
MILES

In the autumn of 1882, after Judge Parker had established the reputation of the federal court as a terror to the lawless, a posse of deputies was chasing six highwaymen out of the Indian country. The outlaws, hard pressed, ran for No Man's Land, hoping to escape in the Canadian River timber. With the deputies in plain sight, hardly more than a mile away, the six came up to the bank of the stream by the signpost. As if by prearrangement they stopped, turned their Winchesters upon the signboard and riddled it. That was their defiance to the Federal Court: they spurred across the Canadian and were lost. Some days later one of them returned to the ford, observed with interest that the "Fort Smith" in the sign had been all but shot away, and, standing in his stirrups, with grim facetiousness, he cut a new legend, so that the chance traveler should read,

500 MILES TO HELL

To his mind the new sign could not prove misleading.[44]

Pale, grim death was indeed stalking abroad. Daniel Evans was hanged for killing a boy whose new saddle and fancy boots he coveted; Jim Reed, with two companions, had tortured old Watt Grayson, a Cherokee, and robbed him of thirty thousand dollars on the promise of ten dollars and a quart of whiskey; William Walker, a negro living in the Choctaw Nation, killed another negro, though the whiskey was the only payment he received.

Crimes like these just noted sent sixty-one men to the gallows in the fifteen years from 1875 to 1890. In September 1895, Judge Parker passed the sentence of death upon Buss Luckey — a negro charged with killing a deputy marshal. In that sentence he summed up his view of the position and his ideas of responsibility. To the condemned man he said:

"You have been convicted of the murder of Newton La Force, a United States deputy marshal of the court in the Indian country. He is one of more than threescore of marshals who, in the last twenty years, have given up their lives in the Indian country while in the discharge of duty, these brave men representing the government and the law in a bloody struggle with outlaws and banditti. They represented peace and order. The banditti represented lawlessness, bloodshed, and crime. The killing of Marshal La Force was but one act in the great war of civilization against savagery which has been waged against the men of crime by this court and its officers for twenty years. The record of this court in its efforts to overcome bloody violence and murder is unequaled in the history of jurisprudence in this country."

Judge Parker was a man to urge his deputies on and inspire them with the same enthusiasm for order that he felt. The men were brave — bravery was taken for granted among the force — and resourceful. Reckless at times, too, they were, with the fine recklessness that stirs the blood. It was a matching of daring against daring, of finesse against cunning, and frequently of brute force against brute force. Among the criminal class there was the strange, wireless, mysterious interchange of warnings and information that puzzles the uninitiated. If a posse rode openly into a neighborhood to arrest a man, the news of its coming was flashed ahead. Deputies penetrated to the most lawless spots under all sorts of guises, acting the spy under conditions to wreck the nerves of a cautious man.

One of these men, Deputy Marshal Fannin, was sent in the summer of 1883 to hunt out Jason Labreu, who had murdered his sweetheart. The crime was a peculiarly revolting one. The criminal fled from Texas to the Chickasaw Nation in the Indian Territory. For several months Fannin trailed Labreu, and found him at length working for a farmer near Red River. The hunted man was known to be a dead shot, and desperate. Arresting him would be no easy matter. As he worked in the field he carried his Winchester strapped to his back; in his eyes was the constantly watchful look of the hounded; and before Fannin showed himself he put away all of his weapons. The deputy was unknown to Labreu, and he hired himself to the farmer for three dollars a month "and board." Then for three months the two men worked together, slept in adjoining bunks at night, ate their meals at the same table, and took their pleasures together. And all the while Labreu was never off his guard.

Gradually, insidiously, Fannin won the man's confidence. From remarks dropped here and there Fannin convinced the other that he, too, was a fugitive from Texas justice. Confidence in his brother in crime brought out a confession from Labreu which was half of what the officer was working for. But the vigilance of the man never relaxed. Once as Fannin came up behind him stepping noiselessly across a fresh plowed field, thinking that here would be his chance if he were armed, Labreu wheeled, with the deputy still twenty feet away, and brought his rifle into position at full cock.

"Oh, it's you, is it?" he laughed. Then he turned and replaced the gun as he went back to work.

Midsummer came with Fannin still awaiting his chance. Then the moment arrived. The two had come in from the field at the noon hour, hot and dirty and tired. A single tin washbasin on a stool outside the kitchen door served them both, and Labreu took his turn first. He leaned his Winchester against the door as he went to the basin, not noticing that Fannin, waiting his turn, stood between him and his gun. The outlaw finished his ablutions, dashed the water from the basin, and stooped forward to bury his face in the towel that hung above the stool. It was only for the briefest moment that the man's eyes were hidden, but in that moment Fannin seized the Winchester and leveled it at the other's head. Labreu looked up with the quick start that the deputy had so frequently noted, and saw the rifle barrel held steady at his head. Without a word his hands went up and Fannin called the farmer out to fasten the handcuffs. Labreu was not hanged, for on the way to Fort Smith he tried to escape and was killed by his captor.

In 1873, Jim Wilkerson, a deputy, with Perry Du Val and Will Ayres as posse, rode over into the Creek Nation and arrested four men wanted for various crimes. At one of their night camps, near the Creek agency, three of the prisoners were chained to Deputy Ayres, while Du Val slept beside him with a pistol in his belt. During the night one of the Creeks, John Billee, slipped his handcuffs and, jerking Du Val's pistol from his belt, shot him through the head. He next fired at Ayres, who was sleeping with his right hand across his breast. The bullet went through the deputy's hand and furrowed his ribs. Wilkerson, who was sleeping some distance away, sat up when he heard the firing, and Billee shot him through the back, the bullet penetrating the kidneys. Ayres, wounded as he was, grappled with the desperado and succeeded in shooting him so that he was disabled. The deputies retained command over the situation and delivered their prisoners at Fort Smith.

In spite of the lawless element over which the Fort Smith court had jurisdiction, in spite of the immense area of that jurisdiction, and with the hot-blooded spirit of the South prevalent over a greater part of it, it was an extremely rare thing for an act of mob violence to take place.

"Certainty of justice brings security" was one of Judge Parker's favorite maxims. In his charge to the grand jury on the opening of court in August, 1895, Judge Parker said:

"I can say, in vindication of these (former) jurors and of these people, that the law has been at least as well enforced by them . . . as it is enforced in any state of the Union. I can say *even more than that.* I can say that there has not been a band of robbers or highwaymen or assassins in the Indian country that has not been, by the officers of this court and by the juries passing upon their cases and finding them guilty, if they were guilty, more promptly broken up, destroyed, and wiped out, than has been the case in the Indian country for twenty years past. . . . You are to teach the people, everywhere, a wholesome lesson, and that is, that they must rely upon the law and upon its enforcement for their protection, and not upon mob violence, not upon that spirit that causes people to degenerate into a mob and become criminals themselves in an effort to seek protection. . . . Sometimes you will find that good men are involved in things of that kind. It is because they have lost confidence in courts and juries. You say to a community that, as surely as a crime is committed, so surely will the party who has committed it be brought to merited justice as the law prescribes that punishment, and you won't find any mobs in that community. There are no mobs in the counties of this State which are in this jurisdiction. . . . And it is a rare exception that mob violence exists in the Indian country. There are cases of it (we have tried in this court three cases of mob violence since I have been here), but there is not the amount of it you would expect from the criminal condition of that country. And it is because the people believe that we will at least endeavor to enforce the law.

"When the history of this court comes to be written; when the passions of the hour, prompted by cupidity, avarice, self-interest, and the desire for gain, shall have all disappeared, those who have been connected with it in upholding the majesty, power, and dignity of the law of the United States shall not suffer from that true history."

From one of his friends, an attorney practicing in his court, came this discriminating estimate of the Judge's work after it was done:

"To Judge Parker the 'Man of Crime' was the enemy of society and civilization, and in his hands was placed the duty of exterminating him within the jurisdiction of his court. He brushed aside the technicalities of the common law which covered and protected the criminal, and laid bare before the juries the real aspect of crime in all its hideousness. The juries responded to his appeals and rarely failed to sustain him. He regarded these technical rules as having grown up under another system, having been built up by the judiciary in the interests of mercy to save defendants from bloody and powerful persecutors and Draconian statutes; and the system having changed, the reasons for the rules having ceased to exist, the rules should cease. Be it right or wrong, it was the stand of a vigorous, strong, and brave man. Necessarily it brought down upon him criticisms from those whose interests it was to criticize; but throughout the Indian Territory the best people — the law-abiding people — regarded Judge Parker's court as the palladium of their liberty."

Working for Fame[45]

> It may be I'll some time be arrested,
> But we're all of us working for fame;
> What care I how that is accomplished?
> For the end of all men is the same.
>
> [From an early unpublished poem by JOHNNIE POINTER, who achieved his ambition indifferently, being hanged at Fort Smith, September 20, 1894]

THERE WAS also the case of Caesar, which is well known. Bob Dalton's history is not so familiar, but it may be said in the beginning that it was an overreaching ambition that led to his downfall. "I'll see Jesse James and go him one better," said the ambitious Bob. The student of poker will understand this, especially if he has in his innocent boyhood devoured the stories of Jesse James, the great, and his band of lawless companions. But should your imagination by chance have been fed only on the tales of Robin Hood and Dick Turpin, you must know that the tribe of Dalton were as brothers-in-blood to those tradition-hallowed cutthroats.[46]

The mother of the Dalton brothers, four of whom fell under the spell of the romantic, was a Younger, and the Youngers furnished some of the most desperate and capable of the Missouri outlaws, co-workers and intimates of Jesse James. The father was a morose, shiftless Irishman, with a huge, if theoretical, sympathy for downtrodden Ireland, and with a practical admiration of its patriots. Two of his sons he christened Grattan and Emmet.[47]

In 1889 the soberer, agricultural element of the Daltons — for among the thirteen children of this vigorous family there was the greatest diversity of taste — joined that spectacular rush which in an hour turned a verdant prairie into the populous Territory of Oklahoma. To the Daltons fell two good quarter sections of land near Kingfisher, and there the family rested after a wandering that had begun in 1860 in Missouri and extended over two counties of Kansas.[48]

The first of the brothers to pay the penalty exacted of the adventurous was Frank, who became a deputy United States marshal in the Indian Territory, and was killed in a fight with whiskey sellers and horse thieves in 1887. Later Grattan was commissioned as a deputy marshal, and Bob joined him as posse until he in turn reached his majority and gained a deputy's badge. Then nineteen-year-old Emmet joined Bob as an uncommissioned officer. The three brothers won reputations as crack shots and fearless, resourceful deputies, acquainted with the habits and haunts of border lawbreakers.[49]

In 1890 Bob, who had established himself as leader among his brothers and their fellow officers by reason of his compelling blue eyes and reckless coolness, became dissatisfied with the meager pay of a deputy. He was familiar with the rich winnings of successful horse thieves and train robbers; he knew their methods, and knew, too, that their own imprudence and stupidity more often brought them into the clutches of the law than the diligence of the underpaid guardians of the peace. To his elder brother, Grattan, and to young Emmet he proposed the formation of a gang which should rival the boldest. The brothers yielded, and the three collected a bunch of other people's horses in the Indian Territory, drove them away to Kansas, and sold them. So the Dalton Boys became outlaws.[50]

As outlaws they were hunted by their former companions, who were acquainted with their hiding places; and to escape this pursuit Bob proposed a visit to California, where another brother, William, had settled some years before.

There, at the little station of Alila, in Tulare County, on the night of February 6, 1891, they entered upon the larger career of crime that Bob had planned by robbing the Southern Pacific express, out of San Francisco to New Orleans. To stop the train at this insignificant station, at which it was due about nine o'clock, the agent was forced to furnish a red light. The telegraph wires on both sides of the switch were cut, and when the red light was swung across the track the train promptly came to a standstill. Two masked men jumped aboard the engine cab and ordered down both engineer and fireman. The latter was commanded to take his coal pick with him, and then the two bandits marched him to the door of the express car. There he was instructed to negotiate with the messenger for the opening of the car. The messenger refused to open or to hold any communication with the robbers. They in turn warned him not to shoot and swore that if he did, they would kill the fireman. After a minute of one-sided quarreling, the fireman was set at the job of battering down the door with the pick.

In the confusion the messenger escaped from the opposite door of the express car, which had been left unguarded, and, running to the bushes near the track, concealed himself. Inside the car the robbers found a locked safe, fastened securely to the floor and too strongly built to yield to hammers and crowbars. They had neglected to provide dynamite; and they did the only thing left to do — they retreated from the train beaten in this first attempt.[51]

Grattan and William Dalton were arrested for complicity in the attempted robbery.[52] William was acquitted, but Grattan was convicted and sentenced to twenty years' imprisonment. On the way to the state penitentiary at San Quentin, his feet bound together with a leather strap and a wrist manacled to the wrist of a watchful officer, Dalton somehow slipped off the handcuff and plunged through an open car window to the water of a stream below. He swam ashore and, cutting the thong from his feet, escaped out of the country. In a short time he joined his brothers in Oklahoma.

On their return from California the Daltons began to steal horses, and a brother-in-law, named Whipple,[53] at Kingfisher, was arrested for receiving an animal stolen by Bob. While awaiting trial in jail at Wichita, Kansas, Whipple delivered to the authorities this notice, received from Bob:

"You are making d——d fools of yourselves if you think you can tackle any of our people without putting yourselves in a hell of a fix. That Ransom Payne" (a deputy who had been active in chase of them) "'ll have to swing for it sure, or have so much lead pumped into his d——d carcass that his own mother won't know him. Let those that are called as witnesses beware." A crudely drawn skull and crossbones adorned the document, and below it in big red letters was written "We shoot to kill!" Brother-in-law Whipple was released, and the injured vanity of the Daltons was repaired.[54]

Immediately after the release of Whipple, Bob Dalton learned that the deputy, Ransom Payne, whom they had promised to kill, would leave Wichita on the Santa Fe express May 9, and that the train would reach Wharton, a signal station in the Cherokee Strip, at ten o'clock that night. With his brother and a companion he descended upon the station half an hour before the train was due, forced the agent to set the signal light to stop the express, and locked him, bound and gagged, in his own bedroom.[55]

Deputy Payne's story of the robbery furnishes the additional details:

"I had been dozing for some time in the last car at the rear, fagged out from my week's stay at Wichita, and was thinking that it would be pleasant to get into my own comfortable bed again when the jerking of the cars as they stopped woke me up. There had not been a holdup in this neighborhood for a long time, and the thought that this was one did not at first occur to me. Then I remembered that the night train which I often rode on was very seldom signaled to stop between Arkansas City and Guthrie,[56] so I raised the window to find out if anything was the matter. Suddenly a couple of shots rang out, and it came over me that here were the Dalton Boys come to carry out their threat to make a sieve of my precious hide. I had received their warning and knew that they had nerve to carry it out.

"I didn't want to fight the gang, so I ran to the rear of the car, dropped to the ground and, keeping in the shadow of the train, walked out to the underbrush by the side of the grade. There I stood waiting, my pistol drawn, swearing to myself that if they found me they'd get all the fight there was in me before I was killed.

"From where I stood I could hear the yells and threats of the rascals as they raced back through the cars looking for me. After they had gone through the train, and Conductor McTaggart had sworn that I was not a passenger, they gave up the hunt. Then they turned their attention to the express car.

"The fireman was brought back from the engine with his coal pick — a trick they had learned in California I understand — and they soon had the door down and the safe open. They got $1,600 in currency but overlooked $5,000 in silver. Perhaps they couldn't manage it.[57]

"No blood was spilled this time, and the whole business was over in half an hour. Then the train pulled out, leaving me alone in the bushes, the moonlight showing me the three robbers plain as day. They passed within a few feet of me on the way to the horses, but I didn't notify 'em that I was watching 'em.

I kept quite still. Pretty soon I heard their horses' hoofs pounding the road and I ran to the station. I untied the agent and we fixed up the north wire where it had been cut. Then I telegraphed to Wichita for a carload of horses and men to join me in going after the gang. Next morning we started on a six weeks' chase that led us all over the Indian Territory and Oklahoma, and resulted in the capture of one of the gang, a man named Bryant.

"Bryant was made prisoner at his sister's home in Oklahoma, and Ed Short, one of my men, started to Guthrie with him. Ed had him handcuffed and the two were riding in the express car. At Enid Ed got out to stretch his legs, giving his pistol to the messenger, who was a friend of his, and telling him to watch Bryant. The prisoner seemed to be quiet enough, so the messenger laid down the pistol to move some packages.

"As he turned away Bryant dived for the gun, his hands tied together as they were, grabbed it, and waited for Short to come up to the car. When the chance came he shot him twice, in the breast and in the neck; but before Short fell he put three bullets into Bryant, who tumbled out of the car almost on top of him."[58]

So the score against the Daltons mounted, resentment was added to the big money rewards offered by the Southern Pacific, the Santa Fe and the Wells Fargo Express Company, and Bob was growing more desperate with each new crime. Their next train robbery was at Red Rock, a small station on the Santa Fe, in Oklahoma, in June 1892. The haul was a poor one, scarcely two thousand dollars falling into the hands of the bandits to be divided among eight men. But the Bob Dalton system of looting, with its ingenious utilization of the fireman, was proving successful. Six weeks later, on July 14, the northbound train on the Missouri, Kansas and Texas Railroad was robbed at Adair, an insignificant station in the Cherokee Nation, and Bob Dalton was credited with the management of the affair.[59]

This robbery was remarkable, because it was carried through successfully in spite of the extraordinary precautions taken to prevent it. For a week preceding July 14 the gang had been in camp on Pryor Creek, five miles from Adair, and the railroad officials had been warned of their presence. So Number 2, the night train up from the south, carried a deputation of armed guards — deputy marshals and Indian police.[60]

On the night of the robbery the eight bandits appeared at the depot nearly an hour before the train was due, and after capturing the station agent looted the station. They sat on the edge of the platform awaiting the arrival of the train. As the engine slowed, two of them climbed aboard to order the engineer and fireman out. The conductor and train porter were captured by others as they stepped to the platform. Following their custom, the robbers conducted the fireman with his coal pick to the express car and placed him ready to smash the door should the messenger object to admitting them.

Upon a refusal to open the door, one of the bandits shouted to the man inside that a huge stick of dynamite had just been placed under the car, and that the seconds were being counted until car, messenger, and express packages should be blown to hell. Then the door was opened. The outlaws climbed in, forced the messenger to open the safe, and piled everything of value in a heap near the door. From out of the darkness appeared a light wagon, which was backed up to the door and into which the heaped-up treasure was hastily shoveled. The bandits piled into the wagon on top of the loot and, with a parting volley, drove away into the night.

In the autumn of 1892 Bob conceived a plan that for boldness outshone the boldest of his predecessors. It was to young Emmet, whom he recruited from a cattle ranch in the Creek Nation, that he declared: "I'll see Jesse James and go him one better." It was to young Emmet, Grattan, Dick Broadwell, and Bill Powers that he revealed his plan to ride into Coffeyville in the open light of day and rob the two banks of the town.[61]

Coffeyville is a quiet, prosperous little village near the edge of Kansas, with a population of three thousand. The farms that surround it are rich and productive. That the two banks, Condon's and the First National, were likewise prosperous and could be made productive Bob had good reason to believe. He knew Coffeyville and the surrounding country as he knew his own home.

October 5, scarcely three months after the Adair robbery, was the day chosen for the raid. The harvest was past, the farmers' wheat and oats sold, and by the economic law of the country the bank vaults should be plethoric. Also, the day was a crisp, clear one, with the frosty sharpness that sets a prairie man's blood to tingling. Men could fight or love or sing lustily on such a day — the air has a quality of intoxication when it blows keen, frost purified, to warn sluggish blood that winter is preparing. It was a day to make boasters of cowards and to quicken the steps of a loafer.

The five men rode into town from the south at half past nine in the morning, swinging from Maple Street, one block away from the public square, into an alley that ran parallel to and between Eighth and Ninth Streets. Here they tied their horses, put on absurd and ineffectual disguises — bristling false beards and fierce moustaches — and marched down the alley. They came out upon the public square opposite to Condon's bank, which occupied an isolated building in the center of the plaza. Somewhat to the north of the alley's mouth and on the eastern side of the square was the First National Bank.

According to agreement, Grattan Dalton, Broadwell, and Powers ran across to Condon's, while Bob and Emmet held on to the First National. The two parties were timed to begin operations at the same moment.

At Condon's, Grattan Dalton was in command. He stationed Broadwell at one of the two doors leading into the bank and set Powers to guard the other, while he, holding out a two-bushel wheat sack suggestively, ordered the cashier to put the whole of the bank's treasures therein. The cashier was a man of quick wit. His reply came instantly, "The time lock is on and won't go off until 9:45." He had made a hasty guess — for the vault door was unlocked — but it was a fortunate one. Grattan looked at the clock, saying:

"The time'll be up in three minutes; we'll wait." He leaned against the railing, his pistol covering the bank officials. The three minutes' delay secured by the cashier's ready duplicity proved fatal to the Dalton ambition, for in that time a score of citizens had armed themselves at Isham's hardware store on the plaza and were shattering the plate-glass windows of Condon's with volleys from Winchesters, pistols, and shotguns.

Meanwhile, Bob and Emmet had robbed the First National Bank, one holding the two officials at the point of his gun while the other stuffed $20,000 of the bank's money into a grain sack. Driving the cashier and teller before them, Bob and Emmet started for the front door; but so quickly had the citizens armed themselves and begun the battle against the outlaws that the two changed their plans and emerged from the rear entrance of the building.

As they turned north in the alley, on their way to Eighth Street and an intersecting lane that led near to the place where their horses stood, a young hardware clerk confronted them, fresh armed from Isham's store. He was ordered to stop, but he did not understand the order, and one of the two shot him. Others in the alley disappeared, leaving the way clear to Eighth Street. Turning into that street and coming up opposite to the square, they saw the battle waging between their companions in Condon's and the citizens. A shoemaker and his friend stood near the northeast corner of the square, armed. Both of them were fired upon by Bob, who was guarding the rear while Emmet carried the sack of treasure.

Bob's shots drew the attention of the cashier and the teller of the First National, who, after being driven from the bank, had armed themselves at the adjoining store. The cashier, within the door of the hardware store, knelt to shoot, but Bob Dalton saw him. There was a quick report, and the cashier fell forward. Continuing west, Bob and Emmet gained the intersecting lane, running through the alley in which the horses stood, as Grattan, Broadwell and Powers, with three thousand dollars, which had been gathered up from the money draws, left Condon's and came toward them under a terrific fire from Isham's store on the east side of the square.

Broadwell had been slightly wounded at the bank, Powers was hit as he ran across the square, and Grattan Dalton got a bullet before he reached the horses. But none of them was disabled, and the reassembled five, somewhat sheltered by a team drawn up in the alley, turned to face the fire that had become too fierce to admit of mounting. The town marshal, coming into the alley west of the robbers, was killed by a bullet from Grattan Dalton's Winchester. The tethered team broke loose and, beginning to plunge, were killed by Powers, whose aim they had blocked.

John Kloehr, whose livery stable cornered on the alley and the square, came out to the rear of his barn armed with a Winchester, not fifty feet from the outlaws' position. Bob Dalton saw the gleam of Kloehr's gun between the cracks of a board and raised his rifle to shoot. But he was too late, for Kloehr's bullet doubled him up before he could fire. Grattan saw his brother fall, then turned to kill the man whose aim had been so true. Kloehr was again too quick, and Grattan fell with a bullet in his throat.

Emmet Dalton mounted his horse, transferred the sack of treasure from Bob's saddle to his own and spurred out of the alley. Powers, as he was vaulting to the saddle, received a shot in the breast from one of the party at Isham's store and, tossing his gun in the air, fell back beside Bob and Grattan Dalton. Broadwell mounted unharmed to race after the flying Emmet.

It was not in young Emmet's nature, however, to desert his brother Bob, who had been his model and hero since he could remember; and before he reached the end of the alley he deliberately turned and rode back to his brother's side. He attempted to raise the limp body to his horse, when a rifle bullet shattered his right shoulder. He tried to lift his brother with his left hand; a charge of buckshot struck him in the back, and he fell unconscious.

As Broadwell raced west through the alley, a young man fired two shots from behind a barnyard fence, almost point-blank into his body, but the outlaw held his seat, swaying and cursing as he urged his horse toward the open country. Half a mile from the town he fell from the saddle, and a pursuing posse found him dead.

Young Emmet Dalton recovered from his wounds sufficiently to be tried for murder and to be given a life term in the Kansas State Prison. Grattan, Bob, Broadwell, and Powers were buried, and Coffeyville went armed for months in fear of the vengeance of the Dalton sympathizers. Kloehr, the accurate shooting liveryman, received a letter threatening his life about the time the Chicago bankers forwarded him a diamond studded gold badge bearing the inscription "The Emergency Arose: The Man Appeared." On the reverse was inscribed "Presented by friends in Chicago, who admire nerve and courage when displayed in defense of social order."

Bob Dalton was a skillful player of the outlaws' game, but the cards "went against him" at Coffeyville, and he "tried to make good" with a bluff. His bluff was "called," and the fame of Jesse James as the greatest of the craft remains to this day undimmed. There were able defenders of the social order to check that terrible ambition, and to illustrate once again that law and order must prevail.

The Fall of King Chris[62]

CHRIS FARRELL was to rope at Bluejacket on the Fourth![63] That was the news that ran about the ranches in the Cherokee country days before June had yielded its verdant freshness to the sultry grip of July. It was sufficient to stir the anticipations of the sport-loving cowboys and urged them to "practice ropin' and throwin'" among their own herds and in the privacy of their own cow pastures. For others — many others — were to rope at Bluejacket; only they were the lesser stars, twinkling in the occasional glory of a chance throw, to set off the brilliancy of the one great planet of the "ropin'" universe.

There had been tales of Jim Hopkins, of his marvelous eighteen seconds' record for the catching and tying of a steer at the Memphis Fair, and young Tom Cochran, "The Indian," had sent up a frenzied yell at Chelsea when he had "tied in twenty-one."[64] However, it was whispered that Hopkins's time was not official, and that it was a pleasantry of Cochran's friends to credit him with such wonder-working. But Chris had earned his title as King of the Bullies and Magician of the Lasso by years of spectacular work. If there had ever been a trace of scoffing when Chris's rope broke, as he wheeled his horse and brought the steer's heels in the air at the end thereof, it had been quieted by the redoubtable puncher's own declaration that, barring the accident, he would have made a record that the world would wonder at and discuss for years. If sometimes his rope had floated gracefully beyond the head of the plunging steer, to fall harmlessly into the grass, there was the cursed prairie hurricane to blame for it, and the devil himself could not be reviled if the rope, falling easily over one horn, was tossed off by a contrary brute.

Chris was a good fellow, with the persuasive way of a comedian. His face was very broad, and his ample mouth, distended to a monstrous grin, shed a prodigal geniality over the just and the outlawed.[65]

He was the friend of the furtive whiskey peddler; he was the companion of the hawk-eyed deputy marshal; he patronized the big cattlemen and bankers who sometimes drove out in buggies to a picnic to see the roping; he loved babies, calling them "bory-eyed little sons of guns" with an eloquence that set them crowing in his face, and to the girls of that unromantic prairie country he was the Galahad and Launcelot, the Dick Turpin and Sam Bass of the West. And above all he was the "king-pin twirler of the snaky manila!"[66]

Chris was no modest, retiring genius, not the man to drag a little girl from before an onrushing engine, then murmur diffidently, "I only done my duty." Not Chris! He would say, with appropriate dramatic pantomime, "I seen the old engine a-comin' hellety belt down the track jest as that pore little kid of a five-year-old child of Berry's comes a-toddlin' onto the ties. I jumps off my bronc' and makes a sprint for little Lizzie. I catches her so, throws her down the bank and rolls after her jest as the snout of that engine grazed my pants!" It was a recital to stir the blood — a man was a fool to ask if it was true.

Who but Chris could have been inspired, in a moment of elation, to throw his rope over the smokestack of a passing express engine, then rebuke the engineer for not coming to a prompt stop? "I sure done it," he admitted, grinning grotesquely through a maze of bandages, and there was nothing surprising in the action. It would have disappointed his friends if Chris had missed the inspiration.

From Paw Paw to the Bluejacket picnic, his rope coiled conspicuously, came Tom Thoburn, who towered above his horse giant-like, angular, and whined droll stories. From Thompson Creek rode JIC-Bert (which was not his name, but a combination of that and his cattle brand), a cool, smooth-cheeked young fellow with a laugh that exploded like a firecracker. From Lightning Creek came Russell Scott, a mouse-colored puncher, his faded moustache and wizened face quite hidden under a spreading white hat. Upper Cabin Creek furnished Henry Jordan, fat, fairly shining with good nature, whose legs came up like stilts when he walked. Then there was "Ras" Lefferts, "Blacky" Goring, and many others, a dozen of whom would rope.[67]

Also there was the New York newspaperman, not quite so green as he appeared. "Who's to rope?" asked the stranger. He spoke to Tom Thoburn. Tom pointed, saying:

"See that stumpy little feller on the dun? That's Chris Farrell. Watch him."

"Two hundred and eighteen contests he's been in," confided Russell Scott, "and the times he's lost you can count on the fingers of your two hands." He spoke as speaks the man exhibiting the "Somnolent Wonder," "sleeping straight through for three hundred days with no other nourishment than warm milk."

If Tom Thoburn was brief, JIC-Bert was laconic. To the newspaperman's query he answered, "Farrell," nodding across toward the chubby wizard slouching over in one stirrup. But the stranger heard, as his back was turned, that sudden "He! He!" — the cool fellow's snort of amusement. He shrugged his shoulders — was the joke to be on him?

The scribe approached the King from the left, the side where Chris's foot did not touch the stirrup, and away from which his eyes were naturally turned. Crowding in on his right came two girls, dodging easily among the restless horses. One was "Tommie" Rogers, Chris's cousin, a girl who liked him and laughed at him. The punchers stared at the other, for hers was a new face. As the newspaperman began to caress that unoccupied left stirrup insinuatingly he heard Miss Rogers say:

"Miss Barton, my cousin, Mr. Farrell." With the quick, cavalier sweep Chris's big hat came off, his smile broadened prodigiously. "Happy to make your acquaintance, Miss Barton." He wheeled his horse quickly to face the new arrival. The newspaperman started in alarm, just escaping the horse's hind feet. Chris saw the stranger's danger and cried out cordially:

"Excuse me, pardner; I didn't know you was anywhere in the neighborhood." Miss Tommie came up to offer the New Yorker her hand. He was introduced to the pretty Miss Barton and formally presented to the sovereign of the lasso.

"Where'd you find him, Tom?" Chris queried genially, heedless of the stranger's embarrassment.

"Oh," replied Miss Rogers, "he's taking a close-to look at the West for a New York newspaper. He wants particularly to see some good roping. That's why he came up here for the Fourth instead of enjoying the fine show at the Vinita Fair Grounds."

"All ready there, JIC?" shouted the judge of the contest, a whiskered man carrying a supple buggy whip which he flourished regally. The cool fellow loped to the starting line dangling his ready loop.

An overgrown two-year-old was separated from the little herd held close in a corner of the big pasture. Down between two lines of expectant cowboys the steer was urged, a hundred feet beyond the waiting roper, then catapulted into the open pasture as the starter's lag dropped. JIC-Bert leaned forward suddenly, clapped his spurs hard to his big sorrel's flanks, and the two were streaking over the prairie before the brute had time to decide which way he wanted to go. JIC-Bert wanted him to swing over to the west, for there was most room in that direction. The sorrel dug out viciously to turn the steer, revolved half round on his hind hoofs, and was racing away at his heels in a brief five seconds.

Away across the grass, toward a distant ravine, the cool roper ran his victim, the great loop swinging round in lazy sweeps until, two hundred yards from the start, he cast that big coil. Down it settled over the steer's head, as inevitably, it seemed, as fate. Twenty yards farther they raced, JIC-Bert paying out slack enough to cast across the brute's rump. Then he stopped, wheeled the sorrel sharply to the left, and waited, straining forward, for the impact of nine hundred pounds of active beef. The shock came, the steer's head doubled down under his forelegs, and his body thumped the earth. The cowboy spurred the horse to a steady strain, then, vaulting down, ran forward tugging at the heel rope fastened about his belt. There was the deliberate ease of perfect coolness in the way the big fellow hauled at the kicking legs, snapping a half hitch over a hind hoof and drawing the two front legs back to form an awkward knot of squirming red legs and shiny hoofs. The last hitch completed, JIC-Bert tore off his hat, sent it spinning skywards with the upward sweep of his arms, and liberated a yell that startled even the sorrel, still straining obediently at the rope.

The judge snapped his watch and raced to the captured steer. He came down from his horse to inspect the work of the cowboy. Safely and well tied the steer was; the judge rode back to announce to the assembled wagons, buggies, buckboards, surreys, and horsemen that JIC-Bert had tied in fifty-eight seconds.

"Looked to me like it was better than fifty-eight," said Chris as he rode up to his cousin and her party.

"I thought it was half an hour, at least," hazarded Miss Tommie, glancing at the newspaperman.

"JIC-Bert's a good hand with the rope," Chris volunteered. "A little slow and deliberate — too slow to break any records, but middlin' certain to catch and tie. But he's young yet." Miss Barton looked as if JIC-Bert ought to bow down to the King and cry aloud his name for an opinion so favorable. She glanced across to where the cool young giant was talking to "Ras" Lefferts and Jordan. She saw his rugged, suntanned face wrinkle into merriment and heard the laugh explode. Fat, good-natured Henry Jordan was afoot, his hand caressing the big sorrel's mane. As he talked to JIC-Bert he assumed a protecting, half-adoring air, as of a parent with a small child — but he did only what most of them felt moved to do with the big boy.

Just before Russell Scott's steer was sent jumping through the cowboy lane and onto the open meadow, Chris motioned for JIC-Bert to join him and the girls. The proper introductions were achieved, and then Miss Barton confided to the newcomer:

"Mr. Farrell said your roping was fine." JIC-Bert looked interested. "He said you were very cool about it usually," she continued; but still the big round blue eyes only looked an absorbed politeness. "But he said you were still young!" There was a challenge in her tone. JIC-Bert's face began to wrinkle, but he subdued the explosion to an impotent "He! He!" that suggested the snapping of the two first grains of corn to pop in a popperful.

"I ain't remarkable old," replied the boy gravely. He was looking over toward the steer, zigzagging down the lane of gesticulating horsemen, and he seemed to be interested in the procession. "There's Scott trailin' out — watch him sift!" JIC-Bert was not so cool and restrained when it was someone else handling the rope. Miss Barton watched the young gaunt giant, with his staring, childish blue eyes. In some ways he was more interesting than the back of the flying roper. She saw a shade of sympathetic disappointment come over the face as Scott threw his rope. It had been too big a loop, and one of the steer's front legs had been caught with the head. Russell swung away to throw, the steer plunged forward, one knee plowing the earth, then rose to stand stolidly. The cowboy straightened the rope again with a jerk, and once more the steer came to his knees, nose outstretched. Three times Russell charged, until at last his gray pony lunged madly ahead, the rope snapped at the saddle horn, and the steer arose to trot away with thirty feet of rope trailing.

"Hard luck!" muttered JIC-Bert under his breath. Miss Barton saw genuine disappointment on the boy's face, and was glad to overhear that ejaculation. Chris's verdict was different, more fully expressed:

"If Russell *will* go ahead usin' twenty feet of rope for a loop, what can he expect? He's so afraid of not catchin' that he jest throws rope corral around 'em — and they jump clean through the bars."

Miss Barton was sorry for the little puncher whose rope had parted — she was disappointed to hear the King criticize. But shouldn't he? For he *was* the King. She liked JIC-Bert's view of the matter, however. Her dark eyes fixed the puncher's blue ones as she asked:

"There is a lot of luck in roping, isn't there?"

"Uh-huh, a right smart." The boy leaned down to twist his bridle rein where it buckled to the bit. His eyes fell before the girl's gaze. "I got to help pen that steer," he said suddenly, straightening up and lifting the sleepy sorrel into a quick lope. He half turned, jerked an awkward salute toward the group, and was soon bending purposefully toward the steer that dragged the rope, as he raced closer and closer. A quick dig with the spurs, a long, downward swoop of his arm, and JIC-Bert had picked the loop from the steer's back where it had been drawn taut. A mighty jerk opened it, the steer stumbled through, and the boy fox-trotted back to hand Russell his rope. It was superbly done. Miss Barton saw the difficulty of the performance, though it had been done with such apparent ease. She saw that it was the short way out of a predicament — any way she considered it, she was pleased. She wished the boy would come back to them; that droop of the big eyes was worth a girl's watching. She could make him lower them, she felt, by praising his last feat. She realized that with a glow of wicked pleasure.

But the boy stayed away from the group at the buggy while eight punchers took turns at roping. Tom Thoburn offered his steer a loop even bigger than Scott's had been, and the brute vaulted through clean. His second throw was too quickly made — the steer had not straightened out when he tried, and his rope only brushed one elusive ear. Thoburn came back to confide to the newspaperman, now wandering at large, his opinion of "little cattle" that dodge.

Henry Jordan's rope broke with the first jar of the captured steer. He trotted back to his fellows holding six feet of remnant and grinning as though he had done a marvelous thing. "Ras" Lefferts missed his first throw, but caught on the second, tying his steer in a fraction over two minutes. Dick Wilson went out silently, threw twice, failing at both attempts, rode back silently to plump into the little pool of cowboys with scarcely a ripple of comment.

"Lefferts might 'a' made a good hand in the milk lot." Chris damned the nervous punchers effectively, but to Miss Barton's untutored mind the wizard's remark did not seem appropriate. Her idea of dairy maids was of groups of inexpressibly dainty, Delft lassies in rustling cloth gowns and clean white aprons and caps. "Ras" wasn't like that. Yes, specialists certainly became over-captious. She wondered what Chris thought of that attractive, stout boy, Jordan, who was laughing still — and melancholy little Dick Wilson.

Miss Barton turned with vague apprehension to watch Sammie Tompkins, whose horse fell, and Keys, who catapulted himself after his steer like a man suddenly gone insane. This time the horse fell at the first jerk, Keys went overboard, and the horse, rising, kicked the saddle free, while the steer snorted and plunged, and the "gallery" howled in delighted appreciation of the spectacle.

Instinctively, the girl shrank from Chris's comment on these two, but she heard it, spoken in the royal manner, "Tompkins ought to know better than to try to run that old plow team wheel horse over level ground — he wants a plowed field!" Chris seemed to consider Keys somewhat before he spoke, "Now you wouldn't think that man could tie a sheep; but he done fifty-one seconds one time when he went up with me and some of the boys at Springfield[68] to rope at the fair." Miss Barton wanted to rebuke the Premier Lasso for his disparagement of all those picturesque young men who seemed to have tried to do their best.

Donnely's time was slow, for he took a second throw, then wrestled his steer almost to exhaustion before he tied. Bill Seymour went out, threw wildly twice, and came back declaring that he saw so many cattle that he couldn't make up his mind which of them to rope. He had drunk, not wisely but too deeply.[69]

"Tight as a fiddler's b——. Excuse me, Miss Barton." Chris's comments were growing bitter. His language needed to be carefully chosen when he spoke of Bill Seymour. Of "Blacky" Goring, who had been reserved to the last but one in the belief that he would do well, but who only succeeded in getting a bruised leg from the horse falling on him, Chris spoke thus: "It's too dog-goned bad that 'Blacky' gets after 'em in such a tearin' hurry — he'd jerk the legs out from under any horse goin' like that!" The King spoke in a broadly impersonal way, including the girls, JIC-Bert, and the newspaperman in his sweeping glance. Then he added, "Blacky's a fine-lookin' fello' on a horse, don't you think?" The newspaperman was decidedly of that opinion concerning Goring's appearance, and edged closer to the King to ask further about him. As Chris's eyes swung round at the stranger's question an inspiration came to him.

The contest, except for JIC-Bert's performance, had been execrable. Broken ropes, falling horses, and inexcusable misses had marred the show. But the finish — that could be made spectacular, historical! In Chris's eyes the proud light of competence burned. Here was his opportunity to show the boys how to do the work — and here was the opportunity to spread that knowledge. For the newspaperman would see and record. His eyes lighted as he beckoned the newspaperman and JIC-Bert aside, excusing their absence from the girls.

"Been writin' some about the Territory in that New York newspaper?" began Chris circuitously. JIC-Bert looked on with interest. The stranger admitted that he had published a number of articles.

"This kind of thing interestin'?" queried Chris. It had much action and color, the scribe thought.

"Sure hits them New Yorkers where they live, don't it!" hazarded JIC-Bert, and his laugh came out unrestrained, startling.

"Now, look here." Chris leaned far over his saddle horn, speaking low and impressively. "Why don't you give me and JIC-Bert a write-up in that paper of yours? You see," he went on, "JIC-Bert's got a cinch on second money—Lefferts only tied in two ten, and 'Blacky' was next with two thirty. An' I reckon I can beat JIC-Bert's fifty-eight" (Oh! modesty, surpassing modesty). The judge was calling out, "all ready, Farrell!" The King squeezed the newspaperman's shoulder genially and rode out to the starting line arranging his rope.

The stranger turned a look of inquiry upon JIC-Bert, but that youth only flicked an eyelid puzzlingly, and rode back to receive the battery of glances from Miss Barton's pretty black eyes. He could stand the fire better now, and once his own great, full-orbed glance, with more than a suggestion of the wondering babe in his face, had sent the girl's dark lashes down and a spot of color into her cheeks. Miss Barton had underestimated the power of those big blue eyes.

The cowboys had trouble in straightening Chris's steer into the course. Once it broke through the line of horsemen and was circled in again. Chris cried out to "sift the son of a gun this way." Then the steer came down past the line, panicky and speedy. The flag fell, Chris's dun jumped forward under the spur, and the flagman hastily retreated to clear the way for the roper's unexpected shortcut.

For the King must not lose time if he would beat that fifty-eight seconds record and win first place in the New York newspaper. JIC-Bert saw Chris's straight-away dash for the steer, saw the loop begin to whirl rapidly, and ventured the comment, under his breath, "Chris has sure gone plum hog wild this time!" Miss Barton leaned over to ask what the boy had said.

"Farrell rides all right, don't he!" JIC-Bert explained gravely, with just a suggestion of a look at the newspaperman, who had heard his first comment. Yes, the boy was older than he seemed.

It was a daring thing that Chris attempted as he crowded close at the steer's left. He flicked the rope across the brute's shoulder, aiming to catch the front feet. But the King was fallible—the loop tightened for a second on one leg, then came off, and Chris was dragging a knot. The King was beaten. "The grass was too long for that," murmured JIC-Bert as the rope was coiled again, Chris's dun still racing close at the steer's tail. "Chance for third money yet," added the blue-eyed boy.

Steer and man had raced fast and far while the rope was coiling. Once they had turned to avoid a wire fence; now, as the loop began to gyrate, the steer pressed in toward the row of teams which were drawn up at the edge of the arena. Chris spurred harder, but he could not turn him out. Closer and closer in they pressed, until it seemed as if the poles of the vehicles would graze the fleeing brute's ribs. But his chance was not come to dodge in yet, and the steer raced madly. Chris rode up until he could have leaned forward and touched the alarmed tail of the two-year old.

Then the King's loop flew forward at the instant that the steer swerved sharply to the left, coming up, to the wire fence between Thoburn's buckboard and the big wagon that held the Roy Green family. The Roy Green off horse, an old-timer on the Roy Green farm, which stood with head down and lower lip working reflectively, snorted and started back in alarm as a swiftly thrown lasso encircled his head. Roy Green had a ready tongue. He called out to the astonished Chris:

"You can catch that old hawss, Chris, without ropin' him!"

Henry Jordan saw the denouement, shrieked once in spasmodic glee, then rolled in the grass. Tom Thoburn began a kind of whining cackle that grew louder and louder, sounding shrill at last above the roar of laughter breaking from the cowboys and spectators. JIC-Bert looked with remarkable self-control at Miss Barton. But the black eyes could not resist the humorous wrinkle gathering on the boy's face. Miss Barton seized the laughing Tommie's shoulder, hid her face thereon, and laughed. Then JIC-Bert laughed, great explosive "He! Hes!" that rose and fell in infectious crescendo and diminuendo.

To think that the King had done it! It was too good to be true. Language failed the cowboys—whoops of pure delight rent the air. Henry Jordan stained every inch of his outer man rolling in the grass; Thoburn had three spells of cackling, whiningly; and it was JIC-Bert who first rode forward, with a grave face, released the Roy Green off horse, and went up to hang the rope over Chris's saddle horn.

The King was silent, his hat pulled low over his eyes. He took the rope from JIC-Bert, grinning just a little glimmer of a grin close down to the boy's eyes. JIC-Bert could approach him now—a cat could look at a King, and this big boy could do more in his irresistible, sympathetic way. At last Chris rode in to join the punchers, a laughing, vociferous group, and the great tension passed.

The newspaperman had remained in the buggy with Miss Barton and Chris's cousin. "Mr. Farrell and Mr. — Mr. JIC-Bert are going down to Vinita with us this evening," said Miss Barton politely. "I hope we shall see you down there." The newspaperman delivered his thanks and went to eat supper at the "Imperial" hotel. As he ate he mused over Miss Barton's last words. Did she really want to see him? Then he laughed aloud at his little vanity as he recalled the way she had hesitated over the big blue-eyed boy's name.

As the waveringly lurid glow of the sunset faded in the west, and, with the freshening night breeze, the crickets took up their grating song, the newspaperman, waiting at the little station platform for the train down to Vinita, saw the fallen King, Chris, and the blue-eyed boy come fox-trotting down Bluejacket's single street close behind a buggy in which sat Chris's cousin Tommie and pretty, black-eyed Miss Barton. JIC-Bert saw the stranger and loped over. Placing a big hand on the newspaperman's shoulder as he looked down from his tall sorrel, speaking quite gravely despite the light in his blue eyes, he said:

"Why don't you give Chris and me a write-up in that New York newspaper of yours!" His left eyelid dropped. "And say," he added after a pause, "you might send a copy up to 5, Fifth Avenue, to the 'Old Man.' I ain't seen him since I was ten, and he might like to know I won that contest."

JIC-Bert leaned over to grip the newspaperman's hand in a mighty grip, then turned his horse, waving a salute. He called back: "Don't forget that write-up — of me and Chris." As the big boy spurred after the buggy, things seemed clearer to the scribe.

"The Quality of Mercy"[70]

MISS VENITA Churchfield took up eagerly the fresh, neatly folded copy of the *Sachem* which a small half-breed Indian boy, with the singular little war-whoop that invariably announced his weekly delivery, had just thrown across the picket fence. Going indoors, she smiled at the three columns of cattle brands displayed on splotchy black cuts of steers, and was irritated anew that Efferts, the editor, should continue to print them. They occupied a considerable share of the four pages devoted to keeping the little prairie town of Black Oak informed of the world's doings in and outside of that small corner of the Indian Territory.[71]

In spite of the editor's declaration that cattle had made Black Oak and that the importance of spreading the knowledge of a brand throughout the country was great, the girl thought the "branding-iron page" distastefully provincial. Fresh from a St. Louis school, she had hoped, two years before, on meeting the editor, that he would be a valuable ally in the work of introducing culture — an exceedingly vague something, meant, for one thing, to suppress the unseemly shooting at signboards when, on occasion, cowboys, full-bloods, half-breeds, and whites came in at night to "paint the town." But the editor had preferred to laugh *with* those who made the place incongruous rather than *at* them. The cattle brands held the front page, and "Missouri Bob," the outlaw, continued to fill space as one of Indian Territory's important men.

"I could write editorials on Ruskin and national politics, and cut out the ugly raw news," Efferts had said once, "but nobody would read the paper. Cattle made Black Oak, and they made the *Sachem*, too."

Miss Churchfield opened the paper at the third, or "local," page. A heading caught her eye, and she began to read:

> "Missouri Bob" has a rival. This time it is a man well known to the country — Dalton, the Englishman. Last Monday, about eleven o'clock, he held up the Hon. C. M. Graybill of Kansas City, who was on his way to Fourteen Mile Creek to buy a herd of cattle from old man Bluefeather, the Cherokee. At the Locust Creek crossing a man came suddenly out of a patch of wild-plum bushes, and seizing the horse, covered Mr. Graybill with his gun.[72]
>
> There was no chance for the cattle buyer to resist, the attack was so unexpected. Robbed of his arms (a pair of handsome pistols), a fine plaited bridle, and $10,000 in currency that he was taking down to pay for Bluefeather's cattle, Mr. Graybill returned at once to Black Oak and telegraphed the news of his loss to his employers, the Great Western Beef Co.
>
> A full description of the highwayman was furnished to our marshals, and under the leadership of Heck Bunner a posse was sent out to try to intercept him before he got to the Grand River hills, where it is presumed he will be safely hidden by certain characters more friendly to lawbreakers than to officers of the law. Bunner returned today (Thursday) without having found a trace of the robber.
>
> How long is this state of affairs to continue? Every lover of order should make it his business to hunt out the desperate characters that infest our country; and now that "Missouri Bob" has a rival in the clever Englishman, who has heretofore borne a fair reputation in spite of the fact that he has never got on, the country has become doubly unsafe.

So far Venita Churchfield read with a growing astonishment. She put down the paper with a gasp, then broke out:

"Impossible! Mr. Efferts must be crazy to print that."

She hurried to a back room, where her mother, a large, shrewd, brown-faced quarter-blood, sat sewing.

"Mother, let me send for Mr. Efferts to come to supper. I must see him."

"What's the matter, dear? Why are you so excited?"

"Read this!"

Venita thrust the *Sachem* into her mother's hand. The older woman moved to the window and read the long account through carefully, never making a sign, while the girl waited impatiently.

"How do you suppose that awful mistake got into the paper?" The question came explosively.

"It may not be a mistake, dear." Mrs. Churchfield spoke quietly.

"But, mother — why, we've known Mr. Dalton for years, and nothing could be further from my thought of him."

"Well, dear," said the mother, folding the *Sachem* carefully as she spoke, "we have known Mr. Dalton a long time, that's true. He worked for your father in Texas when you were so high." Mrs. Churchfield's brown hand went down almost to a level with her knees. "I've never known the man to do a downright dishonest thing; but his family somewhere — Canada, England, or Australia: I've never known — threw him over. Your father, when he was alive, could trust him, and I've done the same."

Mrs. Churchfield hesitated a moment before going on:

"He pulled you out of a bad scrape once about the time we came up to the Territory. You don't remember; you were too young. It was a matter of getting into a corral ahead of some wild steers, knocking down your playhouse, and grabbing you up on his horse. Since that day I've been more tolerant, I think, than I ought with Mr. Dalton's strange notions."

Mrs. Churchfield seemed to speak regretfully. She did not tell Venita of the secret alarm she had felt at the growing friendliness of her daughter for this cowboy Englishman, this irresponsible, clever bit of driftwood, who, after all, had served the Churchfields well until the father died, when he had gone to work for Colonel Clarke.

"Mother," said Venita, in a frightened tone, "Mr. Dalton's coming to supper!"

"Is he?" queried Mrs. Churchfield. "Venita dear, I'm very, very sorry for

Mr. Dalton. He shouldn't have come so often." It was plain that the mother had seen what the girl had hardly considered — that Dalton was deeply in love with Venita. "However, it is best to get these two men together now."

"But do you think I dare to have them both, after this?" She pointed to the newspaper.

"Dear, Mr. Efferts isn't afraid; and Mr. Dalton isn't going to shoot him. Go on, and send Sammy with your note to Mr. Efferts."

After the chore boy, a young Cherokee wearing a broad, umbrella-like black hat shoved far down over his ears, had clattered away on a gray pony to the *Sachem* office, Venita took up the paper once more. There was more about Dalton: his history, as far as it was known to the country, was detailed from the time he began to punch cattle for Colonel Clarke to his disappearance from Black Oak in 1890. His reappearance a year later — a month before the robbery of the cattle buyer — was spoken of as mysterious, and his actions of late as suspicious.

Efferts gladly accepted the invitation from Venita Churchfield. She met him at the door, a well-gowned, tall, rounded girl of twenty, with a dark face and live black eyes. Before going in from the hall she whispered in some agitation:

"Our other guest came in just ahead of you — don't seem surprised." She led the way to the parlor, and before Efferts had time to hesitate was saying: "I believe you know Mr. Efferts, Mr. Dalton."

A tall man, his face bronzed and his light mustache sun-bleached, rose, shifting the opened *Sachem* from his right to his left hand, and came forward to greet Efferts gravely. The editor shook the other's proffered hand, and stepping back, stared frankly. Dalton turned to speak to the girl, dropping the paper on a convenient chair.

For Efferts it was a bewildering moment. Fresh from the press, his words of accusation and denunciation of Dalton stared at him from the newspaper. By every law of probability Dalton should be hiding in the flint hills of Grand River instead of standing here talking coolly to Miss Churchfield within a block of Marshal Bunner's house.

Venita's mother came in to say that supper was waiting. In the girl's appealing glance as she led the way to the dining room both men read the demand for a truce, and the *Sachem* story was not referred to. For an hour Efferts puzzled his brain over the mystery. He was a straightforward, practical sort of man, not given to psychological inquiry. He liked Venita Churchfield, and had hoped that he might someday — But so had a dozen others, and it was no strange thing to see a man flash out with unexpected brilliance in the girl's presence. Certainly the tall, reserved man Dalton, of whom little more was known than that he undoubtedly was English and self-contained, was showing a rare tact and grace in meeting a situation that to Efferts was frankly puzzling. Venita warmed under the fire of the sun-tanned cowboy's talk; a faint red surged up to overwhelm the rich darkness of her cheeks.

Going out to the parlor after supper, Dalton whispered to the girl, who beckoned her mother aside. "An executive session, Mama," she said.

Alone with the two men, Venita stared in some dismay at the editor's uncompromising, grave face and Dalton's half-humorous, silent one. Suddenly she came between them, seizing an arm of each, and cried out:

"Say something, you men — do something, or I shall go mad!"

Dalton laughed, and Efferts, at the touch, felt the blood surge through his veins, a sensation he had thought impossible to a plodding, worldly country editor of thirty-eight.

"What shall we say?" began Dalton, smiling a trifle nervously.

"Say!" echoed Venita. She took up the crumpled *Sachem* from the chair and held it before her. "Tell me," she went on, "how this horrible mistake got into the paper." She turned to the editor. "Tell me that, Mr. Efferts!"

"Why," Efferts began lamely and conventionally, "I'm sure I don't quite understand. I can only quote the *Sachem*'s motto, 'If it's in the *Sachem*, the brand's registered.' Perhaps Mr. Dalton — "

Then the Englishman broke in:

"I suppose I ought to shoot Efferts where he stands, bind you, Miss Churchfield, to a chair, and shut your mother in the cellar, to bear out the reputation I've acquired. But I'm just going to say that the *Sachem* was quite correct in its account of the affair at Locust Creek. The only thing omitted was something that Efferts couldn't have known about. It was a personal matter, and doesn't affect my standing in the eyes of the law — or in the judgment of the *Sachem*. I supposed you'd have the tale from Graybill" — Dalton turned to speak directly to the editor — "but, you see, one can ride safely enough into town in the dusk when everybody thinks you a hundred miles away." He spoke lightly. "My invitation to supper came to me over there" — he motioned toward the east, where rose the Grand River hills — "and of course I came" — he stepped nearer to Efferts and repeated for his ear, tensely — "and of course I came."

Efferts knew then, in a flash, Dalton's real story. He guessed correctly that the blond Englishman had run away from the fascination of the girl, and had been drawn back to her by a poignant memory. Just why the man had adopted this quixotic course Efferts could not quite understand; and it is certain that Dalton would have found it hard to explain the reason back of his robbery of the cattle buyer. It was a wild act, a thing done on the impulse. The need for money had seemed peculiarly strong; the comfort and apparent permanence of the Churchfield home at Black Oak, and the reality of the thousands back of the girl and her widowed mother, had baffled him as an unendowed worker with his hands.

Dalton knew it was a twisted point of view, knew that men as poor as he had aspired and won; but it was an impression he could not get rid of that ten thousand dollars would make a vast difference. He tried to say as much.

"I hope you will both believe me when I say that it was a gamble for a big stake — bigger than the purse I knew the man had. I thought that was a possible first step, but it was all wrong. It was childish. I see it now. I can't explain it adequately to both of you. But I trust you to see the foolish impulse. I'd like you to see it, anyway — you, Miss Churchfield." He turned away for a moment with a little gesture, as if brushing away a dream.

Dalton touched Efferts on the arm, and the two stepped aside. The Englishman said:

"Of course you see your duty, Efferts; do it as soon as you like after we leave the house. But — but if you do see how infernally demented I was" — it was hardly necessary for Dalton to turn his eyes momentarily toward the girl, waiting nervously by the piano — "and want to do a fellow a generous turn, just wait until you can get a telegram to Kansas City. There must be a newspaper there you can reach at this time of evening. Ask if the money I got from Graybill wasn't returned to the Great Western Beef Company. I telegraphed it from Southwest City yesterday."[73]

"Dalton, are you lying to me?"

Efferts looked squarely at the other, but there was no sign of evasion, only a half-contemptuous, half-amused gleam in his eyes, as he answered:

"You've got to telegraph, and the sooner done the better."

"Yes, I've got to telegraph."

The chore boy was sent away again, this time to the railroad station, with a question to the *Kansas City Arrow*.

And the prisoner, the judge, and the sympathetic jailer waited. Just before ten o'clock the boy returned with the answer. Efferts read it and passed it to Dalton. He glanced at the first half-dozen words and gave the message to Venita Churchfield. She read wonderingly:

> Graybill money returned mysteriously — $10,000. Write us immediately full story.

The matter was explained to Venita Churchfield, and again Dalton drew the editor aside.

"I can't ask you to let me off. I can only say that it will be a mistake to bear too hard on me. I'll go out with you — to Bunner's, if you like. It would be foolish to try to play the daredevil and bolt."

To the girl Dalton said, in a voice far from steady: "I wish I had the courage to tell you what drove me to do this foolish thing; but of course you don't want to hear it, and I must not tell you. You see, I'm still too cowardly to ask for more than your pity!" But the avowal was in his eyes, plain, as he held out his hand. "Good-bye," he whispered, and turned hurriedly to join Efferts at the door.

When the two men left the front door and their footsteps crunched down the gravel path together, Venita lingered a moment before shutting them from her sight.

Efferts saw how well the Englishman bore off his broken hope, and Portia's old plea came into his mind.[74] Aside from the bizarre appeal to his sense of the romantic, there *was* the quality of mercy to be considered. At the gate, beside which Dalton's horse stood tied, head drooping comfortably in the warm spring air, Efferts turned to ask:

"Dalton, if you ride away tonight will you go to Texas?"

"I'll catch the midnight train south from Prairie Switch, the next stop from Black Oak. I'll telegraph you tomorrow from Dennison whatever ten words you name."[75]

"Suppose we make it four — 'The quality of mercy.'"

Efferts held out his hand. Dalton mounted with a swing, then rode near to say:

"You'll have the message, old fellow, and you'll find that one fool has had his lesson — a costly one."

He was gone, the sound of his horse's hoofs fading into the night.

A week later Venita Churchfield read in the *Sachem* this brief paragraph:

> The $10,000 taken by Dalton, the Englishman, from the Hon. C. M. Graybill of Kansas City has been returned to the Great Western Beef Co. Dalton is now in Texas, and not likely to win further laurels in the Territory as a rival of "Missouri Bob."

Venita met the editor at the door, the paper in her hand. She pointed to the paragraph as he came up the steps.

"Yes, it is a brief ending," he said, "to an exciting 'story'; but — "

"I know, dear," the girl whispered, coming up to him and slipping her hand into his; "but he was more foolish than bad. It was right to be generous."

Vinita, Indian Territory

The Greater Appeal[76]

SHE WAS no novice at the game and knew Marks for a thief catcher as soon as she set foot on the station platform at Muscogee. No man among the criminal horde that infested Indian Territory in the early eighties knew better than this woman how relentless "Jim" Marks was when once he set up to make a "catch."[77]

Belle Starr's life had been a wild one in the sixteen years since she had, unwittingly at the time, married a horse thief and chosen to follow his fortunes.[78] And though she knew that she, too, had long ago become outlawed, her mission now involved the breaking of no law, and it was not to her liking to fall into the watchful deputy marshal's hand.

One glance at the dark face of the officer, lounging apparently without a purpose on the platform, was enough. Belle Starr stepped unhesitatingly into the single main street of the little town and walked westward as if sure of her purpose. Nonchalantly nodding to a man, inconspicuous in the station crowd, Marks followed to the street a hundred feet behind the woman.

The second officer appeared, crossed to the opposite side of the way, and set out briskly westward as though unmindful of either his chief or the woman walking ahead.

"Well, she *is* cool!" exclaimed Marks under his breath, as Belle Starr passed into the Boston Emporium, Muscogee's biggest store. His partner came across to join him.

"Go to the back door, Thomas," Marks commanded, "and keep her in sight whatever you do." The arrest was not to be made in the town's main street, now crowded with cowboys and half-breeds to whom a pretty woman might appeal with the certainty of enlisting help against even the law's accredited agents. Their work was to follow Belle Starr to whatever haven she was seeking, make the capture, and get her away as quietly as possible to Fort Smith, where she was wanted for horse stealing and robbery.

Marks lounged up to talk to a half-breed sitting stolidly on an empty, upturned goods box. He sat down facing the entrance to the Emporium. Inside, bending over a glass showcase filled with ribbon and bits of cheap lace, he saw his quarry. She was thirty-three, a vigorous woman, too tanned and self-reliant in pose to be beautiful, but alive and magnetic, with snapping black eyes. All unhurried, and with a woman's love for deliberate choice, she picked out at last what looked to Marks like a mere shred of lace. It was made into a small parcel and paid for. She lingered a moment at the counter piled with remnants — that eternal trap for the feminine that lured here as strongly as in the great city shops — fingered a cheap parasol, and, still in the most leisurely way, passed out into the street without the slightest sign that she had seen Marks.

The deputy was sure of his game now, for she turned into a side street that, half a dozen blocks away, ran plump into the open prairie. On either side were the small, one-storied cottages and two-roomed shanties that sheltered the town's poorest citizens. Evidently, Belle Starr was bound for an appointed rendezvous. Perhaps it was her husband, Sam Starr himself, whom she expected to meet in one of these small houses.

"But I could have taken my oath," Marks reflected, "that Sam Starr is fifty miles from here, down in the Creek Nation."[79]

At the second shanty from the straggling street end, where a negro family lived, the woman, still regardless of the two men in the street behind her, turned in. She did not hesitate. Her grip of the latch was that of one who was expected, and who need use no formality. Marks waited until she was inside, then motioned Thomas to come up.

"You cut across lots here," he said, "and go around to the back door of the shack. Don't come in until I've had time to get inside. This looks too easy, Thomas," he added, smiling. "Just keep your eyes open."

He knew that Belle Starr's nerve was good, and knew, too, that she could and would shoot in resisting arrest if she had an even chance. He stepped back into the shelter of a tumbled-down fence and shifted his pistol forward on his belt. In his manner of approach to the cabin there was neither haste nor apparent purpose. Following the woman's example, he lifted the latch of the door and stepped inside. Old Lizzie Burns, the negress who owned the shanty, was at work by the window sorting a pile of newly laundered clothes. Another negress sat before the open fireplace, bonneted and smoking a dingy clay pipe. The early-spring air was sharp outside, and the dying coals gave forth but little heat.

"Hello, Lizzie," was Marks's greeting, "I came in to see your visitor."

"What's that, Mr. Marks?" queried the old negress, leaving her clothes and coming forward.

"I want to speak to your visitor," Marks repeated.

"Susan, Mr. Marks wants to speak to you," Lizzie Burns said to the woman by the fire. "Mr. Marks, that's Susan Sanders, one of my new neighbors."

A grunt was Susan Sanders's answer, as a black face was turned toward the deputy.

"No, no, Lizzie," said Marks, "I want to see that white woman who came into your shanty just now."

"Mr. Marks," declared the old negress belligerently, "that colored woman settin' there is the only soul that's come into my house today. Now, what you want?"

"We'll see," said Marks tersely, as he went to the back door to call his assistant inside.

"Watch these two women while I search this shanty," he commanded. And search he did from corner to corner of the two small rooms. The cramped garret he ransacked thoroughly. There was no cellar, and the windows had been too closely watched to have afforded Belle Starr a chance to escape.

But clearly she was not there. With a threat to have the negress arrested for helping to spirit her visitor away, Marks left the shanty and began a systematic search of the other houses on the street. Then he turned to the outbuildings and fence corners. But the quarry had clean escaped him. Neither he nor Thomas could construct a theory that would account for Belle Starr's disappearance, though the matter was threshed out between them a dozen times.

"It comes to this," Marks confessed at last, "the only way to explain how she got away from us is either to believe that you missed her as she got through the back door, or that she used black magic to make herself invisible.

"That's all right for you," remarked Thomas spiritedly, "but it doesn't satisfy me. She must have got out of the front door; I know she didn't go out the back way. And as for Voodoo work — well, I wouldn't use that excuse to explain things at Fort Smith."

Marks couldn't, of course, report to the authorities at Fort Smith that his game had escaped by dissolving into thin air. As he pondered the enigma he determined to make no report whatever, but to follow the elusive Belle Starr until he could get his grip on her slender wrist and know that she was in his clutches. Thomas was willing enough, since it was demonstrated that he was equally to blame for the fiasco, to suppress all mention of it.

Three days later, dressed in soiled overalls and the worn "jumper" and rusty diagonal coat of an itinerant farmhand, Marks appeared in the Caney Bottoms down on the Arkansas River. His moustache was gone, and he talked with the corrupted drawl of a Texas field laborer. At Pleas. Porter's farm, lying next to the ranch of old Tom Starr, Belle's father-in-law, Marks got employment at fifteen dollars a month harrowing a cornfield preparatory to planting.[80]

The new hand from Texas proved to be a popular addition to the Porter working force. He could "jig" and do a "hoe-down" with a contagious effectiveness that won envious applause. He could call without hesitation the figures of the most complicated country "square dance."

"By Jacks, you got to come over to Starr's next Saturday evening and 'call' for the "rag-out' that's goin' to be pulled off there," said Wes Ferris, as "the Texas Heel-and-toer" (Marks's name in the quarters) finished, in the lantern-lit cabin, a sort of Delsarte rendition of "Sandy Land."[81]

"He sure will!" chimed the other three men.

It was the chance the new hand had waited for. The two weeks in the wet corn land had palled on the deputy, unused to hard physical labor. Now he could go unsuspected to the Starr ranch, and if Belle Starr had gained its shelter he felt sure of getting an opportunity to make the arrest he had failed to make in Muscogee.

The Porter hands were eager to show off their prize prompter after the fiddlers had taken their place in an entry that gave upon two large rooms of the Starr log ranch house, but "the Texas Heel-and-toer" begged them to be patient.

"Boys," he explained, "they got a right smart prompter here already, and I reckon I won't fo'ce mase'f fo'ward too soon. I'll just dance a few numbehs, and then if you-all wants me to, w'y I'll sing off a few like that 'Sandy Land' figger." But when he had sent the Porter hands off to find partners for the sets then forming, he appeared in no hurry to seek a "knock-down" to one of the Caney Bottoms belles and shake a leg in the dance. He was waiting for one partner whom he hoped to take away with him on a first relay to Fort Smith before daylight came to end the dance.

Near the end of the second set, as the shirt-sleeved dancers swung the country girls lustily, stamping the bare floor appreciatively as they twisted in and out through the figures, the face Marks had waited to see appeared. Belle Starr came quietly out from the bedroom that had been turned into a dressing room for the women, and sat down in a chair against the wall.

"Oh! that girl, that pretty little girl,
The girl I left behind me!"

sang out the prompter in time with the two fiddlers who sawed and swayed with the fresh vigor of early evening. Belle Starr's slippered toes began to tap the floor in time with the prompter's sing-song. Porter's new hand laid hold of an acquaintance and whispered a request in his ear.

"Sure, I'll give you a 'knock-down,'" the man nodded. "Come right over now." When the two stood before Belle Starr the new hand was presented:

"Mrs. Starr, let me make you acquainted with Mr. Jackson. Mr. Jackson, this is Mrs. Starr." The master of ceremonies withdrew.

"Is yo' next numbeh engaged, Mrs. Starr?" drawled "Mr. Jackson." "If it ain't I'd like right well to dance it with you."

"Certainly, Mr. Jackson," the woman replied. Following the custom, "Mr. Jackson" withdrew until the dancers in the next set should be called. The man from Texas improved the minutes after sauntering into the open yard to visit his saddlebags and transfer a pair of handcuffs and a small but effective pistol to his pockets.

"She doesn't know me from Adam," he reflected, "but I'd as well be ready for surprises."

Belle Starr danced the set with "Mr. Jackson" of Texas. Two numbers down she promised him another dance, and before that was ended Marks began to understand why men fought for and shielded this woman. She was in the best of spirits — her wit struck fire from the Texan's drawling humor. Her black eyes flashed, her cheeks glowed with the pleasure of rhythmic motion. When the set was ended she cried out joyously:

"Bring my shawl, Mr. Jackson; we must go outside and get cool!"

Events were falling out to fit the deputy's plans. As he followed Belle Starr into the dark dooryard he vowed that he would have her on a horse behind his saddle in half an hour.

"How beautiful and cool it is out here, Mr. Marks!" she said quietly, as the two stood out of earshot of the house. The deputy raised his eyes swiftly to the woman's face, pale and impassive now under the starlight. And he had thought his disguise complete!

"Come with me — no, don't speak yet" — she went on, and led the way to a door that opened into an "L" of the main house. When Marks hesitated she threw the door wide and showed a room sparsely but tastefully furnished. A bed stood over against the wall, and a shaded lamp burned on a small table beside it. Not until Marks was halfway across the room, still following Belle Starr's lead, did he see that a tiny figure, carefully wrapped, lay on the white counterpane.

"Tonight is the first that baby has slept well for three weeks," she said simply, as she bent over to arrange a pretty little face cap about the child's pale forehead. "She was very, very ill, Mr. Marks, and when I got here I didn't think my little one would live. But I've nursed her night and day, and now she will soon get well. I was only afraid you'd come over from Porter's before I could leave her." As Belle Starr stopped speaking she turned to stand before the deputy, docile, her eyes alight. Marks tried to speak, but he could only say weakly:

"I — I — , go on, Mrs. Starr." She took up her story, moving the lamp a little and turning it slightly lower as she spoke:

"I had to get here from Muscogee that day, Mr. Marks, I had to. My baby was calling me, and I tricked you bravely, though my heart was choking me for fear I'd fail. You want to know how I did it? Well, it was simple. I taxed my brain from the time I stepped on the station platform, where I saw you waiting, until I got almost to that negro shanty. The plan came to me in an instant. When I got inside the cabin I collared the old woman and made her swear not to give me away. I grabbed her bonnet and shawl and a big apron from a peg, and had them on before you turned in from the street. I lit that pipe (I found it on the mantel), and as I sat down, I thrust my hands up the sooty chimney and did a lightning change from white to black on hands and face. When you came in I was all ready as 'Susan Sanders,' the old negro woman. Oh! I tell you, it was theatrical, but I just had to get here to see my child. You see?"

Marks nodded. How cleverly she had tricked him! What superb acting she was capable of! But it was neither the actress nor the reckless, criminal Belle Starr who spoke to him. She was now the mother, Marks could see that, altogether human in her joy over the infant's convalescence, trembling at the thought of its late peril. Yes, he saw. Belle Starr took up the story:

"Sam, my husband, is not here — he is away in Texas — and after I came I waited, caring for the baby, and expecting you to come anytime. I should have died before going with you as long as my little girl needed me. Now, she may be left with her grandmother. I suppose you want me to go to Fort Smith?"

For a long time, Marks did not answer. It was not easy to decide this question. At last he queried:

"Mrs. Starr, did you help Sam steal those horses of Bailey's, and help break into the post office at Wagoner?"

"Are you trying me, Mr. Marks, before the court at Fort Smith gets a chance?"

"I wish you would give me a straight answer," he replied.

"Then I will tell you the truth." She looked squarely into the deputy's eyes. "I tried to keep Sam out of both those scrapes, but I did shield him when he'd got into trouble, and I made myself an accessory in the eyes of the law. I'm not trying to justify myself, Mr. Marks. My life has been stormy for a good many years. But ever since I've had my baby I've wanted to settle down to a quiet existence. Oh, I've wanted to so badly!"

Then Marks, the cynical, cool, man-hunting Marks, leaned over to touch the sleeping child's cool forehead and, turning judge and jury all at once, he pronounced:

"Baby, you need your mother more than I or the law." He turned to Belle Starr and asked quietly:

"Shall we dance in the next set, Mrs. Starr, or are you too tired?"

"Oh, let us dance, by all means," she said, and slipped her hand into his with a pressure that conveyed a world of gratitude.

The Problem of Old Harjo[82]

THE SPIRIT of the Lord had descended upon old Harjo. From the new missionary, just out from New York, he had learned that he was a sinner. The fire in the new missionary's eyes and her gracious appeal had convinced old Harjo that this was the time to repent and be saved. He was very much in earnest, and he assured Miss Evans that he wanted to be baptized and received into the church at once. Miss Evans was enthusiastic and went to Mrs. Rowell with the news. It was Mrs. Rowell who had said that it was no use to try to convert the older Indians, and she, after fifteen years of work in Indian Territory missions, should have known. Miss Evans was pardonably proud of her conquest.

"Old Harjo converted!" exclaimed Mrs. Rowell. "Dear Miss Evans, do you know that old Harjo has two wives?" To the older woman it was as if someone had said to her, "Madame, the Sultan of Turkey wishes to teach one of your mission Sabbath school classes."

"But," protested the younger woman, "he is really sincere, and — "

"Then ask him," Mrs. Rowell interrupted a bit sternly, "if he will put away one of his wives. Ask him, before he comes into the presence of the Lord, if he is willing to conform to the laws of the country in which he lives, the country that guarantees his idle existence. Miss Evans, your work is not even begun." No one who knew Mrs. Rowell would say that she lacked sincerity and patriotism. Her own cousin was an earnest crusader against Mormonism, and had gathered a goodly share of that wagonload of protests that the Senate had been asked to read when it was considering whether a certain statesman of Utah should be allowed to represent his state at Washington.[83]

In her practical, tactful way, Mrs. Rowell had kept clear of such embarrassments. At first she had written letters of indignant protest to the Indian Office against the toleration of bigamy among the tribes. A wise inspector had been sent to the mission, and this man had pointed out that it was better to ignore certain things, "deplorable, to be sure," than to attempt to make over the habits of the old men. Of course, the young Indians would not be permitted to take more than one wife each.

So Mrs. Rowell had discreetly limited her missionary efforts to the young, and had exercised toward the old and bigamous only that strict charity which even a hopeless sinner might claim.

Miss Evans, it was to be regretted, had only the vaguest notions about "expediency"; so weak on matters of doctrine was she that the news that Harjo was living with two wives didn't startle her. She was young and possessed of but one enthusiasm — that for saving souls.

"I suppose," she ventured, "that old Harjo *must* put away one wife before he can join the church?"

"There can be no question about it, Miss Evans."

"Then I shall have to ask him to do it." Miss Evans regretted the necessity for forcing this sacrifice, but had no doubt that the Indian would make it in order to accept the gift of salvation which she was commissioned to bear to him.

Harjo lived in a "double" log cabin three miles from the mission. His ten acres of corn had been gathered into its fence-rail crib; four hogs that were to furnish his winter's bacon had been brought in from the woods and penned conveniently near to the crib; out in a corner of the garden, a fat mound of dirt rose where the crop of turnips and potatoes had been buried against the corrupting frost; and in the hayloft of his log stable were stored many pumpkins, dried corn, onions (suspended in bunches from the rafters), and the varied forage that Mrs. Harjo number one and Mrs. Harjo number two had thriftily provided. Three cows, three young heifers, two colts, and two patient, capable mares bore the Harjo brand, a fantastic "H-I" that the old man had designed. Materially, Harjo was solvent; and if the government had ever come to his aid, he could not recall the date.

This attempt to rehabilitate old Harjo morally, Miss Evans felt, was not one to be made at the mission; it should be undertaken in the Creek's own home, where the evidences of his sin should confront him as she explained.

When Miss Evans rode up to the block in front of Harjo's cabin, the old Indian came out, slowly and with a broadening smile of welcome on his face. A clean gray flannel shirt had taken the place of the white collarless garment, with crackling stiff bosom, that he had worn to the mission meetings. Comfortable, well-patched moccasins had been substituted for creaking boots, and brown corduroys, belted in at the waist, for tight black trousers. His abundant gray hair fell down on his shoulders. In his eyes, clear and large and black, glowed the light of true hospitality. Miss Evans thought of the patriarchs as she saw him lead her horse out to the stable; thus Abraham might have looked and lived.

"Harjo," began Miss Evans before following the old man to the covered passageway between the disconnected cabins, "is it true that you have two wives?" Her tone was neither stern nor accusatory. The Creek had heard that question before, from scandalized missionaries and perplexed registry clerks when he went to Muscogee to enroll himself and his family in one of the many "final" records ordered to be made by the government preparatory to dividing the Creek lands among the individual citizens.

For answer, Harjo called, first into the cabin that was used as a kitchen and then, in a loud, clear voice, toward the small field, where Miss Evans saw a flock of half-grown turkeys running about in the corn stubble. From the kitchen emerged a tall, thin Indian woman of fifty-five, with a red handkerchief bound severely over her head. She spoke to Miss Evans and sat down in the passageway. Presently, a clear, sweet voice was heard in the field; a stout, handsome woman, about the same age as the other, climbed the rail fence and came up to the house. She, also, greeted Miss Evans briefly. Then she carried a tin basin to the well nearby, where she filled it to the brim. Setting it down on the horse block, she rolled back her sleeves, tucked in the collar of her gray blouse, and plunged her face in the water. In a minute she came out of the kitchen freshened and smiling. 'Liza Harjo had been pulling dried bean stalks at one end of the field, and it was dirty work. At last old Harjo turned to Miss Evans and said, "These two my wife — this one 'Liza, this one Jennie."

It was done with simple dignity. Miss Evans bowed and stammered. Three pairs of eyes were turned upon her in patient, courteous inquiry.

It was hard to state the case. The old man was so evidently proud of his women, and so flattered by Miss Evans's interest in them, that he would find it hard to understand. Still, it had to be done, and Miss Evans took the plunge.

"Harjo, you want to come into our church?" The old man's face lighted.

"Oh, yes, I would come to Jesus, please, my friend."

"Do you know, Harjo, that the Lord commanded that one man should mate with but one woman?" The question was stated again in simpler terms, and the Indian replied, "Me know that now, my friend. Long time ago" — Harjo plainly meant the whole period previous to his conversion — "me did not know. The Lord Jesus did not speak to me in that time and so I was blind. I do what blind man do."

"Harjo, you must have only one wife when you come into our church. Can't you give up one of these women?" Miss Evans glanced at the two, sitting by with smiles of polite interest on their faces, understanding nothing. They had not shared Harjo's enthusiasm either for the white man's God or his language.

"Give up my wife?" A sly smile stole over his face. He leaned closer to Miss Evans. "You tell me, my friend, which one I give up." He glanced from 'Liza to Jennie as if to weigh their attractions, and the two rewarded him with their pleasantest smiles. "You tell me which one," he urged.

"Why, Harjo, how can I tell you!" Miss Evans had little sense of humor; she had taken the old man seriously.

"Then," Harjo sighed, continuing the comedy, for surely the missionary was jesting with him, "'Liza and Jennie must say." He talked to the Indian women for a time, and they laughed heartily. 'Liza, pointing to the other, shook her head. At length Harjo explained, "My friend, they cannot say. Jennie, she would run a race to see which one stay, but 'Liza, she say no, she is fat and cannot run."

Miss Evans comprehended at last. She flushed angrily, and protested, "Harjo, you are making a mock of a sacred subject; I cannot allow you to talk like this."

"But did you not speak in fun, my friend?" Harjo queried, sobering. "Surely you have just said what your friend, the white woman at the mission (he meant Mrs. Rowell) would say, and you do not mean what you say."

"Yes, Harjo, I mean it. It is true that Mrs. Rowell raised the point first, but I agree with her. The church cannot be defiled by receiving a bigamist into its membership." Harjo saw that the young woman was serious, distressingly serious. He was silent for a long time, but at last he raised his head and spoke quietly, "It is not good to talk like that if it is not in fun."

He rose and went to the stable. As he led Miss Evans's horse up to the block it was champing a mouthful of corn, the last of a generous portion that Harjo had put before it. The Indian held the bridle and waited for Miss Evans to mount. She was embarrassed, humiliated, angry. It was absurd to be dismissed in this way by — "by an ignorant old bigamist!" Then the humor of it burst upon her, and its human aspect. In her anxiety concerning the spiritual welfare of the sinner Harjo, she had insulted the man Harjo. She began to understand why Mrs. Rowell had said that the old Indians were hopeless.

"Harjo," she begged, coming out of the passageway, "please forgive me. I do not want you to give up one of your wives. Just tell me why you took them."

"I will tell you that, my friend." The old Creek looped the reins over his arm and sat down on the block. "For thirty years Jennie has lived with me as my wife. She is of the Bear people, and she came to me when I was thirty-five and she was twenty-five. She could not come before, for her mother was old, very old, and Jennie, she stay with her and feed her.

"So, when I was thirty years old I took 'Liza for my woman. She is of the Crow people. She help me make this little farm here when there was no farm for many miles around.

"Well, five years 'Liza and me, we live here and work hard. But there was no child. Then the old mother of Jennie she died, and Jennie got no family left in this part of the country. So 'Liza say to me, 'Why don't you take Jennie in here?' I say, 'You don't care?' and she say, 'No, maybe we have children here then.' But we have no children — never have children. We do not like that, but God He would not let it be. So, we have lived here thirty years very happy. Only just now you make me sad."

"Harjo," cried Miss Evans, "forget what I said. Forget that you wanted to join the church." For a young mission worker with a single purpose always before her, Miss Evans was saying a strange thing. Yet she couldn't help saying it; all of her zeal seemed to have been dissipated by a simple statement of the old man.

"I cannot forget to love Jesus, and I want to be saved." Old Harjo spoke with solemn earnestness. The situation was distracting. On one side stood a convert eager for the protection of the church, asking only that he be allowed to fulfill the obligations of humanity and on the other stood the church, represented by Mrs. Rowell, that set an impossible condition on receiving old Harjo to itself. Miss Evans wanted to cry; prayer, she felt, would be entirely inadequate as a means of expression.

"Oh! Harjo," she cried out, "I don't know what to do. I must think it over and talk with Mrs. Rowell again."

But Mrs. Rowell could suggest no way out; Miss Evans's talk with her only gave the older woman another opportunity to preach the folly of wasting time on the old and "unreasonable" Indians. Certainly the church could not listen even to a hint of a compromise in this case. If Harjo wanted to be saved there was one way and only one — unless —

"Is either of the two women old? I mean, so old that she is — an — "

"Not at all," answered Miss Evans. "They're both strong and — yes, happy. I think they will outlive Harjo."

"Can't you appeal to one of the women to go away? I dare say we could provide for her." Miss Evans, incongruously, remembered Jennie's jesting proposal to race for the right to stay with Harjo. What could the mission provide as a substitute for the little home that 'Liza had helped to create there in the edge of the woods? What other home would satisfy Jennie?

"Mrs. Rowell, are you sure that we ought to try to take one of Harjo's women from him? I'm not sure that it would in the least advance morality among the tribe, but I'm certain that it would make three gentle people unhappy for the rest of their lives."

"You may be right, Miss Evans." Mrs. Rowell was not seeking to create unhappiness, for enough of it inevitably came to be pictured in the little mission building. "You may be right," she repeated, "but it is a grievous misfortune that old Harjo should wish to unite with the church."

No one was more regular in his attendance at the mission meetings than old Harjo. Sitting well forward, he was always in plain view of Miss Evans at the organ. Before the service began, and after it was over, the old man greeted the young woman. There was never a spoken question, but in the Creek's eyes was always a mute inquiry.

Once Miss Evans ventured to write to her old pastor in New York, and explain her trouble. This was what he wrote in reply: "I am surprised that you are troubled, for I should have expected you to rejoice, as I do, over this new and wonderful evidence of the Lord's reforming power. Though the church cannot receive the old man so long as he is confessedly a bigamist and violator of his country's just laws, you should be greatly strengthened in your work through bringing him to desire salvation."

"Oh! It's easy to talk when you're free from responsibility!" cried out Miss Evans. "But I woke him up to a desire for this water of salvation that he cannot take. I have seen Harjo's home, and I know how cruel and useless it would be to urge him to give up what he loves — for he does love those two women who have spent half their lives and more with him. What, what can be done!"

Month after month, as old Harjo continued to occupy his seat in the mission meetings, with that mute appeal in his eyes and a persistent light of hope on his face, Miss Evans repeated the question, "What can be done?" If she was sometimes tempted to say to the old man, "Stop worrying about your soul; you'll get to Heaven as surely as any of us," there was always Mrs. Rowell to remind her that she was not a Mormon missionary. She could not run away from her perplexity. If she should secure a transfer to another station, she felt that Harjo would give up coming to the meetings, and in his despair become a positive influence for evil among his people. Mrs. Rowell would not waste her energy on an obstinate old man. No, Harjo was her creation, her impossible convert, and throughout the years, until death — the great solvent which is not always a solvent — came to one of them, would continue to haunt her.

And meanwhile, what?

Young Henry and the Old Man[84]

THE RANCHMAN and I were discussing courage. I had that day seen young Henry Thomas mount and ride a horse that had bucked in a way to impress the imagination. I spoke of it.

"Was it the gray?" queried Brunner, and when I said it was, he scoffed. "That horse is trained to buck just the way young Henry wants him, and he hobbles the stirrups."

Brunner's skepticism was disappointing. I ventured to speak of another instance that seemed to illustrate the nerve of Henry Thomas:

"Didn't he help capture the 'Kep' Queen bunch of outlaws[85] a few years ago? I've heard he showed nerve then."

"I reckon you have." Brunner glanced across at me, then stooped to dig a live coal out of the ashes. He held it for half a minute before packing it into the bowl of his pipe, shifting it imperceptibly in his toughened hand as he studied the backlog. When his tobacco was burning steadily, he spoke:

"I can tell you the truth about young Henry—and the old man, too." I thought his tone changed. "Twenty-four years ago I came to this Indian country. For twelve years I rode with the posses as a deputy marshal, and for twelve years now I've been running cattle here on Cabin Creek. I've been all over the Territory. I know every man in the Cherokee Nation that ever handled a hot iron. And I know young Henry Thomas, too.[86]

"It was in 1882 that Queen 'went bad' and began to hold up trains on the 'Katy' and 'Frisco roads.[87] All of that fall and winter we were after him and his gang, but we never got a sight of them. They were 'goers' all right, and when we came up to a two-weeks-old campfire they'd built, we thought we were lucky.

"For six months after the first of the year they did nothing. We heard that Queen was in California. Then, in June 1883, while I was at Muscogee, I got a telegram from 'Cap' White asking me to report at once to him at Red Oak. Paden Tolbert and I caught the eleven o'clock train up, dropping off at Red Oak at one in the morning. 'Cap' met us, told us he had two men ready, and that the five of us would start for Pryor Creek at once.[88]

"It was a fifteen-mile ride. We planned to pick up four men from the ranches on the way down, and get to 'Kep' Queen's camp at daylight. We had been told that there were five men in the camp, that they had been in the Pryor Creek woods for two days, and that it was their plan to hold up the flyer from the north next evening. 'Cap' White was sure of his information, and he had decided upon the men he wanted from the ranches. The two Thomases — old man Henry and young Henry — were picked out, for there was no one else in the family except a younger brother of eighteen, who has since died. 'Bud' Ryder and Jim Kelso were the other two — both good on horses and handy with a gun.

"'Cap' was proud of his posse when he finally got us together. The Thomases came out and joined us like bees a-swarming. The young fellow was all up in the air with excitement, like a boy going to a circus. He was so brash that at first we couldn't keep him from riding on ahead of the rest of us; you'd think he wanted to bring in the bunch all by himself.

"That was all right; brash, eager young fellows ain't always so brave when trouble begins, but they steady into good fighters. It's hard enough to get 'em that want to go after a man like 'Kep' Queen at all."

Brunner told me then of the fight in the woods at daybreak. It was his summary of young Henry Thomas that interested me.

One of the men whom White took from Red Oak led the posse to the camp on Pryor Creek. It was on a ledge on a hillside. The fires had been built under a jutting rock. Only a bush wren could have hidden its nest more completely — Bruce had been lucky in spying it out. He told White that there was but one unprotected approach — a long-unused trail that led down from the cliff-top and ended in a briar tangle fifty feet above the ledge. That trail, it was evident, "Kep" Queen did not know existed.

Young Thomas had ridden with Brunner, seeking him out, as the novice always seeks out the veteran, to practice his valorous speeches upon. For four hours young Thomas talked about bravery, with illustrations. From one incident to another he skipped, for the history of outlawry west of St. Louis, in the last generation, was more familiar to him than many another topic he had gathered from books. Brunner could have set him right on the facts many times, but what was the use?

After a time the youngster's monologue became a sort of soothing hum, for which the other was grateful. "I was cross and sleepy and chilly and nervous," Brunner explained, "and the boy's gabble rested me."

I gathered that the young man was more excited than he cared to confess, even to himself. He talked, as others whistle, to "keep up his courage." Yet the implication that he needed distraction or stimulation would have angered him. Youth and courage are twins, or should be, and a man of twenty-two takes it for granted. At forty, a man may confess to turning tail and yet save his self-respect. I had heard Brunner tell of "back downs" that would have shamed a young village constable, and it had never occurred to me to question his courage.

It was only in the last mile of their ride that the chatter of young Thomas really became audible to Brunner.

"I woke up," he said, "and actually listened to him. I don't remember exactly what he was saying, but this was the idea: 'All of you fellows that chase outlaws make too much fuss about it.' Well, some of us do, though the newspapers and the windbags that follow us around make ten times the fuss we do. He went on to say that the only way to nab a horse thief or an express robber was to go right up to him, don't you know, like the little boy went up to the signpost that he thought was a ghost.

"It's a good theory and generally works. I told him so, and then apologized for doing any other way. The way I thought about this business of a deputy marshal's was the way an old soldier thinks about war. I was hired to get the criminals, and not to be caught by the criminals, to shoot the bad man, if I had to, but not to be shot by the bad man if there was any way to help it. One way to help it is to run and hide. It's a good way, too, for I've tried it."

The young man roused Brunner's curiosity. It was possible that he might be of the exceptional breed that puts a fine theory to the test of action.

"I decided to watch him," the ranchman told me, "and see if he would play up to his big talk. When we left our ponies, half a mile from the camp, I pretended to argue with 'Cap' White, told him he ought to leave young Thomas with the horses and not get such a boy as that all shot up. 'Cap' caught my point and begged him to stay, but, of course, he wouldn't hear of it. 'I'll stick to Brunner,' says he.

"'All right,'" says I, 'come on.'

"When we started afoot, we trailed out single file, and I noticed that old man Thomas waited for the boy and me to pass him, dropping in right behind his son. 'Cap' was in front, then Bruce, then Paden Tolbert, then Ryder and Kelso, and then I and the Thomases. The old man was at the tail of the procession.

"Old man Thomas was the kind that you never think about one way or the other. You said to yourself that he would do his share, whatever it amounted to, and you wouldn't have to bother about him. That's your notion of him, ain't it?"

It *was* my notion of the older Thomas. I don't think a more commonplace-looking man ever lived. Brunner told me that he had not changed in fourteen years.

"'Young Henry swells around and talks big; the old man he says nothing and chaws tobacco.' That's the way people size 'em up around here." Brunner thus confirmed my own impression of the pair.

"What a man can see out of the back of his head," Brunner went on, "is a lot different from what comes in front of his eyes. He feels a lot that don't make a sound and that ain't visible. I did see, out of the corner of my eye, that young Henry Thomas was dropping behind me little by little, but I didn't see why it was he moved up again. I know why, though. The old man had ordered him up — not in words, you understand, for I could have heard a whisper in the still dawn, the way we were snaking it over the trail. From that time on, every foot of the way, the old man drove the boy. You ask me how, and I can't tell you. There wasn't a word, not a motion that I could see, but all the time it was one man driving the other as plain as could be. And it wasn't easy. I felt that young Henry was worse than balky, that he would have broke through the bushes and run off screaming if that old man had taken his eyes off of him for ten seconds.

"A quarter of a mile it was, and we went slow — twenty feet forward picking our way, then the eight of us would stop to listen. If you ever get a chance, ask young Henry how long that trail was. If he don't stop to think, he'll tell you we crawled through the bushes for five miles, but if he remembers his part as the hero of the fight, he'll say, 'Oh we sneaked a hundred yards or so before lighting into Queen's bunch.'"

The trail from above ended in a briar tangle fifty feet up the hill from the ledge on which four of the five outlaws slept. The fifth man, posted as a sentry, was on the lower trail, somewhere out of sight of the party led by 'Cap' White. When the deputies came up to the briars, therefore, they could see no one. As soon as the four sleepers came out of shelter, however, White's men could cover them with their guns.

What had to be done, obviously, was to rouse the four outlaws without revealing the presence of the deputies above. It could be done by someone in the woods below the ledge. But the outpost was down there to reckon with. They could not all be trapped merely by waiting, for they would come out, after waking, one by one; and White wanted the whole bunch.

It was decided that three men should be sent, by a roundabout trail, down to the creek; that they should follow it up until they got opposite to the ledge; and that they should then rouse the sleeping men. They were also to find the sentry and capture him. The risk was that the sentry might discover the three first and spoil the chance to take him. The detail might be dangerous, though with luck it should prove easy.

Brunner was assigned to lead the three. Young Thomas and Kelso were named by White as the other two, but Brunner, who had been aware of that duel on the trail, said he preferred the old man to Jim Kelso.

They beat back for a short distance, then, separating, dropped down the steep hillside to the creek. In open order, they went forward quietly, slowly; they might come upon "Kep" Queen's outpost at any turn. Now and then they came in sight of one another. Each time Brunner saw that the old man was edging closer to his son. Still there was no word spoken — only a grim old man's gray eyes were fixed upon a young man's shifting, over-bright eyes, and the young man moved on, cautiously.

Brunner held close to the creek bank; the old man was twenty yards away and moving farther out as he approached his son. So they advanced abreast, until they came out upon the trail leading up to the ledge. Then Brunner saw old man Thomas run, with short, noiseless steps, to young Henry's side and point up the trail. Hidden from both and out of sight of what had attracted the old man's attention, Brunner yet knew what was happening. Farther up the trail was the sentry, half asleep in the chill dawn.

Brunner saw, as he himself came up cautiously, that the old man was whispering to young Henry. He grasped the boy's arm, half-shoving him forward and pointing with his rifle. The youngster moved a step, then turned with a look of utter panic on his face. His father's eyes glared; a sort of savage anger blazed on his face. From his grip on young Henry's arm, the old man's hand sprang to the boy's throat. There was one fierce, terrible shake, a sort of gurgling scream that expressed terror, and protest, too, but which was scarcely audible to Brunner, twenty feet away. In the tone of a man enraged to the point of madness, old man Thomas snapped out:

"Go on, you confounded whelp!"

Young Henry shook himself free, his terror replaced by a sudden, resentful anger. Fifty yards away the sentry nodded, his back against a tree and his gun across his lap. Brunner saw the man now, and stepped aside to cover him as young Henry approached. But there was no need of that. The boy was swift and noiseless; before the outlaw could wake or move, his gun was in Henry's hand, and he heard the command, "Hands up!"

The sentry was quick-witted. He couldn't shoot, but he could yell. Brunner, however was ready for that. He began to bawl a reveler's song, popular with cowboys on a spree, and old man Thomas joined him. From above, it sounded as if a drunken riot had broken out, in which the outpost's warning shout became only a meaningless discord. The babel brought the four sleeping men out of their blankets. They listened a moment, then stepped out in view of the posse in the briars.

As Brunner came up, old man Thomas turned to face him. On his seamed face the sweat had almost dried, but when he shoved his hat up with his forearm, his sleeve came away from his forehead damp. The compelling glitter in the gray eyes turned to a challenging stare. Brunner met it, then glanced up the trail toward young Thomas and his captive.

"He got him all right," said Brunner.

"Yes," the old man triumphed, "my boy got him. He captured 'Kep' Queen himself."

"I reckon you've heard young Henry's story of how he got 'Kep' Queen," Brunner finished. "If you've ever talked with him when he was out of sight of the old man, I know you have. What I've told you tonight is what old man Henry could tell if he wanted to. But he never will. As I said a while ago, 'Young Henry swells around and talks big; the old man he says nothing and chaws tobacco.'"

Koenig's Discovery[89]

WHEN KOENIG came over the mountains in September, the ugly word concerning Doña Koenig was dropped into his ears. Koenig had first seen Palos two years before, through the dust of a freight outfit that was crawling across the desert to Santa Fe. He had driven the third wagon from the lead. It had been a stiff pull across the Taos Mountains, and when the train arrived at Palos there was some blacksmithing to be done. As the town stood then — that was in the forties — so it stands today: a wide, cool plaza, a looming church, and a group of dignified, one-storied, wide-porticoed adobe dwellings grouped around the plaza. Koenig and his best friend, Schaefer, another driver, fresh from the desert rawness of Kansas and Colorado, were smitten pleasantly with the first sight of the town. Here all at once they entered a ripe civilization. They fingered huge old gate-posts, bleached, rotting, and nodding. They looked with wonder upon houses so old that they sagged. And they both discovered Rachel Garcia.

To them, blond and vigorous and young, moved by the adventurer's and romancer's spirit, black-eyed, flashing Rachel became the instant lure. With them they had brought the traditions of chivalry — its tests, its high fine spirit, its White Knight attitude toward women. Both fell quick whims to her smiles. On the way to Santa Fe both reflected on the beauty and general attractiveness of Palos, and when the wagons were driven into the freight yard both left the train and cut back for the little town.

Koenig arrived first and went boldly to ask for a lodging with Don Enriquez Garcia, Rachel's father. Schaefer was on hand a week later, but as a rival to his friend he was three days behind time.

Don Enriquez kept no strict account of his daughter's actions, and Heinrich Koenig had been an ardent wooer. Schaefer congratulated his friend and promised himself the next most beautiful girl in Palos.

To tide over the time when he should find his beauty, Schaefer hired himself out to Don Enriquez as manager of a part of the Garcia family's widely extended sheep interests. Koenig, it was understood, was to marry Rachel and become head of all the old Don's big organization. It was not to be foreseen that Schaefer would prove a good businessman, or that Koenig should be a flat failure. Though Koenig married Rachel, it was Schaefer whom Don Enriquez made overseer. The old Spaniard intimated to his son-in-law that there was no permanent place in Palos for an incompetent. The end of that quarrel was that Koenig went back to his old job in the freight outfit, and six months after his marriage left Doña Koenig to wait and pine for his rare visits as the wagons came screeching down the mountains or rattling up from Santa Fe. Three trips he had made and quite a year had gone past when, as he came into town, Pedro, the wine merchant, whispered the word he judged ought to be said. Koenig had pried from Pedro many of the details, and now, out in the plaza under the stars, he was going to settle the matter with Rachel.

He began, speaking slowly, and coming round to the subject in an unfamiliar, roundabout way.

"Summer is over, Rachel; that is true." He said this as if feeling for any kind of word to break the silence. Darkness had settled down and the air was chill.

Doña Rachel crowded close to the side of her husband, shivering, but the movement was forced and studied.

"Don Heinrich, I am cold; hold me close."

Perfunctorily and, considering his old ardor, with an absurd stiffness, he took her in his arms.

"Yes, Rachel, summer is finished. It is time now for the chill. I have not yet told you, but I go no more to Santa Fe and Leavenworth. Little girl, I go no more away from you. No more, ever."

"For me, that will be nice — I am glad."

The lie came promptly, but there was no gladness in her voice.

"That is quite right, Rachel; we must both be glad."

Koenig's voice was even. There followed a long pause. At last Rachel ventured:

"I have been very lonely." She looked up at her husband as if she would read the stolid, dimly lit face above her shoulder.

"Yes, of course," he answered. "On my way to Palos this time I have thought much of you and I have decided that it is not good to leave you." Still he used the flat, uncolored tone.

To Rachel the situation was becoming intolerable. Did he know? What did he know? What would happen to Fritz Schaefer? These and fifty other questions crowded up to her lips, but not so much as by an inflection did she dare to probe.

"Soon," she said, "there will be snow up there on the mountains. Was it not cold as you crossed? Did you sleep warm the night you spent at Taos? Were the streams all frozen up as you came by?" These were the questions that she actually framed. Talking about the mountains, Doña Rachel lifted her shawl to point, drawing away from her husband as casually as she did so.

Heinrich answered with grotesque literalness: "It was not warm — that is the truth." Another silence and then:

"I must talk with Don Enriquez about the sheep tomorrow."

"Of course you will work with the sheep once more. Shall you like it now?"

"Yes, I will work with the sheep; this time I will take charge."

Under the clear starlight, in the cool plaza, they stood for a long time. Then the door of Pedro's wine-shop opened and they saw Schaefer come out. Koenig pointed: "I must see Fritz — about the sheep. Good night, Rachel. Do not wait for me." He strode away, leaving his wife staring, wondering. He turned before he had gone twenty steps and called out evenly: "Do not wait, Rachel — it is colder," and she could do nothing except to grope back to her father's house and to bed, shivering. A very long time she lay wide awake. Terrible pictures, cluttered with detail, rose up to beat against her eyelids.

They were all copies of what her imagination told her would happen when Heinrich and Fritz came together — if Heinrich knew. But did he know? There were moments of hope. Perhaps his coolness out there in the plaza was only a reflection of her own heart's indifference. While the pictures came Rachel was desperately unhappy, but at last they grew dim, and her final thought was, before she fell asleep, that whatever happened, surely Heinrich would not kill her, and Fritz should be able to take care of himself.

It was at the moment when Schaefer was turning into the courtyard of the house where he lived that Koenig came up to him. He put his hand on Fritz's shoulder and spoke close to his ear. "Fritz, you were as my brother — once. Now you have betrayed me. It is necessary to talk about this matter — but not here."

"Yes, I have expected you — damn you!" but as he turned, a knife flashing in his hand, he saw Koenig's pistol leveled at his stomach.

"One little shot, Fritz, and you are dead. Better walk on — away from the town." Koenig pointed out toward where the road to Indian Palos ran past the big gateway. "Yes, out there — that's the idea."

Schaefer flung the knife aside and marched. Out of the gate, past the adobe church and the old graveyard, out on the rutted road the two silent figures stepped. Without any further words they went until the last house belonging to Palos had been passed and all the dogs were quiet. Then Koenig called a halt. "You will go on from here, Fritz, and in this world never come back to Palos. We have been too good friends for me to kill you, as one ought to do in this hard country, and besides, it was wrong of me to leave Rachel. Well, good-bye, Fritz, now walk on — clear away."

"Good-bye, Heinrich." Schaefer flung the crisp farewell and moved on. Koenig turned back toward Palos, walking briskly until he could no longer hear the other man's footsteps. Then, suddenly, he turned and began to run back over the road in pursuit of Schaefer. He left the main road after a time and, crouching, sped quietly across the mesa and dropped into an arroyo. From his hiding place he could watch Schaefer pass — a lagging figure outlined against the sky, and when Schaefer was out of sight Koenig took another shortcut. So it went all night — one shadowing the other. Sometimes Schaefer stopped, debated with himself, snatched off his hat, stamped his foot, turned back upon his tracks, started briskly back toward Palos, and, pulling up, resumed his retreat. It was just at daybreak that Schaefer entered the Indian village, ten miles from Palos. Koenig went back to his wife.

There is more to going away forever than a resolve. From Palos the road stretched south sixty miles to Santa Fe. North, ten miles, was Indian Palos; then the mountains barred the way, crossed only by the narrow freight-wagon trail. Schaefer knew that in a few days that way out, seventy-five miles of unpeopled wild passes and high valleys, would be blocked with snow. Still he lingered in the Indian village, an unwelcome guest of old Anselmo. The trouble was, he reflected, that Koenig had driven him in the wrong direction. Had they marched south that night, by now he would be in Santa Fe. Probably Koenig had meant to drive him into the mountains to die. Well, he wouldn't go.

But something must be done. One day old Anselmo's boy gravely told Schaefer that Señor Koenig had said that ten miles from Palos was not a long way and would Señor Schaefer please go away — far away?

What the fugitive decided to do was bold, but unwise. If he must go, why not have it out with Koenig, and, to settle the tangle, take Doña Rachel with him to Santa Fe and then out of New Mexico forever?

Anselmo's boy could have shown him the unwisdom of that plan — only, he failed to ask questions. The boy knew that every day Koenig went up on a hill that commanded the road between Palos and the Indian village, and that every night he lay close to Anselmo's adobe, watching for Schaefer to come out and start back. And the night Schaefer actually started back toward Palos, turning up his collar against the keen north wind, Koenig watched him go. Koenig had not yet wrapped himself in his sheepskins.

There was no uncertainty in Schaefer's walk — he drove directly ahead. Koenig was grateful that only he knew the shortcuts. It was not yet midnight when the outcast walked into Palos. Once in the plaza, Schaefer stopped for a while. Koenig watched from the black shadow of the church. Up and down, for five minutes, Schaefer paced, and then he went straight to the passage that led past Don Enriquez Garcia's patioed old adobe to the stable at the back. Koenig, following cautiously, heard Schaefer unlock the big gate of the corral and then open the door of the stable. In ten minutes the man reappeared, leading two horses. These he brought out and hitched in the plaza.

Schaefer was moving with decision, swift and soft-footed. Koenig climbed to the dirt roof of the house to watch. He saw the intruder pile straw and old pieces of wood at the corner of the stable, then draw from its holster the big army pistol he carried and lay it beside the big gate post — in the shadow. Now the plan was clear: the fire would be started, a shout would cut the dead silence, men would come hurrying, shots would be fired by way of alarm, and, Schaefer believed, Koenig would be first to rush out. As he came through the gate, Schaefer would kill him, drag his body into the stable, and while the men of Palos were fighting the flames, Schaefer would leave, with Doña Rachel, for Santa Fe.

"It is a good plan, my friend," breathed Koenig as he dropped from the roof. "Only, it won't do this time." And before Schaefer could apply the match, Koenig was inside the stable yard. As he entered he picked up Schaefer's pistol.

"Fritz!" Koenig had waited until the match was in Schaefer's hand before speaking. At the word, motion became a rigid silence, one man waiting, cornered, for the flash of a hope of getting away, the other for a movement of resistance.

Doña Rachel, wakened half by a vague stirring of inner alarm and half by the noise of Koenig's scramble upon the roof, had come out of the house. Quite by accident, she stumbled upon the tableau: Fritz, half crouching by the stable, the starlight showing him a fairly clear figure of terror, and Heinrich, so near that she could have flicked him with a whip, bent forward, an armed menace.

"Dios! Don't shoot!" It was not a scream — for Rachel's cry did not rouse even the Garcia servants. But it struck like a swift, stinging blow on Koenig's ears, and it pulled him round to face his wife.

"Now, Fritz, run!" The warning came from her lips, but she was not conscious of uttering the words. It was not needed. As Koenig wheeled, Fritz whipped round the corner of the stable. He was over the gate and on the way to the plaza, running, as Koenig drove Rachel round the corner and back into the house.

Koenig had intended to take Schaefer out to the plaza, mount him on one of the horses, and, in a spot he knew, safe from all but the remotest chance of discovery, end his disturbing existence. Now it would be harder.

As Koenig came out into the plaza, Schaefer was mounting. When he spurred across the open he was leading the second horse. Fritz was a quick thinker.

But Koenig knew that there were only two ways for Fritz to go. He could ride to the Taos Mountains or to Santa Fe. In either case, the road was a devious one, and Koenig had studied all the shortcuts. As he saw Fritz turn into the Taos road, he slackened his pace to a walk. There was no need to hurry now. For a little while Schaefer rode at a gallop, then he stopped to listen. Hearing no pursuing hoofbeats, he brought his horses down to a sober gait. Then the old game of hide-and-seek began again. Just before he came to the Indian village, he swung to the east and climbed to the higher mesa among the cedars. To keep him within hearing then Koenig had to let himself out. Evidently, Fritz had in mind a new plan. Up and up Schaefer climbed, and at last began to turn south. Only then did Koenig understand his strategy. The ride eight miles to the north was a blind: he meant to circle back through the cedars and strike the Santa Fe trail five miles south of Palos. Koenig suddenly remembered the dim trail that threaded in and out among the scrub cedar clumps and made a detour of six miles around the cañon out of which the Rio Hondo came hurtling. It would be daylight at least before Schaefer could come out to the Santa Fe road. And that was all right, too. Koenig could be there in two hours so he dropped Fritz's trail and went stalking down toward Palos.

As he walked, Koenig reflected upon the quality of this border life into which he had so eagerly and zestfully plunged. It was not all romance; it was not even half romantic. There was an unexpected grimness about it. Instead of the blithe, careless, adventurous people that he had pictured while still following the sun over the mountains, he found them close-mouthed and unsmiling — at least those with whom he had been thrown. In them he found a wolfish quality. Life was a matter of the strongest surviving. Surely, there could be no doubt about that. To be effective, in this country, he had learned that a man's hold must never loosen. Prizes were won by the man with the stoutest wrist, and women were among the prizes. They must be won, and held, in the same way that one acquired horses and lands: and if the holder were weak, women were ravaged, just as were horses and lands.

It was a devil's creed, and it had been hard for Koenig to learn: but he knew it now, and knew also that the price of success was the remembering of it every day he lived. It was a lesson that needed to be burned in on his brain. And Rachel should learn it, too. As he plodded steadily forward toward the point that, in his mind, he had chosen from which to end the final chapter of Schaefer's life, he wondered if merely killing the man would be a sufficient cauterization.

In these hours of plodding, Koenig made a true appraisal of the raw West and its people. By the time he came to the bluff-top overlooking the dim trail, just where it came into the Santa Fe road, he was neither troubled nor uncertain. There had been born in his brain a plan to make his warning permanent. In the very early dawn, sheltered from the wind by the projecting rock, lying on his stomach in the sand that still held a suggestion of warmth, he even had a few minutes of sleep.

A long time before Schaefer came into view, Koenig heard the faint clatter of a horse's hoof against small stones. Broad day was there when the rider came into view. Koenig had marked the spot at which, when Fritz passed, he would shoot, and this time there was no hitch. The horse he had been riding shied, snorted, and stood trembling, some yards away. The led horse had merely pulled back, apparently surprised. Koenig clambered down and caught them. Then he lifted what had been Schaefer to the back of the horse that had carried him, and, mounting the other, climbed the stiff, untracked face of the mesa.

For ten miles the mesa sloped very gradually and then merged into the pine-studded mountains. As the little procession moved on, weaving in and out among the cedars, it occurred to Koenig that it was young morning. The air was crisp and intoxicating. The sunlight was lace and silver foam and a dancing thing, but there was something lacking. For a long time it puzzled Koenig, and then, as a fluffy brown bird flitted from one cedar clump across his way to light in another, he found out what it was: there had been no chirp as the bird flitted. That was the trouble — there was no sound here. The birds that lived among the cedars had somehow lost their voices. Perhaps there were rabbits and other small animals exploring the scant grass under the cedar boughs. It was very probable. But even they must have moved silently. Possibly the loose dry soil deadened the sound of their moving.

Under the cedars there was no lush grass to betray, by its waving, a passage. It was a graveyard — a tremendous, wide-extended graveyard — big enough to hold the dead of a continent, and he was taking to plant in the center of it the body of one man. How royally he was treating Schaefer, after all!

Koenig did not return to Palos for three days. And then for thirty-six hours straight he slept. At last, like a hungry animal, he awoke, and was fed. Late in the afternoon he said to Doña Rachel: "We will take a little ride now." And together they started south on the Santa Fe road.

This time, as they threaded the cedars, the sun was going down. Again Koenig noted the voicelessness of it all. He spoke of the matter to Doña Rachel.

"Don't, Heinrich," she said; "the way you say it makes me think of a churchyard."

"I should not say 'churchyard'—I would only say a place for the dead." And then, after a long time: "Now, right away, Rachel, we shall see for whom all this big graveyard has been laid out."

They came upon the sight suddenly. For a moment Rachel did not understand. Then, as she peered tremblingly through the cracks of the barricade, she saw a brown hat that Schaefer had worn. As he sat there, propped against a pile of boulders, the hat was pulled low over his face. Around him, making an enclosure, with a diameter of fifteen feet, were set cedar stakes, ten feet high, their sharpened ends pointing outward. At the base they were buried in the desert floor, and so cunningly had Koenig wrought the woof of this strange fabric that it stood solid as some bit of firm military fortification. Across the top, woven back and forth, was a screen of smaller cedar branches, to keep from the preying buzzards the corpse that was to serve as an ever fresh reminder to Koenig that, in the primitive man's country, to have means to hold.

After a while Doña Rachel could ride back. Heinrich had said nothing, but she had seen the solution of a tangle. One of these days, years after the clothes that wrapped Schaefer's body have been blown away through the cracks of his strange fortress, and even the nails in his shoes are crumbled to rust, someone will find a gaunt skeleton sagging against a pile of boulders and imprisoned in a weather-beaten, rotting stockade of white cedar poles. "A strange Indian custom," someone will say, and wonder, with not much real interest, what the man could have done that induced the tribe to bury him away out there.

Meanwhile, Koenig has become a feeble, garrulous old man, and Doña

Koenig can hardly hobble around the old Garcia house and the path bordering its ancient courtyard. Some of the people who come to Palos are glad to live for a time with the old people. Koenig has a thousand stories of the early West to tell to anyone who will listen. But the story of his first year in Palos is not one of them.

Out of the Night That Covers[90]

SIMPLE JIM of the slow smile rewound the machine vigorously, changed the record, and sat back to enjoy his dream. It came from a tenor ballad sung into the receiving horn in a New Jersey workshop; it stirred the printer of a cow-town weekly in Oklahoma. Editor, proprietor, and pressman, hustler of news and advertisements, bill collector and credit man, simple and sentimental, squat, nearsighted, racked by a devilish cough — an imperfect portrait, this, of Simple Jim Freeman of the *Weekly Round-Up*. Words cannot frame the glow and melody of spirit.[91]

Raw and black, full of clatter from loosed boards blown by the November wind, night came upon Circletown. Supper was over, and the evening drift to Jim's printer shop began. Not merely the music machine drew them, brown-handed, muddy-booted, intent upon the business of picking a way safely across sagging, broken board sidewalks. Some came to read the *Kansas City Star* — a very young man among them turning hurriedly to the sporting page to absorb the football gossip from K. U. One, adjusting a pair of gold-rimmed glasses, studied an auction bill which Jim had printed that afternoon.

"Todd's sellin' out, I see." Two youngish men joined him by the big lamp, set on a flat bundle of newspaper.

"Them three heifers of his is good stock," volunteered one. Number three in the group glanced at the printed bill and went across to Jim's old desk and sat down.

"Why is Todd leavin'?"

Jim blinked behind his spectacles and shook his head.

"I can't tell you, Jep—ever hear this record? It's from the opera *Faust*—'Soldiers' Chorus,' see? Dum-da-da-da—I like that." He coughed. "Todd's coming in for his bills tonight. But, say, don't ask him anything. He don't like to talk about Oklahoma."

Men came in and passed out unnoticed. Two, unromantic in blue overalls, hugged a big stove among the type-racks.

Jep spoke slowly and in a confidentially inquiring tone: "Todd's wife ain't awful spry, I hear?"

"No, I reckon not—hey, Dick!" called Jim, "come over here. I'm going to put on *Lasca*." For four minutes, the youngest cowboy in the world sat rapt before the tin throat of the machine, listening to some old actor's pompous rendering of a flamboyant poem.

Then a wagon rattled across the sandstone slabs that spanned the muddy street at the end of the block. It came slowly, hubs chock-chocking, and stopped in front of the *Round-Up* office.

"Come in here and get warm, Mary, while I go on up to the drugstore." Henry Todd tied the team and led the way to a chair beside Jim's stove.

"Got them bills, I see, Jim." he called. "Jest goin' up to the drugstore a minute; be right back."

"Howdy, Henry," Jim greeted. "It's raw-like outside, ain't it?" When Todd had gone, the editor put a fresh record on his music machine and went across to stoke the fire in the stove. The two inconspicuous men in blue overalls rose and went to stand in front of the machine from which came the blare of band music. To the woman, sitting rigidly on a wooden chair and gripping its edges, Jim spoke scarcely above a whisper:

"I'll go gown to the drugstore and get Henry in a little while; don't you be uneasy, Mary." Mrs. Todd raised her hands from the grip of the chair and held them forward to the stove.

"Jim, this bootleg whiskey and—and the worry about the boy—they'll kill the both of us. Between them they will. I got good nerve, ain't I, Jim?" She was speaking swiftly, under cover of the galloping melody that came out of the machine. "Well, it's most gone — seems to me. I'll never live to get back to Ioway." Down went her hands, and over her face fell the used veil of reticence. Jim finished with the fire, and the machine whirred to a brassy finish of the band piece.

"Cold some, outside, Mr. Freeman," came in the dull tone of the woman Circletown knew as Henry Todd's wife. This was a personality without color, one of the tens of thousands of migratory western women, disappointed homemakers, mothers with no hold on their sons and a passionate hope that their daughters might win the quiet and peace of mind denied to them. Woman in a man's world — servant, sufferer, a piece of the furniture of civilization that grows old and creaky too soon with movings and hard usage — Mrs. Todd at fifty was a type. Todd ruled and ruined his home. Now he was on the road to hell that ran through the back room of Circletown's drugstore.

From out of the black night came a faraway cowboy yelp, then a rollicking song, high-pitched. Dull hoofbeats sounded half a mile away on the sodden road. The middle-aged man with the glasses raised his eyes from an Oklahoma paper he was reading to grin across at Jim, winding his machine again.

"Sure must be Jeff!" He cocked his head suddenly. "Two horses — been up on the Verdigris, I guess. — Say, Jim, I wouldn't give two cents for that there record — what's it called?"[92]

Jim spelled it out — "'P-a-g-l-i-a-c-c-i' — you call it. I know it ain't comic, but *I* like it."[93] Beside the stove, Mary Todd's fingers gripped the chair harder than before.

The sheriff's deputy, "Loud-mouthed" Jeff Thompson, galloped straight up to the board sidewalk in front of Jim's place before he pulled his horse's rein.

"Whoa, you bronc!" he exploded, then turned to the man who had ridden silently by his side. "Come on in, Bud." He held the door open for the entrance of a pale youth on whose face sat plain misery.

"Hello, Jim! Cold *is* the word. A man oughtn't be out after dark in this dog-gone country." Jim shoved his spectacles up to a better focus and turned squarely to face Jeff's prisoner. The deputy started for the stove, but turned back when he saw a woman, a profile of a woman, poke-bonneted, sitting rigid beside it. He steered the pale youth to a place beside Jim's desk.

"Set down there, Bud." Quietly, courteously, the deputy placed his prisoner on the low box at his feet, and then spoke to Jim: "We got to put up somewhere in this town tonight; reckon Jackson'll take us in?" The editor adjusted a record — a lifting, tantalizing waltz — and turned to beam upon Jeff. He nodded his head in time to the music for a minute, then asked:

"Who's this boy, Jeff?"

"Says his name's Rogers, and that he lives up on Big Creek."

"An' don't ye forgit it, my name *is* Rogers!" High-pitched, the youth's voice seemed shrill, almost hysterical, too loud for the low-ceilinged, quiet shop. It startled Mary Todd from her tense stillness; above a type rack appeared her face, shadowed by the bonnet. As she sat down again, Jim's ear caught a sound, hardly more than a whisper, of distress. He grumbled something, seized a blackened stock, and went to open the stove door and poke noisily at the coals. As he poked with one hand, he gripped the woman's outstretched hand in the other. And the wonderful, slow smile of Simple Jim broke full upon her.

"Don't you speak, Mary, it's your boy; I knew him soon as he came in; it'll be all right — he's scared a little." Slowly, as if reciting a piece of gossip, Jim comforted her, and no one else in the shop knew.

"Oh, my God! if Henry comes in an' sees him!" she whispered.

"He won't. You and I will go and get him in a minute." Over on his desk, the record on the music machine had run out, and a brassy discord came from its throat. Jim banged the stove door and went across to stop it. Then, without a word, he returned to the stove and signed to Mrs. Todd. They went out into the blackness. Those who remained heard, while the door was held open, a muffled burst of ribald laughter from the drugstore at the corner of the square. From the middle-aged man with glasses came the sentence:

"Henry's sure getting happy tonight!" Folding the paper he had been reading, he cased his glasses carefully and walked out.

"Pool hall open?" queried Jeff. It was Dick, called in gentle western irony "the youngest cowboy in the world," who answered:

"Pool? Gee! That feller don't know he's livin'; shets up tight at eight o'clock." Dick shook his gray head slowly. Circleville was dead, a regular cemetery for young spirits. Someone else yawned noisily.

"Oh, Jim, I can't stand it! I'm breakin'. My man drunk, my boy on the road to jail! An' I'm forty-six years old, Jim." The two walked under the black night, hand in hand.

"I was fifty-one day before yesterday," said Jim, "and I ain't got woman nor child to worry me, but I'd swap places with you, Mary. My heart's empty. I'm 'Simple Jim,' clown for the boys. I entertain 'em with my music-box, but — "

"They love you for it, Jim! I know. They wouldn't let you know, but it's so. Don't you ever think they don't — Jim, what's Stephen been doing?"

"Well, I heard that he was with that Big Creek bunch of 'rustlers' — I mean, I heard there was a young fellow named Rogers gettin' mixed up in that business, and Jeff says that is what Stephen calls himself . . . I ain't seen Stephen since he was ten years old, I reckon."

"Has he stole? Is he guilty, do you think?"

"Chances are, he ain't. But it's a bad bunch he's taken up with. Being new, he's the easiest one to catch — that's why Jeff Thompson pulled him. You notice Jeff don't tackle the Wilson boys nor their dad — they're the real bad ones, and Jeff's sure afraid of them."

They turned into the drugstore — the drugstore of Circletown, to which the Oklahoma rhyme —

Hush, little drugstore, don't you cry!
You'll be a bar-room by and by

— was locally applied. Familiar with the place, they passed without a word behind the prescription screen and entered the back room. Henry Todd sat with another man — the bottle and two glasses conspicuously half hidden on a ledge under the square table between them.

"All right, Mary, we'll be goin'." Good-natured, better than a caricature of his mildly swashbuckling youth, whiskey could resurrect for the hour the Henry Todd that Jim Freeman knew back in Iowa — the flash and charm of him. Henry came up to the two, linked an arm in each of theirs, nodded to the man at the table, and led the way out, laughing.

"Jim, I reckon them bills is ready? Mary, we mustn't forgit to pay Jim. Goin' to be an open winter, Jim — ducks, lots of 'em, turnin' back north" — a few bars of a cowboy song whistled spiritedly — "Oh, you Bill!" remembering something. He was carrying, consciously and with some pride, the burden of making conversation. After a few moments, however, the fresh air had brought a reaction. He yawned and stumbled.

"Untie the team, Henry — I'll bring out the bills and put 'em in the wagon."

"All right, Jim. Mary, we mustn't forgit to pay for 'em."

"I'll fix it up — don't ye git stepped on, Henry." As Mary Todd entered the shop with Jim, she turned to glance anxiously at her man fumbling with the tie ropes. Under cover of the rustling Jim made as he wrapped the package of auction bills, Mary Todd whispered:

"Is he" — pointing to Jeff Thompson fingering records — "takin' Stephen on tonight?"

"No, I'm going to let 'em both sleep here — Jackson's wife is sick and can't take 'em in. I know you hate to drive on home and leave him, Mary, but it's the best thing to do."

"Seems like I just can't. I'm losin' my nerve. Oh, Jim, I just want to go over there and take my boy in my arms an' tell him his mother don't believe he's bad! I just — "

"Well, now, here's the package all ready!" Jim called out and slid the tied bundle along the bench noisily to drown the rising voice of grief. And as he deftly steered Mary Todd toward the door, he spoke to Jeff Thompson:

"Oh, Jeff! Find 'Summer Roses' — it's a piece by the Empire String Quartet. I'll play it for you."

Outside they found Henry Todd nodding in the wagon seat.

"Climb in, Mary," he grumbled, "an' we'll be a-drivin'."

"He ain't unhitched the team, Jim — will you go around and do it?" Mary Todd took the reins, braced her shoulder against the tilting form of her man, and turned the wagon sharp. Above the grating of a cramped wheel, Mary Todd heard Simple Jim's heartening adieu:

"It'll be all right, Mary — I'll come out tomorrow." For a minute there came back out of the black, windy night a slow chock-chocking of sound, and then Circletown was quiet. A blot on the prairie, a crude reminder of gregarious man's instinct, expressing infinite hope, stirred from time to time by talk of a railroad and a new brick school building, dreams of busy paved streets built into the humpy sandstone crossings, windswept and unpainted, it was the Town that was to be a City — one of the many. Perhaps Jim glimpsed a future that would retire his little hand press into the city's museum, and whose midnights would be stirred with the throbbing of the *Round-Up*'s big web press. Perhaps. But Circletown was sure that Jim Freeman lived in the now, that he belonged to the town and loved it in all its raw uncouthness.

Simple Jim loved the place and its people. No shirking for him — "He's sure the medicine we cain't do without" was one of the aphorisms elaborated by the youngest cowboy in the world. So Jim, sighing, went in to face his latest problem.

Jeff held out "Summer Roses," and, as he wound up the machine, Jim said:

"You two sleep in here tonight. Jeff Jackson's wife is sick. Lots of blankets here."

"Guess I'll roll up then; show me where to bunk." The pale youth was tired — a relaxation from days of excitement and nights of dread.

"Come on, Bud." Jeff saw his prisoner wrapped and stowed among the type racks, one wrist locked to a chain that was looped about a pillar. "Summer Roses" had hardly run out when the boy's heavy breathing signaled that he slept.

Jim began it abruptly:

"You've thought a heap of some one woman, Jeff. No man that's more than half a man but what has. Well you listen to me, 'Simple Jim' Freeman. Don't laugh, don't make any remarks, and forget what I tell you. That his mother is the only woman in the world I ever loved, really loved, so that I'd do anything I could to serve her. One more thing — she is the woman that was in here tonight. And then just one more — no, two more things: she knew her boy soon as he spoke; and Henry Todd, the boy's father, is a poor, weak husk of a man. I've told you I loved Mary Todd — now I tell you I still love her. You see her as a woman getting old and gray and sharp of tongue.

"She's a record, Jeff, that life has made, and she wouldn't suit your taste. You'd ask for something like 'Summer Roses' in a woman. But to me she's the music that stirs — you never heard one of my records; I played it for a few of the boys before you rode up; it's something from an Italian opera called *Pagliacci*; the boys didn't care for it. Well, Mary Todd stirs me and so does that music. And there's tragedy in both, Jeff — hard luck, hunger, reaching out for the things you can't ever get, nobody around to straighten out the tangle."

"What's the answer, Jim?" Into a thumb gesture toward the snoring youth, Jeff threw another question.

"I don't know — yet — I'm for law; it's what saves us in new countries. But Stephen Todd is young, Jeff — twenty-two, that's all. And I don't think — "

"Well, of course, I ain't so sure. Only, I had my orders to go get him." A long silence fell upon the two.

"We'll sleep on it. Pick out your own bunk, Jeff—floor's soft pine all over. Say, maybe we could find one more record that'd rock us to sleep." It was a Strauss waltz he chose, full of gaiety and the rhythm of laughter and joy. Jeff listened for a minute and smiled.

"Jim, you sure keep a fellow guessin'."

Henry Todd fell sound asleep before the wagon bumped over the last cross-walk on Circletown's long street, and his wife eased him down into the hay that strewed the bottom. Slowly, she drove away from the silhouetted huddle of houses, following a road that, unhindered by fences, kept to a high ridge of prairie.

She was driving away from her boy. And he was in trouble. Jim Freeman meant to be good to her—in her heart, that squat, nearsighted man was a song of peace and loyalty. But wasn't it unhuman to run away like that, just to save a row that would involve a drunken man that everybody knew was a drunkard, a brokenhearted woman, and a pale boy who needed his mother? One mile, two miles—Circletown was no longer a silhouette against the sky. Half a mile farther, then, sobbing, Mary Todd turned the team to drive back.

"I just can't help it—oh! my boy, my poor boy!" Over and over again came the phrases, and she urged the horses faster and faster. At the first fence marking the town limits, she pulled up and tied the team. Still weeping, but without noise, she drew a lap-robe over Henry Todd, then walked toward the square. Here and there, a dog marked her passage with perfunctory barks. The clouds were being blown away—tomorrow would be clear and cold; the mud was crisping now.

Through the mud to the edge of the boardwalk that spanned the space between hitching post and front door of Jim's shop, Mary Todd walked so that no sound might draw an inquiring head out of doors. Her first touch of the unlocked door woke Jim from a fitful sleep. He saw the bonneted figure darken the glass, and he knew what it meant.

But Jim could do nothing. Fate had taken the game in charge. Slowly, with infinite caution, moving carefully, Mary Todd came inside, closed the door, and stood for a long time listening. It was the sound of Stephen's heavy breathing that at last gave direction to her next step. As she tiptoed forward in the blackness, Jim rose from his cot and, barefooted, started across to intercept her.

Down on her knees beside the sleeping boy, Mary Todd's hands groped for his face. They struck the chain that led out from his wrist, and the sudden shock of the cold iron broke her self-control. She screamed and fell forward. Jim ran across to her, the boy half rose in terror, and Jeff Thompson, lying at the back of the shop, came awake with his pistol leveled at a running shape between himself and the light that came through the door. There was a finger stab of flame, a roar and an acrid smell. Simple Jim fell forward, gasped for breath, then spoke quietly:

"It's all right, Jeff. Put up your gun and light the lamp. You've shot me. Lock the door and keep out — keep out — the — blame — fools — that — might — come."

Early in the morning, Henry Todd and his wife, Mary, drove across the prairie with a pale boy sitting between them. Mary Todd was busy tearing handbills to shreds and scattering them to the wind that blew cold from the north. When the last one had gone, and the sun was shoulder high from the plain, she spoke:

"Jim Freeman won't die; he's comin' out to our house, soon's they can move him, to get well; it'll be real nice to have him an' his music box."

Walla Tenaka—Creek[94]

Behind the Indian's stoic face there lies
a kindly soul, true to its own traditions,
dignified, aloof, but sometimes, as in this
story, touchingly human and pathetic.

IT WAS a brief item in the morning *Star*, telegraphed to the paper by its Indian Territory correspondent:

> (Special Dispatch to the *Star*)
> Muskogee, June 17, 19—. Walla Tenaka, a full-blooded Creek Indian, was shot today at Okmulgee by the Indian police. He had been condemned to death for killing another Indian in a drunken brawl last December. His execution was set originally for June 3, but the condemned man failed to return from his parole on that date and the tribal officers only brought him in from the hills yesterday.

The paragraph was a tiny item in the day's accretion of news: it was only one of many tablet tales of crime that went out into the world as that day's report of life in a country where full-bloods, mixed-breeds, ragtag whites—men of abnormal appetites for excitement, and women who followed them, loving and hating according to the mood of their men—made rich picking for the correspondent with a nose for sensations. Shortest of all was this item, for its writer saw in the news from Okmulgee only the prosy ending of a story common as rain — or death. An Indian shot to death by authority of his tribal government — positively, the only shadow of interest in it lay in the fact that Walla Tenaka had violated his parole, had overstayed the leave given him by the tribal police in order that he might go home, put his affairs in order, and say good-bye to his family.

The tired, middle-aged man who wrote the one-line caption under which the paragraph was printed took half a minute off to show it to the young reporter sitting nearest him.

"What's this parole thing mean?" the young man asked. As the telegraph form started for the composing room, the headline writer explained briefly:

"Oh, they have a crazy notion down there among some of the tribes that an Indian never fails to keep his word, so they let him go home without a guard when he promises to show up on the day he's to be shot."

"Huh!" — That was all. The *Star* printed the paragraph, under its one-line head, and the world was unmoved.[95]

Down at Okmulgee,[96] a huddle of wooden buildings running out from the crossing of two unpaved streets into a prairie of rank green, Walla Tenaka's execution made scarcely more of a stir. In justice to the people of the tiny tribal capital, it should be said that this Indian was only one of many to pay for his mad, drink-created frenzy with his life.

White men evaded the officers of the law to peddle villainous whiskey to Indians;[97] in that Hell's Kitchen of a country a drunken Indian nearly always meant a fight — often a killing. If the affair was confined to Indians, a trial in the tribal court followed, and, as a final act, the victim of the manufactured whiskey was led out, a little scrap of white paper pinned over his heart, to be shot.

There was a good profit in selling whiskey — what was called whiskey — to Indians if you were not caught.

Down one of the cross streets, ankle deep in dust, two Indian police officers marched Walla Tenaka. They were taking him to the council-house lot, where he was to be kept under guard until next morning at sunrise.

For lockup there was a squat lean-to of corrugated roofing iron: it was attached, a rusty-gray leech, to the south side of the sprawling wooden council house; and in the big lot surrounding the building the long prairie grass was tramped and yellow. In a listless way, a group of boys were playing ball. Midafternoon of a scorching June day had made of the lockup a Tophet. After a sniff inside, the tired Indian guards marched Walla Tenaka round to the shady north side of the wooden council house, and the three sat down to rest. Through the sweat shine of their faces the guards radiated a vast relief at the ending of a wearying task; they were stout men who ate regularly.

Walla Tenaka was thin: he was not sweating. Looking at him, you would think of Indian runners, of brown ascetics, of Oriental fanatics perhaps. He sat upright, at ease, while the tired guards — short, dull-metal rifles across their outstretched legs — shifted and fanned themselves with their wide black hats. The guards had gorged themselves on a twenty-five-cent "dinner" at the Gem restaurant just before bringing their prisoner from the town to the lockup, and they wanted to sleep. One succumbed, and then the other. Walla Tenaka noted that the hat of one had slipped down over his nose, and breathing was becoming a noisy, sputtery affair: he adjusted the hat and sat back, unsmiling, to watch the half-dozen boys as they abandoned the ball game to go off to the creek for a swim.

A little breeze crept round the corner of the council house from the west, and Walla Tenaka shifted slightly to meet it breast on. The marching shadow of the building reached out to the fence posts. Before sunset, thunderclouds were rolling down from the northwest. As the pushing wind, which goes ahead of these sudden summer storms, smote the faces of the sleepers, Walla Tenaka touched them and spoke quietly, gesturing almost imperceptibly toward the storm. The sleepers woke reluctantly, grinned, and the three got up to march solemnly through the public corridor of the council house back to the bake-oven lockup.

Before the thunderstorm broke, the boys had come back from their swim; and one of them had gone near enough to the men to see the rifles across the laps of the Indian police. A conference followed in which the story of Walla Tenaka's crimes, trial, flight, and recapture was pieced out.

"Say, he could git away now!" half whispered one — a light-haired son of an Indian policeman and a towhead white girl from Arkansas.

"Gee!" It seemed to be a signal for the group to break up, though no boy spoke the definite word of fear.

Walla Tenaka could undoubtedly have got away. But, standing close to him so that you could see the serenity of his face, you would understand that he would not break; you would understand it as surely as did the guards. However, orders must be obeyed: the guards would stay by until sunrise tomorrow, and then join the firing squad that was to riddle the scrap of paper pinned over the man's heart.

Hardly exaltation, but surely more than serenity, was upon Walla Tenaka. Men get glimpses of radiant peace sometimes — a content that mortal business cannot affect. To them, so defended, death comes with its bold threat and provokes only a tolerant smile. It was no longer merely a question of an Indian keeping his word; it seemed to be, for him, a sort of glorious, satisfying termination.

Munching the supper brought from the Gem restaurant, the guards seemed weary and peevish: through the night, as they alternately slept and kept watch outside the rusty barred door of the iron coop, they grumbled about the damp heat, the sagging cot they occupied by turns, boots that pinched their feet, and a score of other trifles. Walla Tenaka, stretched flat on his stomach, his head pillowed on his arms, slept the relaxed sleep of the tired and untroubled.

Sitting out in the afternoon shade, alert and wide awake, Walla Tenaka had seemed to want God's daylight to soak into him — maybe he would need — but that is speculation. Cooling night, and sleep, he welcomed. Things of the world had ceased to have importance — so he slept.

He was to be shot at sunrise. Half an hour before, there came four other Indian policemen, a captain of police, an Indian representative of the tribal court, and half a dozen silent, straggling citizens — there was a young, white-faced clerk from the town's dry-goods store among them. Police and officials passed through the corridor of the council house and joined the guards on watch: the fence enclosing the big lot stopped the stragglers. In the dim light that holds between daybreak and sunrise, the stragglers leaned, unreal, against the fence to wait. The fence ran east and west and formed the northern boundary of the council lot: it was gnawed — where the horses of the tribal legislators had stood tied.

Someone had explained the geography of the execution ground to the white-faced clerk, so he knew where to stand to get the best view. If that north fence had represented the line from home plate to third base on a baseball diamond, the execution place would be in a line from first base to second. Walla Tenaka standing on first, and the Indian policemen told off to shoot him standing side by side near second. When the sun came up to shine full on the paper pinned over the Indian's heart, the poor devil on "first" was to be "put out." That was how they explained it at the hotel. It was clear enough to the young clerk — too clear. When he finally dropped off to sleep in the night he dreamed that the great Umpire was crying out, in a voice that shook the hills, "Play ball!" and then the world seemed to come to an end with a crash that made him cry out in terror. It was his alarm clock whirring; he got up, trembling, washed his face, put on his clothes, and went down to join the few stragglers mobilizing for the short walk to the council-house lot. At the fence he found himself beside a man whom he couldn't make out — maybe a Creek Indian. The man seemed to be sure that he had found a good place to stand.

It was full daylight, less than half an hour to sunup. There was a heavy dew on the tramped yellow grass, and the dust wasn't blowing yet. Someone inside the old barnlike council house had lit a fire, and blue smoke was pouring from the stovepipe. One of the guards came out, sniffed the air, picked up some sticks of wood for the cookstove, and went back. That fenceful of men and boys stood there like posts, waiting and speaking in whispers. The clerk began to watch the horizon and speculate as to the spot where the sun would break its soft line; when the spot began to redden and shot out light, he first removed his gaze from it. Soon someone began to talk in a sort of undertone, drawing the clerk's attention. At first he was not quite sure of the speaker: it was hard to swing his mind away from the business of taking in impressions. At his elbow the voice was growing insistent, and the clerk turned to look square into the face of his neighbor. But what the man said he couldn't make out; he felt, however, that he must answer.

"I never saw anything like this before," he said at a venture. "I ain't been here long." Then, after a while: "They say he was a ball player." He jerked his thumb toward the old council house. "They don't play baseball, I understand — it's a kind of Indian game, every fellow with a long stick — "

"Um, I know," the man answered.

"They say he lives west of here eight miles," the clerk couldn't help going on. "I've seen him and his old woman in the store. Seen him in about two months ago and then again last week. They say he run away two weeks ago; why didn't they get him when he was in a week ago? Brought his old woman in the first time I seen him; that was two months ago, just a month after I come here. I was in Dennison, Tex., before that."

By now the man at the clerk's elbow had ceased to talk; the light was getting stronger in the east, and every second it seemed that the edge of the sun might pop above the horizon.

Before the sun actually came up, the clerk turned to watch for it, silent now. He didn't see the procession out of the council house. He had got the idea that the sunrise was the thing to watch. The red disk was more than half over the edge before he turned his eyes upon the council house. Then, in a sudden panic, he realized that he was standing in the wrong place: already the man — he was probably an Indian with no negro blood — had moved along fifty feet toward the east. The clerk looked over toward "first base" and saw why the man had moved: Walla Tenaka stood as though he had taken his place, though he hadn't yet been blindfolded nor turned to face the sun. His back was toward the clerk, and the guards with the rifles were stepping away. Of course, if the poor devil was going to stand that way — the clerk wondered whether or not he ought to move away . . . He walked over beside the other man.

After a minute — perhaps it wasn't a minute — call it the lapse of a perceptible time — the two Indians left with the condemned man, faced him round to the east, tied a red handkerchief over his eyes, and tied his hands behind him with another. Standing again beside the silent, dark man, the clerk saw that their position gave them a half-profile view of Walla Tenaka, standing straight against the clear sunlight to be shot.

The clerk's eyes couldn't focus on more than one man at a time that morning — now he was watching Walla Tenaka. He saw that the condemned man stood alone, but he didn't look at the Indians with the guns until his neighbor broke out with a sort of a frightened grunt as he turned his head toward the sun.

There it was, at last, clearing the horizon! It was red and liquid — whirly and jumpy inside like a pan of water that's just come to a boil, only red. The clerk's neighbor — by now the clerk was sure he was not a negro — turned back to watch the "Lord High Executioner," who had bound Walla Tenaka's hands, raise his hand for a signal. The clerk didn't see it. His eyes would not come away from the sun. But he heard the shots — not quite together, but more like three men firing off both barrels of a double-barreled shotgun. He saw the Indian crumple and come down in a heap. He saw the smoke from the six rifles. The spell was off then, and everything was clear to the young, white-faced clerk. There was a minute's wait among the eight officers who had managed the affair, and then they went back to the council house for coffee.

No movement occurred to draw the attention of the watchers for a little while; then, in the sweet calm of the new June day, there came out of that old council house an Indian woman, a young Indian girl fourteen years old, perhaps, and two Indian policemen without their guns. They walked in that order to where Walla Tenaka's body lay, and then the clerk saw, for the first time, that the Indian woman carried a baby. She passed it over to the little girl and helped to lift up the dead man. Quietly, effectively, she did her part; there was no outcry.

Suddenly into the clerk's mind came the realization of who the woman was; he turned to the Indian at his elbow to verify his guess.

"Who is that woman?" he questioned huskily.

"Him. Walla Tenaka's woman," was the answer from the man, who did not turn his head.

Behind the two men and the wife of Walla Tenaka (carrying that awkward thing that had been a middle-aged Creek Indian) trudged the young girl, silent, making no sign of grief. Across her shoulder, its little brown face, which seemed to be all eyes, looking solemnly into the rollicking sun, lay Walla Tenaka's baby. All the desolation of stricken women, and all the pity of the tender-hearted for stricken children, flooded the soul of the white-faced young man who watched. Though the woman and the girl marched stolidly, the young man swayed as he gripped the fence.

"How old is that baby?" The clerk's voice came thickly, with effort. This time the Indian looked round before he answered.

"Him, she's four days old."

And the clerk broke out, his voice now a high note of hysterical protest: "By God, it's no wonder Walla Tenaka stayed out in the hills two weeks longer than they told him he could!"

One of the stragglers called a guard to come and revive the young clerk when he fainted: they took him into the council house and gave him strong coffee.

Late in the afternoon of the next day the boy who helped him in the dry-goods store showed the clerk the tiny paragraph in the morning *Star*. But there was nothing he could say — it was all so incredible. The world comes to an end, and there are ten lines written about it!

The Apples of Hesperides, Kansas[98]

A COOL, racing wind brought to their ears the sound of the locomotive's whistle. It came to them across ten miles of level prairie, a thin, faint blast. It was the supper call to the graders and track-layers who were pushing the newest railroad across the short-grass country of southwestern Kansas. Darkness was closing down over the wide plain.

Mrs. Marvin met her son at the gate of the feedlot, held it open as he rode in, and followed him to the door of the tiny stable. Dick dismounted, hauled the saddle from his horse, rubbed the sweat marks from its back, and turned it loose to roll luxuriously in the dust.

"Well, mother," the young man smiled and put his arm across her shoulders, "I found out there's plenty of water left for the cattle in Plum Creek. There's one hole I don't think'll ever go dry."

"Whereabouts is it, Dick?"

"Just where the railroad's going to cross—I reckon maybe they're aiming to put in a water tank there." Dick went to feed his horse, and Mrs. Marvin returned to the cabin to fix the supper table.

Five years before, when the boy was a hollow-chested youth of eighteen, they had come from Chicago to the high plains — Richard's doctor had sent them. In that time, the flush had died out of the young man's cheeks and he had padded with solid flesh a consumptive's gaunt frame.

"Dick is getting well, praise the Lord!" It was Mrs. Marvin's daily prayer of thankfulness. Three years ago, she had first uttered it, exultantly — and then she had planned to go back to Chicago. But now the plan was vague, easy for her to put aside. The spell of the wide plain was upon her; she had become a pioneer mother. Dick's little herd of cattle and her own uncertain patch of garden had become important enterprises.

But as she grew more contented, Dick complained oftener of monotony. "No!" he denied, when his mother asked him if it was Chicago he pined for. "It ain't a city I want — maybe it's just people and stir. I'd like to know myself what makes me restless." It was manhood crowding youth in the lusty frame of twenty-three; Mrs. Marvin could have told Dick that, but it would have seemed vague to him.

Beside a window that let in the soft after-sunset light — a window that rattled all day under the assault of the steady wind — the two ate their supper. For a time, the wind died, and the peace of the prairies fell upon them.

From a tin pie plate, Dick lifted a quarter of a fresh-baked pie made of dried apples. He held it in his two hands and measured with his eyes on the crisp, firm crust the boundaries of his first bite.

"Dick, won't you ever learn to eat pie like a white man?"

"Gee, Mother, I never could insult one of your pies by introducing it to a little old three-tined fork!" They both laughed, and Dick's strong teeth closed upon the pie. He finished the quarter, and hesitated.

"One more piece, Dick!"

"Oh, sho! I'll see my grandmother if I do — I'll be dodging apples all night long. Say, mother, isn't this the time of year when they're picking them back yonder? Seems to me about now you can get 'em fresh and juicy from the stands in Chicago."

"October — yes. In New York State, they're lying in windrows between the trees."

"Smooth and juicy, eh, mother?"

"Yes — red and yellow, and you can smell 'em half a mile away!"

"And they feed 'em to the pigs, sometimes, don't they, mother?"

"They used to, when I was a girl—people didn't seem to care very much for apples."

"Gee!" Dick rose and went outside, whistling an unquiet little tune. Mrs. Marvin cleared away the dishes, washed them, and, with a shawl across her shoulders, came out to join her son on the tiny south porch. A young moon was making luminous the west, and far away somewhere in its track a coyote barked. Dick smoked, and his mother sat very quietly with her hands folded in her lap.

"How's the grub holding out, mother?" Dick asked after a time.

"We're all right for ten days."

"Bacon, flour, rice, potatoes, sugar, coffee—and dried fruit?"

"Yes—oh, Dick, why did you bring it into my mind again! Seems to me I just *must* have a fresh apple to eat."

"Now that you mention it, Mother, it sure does sound good. Say, I wonder if a fellow couldn't get some over at the railroad?"

"Can you get away, Dick? I believe I'd rather have a bushel of good juicy apples right now than anything else I can think of."

"I'll ride over tomorrow, Mother . . . Come inside now, it's getting cold out here." The wind had risen again to a steady blast.

"Isn't it lovely, Dick!" Before she went in, Mrs. Marvin stood at the edge of the narrow porch to let the starshine and the faint moonlight beat upon her face.

"I wish there were trees out there," Dick answered irrelevantly.

Next day, Dick Marvin rode to the railroad, a grain bag tied around his saddle horn. He rode past the construction camp and stopped for a time to watch men with stout plows furrow the raw prairie; he joked with other men who, with wheeled scrapers, were piling the dirt in ridges, and shouted greetings to the tracklayers who were putting down on the packed earth-ridge black, creosoted cross-ties and spiking new rails; he rode close to the dingy work-train, where the locomotive's stack was sending up lazy puffs of smoke, and a thin blue ribbon from the cook car's stovepipe rose into the clear air. Whistling cheerfully, Dick rode on. A mile beyond the end of the line, the newest town rose out of the prairie—a switch, a station shack, a group of tents where the construction gang slept, and a combined store and eating-house. This last was the biggest thing in town, its dashboard front standing up fifteen feet from the road and spreading twelve feet on either side of the wide doorway. Across the top of this facade was painted the sign:

MARLOW'S GENERAL STORE AND GEM RESTAURANT

Behind it stretched sixty feet of barn-like interior. Sagging and unpainted board shelves stretched down both sides for forty feet, then gave way, on one side, to a lunch counter. Back from the counter were two tables, each seating ten. The kitchen was a corner, boarded off from the big room by partitions that reached for but never quite attained the ceiling. Marbled oilcloth covered the lunch counter, but on the two tables were fringed and red-and-white checkered cloths, with a glass jar of wooden toothpicks occupying the mathematical center of each.

It was midmorning when Dick Marvin dropped the reins of his horse's bridle in front of Marlow's and went inside.

A girl — buxom, yellow-haired, blue-eyed — had watched him from her post inside one of the big windows. She was Marlow's assistant, from Kansas City; he had brought her from a department store where she had grown weary of using her eyes on the pale young hunters of the streets. She was twenty-six, ripe and sophisticated; and she had no doubt whatever of her motive for coming. It was certainly not for the ten dollars a week which Marlow offered — and might be able to pay. For the first time, in the two weeks she had watched by Marlow's front window, she thrilled at the sight of a man riding; Dick sat his horse with joyous grace. She smoothed her skirt over her hips, put her hands up to be sure of the fluff in her hair, and turned to the shelves.

"Howdy!" greeted Dick. She turned suddenly from the work at which her fingers had been busy. Plainly, she was startled — in the planned moment of recovery, she could size him up at close range.

"He'll more than do!" was her verdict. She saw a strong, young, brown face, white, even teeth, and a powerful body that was carried with elastic ease.

"You ought to knock on a lady's door before you come in!"

"I'm after apples," announced Dick; her blonde beauty struck upon him with a pleasant shock.

"Pippins, or jest plain Ben Davises?" The girl laughed, showing her own strong, white teeth. She lifted her eyes to Dick's, and the rounded, creamy-white throat rising above a plain, collarless waist struck on his senses like a blow in the face from a man's hand. In the past five years, he had forgotten the girl's type. The women of the ranches were high-collared, long-sleeved, and self-effacing.

"Oh!" Dick recovered, "I'm open to argument. Which kind do you recommend?"

"Honest, stranger," she answered demurely, "there ain't an apple in town."

"Gee! I haven't tasted a fresh apple for so long I expect I wouldn't know how to bite into one." They both laughed.

"Marlow went in to Delos yesterday, and he's coming back today — maybe he'll have sense enough to bring back some apples."

"When does the train from Delos get in?"

"It ain't got any schedule — 'most any time from one to five."

"You reckon if I rode on to Cyprus I could get any?"

"I'm sure I don't know." She turned her back and raised her half-bared arms to the shelves again. They were round and creamy-white, dimpled at the elbows.

"How far do you call it to Cyprus?" She finished her task of putting a row of canned goods in perfect alignment before she turned and answered:

"About half as far as it is to Athens. Would you like to ask me anything else?"

"Yes — two more questions. Where's that smile of yours gone? and who names the towns on this road?"

Question one was answered instantly, in a flood of color which rose to the girl's cheeks and a burst of laughter a little too loud.

"I sh'd say they've hired the man that names the Pullman cars." Dick moved aside a plug tobacco slicer to make room for himself on the rough board counter. Seated comfortably, he went on:

"Now, take this town. Who in the world ever thought Hesperides was the proper name for it?" Dick accented the first syllable of the name, and divided it after the r.

"Well, why not, Mr. Man?"

"My name is Marvin — Richard Marvin, or Dick generally — if you ever want to use it."

"Thanks; I might. I'm Clara Cullom."

"What's the name of that town the other side of Athens?"

"Geronimo. Marlow told me it was named by an old Indian trader."

"Some sense in that name. But Hesperides — " Dick laughed.

"Most people call it Hesper and let it go at that."

Until twelve o'clock, Dick Marvin kept his seat on the counter. Three horsemen, and one rancher with his wife, in a rattling wagon, came to buy — staples for nailing up wire fences, canned goods, flour, blue overalls, dried peaches, sugar, bananas, cheese, crackers, molasses, and striped stick candy. Clara Cullom served them swiftly, courteously, with never a softening of the serene contour of her face. It was her acknowledgment to Dick Marvin that today was his. And tomorrow? The blood was racing through his veins, scattering his self-control as the wind outside drove the tumbleweed pell-mell across the plain.

At twelve a negro woman came out of the partitioned kitchen to ring a big handbell. From the steps of a side door, she shook the bell violently, then hurried back. In five minutes, one table was surrounded by hungry men; at the other, the ranchman and his wife were eating fried chicken and conversing stiffly with the station agent. A negro man, some half-grown boys, and a grader from the construction camp occupied the stools before the lunch counter.

Dick was about to slide from his seat on the counter and go to join the three at the table, when he felt the girl's hand on his arm. She leaned close and said:

"They'll all be finished eatin' and gone in half an hour, and then I'll have *my* dinner." Dick rose.

"I reckon I'll go out and see if I can't rustle some feed for my horse — be sure you save some of that fried chicken for me."

"Mammy Thomas'll look after *us* all right, Mr. Marvin. Half an hour — don't be any longer." Dazzling and utterly confidential was the smile that ushered him out. To kill time, Dick rode to the construction camp, where the hungry crew sat in irregular groups about the cook car, and where the mules, released for an hour from the work of dragging the loaded scrapers uphill and outracing them as they came clattering down empty, jerked feedbags from side to side in rhythm with their round, well-sheared tails. Every mouth, of mules and men, was busy with food. A great, out-of-doors hunger was being satisfied. With a boiled potato, peeled and buttered, poised on his fork, the foreman invited Dick to dismount and eat.

"Git you a plate from the cook car and go to it, friend."

"It looks good, all right, but I got a date to eat up at the store at half past twelve," Dick refused. "You boys are sure pushing things along out here."

"Uh-huh," agreed the foreman thickly, as he swallowed the potato, "our boss gits paid by the mile."

"Are you aiming to put in a water tank at Plum Creek?"

"Well, *we* ain't aimin' to do the work, but I guess a tank will go up there just the same. I did hear some talk, though, about puttin' in a pumpin' plant at the creek an' forcin' the water back to Hesper' — that would save a stop, you see." The foreman took up a quarter of an apple pie and stopped the conversation. His mother's affectionate protest, "Will you never learn to eat pie like a white man!" came to Dick's mind as he watched the foreman shove the pie into his face until his thumbs and forefingers struck his teeth. "Well, so long!" He turned his horse and galloped back to Marlow's.

Mammy Thomas spread a fresh white tablecloth for the two; the fried chicken she served them was sizzling hot; the round, light biscuits were fresh from the oven; the baked potatoes broke mealy and turned to delicate gold at the touch of the fresh butter; fresh and fragrant was the coffee. After the chicken, an omelet — light as sea foam and deliciously flavored. And with the second cup of coffee came the apple pie. Dick broke out enthusiastically at sight of it:

"Excuse me, Miss Cullom, but I simply can't — " An instinct made him stop, and, instead of repeating the familiar tribute beloved of his mother, he finished inadequately, "I sure can't help admiring such a cook as you've got here." He ate the pie with the help of the conventional fork, patiently. Clara Cullom ate joyously, with the appreciative discrimination of the clear-skinned, eupeptic human animal.

"I wish *I* could cook like Mammy," she said. "If you got a good appetite and ain't afraid of gettin' fat, I don't know many things that gives you more pleasure than eating. But I've et some fierce meals in my time. Never again, though, if I can help it; and if I was a good cook I'd come pretty close to guaranteeing good eating the rest of the way."

The first effect of this confession on Dick Marvin was depressing, but after pondering it a minute he laughed and recalled the ironical old rhyme:

Sugar and spice
And all that's nice —
That's what little girls are made of.

"This one is, anyway," he reflected, smiling. Firm flesh, built of solid food, exercise, and sound sleep — that's what this blonde girl was made of. It was a new thought to Dick, and one that held allurement. He could picture her meeting the physical strains that men habitually endure — the all-day rides on a roundup, the unbroken twenty-four-hour labors of wrecking crews repairing a washout — and recovering normally after a good meal and twelve hours of sleep. The blood in her full lips and under the skin of her rounded cheeks ran rich and red.

Mammy Thomas, with many an "Excuse me, Honey," mumbled into the ears of both, cleared the table, put back the white and red checkered cloth, moved the jar of toothpicks conveniently near, and returned to the kitchen.

"Have a toothpick!" They both spoke at once, and their hands moved toward the jar at the same time. Neither hand reached its destination; instead, with a swift, eager clutch, the firm white hand met the brown. After what seemed a lifetime of exquisite thrill, Dick heard the girl saying, a bit shakily, "A toothbrush suits me better." White hand and brown clung joyously — the girl spoke again.

"Don't tell me, Dick, you keep your teeth clean with chewin' tobacco!" He shook his head. "Seems to me," she went on, "every unmarried man in this county buys chewin' tobacco just for that purpose."

For a long time the two sat, their hands locked across the corner of the table. From talk, they dropped to whispers, and then to that most eloquent language of new lovers — the straight eye-to-eye messages that none of us have ever learned to put into words. In the boarded-off kitchen, Mammy's dish-washing clatter died out, and the insistent g-r-r-r! of the coffee-grinding machine began. Mammy Thomas, at any rate, knew that time was passing and that supper would have to be prepared and served.

Up from the construction camp, the work train came backing. At the station, it stopped, and the conductor walked hurriedly across to the store. The girl saw him before he entered, and, with a last pressure of Dick's hand and a swift brushing of his hair with her lips, went forward to wait upon him.

"Howdy, Miss Cullom," the conductor greeted her, then exclaimed, "My soul; you're lookin' fine!"

"It's because I'm happy—my grandfather's just died and left me a farm." He laughed.

"Gimme somethin' good to eat—we got to pull right out to Delos without waitin' fer supper."

"Taking the work train in?"

"No, only the engine and caboose—Joe and Henry are cuttin' off now on the switch."

"I got a notion to ride in with you," she offered, and glanced back toward Dick, who was still sitting at the table.

"Sure! Why not," urged the conductor. "Don't *he* want to go to Delos for anythin'?" The conductor grinned and jerked his thumb toward Dick.

"Yes; he wants some fresh apples." The girl laughed her full, rich laugh.

"Well, we'll be startin' in ten minutes—I'll be back for that canned stuff." As he went out, Dick came up to the front of the store, vaulted the counter, and put his hands on the girl's shoulders. There rose in her cheeks a crimson tide, and over her blue eyes dropped a misty veil of desire.

"Oh, Dick!" she breathed, standing quietly.

"Didn't that man say he was pulling out for Delos in ten minutes?" he demanded.

"Yes," her eyes dropped. "Dick, what do you mean?"

"Will he take *us*?" The question was whispered fiercely.

"Oh, what are you saying! Why, I don't know you, don't—"

"Good God! you know enough, girl—I want you!" He shook her savagely, and she put her hands timidly up to his face. "We're going on that train—do you want to take anything, pack anything?"

"No—yes, I must get a hat, and—but, Dick, what do you mean?"

"Mean? I can't mean more than one thing. You're going to marry me as soon after we get to Delos as we can rout a preacher out of bed. Now, you get what you need, and we'll hike for that caboose . . . Oh, girl!" his young boy's voice softened, "this is love—you have put a big fire into me, the kind I thought I'd never feel . . . When do you reckon we get to Delos?"

"I don't know, Dick," the girl answered quietly, and slid her hands under Dick's coat collar and about his neck. She drew him close and kissed his sun-browned cheek.

"Dick, you're my kind — big brown lover!" She whispered it fiercely.

Coming back for the food, the conductor gave ample warning with his loud whistling; he was met by a rebuke:

"Scotty, you didn't tell me what you wanted — now, you just collect whatever it is off the shelves, while I go pack a valise. I'm going with you; and, oh! this is Mr. Marvin; Mr. Marvin, shake hands with Mr. Scott. Say, Scotty, Mr. Marvin says he's going to Delos, too, so you pick out enough for all of us." She went back to see Mammy Thomas, and as she came out of the kitchen the negro woman protested:

"Honey, that's a mighty nice man, and I sorter hates to see you make a fool out o' him."

"Mammy, here's God's truth," the girl cried passionately, "I'd marry that man if I could. But you know the trouble I'd get into if I did — Jake would sure find it out; damn him, why won't he ever get a divorce!"

Across the forty miles of level plain, as the sun slid down the clear blue of the West, turned it to gray, and, after sinking behind the even rim of the prairie, to a dancing, violent pink, the engine raced with its tender in front. The caboose was attached to the cowcatcher — the effect was like that of a terrier hauling frenziedly at a rabbit he had just dragged from its hole. Scott went to ride with Joe, the engineer, and Henry, the fireman, taking food for the three with him.

Under one of the little square windows of the rocking caboose, Dick Marvin sat on the rough-cushioned bench that ran the length of the car. Clara Cullom crowded close to him, and the two watched daytime turn to nighttime and all the light fade from the prairies. At Athens they went on a switch, and the mixed train out from Delos passed them. Clara saw Marlow, dusty and occupied with the Sunday issue of a Denver newspaper, sitting on what had been the sunny side of the one passenger coach the train carried. "Stupid! Just like him," she muttered. There were two closed boxcars in the train — as they were flung past, an odor pungent and exquisite came into the caboose.

"There's your apples, Dick — want to get off and follow 'em back?" The girl laughed happily, and, twisting her head, offered her red lips for the man's kiss.

"Oh, apples," Dick babbled, "I believe you're right. But I'm holding right to the best pippin a man ever tasted."

"Holding tight is just what you're doing, Dick, lover; you're killing me, you bear — but I like it," she giggled.

An hour before the engine and caboose crept over the temporary wooden trestle-bridge across the wide, dry river and stopped at the station, lights had appeared to draw the eye to the spots of denser black where the scattered ranch houses dotted the level plain. For Dick, that two hours' flight, holding in his arms the throbbing, responsive form of the girl, became a literal, deep intoxication. They got down from the caboose dazedly. Clara was carrying a roughly tied parcel — their untouched share of the supper. She showed it to Dick and laughed.

"Ain't we the sillies!"

"Ain't we!" Dick rubbed his hand across his eyes. "Say, let's ask Scott about a preacher." But the conductor had disappeared, and the engine was clattering away to the yards. Before them stood the pretentious Harvard-brick hotel and eating house which had been built for the convenience of the great transcontinental road's patrons. In the center of a tiny plaza, between the tracks and the hotel, a fountain played, and a patch of vivid green grass was bordered by flaming salvia.

"Ain't that lovely!" sighed Clara, pressing close to Dick. "Say, Dick, lover, I'm hungry!"

"Why, sure — so am I — you poor thing! Come on in and let's eat. I reckon we can get that preacher after supper."

At the door, a young Indian boy, in uniform, took the satchel from Dick and led the way to a desk.

"Yes, we'll want a room," the girl answered the clerk's query — "away from the tracks — my husband can't sleep on the noisy side."

Dick signed the register, breathing, "it will soon be true, anyway," when he wrote, "and wife."

They ate supper at a tiny table screened by palms, laid with smooth, rich linen and heavy silver, and lighted by a mellow, shaded electric candle. Noiseless and perfect service, excellent food cooked to please the finicky palates of jaded transcontinental travelers, a feeling of long-established intimacy between them made the meal a dream-feast to Dick.

"Did you notice the little balcony off our room, Dick — we'll sit out there while you smoke. There's a lovely moon!"

"But — " Dick was finding it hard to remember the preacher.

"Let me pick out a cigar for you, big man. I'll bet I know the kind you like." She chose three, with discrimination, and Dick paid half a dollar for them.

Out on the balcony, with the young moon shining on their faces, with the lights and noise of Delos pleasantly remote, and with the girl in his arms, the cobweb chains of enchantment held them motionless for a long time. Dick flipped his half-smoked cigar over the railing and buried his face in the girl's thick, yellow hair, orris-scented. After a while, a waitress, free for the evening, passed under the balcony on her way to the town — she sang as she went,

"Darling, I am growing old — "

Dick heard, laughed, and set the girl down from his knee.

"Come on, girl — my goodness! I'd sure hate to wake a preacher out of sound sleep. Cover up that wonderful gold hair of yours with a hat and follow little Richard." He turned to go back into the room.

But Clara was at the door ahead of him, barring his way. To stop him, she put up her arms and locked them about his neck; Dick saw that she was weeping — her tears moistened his cheek while she whispered, vehemently, in his ear:

"Dick, we can't! Oh! I had ought to have told you — I'm sorry, now, I didn't. Don't leave me! Don't leave me!"

"Why, sure I won't leave you, Gold-Hair! What's your trouble?"

"We can't be married, Dick — I've got a man somewhere."

"You're married already!" Dick's hands dropped to his sides, but the girl clung close to him and wept, wetting his cheek with her tears. "Good God!" For a long time she clung, saying nothing, weeping hysterically. "Why — why" Dick spoke again with an effort — "stop crying, girl — it hurts me." His fingers came up to caress the thick, yellow hair. Clara released her grip, turned to put her white, plump forearms against the doorjamb as a cushion for her forehead, and began to speak brokenly, through her tears:

"Yes, go and leave me, Dick — it's best — Oh, my God — I was just a kid when I married Jake — I didn't know what I wanted, and he was a big brute — but you don't know — and I thought — Oh! my God, I don't know *what* I thought — But, Dick, you made me crazy — I did want you; and I still want you — more than anything in Christ's world — Leave me, Dick!" The man did not stir, and Clara knew that she had won. She became quiet, a figure of sorrow in the pale moonlight. Dick came up and turned her to face him.

"Gold-Hair, you're mine! Don't you cry anymore — I'm going to telephone that young Indian bellhop to bring up some ice water." He crushed her in a fierce embrace, laughed, and went into the room.

Two hundred miles to the east, in a fat, drowsy town of eastern Kansas, Jake Thompson, competent mechanic, was at work in the railroad repair shops. A hustling, spectacled foreman came into the shops, stopping for a moment at this bench and that. He came and touched Jake's elbow.

"You get ready to go out with me to Delos on number four — we got a pumping plant to install on that branch road, and I need good, sober men. You can go all right, can't you? Got a wife and kids, eh?"

"Free as air," said Jake, and turned back to his work. That night, as the pump-erecting crew in the chair car were speeding to Delos, two of Jake's friends gossiped:

"Say," inquired one, "what you reckon Jake'll do when he sees Clara and that young ranger at Delos?" For more than a week, the man's friends had known that Jake's yellow-haired wife was living in Delos with a man from the short-grass country — it was common gossip among the train-men on the division, and it flowed into the repair shops as naturally as Hertzian waves agitate the antennae of a wireless station.

"Huh! I bet you he knows already."

"Jake ain't no man fer a gunplay."

"Over that woman of his! You're sure right about that."

"She was in a store at Kay See when Jake got her — and back she went when Jake dropped her. Say, the store girls is sure the stuff! How many men you reckon she's throwed her spell over since Jake quit her?" The conversation trailed off into a region of vague, murky surmises. Four seats ahead, Jake slept peacefully.

In ten days, Dick's bank account at Dodge had suffered — and Clara's wardrobe was richer by every bit of feminine gear that had taken her fancy. She was proud of her clothes, vain of her full-blown beauty. And Dick, uniformed for the streets from Delos's biggest store, was a man she could parade proudly. Early in the morning, just before number four, from the east, pulled in, they had acquired the habit of coming down to breakfast — Clara liked to show herself, fresh-bathed and spotless of dress, among the jaded women from the sleeping cars.

Jake Thompson had finished his lunch-counter breakfast of ham and eggs, wheat cakes, syrup, and coffee. He was sitting on the edge of the hotel porch, chewing a toothpick and waiting for the mixed train out to Hesperides. Clara led Dick plump into him before she knew anyone was sitting there.

"Hello, Clara!" Jake greeted her without embarrassment. She turned as if to go back, then stopped, flustered and uncertain. Dick had stopped, and was watching the man chew his toothpick unhurriedly.

"Who's — " Dick began pleasantly, and old habit conquered Clara.

"Jake," she stammered, "shake hands with Mr. Marvin. Mr. Marvin, Mr. Thompson."

"I don't reckon I'll shake hands with him, Clara," Jake observed quietly, "I'm kind of particular about who I touch." His words cut her, like a lash across the face.

"Say, you big boob!" Clara broke out, "don't you make any passes like that around here; Dick, here, is the kind of a man to whirl you round his head and beat your brains out against the doorjamb for talk like that. What the hell you doin' round here, anyway! I thought I'd seen the last of you." Clara was caught up in a whirlwind of reproaches, hysterical curses, and angry sobs. Passengers strolling back to the Pullman from the dining room stopped to stare frankly. "Gee!" exclaimed one youth delightedly, "it's real old meelo-drammer, straight from Third Avenue."

A grin froze on Dick's face, then settled into faint gray lines that spelled nothing suggesting humor. Something that tore and throbbed crept under his skin, rising from spine to scalp, damming the blood-currents and paralyzing thought and speech. Clara's curses, her frenzy of anger, the whole grotesquely coarse outburst seemed a sudden, horrible illusion. He drew his hand across his eyes to drive away the vision, but it persisted. After what seemed a long time, he was astonished to feel Clara's hand on his arm, to hear her angry voice close to his ear saying:

"Kill the ——, Dick! He's laughing at me." Dick shook himself and turned his gray, set face to the girl.

"Didn't you hear Mr. Thompson say he was particular about people? Maybe he wouldn't like me to touch him — I couldn't blame him." The exquisite humor of Dick's speech, born out of a stiffening agony of self-reproach, was lost on Clara. She screamed an epithet at the two men and ran into the hotel.

"Gee!" muttered the youth from the Pullman, "wouldn't that curl your hair!" He referred particularly to the word that Clara had flung into the faces of the two men.

After a little while, Dick addressed the man sitting on the edge of the porch, still chewing evenly at the toothpick:

"Maybe you and I'd better have a talk." He spoke mildly, courteously.

"Go ahead, I'm listenin' — only make it short, fer I got to catch a train out to Hesper' in a few minutes."

"Oh!" Dick took off his hat and wiped the sweat from his forehead. "'Hesper' — you mean Hesperides?"

"Uh-huh," the man agreed.

"I — I came from out that way." It was as if he had been asleep a long time and the waking was difficult. The world he had left was coming back into being.

"That country any good?" queried the man perfunctorily.

"How's that?" Dick was recalling it better, now. "I live ten miles south-west of Hesperides, and I rode my horse in to get a sack of apples for my mother." He paused and searched his mind again. "Say, *I'm* going out on that train, too — you wait for me."

"They ain't no law ag'in' it that I know of," was the man's stolid comment.

Clara came downstairs and out of the door, a bag in either hand. She put down the bags — shining new and bulging — and came up close to Dick. Her cheeks were aflame with anger, and she spoke rapidly, with brutal scorn, utterly unmindful of the curious passengers:

"Say, you good little boy! I'm through with you — and damn glad of it. You've made me tired, see! and I won't stand for it. A boob and a mammy's boy! Ain't there no *men* left in the world?"

Watch in hand, the conductor of number four began calling, "All aboard!" His hand was lifted as a signal to his engineer.

"Wait!" screamed Clara, and ran toward the train. A negro porter took her bags, and the last of her that Dick saw, as he stared dazedly, was the flutter of a violet silk petticoat as Clara flung herself up the steps of a Pullman.

The mixed train to Hesperides was coming to a stop, and Jake Thompson was tacking on a moral to the story of his courtship and marriage:

"Clara's wild an' full of life — maybe sober, steady-goin' men *do* make her tired, like she said. I reckon she don't belong in this slow, dog-trottin' age — anyway, such as you an' me can't hold her. Lord! I done got over rampin' an' prayin' on account o' her; maybe, someday, though, she'll git tired of whoopin' it up, an' want to come back an' say, 'Jake, I'm through.' Then I'll give her a home — damn me, if I don't!

"You ride straight home to that good mother o' yours, Dick Marvin, an' forget all about this last ten days. I'll be workin' over here — Plum Creek crossin', they tell me it is — for a month, maybe. Be glad to see you any day." They shook hands, and Dick went across to Marlow's.

As he entered the long store, a pungent, pleasant odor came to his nostrils. Marlow came forward, smiling.

"Going out to the ranch today, Mr. Marvin?"

"Yes."

"Your mother was in the day after you left, and I told her you were called to Kansas City suddenly . . . I been keeping your horse for you in my stable — he's kind of frisky by now."

"Say — " Dick sniffed, and smiled gratefully at the store-keeper — "sack me up a bushel of those apples, will you, Mr. Marlow."

"You spoke just in time — I never did see such a call for apples! Every ranch in three counties sent in for some of that two carloads I brought in. Surprised *me* — I thought I'd got enough in to last all winter."

"People get awful hungry for such things out here."

"I reckon that's so — they work up an awful, what you might call an unnatural, taste for something that's fresh and kind o' sweet and sour, too."

"That's right — you ought to make a good thing out of apples here, Mr. Marlow . . . Well, I'll be riding — you can hand up that sack when I come round."

Dick's horse bucked and plunged, thrilling its rider with the joy of violent motion. At the front door of the store, Marlow gingerly hoisted the apples to the saddle.

"For your mother, Mr. Marvin, with my compliments." Dick slackened the rein, and in three minutes he and his horse had become a bobbing speck to the shortsighted vision of the contemplative Marlow.

The Man Who Interfered[99]

UNTIL LONG after midnight Jim Freeman sat reading a battered,[100] graceful old volume containing *Troilus and Cressida* and *Julius Caesar*—a book bound in leather for a gentleman of Virginia in 1771, and strayed from its mates of the set generations ago. Its type was bold and clear, fit for failing eyes to peruse.

Hoofbeats sounded in the square, clattered across the frozen mud; a horse stopped at the sidewalk; Jim put down the book, changed his spectacles, and waited. The rider dismounted, crossed the sagging boards outside the door, but there came no knock. Jim threaded his way among the type racks and piled miscellany of his small printing shop to confront his visitor.

As he came into the starlight, he could discern only that it was a woman who stood there.

"Howdy!" he greeted. She shifted a little, but did not answer.

"Step inside—seems chilly out here, but I've got a little bit of fire left in the stove." Jim opened the door wide; in his words had been neither surprise nor question.

The woman came in and sat down on the other side of the battered walnut desk from his own. Jim sat down, too, and began to finger the book.

The editor of the *Circletown Round-Up* was fifty-four, spectacled, and dingy. He lived alone in a room partitioned off from his printing shop, and after supper every evening, by the yellow glow of a big oil lamp, he gave a concert on his fifteen-dollar music machine for the men who came to the post office next door for mail — every evening except Friday. On Friday the *Round-Up* was printed; and the job of wrapping it ready for Saturday's distribution to its four hundred subscribers lasted into the night.

He was a pioneer of the tiny Oklahoma town; he had come upon it when it was first taking shape as a yellow, pine-board blot on the prairie, and he loved it. To the editor, Circletown was not what it seemed — merely a forlorn, drab outpost of civilization. Rather, it was a spot of splendid promise. Someday a railroad would come, and someday, too, twenty-five hundred feet or so below the grass roots, somebody's oil rig would strike the black, saturated sand that spells wealth and excitement. Meanwhile, in his heart dwelt a troubled consciousness that among his neighbors were some who failed to find peace and prosperity in Circletown and the district of which it was the center.

"Sometimes I sit up late reading," Jim remarked after a long silence.

"I am Lizzie Squirrel," said the woman finally. She spoke very quietly. "I am 'Wolf' Harper's wife."

"Yes; I knew you as soon as you came into the light. In trouble?"

She nodded.

"About 'Wolf'?"

"Yes — I am leaving him."

"I saw him going out of town this evening." Jim opened the book, fingering the leaves; after a moment he spoke:

"You got to the end, I reckon?" She nodded. "Well, it had to come. Where you bound for?"

"Back to my home — my people live over yonder." She bent her head toward the East.

"In the Spavinaw Hills[101] — yes. It is thirty-five miles — a long ride."

"First I want to speak to my brother. I saw your light, and I thought maybe you would go and wake Billy. He is hard to wake."

"Yes, Billy *is* hard to wake!" Jim's mind held a picture of Lizzie Squirrel's brother, the Indian pool-hall loafer, as he had lurched home to his shack that evening.

"So, you put 'Wolf' to bed and pulled out?"

"No." Lizzie Squirrel turned to study Jim Freeman's face by the light of the big lamp. She was of the erect Indian breed, strong and comely; at thirty she still bore herself proudly and, in spirit, all but unscarred by the brutality of her husband. Six years of alternate joy and humiliation had driven the light back from the front of her eyes, but had not extinguished it. She wore a man's heavy overcoat, buttoned close under her chin, and a thick woolen scarf was wrapped about her head, almost concealing her black hair.

"Listen!" She loosed the coat at her throat. "When 'Wolf' got home this night he tried to beat me, but I fought with him; and because he was weak from drink I choked him until he lost his senses. Then I tied his hands and locked him in the stable. In one hour he came back to his senses and called to me to come and let him out. But I did not—I was afraid. So, I sat and thought what to do."

The woman's tight-balled hands were resting on the desk; she was leaning forward to watch the effect of her words on Jim Freeman. He did not speak, but in his face Lizzie Squirrel read sympathy and a wish to understand. Presently her hands relaxed, and she spoke calmly.

"So, I thought and thought about what to do, and at last I could only see one way—I will go back to my people in the hills. There I will have peace. Though I have not lived with my people since I went away to school as a young girl, I know that they will take me in. They will take back the 'white girl'—you know they call me that because I went away to school among the whites and married a white man. But they are good people, and they will give me peace anyway!"

"Peace!" echoed Jim Freeman. "Yes, that would be good—but only for a while."

"Will you go and wake Billy now? I must tell him to ride out and turn 'Wolf' loose."

"Yes, in a minute." A conviction that he ought to stop this woman from going back to the hills, and to a family who would not understand her failure to find a niche in the white man's world, was in Jim's mind, and he was searching for the reasons that lay behind it. There was, of course, the general good which comes from preserving the social order; but beyond that was another argument, if he could only get it. He looked across at Lizzie, at her puzzled, unmarred face. Suddenly the argument came to his mind; she had not been beaten.

"Tonight," he asked, "did 'Wolf' hurt you?"

"No; I told you I whipped him and choked him — it was easy."

"Why then, you're leaving just when you don't have to!" Jim Freeman smiled, as if a great load had been lifted.

"But 'Wolf' would kill me if I went back!" Lizzie said it calmly.

"Maybe — this time. But never again."

The woman's face lighted, and she laughed.

"Once would be enough!"

"No, no," Jim protested, laughing too, "I mean, he might try this time, but never again. And I will go with you."

She shook her head.

"Don't you see! You beat him this time; you've got him tamed. He'll be a good old workhorse after this. After this, when he wants to go out and kick up his heels, go along with him and see that he don't bust things. In your place, instead of running away, I'd sure stay and make a man out of 'Wolf' Harper."

Again the woman shook her head and spread her hands in a gesture of despair.

"Anyhow," Jim Freeman went on, peering at Lizzie earnestly, "you ought to go back with me, and tell him why you're quitting him. Going off this way won't do — he'll follow you and make trouble for your folks. What do you say — we'll not bother to rouse Billy, but you and I'll ride out now?"

Lizzie's gaze met Jim's steadily, then she rose, buttoning the coat with shaking hands.

"Yes, I think I ought to tell him."

"Good! We'll go and get a couple of horses out of Dick Grayson's barn."

Jim scrawled a note to be pinned to the door of Dick's stable, put out the light, and the two went into the cold, starlit night.

Inspired by the dingy, lonely man who rode beside her, a battered derby crushed down almost to his spectacles and a knitted scarf about his throat to keep out the cold, Lizzie rode toward her home with the first genuine uplift of hope she had felt in years.

It was a raw November night, with high clouds driving before the wind.

Jim was cold and uncomfortable; he hated horseback riding. He preferred a double-seated buggy, with two sedate horses jogging along at six miles an hour. Astride Grayson's big sorrel, he looked grotesque and old and frayed, the literal Jim Freeman; but, underneath, lived another Jim Freeman, one who talked gaily, wisely, to Lizzie Squirrel, and who seemed to her as peaceful as the hills for whose shelter she yearned. Jim spoke of the stars, in a strain to outrage an astronomer:

"Now, you take the 'Dipper' — it's my special, favorite constellation. Round and round the North Star it goes, like a cup on a chain pump, dipping up a little drop of life every day and spilling it out over the world. One day it's a storm, or a big fight somewhere in heathen parts, and next day it spills over us such a cupful of good luck (sunshine, or a baby boy, or a good price for the fat hog we've got to sell) that we forget the sorrow it brought up yesterday. That's how it seems to me — it's a symbol of life."

Other constellations and particular stars Jim pointed out as they jogged over the frozen road. After a time Lizzie interrupted:

"I do not know the stars; maybe I do not look up enough."

"You've got to look up if you take the 'Dipper' for a mascot. What it has for you must be spilled in your face, not on top of your head! Study it if you want to find out what comes up out of the well of the world."

They rode through a depression, where the cold struck in and set them shivering; they crossed a mile of prairie which rose like a backbone — over it the wind blew dry and stimulating. Once Jim Freeman lifted his derby to let such a breeze tumble his thinning hair.

As they came close to the little weather-beaten house on the prairie where "Wolf" Harper and his Indian wife lived, Jim Freeman heard maudlin sounds coming from the log stable. They were the cries of the enraged brute, sickeningly familiar to the man who had spent his life among people of primitive passions. Men like "Wolf" Harper had almost shaken Jim Freeman's faith in his fellows — almost.

"I'm cold," said Jim Freeman, as they rode up to the gate of the wire-fenced enclosure, in which the house and barn stood, and dismounted. "Could you just make a cup of coffee, while I go down and let 'Wolf' out?"

"Maybe I better go, too," suggested Lizzie, but Jim Freeman shook his head and said:

"No, you stay here; and while we drink some coffee, you and I and 'Wolf' can talk things over."

"Then you take the lantern," advised Lizzie as she lighted it.

A ludicrous sort of a whistled tune marked Jim Freeman's progress toward the stable. Hearing it, "Wolf" Harper broke into a spasm of shouted profanity; before Jim's hand touched the heavy wooden bar which Lizzie Squirrel had fastened across the door, he made out the words of the drunken man's tirade:

"I'm a wolf—that's what they call me! And it's my night to howl! Stand back there, an' let me at him! Let me at him, I say!" Then the man laughed, wildly. Jim Freeman was not fit to tackle a drunken man—he wasn't even sure that he had the courage to tackle one. Sweat stood on his forehead as he fumbled with the bar—Jim Freeman knew that it was the sign of fear! He trembled as the bar was thrown clear and the heavy door of the stable swung open. He understood that he had to go to the drunken man, untie his hands and feet, and then deal with him as the fates directed. He forced himself forward.

The lantern's light flashed in "Wolf" Harper's eyes, and he made a grotesque, squirming effort to leap upon the bearer of the light. Then he saw that it was Jim Freeman who had come. Snarling, he babbled:

"So, it's you, 'Old Four-eyes.' Well, what you goin' to do to me?"

"Going to turn you loose, 'Wolf,'" said Jim Freeman; and by some miracle of self-control the editor's voice was held steady.

"All right," promised "Wolf" Harper thickly, "an' then I'm a-goin' to kill you! Let me at you, you old, four-eyed, interferin'—"

"Keep still till I get these ropes off you!" Jim Freeman bent over the struggling man and began to drive unwilling fingers to the task of freeing him.

First, Jim took the ropes off the feet of the man on the ground; and instantly he had to dodge a sharp bootheel swung blindly at his head. "Wolf" got to his feet then, standing unsteadily and holding out his hands. Jim got the rope free and stepped back, picking up the lantern that he had set down close by.

"Now, —— you, I'm goin' to clean you up!" cried "Wolf"; he sprang toward the battered man who stood with the sweat of fear beading his forehead. But Jim Freeman did not flinch.

"Wolf" Harper bore the editor to the floor of the stable; as they went down, the lantern rolled out of Jim's hand, but, freakishly, righted itself near the door. Its feeble glimmer shone upon the two as they struggled.

A crashing blow from "Wolf" Harper's fist shattered the editor's spectacles; but a cut on the cheek was the worst of that. "Thank heaven, they didn't get into my eyes!" muttered Jim. He was holding onto the arms of the drunken man with all his strength. And with all the strength and frenzy of the drunken brute, "Wolf" Harper was struggling to get his fists free.

Jim Freeman was a battered man of fifty-four, unused to physical strain; the sweat on his forehead became a sign of exhaustion within a minute. Suddenly he loosed his hold on "Wolf" Harper's arms, and, plunging swiftly, succeeded in getting from under. His fingers sought the other's neck — sought and found an uncertain grip.

He held that grip with the desperation of a great fear and a great necessity. "Wolf" Harper tried to beat him off, tried to fling him off with brutal kicks, tried to brain him with deliberate swings of his doubled fist. But, battered, bleeding, with all but a flicker of consciousness gone, Jim Freeman contrived to hold on until the other was staggering and gasping for breath.

Lizzie Squirrel had lighted a fire in the stove and had put water on to boil before it occurred to her that the two men ought to be there. She went to the door to listen, but heard no sound; she ran swiftly to the stable.

Just inside the door she found the lantern, shining feebly, peacefully, upon two unconscious men. She swung its light across them and fell back with a startled cry at the sight revealed. She went to hang the lantern on its accustomed nail, then stooped to loosen the grip that Jim Freeman had never relaxed on the throat of her husband. She sobbed as she tugged at the battered man's fingers; and when she pulled him free from "Wolf," the older man rolled inertly to her feet, his bruised and bleeding face upturned in the dim light.

Lizzie Squirrel dragged the two men into the cold air and went to fetch water. It was not a time for wailing; she worked with quiet effectiveness. But when the clean, cold dawn came and the sky grew pink where it met the prairie, only one man saw it.

"Wolf" Harper, sober and shaken, sat against the wall of the log stable gazing fearfully at his Indian wife as she worked over the battered form of the man who had interfered. He said nothing, but, burning deep into his primitive soul, he heard the words that came like a prayer from his woman's lips:

"Freeman—he has done it for me—and I was nothing to him!" As the sun rose and showed her the truth beyond the possibility of questioning, she went to lean her head against the door; over her tired, gray face the tears streamed.

Jim Freeman had believed in people. To Lizzie Squirrel he had said:

"After this night, 'Wolf' will never beat you again—if I were you I'd sure stay with him and make a man out of him!" Well, she could do that now; and the reconstructed life of a cow-country bum and wife beater was perhaps the fittest memorial the editor of the *Round-Up* could have wished.

The Other Partner[102]

THOUGH THE night was young and Mrs. O'Field's bootleg joint—where the bottles were cached under mattresses and the drinkers held cards in the "Boost Remus, Oklahoma's Hope!" Club—was not yet crowded, Ben Wardall could no longer suppress his desire to praise the twisted little man on the other side of the crap table. Ben had been celebrating since noon, when the mail from Lolita, combined with the radiant April day, had provoked in him a mood of jubilant, generous appreciation.

"He sure beats the world," Ben announced unreservedly, leaning back in his chair and pointing to his law partner. "Lookit th' facts—I'm goin' to be pers'nal, gen'lemen: he don't know who his parents were; named Woods for th' county he was born in; first name—gen'lemen, I won't say Christian—Alva for th' county seat; twin to th' immortal Topsy, only while he was still soft—no, gen'lemen, there's a better word. Mr. Tims says *plastic*—while young an' plastic, somebody took an' worked him over. Lookit th' result: wicked crossed eyes, dished face, knobby bald head, droop in left shoulder, mosquito biceps, warped sycamore saplin' legs, an' th' disposition of an angry centipede!"[103]

Woods interrupted the big, comely man, favoring him with a crooked, sardonic grin.

"Don't pick on me, you hippopotamus," he whined softly, and Ben exploded in loud laughter before adding other strokes to his picture:

"Early education picked off th' plank sidewalks of his native town — say, Alva, that's right, ain't it?" He put the question accusingly.

"Yeh." Woods glanced in Ben's general direction as he warmed the dice between skinny hands.

"Now lookit!" Wardall triumphed. "Best little ol' criminal lawyer in th' State of Oklahoma . . . He'd ought to be pres'dent of Boost Remus Club, 's what I'm gettin' at. Don't you agree?" Ben's tone was belligerent as he swung in his chair to face the room.

Mrs. O'Field caught Woods's cockeyed glance, nodded, and waddled to the locked inner door; with an irritated whine the little man rounded the table, put a claw on the exuberant Ben's arm, and commanded:

"Come on, Hippo, let's beat it!"

Wardall glanced up at the malevolent face, thumped the crap table violently, and shouted: "I'll do it for you, Alva!" He rose and defied the others: "But I wouldn't stir one inch — no, not one inch — for anybody else!"

A gray-bearded, stooping, tobacco-stained man who had sat at Ben's elbow got up at the same time, informing no one in particular that he reckoned he'd have to mosey along too. Wardall took his arm, stopped when near the door, and turned to say impressively:

"Gen'lemen, this ol' man loves me." He paused. "D'you know why?" No one paid the slightest attention until he boasted dramatically: "I saved his boy from hangin'!"

Eyes came round to the big lawyer and the embarrassed old man to stare, not because of the revelation of a fact that was no secret, but in astonishment at the shameless boast.

The old man shrank visibly, dropped his eyes, and Woods snapped:

"Getell outa here!" Mrs. O'Field let them out and locked the door.

"It's the last time *he* gits in," she told the club members in virtuous wrath. She had said it three times before, on occasions when Ben had celebrated legal victories, and her words got a laugh.

Mrs. O'Field, who in friendlier moments thought of Ben Wardall as

Remus's prize bachelor, would have been interested to know that this time he was not rejoicing over a law-court victory. His exuberance was due to the letter in his inside coat pocket that had come to him at noon — "I love you, Ben!" the letter said, among other pleasant things.

Leaving Wardall asleep on the huge leather-covered lounge in the library of the Wardall and Woods office, the twisted little man and the drooping-eyed old man came down the wide wooden stairway to the street.

"Now beat it, Pap; he'll be OK." Woods dismissed the other briskly, and by the light of a full moon consulted his watch. "Ten o'clock," he noted. "Dave ought to be at the club in a couple of minutes." His return was timed accurately, for he and Dave Smith came together in Mrs. O'Field's "coat-room."

"How about our game?" Smith put his customary question truculently. Woods nodded, and they went in to make up their usual poker table.

From noon until ten at night, Dave Smith was in charge of the telegraph office, and from ten to midnight he was a dependable patron of Mrs. O'Field's joint. A consistent loser, yet believing himself always on the point of getting adequate revenge on the little lawyer, Smith's excitement and irritation marched abreast as he played. Woods handled him cleverly, allowing his mind to dwell upon the devastating blow he was even then aiming at the narrow, mean head of the slab-sided man who had been his first employer in Remus.

"He sure made life hard for me," Woods summed up bleakly, "and he's got it coming to him!"

Playing his hands swiftly, almost automatically, the little man thought over his ten-year hitch with Dave Smith, beginning as a boy of fourteen, victim of kicks and curses and threats, pedaling a creaking old bicycle about town delivering messages, thrust into horrid hidden dens, nauseated by the dregs of a small town's fast life. He had begged Smith for part-time work, a chance to go to school, and had been told to getell out of there if he wanted to go fooling with books.

He tried to find a crack in Smith's armor of contemptuous selfishness, sought some human response; failing there, he attempted to make friends with his little girl, Cora, who was six when she began coming to the office sometimes with her mother, and Smith went at him savagely, growling, "Let my girl be, you dam' little rat!" That hurt! And the boy was hurt worse when Cora herself, parrotlike, chided: "Go 'way, dirty bad boy!"

At fifteen, undersized, undernourished, friendless, he fought a terrific battle with spinal meningitis. The drug-soaked doctor whom Smith reluctantly brought to attend him in the dirty back room of the telegraph office pulled him through, but it was a long, long pull up from the shadows, weeks when the waif was learning again to walk and to breathe consecutively. In that mellow autumn time he acquired the habit of dragging himself to the sunny south side of the brick railway station building and studying the pictures in the pink pages of a New York weekly paper to which Smith subscribed. Curiously, this sheet had served as the spur to ambition . . .

One day, as he sat there in the sun contemplating pictures of prizefighters and actresses, Ben Wardall saw him and stopped. Woods would never forget that first movement of compassion on the part of smiling, handsome young Ben!

"Hello, sonny," he said cheerfully, "how you comin'?" Before Alva could answer, Ben had taken the paper from his weak claw. "Say, that's strong stuff for a kid!" Ben was twenty-three then, just through his bar examination, content with the world, wise to the records of prizefighters and big-league ball players.

"Can't make out much of the printin'," the boy complained. "Say, Mr. Ben, what's that feller's picture in it fer?" He pointed out the cut of a flashily dressed, full-fed, and block-shouldered man sitting behind a broad table-desk. Ben studied the long explanatory caption under the picture, laughed, and answered:

"Sonny, that's interestin'. It says that Mr. Moe Heimel, the best-known lawyer in New York, has won more criminal and divorce court cases than any other man in America because he knows more underworld history than the police department. He's got the goods on thousands! Some lawyer, I'll say!" Ben laughed again, hesitated, then handed back the paper folded over a five-dollar bill, saying: "Boy, you sure look hungry; how about it, hey?"

Catching sight of the bill, Alva burst into tears and blubbered: "Say, Mr. Ben, I can't take this — all this!"

"All right," Ben grinned, "get it changed and bring me a nickel; bring it up to the office when you can navigate the stairs." Ben left him with an exquisite choking sensation in his breast and a renewed interest in the picture of Moe Heimel of New York. He shaped his dream of destiny sitting there in the sunshine.

He climbed painfully to the office of Wardall & Wardall — Ben's father had been alive then, and had just put out the proud new sign indicating his son's partnership — and attempted to return the five dollars to Ben while begging for a chance to study law. Ben, swearing that he'd be damned if he'd take more than a nickel, went in to talk with his father. He came out beaming and said:

"Sonny, here's a key. Come in anytime, only don't get in the way. I'll help you now and then."

Ben helped him too — redeeming his promise casually, cheerfully, offhandedly — loaned him old schoolbooks, taught him to write, directed his first feeble assaults on the law books.

It had been a long, stiff pull! Eight years and more of Dave Smith's brutal driving by day — for now he wouldn't quit the job that was to be a steppingstone to power through knowledge of men and their devious ways — and eight years of evenings in the Wardall office library, digging.

Running like a red thread through the toil of his days and nights was his hatred of Dave Smith. One day, after her mother's death and while she was in Remus for one of her periodical visits to her father, Cora Smith came in and found him alone. While waiting for her father, she consented to be entertained by watching Alva turn the pages of a state atlas and proudly air his knowledge of the populations and officials of any city or town Cora cared to name.

Smith came in and found them absorbed in the game.

"Come in here!" he ordered, leading the way to the back room. He turned upon the boy to say in a gray fury: "You let my girl be, you miserable little whelp! Ain't warned you? If you try to double-cross me again, I'll skin you alive!"

Then Alva had shrilled defiantly: "Oh, I guess you never double-crossed anybody, you an' Jim O'Field! How about holdin' up that wire on the sixth race at New Orleans last tenth of February, when Jake Drummond was playin' Fairy Ace in Jim's rooms?" That had been while Mrs. O'Field's good man was living and gathering fleeces in his small way.

Dave pounced upon him, knocked him about, threatened to kill him. But he didn't whimper, and the unsuspecting Cora never knew what happened in that back room.

Smith was afraid to fire him after that, and Alva determined to endure the persecution for the sake of the job's opportunities. Meanwhile, he made himself useful to the Wardalls.

Finally he managed to skin through the bar examination, and Ben Wardall, overcoming his father's objections, made a place for him in the law office at thirty dollars a month. On that memorable day, with no word to Smith, he moved out of the old back room, took a tiny cubicle at the Western Hotel, and dedicated his whole mind and talents to the affairs of Wardall & Wardall.

He was made junior partner at old Wardall's death—when he was thirty and Ben was thirty-eight—and the firm became Wardall & Woods. He was its new balance wheel, the silent check on Ben's exuberance, keeping that imaginative, impulsive, oratorical lawyer down to earth, down to the hard, cold facts about their clients, their lives and wives, their clients' enemies' lives and wives. The discriminating few who looked below the surface for an explanation of Wardall & Woods's prodigious success in criminal cases began to say: "Oh, Ben's brilliant and able, all right, but it's the *other partner* that's got the brains!"

Woods heard it, but it didn't flatter him. He said to himself: "Maybe Ben can't always see through a stone wall, but without him I wouldn't go far. We're a team!" Now they were "settin' pretty," Handsome Ben in the prime of life, magnetic, persuasive with juries, a good fellow; himself, at thirty-four, matured and with a headful of profitable information and the wit to use it.

And now at last the time had come for Dave Smith to "get his"! Stabbing him with infrequent cockeyed upward glances, Woods meditated the knock-out he had prepared for the man who had ridden him so cruelly and who still felt contempt for him—only now it was mixed with fear!

At eleven o'clock Woods rose abruptly. "Dave," he taunted, "I'll take that last fifty cents of yours the next time; keep it for me."

Returning to the office, he softly removed Ben's shoes, loosened his collar, settled him more comfortably on the sofa, and threw over him a long coat that he found on the rack. He closed the door, entered his own workroom and, with a green shade over his eyes, dragged his desk aside to reveal a wide, squat, shallow cabinet.

This cabinet was his treasure chest. Inside its seventy-two labeled drawers were seemingly chaotic piles of jottings on scraps of legal cap paper, crabbed, nearly illegible letters, numbers, cabalistic signs, an occasional word. Pulling a chair up, he opened a drawer marked *19+a* and took from it five fragments, greeting the topmost with a faint whine of satisfaction. It had been completed late that very day, just before supper, the final trump card of the hand he had waited a long time to fill. Its scrawls represented the recent history of Cora Smith.

Rw—312—3—19. 24—S—Pn, the cipher began, and then ran on to a second, third, fourth, and fifth jagged sloping line; the ink was scarcely five hours dry on the last entry, *K12ta6 ↔ 13+a 5–6*.

Only he and Ben Wardall knew about the contents of that squat cabinet, and only he knew how to use its riches. He had begun it nine years before by scribbling a cryptic memorandum on a bit of paper and putting it into a drawer; and now the record had grown to a formidable, apparently complicated and yet simple, mass of information based on verified gossip, personal knowledge, and rows of filed official rosters, city and town directories, telephone books, county histories, fair programs, pasted newspaper clippings, and so on. It concerned men and women in every corner of the state: the governor, members of the legislature, federal, state, and county judges, sheriffs, court clerks, prosecuting attorneys, road commissioners, county agents, school superintendents, mayors, councilmen, club leaders, church workers—everybody who had stepped even momentarily into the light of publicity.

Folded into a top drawer was a large-scale map of the state, cross-hatched into tiny squares lettered at top and bottom and numbered at the sides; and his notations on the filed scraps of paper included the square on this map in which the "subject" could be located.

Woods kept his strange index and the sources to which it pointed—rosters, directories, pasted clippings, etc.—even with the latest developments, using the hours from eleven to one or two in the morning for his reading and memory notes; then, shutting the cabinet and wheeling his desk back into place, he would go to his room at the Western to sleep until nine. Waking, he would dance about for fifteen minutes in a curious set of light exercises, drink a bowl of half coffee and half milk, and report, energetic and grinning crookedly, to Handsome Ben.

He loved the life: days of hurried, definite work in the office, roughing out briefs, agreements, depositions for Ben and Miss Sartwell to put into presentable form; sessions with witnesses, Ben sitting by, in which memories were purged, refreshed, adroitly fed; casual calls on judges, sheriffs, county, state, and federal prosecutors, prosecuting witnesses, bankers, loan brokers, conveying subtly in the cracked tenor of his high-pitched voice hints of lightly buried social or legal dynamite; scandal-provoking luncheons with Mrs. O'Field or "Madame" Leary, her more retiring and sinister rival in Remus for men's after-supper leisure and dollars; sudden journeys to the capital, to Tulsa, to Muskogee, Ardmore, Lawton, or to some crossroads speck on the map; sometimes into neighboring states.[104]

He built up Ben's cases, put into the big fellow's hands the materials for use before judges and juries in matters that could not be settled in conference and must go to trial, but himself never entered a courtroom. As he said, he was no blooming Daniel Webster! On his partner's solid foundations, Ben built gloriously, with flourishes that attracted eyes in all sections of the state, and Woods was content that he should.

Now, while Wardall slept fitfully, as the frequent squeakings of the leather-covered couch informed Woods, the other partner went over for the fiftieth time the story of the family, friends, and roiled currents of Dave Smith's life. Briefed on the five scraps of paper under his eyes were the facts — ample for his need, proved, airtight, checked, and rechecked.

Woods's slips picked Dave Smith up at birth, back in 1865, carried him through school at Albany, NY, his marriage to Clara Watson of that city, his wanderings from job to job before coming to Remus in 1903 to take charge of the telegraph office. They recorded Cora Smith's birth, at Albany, and Dave's hasty flight when a woman named Myra Bell appeared and threatened the peace of his little home. Myra Bell followed him, apparently after due deliberation, to Fort Wayne, Ind., and then to Homeville, Kan., where she showed up with a ten-year-old nephew.

While at Homeville, Smith inherited money from his father's estate and invested it in a house and ten acres of land near the little Kansas town. His fear of Myra Bell drove him to make over to her a long lease of the property before pushing on to Oklahoma.

Soon after Smith arrived at Remus, Alva Woods dropped off a freight train and began working for him as a messenger boy. From that time forward, the Smith history developed under his own increasingly observant eyes. He watched Dave's slow disintegration since his wife's death in 1906; he noted with satisfaction Cora's gradual distrust and coolness toward her father as she grew up and spent more and more of her time with her aunt; two years ago, he witnessed the descent upon Smith of Myra Bell and her nephew, young Paul Steif, grown into a shrewd small-town sport and oil-lease speculator. The two had come to force Dave Smith to sell his ten acres to them, because it seemed probable that a new oil field would include it. There was a terrific row. Dave held out, determined to keep the property for Cora. Myra Bell told Cora everything she knew about Dave. Cora fled to her aunt, where she stayed for six months before returning to her father. She came back thoroughly disillusioned and began earning money by giving lessons in embroidery (for she could accomplish wonderful things with her needle).

Cora's industry enabled Dave to spend more money at Mrs. O'Field's, but the girl never protested against his profligacy; only she went for frequent short visits to her aunt at Homeville.

Paul Steif acquired a pool hall in Homeville and induced his aunt, Myra Bell, to open a millinery shop in the little town of Lolita, Okla. The shop prospered for a time, then Myra Bell began taking drugs; and two weeks ago, on the last day of March, her troubled, sordid history ended with an overdose of veronal and —

Here was the last slip of paper, containing Cora Smith's movements during the last fourteen days. It showed the symbols, *Rw — 312 — 3 — 19. 24 — S — Pn*, etc. Decoded, this read:

"Reference: Remus telephone directory, No. 312. Cora Smith, twenty-four years of age, single, member Presbyterian church, Sunday-school teacher, left Remus April 2, 1924, for Homeville, Kan. Went to her aunt, Mrs. E. F. Boone, 764 Oak Street, where on the same day she saw Paul Steif on his return from Lolita, Okla., where he had buried Myra Bell; saw him daily thereafter; drove about the country with him in his flivver. April 10th they drove to Lolita and stayed overnight, the two occupying adjoining rooms at the Palace Hotel. Paul Steif was half drunk, had been drinking moonshine for two weeks.

"Informant's name, Henry Bates of Lolita. Charge to be made against Steif in the federal court at Tulsa, violation of the Mann Act.[105] Witnesses to be summoned: Bates; Mose Galey, proprietor of the Palace Hotel; and Gussie Shaw, chambermaid. Prosecuting witness, Bates (whose history and the reasons why he would consent to bring the action against Steif would be found on two scraps of paper in the drawer marked *2+a*). Federal prosecuting attorney, C. R. Mays (his record would be revealed by slips *5* and *6* in drawer *13+a*)."

An excellent case! A double-barreled revenge: not only would the sanctimonious, hypocritical Cora, who had regarded Woods as dirt under her feet, bring disgrace and grief to Dave, but Dave would certainly be compelled to sell that Homeville property in order to help Paul Steif, whom he hated and feared, hire counsel for his defense. As he contemplated the facts, Alva Woods thanked the ironic gods for their favor.

Another perfect touch: in no way would the firm of Wardall & Woods be openly identified with the smash. In fact, Ben would know nothing about it until the complaint was filed and the newspapers disclosed it . . .

As a matter of form, Woods turned up the slips concerning Henry Bates and C. R. Mays and studied them once more. Then, setting a pitcher of water and a glass convenient to Ben's hand when he should wake, he departed for bed. His final thought was that he would call Bates on the long-distance at a quarter to ten and tell him to get busy.

Thirst and a troubled conscience assailed Ben Wardall as he kicked off the protecting overcoat and set his stockinged feet on the cool floor. Gratefully he gulped the water and noted his shoes set near at hand.

"Good old Alva!" he said, put on his shoes, and arranged his collar and tie, thinking of the awaited shave, the leisurely soaking bath, fresh linen, the newly pressed suit, grapefruit, eggs, coffee, and the customary scolding of Aunty Mullens, the old woman who had served the Wardall family for forty years and who now kept his bachelor home. But before leaving the office he reread the letter that had come to him yesterday and sent him out to celebrate. Thrusting it into his coat pocket with a sincere whispered plea to its writer not to hold last night's outbreak against him, but to understand the reason, he crooned:

"She loves me. By the eternal, that'd ought to satisfy me! She loves me." The three words became a refrain as he emerged to face the soft April sunshine; and he managed to whistle as he shaved.

"Wish I could announce it," he murmured regretfully as he drew the bath. He wanted his friendly world to know of his incredible luck. Victim of love at forty-two, for the first time hopelessly, heels-over-head in love, with a comfortable home all ready, it was hard to wait in silence until she could make up her mind to say yes — even if she had the best of reasons for putting off her definite promise. But she would tell him her troubles, and he would persuade her . . .

Vaguely, while he gave himself to the soothing hot bath, he sought adjectives fit to describe his lady: sweet, sympathetic, intelligent, quiet, sort of serene, like a saint. Beautiful, too! Not in the new bobbed-hair, jazz-animated way, but with poise and dignity: black hair parted in the middle and drawn to the back of her head in a heavy, fascinating mass; the clear oval of the face like some old Italian painter's idea of — what was the name of that picture somebody stole out of the Louvre? Mona Lisa, yeh. There was in his lady something of the same hint of mystery, a charming hint of mystery, promising, thrilling![106]

The wooing had been a strange, quiet attack; and, come to think of it, why had he been so quiet about it? Oh, the influence of the girl herself, of course. She could do anything with him! . . . Anyway, he'd like to be able to tell Alva, hear the little man's jeers at love, his cynical comments on marriage, his acid rebuke, "You're a big fool, Ben!" and then feel the quick, hard pressure of the two claw-like hands on his as Alva wished him happiness . . .

Ben had finished his first cup of coffee when Miss Sartwell rang the front-door bell, came in, and followed Aunty Mullens to the dining room.

"Well!" she taunted, aware that she was not overstepping any boundary of privilege with him (both of those poor men would have been helpless at the office without her, and she had to speak freely if kindly!). "Pretty soft. Say, Mr. Ben, Mr. Alva says he don't expect you at the office before noon, but he would like that Holton deposition in the Means manslaughter case. You know, you took it away with you yesterday. The case comes up next week, and Mr. Alva's goin' to see Holton this mornin'."

"Sure thing, that's right." Ben called his housekeeper: "Aunty, will you do me a favor, run up to my room and get that long folded paper out of the inside pocket of my gray coat?" He laughed as the old woman left the room growling, "Git your own papers, lazybones!" He turned a radiant, impersonal smile on Miss Sartwell: "Have some coffee, Miss Emma?"

"No, thanks, I've had mine. I got to beat it right back."

"Alva cross?" he asked, grinning.

"As usual; and busy as a pup with his first flea!"

Aunty Mullens came down with the paper.

"Thanks, Aunty, I knew you'd do it for me—just give the thing to Miss Emma." To the rapidly retreating back of the firm's secretary Ben called: "I'll be along pretty soon."

Pulling down the blinds to shut the sunlight away from the davenport in the wide bay of the dining room, Aunty Mullens stole quietly out to her work in the kitchen. Ben rose, stretched, and muttered ruefully:

"No matter what they say, you don't get back your pep as quickly at forty-odd as you did at twenty-five. Ho, hum!" He was feeling fine, but there did remain a certain lassitude to remind him of Mrs. O'Field's mattress-warmed whiskey; he hesitated toward the comfortable couch, and the faint squeak of a cool leather cushion as he fitted it under his cheek reminded him:

"I'd like to read that letter again." He half rose to go upstairs and fetch it, then sank back. "Nev' mind," he said sleepily, "I know th' important parts by heart: 'I do love you, Ben.' . . . 'I loved the way you came to me, like a shy boy, who—' . . . 'I loved your letter, so lawyer-like on the first page, then so human and thrilling, writing things you hadn't dared to say.' . . . 'If I only could.' Well, whatever 'tis holdin' her back, she'll tell me an' we'll fix it . . . Folks get married in June, an'—" His pleasant reflections were continued to slumber.

As Miss Sartwell slipped in and laid the folded Holton deposition at Woods's elbow, he was speaking into the telephone:

"Bates? Alva Woods talking . . . Yeh, I'm all right. How're you and *Mrs.*

Bates?" He laughed knowingly and paused to allow his listener at Lolita to get the flavor of his emphatic insinuation; "Mrs. Bates" indeed! What Woods knew about her — His free hand reached for and unfolded the Holton deposition, and a smaller, note-sized enclosure fell out. "Something of Ben's that got folded in," he thought, and thrust the smaller pages aside with the intention of putting them on his partner's desk. He spoke to the waiting Bates:

"In that Palace Hotel matter, the word is 'shoot!' . . . Yeh, right now. Get the ten-fifteen train to Tulsa; see Mays, he's waiting for you; the papers ought to be filed by noon. Then go to the *Evening Journal* office and see Colter . . . Yeh, Colter, they call him city editor. He'll send a man to the court house to copy the complaint . . . No, don't say anything, just act like a man that's seen his duty and done it, guardian of the morals of a community, see . . . Yeh, ha, ha . . . Sure, Colter has the dope on the whole outfit . . . No, don't say a word to anybody else; keep mum until you're called to testify . . . Call me up from the *Journal* office after the paper goes to press, and get six copies for me on the afternoon train for Remus . . . 'Sall; hop to the depot now!"

Hanging up the receiver, Woods consulted his watch. With Bates on the way, it was time to think of the Means case and Holton's deposition, which required strengthening. In two minutes Holton would be at the bank. He picked up the document, grabbed his hat, flung a hurried explanation to Miss Sartwell, and streaked for the door, leaving Ben's precious letter lying beside his telephone — four loosely folded sheets of notepaper.

Woods found his man at the bank, arranged to lunch with him, and recast the faulty deposition afterward in the office, then circulated in a mood of high geniality about the streets. He spent an hour at the club, shot craps and played the wheel leisurely — today was as near to being a holiday as he was ever likely to achieve. He was induced by Holton to prolong the luncheon; and he sat chewing toothpicks and tasting in advance tomorrow's triumph while his companion enjoyed a second cup of coffee and smoked.

Tomorrow would be his big day, when the *Remus Eagle* came out with a reprint of the "Journal's" story; he was sure that Otis, the *Eagle*'s editor, would copy it, with a note at the head calling attention to "the shocking action taken in connection with the family of one of our respected townsmen." Dave Smith would open his copy of the *Eagle* — but somebody might get a copy of the *Journal* this evening and have the nerve to thrust it into

Dave's hands at Mrs. O'Field's, and Alva could catch him shrivel! He had a momentary regret that he hadn't asked Bates to come on to Remus with the copies. However, that might be risky, involve him openly, connect the firm with Bates's action, and that wouldn't be fair to Ben. This vendetta with Smith was his own; and he'd find a way to let Dave know whose finger had pulled the trigger . . .

At five minutes past two Woods interrupted Holton's discursive talk, and at 2:15 he led him into the office to meet Miss Sartwell's mocking welcome: "Well, stranger! Thought I was to have the office to myself today."

"Sorry, Miss Emma," the little partner grinned crookedly. "Ben's not here yet? Will you bring your notebook, please?" To Holton he recommended: "Move your chair up closer." With his habitual gesture, he swept a hand across the desk top to clear it, ruffling the loosely folded sheets of the letter he had forgotten to put on Ben's desk. His eye caught the greeting, in a woman's large, clear handwriting:

"Ben, dear!"

He couldn't help it—he simply had to read the next words, so surprising it was to know that some woman was "dearing" his partner. Was it sister or aunt? No; "I do love you, Ben . . . I loved your letter," sprang out from the page to startle Woods . . . And the handwriting—where had he seen it before? "Fold this thing up and put it on Ben's desk!" he swiftly slipped the bottom sheet out and saw the signature:

"Cora."

Something inside Alva Woods seemed to explode, sending a terrifying, nauseating shock through his frail body, setting his limbs trembling. A tremendous effort of will was required to rise, holding the four sheets in his hand, and walk slowly to his partner's room.

"'Scuse me, Holton," he muttered before closing the door and sitting down in Ben's chair to read Cora Smith's confession of her love, her April song of joy, her sentences hinting at difficulties ("Ah," Woods raged silently, "if Ben only knew what a pickle she is in!"), her appeal for time in which to make up her mind ("Time to get rid of that young pool-hall sport she's fallen for!"), her clever, flattering characterizations of Ben ("She knows the value of the prize she's after, all right!").

"Jezebel, Delilah!" Then suddenly Woods's fury was drowned in the black pool of grief opened by the closing paragraphs:

"Oh, Ben, you scare me when you say that I am everything to you! I know you mean it, mean it so hard that if I should say yes and then ever fail you in any way—

"And you've never really been in love before? I believe that too. I really do, Ben. It's terrifying, and—"

How accurately she reflected Ben's exaltation, his sincerity, his deep passion! Woods stretched his twisted neck, shaking his head in the effort to clear his muddled brain. He must do something! But just what? He put his queer, distorted face in his hands, leaned his knobby head on the edge of Ben's desk, and tried to quiet the fierce, hot tumult that racked his body and sent the blood pounding in ears and temples. "Poor old Ben!" Colter's story would nearly kill him. It would wither that ripe, human, optimistic, lovable old fool of a partner of his! The one human being that Alva Woods loved! . . . He must think fast; he couldn't conceive of Ben turned bitter and cynical, as he must be by what was coming.

Without knowing it, Alva Woods began to cry; the long-maturing and overpowering affection for his big partner welled up and overflowed his eyes. "I can't let it happen, Ben," he whispered. But if he should marry her? "Maybe it won't get that far, after all."

Woods sat up and rapped imperatively on Ben's desk, the summons to Miss Sartwell.

She came in, cried out sharply at sight of the little partner's tear-wet, agonized face, closed the door, and ran to him. "Why, Mr. Alva—poor boy!"

Woods spared half a second to comprehend the swift sympathy of her tone, then snapped: "Get Colter, *Tulsa Journal* office, on the phone."

"Mr. Holton?" she was retreating rapidly.

"Tell him to get out. Tell Central to hustle!"

No, he couldn't let the blow fall on Ben . . . When he had made Colter kill the story—if he got through to him in time—he must call Mays and have the Bates complaint buried . . . When did the first edition of the *Journal* come out? 2:15? 2:30? It was 2:20 now; God, but Central was slow! He'd heard Holton go out; he'd heard Miss Sartwell's insistent but good-tempered reminders to Central: "A little speed, Dot; you know we ain't got all day to wait for this call!" Woods's fingers were working, flexing in a spasm of impatience. The bell tingled, and his claws pounced upon the telephone.

"Colter? Alva Woods — yeh, Woods. Listen: about that Bates matter." He was speaking clearly, rapidly, responsive to the spur of necessity. "Is your paper out yet? . . . First edition just gone!" His hand shook so that he nearly dropped the receiver, then: "Oh!" in a great gasp of relief: "Didn't get in the first edition, eh?" He permitted himself a more deliberate, friendly manner: "Say, Colter, do something for me now and wait for the explanation — kill that Bates story . . . Yeh, it's OK, safe . . . Yeh, it's a peach of a story, it's all you say, but kill it . . . You've just passed the proofs, and it's about to go into the forms? Well, rip it out . . . Yeh, it's too bad! . . . What'll you put in its place?" Woods's clearing brain caught a flash, a remembered fragment from one of Ben Wardall's jury pleas that he had tried out on the little partner, and he said with sardonic lightness: "Say, Colter, why not print that Bible parable about 'Who among you is fit to cast the first stone?' . . . Sure, get 'em guessing . . . Well, good boy, Colter, you won't be sorry! When you see Bates again, tell him to call me . . ."

Woods was talking with Mays when Ben came in, smiling, refreshed, glowing. The sight of him sent a sharp, strange twinge through the little man, a compound of relief, anger, and compassion. Ben reached across his shoulder for Cora Smith's letter, a smile lighting his face.

"No, Mays," Woods explained patiently, "there won't be any prosecution, nix. Lose the papers, see, and forget the matter too — absolutely . . . Yeh, Bates will . . . Mistake? Yeh, Bates was a fool." He put down the transmitter with a bang.

"Bates?" Ben echoed. "At Lolita? What's he been up to?"

"Oh, he's been bothering Mays about some bootleg joint he *thinks* is hurting his ice-cream business," Woods extemporized. "No evidence."

The other partner got out of Ben's chair, looked up with his malevolent, crooked grin, and broke into his own peculiar hymn of joy:

"Well, you drunken bum! Decided to come to life at last, did you? You big simp — Come along, Ben, let's hop over to Widow O'Field's and get a shot. Do you good." His hand was on his partner's arm, and he went on in a whining cackle: "Drink and be merry, my boy, tomorrow's — another day!"

"No, nix, Alva," Ben protested. "I'm off booze. Cuttin' it out. Quittin', see! There's a reason — tell you someday, Alva, durn you little ol' soul anyway!" He grabbed Woods's narrow, bony shoulders with his big hands, shook him, roughed him joyously, swept a palm affectionately across the knobby, bald head.

Shaken by a great gust of pity, trembling from the touch of Ben's hands, the little partner turned away to his own room . . . His hand went to the edge of his desk, to pull it aside, to check over once again the five scraps of paper in drawer *19+a* . . . Dynamite? Yeh, and he'd come darn near blowing up his beloved partner, Handsome Ben, with it!

Cora Smith, back in Remus eight days later, told Ben her troubles as he held her in his arms. Ben begged her to allow him to enlist his partner's help in settling them.

"All right, Ben," she assented at last. "You know, I've always been afraid of Alva Woods, but he must be all right if you like him."

Ben's session with his partner took the place of the abandoned after-supper visit to Mrs. O'Field's rooms . . .

"It's that half-brother of hers, Paul Steif," Ben was saying.

"What!" Woods interrupted.

"Yes," Ben explained calmly. "He's Dave's son by — but the story starts a long way back, and it's been the secret of only five people, three since August Steif and Myra Bell died. Myra was Paul's mother . . . It was an early marriage, form of marriage rather, when Dave was hardly out of school and went on a visit to Rome, NY, and fell for Myra Bell, who was cutting a dash as a gay young widow — grass widow. A year later, just before Paul was born, Myra's real husband, Steif, turned up, ran Dave off, and took Myra back. He threw her over again after Dave had married Cora's mother, and Myra showed up and demanded protection from Dave on account of baby Paul. It's a long story . . . Here, two years ago, the time Myra showed up in Remus, Cora learned about it . . . But the matter's all wound up now except for Cora and Paul. He's half cracked on account of his mother's death, coming as it did after a long spell of taking drugs. He's a sort of flighty kid, I expect, though he's got ability and hustle. Dave's afraid of him, but Cora's fond of him and thinks she can keep him straight if she sticks by him . . ."

Woods roused himself from the huddle he had become at Ben's opening statement, the look of the stricken creature passed from his face, and his familiar crisp whine, in response to Ben's "What about it, Alva?" lighted the big man's eyes:

"We'll take the case. Marry Cora as soon as she'll have you. Get Paul Steif to sell out that Homeville pool hall, settle his mother's estate at Lolita, if there's anything to settle, then bring him down here. We'll make him handy man in the office. He knows a lot of oil people, and that property of Dave's ought to be developed. Good thing all round, and profitable too — what say, Ben?"

"Sure sounds all right, ought to work. I'll put it up to Cora."

"Now!" Woods demanded. "No time like the present. It's early yet; I bet she ain't gone to bed. Better beat it! And give her my best, Ben."

As the sound of his partner's feet on the wooden outside stairway ceased, Woods wheeled his desk aside and drew his chair up to the cabinet. Then he set his own, Ben's, and Miss Sartwell's wastepaper baskets handy and dumped the contents of the seventy-two secret drawers into them. One by one he carried the crammed baskets down to a vacant lot behind the Wardall building, lighted the piled heap, and saw it burn to a tiny mound of ashes. His requiem was brief:

"One little missing link, and — they ain't no good now; I ain't sure of 'em!"

The Singing Bird[107]

"NOW WE talk, me and these Kee-too-wah fellows. Old woman, go to bed!"

Thus Jim Blind-Wolfe dismissed his wife, Jennie, who was not old. With the fleetest glancing look he pushed her gently toward the back door of the firelit cabin, one huge outspread hand covering both of her erect shoulders.

Big Jim, old Spring Frog, Panther, and The Miller made up this inner, unofficial council of the Kee-too-wah organization that had met at Jim's cabin.[108] Self-charged with the duty of carrying out the ancient command to maintain among the Cherokees the full-blood inheritance of race purity and race ideals, they would discuss an alarming late growth of outlawry in the tribe, an increase in crime due to idleness, drink, and certain disturbing white men who had established themselves in the hills. Paradoxically, as they talked and planned secret pressures here and there, they would pass a jug of honest moonshine — but they would drink from it discreetly, lightly, as full-blood gentlemen should!

"Jim," old Spring Frog opened, "I hear my friend say something about that fellow you hit that day at Tahlequah — "

Jim's sudden, loud guffaw interrupted the old man.

"Him!" and Jim's scornful rumble summed up the case of Lovely Daniel, a wild half-breed neighbor.

Smiling at the muffled sound of Jim's laugh, Jennie Blind-Wolfe drew a gay shawl over the thick black hair that made a shining crown for her cleanly modeled head and oval brown face and went across, under the brilliant September starlight, to the out cabin where she was to sleep. It was an inviting pine-log room, pleasantly odorous of drying vegetables and smoked side meat hung from rafters.

She stood for a minute on the solid adz-hewn step listening to the faint, unintelligible murmur of her husband's voice, the occasional comments of the others whom she had left crouched in front of glowing wood embers in the wide stone fireplace; to the music of Spavinaw Creek racing over its rocky bed to Grand River; to the incessant, high-pitched chirring of crickets in the grass, the hysteric repetitions of katydids, and the steady clamor of tree frogs yonder at the edge of the clearing.

A maddening sound, this all-night chorus of the little creatures of grass and forest! For ten nights, as she lay beside the relaxed bulk of her giant husband, she had strained her ears in the effort to hear above their din the sound of a horse's tramping at the timber edge and the sound of a man's footsteps coming across the dead grass of the clearing.

"Oh, why don't they stop! Why don't they stop!" she had cried, silently, in an agony of fear. But tonight—

No fear, no resentment of the chirring voices in the grass, the forest clatter; tonight she knew what was to happen. Tonight she would know the shivery terror, the illicit thrill of the singing bird, but she would not be afraid. Lovely Daniel had promised to come to her. Sometime before dawn he would come to the edge of the clearing, repeat twice the call of the hoot owl. He would come to the tiny window of the out cabin, and then—

Lovely had made a wonderful plan, a credit to his half-breed shrewdness, if not to his name! It had been born of his hatred of big Jim Blind-Wolfe and nourished by a growing fever of desire for Jennie. Enough of it he had revealed to Jennie to set her heart pounding, hang a fox-fire glow in her eyes.

She undressed in the streaming light of a moon just past the half and diamond bright stars that laid a brilliant oblong on the floor in front of the open door. Standing on a warm wolf rug beside the wide home-made bed, she stretched her lithe brown body. Then, comfortably relaxed, she recalled the beginning of Lovely's clever plan; a ripple of laughter, soft, enigmatic, rose to her lips.

The beginning dated from a torrid day of midsummer. The Cherokee tribal council was meeting in the boxlike brick capitol, set among young oaks in a fenced square. In the shade, on the trampled grass of this capitol square, lounged a knot of councilmen, townsmen, gossips from the hill farms. Jim Blind-Wolfe — huge, smiling, dominating — was of the group, in which also stood Lovely Daniel. Alert, contentious, sharp of tongue, Lovely was sneering at the full-blood gospel that was being preached. Men grew restive under his jeers and mocking flings until at length Jim demanded the word. In slow, measured terms, as became a man of his impressive presence and bull-like voice, he summed up their drawn-out discussion:

"I tell you, Kee-too-wah fellows don't like this lease business. You lease your land to white man, and pretty soon you don't have any land; white man crowd you out! This here country is Eenyan (Indian) Country, set aside for Eenyans. We want to keep it always for Eenyans. Such is belief of Kee-too-wahs, and I am Kee-too-wah!"

These were the words Jim repeated when he told Jennie of what followed. He described Lovely Daniel's quick, angry rush toward him, and mimicked his sharp retort:

"Kee-too-wah fellows — hell! They think they run this here country." Jim could not reproduce the sneer that twisted the half-breed's mouth as he went on: "Kee-too-wahs are fools. White man goin' to come anyway. Jim Blind-Wolfe — huh! Biggest dam' fool of all!" He ended with an evil gesture, the sure insult, and Jim's sledgehammer fist swung smoothly against the side of his head. Lovely's body, lifted by the blow, was flung sprawling. He lay motionless.

"Jim!" cried old Spring Frog, "maybe so you kill that fellow. Bouff! — My god, I don't like."

Jim carried Lovely Daniel across the road to the porch of the National House, while young Hunt ran for Dr. Beavertail. That grave half-breed came, rolled up his sleeves, and set to work. His native skill, combined with his medical school knowledge, sufficed to bring Lovely back to consciousness by late afternoon.

Next morning, with the memory of Jim's devastating and widely advertised blow fresh in their minds, the councilmen — after much half-jesting and half-serious debate — passed a special Act and sent it to Chief Dennis for signature:

"*It shall be unlawful for Jim Blind-Wolfe to strike a man with his closed fist!*"

It was promptly signed and posted in the corridor of the capitol. Jim read it, and as he strode out into the square the thin line of his sparse mustache was lifted by a loud gust of laughter. Hailing the chief, fifty yards away, he roared:

"Hey, Dennis, must I only slap that Lovely Daniel fellow next time?" The chief met him at the center of the square. In an undertone, he undertook a friendly warning:

"You want to watch out for that Daniel fellow, Jim. You mighty nigh killed him, and — I kind of wish you had! He's bad. Bad — " the chief repeated soberly, and came closer to impress Jim by his words — "We ain't got sure proof yet, but I'm satisfied it was Lovely Daniel that waylaid Blue Logan on the Fort Gibson road and killed him."

The chief's low-toned confidences went on, and before he mounted the steps and went in to his battered old desk, he recalled:

"You have seen that Yellow Crest woman sometimes? She comes into town from the hills with stovewood and sits on her wagon, with a shawl across her face. She was a pretty young woman six years ago, wife of Looney Squirrel. This Lovely Daniel took to hanging round, and Looney caught 'em — Yellow Crest and him. You are Kee-too-wah, Jim; you know what the old fellows do to a 'singing bird'?"

"Yes," Jim admitted, "they cut off the end of her nose!"

"Yes, they punish the woman so, and — " the chief's face showed a shadow of passionate resentment — "they do nothing to the man! The old fellows, the Kee-too-wahs," he repeated, "still do that way. It was what Looney Squirrel did before he sent Yellow Crest from his cabin."

"Yes, I know," Jim assented.

"This Lovely Daniel is bad for women to know; a bad fellow for any woman to know, Jim!" The chief eyed him shrewdly, pressed his piston-like arm in friendly emphasis before he walked slowly away.

On the long drive to his clearing beside Spavinaw Creek, Jim weighed Chief Dennis's words. He thought of Jennie's fond care of Lovely Daniel's frail sister, Betsy, who was fighting a hopeless battle against tuberculosis in the cabin across the Spavinaw where she lived with Lovely.

"A bad fellow for any woman to know!" Jim repeated, with half-closed, contemplative eyes as he urged his tough pony team along the stony road. He would have to think about that. He would have to take more notice of his wife, too — that gay, slender, laughing young woman who kept his cabin, clung adoringly to him, her eyes dancing, and flashed into song with the sudden, clear burst of a red-bird in early spring —

Lovely as a menace to himself was one thing, he considered; foolishly, he refused to believe that he might be in serious danger from the half-breed; he believed that Lovely was a boaster, a coward, and that he would be afraid of the prompt vengeance of Jim's friends. But Lovely as a menace to Jennie — well, no friend would serve him here, either to warn, fearing his wrath and the tiger-swipe of his great hand, or to avenge!

In direct fashion, Jim spoke to Jennie of his encounter with the half-breed and repeated the chief's words of warning. A passing gleam of fear rounded her eyes as she listened; it changed to a gay, defiant smile when her man added:

"I think you better not go to see Betsy anymore."

"No?" she queried, then very gravely, "She is awful low, Jim, and I am her friend." She sat studying her husband's face for many minutes, turned to the pots hanging in the fireplace with a tiny, secret smile. "I am Betsy's best friend," she reiterated coaxingly.

"Well," Jim conceded, stretching his great bulk negligently, "you watch out for that fellow, her brother!"

Some days later, Jennie rode to the capitol, sought Chief Dennis, and asked:

"Is Jim in real danger from Lovely Daniel?"

"I think maybe he is in great danger, Jennie; but Jim does not agree with me on that!" The chief's slow smile was a tribute to her husband's careless bravery.

"Ah, that would make it easier for Lovely," she said to herself softly.

Jennie's thoughts drifted back to various occasions when she had visited Betsy Daniel. Sometimes, but not often, as she sat with her friend or busied herself sweeping and airing the cabin, preparing a bowl of hominy, putting on a pot of greens and bacon, stripping husks from roasting ears, helping on a patchwork quilt, Lovely would come in. He would squat, a thin handsome figure, in front of the fire, sniff eagerly at the cooking pots, rise, move restlessly about. He would speak with Jennie of his hunting; he would talk of the white men he knew at Vinita, some of whom came to the Spavinaw Hills in the late fall to chase deer with him and encourage him to become active in tribal politics. These men wished to spur him to active opposition to the reactionary full-bloods, the Kee-too-wahs, who bitterly resented white intrusion.

When Jennie was ready to leave, he would bring her pony to the door, hold his hand for her to step on as she mounted; and he would turn glittering black eyes and grinning face up to her as she gathered the reins to ride away. She had known of Yellow Crest's punishment; she knew that the full-bloods called the deceiving wife a "singing bird," with notes to lure others than her mate; and in Lovely Daniel's eyes she had read an invitation to sing!

When Jim had thrashed the half-breed, she wondered if that invitation would still hold good. The end of her wondering and weighing was a resolve to find out.

Two weeks she waited and planned before riding across Spavinaw Creek, and during that time news of Lovely Daniel drifted to her ears. He had crossed the line into Arkansas with one of the reckless Pigeon boys. They had secured whiskey, had rioted in the streets of a border town, had been chased home to the hills by peace officers. The half-breed had brought back a new pistol from Maysville, and up and down the Illinois River and among his friends on Flint Creek he had sprinkled ugly threats against Jim. In mid-August, when she knew that he was at home, Jennie rode across to Betsy.

For half an hour, as Jim Blind-Wolfe's wife made Betsy comfortable in a big chair beside the doorway and put the cabin to rights, Lovely sat on the doorstep digging at its worn surface with a pocketknife, saying nothing. Then he disappeared in the brush, to return presently with his saddle horse. At sunset, after Jennie had cleared away the early supper dishes and tucked Betsy into bed, he was waiting to ride with her. Eyes lowered, fingers nervously caressing her pony's mane, Jennie rode in silence. They crossed Spavinaw at the lonely ford, where she had often seen deer come down to drink, and went slowly up the steep, pine-covered slope. Near Jim's clearing she stopped. Without raising her eyes, she put out her hand.

"Now you go back," she half whispered. "I see you again." Lovely crowded his horse close, took her hand, muttered:

"Look up, Jennie, let me see what is in your eyes!" But she turned her head away and answered:

"I am afraid of you, Lovely—goodbye." She pressed his supple, eager fingers, urged her pony forward. He dared not pursue, and turned back; at the ford he whooped, uttering the primitive burst of sound that expressed for him hatred, lust, exultation. His wildcat eyes glowed. Back at his cabin, when he had loosed his hobbled horse to browse in the brush, he sat in the doorway conjuring up pictures of the evil he meant to do Jim Blind-Wolfe and his young and foolish wife. First, he would make Jennie a sinister, branded outcast in the sight of the tribe, and then after Jim had tasted that bitterness he would lay for him. There would be a shot. Someone would find him a stiffening corpse, beside a lonely road! Until long after the new moon had sunk he sat, at times crooning fragments of old Cherokee songs, or flinging an occasional gay word to Betsy.

At Jennie's next visit, Betsy sent her brother to the Eucha settlement store for medicine. He had scarcely gone when Betsy called Jennie to her side, looking searchingly into her face.

"You are very dear to me, Jennie," she said in Cherokee, her hand stroking the other's face, fever-glowing eyes and a strain of telltale red on her thin cheeks emphasizing her anxiety. "Will you promise me that you will be wise, and careful—with Lovely? I do not want to lose you for the little time left to me!"

Jennie put her arm about her friend's wasted shoulders and leaned to whisper:

"My sister, you will not lose me."

"But Lovely—he is wild—he is Jim Blind-Wolfe's enemy—and I am afraid." Her words were hesitant but suggestive.

"You are my friend," Jennie assured her quickly. "What I do will be best for both of us—and Lovely too! You will trust me?"

Betsy nodded, fell quiet under Jennie's gentle caresses.

Again Lovely rode across the ford with Jennie, rode close, begging for the promise that seemed to hang upon her lips; and before they parted she gave it, in a soft rush of speech:

"That will be hard, what you ask, Lovely, but sometime when Jim is not with me I will let you know!" The half-breed's whoop at the ford punctuated a snatch of song.

Jennie was committed now. She quieted Jim's vague uneasiness at her visits to the cabin, by emphasizing Betsy's need of her care and asserting that Lovely's behavior was correct. By cunning degrees, she led the half-breed to reveal his plan for squaring accounts with her husband — that is, the part involving Jim's assassination. To Lovely's passionate outburst of hate she replied crooningly:

"Yes, I know. He hurt you, Lovely!"

By late August, when dying summer had released upon the night myriad insect sounds, above whose clamorous fiddling and chirring casual noises were hard to distinguish, she had stirred Lovely to a very frenzy of impatience. More than the desire of vengeance drew him now. He wanted Jennie for herself. He had sworn to come to her when the new moon was as wide, at the center of its crescent, as the red ribbon that bound her hair. He would come to the edge of the clearing sometime before dawn — Jim would be asleep — and twice he would utter the hoot owl's cry. She must slip out to him. If she did not, he swore that he would cross the clearing cat-footedly, open the door very slowly and quietly, come in, and shoot Jim as he lay asleep. And then —

"Oh no, not blood!" she cried, fighting desperately to alter his determination. He raved, boasted. She held out, pleading:

"No, no, not blood, in my sight! Wait until I come to you." As he persisted, she threatened: "If I hear you coming to the door, I will scream and Jim will rise up and kill you!"

Night after night she lay, sleeping fitfully, listening for the double owl cry, straining her ears to catch, above the high-pitched monotone of the insects' singing, the sound of footsteps in the dead grass. Twice during that time of waiting she visited Betsy and fought off Lovely's importunate advances with the warning:

"It must be safe — no blood. I will let you know."

The moon had filled its crescent, was swelling to fullness, before the opportunity Jennie had waited for arrived. Then Jim told her of the coming secret council in his cabin of the leaders of the Kee-too-wahs. They would eat supper and talk all night. She would prepare a pot of coffee for them, set it beside the fire, and go to sleep in the out cabin. She weighed the peril, decided, and slipped across to Spavinaw to tell Lovely Daniel:

"Come to the out cabin before dawn, as you have said. Come to the little window that looks toward the creek. Tap, and I will open and say if all is safe." In a quick upward glance from her lowered eyes, Jennie saw the half-breed's grin of triumph. Trembling, she sent him back to the ford and his whooping rush up the opposite slope. In his eyes she had read — love of her? Yes; and death for Jim! Lovely's hatred of the giant who had all but killed him with a blow of his fist had become a crackling blaze in his breast.

Ten days of strain and nights of broken sleep had fined the edges of Jennie's nerves. She lay quite wide awake now, certain of herself, confident, and now she did not care about the foolish insect noises. She leaned out of bed to place her deerskin slippers at just the spot she desired to have them and hang a warm shawl over a chair where she could seize it with one movement of her hand. Fingers clasped behind her head, she lay watching a little square of starlit and moonlit sky through the window.

A rooster's crowing announced midnight; a little later she heard Jim's heavy step on the east porch of the main cabin as he emerged to sniff the fresh air, and then the slam of the door as he went in; she was aware of the pleasantly nipping coolness of the period before daybreak; again there was a stir on the east porch.

Cold, passionless men's business Jim and his three companions were busy about now. Impersonal, free from individual angers, jealousies, attachments, they sat, like remote, secret gods, in judgment on the conduct of a community, the policy of a tribe. Kee-too-wah tradition, the old conception of tribal integrity, the clean spirit of ancestors who had successfully fought against race deterioration and the decay of morale in the long years of contact with the whites in Georgia and Tennessee — these were their preoccupations. They harked back to legendary days, to the very beginning, when the Great Spirit had handed over to the tribe a sacred fire, with the injunction to keep it burning forever; and they strove to keep alive in the minds of an easy-living, careless generation the memory of that road of Calvary over which their fathers and mothers had been driven when the then new Indian country was settled.

Jennie could understand but vaguely the purpose that dominated the four. It seemed shadowy, very different from the flaming, heart-stirring enterprise that concerned her! She lay taut-strung, like a bow made ready, thinking, feeling. Soon now, perhaps when the talk in the cabin had thinned and sleep was close to the eyelids of the four, she would hear a tapping at the window. She began to listen, to watch for a shadow at the little opening.

It came. Lovely's head and shoulders made a blur against the small luminous square; his tapping was as light as the flick of a bird's wing, insistent as the drumming of the male partridge in spring. Jennie stepped into her slippers, flung the shawl about her shoulders, flitted silently to the window.

She would not let him in at once. She knew the steps she must take in order to test his ardor, stir him to impetuous frenzy. She knew the privilege of her who turned singing bird to savor the preliminary delights of song! She pushed the tiny sliding window aside a crack and whispered:

"Who has come?" At Lovely's fatuous answer, she laughed a faint ghost laugh and breathed, "Why have you come?" Then, before he could speak, "No, don't tell me; wait and let me talk with you here for a time."

In throaty whispers, only half coherent, the man pressed his suit. Jennie went silent in the midst of his jumbled speeches, so stirred by inner turmoil that she scarcely heard his pleading. Then her trembling voice insisted:

"You must wait a little while longer, Lovely. I am afraid. But I will let you come in before it is light. I promise!" Her shawl was drawn across her face, and as she put timid fingers in his reaching hand he felt them shake. Again, in maddening repetition, she sang the refrain:

"Wait; and tell me once more what it is that you and I will do after tonight. Wait a little. I will not be afraid to let you in after a time." When he threatened to leave the window and go round to the door, she protested in great agitation:

"No, no. The bar is up against you, and if you rattle the door Jim will hear. He will come and spoil everything. He would — " her voice all but faded in her throat — "he would kill you, Lovely!"

At length the last note of the singing bird had been sounded, and Jennie answered to Lovely's frantic entreaty:

"Come now to the door swiftly and silently, in bare feet. Leave your coat there." She pointed, and stood breathless, watching his movements. He dropped shoes, coat, belt, and pistol holster in a heap. With a gasp of relief, she ran to unbar the door.

"Quick!" she urged, pulling him into the blinding darkness. Then, close to his ear, "wait for me here!" She flashed by him, stepped through the doorway, closed him in, and reached up to trip the stout greased bar that she had prepared. It slid noiselessly across to engage iron stirrups fixed in the heavy door and the massive logs of the door frame. Clasping her shawl tightly about her body, she ran to the cabin where Jim and his three friends sat in silence, cross-legged in front of the fireplace. She opened the door and called:

"Jim!" He jerked his head up, rose. "Don't be troubled," she told the others. "Jim will be back soon." She shut the door as the great bulk of her husband emerged.

"Quick, Jim, come with me." She seized his big paw and dragged at it. "Quick! quick!" He followed at a lumbering trot, dazed and uttering fragments of questions. To the back of the out cabin she led him, ran to the dark heap of Lovely Daniel's clothes, seized belt, holster, and pistol and thrust them into Jim's hands.

"Here, what's this!" he bellowed. Inside there was the sound of bare feet rushing across the floor, an ineffectual yank at the door, a snarl of disappointed rage — then silence.

"Jim!" His wife was on tiptoe in the effort to bring her lips nearer to his ear.

"In there is Lovely Daniel. He came to kill you, Jim — Listen, Jim; he came to kill you, do you understand? I knew why he was coming and I — I made him believe I was a — a singing bird, Jim! And he came to me first. But I did not, Jim — I put down the outside bar that I had fixed, as soon as he came in, and ran to you. Come and see. Come and see how I fixed it." She pulled him round to the door, showed him the bar firm in its place. "See, I fixed it so to trap him. You see, Jim?"

A faint glimmer of daylight had come, and big Jim stooped to look into the shining eyes of his wife. His gaze was like a downthrust knife, cutting clean and deep into her soul. It found there only a turbulent fear for him, a sunburst of adoration that excited in him a surge of primitive joy. He came erect.

"Ah, you Lovely Daniel!" he shouted savagely. "You try to make singing bird out of my wife!" He broke into the old Cherokee killer's dread warning, the wild turkey's gobble.

With his hand on the door, and before he could lift the bar, he saw his friends emerge from the main cabin. Old Spring Frog peered round the corner from the east porch. He had heard the turkey gobbler signal! Jim thought swiftly; these men must not know that Lovely Daniel was in the out cabin, where his wife had slept. In a voice forced to calmness, he called to Spring Frog:

"I just now hear a big old gobbler, yonder." He pointed across the clearing toward the creek. The three returned to their places in front of the fire.

Jim flung up the outer bar, swung the door wide, and struck aside the knife-armed hand that leaped toward his breast. The weapon dropped, and Jim grabbed Lovely by the shirt to drag him forth.

"Put on your clothes," he ordered. With one hand helpless from the force of Jim's blow, the half-breed made slow progress with his dressing, and Jim had time to think, to make a little plan of his own. With shawl drawn closely about her body and over her head, Jennie stood waiting at the corner of the out cabin, watching the dawn change from gray to pink-shot silver.

Dressed, Lovely Daniel stood still, in a sort of frozen apathy, awaiting he wondered what terrible retribution. Jim grasped his arm, turned his head to speak to Jennie:

"Stay in here until I come." She disappeared into the shadowy cabin, closed the door, ran to crouch against the thick pillow and the rude headboard of the bed — and waited.

Jim led the half-breed round to the east porch of the main cabin, opened the door and thrust him into view of his friends. They looked up, curious, expectant.

"Ah," muttered Old Spring Frog, "I did hear what I heard!" — Jim's warning gobble.

"This fellow — " Jim shoved Lovely Daniel close to the cross-legged group—"come to kill me. My wife, she hear him coming and she run to tell me just now." He fell silent, waited for a minute, then:

"You know this fellow, what I done to him. You know this fellow, how he kill Blue Logan, how he make Yellow Crest outcast woman, how he make Looney Squirrel a man ashamed—We get rid of this fellow?" The last words were more a statement than a question, but his friends nodded assent.

"Let that be done." Old Spring Frog, staunch Kee-too-wah defender of Indian probity, made a sign; it was repeated by Panther and The Miller. The three rose to stand beside Jim Blind-Wolfe. Sure of his friends now, Jim's face framed a smile, a kind of savage radiance. He spoke rapidly for a minute, reached for the brown whiskey jug that was a blob of darkness on the wide, lighted hearth—the jug from which the four had drunk sparingly throughout the night. Still smiling, he handed it to the half-breed.

"This fellow like whiskey—drink!" Lovely Daniel took the jug, tilted it, and drank deep, the Adam's apple in his lean throat working rhythmically as he gulped the raw, hot liquor. When at last he removed the jug from his lips, he shook it to show how little remained. They would not say that he had been afraid to drink! Jim's smile turned to a low laugh as he spoke to his friends:

"I take this fellow outside now; you wait here for me few minutes."

The two stepped out to the east porch, facing a fast-mounting radiance that presaged the coming of sunrise. Jim carried the half-breed's pistol. He had Lovely Daniel to the end of the porch; they stood in silence, Jim's eyes fixed on the other's face. At the edge of the clearing they heard a crow's awakening "caw! caw!" and the jarring call of a jaybird.

Jim spoke musingly, earnestly:

"Listen, Lovely Daniel: If you want to do that, you can go away from here—clear away from all Cherokee people, and I will not kill you!" Jim's stunning speech hung suspended, and Lovely's eyes sought his face; he resumed: "If you go away, it must be for all time. You must be outcast always. You try to come back, Kee-too-wah will know and I will then kill you. You know that?" The other nodded somberly. Jim spoke again, his gaze boring into eyes that wavered. "But I don't think you want to go away, like that, to stay always, lost man. Well, then?

"Listen, I will tell you one other way. Like this, Lovely Daniel—you can go up yonder, if you are brave man"—solemnly Jim pointed to the crimson-streaked sky—"on the back of the sun! Old Cherokee folks tell about how Eenyans go home to Great Spirit on the back of the sun. I don't know; maybe so; you can try. You try?" His face had become stern now, and menacing; he bent close to peer into the drink-flushed face of the half-breed.

Lovely Daniel weighed the alternatives swiftly. Reeling, aflame with the fiery liquid he had drunk, his mind seized upon Jim's suggestion.

"I go with the sun!" he cried, swaying toward the edge of the porch. Boastfully, exultantly, he demanded, "Give me my gun." Jim handed him the pistol, stepped backwards noiselessly, his eyes holding Lovely. His hand on the latch, he stopped.

Lovely Daniel's uninjured hand, loosely gripping the pistol, hung at his side as he watched the full daylight spread down to the edge of the clearing. Out of some deep, long-hidden spring of memory rose a fragment of wild song, a chant of death. It mounted to a fervid burst, as the sharp red edge of the sun appeared; it ended in a triumphant whoop—and the roar of the pistol, pressed against his temple, sent a perching crow whirling upwards with a startled "caw!"

Jim stepped inside.

"What was that?" Spring Frog questioned perfunctorily.

"Lovely Daniel was making answer," Jim responded enigmatically.

"Making answer? To what?"

"Oh, a singing bird, I think—early morning singing bird, I think." He looked into the faces of his friends until he knew that they understood, then turned to go out. He lingered to say:

"If you fellows go look out for that which was Lovely Daniel, I get my wife to come and cook breakfast for us."

He found Jennie still crouched on the bed, hands still clapped tight against her ears. He gathered her into his arms, a vast tenderness and a fierce pride in her courage thrilling through him. With her face buried beneath his cheek and her arms tight about his neck, he sat on the bed and whispered:

"All is well now, all is well!" Her convulsive hold on him tightened.

"Oh, my Jim!" she breathed fiercely and, after a minute, "I can go now and care for Betsy without fear."

"Yes." Jim's eyes sought the brilliant oblong of daylight that was the doorway, and his voice was tender and solemn as he added:

"You can go to Betsy now, and tell her that Lovely went home without fear, on the back of the sun. I think she will understand what you say — Pretty soon you come and cook breakfast?"

"Pretty soon, I come," she echoed and, shivering, settled even closer to the great bulk of her husband.

« PART THREE »

Essays

Cherokee Migration[1]

IN ACCORDANCE with the policy of the United States in dealing with the Indians, and in pursuance of treaty stipulations entered into with a small fragment of the tribe, it was determined by the general government in 1838 to remove the Cherokees from the lands occupied by them in Georgia, Alabama, North Carolina, and Tennessee.[2] Lands west of the Mississippi, within the boundaries of the present Indian Territory, had been set aside for them, and a considerable number of their brethren had voluntarily migrated to the wild new country in response to inducements held out to them by the treaty of 1817.[3]

On April 10, 1838, General Winfield Scott was commissioned to proceed to the Cherokee country and put in motion the whole tribe, amounting to more than fifteen thousand persons, toward the new reservation west of the Mississippi, "peaceably if he could, forcibly if he must."

In 1802 Georgia had obtained from the United States an agreement to extinguish, as soon as it could be done by treaty stipulation, the title to all Indian lands held within the state; and from 1785 seventeen separate treaties had been concluded, thirteen of which followed the agreement with

Georgia and provided for the cession of tribal lands. Georgia professed an utter inability ever to assimilate a body of Indians, declaring that she would never rest until they had been sent out of her boundaries. It was this hostility that spurred the general government to hasten the removal.

Cattle and Horses

In spite of Georgia's claim, an agent of the War Department, as early as 1825, reported, after an extended tour in the Cherokee country, that numberless herds of cattle grazed upon their extensive plains; horses were numerous, many and extensive flocks of sheep, goats, and swine covered the hills and valleys; the climate was healthy and delicious, and the winters were mild; the soil of the valleys and plains was rich and produced corn, tobacco, cotton, wheat, oats, indigo, and potatoes; considerable trade was carried on with the neighboring states, much cotton being exported in boats of their own to New Orleans; apple and peach orchards were quite common; much attention was paid to the cultivation of gardens; butter and cheese of their own manufacture were seen upon many of their tables; public roads were numerous in the Nation and supplied at convenient distances with houses of entertainment kept by the natives; many and flourishing villages dotted the country, cotton and wool cloths were manufactured by the women and homemade blankets were very common; almost every family grew sufficient cotton for its own consumption; industry and commercial enterprise were extending themselves throughout the Nation; nearly all of the merchants were Cherokees; the population was rapidly increasing, a census just taken showing 13,563 native citizens, 147 white men and 73 white women who had intermarried with the Cherokees, and 1,277 slaves; schools were increasing every year, and indolence was strongly discountenanced; the Nation had no debt, and the revenue was in a flourishing condition; a printing press was soon to be established, where their own and the English language were to appear side by side in newspapers and books; and a national library and museum were in contemplation. These were the people whom Georgia held in contempt; and this the Arcadia that General Scott was sent in 1838 to destroy.

Stationed Forces

Prudently, Scott stationed his forces—a regiment of artillery, one of infantry, six companies of dragoons, and four thousand volunteers from Georgia and Tennessee—in the passes of the Smoky Mountains, occupying every available fastness and point of strategic advantage. Then he sent out an address to the Indians, advising them to come voluntarily into camp at Ross's or Gunter's landing on the Hiwasse River. In part, he wrote:

"Cherokees: The President of the United States has sent me, with a powerful army, to cause you, in obedience to the treaty of 1835, to join that part of your people who are already established in prosperity on the other side of the Mississippi. Unhappily, the two years which were allowed for the purpose you have suffered to pass away without following and without making any preparation to follow, and now . . . the migration must be commenced in haste, but I hope, without disorder. . . . The full moon of May is already on the wane, and before another shall have passed away, every Cherokee man, woman, and child . . . must be in motion to join their brethren in the far west.

"I am an old warrior, and have been present at many a scene of slaughter," General Scott added feelingly, "but spare me, I beseech you, the horror of witnessing the destruction of the Cherokees."

Ross enrolled for removal in October the names of 13,149 persons. Captain Stevenson, the agent who received them on their arrival [in the] West, accounted for 11,504, and the disbursing officer, Captain Page, paid Ross for the removal of 11,721. That is the brief story of their losses. Two hundred went down with the sinking of a rickety old steamer in the Mississippi; the rest of that list of 1,428 unaccounted for either died on the road, were lost in accidental upsettings of boats, or deserted to make their way back to their old homes in the Georgia hills and in the mountains of Tennessee.[4]

Immediately upon the arrival of the Eastern Cherokees in the Indian Territory, violent quarrels broke out between the two sections of the tribe. Three leaders of the "Treaty" party—Major Ridge, John Ridge, and Boudinot—who had moved west two years before—were murdered by the Ross faction, and it required all the influence that Ross and the more level-headed leaders could command to effect a formal unification of the Eastern and Western Cherokees in 1859.

Final Settlement

Peace finally settled upon the nation, and the progress toward the higher civilization resumed. Then the civil war came on to devastate their country and set them back another ten years in the race. But the power to recuperate, the habit of industry enabled them to meet even this catastrophe with a certain philosophical calm. They have brought their country up to a high state of cultivation; they have developed anew schools, churches, and printing presses; they have encouraged industries to such an extent that the traveler today will be puzzled to know where the Kansas, Missouri, or Arkansas boundaries cease and the Cherokee country begins.

The general government now considers the tribe fit for citizenship. The long series of negotiations, during which the Cherokees have, by various treaties, ceded 81,000,000 acres of land to the United States, and retain of their Western reservation but 5,100,000 acres, will soon be concluded forever. Indian Territory is quite ready and fit for statehood. The 35,000 Cherokee citizens recognize the impracticability of maintaining longer a separate government, and are seeking now only to obtain a wise and just basis for settling their long last account with their Great Father at Washington.

The President and the Indian

RICH OPPORTUNITY FOR THE RED MAN[5]

PRESIDENT ROOSEVELT'S word about the Indians in his message to Congress is an exceedingly intelligent one.[6] In the necessarily limited space at command for a discussion of their affairs he hints at an unusual familiarity with Indian needs and a wise sympathy for their shortcomings. He has an intimate firsthand knowledge of them; as a young man he was made a special commissioner to visit and report upon a number of Indian schools in the Midwest; as a rancher he lived in neighborly proximity to some of the reservations; as a soldier he recruited a considerable part of his regiment from among them; and as governor of New York he took up the problem insofar as it related to those tribes whose reservations are within the state.[7]

"In portions of the Indian Territory," says President Roosevelt, "the mixture of blood has gone at the same time with progress in wealth and education, so that there are plenty of men with varying degrees of purity of Indian blood who are absolutely indistinguishable in point of social, political and economic ability from their white associates." Then the problem is working itself out in an interesting way; and there the government has labored long to make the transition from tribal superstition and prejudice to national citizenship as smooth as possible.

As early as 1893, when the "Dawes Commission" was created to treat with the Five Tribes, the proportion of white residents to citizens, even including those by adoption and of the thinnest dilution of Indian blood, was greater than two to one. These aliens, having no standing under tribal jurisdiction, had begun to complain of the crudity and inefficiency of Indian courts. They besought the protection of the United States court, and one was established at Muscogee. Under the new arrangement, all matters in dispute between citizens and noncitizens had to be taken to this newly created district court.[8]

Then the question began to be agitated by the lawyers who flocked in to get their share of business at the new court — and the movement had substantial backing in the tribes — of abandoning entirely the Indian courts, and extending the jurisdiction of the United States tribunal over all aliens and citizens. Naturally, there was much opposition from the full-bloods and the Indian lawyers. That was a long fight, but it was won in 1898 by the inevitable winners, those who favored the abolition of Indian courts. In a surprisingly short time, the new system was working smoothly. The memory of the tribal courts [having] faded, the Indian lawyer took up the practice in the new court successfully.

Meanwhile, the commission from Washington was working in the territory, going from tribe to tribe, hearing objections and urging the giving up of tribal organizations. "Why not," they asked, in substance, "give up the pretense of government and allot your land, join Oklahoma, and become a territory until such time as you are ready for statehood?"

The answers at first were short and decided: "The country belongs to us, and we don't want to make any change in our method of holding it." Patiently the commission pointed out that the tribes were wrong in thinking they could keep to themselves, holding rich country unproductive that the white homekeepers would be glad to use. It was manifestly unfair, they said, to tie up from 160 acres of land for every man, woman, and child of Indian blood or citizenship when a whole white family might live on a single share. At the same time it was pointed out that the whites were pouring into the country, willy-nilly, and, as lessees or citizens, using the greater part of the land.

Year after year the commission went about from town to town among the tribes, arguing and exhorting. But nothing seemed likely to come of their efforts, though the persistent purpose of the government was revealed. Then, in response to urging from Washington, the commission stated plainly that the tribes must come to some agreement, as the government had determined to end their existence, as separate and utterly anomalous political organizations.

Following this informal ukase, the more hotheaded among the native leaders talked somewhat vaingloriously of armed opposition, hinting at possible martyrdom to ancient rights. A certain Cherokee secret society was credited with the actual beginning of the arming and organizing of a resisting force.[9]

The magnitude of the work ahead of them may well have caused impatience among the commission's members. In a review of the work recently published, this adjusting commission spoke of the talks in this way:

"Instead of an arid Western plain occupied by the savage of tradition, as many suppose, the commission found a territory not greatly smaller than the state of Maine, rich in mineral and agricultural resources and invaluable timber; a country which has been occupied and cultivated for over half a century, whose fertile valleys yielded bountiful harvests of southern products, and on whose prairies grazed a quarter of a million cattle yearly; where cities had sprung up; through which railroads had been constructed; and where five distinct modern governments existed, independent of the sovereignty of the United States.

"For diversity, the social and political conditions found here were unexampled. Thousands of white children without the meanest of educational advantages, yet no one of the nations without an institution of learning that would have been a credit to a more advanced civilization; men of Indian blood whose genius would have adorned the halls of Congress or challenged admiration in the business world—high-minded, able, and politic; within the tribes, in no small numbers, those who, when in normal conditions, had scarcely sufficient intelligence to realize or express the ordinary waste of man."

So it was throughout—saintly women and God-fearing, honest men knocking elbows with the worst criminals in the whole world. Intense industrial activity was found bordering upon utter indolence and primitive makeshifts. For the last half dozen years Ardmore, a town in the Chickasaw Nation, has been known as the greatest primary cotton market in the United States. This means that more cotton is hauled there in wagons than to any other town. During this same period some of the worst gangs of outlaws that ever ravaged a country have found refuge in that nation.

Vinita, in the Cherokee Nation, has long been one of the country's leading cattle-shipping towns, and its neighbor, Claremore, forty miles west, called a statehood convention for December 8 this year.[10] In that same Cherokee country, hidden in the rough, flinty hills that border Arkansas, live full-bloods who cannot talk English and who still gain a precarious livelihood by hunting.

From 1893 to 1902 the commission has labored. Its members have seen the Indian population in the Territory rise to a total of more than 80,000, while more than 350,000 whites have settled within its boundaries. In 1898 the Choctaws and Chickasaws concluded a treaty with the commission, a year after the small Seminole Nation had treated. In August 1902 the Cherokees and Creeks finally agreed to give up tribal existence as soon as the details of allotment and rearrangement could be completed.

The commission's work, however, is by no means completed. Puzzling questions remain to be settled. A work of great magnitude that is not yet finished is the making up of the tribal rolls. Here have been met fraud, ignorance, and hindrances. Citizenship has come to have a tangible commercial value, where a citizen is likely to come into possession of from one hundred to five hundred acres of land, and those whites who have long been settled in the Territory are reluctant to depart. Some of them have brazenly claimed citizenship and have attempted to prove it. The freed slaves of Indians were given citizenship in the tribes after the civil war, and now some hundreds of negroes are trying hard to prove that their parents were freedmen under the citizenship provision.

Besides this, there are grave matters connected with the establishment of a territorial government to be established. What shall be done with the valuable land and asphalt deposits now held and leased by the tribes acting as commercial organizations? What embargo shall be laid on the sale of the lands when they are transferred to the individual owners? How are the school and taxation systems to be rearranged to serve both Indians and whites to best advantage? Supposing the Indian Territory and Oklahoma to be included in one Territory, how are the peculiar needs of those who still live in the old full-blood style to be met? And where is the seat of territorial government to be established? Will the imposition of a territorial government at the present time result in forcing these tribes toward United States citizenship too fast and result, as the president has wisely warned, in preventing their going forward at all?

The leaven of education is spreading among the tribes. Graduates of the great government schools, and mixed-bloods who have penetrated to the universities are taking their places as leaders in the movement toward amalgamation. Born to the Indian prejudice against white influence and ways, then trained to see the point of view of the whites in their colleges and universities, these men are standing by eager to help forward any movement that tends to advance their people toward economic independence. To them the president looks for material aid and practical suggestions. The time is past when the Carlisle graduate is permitted to go back to his people and discard sack suit, derby hat, and patent leathers for the blanket, feathers, and moccasins.

The Outlook for the Indian[11]

> The first and most important step towards the absorption of the Indian is to teach him to earn his living.
>
> PRESIDENT ROOSEVELT, in his last message to Congress

FORTUNATELY FOR the white race that has extended our frontiers, the "bad" Indian has long ago ceased to exist; fortunately for the Indian who must still face the problem of living, the time has passed when the lawless, cynical white man can appropriate his reservations with impunity and have him "suppressed" when he begins to ask for justice. We are far enough away from the crunching of cavalry hoofs and the rallying yell of warriors to see that there are two sides to the question. Only the most rabid and ignorant enemies of the Indian still maintain that unfortunate, cynical doctrine that "the only good Indian is a dead Indian." And only the most obstinate of our Indians still rail against the domination of the white race.

It is a hopeful fact that the leaders among the various societies formed to protect and befriend the Indian have substituted personal knowledge and close observation for an enthusiastic but ignorant sympathy. They have come to understand that an Indian is a human being with a long and significant history behind him, with a very well-worked-out moral law, and with a tradition of living that is not easy to give up. Likewise, the Indian has come to understand that the white man has a tradition of living to maintain and that it is not altogether greed and hatred that have sent him forward across frontiers. Tolerance increases.

Now that the races have come to know each other better and have laid aside the old distrust and fear, we hear those who are qualified to speak with authority say that the next inevitable step is the complete absorption of the Indian into the white race, which will result in an ultimate amalgamation of the two. This is an idea that is worth considering. The sooner all the foolish talk about the impossibility of uniting the two people ceases, the better.

Commissioner Jones, in a recent report, calls attention to the fact that the nation has expended over a billion dollars in subduing and attempting to educate the Indians, only to learn of the absolute failure of the "ration system" as a device for making useful or productive citizens of them. That the policy of feeding the Indian at public expense on reservations was the outgrowth of a mistaken philanthropy and was foolish in that it exempted the Indian from the natural and inexorable law that man must earn his living by labor of some kind is now universally recognized. How to rectify the errors growing out of this policy and supplant it by a system that would ultimately induce the Indian to put his hand to the plow is a problem that has engaged the study and activity of Commissioner Jones since his induction into office.

The most radical change inaugurated was the departure from the custom of dealing with the tribe to that of dealing with the individual. The results attending this change, according to Commissioner Jones, have been most gratifying. The manhood of the Indian is appealed to, and he is taught self-reliance and self-respect. As a result of this policy, over twelve thousand have been dropped from the ration roll, being wholly self-supporting, and others not yet self-supporting have been put to work. The Indians will become self-supporting, and will adapt themselves to their white neighbors' way of life — there is no doubt of it. But they are not yet ready for the struggle on equal terms; they must be protected from speculators and land-grabbers; they must be led to see what economic independence really means; and their education must be adapted to the needs of their future life. Think of them how we will, we cannot close our eyes to the fact that they are still children, with all of the child's ignorance of modern life, with the child's helplessness in practical affairs. For a little longer the "Great Father" at Washington must direct them.

How constant must be the "Great Father's" vigilance is shown almost every day. It is interesting to compare a part of Mr. Hamlin Garland's last novel, *The Captain of the Gray Horse Troop*, with the story of the Standing Rock cattle leases.[12] In the course of the contest over the Standing Rock land leases, now more than a year ago, it became necessary for the Indians to send a delegation of Sioux chiefs to Washington, where, after waiting two weeks, they met the Senate committee on Indian Affairs. They convinced the senators that the cattlemen's contract, if carried out, would amount to robbery, and would delay the time when the tribe could take up the work of grazing and farming on their own account. The publicity given the matter by the visit of the chiefs led to its being referred directly to President Roosevelt, who sent Dr. George Bird Grinnell[13] to Standing Rock. The matter gained wide publicity, and it is not improbable that the disclosures made by the Grinnell report will result in the appointment of another agent at Standing Rock. Here is Mr. Garland's tale worked out in actual life almost before the book was off the press. And, as in the novel, there is a distinctly hopeful ending to the story. Everywhere it is true that eternal vigilance is still necessary to ensure the Indians a chance even to earn a living. Moreover, they must be taught how to work. It is not yet enough to say, "Here are lands well protected and productive: take them and develop their resources." The Indians do not know how to do it, and they must learn.

The founders of the new Sherman Institute at Riverside, California, have set an excellent example.[14] Here a farm of one hundred acres has been purchased, all under irrigation; ample buildings have been erected to accommodate over three hundred children from the Pacific Coast tribes and those in the Southwest where irrigation must be resorted to in order to raise crops. The idea is to train them in this peculiar method so that the graduates may return to their people equipped for the task of turning deserts into rich fields with the aid of precious water. For the girls there is to be instruction in lace making, dressmaking, fine needlework, basketry, plain sewing, and housework—with all that ranch housekeeping implies. And the peculiar value of an institution like this is that its members can go out of the school to the reservation and take up the work of making a living without readjusting themselves to different methods of work from those prevailing at the training school in a faraway state. If a man is to grow alfalfa to make his land yield a living he is not likely to appreciate half a dozen years of instruction in the planting and cultivation of corn and cotton. For this reason the neighborhood school for industrial training is of the greatest value.

In the Indian Territory, where, for more than twenty years, the tribes have come into competition with the whites as farmers, stock-raisers, teachers, lawyers, and tradesmen, the process of absorption is far advanced and education has also advanced rapidly. The Cherokees maintain three boarding schools and one colored high school. The enrollment in these four schools is something under five hundred, and the expense of maintaining them amounts to about $140 a year per capita. For seven months in the twelve, 124 day (or neighborhood) schools, are run, with an average enrollment of 2,200, at a cost of about $14 per capita. It is estimated that there are some 8,300 children of school age in the tribe. In the Creek Nation, 9 boarding schools and 55 neighborhood schools are maintained, with an average attendance of over 1,500. The figures for the Choctaw Nation show 6 boarding and 110 day schools, with an enrollment of more than 2,100. Five academies and 17 primary schools with an approximate enrollment of 850 are supported by the Chickasaw Indians.

Mere figures, of course, have little meaning in themselves, but when it is known that all of these children are coming out of the schools to enter upon a course of life that brings them into contact with the whites — many of the girls to become the wives of white men — they assume importance. They mean that the Indian problem, so far as the tribes of the Territory are concerned, is being solved by extinguishing the Indian as a distinctive individual and merging him with his white neighbors and competitors. They mean that this process is going on more and more rapidly, and that when the Territory is brought into the ranks of the states, Indians and whites alike will be ready to take up the everyday work of a rich and prosperous commonwealth and do it successfully. And that, after all, is the problem in every tribe.

Friends of the Indian[15]

AT LAST year's "Lake Mohonk Conference of Friends of the Indian and Other Dependent Peoples," Mr. Bonaparte quoted a naval officer as once declaring that "the service would never be worth a —— until all the well-meaning people in it had been hanged."[16] He hinted that something of the same tenor might have been said with equal justice of the activity of champions of the Indian who are merely well-meaning. Knowledge and discretion in those who have undertaken unofficially to influence the conduct of Indian affairs would have tempered their zeal usefully in the years when service was most needed; and, though little fault can now be found with the methods and personnel of the Indian Rights Association[17] and similar bodies, there is still a too noticeable tendency to let good intentions evaporate in earnest, purposeless talk. That "court of final appeal, public opinion," has been appealed to so often that the last advocate must needs be silver-tongued indeed to rouse more than a momentary interest. The Indian Service, bad as it has been at times, has accomplished more for the disappearing natives than it has been credited with in the popular mind. It would have done still more if its critics had been inspired by accurate information and good judgment.

Suppose some well-informed, persistent friend of the Pimas in Arizona had taken up the matter of white encroachment on the tribe's water rights along the Gila River eighteen years ago.[18] Is it conceivable that he would have advised the poor Indians to take the matter to the Department of Justice? If he had done that, he would have gone contrary to the teachings of history. He might have foreseen exactly what happened last year when the district attorney in charge of the case recommended that the suit begun in 1886 be dropped on the ground of the excessive costs of pushing it to a favorable conclusion, and the impossibility of enforcing a decree "because of the varied interests involved."[19] The moral of Indian litigation against the invading settler could have been read as plainly in 1886 as in 1876 or in 1905: The Indian, "not taxed, not voting," has no real standing in the courts organized by and for the American people. The "varied interests involved" was a phrase in common use long ago to explain away apparent miscarriages of justice. Those 960 white settlers using the water from the Gila River which for generations had irrigated the Pimas' wheat fields were as confident of holding their ditches when they built them as it is in human experience to be. Why, then, did the Indians go to court and patiently watch their fields revert to desert land while the proceedings dragged along for half a generation? Simply because some well-meaning, unhanged friends advised them that they had a good case.

It is not the despairing cynic who advises the Indian, "For God's sake, get the ballot in your hands as soon as possible." Thirty years ago, a commissioner of Indian Affairs, commenting on the twenty-five years' struggle of the California Mission Indians to preserve themselves, said: "This class of Indians seems forcibly to illustrate the truth that no man has a place or a fair chance to exist under the government of the United States who has no part in it." It is such elementary considerations as this that have been overlooked by the friends of the Indian. In Congress, the final court where the cause of a dependent people is decided, the white invader has representation, and the Indian has none. Bishop Whipple, in 1863, said: "I submit to every man the question whether the time has not come for a nation to hear the cry of wrong, if not for the sake of the heathen [Indian], for the sake of the memory of our friends whose bones are bleaching on our prairies."[20] In 1877 the white settlers of the Northwest prevailed upon their representatives in

Congress to remove the small Ponca tribe of Indians from their old home in southeastern Dakota, where they had built comfortable houses and opened farms, to the Indian Territory, where in a year a third of their number died. The Ponca reservation was wanted for those troublesome Sioux who were keeping the gold hunters out of the Black Hills. The nation "heard" the cry of wrong, as uttered by Bishop Whipple; but Congress drove the Poncas from the Niobrara in obedience to the demands of a handful of constituents in Iowa, Minnesota, and Nebraska.[21]

On the whole, the Audubon movement[22] has succeeded better than that to protect the Indians. Bishop Whipple and those who meet annually at Lake Mohonk have insisted, and do insist, that the government deal with the Indians as with human beings whose rights are coextensive with those of the whites. Theoretically, their attitude is correct. Public opinion has approved them and applauded their sentiments. Practically, they have plodded along without accomplishing as much as could an obscure western member of the House of Representatives with a vote on a harbor-improvement bill to trade for a vote to dam Salt River and irrigate Grass Valley. The Indian, until he is absorbed and enfranchised, is not a "person." That was settled in California in the course of the degradation of the Mission tribes. Treaties and agreements with Indians may be abrogated at the pleasure of Congress. That was finally and formally decided by the Supreme Court in the Lone Wolf case, two years ago.[23] The attitude of the settler, at whose request every Indian removal has been made and every tribal reservation extinguished, has been plain and consistent from the beginning. It has been equally plain that the settler, with a sympathetic and industrious representative in Congress, would decide the attitude of the Indian Department.

The need for friends with discretion and detailed knowledge of the economic and political history of the tribes is, of course, obvious at this day. It should be just as obvious in the case of the other "dependent peoples" whose welfare under the guidance of our government is becoming more and more the subject of friendly discussion at Lake Mohonk. The promoter of an inter-island steamship line for the Philippines has his champion in Congress, while Secretary Taft[24] has no vote to trade, and can only offer a trip to Manila for a vote to reduce the duties on imports from the islands.

Lake Mohonk Conference[25]

THE PRESIDING officer of the twenty-third annual "Lake Mohonk Conference of Friends of the Indian and Other Dependent Peoples" in his opening speech foreshadowed the course of the discussion.

Dr. Abbott said that "we can, here at Lake Mohonk, lay before the Christian churches their opportunity and summon them to enter upon their duty." He added: "The Indians need the institutional church — the Christian school, the social settlement, the boys' club, the girls' club, the mother's club, the YWCA, the YMCA, the societies of Christian Endeavor, pure literature, and above all the living men and women carrying to them that life which always must be personally carried, which never can be impersonally sent."

This note was struck again and again in various speeches in the three sessions devoted to a discussion of the Indian. Mr. S. M. McCowan, superintendent of the Indian School at Chilocco, Okla., provoked the most earnest discussion of the conference by criticizing impatiently the government's methods of educating its wards. His gloomy picture of the adult Indians — the incorrigible Indian, fiercely opposed to sending his children to school — was declared to be unfair. Dr. Frissell of Hampton, Mr. H. B.

Peairs of Haskell Institute, and Mrs. Walter C. Roe of Mohonk Lodge at Colony, Okla., testified to the readiness of Indians of all ages to respond to the advances of educators and religious workers when they came with the true missionary spirit. The practical outcome of the discussion was the adoption of the platform agreed upon at the last session on Friday evening, October 20, of these resolutions:

We are gratified with the progress made by the government for doing away with Indian agencies and reservations. We heartily commend the effort made in the last Congress to provide for the distribution of tribal funds in accordance with recommendations made by President Roosevelt in his first annual message to Congress, and we recommend the passage by the present Congress of an act whose object shall be that sought by the Lacey Bill for the division of such funds;[26] and we farther believe that an early date should be fixed by law on or before which the registration of Indians and of their family relationships at each agency and sub-agency (already required by regulation of the Indian Office) shall be thoroughly completed, and that each Indian so registered shall then be enrolled as a shareholder of tribal property, and that no Indian child born after that date shall have a right to any share in Indian lands or Indian funds in his own name, but shall have such rights as shall be his by descent or relationship under the laws of inheritance for citizens of the state or territory where such child may reside or such lands be situated.

We strongly recommend an enactment in the early days of the coming session of Congress to provide for the continuance of existing schools in the Indian Territory.

This conference respectfully petitions Congress by legislation to pass upon the question whether any funds held in trust by the United States should be used for the support of any schools under denominational or ecclesiastical control. And the conference records its conviction that the decision repeatedly embodied in the legislation of Congress against the appropriation of any public funds for the support of such schools, should also be by law enforced against the use of Indian tribal funds of which the United States government is the trustee.

We recommend to the secretary of the interior and to Congress that such measures as are necessary be taken to make possible the admission of full-blood children of the so-called Five Civilized Tribes residing in the Indian Territory into the government Indian schools of the country.

We believe that Congress at an early date should enact legislation requiring all Indian children of school age and in good health to attend such school.

This conference expresses the hearty appreciation and approval of the very decided stand taken by the Senate of the United States at its last session in favor of the continued maintenance of prohibition in the state of which it was proposed to make Indian territory a part, and urges that there shall be no receding from the position upon prohibition then taken by the Senate.

Perhaps the most significant action, taken at the suggestion of Dr. Abbott, that the conference committed itself to regarding Indian matter was summed up in this paragraph of the platform:

The conference hereby resolves that a committee of five be appointed by the chair with power to increase their own number, with authority to issue an address to the churches on the necessity of more of Christian work among the Indians and in the Indian neighborhoods.

In accordance with this resolution, Dr. Abbott asked the Rev. Dr. William F. Slocum Jr., Dr. Merrill E. Gates, the Rev. Paul de Schweinitz, Mr. Daniel Smiley, and the Rev. Dr. Teunis Hamlin to serve on the committee.

Another committee was authorized by the conference to examine into the proposition submitted by Mr. T. H. Tibbles of Nebraska, to secure for Indian reservations where the period of protected allotments was about to expire, a government probate judge before whom should be tried all cases arising from disputes as to the heirships of Indian lands. The object of such appointment would be to frustrate the efforts of unprincipled lawyers, working in connection with county judges elected through their influence, to get possession of the Indian estates by pressing litigation and piling up costs against them. The committee, composed of Hon. Charles Andrews of Syracuse, Mr. Tibbles, and Hon. John J. Fitzgerald, members of the House of Representatives from New York, was asked to report to the conference next year.

The conference noted with gratification the rapid progress of the educational work of the government in the Philippine Islands, especially along agricultural and industrial lines, and the efforts made to further industrial progress by the building of harbor works, and the next step toward the furtherance of Philippine prosperity by the adoption of the recommendations of President Roosevelt that the United States grant free trade with the Islands.

The speeches of Mr. Robert Lincoln O'Brien of the Washington bureau of the *Boston Evening Transcript*, of Prof. Jeremiah Jenks of Cornell, of Dr. Roland P. Falkner, commissioner of education in Porto Rico, of Prof. Frank A. Hosmer of Amherst, of Prof. Jacob H. Hollander of Johns Hopkins, of Prof. C. H. Hitchcock of Dartmouth, of the Rev. Dr. Doremus Scudder of Honolulu, and others concerning the Philippines, Puerto Rico, and Hawaii were crystallized into this platform utterance:

We wish particularly to urge upon the attention of the government the wisdom of considering the difference between the civilization of all our insular territories and that of the United States, with the resulting need of giving especial heed to the recommendations of the men there in charge, even as concerns matters so important as those of forms of government, coastwise traffic, or immigration.

The need for general primary education, not only among the Indians but in our dependencies, was urged by all the speakers and agreed to by the conference, which declared that:

All those who would be of real service to the people of different races and religions with whom the events of the past decade have brought us into close political relations, should study sympathetically the national life, the history, the ideals, and the racial characteristics of those whom they would help.

The absence of Hon. Francis E. Leupp, commissioner of Indian Affairs, and of Gen. Frederick D. Grant, both of whom were to have addressed the conference, due to imperative engagements elsewhere, was regretted by the conference. Nevertheless, the attendance of the conference, which ran up to more than two hundred, was the largest in the history of the Lake Mohonk fall meetings.

The Need of Publicity in Indian Affairs[27]

YOU ARE all ready enough to act as religious instructors, teachers, and doctors, if necessary, to the Indians; now would you like to become press agent on behalf of the Indian?

I read a book published last year which went over a certain interesting period of Indian history, but which ended, I should say, about ten years ago. This book recited very graphically a series of wrongs suffered by the Indians. The Indian part of my nature boiled up when I read that book, but the white part said, "Now, that is only one side of the case; the other side ought to be presented." Then I thought of a newspaper story that had been sent to our paper by its Washington correspondent a little while before about Quanah Parker, one of the old Comanche chiefs.[28]

Parker had been extremely valuable in bringing the Comanches into friendly relations with the whites. He found himself getting on in years but without any property, and his white neighbors thought it would be a good idea to collect money to build him a house. They did this, and when the house was ready they told him, and he went to see it. "There is no furniture here," he said. They asked, "What do you want?" He replied that he wanted this and that, and added, "I want a big desk, a great big desk." "What do you want that for?" "Well," he said, "I want to go in there and sit back in my chair and put my feet up on that desk and someone will come in and knock at the door and say, 'Is this Mr. Parker?' 'Yes.' 'I want to speak to you.' And I will say, 'O, go 'way, I'm busy today.'"

Well, that story struck me as a great deal more promising than this whole book that I spoke of. It is really no use going over things that are past in our Indian history. What seems to me is required is a general knowledge of specific facts concerning the status of the Indians today.

People generally should know how the Indians are getting on and what they are doing. We who come to this conference know it, but the average person does not. Men and women still turn to Mrs. Jackson's old story and say, "That must be the truth today, *Ramona* is an authority."[29]

The average person I have in mind is the newspaper editor — there are about twenty-five thousand periodicals in the United States, and twenty-five hundred daily newspapers, practically all edited by men of ordinary intelligence, without expert knowledge of the Indian question. If anything in connection with the Indians requires comment, where do they turn? They go to the library and the first thing they think about is Mrs. Jackson's story. "Have you anything later than that?" they ask the librarian. "Yes, we have this other story." And they depend upon this material for the basis of their comment. The comment is, of course, out of date, it lacks foundation in specific facts.

If you want to become press agents, would it not be a good idea to acquaint yourself with a lot of facts? You can get many of them out of the Mohonk Conference Reports, and spread them around. The average editor is an overworked individual, without any extraordinary knowledge of Indian history, and with a very broad point of view. He would be glad to get hold of a new set of facts as a new basis for comment, which would show that the white people are not all villains in their treatment of the Indians. He is in sympathy with the whites, you know, because the average editor is a white man and believes thoroughly in his race. The facts are there; there is no trouble about that. The Indian question is nearer settlement than ever before, the development is satisfactory, and the head of the department is satisfactory, as everybody agrees in saying. But your editor, of course, cannot state this in general terms; he would like to be specific. He would like to tell about Quanah Parker, or Pleasant Porter, or W. C. Rogers, or half a dozen men down in the Indian Territory who have made fine records as tribal chiefs.[30] He would like to tell how they are going into politics, and being mentioned for senators, and all that sort of thing. If he gets these specific facts he will use them.

I have no plan to suggest as to how you shall proceed as press agents, but I think you have the spirit. I think you are perfectly willing to tell your neighbors and everybody with whom you come in contact that there are promising things to be said about the Indian, and, along with a lot still left to complain of, there is a lot of praise. Do not spare praise, do not spare blame. Be as convincing and specific as possible. Tell about an interview with somebody who comes from the field; find out what is doing at Rosebud, in Arizona, in California, remember the facts and give them to your editor. He will be very glad to use them.

Remaining Causes of Indian Discontent[31]

WHEN THE White River Utes left their reservation in Utah recently in angry protest against the government's allotment of their land, they attracted attention to a vanishing type of discontented Indian.[32]

Only one big distinctively Indian problem — the distribution of Indian Trust and Treaty Funds — remains to be settled by Congress. Others, such as irrigation for arid and semi-arid lands occupied by the tribes, the menace of tuberculosis, the supplying of good day schools, the blight of the liquor traffic, and the overreaching arm of the speculator in oil, mineral, and grazing lands, are in some measure the problems of all the West. Continued urging by the Indian Office and the friends of Indian progress is resulting in a merger of the tribesman with his white neighbors and a sinking of the reservation problem in the community problem. Nine out of ten "reservation" Indians are self-supporting. Five of these nine are working in competition with white laborers, mechanics, farmers, and stock raisers of the West. The other four are doing work, more or less well, provided by the government in place of pauperizing rations. Except for the children in government schools and the old, sick, and infirm, few Indians now live on the direct bounty of Congress.

The Indian as a landholder is familiar, but as a capitalist he is not so well known. Yet there is in the United States Treasury to the credit of some fifty-three thousand Indians of sixty tribes more than $35 million. Nearly all of this is in the form of Trust Funds, held, in varying amounts, for these tribes, only the interest being paid from year to year. The money has come from the sale of land from time to time.

When the land allotment law was passed, in 1887, it was bitterly opposed by the tribes. Later, it became a popular measure with the progressive Indians who were ambitious to distinguish themselves as individuals. This ambitious Indian wants the Trust Funds segregated so that they may be paid, in proportionate share, to every individual who is qualified to use his share. Next to the Dawes allotment law of 1887, this legislation will do most to break up the old communal life that has been nursed by the government's reservation policy. Holding vast areas of land "in common," with no opportunity to secure private ownership, made the Indians feel as if they were heirs to an estate in chancery. There was no incentive to develop a community holding; reservations were leased to cattlemen and farmers who had no interest in their ultimate improvement. Upon the allotment of tribal lands, this prop is knocked from under the Indian: the problem of getting a living becomes a personal problem.

That other prop, the tribal fund, should be removed. To illustrate: So long as a member of the Osage tribe knows that he is one of 2,000 heirs to a fund of $8,360,000, and that his proportionate share of interest at 5 percent on this tribal fund will be paid to him regularly, he feels no spur to become a producing member of his community. If it were permitted, however, to set aside Frank Corndropper's share of the $8,360,000 and pay it over when he could convince the government that he is qualified to use it, Frank Corndropper would bestir himself. His example would be followed by Fred Labadie, and by Black Eagle, and by others, until every separate account between the United States Treasury and the Osage Indians would be closed out. Until that is done, no Osage can be made to realize that he is a competitor of the white man in any vital sense.

Legislation designed to segregate Indian funds has been urged upon Congress for years. At Washington, however, the fear of opening a way for exploiters of the Indians has blocked this needed measure. The conscience of their guardian is as tender toward these wards now as it once was lethargic. Last year Representative Lacey of the House Committee on Indian Affairs introduced a bill into Congress authorizing the president in his discretion to allot tribal funds and open separate accounts with individuals. The bill was amended in the Senate to allow the president to designate individuals of a tribe who had shown the capacity to use money wisely as allottees of tribal funds. But this would leave a common fund to be divided later, and would not meet the views of the Indians' well-wishers. Unsatisfactory as the amended bill was, however, the Indian Office urged it as a first step. But the measure failed of enactment.

Certain "Treaty" funds, derived usually from "agreements to be good," the income from which is available, but the principal of which has never been appropriated by Congress, should also be capitalized and segregated. Periodical payments of interest on these funds, usually in trifling sums, serve to remind the Indian that he is still a dependent. For example, the Oneidas of Wisconsin, more than two thousand in number, are entitled to the annual payment of $1,000. The majority of them are farmers. They live well, in neat houses, and their children are at school. In no way do they require the material help of the government. Yet once a year the whole tribe is called away from home to draw forty-eight cents apiece!

Whether the yearly dole be forty-eight cents, interest on a Treaty Fund, or $350, earned by the large Osage Trust Fund, the objection to it holds. The commissioner of Indian Affairs has clearly indicated that as long as tribal funds remain undivided "the government has no way of setting free and closing the door behind any Indian who is able fully to care for his own." That the way back to idleness and dependence should be left open is a legitimate cause for complaint among the modern Indians.

Of the 51.5 million acres of land occupied by the "reservation" Indians, nearly 32 million lie within the states and territories of Arizona, New Mexico, California, Nevada, Utah, Oregon, Idaho, Wyoming, and Montana. Ten and a half million more are included in the Dakotas. In all these eleven states and territories irrigation is a vital subject, and in most it is counted upon to make whatever future lies before them. Nearly 17 million acres of Arizona's huge area are owned by Indians; not one acre in a thousand is arable without water. The same is true of the 1.7 million acres of Indian land in New

Mexico. Most of the 7.5 million acres held by the Montana tribes will not be productive without irrigation. Idaho's 950,000 acres, and Wyoming's 1.75 million acres of tribal holdings are mainly arid and semi-arid. The 10 million acres in the Dakotas include great tracts of drought-smitten land. How vital, therefore, to the modern, progressive Indian a vigorous irrigation policy is can be understood from these figures.

The white man with whom the Indian must expect to compete in the West is having his irrigation needs attended to by the government; the Reclamation Service is working at top speed, hampered only by the difficulty of getting workmen, and its plans are enlarging marvelously. But the Reclamation Service has nothing to do with putting water on Indian lands except in a half-dozen instances where a part of a reservation happens to fall within a big project. To the Indian Office is left the task of making arid Indian lands productive, and the Indian Office is severely handicapped for the task. Until two years ago only Indian funds could be used to construct irrigation works; last year and the year before, Congress appropriated $185,000 "for construction of ditches and reservoirs, purchase and use of irrigation tools and appliances, and purchase of water rights on reservations." The sum is a paltry one. It will be needed to outfit surveyors and to "begin to get ready to dig."

Thus far the government's work in supplying water to the reservations has been of a haphazard character. It has been undertaken, not primarily to make the cactus desert and the sagebrush plain blossom, but to provide work for able-bodied Indians in lieu of rations. Whole systems built under this policy have been swept away by floods. In the cases of the Mission Indians of California and the Pimas of Arizona, the Indian Office has not been able even to protect the tribesmen in their use of water that had been theirs for years. White settlers above the reservations calmly appropriated the flow that had made the Mission Indians and the Pimas prosperous and self-supporting, and the Indian Office saw these people beggared. With the best intentions in the world, the Indian Office can make only the weakest showing with its own Reclamation Service. In the last report of the commissioner of Indian Affairs, eleven separate projects for putting water on reservations are described; in but a single instance was it possible to record more than the merest beginning.

Seven years ago the agent for the Pine Ridge Sioux in South Dakota reported that the annual average death rate on the reservation was fifty-two per thousand. Last year, Dr. J. R. Walker, one of the two agency physicians, reported that this rate had been reduced to thirty-two per thousand. The difference represents a saving due to Dr. Walker's long campaign against ignorance of sanitary laws. So successful has this campaign been that last year the Indians themselves collected all but a small fraction of the money needed to publish in their native Dakotah language a pamphlet describing a clean, well-regulated home and instructing home builders in drainage and ventilation.

The change from tepee to cabin has cost scores of lives and is likely to cost thousands more. The old Indian camp was frequently changed; the wind blowing through the tents counteracted the effects of lax sanitation. When the cabin was built and the permanent home on the allotment established, the Indian did not realize the necessity for changing his habits of life. Filthy, overcrowded, overhot shanties breed tuberculosis. Ignorance of "civilized" clothes, leading to the wearing of thick garments in summer and thin garments in winter as often as the other way about, makes pneumonia a serious menace. Ignorance of the meaning of quarantine leads to epidemics that carry off a much larger percentage of victims than among the whites.

It has been impossible for the government's physicians to teach the newly housed Indian how to live. Their time is fully occupied with the urgent cases. On the Pine Ridge Reservation, for example, which is approximately the size of Connecticut, there are two doctors to look after the health of seven thousand Sioux. Neither of these has been supplied with surgical instruments; indeed, surgery, so far as the Bureau of Indian Affairs is concerned, might never have been practiced. Still, the modern Indian does not complain that doctors are scarce, for in all of the thinly settled West the doctor is a rare visitor. His just cause for discontent is that he has been urged to build a house and wear "store clothes" without being told how to live under a roof and save woolen underclothes for cold weather. Agents, agency physicians, school superintendents, and field matrons continue to send in alarming reports, showing the spread of the "white plague" among the tribes. They emphasize the importance of a campaign of instruction, and they point out the immediate need of a sanitarium and school in the Southwest where all consumptive Indians, adults and children, may be sent.

It is important, if the "white man's West" and the Indian's West are to merge, that the children of Indian parents shall be educated, wherever possible, in the same schools with white boys and girls. A few of the progressive men in the tribes realize this, though the average Indian does not. From reports made to the bureau at Washington it is found that about 450 public schools are either on reservations or near enough to permit Indian children to attend. In case a public school takes a reservation pupil, the government agrees to pay to the county authorities the proportionate cost of its teaching. Last year, however, only ninety-four contracts of this kind were made — ninety-four Indian children enrolled in the common public schools out of a total, in government, mission, and non-reservation contract schools, of 29,500. To the Indian's own indifference this small showing is mainly due, but there exists in the West, besides, a strong prejudice against seating an Indian child beside a white child.

The westerner's aversion to the reservation pupil is unfortunate. It discourages the newer type of Indian, for no one sees clearer than he the need for beginning the process of merger at the earliest possible moment. He has accepted in good faith the doctrine that his tribal life must be changed, that he must become in every sense a competitor of the white man. The logical result of such a recognition of superior wisdom would be to secure that wisdom, along with the white man, at a common source. In theory, the public school authorities of the West agree; in many cases Indian children are included in the state scholastic census, and funds are apportioned as though the doors of the schools were not shut to the little shy people. A small cloud now, this prejudice will assume a very real importance as the tribesmen come to closer grips with their white neighbors.

In the bill of complaint filed against their white neighbors and the government by the modern "reservation" Indians, the usurer and the trickster, familiar pests in the white man's West, are cited as defendants. These have succeeded the conscienceless old traders. Their methods are different, but their aim is the same — to strip the ignorant Indian of everything that can be obtained. In his report to the Indian Office in 1905, Colonel Randlett, one of the best Indian agents in the service, in charge of the Kiowa Agency in Oklahoma, cites an interesting case. An Oklahoma bank official was arrested for trespassing on the reservation. His business there, he explained, was to collect interest on loans made to Indians. On inquiry, it was found that these loans bore interest at any rate between 150 and 3,360 percent.

The case was not an isolated one, wrote Colonel Randlett. "This practice of extorting usurious rates of interest (from the Indians) is not confined to the despised professional gamblers, but is generally found to be a habit of senior officials of National as well as State banks." Wherever periodical payments are made to tribes, or where personal property can be secured as pledges, loan sharks thrive, and it is not an unreasonable demand the Indians make who want to be protected from them.

Trickery of another kind is reported by the agent in charge of the Shawnee, Pottawottomi, and Kickapoo reservation in Oklahoma. In an act of Congress approved March 3, 1905, restrictions were removed from the allotments of seven Kickapoo Indians. Six of these lay adjacent to the growing town of Shawnee, and are of exceptional value as townsite additions. The agent declares that "unless some legal steps are taken to prevent the passing of title from the Indians interested, they will soon have lost property worth no less than $100,000. This matter certainly represents a gigantic fraudulent scheme." It is accepted by the intelligent Indians as well as their well-wishers among the whites that the only way to teach the tribesman the value of land and money is to let him use it. But this does not mean connivance with sharpers. It does not mean, as in the case of the Colville Indians in Washington, allowing white men to go upon a reservation and "locate" a farm under pretense of working the claim as a placer mine. Captain Webster, in charge of the Colville Agency, hints that "here is a fine field for an expert to trap a conscienceless lot of individuals and corporations who regard government holdings as legitimate prey."

Between the liquor seller and the government the old quarrel over the right of an Indian to buy whiskey has reached a threatening stage. The Supreme Court held, in a recent decision, that it is not against the law to sell liquor to an Indian who has taken his allotment and, by that act, become a citizen of the United States.[33] An act of Congress, long relied upon by the Indian Office to keep the Indian and whiskey apart, was by this decision declared unconstitutional. It was declared to be an infringement upon the rights of citizens. In spite of the decision, the Indian Office has declared that an allotted Indian must go outside the reservation, or off his allotment, to buy liquor. It is anticipated that the whiskey sellers will keep up the fight and attempt to secure the removal of the remaining restrictions. No one is more interested than the modern Indian in the efforts of the Indian Office to put off the time for letting the tribesman have free access to the saloons until he has become a competing factor in the life of his community. No one is more concerned over the victories of the liquor sellers. Whiskey flows toward all frontiers and is one of the "civilizing influences" that is resisted by white men as vigorously as by the shrewd Indian who wishes to preserve his race as industrial competitors.

When the trust periods begin to expire on allotments already taken by the Indians, as they will in five years, there will be confusion. Questions of heirship that should have been settled long ago will involve Indians in costly litigation. A majority perhaps of the allottees will have died in the trust periods. Who is to inherit? Registers of marriages and records of family relationships are woefully incomplete, and there looms ahead endless costly suits among claimants, with only the lawyers to profit thereby. Left to themselves, the Indians had no incentive to record their family histories. It is a necessity imposed upon them by the adoption of our laws, and it is a just cause for complaint that the making of these records has been neglected.

The bill of complaint contains many minor counts, such as the new greed of the monopolists who are allowed to trade with the Indians, the costly restrictions on the sale of inherited Indian lands, and the demoralizing "work system." Certain of these counts are directed against a government that is striving with honesty and vigor to satisfy its wards, and some against the white civilization that surrounds the Indian. In its body, the bill is in striking contrast to those so often drawn in the last half-century. To an extraordinary degree, it embodies the complaints heard by the alert traveler in any part of the sparsely settled West, whether Indian reservation or white settlement. It is significant as indicating the practical disappearance of the old "Indian question," and more significant as a sign that the tribesman is becoming a factor in his community.

Making an Individual of the Indian[34]

A NEW series of Indian portraits is needed. The "noble red man" of Fenimore Cooper and of Catlin, the fierce figure in war paint and feathers, lost his romantic interest when he was confined to a reservation and fed on rations. He became of no more interest than any other stall-fed creature. Admiration of the untamed savage gave way to contempt for the dirty beggar in the streets and under the car windows. This period did not have its picture makers, yet the public got a vivid impression of it, nevertheless.[35]

Now the stall-fed reservation dweller has been supplanted in turn by the new man, Indian only in blood and traditions, who is stepping up to take his place in the life of the West. The pictures that are to represent the new Indians will include a short-haired, dark-faced man dressed in black slouch hat, dingy white cotton shirt, blue overalls, and hobnailed shoes. He may be a Kiowa farmer who gathered six hundred bushels of corn from twenty acres of cultivated land last year, or one of the 391 Pine Ridge Indians who put up sixty-seven hundred tons of hay to carry their stock through the winter. Or he may be Plenty Buffalo, who has worked with team and scraper on the Huntley irrigation project in Montana for six months; or

Bert Fredericks, the Hopi night foreman on the tunnel at the Zuni dam in Arizona.[36]

The pictures will also depict the Indian woman as mistress of a prairie cabin, feeding the chickens or carrying food to the calves and pigs. They will include a group of children, dressed very like white children, trotting off to day school at eight o'clock with their noon lunches in packages under their arms. A big canvas to hang beside the old painting of the war dance will show two thousand Sioux attending a convocation of the Episcopal Church at White Swan, South Dakota, and listening to addresses from Bishop Hare, or from their own clergyman, Amos Ross, a full-blood.[37]

The point is that the modern Indian must be thought of as an individual, not merely as a unit in certain tribal groups. For of the eighty-one tribes of "reservation" Indians now in [the] charge of agents and superintendents, comprising 190,000 individuals, sixteen tribes, with some 53,000 members, are self-supporting, in the sense that they are provided by the government with neither work nor rations. Except for two Sioux groups and the aged, sick, and infirm, only a few hundred adult reservation dwellers receive rations regularly. Even taking into account the children in government schools, nine out of ten Indians of all ages have been weaned from this pauperizing source of supply. In certain of the tribes 80 percent are judged to be capable of using their individual shares of the tribal funds held in trust by the United States. All of the members of six tribes are occupying their allotments, and from 60 to 90 percent of six other tribes are doing so. At fifty of the eighty-one agencies, complete registers of the family and marriage relationships existing among the Indians have been completed.

Every effort of the Indian Office and of the Indian's friends since the Dawes Land Allotment Act was passed in 1887 has been directed toward getting every tribesman into his own house, on his own land, and at work for himself. The effort has begun to tell. At first cabins replace the tepees on the northern reservations and the brush shelters of the Southwest; millet is then sown and cut for cattle feed. The following year the land produces wheat or corn. Near the cabin a garden is started, where squashes, melons, potatoes, beans, carrots, and the other familiar vegetables are grown. Indian women make quilts and jams, and the children learn at school that the clever worker with the needle or the patient handler of the hoe is the one who is popular with the teacher and among the white people who are crowding in on every side. The attempt to make the Indian realize his individual responsibility has indeed begun to show result.

The County Fair that was held from October 3 to October 6, 1906, at Black Pipe, on the Rosebud Reservation in South Dakota, clearly reflected the "new" Indian. Reuben Quick Bear, a full-blood Sioux Indian, provided the site, a clipped pasture big enough to include a mile racetrack, and invited entries for a list of "events" long enough to satisfy any hardworking committee on arrangements. The "large and enthusiastic attendance," usually reported on the occasion of a county fair, was described by an Indian reporter for the *New Era*, "the only magazine published on the reservation" — a monthly edited by the students of the Rosebud school.[38]

The Indians camped in a great hollow square surrounding the track. Near at hand was a fine, running stream that furnished water for the horses; there was good pasturage; and plenty of fuel for the camps could be obtained in the woods bordering the creek.

For two days the races, the exhibits, the games, and the "Farmers' Institute" engaged the attention of the visitors. On the third day Reuben Quick Bear announced the prize winners among the exhibitors and distributed the prizes. To Zander Big Crow was awarded a clock for owning the best-improved and best-equipped allotment on the reservation. Wooden Ring won a watch for showing the best collection of domestic animals. Minnie War Bonnet carried away a lamp as evidence that she is the best housekeeper and cook among the women of Rosebud. An appropriate prize was that won by Andrew Long Warrior, the champion vegetable grower, for the committee awarded him a spade. Plenty Bull has the largest area of cultivated land on his allotment; the committee gave him a file to sharpen his plowshare. John Elk-Looks-Back grew the largest melon, and his reward was a long-bladed jackknife. The best colt and the best calf of 1906 were shown by Willard Standing Bear and Charles Stands-by-Him, respectively. A cane was presented to the tallest man present, named Jumbo Stands-at-Him, and a dollar in cash went to Alice Search-the-Enemy because she was judged to be the prettiest girl in camp.[39]

The enterprising reporter for the *New Era* sought an interview with Reuben Quick Bear after the fair was over. Mr. Quick Bear was enthusiastic.

He said that the fair had served to bring to the notice of hundreds of Indians what was being done by their neighbors, and that it would stimulate competition. He had not observed a single case of drunkenness; there had been no disorder. The games and races had been keenly contested, but no bad feeling had resulted, and no gambling had been discovered.

Reuben Quick Bear is a "returned" Carlisle student who has not "gone back to the blanket."[40] He is forty years old, lives in a five-room cottage, owns thirty head of horses and cattle, and has money enough to outfit his five children when they shall be ready to go to school. Mrs. Quick Bear is a "mixed-blood" Sioux and a graduate of the Indian school at Genoa, Nebraska. Quick Bear represents a rapidly increasing proportion of the 190,000 reservation Indians who are being pushed out and away from their old community life into active individual competition with white men.

But the "middle-period" idea of the reservation Indian as an overfed loafer is a persistent one. Thus, the agent in charge of the Rosebud Sioux, among whom Reuben Quick Bear promoted his County Fair, reported last year to the commissioner of Indian Affairs that the Indian laborers he employed shirked their work. The agent wanted additional white "assistant farmers" hired to take charge of working gangs; he has had four years of experience with Indians at work, and he fears that "it will be several years before they learn to labor as white people do."

"But what of that?" asks Reuben Quick Bear. "How long has it taken the white laborer to learn to work as he does?"

An office engineer at Washington, with a brown, seamed face, who has been working in the Reclamation Service of the United States since its establishment in 1902, also has theories about the efficiency of Indian labor. He says that the red workmen employed by the government and by contractors on various reclamation projects are fitted only for "pick-and-shovel work." They can't manage teams, he says, and complicated tools "stump" them. Now, the Reclamation Service keeps a photographer in the field, and some of his most telling pictures show the Crow Indians in Montana and the Apaches in Arizona handling scrapers, driving teams, and working in the concrete mixing beds. The engineer in charge of the construction of an irrigation system for the Zunis reports that a considerable number of this tribe have become fairly skilful drillers, quarrymen, and derrickmen.

Missionary workers say that Indian women make lace quite as beautiful as any made in Italy. Miss Sibyl Carter, who has worked in the Northwest for years, sent some Indian-made lace to the Paris Exposition in 1900, and it was awarded a gold medal. She sent more to the Buffalo fair; it also won a gold medal. A still better exhibit at the St. Louis fair was judged worthy of a grand prize. One of her acquaintances while in Italy watched some young Milanese girls being trained to work the beautiful Venetian patterns.[41]

"How quick they are!" this friend exclaimed. "They learn nearly as fast as Miss Carter's Indian girls."

Down among the Cheyenne and Arapahoe Indians in Oklahoma, Mr. and Mrs. Rowe are conducting, in connection with a missionary station, a workshop called the Mohonk Lodge.[42] In one year the sales of beadwork, leatherwork, and baskets amounted to $5,200. Mrs. Greatnose earned $107.95 and Little Woman $98.50. The Navajo women retain their old skill in making blankets, though they can hardly hope to rival in brilliancy of color and weirdness of design the output of the "real Navajo blanket" factories of New Jersey.

In isolated cases, Indians from the reservations have entered professions; more have become skilled, highly paid workers; a few have gone from the higher, non-reservation schools into the army, where they make satisfactory soldiers and are well liked; and the Indian Service, in its higher branches, is absorbing an increasing number of those who win through such an academic training as may be had at Carlisle or Hampton Institute.

Dr. Charles Alexander Eastman, a full-blood Sioux, who is the author of two or three books descriptive of Indian life, is engaged in registering various Sioux tribes and renaming their members. Francis La Flesche, an Omaha, who has done valuable work in preserving Indian music, and has also written a book, is employed at Washington. Angel de Cora, the Indian artist, is now an instructor in Indian art at Carlisle School. Charles Doxon, an Onondaga from a New York reservation, is a teacher and director of manual training work at Hampton Institute.[43]

The roll of these efficient workers is, of course, lengthening. It includes Jim Stewart of the Nez Percés, a good civil engineer, who finds work not only among his own people but among the white settlers of Idaho. Cut Bank John, a Blackfoot, and Henry Jacobs of the Klamath are skilled workmen.

One would be tempted to strike a special medal for Charles Dagenett, the young Indian employment agent, who has undertaken to find work for all of his tribesmen who want jobs in the Southwest. The Indian Office calls him an "outing agent," but he is really an industrial missionary who has the knack of making the Navajo workmen understand that they are more efficient than the available white "hobo" laborer in the West, and that they can get better wages. He brings the Indian and the job together, but he does not stop there. From time to time he visits the labor camps and notes progress, hears complaints, and leaves papers and magazines for those who can read.[44]

Plainly, so far as providing employment is concerned, the government has fulfilled its obligation to fit the Reuben Quick Bear type of Indian to compete with his white neighbor as an individual. The schools that Indian children attend are also, as a rule, admirably fitted for the work that they must do; and if few boys and girls from the reservation are permitted to attend the district schools of the states, it is not the fault of the government, but of frontier white prejudice. In the matter of teaching Reuben Quick Bear how to live in a cabin instead of a tepee, however, the government has failed to do its plain duty. And its neglect is the cause of perhaps the gravest danger now threatening the Indian.

The modern reservation Indian has left the shifting camp for the small cabin at the urging of the agent or superintendent. Now he finds that 26 percent of the babies born in his family and in the families of his neighbors die before they are a year old, and that before the age of five, 17 percent more are carried off by disease. He finds that pneumonia is a terrible thing, and that epidemic fevers kill more of his people than they once did. Worst of all, he finds that tuberculosis is increasing at an alarming rate. It is the most serious danger that threatens him as he steps up into the ranks of the country's productive citizens. An increasing number of Indian children are being kept away from schools because of it, and it is killing and disabling hundreds of adults. From the great volumes of reports of agents, agency physicians, and school superintendents are taken such significant statements as these:

Leech Lake, Minn.: Out of an enrollment of 122 in the government boarding school, ten children were sent away during the year because they had developed incipient tuberculosis.

Pembina, Minn.: Forty-two deaths occurred during the year, twenty-seven of them due to tuberculosis, which "in its many forms continues to be the greatest menace to the health of these people, seeming actually to portend extinction if we consider the full-blood only."

Jocko, Mont.: The physician at the government school examined carefully the fifty-two pupils enrolled, admitting only those who appeared to be healthy. Yet two boys in the school died of tuberculosis within the school year.

Harlem, Mont.: "The Indians are peculiarly susceptible to the ravages of tuberculosis, and a large percentage of the mortality is due to this disease. Instead of awakening them to the danger of close herding, familiarity with consumption has caused a stolid apathy among them which makes cleanliness, isolation, and ventilation very hard to enforce."

Mescalero, New Mex.: Of the five hundred Indians on this reservation, twenty-six died in the year, and there were only twenty-one births. "The Indian's susceptibility to tuberculosis is well known, and this dread disease is directly responsible for by far the larger proportion of the deaths, as well as the cause of many physical wrecks still living."

The theory that the Indian is peculiarly susceptible to this disease is not sound. It is based on observation of tribes that have given up the open-air life of the camp for cabin homes. The death rate would be quite as high among whites who made such a radical change in living with no training in adapting themselves. Occupying well-ventilated tepees, changing their campsites frequently, and observing tribal laws against the fouling of springs and small watercourses, the old Indians could ignore ordinary laws of sanitation without serious results. When they introduced camp habits into the cabin, however, there was a swift, sure penalty, against which they had not been sufficiently warned.

Agency physicians, few in number and already overtaxed by calls to urgent cases, are supposed to look after the sanitary condition of reservation homes. Naturally, the task is left undone. Here is the result on one reservation, as reported by the teachers and field matrons at Pine Ridge:

Of 393 families visited, 271 occupied one-room houses, 30 of which had but one window. Only 8 were without beds; 265 had tables; 389 were provided with chairs; 86 owned sewing machines; 218 women belonged to church sewing societies. Yet only 76 of the 393 families were reported as having proper ventilation in their houses; many of the windows were nailed down and had never been opened.

The immediate need is for a school and sanitarium in the Southwest to which consumptive Indians, children and adults, may be sent from all of the reservations. Another plan, to be put into effect next year if the appropriation of Congress is large enough, is to establish at agencies and schools open-air camps in charge of directors who shall enforce strict sanitary regulations and teach elementary hygiene. So much must be done as emergency measures, and the broader work of teaching the average Indian how to live in a house as a white man does should not be long delayed.

The segregation and allotment of the Trust Funds now held for the Indians by the government is the necessary next step in the individualization of the tribesmen. This will remove the last great prop upon which even the most progressive Indian has unconsciously leaned. It will, within a period shorter than that which has elapsed since the Dawes Land Allotment Law was passed, do as much as that act has done to give the red man a sense of personal responsibility. With the help of these funds he will build houses and barns and fences; he will buy cattle and horses; he will open stores; he will send his son away to learn the carpenter's trade; he will have his daughter trained as a nurse; he will drain his land, or clear a wooded tract of fertile soil. In many instances, of course, he will spend his share for whiskey, at the gambling table, for organs and folding beds and phonographs and crayon portraits. But many a young white American in the West who inherits a sum of money from his father disposes of his legacy in exactly the same way; and there is no paternal government to stay his extravagance or to guide his investment.

A total of more than $35 million is held by the Treasury of the United States in trust for about fifty-three thousand reservation Indians. But this does not mean that each individual has a $660 share in the big fund to encourage him to live on his expectations. In varying amounts, it is held to the credit of many tribes. To illustrate: the fifteen hundred Nez Percés of Idaho have but $3,900, while the two thousand Osages of Oklahoma own nearly $8.5 million. These tribal funds, whatever their size, cannot, under the law as it now stands, be apportioned to the individual Indians. It is becoming more and more desirable that an act, such as was urged upon Congress last year by the Indian Office, shall be passed, allowing the president in his discretion to designate tribes whose funds are to be segregated, and then paid to individuals as fast as they show themselves fit to use money.[45]

Among the Lower Brule Sioux a Returned Students' and Progressive Association has been formed. It is made up in part of graduates of Carlisle, Hampton, Haskell, and other non-reservation government schools. It exists primarily to encourage the Indians to stick to their homes and to develop their allotments. For one thing, it is opposing the "work system," inaugurated for want of a better plan when the Bureau of Indian Affairs decided to furnish work instead of rations to able-bodied "reservation" Indians. "For instance," says Henry Leeds, a Hampton graduate and the secretary of the association, "I take my allotment of land, 320 acres. I am without tools and money. I work on some job provided by the government until I can buy horses and a plow and materials to build some sort of house. Then I start my improvements. I get the house up, a garden planted, some pigs and chickens about my house, and — then I have to go back to work again to get money to buy food. The job and my allotment are many miles apart. If I leave my wife and my small child at home and go away to work, I am not sure that they will not be bothered by loafers. If I take them with me, then my garden grows up into weeds, cattle break into my crops, and my pigs and chickens are killed and stolen.

"All the time in Washington lies a sum of money to the credit of my people. A little comes to us every year from the interest, but my share is hardly worth driving to the agency for. Now, if I could get my share, my wife's share, and my child's share of the tribal fund, I could afford to stay on my allotment and take care of it until I could make my living from the land." Henry Leeds is typical of an increasing number of Sioux and Crows and Blackfeet and Osages who are trying to practice the theory that a man has to stand on his own feet. They wonder why the government insists upon keeping this Trust Fund prop under them.

Congress has not been sufficiently impressed by the necessity for apportioning the Indians' money as well as their land. Certain congressmen, in charge of Indian affairs in the House, have objected on the ground that, since the decision as to when an individual Indian is capable of using his money must rest with the agent, too great an opportunity for graft would be offered. Economical-minded objectors point to the vast increase of bookkeeping necessary if the Treasury Department should open an account with each of these fifty-three thousand Indians. Others invoke the old paternalistic argument that by giving an Indian his share of money and land and conferring citizenship upon him, the government is leaving him exposed to the danger of having his farm sold for taxes and his money taken by process of law to pay outrageous claims. Everywhere there is a general distrust of the power or the inclination of local courts to protect the Indian from the spoiler. But the Indian must take his chances with the whites at some time, and, considering the personnel of the Bureau of Indian Affairs since it was taken out of politics,[46] this appears to be an appropriate time for this further step.

Certain whole tribes, like the Iowas and Sacs and Foxes of Kansas, the Oneidas of Wisconsin, and the Omahas of Nebraska, some of whom are now members of the local common school boards of the state, are ready to receive their proportionate shares of the tribal funds. Other tribes, like the Kiowas of Oklahoma, where not 3 percent know the value of money, or the Piutes of Nevada, where the percentage is even smaller, must defer any general payment to individuals. But even among the Kiowas and Piutes it is desirable that the fit minority shall be given the chance to use their money for developing their property.

The commissioner of Indian Affairs has suggested that it will help us to understand the condition of our Indian if we can imagine that, three centuries ago, the Chinese had invaded North America and driven the white settlers back and back, and had finally penned them on reserved tracts and fed them rice for thirty years. "To what condition would the white Americans of today have been reduced?" he asks. "In spite of their vigorous ancestry they would surely have lapsed into barbarism and become pauperized. That our red brethren have not been wholly ruined by our treatment of them is the best proof we could ask of the sturdy traits of character inherent in them."

The Indian has not been ruined, but he has deteriorated. His body is not the thing of steel and sinew it once was. His sense of humor has suffered, and his imagination has taken on a somber tint. But good food, hard work, and a sense of self-respect that comes from owning a home and seeing a family dependent on its head will restore the tribesman's efficiency. Indian workmen who have been employed for some time are placed alongside fresh recruits to the job. The comparison is eloquent—"the men who have done some work are found to be fully twice as valuable as the newcomers." Indians learn to work with unusual quickness; they have grasped the idea that there is to be competition between them and the white men of the West. They know that in the future they must enter the lists, not as tribal groups with an agent at their back, but as individuals with only the government's goodwill and godspeed behind them. It is the government's part first to grant the Indian his full individual rights and then to safeguard his interests and to insist that no unfair advantage be taken of him until he is able to care for his own in every way.

A Carlisle Commencement[47]

AT THE government Indian school at Carlisle, graduation week began this year with a baccalaureate sermon by President Faunce of Brown University and ended with the public performance of a comic opera in Harrisburg, Pennsylvania.[48] Between came school drills, exhibitions of shop work, a lacrosse game, a track meet, three home performances of the comic opera, and a unique program of graduation exercises. Among the thousand students ran a contagious spirit of holiday and spring. Early green and the soft air of the Cumberland Valley tempted the visitors to believe that the calendar had somehow gone wrong, that these were June days instead of end-of-March days. And throughout the week the school added one demonstration to another to prove its right to live.

Farms' and Kitchens' Call

They have their commencement at the end of March because five hundred or more of the boys scatter to farms of Pennsylvania, Maryland, and New Jersey every spring in time to take a hand at the plowing and planting. At the same time, scores of housekeepers in Jenkintown, Wilmington, and less important centers of good living prepare to take in the Indian girls who want to supplement, with practical household work, their school training in sewing and cooking. Those graduates who turn back to their allotments want to arrive in time to sow oats; those who have learned to lay brick or do plastering want to catch the building boom at the top; and the graduate in blacksmithing knows that spring means many plowshares to sharpen and horses to shoe.

It is a prosaic enough explanation, and throughout the commencement program this year strong emphasis was placed on the practical training given the boys and girls.

"Outing" System and Its Results[49]

Said the superintendent, with calls for his attention coming in ceaselessly: "I must talk with you about the industrial side of our work." I suppose if Mr. Friedman[50] ever leaves the service and gets an hour to himself, he will be able to talk entertainingly and to the point about teaching Indian boys to paint carriage bodies, and the Indian girl to sew and do typewriting. But why wait for this exposition when the graduating exercises, the shops, and the classrooms show so plainly the result of the school's system of combining work and study?

Three thousand assorted visitors crowding two-thirds of the floor space of the huge gymnasium; the smiling young commissioner of Indian Affairs, the governor of Pennsylvania,[51] and a small company of earnest friends of the school, sitting up close to the stage; a thousand Indian students—boys in smart blue uniforms and girls in conventional white—massed at the end of the long room; in a hollow square, dominated by the music director's dais, the school's orchestra, supplemented by a girls' mandolin club in white satin; a wide, shallow stage resembling a cross section of the upper floor of somebody's suburban villa; outside, the swelter of the hottest March 31 in the memory of Carlisle. The class of 1910 was about to graduate.

Following the opening prayer and the big orchestra's playing of the stirring overture, *Nabucodonosor*,[52] Alex Arcasa, who would strip at about 165 pounds, stood beside a roll map stand on the stage and told how he intended to farm his land when he went back to the reservation at Colville, Wash.

His talk was a fine advertisement of the "outing" system. Last summer he worked for a farmer in New Jersey whose land was laid out in such and such a way — thirteen acres of potatoes, for one thing, that produced sixteen hundred bushels, which sold for sixty-five cents a bushel.

Talk and Walk — A Contrast

In detail, he gave the program of his summer's work; to illustrate, he pulled down a map showing the geographical divisions of the farm. From New Jersey he jumped to his own allotment in Washington, and flashed before his audience a map showing just how he planned to devote a quarter of his land to pasture; an eighth each to wheat, alfalfa, and timothy; about one-eighth to orchard, potato field, and garden; and the rest to forest.

When the rehearsed speeches were delivered and the practical demonstrations were undertaken, self-consciousness left Arcasa, Peter, and the rest. A certain cool young competency, a reflection of their shop training, marked their handling of tools.

Staging the Carlisle Industries

Peter was one of a small typewriter chorus that Libby (something of a football player himself) put through its paces. First, three boys — Peter Hauser, Morgan Crowsghost, and Joe Libby — were put up in front of the ruled blackboards. Then Libby read off at a fair speed three or four sentences about the value of integrity in business. These were written down in shorthand, then read off to the typewriter chorus, which transcribed them neatly and speedily.

There is a normal department at Carlisle — and fine material for the students to work with. Two of its graduating members, Sarah Hoxie and Evelyn Peirce, showed how the stagnant mind of the just-caught Indian boy is awakened. A wooden frame, on which was draped a set of harness, was carried on to the stage. Each of four Pueblo boys, seated at desks in full view of four thousand, was asked to name five parts of the harness. One after the other they rose and walked rapidly to the wooden horse, touched and named five separate parts: Bit! ham! back and lines! winker! smiling somewhat nervously at the audience as they called out each word. "Now make a sentence with the word 'back-hand' in it," commanded Miss Sarah Hoxie, and a boy who, when he arrived at Carlisle last September, could speak no word of English, answered, "Dis ees a back-hand!" After that each boy was asked to write a sentence on the blackboard containing the words he had pronounced.

Many of the three thousand visitors had toured the school shops in the morning and watched the young blacksmiths, cabinetmakers, bricklayers, plasterers, wagon makers, silver workers, and rug weavers at work. For those who had not, the final feature of the commencement program contributed by the students was a bit surprising, and very convincing. Up on the stage marched Levi Hillman and began to speak:

"It was in the year 1904, on February 16, that I arrived at Carlisle from the Onondaga Reservation. My object in coming was twofold: first, to improve myself in every way possible, so that I might return to my people and give to them the benefit of the training which I received; second, to fit myself to compete, on equal terms, with the white man. The demonstrations which are now being made will give you a picture of everyday life in the industrial departments of Carlisle." Thus the beginning and the end of his rapid and specific talk.

While Levi Hillman talked, nine young men in white canvas overalls worked on the stage. One plastered over a section of lathed wall; two worked swiftly with brick and mortar to erect a low brick wall across one end of the stage; two others varnished the body of one of "the famous Carlisle Concord buggies" until it threw back reflections of the thousand hat plumes out in front; two put together a heavy oak study table; and two erected from a formless pile of sticks a "mission" chair that was a pleasure to the eye.

Priscilla, John Alden and Co., in Comic Opera

Eighty-nine years ago, Sequoyah, a half-blood Cherokee Indian, perfected an alphabet and taught his small daughter to read and write the new language. Worse luck attended his efforts to teach the older people. They would not believe that Sequoyah's syllabary was either practical or desirable. Indians, they said, had no business with written language. Long ago the Indian and white man were created, the Indian first, and he, being the elder, was given a book. To the white man was given a bow and arrows. Each was instructed to take good care of his gift and to make the best use of it. But the Indian became neglectful of his book, and the white man stole it, leaving the bow and arrows in its place. So, Sequoyah's critics argued, books and reading belong of right to the white man, while for the Indian the hunt must suffice. It is to the credit of the Cherokees, however, that only two years later they struck a medal in honor of Sequoyah, and for years maintained a book and newspaper press.

At Carlisle, not only have the students from two-score tribes won back books and tools of trade, but they are making long strides toward the recovery of music and arts. Mr. Harry C. Eldridge, of Columbus, O., some years ago wrote the music of a comic opera called *The Captain of Plymouth*. It tells the old story of Miles Standish, John Alden, and Priscilla, tunefully and with humor. Into it Seymour S. Tibbals, the librettist, introduced an Indian chief, a puritan elder, a chorus of soldiers with bell-mounted guns, a chorus of sailors, "sextette of Plymouth daisies," twelve squaws, twelve Indian men, ten Puritan men, and sixteen maidens, besides the fourteen principals. The opera is in three acts and calls for elaborate scenery and costumes. Rather a stiff undertaking for amateurs altogether, yet the performances of *The Captain of Plymouth* given by the Carlisle students this year would rank in dash and color with those of any non-professional company. Miss Carlysle Greenbrier, who took the part of Priscilla, is a real prima donna.[53]

It was the third performance that I heard; in the afternoon I talked with Mr. Stauffer, director of music at the school, under whose direction the opera was produced. He praised Miss Greenbrier's ability, introduced her to me as she sat on the green grass of the school campus, and told me that at the end of the second act, the night before, she had fainted. But she rallied and came on for the long scene in the third act, taking her recalls with all the smiling self-assurance of a Geraldine Farrar, or a Mary Garden.[54] "Plucky, wasn't it?" said Mr. Stauffer. During act 2 I thought of it through the long and rather difficult spinning song, the interpolated "To the End of the World with You" solo, and "Love Thy Neighbor," a duet with John Alden, which Priscilla sang almost without taking a breath between.

In the interest of justice, it should be said that the boys generally were not as good as the girls. Miles Standish, "wonderfully like Caesar," played by Montreville Yuda, a French Indian boy, was the one exception. Into his performance Yuda put swagger and bluster. He sang well, and the comedy scenes between him and Katonka, daughter of Wattawamut, chief of the Pequots (a part played by Rose La Rose), helped to make a fine second act. Before coming to Carlisle to take up serious study, Yuda had spent a time as a mountebank performer in some sort of a small circus or medicine show. To the students he is a sort of O. Henry character, reminiscent of adventure — his swaggering manner, self-confident singing, and ease on the stage confirmed their judgment.

Athletics for Students

If anybody thinks that athletics are the chief business of Carlisle and its invaluable advertisement, he should hear "Pop" Warner tell about why they have cut intercollegiate baseball out of the school's schedule. Two Carlisle students are playing on professional baseball teams — the only two to make good out of a half dozen or more who have been lured away by managers with promises of thorough tryouts and an idea of the value of an Indian player as an advertisement. So baseball, except class and shop games, was abolished this year. Lacrosse has been introduced as a substitute; a feature of the graduation-week program was a school game — the reds versus the blues. No one with an eye for grace and dash in athletics will regret the change.[55]

"Athletics at Carlisle," said Mr. Warner, when forty-five young men were given their "C" a few weeks before, "are here for the students, not the students here for athletics." See how the forty-five letters were distributed: fourteen to football players, fourteen to the track team, eleven to the baseball players, and six to the cross-country runners. In Lewis Tewanima, says Mr. Warner, Carlisle has the greatest ten-mile runner in the country.[56]

That was a joyous afternoon — the lacrosse game and the dozen track and field events moved along smoothly. Nobody seemed to care about records, and yet the high hurdles were run in 15$\frac{4}{5}$, the mile in 4:35$\frac{3}{5}$, and George Thomas, alternating between the jumping ground and the shot-putting circle, cleared 5 feet 10½ inches in the high jump and put the shot about 40 feet.

The only general comment among the boys on the afternoon's performance was when a rather pale-faced, thin-shanked boy, on scratch, a newcomer evidently, was beaten in the mile run. Then it was not a criticism, merely an observation: "So, the great Michigan runner didn't come in first!"

Besides the twenty-three young men and women of the Cherokee, Menominee, Chippewa, Sioux, Klamath, Nomelaki, Seneca, Arickaree, Sac and Fox, Puyallup, Hoopa, Oneida, and Pima tribes who were graduated, thirty-eight other received Industrial Certificates. These were guarantees of efficiency in baking, cooking, laundry work, tailoring, job printing, plain dressmaking, and so on and so on. Hearing the list read recalled the widely held theory that it is folly to train these boys to do a white man's work and send them back to the blanket and the reservation, where their training is wasted.

On this point I beg to reproduce some statistics from the last report of the superintendent of Carlisle. Of the 4,080 returned students sent out in the thirty years of the school's existence, a record of the present employment of 1,675 has been made. Of these, 364 are farmers and ranchmen; 170 are in the Indian Service as teachers, clerks, matrons, industrial instructors, and other capacities; 321 are housewives; 20 are clerks; 3 are band musicians; and (those who have "gone back to the blanket," in the ordinary understanding) 34 are at home with their parents. Others are cowboys, merchants, ball players, laborers (141),[57] hotelkeepers, circus performers, in the army and navy, and so forth. An older generation of graduates is represented at Carlisle by 29 sons and daughters, and 488 former students have at some time sent relatives to the school.

"The School-Room Road"

Why should the Carlisle graduate revert to his old life? He can make money and win a higher place in the world — ordinary vanity would lead him to do this much. At Carlisle last year, besides the vast amount of routine labor done by the students, work to the value of nearly seventy thousand dollars was turned out of the shops.

Raymond Hitchcock, a Hoopa boy, is the poet of the graduating class. In the commencement number of the *Carlisle Arrow*, the school weekly, he published eight stanzas called "The Web of Life." Not for its originality or technique, but for its spirit, I reproduce one:

The toilers that travel the school-room road
No idle loiters are;
They weave each day their web of life,
With threads both dark and fair.

It was the unanimous feeling of the graduates and underclassmen, the superintendent and his seventy-five assistants, the governor of Pennsylvania, and two thousand visitors, as the students marched out of the big gymnasium on the afternoon of March 31, that this year's bunch of weavers, like those who have gone before, would go on with the job and turn out a fabric altogether creditable to the school and to the country.

The Indian in the Professions[58]

MY BUSINESS, or profession, is writing and editing. In my small way, I've tried to make myself an interpreter to the world, of the modern, progressive Indian. The greatest handicap I have is my enthusiasm. I know a lot of Indians who are making good; I know how sturdily they have set their faces toward the top of the hill, and how they've tramped on when the temptation to step aside and rest was strongest. When I try to write about them I lose my critical sense. Then the editors sympathize — "Too bad he's got that Indian bug" — and ask me about the cowboys. Now, I'll write fiction about cowboys, make 'em yip-yip and shoot their forty-fours till everybody's deaf, but I will not repeat [I'll be hanged if I'll repeat] the old lies about the Indian for any editor that ever paid on acceptance!

"Most of the Indians that go through Carlisle really *do* go back to the blanket, don't they?" It was an assertion rather than a question, and a modern magazine editor made it to me not a year ago.

"You're wrong," I said. "I can send you accurate statistics compiled by Mr. Friedman, superintendent of the school, which show exactly what has become of the Carlisle graduates. They go back to useful, serviceable lives. They plow and trade, become soldiers and mechanics, enter the professions — teaching, nursing, the law, the diplomatic service, the ministry, medicine, politics, dentistry, veterinary surgery, writing, painting, acting. If you want me to do it, I'll assemble a gallery of individual Indians who are getting to the top of their professions in friendly, honorable competition with 90 million white Americans that will fill half of your magazine."

Did he want me to do it? Not he! Better for him one Indian who had slumped than a hundred who had pushed ahead. If only Congressman Carter or Senator Curtis would go back to the tepee and the blanket! That would be a story worth telling![59]

[The other day there came to me in the office of *Collier's Weekly*, of which I am associate editor, a package of papers from the Council of Santa Clara Indians at Espanola, New Mexico. The letter from the council, signed by Santiago Naranjo, opened in this way:

"Lately we observed your comment upon the Pima Indians. Encouraged at the display of fairness, we are submitting to you a few carbon copies of some correspondence which will in a slight measure indicate the maladministration of the affairs of the Pueblo Indians, which is even yet in no measure relieved after eight or more investigations."[60]

To a copy of a memorial addressed to the secretary of the Interior were signed the names of the governor, lieutenant governor, the war captain, and the principal. Signing as principal for San Felipe, I noted the name of Harvey Townsend. I recalled a long drive up the Rio Grande with Dagenett two and a half years ago when we stopped on the edge of the village of San Felipe and asked for Harvey Townsend. Harvey and Dagenett were at Carlisle together — in the same military company. As we drove on from San Felipe to Santo Domingo, the supervisor made some scattered observations to the effect that the white man would certainly say that Harvey Townsend has gone back. But he hasn't. He has been governor of the Pueblo, he is now principal, and he is one of that Rio Grande Indian Tea Party that is out to get a square deal from their agent and to break up an illegal traffic in liquor that is ruining many of their young men.

Professional reformers they are — I pity the shortsighted official who thinks he is dealing with a lot of ignorant and pliable children when he goes against the fifty-two Pueblos who signed that letter to Secretary Fisher.

Everywhere the Indians are getting back their voice and speaking out for their rights like men and women who mean to get them. We know the meaning of worry these days at Yuma, at Sacaton, at Santa Fe. And government officials know it, too. Our commissioner of Indian Affairs is honest and efficient. Neither his tongue nor his mind is crooked. And he is having the devil's own time to keep pace with the Indian recruits to this profession of reforming. I don't think he'll ever catch up: I hope not!]

Let us develop this profession of reformer; let us develop self-confidence — make ourselves effective, sane, and scientific. Cut out mere complaining, and develop the lawyer's habit of investigation and clear arrangement of facts.

Last spring, at Carlisle, I heard a Siceni Nori, a graduate of the school of 1894, [make a] talk to the graduating class of 1911. Mr. Nori is, I believe, a Pueblo Indian, and is a teacher [the chief accountant] at Carlisle. I should like to quote all of that good speech to you, changing it here and there to make it fit you. The gist of one paragraph I cannot resist using. It is one in which Mr. Nori ran over a list of Carlisle graduates who are making good in business and the professions:

"If it shall be the pleasure of anyone here to take a trip to Cuba and it becomes necessary to have the assistance of a dentist, just look up Dr. James E. Johnson, who is enjoying an annual income of $4,000, and his wife, also a graduate, employed by the government at a salary of $1,500 [$1,200] per annum; or, if you do not desire to take the water trip, take the Pennsylvania Limited and go to Tiffin, Ohio, where you will find Dr. Caleb Sickles, another graduate and a prominent dentist who is equally successful; then, if you have time, go to Oneida, Wisconsin, where you will find Dr. Powlas, a prominent physician who has the largest practice at his home at DePere, Wis., and is a real leader and missionary among his people. Then proceed to Minnesota and find Carlisle graduates practicing law and other professions in the persons of Thomas Mani, Edward Rogers and Dr. Oscar Davis. Or, if you took the southern way you would find along the Santa Fe route Carlisle graduates and ex-students working in the various railroad shops and taking care of sections of that great railroad system, preferred above all other kinds of skilled labor, for they have shown their worth as good workmen. Or, you might meet Chas. A. Dagenett, a graduate, who is national supervisor of

Indian Employment, and who has by experience gained here at this school under the Outing System, been able by untiring effort, to systematize and build up what is really the Carlisle Outing System for the entire Indian Service, and for three hundred thousand Indians. It is not often possible to find a man who can be equally successful in everything that he attempts, but we have in a Carlisle graduate, Charles A. Bender, the world-famous pitcher of the Philadelphia Athletics, a crack marksman and a jeweler by trade, and a past master in all."[61]

Every month I get the *Southern Workman*, the school magazine published at Hampton. Over in the back is a department of "Indian notes" which is inspiring reading. Here are printed bits of news of Indian graduates who are busy in the world. In one paragraph you will read that Elizabeth Bender is taking a nurse's training at the Hahnemann hospital in Philadelphia; in another that Eli Beardsley has gone to take a job as engineer at the Grand River School in South Dakota; in a third, that Jacob Morgan, a Navajo, is working as a missionary among his people in New Mexico.[62] Month after month the list of those who graduate into the professions lengthens. And not only at Carlisle and Hampton are the professions recruiting Indian members, but Haskell and Sherman Institute, the high schools of Oklahoma, and scattered colleges from Dartmouth to the University of Washington are turning them out. With me at Stanford University was an Indian named Jeffe, from Washington. Not only was he a good football player, but one of the best students we had in our law department. Another law student who came to Stanford in my time was a Cherokee named Hughes.[63] He had previously spent two years in Dartmouth. Last fall at Muskogee, I had a good talk with a young Cherokee named Bushyhead, son of a former chief of my tribe. He had just come back from six months in Mexico where he went to learn Spanish. He was fitting himself for an appointment in the Diplomatic Service.[64]

How many here know Little Bison, that thin-faced, keen-eyed Sioux who wants to colonize Nicaragua with American Indians? There's the type of professional man who stirs the imagination! Professionally, Little Bison is a veterinary surgeon — very modestly, he told me once that there isn't a better horse doctor in the country — but he has also been a showman, an artist's model, a companion for an invalid man who wanted to see the ends of the earth before he died. Now he is a colonizer, a practical diplomat having business with the Estradas and the Zelayas of Central America. He comes to my mind, a figure of adventure, out of a tropical upland where the bright-plumed parrots screech. He brings the bright feathers and stories about curing a mule for a native of Nicaragua; about the fine land waiting for development, and about the power five thousand Indian men would be down there when a revolution broke out.[65]

To my mind Little Bison is a type of promise. He lives by his wits. And that is my definition of a professional man. Not to follow worn trails, but to be ready to break out new ones — let this be the aim of those of us who enter the professions — whatever they be.

The professions are wide open to us. We have the strength and the steadiness of will to make good in them. Prejudice against the Indian simply does not exist among the people who can make or mar a career. Always the climb for the top will be going on. The Indian who fits himself for the company of those at the top will go up. He will go as swiftly and as surely as his white brother. There is no easy, short road up — either for the Indian or for the white man. Conscientious, thorough training, character, hard work — the formula for success in the professions is simple. I believe the average Indian would rather work his brain than his hands. That has been accounted our misfortune. *I* think it will be our salvation. There is room for us in the professions, there is a wide market for brains.

The Enduring Qualities of the Indian[66]

MY FRIENDS, I am an Indian; I was born and raised among them; but it has taken me a long time to figure out a satisfactory explanation of my interest in them. Naturally, we are not very much interested in people we are familiar with. I find this interest growing all the time. For an explanation my mind has gone back to a process of building up an ideal which went on in my youth.

I never read very much good literature when I was young—mostly the novels that you can buy for five cents and which are published in Augusta, Maine. They were not usually standard works, however full of romance and blood they might be, so it happened that I did not read *Aesop's Fables* until I went to college. Doubtless, there is a craving in every child's mind which *Aesop's Fables* satisfies. I did not find them, so I built up a sort of symbolism of my own to take their place.

I remember when I was quite small the family acquired a gray mule about 15½ hands high. He was a solid, square-rigged type of mule. I grew up alongside that mule, and had a lot to do with him personally. At first, I thought he was about the meanest and laziest and orneriest mule I ever heard of. Every time I turned away or dropped the whip, that mule would slow down. It happened that it was I usually who had to make him hustle; one day I would be driving him to the plow, the next day I would be driving him to town for something. Later on, the family acquired some cattle, and I was promoted to the job of cowboy. My first mount, as a matter of course, was that obstinate, lazy gray mule. For a long time I felt that heaven for me would be to get rid of that mule forever. No such luck. The mule flourished, and grew more vigorous with age.

After awhile, I began to ask myself what there was about this mule that was enduring, what it was that was turning my impatience into genuine liking. It seemed to me that he grew more desirable, a little more of a friend; and it came to a point when I would rather have that gray mule assigned to me than any other animal on the ranch. When I grew older, about sixteen or seventeen, the mule about the same age, I found that he had survived a great many of the horses we had acquired at the same time we bought him. I don't know whether that mule is dead yet. When I left the ranch, and went to college, he was still a pretty good mule, still going strong.

Very slowly, as I have battered away at the world with my pen, an Aesop's Fable of my own has been worked out in my mind. I learned that in the story of the gray mule was a moral, and it was up to me somehow to utilize that moral. Since taking my farewell of him, I have held six positions as writer and editor, each a little better than the one before. I am about to go on to number seven. There was a lesson in that plugging, enduring gray mule that I tried hard to learn. I have tried to apply it, not only to my own life, but also, by way of explanation, to other Indians who have grown up under my eye and are doing the work of grown-ups. I have thought to myself—and this is a tribute to the Indian—we are a great deal like that gray mule. We are lazy. You have got to spur us on, but we are dependable. You know we are there.

That gray mule could not outrun a pampered yearling, but he always got the yearling! The more I go about among the Indians, the more firmly convinced I am that you can depend on them. They are there. They deliver the goods in the end.

From many schools throughout the country, trained Indians have gone out to show their quality. I know a good many of them who have not been at Carlisle or any other Indian school. Indian friends of mine, too, are graduates of Princeton, Harvard, Dartmouth, Columbia, Stanford, and of other colleges, and they have always panned out. School-trained or not, it is a habit of theirs to make good. They have always justified my reading of the gray mule fable.

On behalf of the gray mule, and on behalf of these Indians from other schools and all sorts of trades, I thank you very sincerely for this opportunity to speak to you this evening.

The Little Mother of the Pueblos[67]

TEN YEARS ago Clara D. True went to teach an Indian day school at the Santa Clara Pueblo, in New Mexico. Six years she labored there, under the direction of the Bureau of Indian Affairs, and was then sent to Morongo, in southern California, as agent for a number of groups of demoralized "Mission" Indians. After two years of regenerative work, under conditions so difficult that they could no longer be endured, she resigned from government service and went back to Santa Clara. There she is living now, on a small fruit ranch, and working at the job she has made for herself—being the Little Mother of the Pueblos.[68]

Up and down the Rio Grande for a hundred miles these ancient, orderly pueblos are scattered—from Isleta to Taos. Eleven villages lie between Isleta and Taos. To you, if you go through New Mexico as a tourist, they will appeal as picturesque survivals of the oldest civilization this country can show. Their crowded adobe community houses, their guarded underground chambers of native worship,[69] maintained through the centuries within a stone's throw of the Catholic churches whose priests they hear with quiet tolerance, their ceremonial dances, and the highly perfected social system they have worked out, will interest you. But you are apt to go away with a feeling that you have been through a museum. For your gaze, history has turned back five hundred years.

In those thirteen pueblos, however, live about four thousand human beings, with peculiarly difficult problems to face. White civilization is pressing upon them; in some way they must be made to pass from medieval to modern America—and the transition cannot long be delayed. To the Indian Bureau the Pueblo Indians are but a tiny factor in a big problem; there are in this country three hundred thousand native Americans to fit for the grapple with modern life.

The Indian Bureau does what it can; often, however, it stands helpless, moves too slowly, blunders sadly, obstructs justice through no motive of malice. Patiently, silently, the Pueblos have endured the bureau's intrusion—the introduction of schools badly taught, the replacement of their orderly self-government by the unfamiliar civil law of New Mexico, stupid interference with religious ceremonials and family practices.

They needed a voice. Miss True has supplied it. Early in her service at Santa Clara she found that school teaching was but one of the many services to be rendered if she meant to satisfy her conscience. There was an outbreak of diphtheria, ten babies were dead, and the women of the village were hiding their young from the death that walked among them unseen. It was a time for a thorough sanitation, and Miss True acted promptly. She spent sixty dollars in buying from the Indians infected clothing and bedding, which she burned, and in cleaning out the pest places.[70]

As reward for that she was reprimanded by the superintendent, who should have done the work himself but was afraid to enter the village. But the Indians were grateful, and ever since they have turned to her in time of trouble.[71]

It seems inevitable that a superintendent in the Indian Service should seek to avoid trouble, to ignore wrongs when their righting is likely to involve him with men of political weight. He settles into his job and doesn't want to lose it. The man who reprimanded Miss True for an unauthorized expenditure of sixty dollars for ending an epidemic of diphtheria has been transferred to another post, and it is no libel to say that he was a skilled shirker of moral duties. Under his administration the Santa Clara Indians lost eight thousand acres of land to a white man who told the Indians that they were only signing a grant of a right-of-way for a road; in the time of his stay at Santa Fe, the Pueblos under his charge were overrun with the cattle of white ranchers, and Mexicans appropriated Indian land with impunity. And he watched the debauching of Indian youths by whiskey sellers without lifting his hand; indeed, he held stock in a Santa Fe drugstore that, in violation of the law, sold whiskey to Indians.[72]

As a teacher at Santa Clara, Miss True saw these things and reported them to Washington. Investigation confirmed her reports, but the superintendent stayed on and made life as miserable for her as he could. There came a respite when Miss True was sent to California. Conditions grew worse, and when she returned to Santa Clara two years ago, no longer in the pay of the government, she took up the Indians' fight in earnest.

One of her first acts was to send for "Pussyfoot" Johnson, the chief special officer of the Indian Bureau for the suppression of the liquor traffic among the Indians. Johnson came willingly; they two had fought effectively against the "boot-legging" whiskey men in southern California. Johnson worked with characteristic energy and skill to jail violators of the law against selling whiskey to Indians, and the superintendent reported to Washington that Johnson was stirring up trouble among the Indians. One night, at Chamita, there was a fight. Four drunken Indians pounced upon Juan Cruz, a young Indian deputy appointed by Johnson, and Cruz fired. One of the four was killed. Cruz was arrested by the territorial authorities (this was before New Mexico became a state) and promptly put to trial.[73]

Here was a chance for the superintendent which he did not neglect. To Washington he sent such a report of the shooting that telegraphic orders were sent to Johnson forbidding him to take any steps to defend Juan Cruz.[74] Promptly the stage was prepared for a drama entitled "The Doom of the Meddler." It was to end with the hanging of Juan Cruz — a realistic and terrible scene when you consider the drama's inspiration.

Miss True didn't believe that the young Indian ought to be hanged; she knew how passionately the fathers and mothers of all the Pueblos desired the stamping out of drunkenness among their young men, and knew that Juan Cruz was a clean crusader for sobriety and order. She organized, among the women of the Rio Grande Valley and Santa Fe, a Juan Cruz Defense

Committee, and Johnson, facing certain discharge, made her his deputy in order to help her gather evidence.

That Defense Committee became one of the most active bodies that you ever heard of. They prepared a statement and wired it to Washington; back came an order to Johnson to get busy instantly in Juan Cruz's defense.[75]

That was followed by an inspector, whose report you are not allowed to see at Washington. Juan Cruz was freed, Johnson lost his job, the superintendent was transferred — and the Juan Cruz Defense Committee inspired by Clara D. True has taken up the other work which must be done if the Pueblo Indians are to become contented and useful citizens of New Mexico and the United States.[76]

This Little Mother of the Pueblos comes from an old Kentucky family. Before entering the Indian Service in 1893 she was graduated from the Mayfield-Smith Academy, in Missouri; the principal's letter of recommendation said that she stood "high in the classics" and that she was "cultured and refined." I suppose she weighs about 105 pounds, and every ounce of that is fighting brain and bone and muscle.

Courage and sanity and great-heartedness are her equipment. And the Indians love and trust her.

An Apache Problem[77]

GERONIMO, THE old war chief of the Apaches, died at Fort Sill, Oklahoma, two years ago.[78] With his passing, public interest in the prisoner Apaches at Fort Sill died to gray ashes. A few months ago, through certain newspaper stories, it was fanned to a feeble glow. Those stories said that at last the Apaches who have been held, technically, as prisoners of war by the United States military authorities since 1886 were to be set free and given a home in New Mexico. After twenty-six years of bondage and exile, they were to be set free and sent home.

All very fine — in the inspired newspaper dispatches! Justice comes if we wait long enough, sometimes; so we reflected, tritely, when we read.

But let us look behind these reports, let us search for the motive of those who blew upon the gray ashes of public interest in the prisoner Apaches. There is something that needs, urgently, to be said.

That period from 1880 to 1886 was full of drama — call it bloody melodrama, if you will — for the Apaches of New Mexico and Arizona. There were five clans of them: the Warm Springs clan on the Rio Grande in New Mexico, who were cultivating fields, raising stock, and living in peace with their white neighbors; the Chiricahuas, on a reservation in Arizona near the Mexican border; the White Mountain clan, a nomadic, numerous tribe occupying a big reservation at San Carlos near Fort Apache, Arizona; and the Yuma and Mojave Apaches, who lived near one another on the Colorado River in southwestern Arizona.[79]

In certain places, trouble arose between the whites and the Apaches. There was murder, destruction of property, and retaliation by both Indians and whites. The War Department took a hand. One of the measures was to order all Apaches to the San Carlos Reservation.[80]

For a long time, months in the case of the Warm Springs clan, and nearly three years in the case of the Chiricahua Apaches, there was no attempt made to force the Apaches to go to San Carlos. When word came, however, that they must go, the Warm Springs band went. They went peacefully, and they found San Carlos a rocky, desert waste.[81] They refused to stay, and in a few hours started back to their homes and half-grown crops at Warm Springs. Soldiers followed the Warm Springs Indians to bring them again to San Carlos. Chief Victorio counseled with his people, and with the whites who were his friends and neighbors. All advised him to fight for the Apache Indian homes at Warm Springs. That was the spirit of the West! So, with five mules laden with ammunition which was largely supplied by the whites, Victorio went out with a picked body of fighting men to meet the troops. He was surrounded by the soldiers; he and his men fought until their ammunition was gone and then threw down their guns. They were all killed, shot down by the troops from Fort Apache.

That was in 1880. In 1883 the soldiers sent word that the Chiricahua Apaches must come to San Carlos. Geronimo was their chief; he had succeeded Cochise, one of the great old leaders, after whom a county in Arizona is named.[82] Geronimo would not take his people to San Carlos; instead, he led them on the warpath. He did come to San Carlos, but only to persuade as many of the Warm Springs clan, who had been forced to go to Arizona after Victorio's band was wiped out, as he could to join him.

Probably a third of the Warm Springs Apaches joined Geronimo, and then there followed the fierce fighting when Crook and Miles and Lawton attempted to round them up.[83]

Those two-thirds who would not join Geronimo stayed at San Carlos, and the men joined the United States troops as scouts and helped to run down Geronimo and the "renegades." As a matter of sober history, the friendly Apaches were the leaders in the chase, and it was due to four of them, Chato, Noche, Kuta, and Martinez, that the final plan to induce Geronimo to surrender was carried through.

In 1886, Geronimo and the renegade Apaches were brought to Fort Apache. A delegation was sent to Washington to confer with the president and the commissioner of Indian Affairs. While this delegation was in Washington, Chato, one of the number, was given a medal by the secretary of war. That was for his services in bringing in Geronimo. Both the Indian commissioner and the president told these Indians that they could go back to their old homes at Warm Springs and Chiricahua. It was good news.

But on the way back to Fort Apache, at Fort Leavenworth, Kansas, this delegation was arrested and shipped to St. Augustine, Florida. There at Fort Marion, they found all of the other Warm Springs and Chiricahua Apaches, men, women, and children, hostile and friendly, those who fought with Geronimo and those who had helped capture him; Noche, Kuta, and Martinez, who were promised a reward of thirty thousand dollars by General Miles if they would bring in Geronimo, dead or alive; Tockany, whom Geronimo tried to kill because of the part he took in his capture, along with Geronimo's lieutenants, Mangus, son of old Mangus Colorado, and Naiche, son of old Cochise. All were prisoners.

For twenty-six years the Apaches have been kept, actually and technically, prisoners. They did not stay long in Florida, too many were dying, and there was much talk. From Fort Marion, in 1887, they were sent to Mount Vernon Barracks, thirty miles from Mobile, Alabama. That was no fit place for them either; it was low and unhealthy, and they kept on dying.[84] Look up what Captain Witherspoon (now major-general and head of the War College) said about conditions there. When the government refused to send the Apaches away, Captain Witherspoon would not stay in charge and was transferred. Captain Scott (now Colonel Scott) took his place.[85]

From 1887 to 1894 the Apache prisoners remained at Mount Vernon Barracks, and then they were sent to Fort Sill, Oklahoma. There the Comanche, Kiowa, and Kiowa-Apache Indians gave up about thirty thousand acres of land for the use of prisoner Apaches. This land adjoins the military reservation of Fort Sill and is near the city of Lawton. The Apaches had always understood that this was to be their permanent home, and so, there they have worked and made homes. They have stock, they have schools, and most of them are useful citizens.[86] There has always been some talk about going back to their old homes in New Mexico, but those who talk that way have not realized that all the Warm Springs land was taken up by settlers a long time ago. They cannot go back there.

Oklahoma is the right home for the Apaches, but they are likely to lose it, and this is the plan that was made to get them away:

A bill, backed by one of the United States senators and one congressman from Oklahoma, was introduced last year to turn all of the land occupied by the Apaches at Fort Sill into a military reservation as an artillery practice ground.[87] In October 1911, Colonel Scott (the officer who took Captain Witherspoon's place at Mount Vernon Barracks) selected six Apaches from Fort Sill to go with him to New Mexico and look over the reservation of the Mescalero Apaches, and also the old Warm Springs reservation. The tribe had nothing to do with the selection of those men who went with Colonel Scott.[88]

Of course, they found all of the good land at Warm Springs taken up by white settlers, so there was only the Mescalero reservation left to consider. They went all over it, carefully, and when they got back to Fort Sill, the Apache delegates called the Indians in council. These delegates told the Apaches that the Mescalero reservation was not the right place for them; they said that it was not any good for farming; every little piece of farm land in the deep cañons of the Pecos River, where the sun shines only a few hours each day, was taken by the Mescaleros, and the rest of the reservation was rugged and rocky. The Mescalero boys are not sent to school, but run wild in the hills.[89]

To go there would be a step backwards for the Fort Sill Apaches. And at that council, the Indians said they would not go. Afterwards, Colonel Scott and the congressman who is backing the bill for their removal called a meeting of some of the old men of the tribe to talk about going to New Mexico. Those Indians who went with Colonel Scott did not know about this meeting. When he got the old men together, Colonel Scott told them that he had found a good home for the tribe on the Mescalero reservation.

To catch the old men, he said that there was good hunting there; he saw lots of deer tracks and plenty of wild turkeys. He said that the Mescaleros wanted them to come, and then gave them a piece of news which he thought would help them to make up their minds: the Mescaleros were going to sell their timberlands for $1,335,000. If the Fort Sill Indians would go down there right away they would share in the distribution of this money. Besides, Colonel Scott told them the War Department and the white people of Lawton didn't want them in Oklahoma.

What Colonel Scott said pleased these old men, and they said that they wanted to go back to New Mexico. But the younger generation are against going back, strongly against it, and they will hold out against the move. And they are right! The modern Apaches have nothing to do with hunting. What the new generation must do is to learn trades, learn how to farm, and have good schools for the children, and learn just as fast as they can how to live like the white people around them.

There is another objection: *That land which was given up by the Comanches, the Kiowas, and the Kiowa-Apaches was given only for the use of the prisoner Apaches, and not for military reservation.* Already the government had twenty thousand acres — as much land as they have ever used, or ever will use for military purposes. You will see that when the Apaches are sent away and the land they now occupy is turned into a military reservation, it will not be long before the thirty thousand acres is thrown open to settlement. For that thirty thousand acres is good, level land, it lies near a growing city, and let me tell you something: Not long ago, in a dry spell, an Apache dug a well near the creek that runs through their land. Down about twenty feet, he struck a thick black stuff that bubbled up. It was oil! He covered up the hole, quick, but it is known the oil is under the land.

In the last days of the last session of Congress a characteristic compromise was arrived at. Tacked to the Appropriation Bill was an item setting aside $200,000 to buy land in Oklahoma for those Apaches who do not care to go to New Mexico. The money is to be used to buy dead Indian allotments among the tribes nearby, one piece of land here, another there. Out of nearly three hundred survivors at Fort Sill, about eighty-eight say that they will stay and take these allotments. The rest will go to New Mexico and cast their lot with the Mescaleros. The reason is plain — they want to stay together.[90]

It is a solution that ought not to stand. No settlement that does not deal out to them justice in full measure can be right.

This other side of the prisoner Apaches' story ought to be made known to everybody. It is up to Congress either to push the bitter force to the end desired by the schemers of Oklahoma, rounding out a disgraceful take to its sordid end, or to recognize the real needs of the group of people to whom an overflowing measure of injustice has already been meted. If you want to help, take this matter up with your own congressman. Let him have the true story, and if he won't promise to help, let every newspaper in that congressman's district know it. The ancient fight of the Apaches for their homes is not over yet; and it ought not to be ended until a juster settlement is obtained, a settlement that is not a compromise.[91]

Acquiring a Standard of Value[92]

THE INDIAN wins success—and I am thinking more especially of material success, money success—by coming into contact with people who can give him a *standard*. I think the "Harveyizing" process along the Santa Fe Railroad, from a commercial standpoint, a material standpoint, is going to be a mighty good thing for the Indian.[93] I don't care especially to see them squatting out in their picturesque rigs when the trains come in, and all that, but they do get a chance to acquire a standard of value. As soon as an Indian can get close to a standard of value and can adopt it, he loses that prehistoric idea concerning value. As soon as he has reached that point, I have personally ceased to fear for him. My only disquietude comes for fear he is going to overdo it, because I have noticed a certain trait among Indians, when they come into contact with civilization and get this standard of value, and that is that they are shrewd bargainers, who are apt to overdevelop that bargaining instinct. It is rather oriental in character. So I don't fear so much that the Indian will not set a proper value on what he does, what he can produce or what he has to offer to the world, as that he will be tempted to overvalue it, and when he finds this valuation is too high and cannot be accepted, generally he is apt to retreat into himself and think he is being badly treated. It is difficult, and it will be for a considerable time, for these Indians who are merging, to learn exactly what square dealing is. There is a great opportunity for someone who knows what square dealing is, commercial, legal, moral, to elaborate standards, so that the Indians can understand.

I have been down, within a few weeks, to the Pima Reservation, in Arizona, and I saw there a gradation of opportunity that seemed to me exceedingly interesting. The first group of Pimas that I went to lived near Mesa, in a section that is highly developed and all under irrigation. I found it difficult, with my lack of knowledge of the irrigation technique, to follow their talks. They had a series of grievances about their water supply, and it all hinged on certain degrees of service. They were A, B, and C users under certain contracts with a certain water users' association. They got so many acre-feet, and got the water on the land at a certain time. From there I went over to Sacaton, and there found a different set of grievances. The men at Sacaton wanted to talk. They seemed at Sacaton to understand less definitely what they wanted. From Sacaton I went to Black Water, and at Black Water it was a whole lot of petty details, like a bunch of children complaining that their teacher favored somebody else; there were internal dissensions based on what seemed immaterial things. Then I went to the McDowell sub-agency, where some of the Apaches lived. They all thought that I and the people who were with me were powerful enough to fix anything that was wrong, so they wanted to talk to us about it all, so they spent two hours telling us about this policeman they had, and how the farmer went around in his automobile, and did not show them how to farm, and how this fellow was charged with beating his wife, and he was not guilty of that, and how they put him in jail anyway and sent his wife to school—little, little, little details; their minds were not on the big things, and it was all one-sided; that is, they could consider no other idea than their own. And then we went to San Carlos among those Apaches, and they had various little troubles that they were excited about; and then to Fort Apache.

This may sound like a travelogue, but I don't want it to be one. In each of those places was opportunity for some Indian who could see clearly, who could talk sanely and moderately, to take a place of leadership; to take from the shoulders of the agent and superintendent a lot of work which he was not equipped to do, which he was too busy to look after, even if he had the best intention.

For instance, the San Carlos and the Fort Apache Indians, about five thousand in all, own a great reservation — the White Mountain Reservation. A lot of that is good grazing land. The superintendent leases that grazing land, and the money, of course, which is received belongs to these two groups of Indians. The superintendents are supposed to use that money for the benefit of the Indians, pay it out to them and give them rations — anything that seems feasible. There is a project afoot to build a dam on San Carlos Reservation. This dam would flood considerable of the land under cultivation and would back the water up to certain points on two rivers. Now the people of Arizona, through their representative in Congress, wanted to build bridges over these two rivers back of the point where the dam water would extend, and he succeeded in having put into the Indian Bill — I am not sure it was the Indian Bill, but at any rate a bill that was pending — a provision for the building of these two bridges, and having them built in large part out of the funds belonging to the Indians of these two reservations. I talked to the superintendents at San Carlos and at Fort Apache, and they agreed that these two bridges would in no sense benefit those two tribes of Indians.

They made their protest, and the provision was cut out of the bill, but at the last moment it was restored there by the congressman from Arizona. The superintendent at Fort Apache, in talking about this, said: "All I can say is that the congressman from Arizona had better never come onto the Fort Apache Reservation. If he ever comes over here he will sure be killed, because those wild fellows over at Sibicue know these bridges are going to be built, that those bridges are going to be of no service to them, and it is simply a plan to get the bridges built for the white people of Globe and southern Arizona who want to go over that road, and they know the congressman from Arizona is responsible for it, and what they will do when he comes over here is perfectly plain." Well, it is very likely that the congressman from Arizona will go there. I know him personally very well. He would not believe anything of that sort, and I think if he heard that he would directly go. It is just possible he might be killed. The superintendent realized that he was saying a very sensational thing, and he realized he was saying it to a newspaperman and all that, but I have no reason for doubting it. Now if that happens, it is going to set back the whole Indian business a long way; it is going to block the progress of those twenty-five hundred Indians at Fort Apache indefinitely, and give the whole business a black eye; and yet it is up to that superintendent — who is overburdened with details, who has half a dozen things that he wants done, who has no clerk to help him, even at this time — it is up to him to tackle that situation and prevent anything of that sort, and to try, if he can, to stop the building of those bridges to save the money that belongs to these Apaches, and it seems pretty hopeless.[94]

Such situations, of course, exist. Any of the other men who have gone around can give you instances. I have heard it from dozens of sources. That is the specific opportunity. Somewhere among those Apaches there ought to be some Indian who can take hold of that and get a hearing; somewhere in our society there ought to be somebody who can help; somewhere in their tribe, in their reservation, every group of Indians, there ought to be somebody who can get a clear understanding of situations of that sort, and who can prevent them. This society would be, to my mind, the ideal medium through which to bring such matters before the attention of the proper authority.[95]

Mr. Coolidge has read the telegram from the commissioner.[96] He has told you that we have free access of investigating conditions in the Interior Department, and he has shown you how cordially we are likely to be received by congressional investigating committees. They are all friendly. It is our opportunity, therefore, to gather the facts; to gather them in a coolheaded sort of way, so that we can go before these committees and lay facts before them on which they can act. That is to my mind the biggest opportunity the Indian has today for helping himself, and, incidentally, for getting the country straight on the Indian question.

I am speaking more especially of material things — the questions of land, water, coal, oil, timber, and all things that belong to the Indian, and which he can capitalize and which he will find a tremendous advantage later on. It is a matter of conserving his material resources and using them properly. I am not much of a preacher. I think the same opportunity exists along educational lines and along ethical lines generally. *It all means getting a standard of value fixed into the minds of the Indians, a standard that is fair to him and which is fair to his neighbors*, and which is fair to everybody, and to insist that that standard be recognized. That will be the greatest service an Indian can perform for himself and his people.

Arizona and Forty Thousand Indians[97]

IT CAME upon me gradually, as I made my first pilgrimage last fall among the western Navahos, the Pimas and Maricopas, and the Apaches of Arizona, that this western state has the greatest variety of live Indian problems on its hands that confront any of our organized communities.

Only in one other state (Oklahoma) is there a greater Indian population; and in Oklahoma the Five Civilized Tribes, which make up 101,000 of the state's 117,000 Indians, are no longer thought of as Indians requiring special guardianship. Arizona holds 40,000, and the state is deeply concerned about all of them. For these 40,000 are real Indians, not "mixed-bloods"; they are reservation Indians, among whom the allotment idea is new; they are just beginning to feel the pressure and the irritations that follow from a first sharp clash with the white man.

"They've been dancing more this summer than I've ever known before," said the traders among the Western Navahos, as I talked with them in September. "I don't know why — they just seem to be restless. No, we don't expect any trouble; we're long past the time, of course, of 'uprisings.'"

Then, two and a half months later, came the widely advertised break of a few renegade Navahos to the Beautiful Mountains, and the expedition of General Scott, the famous Indian tamer. You couldn't blame the citizens of Arizona for getting nervous about the Navahos! Not unless you knew all the facts — and the average citizen of Arizona certainly couldn't be expected to know them.[98]

For a number of years, the Navahos have been spreading outside the boundaries of their 12-million-acre reservation. Between five thousand and nine thousand of them are on public land; the growth of their herds and flocks has forced them to seek pasture outside the limits of their mountain and desert reservation. For perhaps half of those who live off the reservation, allotments have been scheduled (though not yet confirmed); but there is a hitch in the proceedings, and no one knows when the rest of them will be assured of their right to government land.

Why the hitch? Grazing land is precious in Arizona, and the white stockmen are unanimous in the belief that they can make use of it all. White men are voters and pay taxes; the three men who represent Arizona in Congress have been sent there by the whites. They prefer to see the wealth-creating resources of the state in the hands of white voters and taxpayers. The matter is simple![99]

Simple as it is at bottom, the problem of the Arizona Navahos is perplexing and highly interesting on the surface. It is going to offer a pretty study in tactics; and the white men of Arizona have beaten the Indian Office to the first move.

Their nearest neighbors like and trust the Navaho stockmen. I rode for half a morning with a blue-eyed, drawling cattleman whose range, north of Flagstaff, lies at the edge of the public-land ranges used by the Navahos. His friends say that this man has held cattle on this same range for nearly forty years. They call him "Rimmy Jim," because he rides the rim of the canyon through which the Little Colorado River twists.

"Shucks! these Indians are the finest people in the world to get along with," said "Rimmy Jim" when I asked him if he had ever been troubled. "They'll look after my stock, when any of it gets over on their range, just like it was their own; of course, they know I'll do the same for them. I ain't never had a bit of trouble — don't ever expect to have any!"

But "Rimmy Jim" plays his hand alone — the big cattle companies are vastly more concerned over the question of making profit than this blue-eyed neighbor of the Navahos. They have no sentiment, and they want the Navahos kept on their reservation. If the reservation is not adequate to support the Navaho herds and flocks, the Arizona cattlemen and sheepmen don't feel that they are responsible.

So (I am going to quote the president of the Indian Rights Association), "the national policy of allowing the Indians to locate on the public land was held up in Arizona and New Mexico by the indirect method of introducing an amendment into an appropriation bill, whereby the Indian Office was forbidden to use any of the money appropriated for the current year to effectuate such allotments. This amendment was championed by certain senators from New Mexico and Arizona because they claimed that the reservations, which Senator Fall[100] describes as 'immensely rich reserves,' are the proper place for the Indians, and that the states of Arizona and New Mexico are entitled to have these public lands settled by white people, who will be voters and taxpayers."

Naturally, it would help to get the Navahos back on the reservation if the public were convinced that they were troublemakers and not fit to be trusted to live alongside the whites.

With Dr. Montezuma of Chicago, I started, early in October, on a round of visits to the Pimas and Maricopas and the Apaches. So far as the Pimas and Maricopas are concerned, it was only a start. We attended one meeting at the small settlement of Lehi, near Mesa, but when we drove, next day, to listen to the talk of some hundreds of Pimas and Maricopas who live under the Sacaton Agency, we were met by the superintendent's Indian police and asked to come to the agency to explain the purpose of our visit. Dr. Montezuma was charged with being a troublemaker and a contract seeker, and we were ordered not to hold any meetings with the Indians.[101]

Now, the superintendent who chased us with his police from Santan to Blackwater and back again, zealous in carrying out his purpose to prevent a meeting, was merely reflecting a state of acute strain. There exists, among the Indians of Lehi, of Santan, of Sacaton, of Blackwater, and of Gila Bend, problems so acute that every man who touches them becomes excited and suspicious of every other man. There are factions among the Indians that have split on matters of water and the question of allotment, on the sale of surplus land, on the building of the storage reservoir at San Carlos; and we who went to listen and learn (and add, if we might, our influence toward harmony) were bundled off the reservation as meddlers!

At the Lehi meeting I heard talk so specific and so convincing as to the injustices suffered at the hands of white water users that I do not wonder the superintendent doesn't want the Indians to talk to outsiders. That superintendent believes the Indian Office will be able to settle the matter satisfactorily; and he has his faction among the Lehi Indians who counsel patience, who favor allotment on terms that do not please the older people, and who are optimistic in the face of dry irrigating ditches and withering crops. These Pimas and Maricopas are truly at close grip with the problems that follow the whites into any Indian country.

The impression was forced upon me that the Indian Office was arranging compromises on behalf of the Salt River and Gila River Indians that will prove too costly. For instance, I was told by Indians who supported his policy that the superintendent at Sacaton is going to have restored to the Pimas their ancient rights in the natural flow of the Gila River. Meanwhile, he urges the Indians to use the well water (which most of them don't like) and to refuse to push their claim for a proper share of the water that will be impounded by the San Carlos dam.

I don't know, of course, that it is beyond the power of the superintendent and of the Indian Office to have restored to the Gila River Indians their old rights, but for thirty years the fight has been going on without result. I don't believe it will ever be done. If it can't, the Indian Office is wrong to encourage its representative to make such a promise in order to avoid facing a troublesome alternative — that of securing from an organized association of white water users the Indians' fair share of the water that is expected to make fertile the Gila Valley when the San Carlos dam is built. For not only will the whites who have usurped the natural flow of the Gila keep what they have been using for a long time, but those newcomers who are already building their ditches in anticipation of the completion of the San Carlos project will demand that the Indians pay their proportionate share of the cost of the project before they take water from the dam.[102]

So far as these newcomers are concerned, that is a perfectly fair attitude. Now, the question comes, Who is to pay — the Indians or the government?

The Indians don't feel that they ought to be compelled to sell any part of their land (they say they have no more than they need) in order to raise the money to pay for water from the San Carlos dam. They feel that they can stand pat on the plea that the government owes them restoration of the water they lost.

On the other side, the government (represented by the Indian Office) finds it hard to get money from Congress to meet the bill. As a result, there is dissention within the reservations. One faction believes that the superintendent's promise will be made good; another does not. One faction is for immediate allotment, in five- or ten-acre tracts, of the land, and the sale of what is left over; another says that this is a government scheme to saddle upon the Indians the cost of securing for them an adequate water supply.

Few of the Arizona Apaches have yet come to close quarters in the conflict between their interests and those of the whites. But the little band of 270 at Fort McDowell constitute an exception. I accompanied Dr. Montezuma on his flight from the Gila to the little reservation of the McDowell Apaches on the Verde River; and there I heard the story of the attempt that is being made to transfer this band from their lovely old home on the Verde to a flat stretch of desert under the main ditch that comes from the Roosevelt dam.

Here it is a question of another compromise between the government and the hungry white water users. If the McDowell Indians will give up their little twenty-four-thousand-acre reservation and relinquish their rights to the flow of the Verde River, they will be given allotments on a bare desert under the Salt River ditch and a right in the water of the Roosevelt dam. And if the Indians will get busy, build houses, plant trees, clear off the sagebrush and greasewood, and open up fields, this Salt River water will enable them to make homes just as attractive as those they now occupy — in time.

All this will result — if the Roosevelt reservoir doesn't go dry! And throughout the Salt River Valley last fall, I heard many prophecies that this is exactly what will happen if the winter of 1913–14 stores as little snow in the mountains as did the winter of 1912–13, or if there is any further great extension of ditches in the valley.

But the government's advocates of this compromise say that if the McDowell Indians move under the Salt River ditch, they will take along their priority of right in the water. That is what the Pimas and Maricopas who live in the

Lehi settlement near Mesa thought when they abandoned their old ditches and took a share of the water from the Roosevelt dam through the ditches of the white users in the valley; and now they must see their crops wither because they are classed, through some manipulation of the contract that they do not understand, with those users who are supplied after the rest are satisfied. They are in class C — and they can't get water until the users in classes A and B are supplied.

The McDowell Indians know this, and they prefer to stick to the reservation on the Verde. They want to stay there, and they want a permanent irrigation system installed there. But that would cost about $90,000; and how is the Indian Office to get the money?

And vital to the whites who are crowding the Salt River Valley to suffocation is the question: Won't the McDowell Indians block the plan to build a great storage reservoir on the Verde to supplement the Roosevelt supply if they are allowed to remain on their present reservation? As a guardian, the government is certainly having its troubles with the Indians of Arizona.

If the Fort McDowell Apaches are like children just emerging into a faint understanding of what is meant by bucking white civilization, the five thousand Apaches of the White Mountain Reservation, under the San Carlos and Fort Apache Agencies, are still real infants.

Their nursery is a great body of mountain country, with strictly limited areas of land capable of cultivation when water is led on it. At San Carlos, on the upper reaches of the Gila, and on the San Carlos River, a good many of the Indians do support themselves by farming. Many of them own some cattle and horses, but the greatest part of the excellent mountain pasture belonging to these Apaches is leased to white cattlemen;[103] and so long as the government can't, or won't, induce the Indians themselves to make use of the range, there is no reason why the white cattlemen should not be permitted to lease it. But it is hard to see why the government permits the use of money received by the Indians from the cattlemen in a way to benefit only the whites! For example:

There is a public highway from Globe to southern Arizona that runs across the White Mountain Reservation, crossing the Gila and the San Carlos Rivers. Bridges over these two streams are needed, and Arizona's representative in Congress set out to get those bridges built with money collected by the Apaches for grazing fees. His argument was that the bridges would be on Indian land and would be of beneficial use to the Indians, therefore the Indians ought to pay for them. But the fact is that the bridges would not be of the slightest use to the Indians. The nearest of the Fort Apache Indians lives at least fifty miles away, and to use the bridges to cross the two rivers, the San Carlos Indians would have to make a twelve-mile detour! Yet that authorization of the use of Apache money was successfully included in a bill that went through Congress.[104]

San Carlos faces a situation a good deal more serious than the misuse of grazing fees, however. If that storage reservoir is built at San Carlos (and the site is an ideal one), practically every one of the San Carlos Indian farmers will be flooded out. While I was at San Carlos, surveyors and reclamation engineers pushed their work, and a government man was there to assist the superintendent in appraising the value of the property that will be covered by water when the dam is built. It certainly looks as if the project, which has been delayed a very long time, is going through.

What provision has been made to take care of the San Carlos Indians who will lose their land? I asked the superintendent that question, and he replied:

"No provision has been made; I have no idea what will be done."

It certainly would not be fair to ask the thousands of settlers on the Gila below the dam site to forego indefinitely the chance to put water on fertile land because a handful of Indians would be flooded out. They would resent being held up by a handful of white men in the same way.

What is the Indian Office going to do with those San Carlos Apaches? Both the Indians and the people of Arizona are anxious to get an answer to that question.

What is going to become of the six thousand Papago Indians down in the southern part of Arizona? These industrious and always peaceable people have been shifting for themselves, living on public land, getting crops from the desert by an ingenious system of conserving the scanty rainfall, and grazing their stock over immense areas of poor range. Now, are they going to give way before the demands of the white stockmen for all the public range, and be crowded into a reservation to become dependents and drawers of rations? If they are not, it devolves upon the Indian Office to find a way to insure them in the possession of their water holes and their widely scattered fields.

In Arizona I did not find any general sentiment hostile to the Indians. What was evident was a strong determination among the whites to push the state along the road to prosperity as fast as possible. It is regarded as a very great handicap that so large a part of the state's resources are either in the Indian reservations or in the national forests. The people of the new state who have to support its government feel unjustly burdened by taxes, and they see little relief ahead as long as conditions remain as they are.

No one can blame the citizens of Arizona for thinking of their own welfare. But this very determination to save for taxpaying whites every resource of the state it is possible to save is making the Indian problem of Arizona one of the most acute and one of the most interesting we face today.[105]

The Closing Chapter

PASSING OF THE OLD INDIAN[106]

THOUGH THE reports of agents and superintendents confirm the census figures which show that the number of Indians in the United States is slowly increasing, the real Indians are disappearing. There are 305,000 individuals classified by the Bureau of Indian Affairs as Indians, though the number claiming Indian citizenship by blood is not above 276,000: of that number only 130,000 are known as full-bloods — and a considerable proportion of the so-called pure-bloods have some admixture of white blood.

Within historical times the Indian population of the United States decreased from a total of 850,000 (the estimate of the most reliable researchers) to about 250,000;[107] and then, within the last thirty years, there has come a slow increase — not of the old, pure-blood Indians, but of the mixed-bloods who make up the larger portion of the race as it is constituted today.

The Indian birthrate is lower than for all races (the figures are 30.2 and 35.1 per thousand), and the Indian death rate is much higher (24 as compared with 15 per thousand). This is true of the birth- and death rate of today. Of course, after their first contact with the whites, epidemics of smallpox and other contagious diseases, tuberculosis, whiskey, starvation, and the results of warfare swept the Indians away at a rate ten times higher than the normal.[108]

Making up his estate today, the Indian holds possession of 161 reservations with an area of about 55 million acres; the government holds in trust for him $42 million; his timberlands are valued at over $84 million; mineral wealth on the reservations has been as yet only roughly estimated — it probably exceeds $100 million. In land and personal property, the Indian is worth about $680 million.[109]

Ninety tribes have survived the quick changes that have come over the Indians since they have been compelled to adjust themselves to another civilization. They are scattered over thirty-six states, but twenty states hold nearly all of them. With something more than 30,000 members, the Navahos of Arizona and New Mexico are today the most numerous tribe of pure-bloods. In the last twenty-five years, their increase has been rapid and their prosperity great; and their contact with the whites has been slight.

Among the various Sioux groups are counted about 28,000 — and comparatively few are of the mixed-blood class. The Chippewa groups, more mixed in blood than the Sioux, number 17,000; on half a dozen reservations live about 6,000 Apaches and the same number of Papagos, both tribes still retaining practically untouched their Indian traditions and blood.

Largest of all in actual numbers, the Cherokees of Oklahoma are the most advanced in the process of amalgamation. Of the more than 30,000 blood members of that tribe, a liberal estimate of the full-blood population does not go beyond 5,000; and an educated Cherokee who has made a careful study of the histories of the principal families in the tribe says that there are not a hundred Cherokees in whose veins some white blood does not flow. Nearly as much mixed are the others of the Five Tribes — the Choctaws, with a membership of 26,600, the Chickasaws, with 11,000, the Creeks, with 18,700, and the Seminoles of Oklahoma, with 3,100.

What a century of close association with whites has done to destroy the Indian identity of the Five Civilized Tribes, another half-century will have accomplished with practically every tribe in the United States.

Already the old type of Indian — the plains leader and campfire statesman, the mighty hunter and the poet-keeper of legends — has gone; and in two more generations the Indian as a distinctive person will be all but a memory.

Thirty years of the reservation system has seen the inglorious passing of the old Indian. He was rounded in from the plains and the mountains, a man of resources, of energy, of character. He sat idle on the reservation for a generation and more, and the stages of degeneration he passed through left him a soiled relic of his old self.

But out of the corrupt soil of the reservation system has grown a new type of Indian — the one who intermarries with white neighbors, who goes to school, raises cattle and horses, opens up and cultivates farms, learns a white man's trade and works at it. More than 200,000 Indians live on individual allotments of land, more than 40,000 are voters and 104,000 are taxed and occupy permanent homes. Today the government agents report that 70,000 Indians are farmers and stock raisers; and 8,700 are in government employ. Fewer than 50 percent of the whole Indian population are illiterate, and not quite 25 percent are as yet unable to talk or understand English. For the education of the rising generation of Indians the government spends $4 million a year and supports 111 boarding schools and 223 day schools. Various churches and religious societies conduct 57 Indian schools; in all, 58,000 Indian children are in school; and more would be if there were more schools.[110]

In another ten years 90 percent of all our Indians will have become taxpayers; politically, the absorption into American life will then be nearly complete. Another generation ought to see the end of the reservation system.

So, the American Indian is entering upon the final stage of his history; and what a lurid picturesque history it has been!

His very origin is deep hidden in the mists of guesses and traditions. The romanticist has had his turn in explaining the presence on this continent of the Indian, and the scientists have delved to no purpose.

First of those who published their speculations about the origin of the Indians were those who sought piously to discover among them traces of the "lost tribes of Israel" — and that theory was promulgated as early as the discovery that the newly found continent was not connected with Asia.[111]

How could they get here, and who were their ancestors? Two intensely interesting questions. Explorers found customs, scraps of ceremonials, fragments of speech that seemed to point to an Oriental origin; very early in American history a Welsh preacher said that he had found certain Indians who knew his language, and an attempt was made to trace across the continent the evidence to establish a claim that Prince Madoc established a Welsh colony in America as early as 1170, and to show that the Indians came from that stock. By other explorers and theorists their origin has been traced to the Irish, the Greeks, Phoenicians, Polynesians, Australasians, the Japanese, the Chinese.[112]

One of the theories that has persisted is that the Indians are of Asiatic origin, that they crossed the Bering Strait and flowed down across what is now Alaska and the Dominion of Canada. Among various tribes, traditions tell of migrations from indefinite directions at periods so remote that nothing but vague memories have survived. But at the end of every path of investigation the scientific searcher has found — nothing but theory! Similarities of language are wholly accidental; and the world-student of racial development finds that similar institutions and even industrial products develop among similarly placed people at opposite ends of the earth. Whatever his origin, the old Indian became an individual forceful and picturesque. He appealed to the sympathy and to the imagination alike. From Dekanawida, who with Hiawatha founded the confederation of the five Iroquois tribes in the fifteenth century, to Red Cloud, last survivor of the strong Sioux leaders, who died in 1909, the race has furnished real statesmen and strong war captains. In the American Revolution, the names of Red Jacket, Cornplanter, and Joseph Brant (Thayendanega) became known as those of a great orator, a great war chief, and a great peacemaker, respectively.[113] It was Red Jacket who said: "The Indian can never be civilized; they are not like white men. We are few and weak, but may for a long time be happy if we hold fast to our country and the religion of our fathers." Throughout his life, Red Jacket stood firm for the right of the Indians to go on living as their forefathers had lived.[114]

A century earlier (in 1675–76), Metacom, son of Massasoit, led the Indians of New England against the colonists in a desperate and all but successful attempt to exterminate the whites. Because of his qualities of leadership he came to be known to the whites — and to later history — as King Philip. For nine years before King Philip opened his campaign against the colonists, whom he regarded as hostile invaders, he remained friendly in order to study with care the strength, resources, and location of every settlement. When his plans were ready and he had completed the formation of a confederacy of tribes, he struck swiftly and hard. Almost simultaneously, fifty-two of the ninety towns of the colonists were attacked, and twelve were completely destroyed. Philip's failure to exterminate the colonists was due to treachery among his followers — through that one failure, he missed setting up for a time a real Indian kingdom on the ashes of the destroyed towns.[115]

Osceola, the Seminole leader in the war of 1835, was seized under a flag of truce by the soldiers of the United States who had been driven back time after time by his warriors; and after three years of imprisonment he died at the age of thirty-five — not before a blaze of public indignation was kindled against his captors and his own name made an inspiration to the Indians who later fought to drive back a civilization they hated and feared.[116]

Tecumseh, like Philip, was another Indian who dreamed of a great confederation of tribes that should be powerful enough to sweep back the tide of white settlement that was drowning his people. His plan was frustrated by the premature action of his brother, Tenskwatawa the prophet; and thereafter he fought with the British against the Americans in the war of 1812. He was killed in battle at the age of forty-five.[117]

Another Indian of marked ability as a war leader who undertook to gather into a confederation the tribes of the Mississippi Valley was Black Hawk, the Sauk. For five years, in his early manhood, he abstained from intertribal warfare in order to fit himself for spiritual leadership; but, when the crisis in the affairs of his people came, he ranged himself among the enemies of the Americans and took the leadership of his people away from the "friendly" Keokuk (a chief of undoubted power who was of great service to his people after peace was declared).[118]

Down the line of great war leaders, as the nineteenth century wore on, the reader of Indian history comes upon that group of Sioux chiefs whose power was not broken until after the Custer Massacre of 1876 — Sitting Bull, Spotted Tail, Two Strikes, Little Crow, and the rest.[119] So effectively were the Sioux led in their long warfare with the whites that a saying has grown up in the Indian Service that the tribes, like the Sioux, that fought hardest against the government have won better treatment than those who were friendly. "Homeric children" is a term applied to the old Indians by a United States commissioner of education.[120] It is a description to captivate the imagination, and more accurate than most. With their sudden, vast angers and their fierce, swift reprisals, the Sioux particularly earned the title of "Homeric children." The mysteries of their medicine lodges, dependent for their effect on the childlike faith of the people, became bound up inextricably with the matter of leadership in the hunt and in warfare.

Last of all the great war leaders came the Apaches Cochise, Mangas Colorado, and Geronimo in the Southwest, and Chief Joseph of the Oregon and Idaho Nez Percés. Cochise, who gave his name to one of the counties of Arizona, made peace in 1872, ten years after his associate, Mangas Colorado, was killed. Geronimo carried forward the reckless warfare of the Arizona and New Mexico Apaches until 1886, when he was taken. He died a prisoner of war, though not confined, in 1909.[121]

Worthy to be remembered with the retreat of Xenophon's ten thousand was the retreat led by Chief Joseph in 1877, when with Miles in front, Howard behind, and Sturgis and his Indian scouts on his flank, the Nez Percé chief led his people (a small band, incommoded with women and children) a thousand miles toward the Canadian border. It is from the lips of the men who fought against him that the strongest tributes to his ability as a great leader were paid to Joseph. With Chief Joseph, who died in 1904, passed the last of the great war leaders of the Indians.[122] When the reservation system was firmly established, their occupation was gone. A few professed a mild faith in the white man's civilization, and when they were convinced that it was hopeless to try to turn back the advance of the settlers they became effective keepers of the peace among their younger and more hotheaded tribesmen. In this employment most of them spent their last years.

Great leaders of peace, real statesmen were not lacking among the old Indians. Among the first to welcome the English colonists as early as 1621 was Massasoit, of whom Drake wrote: "He was a chief renowned more in peace than war, and was, as long as he lived, a friend to the English, notwithstanding they committed repeated usurpations upon his lands and liberties." In the history of the settlement of Ohio the name of Logan (Tah-gah-jute), a Cayuga or Mingo chief, is written large as a friend of the whites until his family was massacred; and then, he turned against the settlers. Rum was the fatal gift of the whites to Logan, as it had been to Tedysking, the great Delaware chief, diplomat, and friend of the Americans a few years before, and to many another before and since.[123]

Debarred from following the life of a hunter by a crippling accident, a

Cherokee named Sequoya (born about 1760) became a trader and silversmith. He came into contact with the whites, was impressed by their ability to make themselves understood by writing, and sat down to work out an alphabet or syllabary for his own language. Twelve years he labored at it, in his intervals of leisure, got a system that satisfied him, then set out to teach his people. They responded eagerly, and in two years (this was in 1824) a part of the Bible was printed in the Cherokee characters Sequoya had elaborated. By 1828 the Cherokees had a weekly newspaper — half of it printed in English and half in the character that this Indian Cadmus had made familiar to his people. In his later life Sequoya became a man of power and influence in his tribe, and his counsel was potent in the settlement and political organization of Indian Territory.

Sacagawea (Bird-Woman), the calm Shoshone wife who guided Lewis and Clark across the Rockies in 1804, has been honored by the erection of two statues — one in the City Park of Portland, Oregon, and another in the state capitol of North Dakota. A monument at Fort Washakie, Wyoming, marks the grave of another Shoshoni, Chief Washakie, who was the strongest war leader among his people in the intertribal campaigns and the strongest friend of the whites in the years when other Plains Indians were embroiled with the soldiers. Fit to stand with those old statesmen among the Indians were three whose fame reaches up to our own generation — Red Cloud, the Sioux chief, who fought as hard for peace as any of the others for conquest; Ouray, the Ute leader whom Carl Schurz, while secretary of the interior, described as being the most intellectual man he had ever met; and Standing Bear, the Ponca chief whose tragic story stirred the country and whose pleas for just treatment led to the famous court decision that established for the first time the Indian's right to be recognized in law as a "person."[124]

No generalization is quite true. Here and there among the older Indians you may still find men of real influence in their tribes — like Francisco Naranjo, chief of the General Federation of Pueblo Indians in New Mexico, who has met with courage and intelligence the problems of land tenure, of taxation, and the unlawful traffic in whiskey among his people. When Francisco Naranjo dies there will pass from the scene not a hopeless old man degraded by the idleness of the reservation and muttering against the injustices of the whites (a characteristic type) but one who saw clearly and tried sanely to shape the destiny of four thousand Pueblo Indians.[125]

"Four things you must know to be a leader" said the old medicine men (who were not "healers," but moral and spiritual guides for their people). "You must know that human life is sacred; you must know how to walk straight in the path of truth; you must know patience and forbearance in action; and you must know deliberation and prudence in speech." Those old ones met that test. They have passed, but their memory is left. To their successors they have handed on a wonderful standard of leadership, and to America something distinctive and admirable in type.

A Bigger Load for Educated Indians[126]

MUCH OF the trouble between the superintendent, the Indian Bureau, and the Indian is due to the fact that the Indian, whose human and property rights are so vitally affected, has no accurate information. He has not been given, or has had no access to, a reliable and complete account of his tribal rights and claims. Most generally, it is affirmed, he is not notified of agency or of federal rulings, awards, or projects. The first thing he knows is that something happens. An irrigation ditch is dug, a new herd of cattle is distributed, his children are ordered taken from a mission school, his surplus land is sold, his land is leased, a system of roads is built, his money, or public money, is expended ostensibly for his benefit, his timber is sold, his sheep are subjected to a new blood strain — and in all this he has been neither consulted, counseled with, or been allowed to express an opinion. He is the victim of actions, beneficial or otherwise, in which he has no part. He considers that he is not sufficiently important to be notified. Yet he is told he is being educated for American citizenship!

It is quite likely that the government does not think it needs to consult "ignorant Indians" or that as a guardian it needs to let its wards know the reasons for its acts. That may be, but good citizens are not made that way — at least not in America. This is a democracy and not an autocracy.

To give educated, capable Indians a larger part in the administration of Indian affairs, and to let the Indians generally know more about what is being done for them — these are the two details of bureau business I want to speak about.

First, as to letting the capable ones in on the job of formulating policies as well as doing the work. I have no complaint to make against the spirit of the bureau, nor do I think the showing of Indians already employed, in numbers, is anything but creditable and encouraging. But this criticism I do want to make in friendly earnest: So far as I have observed, it seems to be all but impossible for the sort of educated Indians I know best — the leaders in our own Society of American Indians, for instance — to work for the Indian Bureau. Either they do not go in, or they go in to become (in the phrase of a speaker here) troublemakers. In the latter case they do not last. Why? Frankly, I do not know. When they talk with me they seem to be balanced, rational men and women; the detailed stories they tell me of their experiences convince me at any rate that the troubles they start ought to be started. I can't help feeling, in their cases, that the bureau has taken the easy way of branding them troublemakers and, at the first opportunity, of getting them out.

Isn't it worthwhile to make special efforts to use these men and women of the race who are educated, not merely to be policemen and clerks but to shoulder some of the real responsibilities of administration? Troublemakers are certainly interested; they have energy at least? Can't the bureau utilize their interest, sympathy, and energy to break down the distrust that certainly exists on many reservations toward the office and its workers?

If it shall be judged, in the future, that an Indian commission ought to take the place of the present system, I want to see as a member one of our race. I want to see the sort of Indian I have in mind tested with real responsibility. I believe the test will be met.

Let me emphasize one item of the platform of the Society of American Indians, which was read to you on Wednesday by Mr. Parker. One section, you will recall, is this:

"The present confusion of reservation Indians as to their legal rights is due very largely to their lack of essential information. They have no means of knowing what their tribal claims are or the letter of the law and rulings governing them. This information should be commonly available, as also should be a report of the wealth income and the disbursements of the tribe through and from rents, leasing or trust funds or other assets.

"If the government is sincere in its efforts to bring the Indians to citizenship, the Indians must know the details that affect their progress to this point. We therefore call upon the Interior Department and the Indian Bureau to prepare a set of simple booklets giving digests of the laws governing reservations and to publish the special rulings of each agency. To these should be added the financial accountings in order that the Indians most affected may be given that confidence in the government's intent that is so necessary for good citizenship."

Here is a suggestion to let in light, a practical step to take if we believe that the Indian is becoming more and more capable of understanding the details of his own problems. Certainly, if we believe him capable of taking some part in solving these problems, we ought to let him know the actual laws and Indian Office rulings under which he must act.

Very jealously, and properly, the Indian Office has refused to make public the financial condition of individual Indians. I do not care to have that old caution abandoned. But when it is possible for Indians to be deceived as to the source of money expended for their tribal benefit (believing it to come from the government as a gift, for instance, when, in fact, it is taken from Indian money), it is time at least to publish fully the facts as to tribal funds!

Allow me to plead also for a further extension of this plan of letting the Indian know. I would welcome a regular bulletin service in the Bureau of Indian Affairs. Let these bulletins be issued at regular intervals. Let them be of the character of the Daily Consular Reports of the Department of Commerce, gathering up from the vast amount of material that comes into the Washington office all suggestions for the betterment of the service.

On a certain reservation, for instance, a day school teacher (an Indian teacher) has succeeded in making the school a community center for the Indians. He has held a series of evening meetings with the men. At the meetings, home problems, crop problems, fencing problems — the matters that puzzle Indians in their daily living — come up for discussion. The idea has succeeded beyond the hope of its originator.

Now, an idea like that is worth trying at a good many schools and agencies on the reservations. On many of them, it will work if the teacher or other government employee is told about it and about the details of stirring up interest and holding it.

Into the office at Washington comes a great mass of correspondence, of special reports, of regular reports, from agents and superintendents. Before committees of Congress, regular and special, appear many persons during the year who are charged with plans and suggestions. Among the letters and reports in the great mass of testimony (all duly recorded) appear many specific suggestions that everybody in the Indian Service ought to hear. Those in the office to whom they come get into the habit of believing everybody must know about them. But that isn't a fair assumption. A great number of employees in the service are ambitious enough, interested enough, to take up whatever plan for making his work more effective that he can use.

I would not even limit this bulletin service to field officers of the service. Let these regular hints, news items and reports of progress go to as many of the Indians as can read them. Give the intelligent Indians on the reservations a chance to know what is being done in the reservation world. Give them a chance to take the initiative in putting some of the plans into practice. Give them a basis for constructive criticism of the superintendent.

I would have this bulletin service prepared, not by any clerk bound by the routine of the office nor by an overworked commissioner, but by a person trained to sift material for the significant and interesting grains and to put his in simple, readable form. I would have a trained newspaper writer to establish and maintain this bulletin service under the direct supervision and with the hearty cooperation of the bureau.[127]

In Governing the Indian, Use the Indian![128]

ONE OF my fellow tribesmen, now a member of Congress from Oklahoma, helped me to form my ideas of the ability of the Indian to understand his own problems, and to fight effectively for their right solution. He was the attorney of my people in the days when the Dawes Commission was at work on the complicated business of settling the affairs of the Five Tribes.

I was very young then, and "Bill" Hastings was no graybeard either, having arrived at about the age of twenty-eight. I remember with something of a thrill the curt, pouncing manner of the young Cherokee attorney. In the particular session I remember, Hastings was fighting the claims of certain descendants of negro slaves owned by Cherokees, and he was battering down the structure of proof reared by the negro claimants' white attorney. There was a certain cool, sarcastic quality in the Cherokee attorney's questions and comments — the assured manner of the man who knows exactly what he is talking about and is out to puncture the other fellow's vague claims and theories. So far as I could see, the fact that Hastings was an Indian created no prejudice in the minds of those white men who were sitting to hear the arguments.[129]

A good while I carried that impression. Then I began to come in contact with young and educated Indians of other tribes, who told me that at home, on their reservations, they were merely subjects of the white man put there by the government to administer Indian affairs.[130] They had no standing, no voice, no influence — unless they chose to follow unquestioningly the policy of the agent or superintendent. Usually, these young men and young women had specific proof of incompetence or graft in certain features of reservation administration — not difficult to find in view of the miscellaneous character of the men sent out to take charge. But they found it difficult to get a hearing anywhere.

My new Indian friends opened up to me another vision of the Indian from that I had known. To me, Hastings, university trained, fighting before white men for the interest of his tribe, seemed perfectly logical. I had been told that the legislature of my tribe as early as 1819, a quarter of a century before any such laws were enacted by the whites, had prohibited traffic in liquor. Of course, the Indians knew their own problems! I have had to give up much of my early pride in the work done for Indians by Indians; what has been true of my own tribe is not typical of the reservations. There has been a thirty-three-year period of suppression that has done infinite harm to the theory of Indian leadership. It began about 1883, when Grant's policy of placing the agencies under missionary control was abandoned in favor of the spoils system. Under the guidance of church workers, the reservation Indian was encouraged, not merely to become a religious leader, but also a leader in the industrial education of his people. Missions could grow fastest when they could count upon active help from those men and women who were natural leaders.

However, it was no system for the spoilsman agent! He was a politician, ignorant of Indian government methods. He knew what a white community of the size of the reservation over which he was given control would expect in the shape of government, and he tried to give that system of regulations and that theory of industrial organization to the Indians under his jurisdiction.

The political agent has seldom been in sympathy with the Indians. Unlike the agent working under the stimulus of missionary zeal, he has regarded his exile to the reservation as a real hardship. So he tackled his job in a spirit of "let-me-alone-if-you-don't-want-to-get-into-trouble!" Such was the attitude of the average honest agent after 1883. Of course, the grafter was even more intent upon getting into his own hands control of all reservation activities. So, the old men and women who used to exercise authority over the practical affairs of their people, and guide their moral development, were shoved into the background—into a permanent obscurity. Councils continued, but more and more they were spoken of by the agents as long-winded, time-killing powwows. Almost any commissioner of Indian Affairs, after six months in the office at Washington, felt qualified to act on any reservation as a wise representative of the "Great Father." Of necessity, he had to back the authority of his agents—and that meant stilling the voices of those Indian leaders who dared to disagree with the agent's policy.

True enough, tribes continued to send delegations to Washington, and the president heard them. But what could he do except to refer their bill of complaint to the Indian commissioner with instruction to look into it? What could the commissioner do except to refer it to his appointed agents and inspectors? And finally what could they do except to insist that their original acts or policies were best for the Indians?

Old-time Indian leadership and wisdom fell under the ban along with long hair and the shoulder blanket.

It has been forty-five years since General Ely Parker, a Seneca Indian who had been on Grant's staff and acted as his secretary in the Civil War, left the office of commissioner of Indian Affairs. No one of Indian blood has since been found worthy to hold that office! The roll of Indians chosen to fill subordinate positions of responsibility in the service is pitifully short.

Yet education has gone forward—through many mission schools, through government reservation schools and such outside institutions as Carlisle, Haskell, Hampton, and Sherman Institute. A large number of young men and women of Indian blood have departed from the reservations to pursue college and technical courses. They have become able professional men and women in the large cities of the country. When I go to the annual meeting of the Society of American Indians (organized to bring such as they into cooperation) I meet them from about every corner of our country, except the reservations.

This is not written merely as a lament over lost opportunities. I suppose most readers are fairly familiar with the theory that Indian affairs in this country have been badly managed; and they do not lack knowledge of the evidence. What I want to say now is that there is yet time to revise our theory.

In the states of Arizona, New Mexico, California, South Dakota, Montana, Minnesota, North Dakota, Idaho, and Washington are some 128,000 of the least advanced of our Indians. Thus 95 percent of Arizona's 30,000 Navajos, Apaches, Pimas, Papagos, and smaller groups are full-bloods; of New Mexico's 21,000 the percentage is 99; about 13,500 of South Dakota's 19,000 are full-bloods; while in Nevada and Idaho the proportions are 87 percent and 84 percent. Here live our real "problem": the pure-strain Indians who do not talk English, whose education is hardly started, who are still vague about the meaning of white civilization.

In such tribes as these you may find survivors of the old generation of leaders — mature people upon whom the hand of the agent has as yet fallen only lightly. If you want to know about the government of the vital affairs of the Navajos, go back into the mountains of Arizona and New Mexico, not to the office of the superintendent! So, with the Apaches. So, with the Oglala and Teton Sioux of South Dakota, the Utes of Colorado and Utah, the Assiniboin, Cheyenne, Crow, and Piegan tribes of Montana.

These people have a long march ahead — many years of effort to understand white government, of difficult adaptation to white civilization. Consult any recent report of the Indian Bureau to get an idea of what bewildering questions of irrigation, assisted stock raising, leasing, school administration, timber utilization, and modern farming are being thrust upon them for action. And the multitude of problems affecting the personal life of the families.

One would think that our government would bid eagerly for the help of the old people in these tribes, try by every means to make them allies, give them as full measure of responsibility during the transition time as they could be induced to shoulder. One would suppose that the few young Indians from those tribes who have had training in the higher non-reservation schools and in the white man's colleges would be drafted into the service and set to work.

They are not. The few exceptions may be listed on the back of an envelope.

I recall the talk of an enlightened member of the Board of Indian Commissioners (an unpaid body of men established by President Grant to act as advisers to the Bureau of Indian Affairs, but with no administrative authority) some years ago. I refer to it here to illustrate the waste of ability under our thirty-three-year-old system of Indian management.

Dr. Gates had made a trip from his home in Massachusetts across the country to California; and on his way back (as a representative of the Board of Indian Commissioners) he had visited the Modoc and Klamath tribes in Oregon, and the Blackfeet and Fort Peck reservations in Montana. They were very brief visits, yet in his talk Dr. Gates mentioned Henry Jackson, old Chief Lalu, Henry Wilson, Jesse Kirk (of the Oregon tribes), and three old Blackfeet judges of the court of Indian offenses—presiding judge Shorty White-Grass and associate judges Little Plume and Wolf Tail, besides the 150 Northern Yanktonai Sioux and Assiniboines who met him in council at Fort Peck. These pure-strain Indians had impressed him in a way to make him hold them in mind for months after his return to a busy schedule of duties as president of Amherst College.[131]

A sitting of the court of Indian offenses at the Blackfeet agency was described with too great detail to quote here, though it makes a fascinating picture of Indian justice in operation. One case that Dr. Gates heard through was that of *Cowbedding v. Cowbedding*, man and wife. Under a more developed civilization, the action would probably have been for a separation, with an allowance to Mrs. Cowbedding. There had been a quarrel, a blow, and both parties had made application, through the Indian police, to the court for a determination of the rights of the case.

Very patiently and solemnly, Judge Shorty White-Grass ("immense head, strongly marked features, a deep chest and powerful arms and shoulders, and a voice which would fill easily the chamber of our House of Representatives at its noisiest," with a green parrot perched on his left arm and whispering into his ear from time to time)[132] and his two associates listened to the stories of both man and wife. They agreed exactly except upon one minor point. When both had finished, the judges went into consultation; and Shorty White-Grass rendered the decision. It was preceded by a lecture, "as kindly a mingling of paternal and neighborly advice with the administration of rudimentary justice as one could ever hope to hear." The two would not be punished in any way; they must sit together there in the courtroom and think over the right thing to do. Personally, the judge thought the right thing was for them to forget their quarrel and go home. Still, he would leave the decision to them. They sat silent for half an hour, then looked round at one another and "quietly rose and went out together. As I looked out the window, I saw an almost unheard-of sight — an Indian man helping his wife to mount her saddle horse!"

At Fort Peck, one of the oldest chiefs among the Assiniboines was quoted to Dr. Gates by the interpreter in these words:

"When I was a young chief, all the young men kept silence and the old men talked in council; and that was right, for the old men knew, and we did what the old men said. But I have lived to see a time when the other thing must be done. We old men must be silent, and we must hear the young men speak. For we must all go the white man's way. There is no other way now. The buffalo are gone. There is no game. And the old men could not go East. But our children have gone East, and they know the white man's way. A light comes from the East, and our young men have seen it. We old men must listen to them. We must keep silent and go as the young men tell us — in the white man's way."

This speech was the summing up of recent history for those Indians; it came after a number of returned Carlisle students had been called upon by the old people to talk of what they had learned about the "new way" in the East.

In the administration of tribal business of real importance none of these men who impressed Dr. Gates had any part. To be sure, Shorty White-Grass, Little Plume, and Wolf Tail sat there as a court of Indian offenses, but in any case of actual importance their decision would have amounted to nothing without the OK of the agent.

Those young men, home from Carlisle, to whom the old men listened, were not in the Indian Service — or, if they were, their jobs were agency tailor, police, blacksmith, or herder. Every clerk or teacher or other employee who was called upon to exercise discretion was a white appointee.

To some genuine friends of the Indians — that is, a gathering of representative Americans — I recently made the plea which I take the liberty of repeating here:

"To give educated, or otherwise capable, Indians a larger part in the administration of Indian affairs, and to let the Indians generally know more about what is being done for them — these are two essentials of reform in our Indian Bureau.

"I have no complaint to make against the personnel of the bureau. The days of the wholly incompetent political agent are safely past, and in aggregate numbers Indian employees of the government make a fine showing. But in friendly earnest I want to say this: So far as I have been able to see, it is all but impossible for the sort of educated Indians I know best — leaders in our own Society of American Indians — to work for the Indian Bureau, and therefore for their people. Either they never get a chance at any responsible position, or they get into hot water and are turned out as 'troublemakers,' — a phrase much used in the Indian Service.

"Why are they branded as 'troublemakers?' I don't know positively, but I have a very good idea. Being Indian, and sympathetic, they find out a great many things that need attention — matters involving neglect, inattention, petty criminality, and immoralities. They bring these matters to the notice of the agent or superintendent. He is working hard, and convinced that he is doing well as an administrator. He resents having criticisms of his policy thrust under his eyes. He sends a complaint to Washington, and the Indian employee is either transferred to some unfamiliar work or dismissed.

"I have talked to a number of these 'troublemakers' at great length; I think they are exceptionally alert and balanced individuals; the detailed stories they tell me of their experiences convince me that all the troubles they ever started ought to have been started.

"Isn't it worthwhile for the government, through the Bureau of Indian Affairs, to make special efforts to use the capable men and women of the race — not merely as policemen and tailors and cooks and laundry helpers, but in positions of leadership? 'Troublemakers' cannot, at any rate, be accused of indifference; they have energy. Can't their interest and energy be utilized? Must it continue to be impossible for such young Indians as are making their way as doctors and lawyers and businessmen and trained nurses and singers and members of Congress to serve their race by taking some share in the administration of Indian lands equal in area to New England plus New York, New Jersey, Delaware, and Maryland; and in the settlement of money and human problems vital to some 270,000 of their fellows? Shall we go on excluding from our governing councils those who know the hearts of 150,000 full-bloods who still must be shown how to walk in the white man's way?"

Why not try, in governing the Indian and in administering his affairs, to use the Indian?

The New Indian Leadership[133]

THEY DON'T even call it a council anymore! Today when you go to talk with the Indians, and listen to what they have to say, you simply attend a "meeting." First, the old man who bears the now purely honorary title of chief walks solemnly over to speak a few words to some Indian under forty who wears a black suit, more carefully brushed perhaps than those worn by the others. Standing aside, the chief takes off his hat; all the men crowded around the brush arbor uncover, quiet the children; and there follows an impressive pause before the man in the neat, black suit, with eyes closed and face upturned, begins to speak.

"We pray to our Father in Heaven — " The man's English is halting; you realize that you are listening to an alien whose tongue fumbles the language. Yet you are able to sense, in that brief, stiff prayer, a giving up and a reaching forward — the old Indians giving up their ceremonial pipes and their right to speak the first word, and the younger people, equipped with the white man's language and instructed in his ways, reaching forward timidly and awkwardly for the leadership.

The manner of that opening prayer will show you how poorly equipped as yet these younger men are to take the place of the old men as counselors. Only because the old men know that new leadership must come do they give way. As the meeting goes on, you see the change dramatized.

The old men speak—first of all, one whose face is much wrinkled, whose eyes have retreated to vague slits through which now and then flashes an apparition of command, whose voice is first a mumble and rises later to a quiet eloquence. Your alert, unsmiling interpreter (who was graduated from Carlisle only last year, and who has left his tailor shop for the day to help you out) catches your inquiring eye and leaves his place beside the old man to come and whisper.

"His name is Maricopa Sam." It is an ill-fitting name, lacking proper dignity—you would have preferred to hear the old man's Indian name.

After a minute of talk, the old man turns his face ever so slightly toward the interpreter. That youth, with arms straight down at his sides, his face mask-like, speaks.

"He says he is glad to see you here today; he is glad to shake your hand; he says all of us are glad to see you here today; we are glad to have you see with your own eyes how we are living."

Again the old man takes up the tale, and more than once you catch from those slits of eyes among the wrinkles a disturbing flash. Then the interpreter:

"He says he can remember when the first white man came into this valley. He can remember the words that first white man spoke. He says that first white man spoke different from the way they speak today. In that day, the white man said all he wanted was a place to rest for awhile; the white man said he would go on, after he was rested, on toward the West, where many other white men had gone ahead. But he did not go on. That time was more than fifty years ago; he says he was a young man then, about as old as I am now."

You had noticed the old man's slight gesture toward the young interpreter, and had wondered what it meant.

For half an hour, the old man goes on, telling over what he has told many times. At the end, he says earnestly:

"We are not satisfied with the way things are going here; we hope you can find a way to help us. For me, it does not matter anymore—I am an old man, and I will soon pass away. But for these young people it does matter! I am speaking today for these young people who must go on living with the white men." He steps back.

Even through the colorless rendering of the young interpreter, the old man's words get you by the throat, and you wonder at a power of self-control that permits of quiet talk of the day when he shall have "passed over the border," leaving a great weight of trouble for his people behind.

Other old men speak, in the same strain, but less eloquently and less hopefully.

Toward the end of the day (for there is vast leisureliness, as well as dignity, in the proceedings), the young men are heard; and what a contrast they make with the old fellows!

First among the young men to speak is a "black-coat," who has been persuaded by missionaries to come forward and assert himself in tribal affairs. Looking straight at you, he talks for a little while in halting English; as he pauses, you hear mutterings among the old people who understand no English — those of the 25 percent who know no language but their own — and then, facing away from you, the young "black-coat" speaks to his people. He tells them that he is speaking in favor of immediate allotment of the tribal land; he says that they ought to know their boundaries, so that they can begin at once to build the better houses they all ought to build.

Young "black-coat" is friendly with the superintendent of the reservation — the same arguments he puts blunderingly before you have been made to you already by the man at the agency. Some of the superintendent's very phrases you hear repeated; and in the talk of the young "black-coat" is reflected that white man's impatience of the "conservatism" of the old men.

That night, before they sleep, some of the young men go to the agency to report to the superintendent what has been said. Next day, that official sends a summary to the Indian Office at Washington, with a recommendation that he be given authority to forbid any more meetings of the sort.

He is an honest, vigorous, and conscientious official, this superintendent. He believes that meetings at which the old men talk over their grievances and recall their old life only serve to delay the carrying out of the government's wise policy. He thinks of you, who have gone to listen to the talk of the old men, as a meddler.[134] He is frank to tell you that you can't understand the situation on that reservation, and that every bit of encouragement the old people receive makes his own job more difficult.

On every reservation — there are 161 of them, large and small, in the United

States, embracing a total area of over 55 million acres — the superintendent is supreme. To the Indians, he is the voice of Washington — one who must be obeyed. Through him, meetings of the old people are frowned upon and their traditional spiritual practices discouraged; Indian dances are forbidden; long hair must be cut short; allotment of tribal land to individual Indians is pushed; tribal land is traded to whites for water rights in irrigating ditches; Indian money is used for building irrigating systems, bridges, and roads.[135] It is the superintendent on the reservation who determines what the 90 million whites want done with the 300,000 Indians.

In every move this conscientious superintendent makes, he calls upon the younger people of the reservation for support. He gives them arguments and sends them out to do missionary service among the old people. His young men of the Indian Police are more than keepers of order; they are the eyes, and ears, and (so far as they can be used with discretion) the tongue of the superintendent.[136]

After the Civil War, the government turned with vigor to the settlement of Indian troubles. As a solution, the reservation was chosen; from all corners of the western country the government troops rounded up the Indians and segregated them on tracts of land widely scattered over twenty-five western and midwestern states and territories.

That policy amounted to imprisonment; and as soon as it was settled upon, the old Indian was doomed. More than thirty years of imprisonment have served to destroy his power and influence.

For ten years or more after the Indians were imprisoned in idleness on the reservations, the government was content merely to feed them and keep them peaceable. Then it was thought desirable to get the children into schools to learn the white man's language and ways. Agents were sent to the reservations to induce the old men and women, who sat idle and hopeless and discontented, to send their children and grandchildren away to the schools. It is wonderful, but true, that these old people consented.

Then the school-trained young men and women — Carlisle School alone has graduated over six hundred, and sent back nearly forty-eight hundred — returned to find in the eyes of the old people a question: What are you going to do to help our people? Fifteen years ago, a man in the Indian Service[137] held a council with the Northern Yankton Sioux and the

Assiniboines at Fort Peck; and at that council the old men called upon three young men who had been to Carlisle to speak about the white man's way. One old chief said:

"When I was an old chief, all the young men kept silent, and the old men talked in council; and that was right, for the old men knew what was best, and we did what the old men said. But I have lived to see a time when another thing must be done. We old men must be silent, and we must hear the young men speak. For we must all go the white man's way.

"There is no other way now. The buffalo are gone. There is no game. And the old men could not go East — they could not go to school. But our children have gone East, and they know the white man's way. A light comes from the East, and our young men have seen it. We old men must listen to them. We must keep silent and go as the young men tell us — in the white man's way."

The old man was right — leadership in the white man's way was needed, for there were vast estates to administer. Today, after the process of allotment has gone on for twenty years, the Indians own land and property worth nearly a billion dollars.

After the young people began to come back to the reservations from the schools, the government faced a new problem: How to cure the evils of the reservation system? Drink, disease, and idleness were destroying the Indians faster than the bullets of the soldiers ever destroyed them. It became the new policy of the government to break up the reservation system. Congress passed an Allotment Act; schools were multiplied on the reservations (there are 114 boarding schools and 223 day schools now); farmers and work-teachers were sent to the Indians; the health of the Indians became a matter of concern; and the fight to keep liquor away from them was pushed with energy.

Quickly the Indians responded. Today, less than 50 percent are illiterate, and fewer than 25 percent are unable to speak English. Some 200,000 of them are living in permanent homes on their own land; nearly as many are subject to taxation; and 8,700 of them are employed in government service. Of the $10 million a year spent for the support of the Bureau of Indian Affairs, $4 million goes to educate the Indian children.

Truly, a new spirit entered the Indian Service when it was decided that the reservations must be broken up; and under the new order the Indians themselves were asked to cooperate. But — and this was the tragedy of the change—the old Indians were not asked. It was assumed that they would not be in sympathy with the new program, and that, even if they were, they could not help effectively in carrying it out. They had been neglected, debauched, and broken by the government—and when the government got ready to do some of the things these old men had been urging for years, it wasn't thought worthwhile to ask them to help.

Well, it really wasn't—that was the bitter truth! Self-confidence, the power to command, were gone from most of the old men—the government had killed it, deliberately. It was a mockery that the chiefs among them were allowed to keep their nominal titles.

What real power, understanding, and influence has been wasted! I have before me some notes made among the Blackfeet Indians of Montana fifteen years ago by Dr. Gates, secretary of the Board of Indian Commissioners.[138] Among the notes is a description of the meeting of the "court of Indian offenses," where, on that reservation, minor troubles arising among the Indians were threshed out and adjusted by three old men. The case of a man who had quarreled with his wife was before the court, and Dr. Gates wrote:

"Judge 'Shorty' White-Grass presided. The two associate justices were Little Plume (a son of Chief White Calf) and Wolf Tail. Let me give you some notion of the presiding justice: He has an immense head with strongly marked features; his chest is deep and he has a voice which would easily fill the chamber of our House of Representatives at its noisiest; he has broad, powerful shoulders, and long arms—sitting, he seems a man of more than six feet, though he measures only four feet, eight. His still-black hair is worn long. He is fond of carrying a green parrot on his left arm (many of the Indians think the parrot whispers wisdom into the old man's ear!). He is a great medicine man among his people, and with old chief White Calf, Lone Plume, Mad Wolf, and other 'conversatives,' he spends his Sundays worshipping and praying to the beaver god."

Behind a table in one of the buildings of the agency sat those three old men hearing evidence, arbitrating disputes with success (as in the case which Dr. Gates heard), dealing out just punishments, and maintaining the dignity that properly belongs to a court. Yet as they sat there, helping to keep their people in the right path, all three of those old men knew that a word from the white men in charge of the reservation could nullify every act of theirs, could reverse every decision they made.

Now, what about this new generation — the Carlisle-trained, the literate, the "mixed-bloods"? Few of them are yet proved as leaders — and, after all, they are the creations of yesterday. But one need not become pessimistic about the new Indian leadership.

Some of them think straight and talk effectively; they see with clear vision what lies ahead of their people, and they work intelligently to shape the future. In their speech is an acid quality that makes you sit up and grit your teeth — just as the eloquent old fellows wrung your heart with their simple language, their poetry, their moving stories of wrongs patiently endured.

There was an old Apache chief named Victorio, who went on the warpath in 1880 to fight for the homes of his band. With Victorio and his family when that warfare began was a baby boy — carried strapped to a board on his mother's back. He was Natalish, grandson of Victorio. Before his people stopped fighting for the right to live on land they believed had been given them for their own, he was big enough to go a little way out on the battlefield with his uncle (both father and grandfather were killed in the years of warfare) and learn something about how to fight in the old Apache way.[139]

The boy became one of the famous band of prisoner Apaches that was held in Florida and Alabama from 1886 to 1894, and then sent out to Fort Sill, Oklahoma.[140] From the military prison in Florida, Natalish was sent to school at Carlisle: he studied civil engineering; he had held a place in the Bureau of Highways of New York City; and he is now in the employment of the government making a family census of the Arizona Apaches.

Within the last two years, that young man has demonstrated the possibilities of the new leadership. He and Henry Roe-Cloud[141] very largely organized and directed the fight made on behalf of that band of prisoner Apaches to be given allotments of land in Oklahoma, where they might soonest become self-supporting and qualified to stand side by side with the whites as citizens of the state. When you understand that the fight had to be made against the influence in Congress of most of the Oklahoma delegation, backed by thousands of scheming whites who had set out to get the Apaches removed from the state, as well as by the War Department, which wanted for an artillery practice ground the land the prisoner Apaches in Oklahoma occupied you will appreciate the fact that Natalish and his friends were able to force a compromise upon the government. According to this compromise agreement, instead of the whole band of 270 prisoner Apaches being removed to the unfertile and mountainous reservation of the Mescalero Apaches in New Mexico, most of them were given the choice of going or staying in Oklahoma.

Natalish and Roe-Cloud wanted them to stay in Oklahoma. They went among them and urged them to resist removal; and it was largely due to their persuasion that seventy-eight (mostly the younger and better educated) decided to remain in Oklahoma.

Such fights to carry out obviously wise policies among the Indians are still ahead — and the need for strong leadership in the tribes is great. Take the case of the Arizona Navahos and Papagos.

We think of the Navahos as a peace-loving and pastoral people, yet for four years (from 1863 to 1867) they were herded at Fort Sumner, New Mexico, as prisoners. A third of their number died in that time, and there were fewer than eight thousand of them when they were sent back to their old land.[142]

After four years of confinement and idleness, they were sent back to the desert and the mountains — and a sheep apiece was given them by the government. An old Navaho who now owns fifteen hundred sheep has told about that issue:

"They gave one sheep to me and one sheep to my wife, and they gave a sheep to my little boy." He stopped for a little while, and laughed. "So, we started out and drove our sheep across the desert — three of us, and three sheep. From Fort Defiance way out here beyond the borders of our reservation we drove our three sheep; and that is all the government has done for us."

Now, the Navahos were used to the desert and the mountains, and when they were sent back there they prospered. From fewer than eight thousand they have increased to more than thirty thousand — they are now the largest pure-blood tribe in the country. Their reservation embraces over 12 million acres of mountain and desert land; and it is fully stocked with cattle, sheep, and horses.

Also, outside the boundaries of the reservation, between five thousand and nine thousand Navahos are occupying public land. Many of these outside Navahos have been given allotments of public land, but several thousands (no one is sure of the figures) are not yet assured of their title or right to go on occupying government land outside the reservation; and there is a stiff fight ahead before they will get that assurance. Strong opposition has been aroused by the cattlemen and sheepmen of Arizona — these white men want the unallotted Navahos driven back on the reservation, though they know that the reservation is not adequate to support their herds and flocks.

In southern Arizona, six thousand Papago Indians are supporting themselves on public land outside any reservation, and they are up against practically the same problem.

There is work in Arizona for strong Indian leaders of the new generation, and at a score of other points acute problems are demanding the best cooperative effort of the government and the educated young men and women of the tribes.

Source Acknowledgments

PART 1. AUTOBIOGRAPHY

"A Tale of the Old I.T.: An Autobiography by John Milton Oskison" is held in the Western History Collections, University of Oklahoma Libraries.

"A Trip to Yosemite Valley: Graphic Picture of Grand Scenery Drawn by a Vinita Boy" originally appeared in *Indian Chieftain* 8 Aug. 1895.

"A Letter to His Father: John Milton Oskison Writes of His Visit in Europe" originally appeared in *Indian Chieftain* 9 Aug. 1900.

"An Autobiographical Letter to Journalist Frederick S. Barde" originally appeared in *Native Press Research Journal* 6 (Fall 1987): 1–7, under the title "A Letter by John Milton Oskison (1874–1947), Cherokee Journalist."

PART 2. FICTION

"I Match You: You Match Me" originally appeared in *Indian Chieftain* 27 May 1897.

"Tookh Steh's Mistake" originally appeared in *Indian Chieftain* 22 July 1897.

"A Schoolmaster's Dissipation" originally appeared in *Indian Chieftain* 25 Dec. 1897.

"'Only the Master Shall Praise'" originally appeared in *Century Illustrated Magazine* Jan. 1900: 327–35.

"When the Grass Grew Long" originally appeared in *Century Illustrated Magazine* June 1901: 247–50.

"The Biologist's Quest" originally appeared in *Overland Monthly* 38.2 (1901): 52–57.

"I Saw an Eagle Strike" originally appeared in the *San Francisco Chronicle* 1 Mar. 1903.

"To 'Youngers' Bend'" originally appeared in *Frank Leslie's Popular Monthly* June 1903: 182–88.

"A Border Judge and His Court" originally appeared in *Frank Leslie's Popular Monthly* July 1903: 18–23.

"Working for Fame" originally appeared in *Frank Leslie's Popular Monthly* Oct. 1903: 372–82.

"The Fall of King Chris" originally appeared in *Frank Leslie's Popular Monthly* Oct. 1903: 586–93.

"'The Quality of Mercy'" originally appeared in *Century Magazine* June 1904: 178–81.

"The Greater Appeal" originally appeared in *Black Cat* 11. Boston: Shortstory, 1905. 28–35.

"The Problem of Old Harjo" originally appeared in *Southern Workman* 36 (Apr. 1907): 235–41.

"Young Henry and the Old Man" originally appeared in *McClure's* June 1908: 237.

"Koenig's Discovery" originally appeared in *Collier's Weekly* 28 May 1910.

"Out of the Night That Covers" originally appeared in *Delineator* 78 (Aug. 1911): 80, 125.

"Walla Tenaka — Creek" originally appeared in *Collier's Weekly* 12 July 1913: 16–17, 32–33.

"The Apples of Hesperides, Kansas" originally appeared in *Forum* 51 (March 1914): 391–408.

"The Man Who Interfered" originally appeared in *Southern Workman* 44 (October 1915): 557–67.

"The Other Partner" originally appeared in *Collier's Weekly* 6 Dec. 1924: 14–15, 30–32.

"The Singing Bird" originally appeared in *Sunset Magazine* Mar. 1925: 5–8, 87–89.

PART 3. ESSAYS

"Cherokee Migration" originally appeared in *Tahlequah Arrow* 31 May 1902.

"The President and the Indian: Rich Opportunity for the Red Man" originally appeared in the *Vinita Weekly Chieftain* 25 Dec. 1902.

"The Outlook for the Indian" originally appeared in *Southern Workman* 32 (June 1903): 270–73.

"Friends of the Indian" originally appeared in *The Nation: A Weekly Journal* 81 (October 1905): 332–33.

"Lake Mohonk Conference" originally appeared in *The Native American* 4 Nov. 1905: 391–93.

"The Need of Publicity in Indian Affairs" originally appeared in *Proceedings of the Twenty-Fourth Annual Meeting of the Lake Mohonk Conference of Friends of the Indian and Other Dependent Peoples*. Lake Mohonk Conference, 1906. 38–40.

"Remaining Causes of Indian Discontent" originally appeared in *North American Review* 1 Mar. 1907: 486–93.

"Making an Individual of the Indian" originally appeared in *Everybody's Magazine* June 1907: 723–33.

"A Carlisle Commencement" originally appeared in *Collier's Weekly* 4 June 1910: 21–22.

"The Indian in the Professions" originally appeared in *The Red Man* Jan. 1912: 201–4, published by the Carlisle Indian Press, Carlisle, Pennsylvania.

"The Enduring Qualities of the Indian" originally appeared in *The Red Man* May 1912: 396–98, published by the Carlisle Indian Press, Carlisle, Pennsylvania.
"The Little Mother of the Pueblos" originally appeared in *Delineator* 81 (Mar. 1913): 170.
"An Apache Problem" originally appeared in *Quarterly Journal of the Society of American Indians* 1 (Apr. 1913): 25–29.
"Acquiring a Standard of Value" originally appeared in *Quarterly Journal of the Society of American Indians* 2 (Jan.–Mar. 1914): 47–50.
"Arizona and Forty Thousand Indians" originally appeared in *Southern Workman* 43 (Mar. 1914): 148–56.
"The Closing Chapter: Passing of the Old Indian" originally appeared in *The Indian Leader* 17 (May 1914): 6–11.
"A Bigger Load for Educated Indians" originally appeared in *Report of the Thirty-Third Annual Lake Mohonk Conference on the Indian and Other Dependent Peoples*. Lake Mohonk Conference, 1915. 174–77.
"In Governing the Indian, Use the Indian!" originally appeared in *American Indian Magazine* 5.1 (1917): 36–41.
"The New Indian Leadership" originally appeared in *American Indian Magazine* 5.2 (1917): 93–100.

Notes

INTRODUCTION

1. Frederick Samuel Barde (1869–1916) was a newspaper journalist and a naturalist. He was born in Hannibal, Missouri, but moved to Guthrie, then the capital of Oklahoma Territory, in 1898, where he served as a correspondent for the *Kansas City Star*. He wrote numerous articles on Oklahoma Territory and Indian Territory and the movement toward statehood. He also contributed to the *Oklahoma City Times-Journal* and the *New York Sun*, among others. In a 1965 tribute, Larry Phipps wrote of Barde that "he is the acknowledged dean of Oklahoma's first journalists" (1). À la Henry David Thoreau or John Joseph Mathews, he lived in a natural sanctuary, which he called Doby Walls, where he could observe Oklahoma fauna and flora. As a naturalist he published *Field, Forest, and Stream in Oklahoma* (1912) and *Outdoor Oklahoma* (1914) (Phipps).

2. Before 2007 only a handful of articles and book chapters about part of his work were published: Arnie Strickland, "John Milton Oskison: A Writer of the Transitional Period of the Oklahoma Territory," was the first, in 1972; Charles Larson included analysis of Oskison's novels in his *American Indian Fiction*, in 1978; Littlefield and Parins, "Short Fiction Writers of the Indian Territory," dealt with Oskison as a regionalist writer along with Sac and Fox William Jones and Creek Alexander Posey, in 1982; Gretchen Ronnow, "Cherokee Journalist," in 1987, dealt with Oskison as a journalist. The most complete analysis of Oskison's work is Ronnow's PhD dissertation, "John Milton Oskison: Native American Modernist" (1993). Much more scholarly analysis of Oskison's writings remains to be done.

3. It is, however, probable that the first novel Henry Odell refers to as "a mess, misty, sentimental, badly knit," etc. and "a prize-amateur effort" is a novel Oskison never published and one he describes in a letter to journalist Fred Barde published in this volume in the following way: "In spots, it was so good that the rest of it seemed depressing."

4. Littlefield and Parins called Oskison a regionalist, or a "local color" writer of Indian Territory ("Short Fiction"). Arnie Strickland called him "A Writer of the Transitional Period of the Oklahoma Territory."

5. In the introduction to her PhD dissertation, Gretchen Ronnow proposes an analysis of Oskison's fiction that attempts to demonstrate that "the charges of melodrama, sentimentality, stereotypical characters, absence of Indian characters, or lack of interest in Indian issues in the consideration of Oskison's short fiction apply only so superficially as to be, ultimately, grossly inaccurate" (25). She notably argues that "his stories are permeated by a sub-structure of Cherokee myth and mythological worldview. Ultimately it is this mythological influence which produces the sense of strangeness — the peculiar but signifying twist — prevalent in Oskison's stories. Ultimately to a careful reader, Oskison is a writer clearly influenced by his Native American experience in all its ramifications" (27).

6. The Cherokee Outlet, also commonly but wrongly called the "Cherokee Strip," was a 6-million-acre tract of land lying west of the 96° meridian. It was unoccupied but was supposed to give the Cherokees access to buffalo hunting after they were removed to Indian Territory. After the Civil War, the Outlet became the center of attention for many until the cession of it to the United States in 1893 became what some historians called a "pivotal moment" in Cherokee history (Miner 121). After the Civil War, the Cherokee Nation, which had signed a treaty with the Confederacy, was in a weak position. The treaty signed with the United States in 1866 forced them to accept the relocation of tribes in the eastern part of the Outlet. In the aftermath of the war, Texas cattle began to invade the Outlet. With its fertile soil and high-quality grass, it was ideally located between the cattle herds in Texas and the cowtowns of southern Kansas. Besides, it was distant from its owners and separated from them by the tribes removed to the Outlet after the 1866 treaty. As they were driving their herds to the Kansas railroad towns where the animals would be shipped east, Texas cattlemen would let them fatten for weeks in the Outlet. At the end of the 1860s about 600,000 head were driven through these Cherokee lands (Milam 269; Dale 61). Although these cattle were there illegally, the cattlemen felt so comfortable that "they established themselves upon ranges the boundaries of which the various men determined among themselves under that common law of the range known as 'cow custom'" (Dale 62). Since the cattle disturbed no one in this unoccupied territory, the Cherokee Council tried to make good of this intrusion and decided in 1879 to try to collect revenue from the cattle owners (Milam 269). This task was made easier in 1883 when the cattlemen organized themselves into the Cherokee Strip Live Stock Association, to which the Cherokees leased the Outlet for the modest sum of $100,000 a year, later to become $300,000 a year (Miner 131). Investigating for the Indian Rights Association in order to determine "the effects, prejudicial or otherwise, of the herding of cattle on the reservations" and "the propriety of leasing Indian lands to companies of white men, often strong

in political influence, whose hold on the land may never be broken" (20), Friend of the Indian Samuel Armstrong gave his opinion on the issue in a report published in 1884. He wrote that "there is an increasing demand for grass. The Indian Territory is a splendid pasture ground in relief against the nearly exhausted pastures of Texas. Experience shows that outside herders will drive their cattle upon unused pastures. Indian policemen and United States soldiers have failed to keep away Texas cowboys with their flocks; if driven back, they at once return. It is best, on the whole, I believe, to rent to the highest bidder the privilege of grazing cattle on Indian lands, for it hardly increases the consumption of grass and it creates a revenue" (21). The lease was in effect until 1891, when the Cherokees agreed, on 19 December, to sell the Outlet to the United States. The sale was confirmed by Congress on 17 March 1893 for the sum of $8,595,736, and in September the last land run in the history of the Twin Territories took place.

7. In *Wild Harvest: A Novel of Transition Days in Oklahoma* (1925), Oskison has one of his characters, Billy Dines, tell his niece Nan that "the Indians are talkin' about enforcin' quarantine against Texas cattle that are shipped in durin' the summer an' fall. They ain't decided yet, though they ought to do it, the way them Texas steers give our native stuff the fever" (33). Later, the narrator says that "the Indian tribal authorities clamped down quarantine restrictions. No more Texas cattle would be admitted until cold weather, when what was known as 'splenetic fever' was no longer to be feared" (48).

8. For a study of the development of Native American studies, see Kidwell and Velie, *Native American Studies*.

9. For studies of Grant's Peace Policy, see Whitney, "Grant's Indian Peace Policy"; Utley, "The Celebrated Peace Policy of General Grant"; for an early study, see Tatum, *Our Red Brothers and the Peace Policy of President Ulysses S. Grant*.

10. Hazel Hertzberg published a very interesting history of the SAI in *The Search for an American Indian Identity* (1971). Lucy Maddox offers a meticulous analysis of the philosophy held by Indian intellectuals of the SAI in *Citizen Indians*. Although she does not deal much with Oskison in particular, what she writes about his fellow members Arthur Parker, Charles Eastman, and Gertrude Bonnin, among others, is very useful to understanding Oskison as well.

11. For a complete study of the Pueblo Indians and their interaction with the federal government, see among many others Edward Dozier, *The Pueblo Indians of North America*.

12. Many studies have been dedicated to the boarding schools. See, notably, Brenda Child, *Boarding School Seasons*. For personal renditions see, notably, the first chapter of Wilma Mankiller's autobiography, *Mankiller: A Chief and Her People*, in which

the former principal chief of the Cherokees evokes Sequoyah Training School, near Tahlequah, which several members of her family had attended: "At Sequoyah School, south of Tahlequah . . . my father and his little sister were forbidden to speak their native language. They could not speak a word of English when they first went there, so they were whipped for speaking Cherokee" (7). See also La Flesche, *The Middle Five*. Many other firsthand testimonies, from other schools and tribes, can be found in Bensen, *Children of the Dragonfly*; Archuleta, Child, and Lomawaima, *Away from Home*; and Lomawaima, *They called It Prairie Light*. Useful documents can also be found in N. Shoemaker, *American Indians*.

13. On the very complex issue of allotment policy, see the following, among many other studies: Conley, *The Cherokee Nation*; Hagan, *Taking Indian Lands*; LaVelle, "General Allotment Act." Holm, "Indian Lobbyists," in particular, touches on the support given allotment policy by the reformers. A very recent analysis of the consequences of allotment is Ruppel, *Unearthing Indian Land*.

14. William Wirt Hastings (1866–1938) was a very active Cherokee leader and a nationally recognized politician. He graduated from the Cherokee Male Seminary, in Tahlequah, in 1884 and obtained a law degree from Vanderbilt University, Nashville, in 1889. At the Cherokee Male Seminary he had been a student under Robert L. Owen, who was to become one of the first United States senators from the new state of Oklahoma. After holding several offices in the Cherokee Nation — tribal education superintendent (1890–91), attorney general (1891–95), and Cherokee national attorney (1907–14) — Hastings was elected to the U.S. House of Representatives. In all, he served in Congress for eighteen years (1915–1921 and 1923–1935) (J. B. King). In 1905, Hastings had been chairman of the Constitution Committee that was to organize the Indian Territory as the state of Sequoyah separate from Oklahoma (Maxwell 70, 86–87, 133). Oskison wrote of Bill Hastings in his autobiography and in "In Governing the Indian, Use the Indian." Hastings was also, on 22 January 1936, one of the "Chiefs for a Day," the six principal chiefs of the Cherokee Nation that were appointed by the president of the United States between 1919 and 1936 (Conley, *The Cherokee Nation* 204). Conley considers that the "Chiefs for a Day" remained "often in office only long enough to sign some documents" (*Cherokee Thoughts* 43).

15. For a detailed study of the Jerome Commission, see Hagan, *Taking Indian Lands*.

16. Indications of his position on allotment could arguably be gleaned — although not definitely assessed — from a dialogue between Nan and Tom, the two protagonists of *Wild Harvest*. Talking of his future as a farmer, Tom says: "One of these days, the Indians'll be argued into allottin' all these miles an' miles of prairie, like them Kansas politicians are tryin' to make 'em do now. Then there'll be land for

sale, an' the Indians'll have to buckle down to farmin' an' cattle raisin' to keep even with us white folks. Good thing for 'em, too." Nan agrees and adds: "Uncle Billy says Indians like Chief Littlespring, Ross Murray and 'Sofkey' Horseford are already showing the way to the others. Uncle Billy likes these Indians; he says they're as smart as anybody—no reason why they shouldn't move ahead with the rest of us." Tom concludes: "An' they sure will . . . At the bank in Big Grove they're already beginnin' to open accounts, make loans an' carry on like regular fellows" (295).

17. "Illogical" is the word Debo uses when she quotes Dawes (*And Still* 21). Senator Dawes reported to the Lake Mohonk Conference what he had heard and seen during a visit he made to the Indian Territory: "The head chief told us that there was not a family in that whole Nation [presumably the Cherokee Nation] that had not a home of its own. There was not a pauper in that Nation, and the Nation did not owe a dollar. It built its own capitol, in which we had this examination, and it built its schools and its hospitals. Yet the defect of the system was apparent. They have got as far as they can go, because they own their land in common. It is Henry George's system, and under that there is no enterprise to make your home any better than that of your neighbors. There is no selfishness, which is at the bottom of civilization. Till this people will consent to give up their lands, and divide them among their citizens so that each can own the land he cultivates, they will not make much more progress" (Dawes 43). To Dawes, then, lack of selfishness, homelessness and pauperism were reasons to pass his famous bill, the purpose of which he also explained in clear terms to the conference: "The purpose of the bill is to clothe the Secretary of the Interior with all the power he needs to do everything in respect to the Indian that every one of you said to-day he wanted to have done. It is, first, to put the Indian in severalty on a farm; next, after having done that, to sell all the rest of his reservation; next, to give him all the rights and privileges of any white man in the courts. When it was drawn, it was supposed he was a citizen, and if it is ever introduced again it will have a provision that makes him a citizen" (Dawes 38–39).

18. The white citizens of the Cherokee Nation took the rivalry between cattlemen and farmers into the political arena. In Oskison's *Wild Harvest*, a white farmer named Vergil Stokes, believing in "the Shorthorn yearlin' an' the steam plow layin' down together in peace" (157), runs for a seat in the tribal council. He is said by another character to want "to show what a 'squawman' can do down there in the timber about makin' laws that'll suit Indians an' whites, too" (158). Later, as he launches his campaign, "Vergil's mid-July meeting was welcomed by farmers and haymen as a brief respite in the busy season's grind of hard work; and it drew the Indian and negro voters (negro 'freedmen' voted by virtue of membership in the tribe granted when they had ceased to be slaves of Indian owners) who were curious to 'size up this white man that wants to help make laws for Indians'" (165–66).

19. For praises of industrial tycoons or innovators, see "A Less Known Edison," "A Chemist Who Became King of an Industry," and "The American Creator of the Aluminum Age," all published in *World's Work* in 1914. For financial advice, see, among others, "The Spider and the Fly" (*Woman's Home Companion* Oct. 1911), in which the spider is some of "the financial sharks that infest New York waters" and the fly is a widow whose husband died leaving "a modest fortune"; and most of the articles he published in *Collier's Weekly* between 1909 and 1914: "Exploiters of the Needy," "Competing with the Sharks," "Round-up of the Financial Swindlers," "Boosting the Thrift Idea," etc.

20. As the Dawes Commission was accomplishing its mission, some Cherokee actually considered a move to Mexico. "In 1895, Bird Harris proposed that the Cherokee Nation go ahead and sell all of its land to the United States, use the money to purchase land in Mexico or South America, and then remove the entire Cherokee Nation once more, this time completely beyond the long and greedy reach of the United States" (Conley, *The Cherokee Nation* 196).

21. Circe Sturm uses the term *multiracial*. Although she uses it to talk about individuals "to avoid the negative connotations and biological fictions associated with the more familiar expression *mixed blood*" (213), the term can make sense to refer to the Cherokee Nation, or the Indian Territory at large, in Oskison's day. I understand and share Sturm's reservations about the term *mixed blood*, but I have mine as far as the term *race* is concerned in its everyday use in American English. I have always found it very problematic—probably because its literal translation in my mother language, French, is unacceptable because it is clearly racist—since it directly comes from the old lie that mankind is composed of human races. Even if the term today is not used only by proponents of racist theories, of course, the history of the signifier is too heavy a burden not to weigh on the signified. In the words of the American Anthropological Association, "race" as it is used in the United States is a European ideology: "As they were constructing U.S. society, leaders among European-Americans fabricated the cultural/behavioural characteristics associated with each 'race,' linking superior traits with Europeans and negative and inferior ones to blacks and Indians. . . . Ultimately, 'race' as an ideology about human differences was subsequently spread to other areas of the world. It became a strategy for dividing, ranking, and controlling colonized people used by colonial powers everywhere" (American Anthropological Association Statement on "Race," 17 May 1998, qtd. in S. Russell 107). I share Sturm's view of "race as a Western social and political construct around various biological fictions that is nonetheless 'real' because of its impact on lived experience. It is created to explain social difference and justify inequality, and its meaning varies over time according to shifting relations of power

and struggle" (213). For these very reasons, because "race is not a natural, biological, or scientific category" but a "social, historical, and political category defined in biological terms" (14–15), I avoid using the term. If the term *multicultural* can appear anachronistic to describe a situation at the end of the nineteenth century, I think it better reflects the reality. Even if the term becomes common with the beginning of multicultural policies in Canada in the 1970s, taken etymologically, it signifies social realities that had existed for a long time before then, notably in the "Old I.T."

22. For more on this subject, see Conley, *The Cherokee Nation*, especially the chapter entitled "Jurisdictional Confusion." See also "Autobiography" nn. 21 and 60 and "Essays" n. 8.

23. For assessments of pre-contact Cherokee life, see the first chapters of Conley, *The Cherokee Nation*; Perdue and Green, *Cherokee Nation*; E. Starr, *History of the Cherokee Indians*; D. King, *The Cherokee Indian Nation*; Mooney, *History, Myths, and Sacred Formulas*.

24. "The trail where they cried" is the literal translation of *Nunnadautsun't* or *Nunna daul Tsuny*, the Cherokee expression that refers to the Trail of Tears (Byers 47). In *The Singing Bird*, the protagonist missionaries live with the Western Cherokees in Arkansas first, where they moved in several groups in 1810–11 and in 1819. From there, and then from Indian Territory where they moved in 1828, they see the arrival of the Cherokees who left after the Treaty of New Echota, and then the Cherokees who were removed on the Trail of Tears.

25. Histories and studies of the intricacies of these clashes are numerous. Among many works, see the following: Conley, *The Cherokee Nation*; Perdue and Green, *Cherokee Removal*, which contains essential historical documents written by the protagonists; Perdue and Green, *Cherokee Nation*; Confer, *The Cherokee Nation in the Civil War*; Reed, "Postremoval Factionalism in the Cherokee Nation." See also earlier accounts: E. Starr, *History of the Cherokee Indians*; Wardell, *Political History of the Cherokee Nation*.

26. About the seminaries and the Cherokee Nation educational system in general, see "Autobiography" n. 4.

27. Here is an interesting paradox of the time: blood quantum rhetoric was commonly used, yet that kind of information was taken rather loosely when defining someone. On the one hand, the final rolls of the Cherokee distinguish the Cherokees by Blood from the Cherokee Freedmen and the Cherokees by Intermarriage and give the amount of Cherokee blood flowing in the veins of the Cherokees by Blood. On the other hand, Oskison, for example, appears on the rolls as a one-quarter Cherokee when he defines himself as a one-eighth and is defined in many different ways by the publishers of his texts and by the journalists writing about

him. The *San Francisco Chronicle*, in a 1906 article, dubiously defined Oskison, "in whose veins runs a half strain of Indian blood," as "a Half-Indian." The paper hardly redeemed itself by also calling him a "brilliant writer" under a headline that read "Did he Heed Call of Wild?" (5 Sept. 1906). *Southern Workman* defined him as "a member of the Cherokee tribe in Indian Territory" in the issue publishing "The Outlook for the Indian" (1903). The *Quarterly Journal of the Society of American Indians* defined him simply as "Cherokee." So did *The Indian Leader* and *Case and Comment* in the issues featuring "The Closing Chapter" (1914) and "In Governing the Indian" (1917), respectively. The *New York Times* wrote that he "was partly Cherokee in descent" in the article reporting his death (26 Feb. 1947). Barde called him "an Oklahoma Indian." *The Oklahoman* reported him saying that he wrote a biography of John Ross (never published) because the chief "was of the same degree of Cherokee blood as himself" (28 Dec. 1930). On the title page of that biography's typescript, which he submitted for publication in 1933, Oskison had typed "Tsalagi" (meaning *Cherokee* in Cherokee) under his name, before crossing over it with a pencil. If some texts are signed "Lieutenant John M. Oskison" ("Back-firing against Bolshevism"), the most common title following his name, though, is "Financial Editor of *Collier's Weekly*," although the *Indian Chieftain*, at the beginning of his career, often affectionately and proudly refers to him as "a Vinita boy" — when publishing "A Trip to Yosemite Valley" (Aug. 1895) and "I Match You: You Match Me" (May 1897) — or "Vinita's Representative at Leland Stanford University" when publishing "A Schoolmaster's Dissipation" (Dec. 1897).

Arguing that because they "sensed a general disinterest in fiction by Native Americans," Charles Larson claimed that publishers often "tried to conceal the racial identity of the author — perhaps with the encouragement of the author himself." Larson asserted that Oskison's "racial identity was . . . thoroughly camouflaged" (3). To prove his point, he noted that "the dust jackets of his three novels . . . make no reference to Oskison's Cherokee heritage, though the one for *Brothers Three* goes so far as to state that the author was 'born in the old Indian Territory, near the capital of the Cherokee Nation'" (3–4). I disagree with Larson's conclusion. First, the publishers did not advertise the "racial identity" of their European American authors either. Then, the dust jacket of *Tecumseh and His Times*, published a year after *Brothers Three*, stated that the author "inherits from his mother a strain of Cherokee blood" and reminded the reader of his previous works. This seems inconsistent with a "camouflaging" of Cherokeeness. Besides, by the time Oskison published his first novel, in 1925, he was already a well-known Indian activist and short fiction writer. In a short biography from the "Author! Author!" page of an October 1927 issue of *McClure's*, in which "Yvonne the Terrible" was published, a national audience could read that Oskison "has in his veins a strong strain of Cherokee Indian blood." The story is captioned "A Love Episode of the Great War" and has so little Indian content that the publisher could have hidden Oskison's Indianness if it had seen fit.

28. In a monologue that Oskison obviously uses to counter clichés about the Indians, Gabe Horner continues: "Here they've got a regular government: chief, second chief, a senate, a council, courts, schools, asylums, churches an' preachers. They've got plenty of educated men an' women; they've got lawyers an' doctors an' traders; they've got their political parties an' tribal newspapers an' public men that have growed up thinkin' an' talkin' about their own problems till they can hold their own with Congress when they go to Washington as delegates." He then concludes: "The way I size 'em up — if you ain't tired of hearin' a windy old timer like me shoot off his mouth — these Indians have got to be mighty like regular folks that know what they want an' know how to get it" (255)

29. It is remarkable that this early guide gives quite a significant acknowledgment of the roles the Indians played in shaping the state politically, socially, and culturally. In an opening chapter, titled "The Spirit of Oklahoma," for example, historian Edward Everett Dale wrote that the "long Indian era has profoundly affected present-day Oklahoma," that the long diplomatic training of the Indians, as well as "the experience of administering the affairs of their tribal governments after reaching Oklahoma, gave the Indians of the Five Civilized Tribes a knowledge of diplomacy and politics equal to that of any people in the world" and contributed to producing outstanding statesmen. "Steadily there is being woven into the fabric of Oklahoma's citizenship this red thread of the Indian," Dale concluded (3–4).

1. AUTOBIOGRAPHY

1. In "When the Grass Grew Long," Oskison writes of his cowboy protagonist: "It was when the puncher was seventeen years old that he came to the Territory, leaving a rather miserable Indiana home."

2. In *Brothers Three*, though, Oskison gives a romantic explanation: "Disappointed of quick wealth from the worked-out placer diggings of the Sierras, and tired of California's sun-hot wheatfields, he had been adventuring eastward by slow stages. Keith Prairie seemed to say, 'Stay, restless spirit, and find peace'" (8). The narrator refers to Francis Odell, a fictional character that Oskison obviously modeled on his father. Keith Prairie is a fictional place where Francis meets his part-Cherokee wife, Janet Keith. Details are different, of course, but *Brothers Three*, Oskison's third novel, published in 1935, is replete with autobiographical references. The three brothers — Timmy, Roger, and Henry — are modeled on Dick, William, and John M. Oskison himself, respectively.

3. The Texas Road was the main emigrant route passing through Indian Territory before the massive migration to California. This route was largely used by emigrants traveling to Texas during the Mexican War. One branch of this route came from Baxter Springs, in the southeast corner of Kansas, and went through Fort Gibson. The other branch came from St. Louis through Springfield, in the southwest corner of Missouri, and entered Indian Territory through Fort Wayne, near the Illinois River. From Fort Gibson, the Texas Road went southwest to Fort Washita and on to Texas. Grant Foreman quotes an army officer who traveled the Texas Road in October 1846: "The way from Fort Gibson was literally lined with wagons of emigrants to Texas and from this time until we arrived at Saint Louis, we continued daily to see hundreds of them" (qtd. in "Early Trails" 117). Foreman praises the pioneers and emigrants who "discovered the easiest and most practicable route through this country . . . ; and it is a remarkable fact that when the Missouri, Kansas & Texas Railroad was surveyed through eastern Indian Territory the route adopted was almost identical with that of the Texas Road" (118).

4. From the very beginning of the nineteenth century, the Cherokee Nation had encouraged an education that would enable the Cherokee to understand the white man. As early as 1801, Moravian missionaries were invited to establish a school in the Nation in Georgia. In 1803 the Presbyterians followed (J. B. Davis 168). Section 10 of the 1827 Constitution stipulated that "religion, morality, and knowledge being necessary to good government, the preservation of liberty, and the happiness of mankind, schools and the means of education shall forever be encouraged in this Nation." After removal, a public school system was created. At the end of the century the Cherokee Nation counted at least one hundred Cherokee elementary schools and fourteen schools for colored people (J. B. Davis 171). In the West, the first school established among the Cherokees was the Dwight Mission, founded in 1819 in Arkansas by Cephas Washburn. According to Powell and Mullikin, the Dwight Mission inspired Oskison's Wear Mission in *The Singing Bird* (xliv).

The 1835 Treaty of New Echota as well as the 1846 treaty signed in Washington both made provisions for the establishments of two higher education schools in the Cherokee Nation. The Male Seminary and the Female Seminary were the two "first nonsectarian school[s] of higher learning to open west of the Mississippi River" (Mihesuah, "Out of the 'Graves'" 503). The Male Seminary, located southwest of Tahlequah, and the Female Seminary, located three miles southeast, were completed in 1850 and opened in May 1851. The Female Seminary was destroyed by fire in 1887 and built again two years later. The Male Seminary burned in 1910. The two seminaries combined and formed Northeastern State College. While the seminaries were under construction, Chief John Ross sent for some highly qualified teachers from Mount Holyoke Female Seminary (in Massachusetts), Dartmouth, and Princeton. The curriculum, modeled on Mount Holyoke's, included German, French, Latin, mathematics, moral philosophy, English, the sciences (such as botany, chemistry, geology, etc.), music, and home economics, among others (Abbott 188, 191; Tinnin 64–65). In an 1893 decision called *Mehlin v. Ice* (see "Autobiography" n. 43), Judge Caldwell of the Circuit Court of Appeals, attempting to demonstrate that the Cherokee were a "civilized" tribe, cited the quality of the Cherokee schools and stated that the Cherokee's "opportunities for religious instruction have not been at all inferior to those of the frontier white settlements." Debo writes that "as a result of this boarding school and college training there was a larger proportion of educated people among the Cherokees, Choctaws, and Chickasaws than among the white people of the neighboring states" (*And Still* 8).

5. The principal chief at the time of John Oskison's arrival in Cherokee Territory was William Potter Ross, nephew of Chief John Ross, who indeed had provided for his education at Princeton. W. P. Ross was appointed by the council in 1872 to replace Lewis Downing after the latter died in office.

6. The *Cherokee Advocate* was a successor of the first Cherokee newspaper, the *Cherokee Phoenix*, first published on 21 February 1828. This newspaper "was a direct product of Sequoyah's great invention of a Cherokee alphabet" (Debo, "Cherokee Paper"). The *Cherokee Phoenix* was published with the assistance of missionary Samuel Austin Worcester, and its first editor was Elias Boudinot. In 1821, Sequoyah (George Gist) created a syllabary to put the Cherokee language to writing. Debo wrote about the enthusiasm with which the Cherokee welcomed Sequoyah's invention: "The whole nation was swept by the exhilaration of learning to read and write their language. Travelers passing through their country found the characters marked on tree trunks and fence rails or scratched in the dust as the people joyfully practiced their new literacy" ("Cherokee Paper"). In *And Still the Waters Run*, Debo writes that Sequoyah was "one of the greatest geniuses ever produced by any race," whose alphabet "enabled the whole tribe to become within a few months a literate people" (4). Oskison would include Sequoyah as a character in *The Singing Bird*.

7. On 25 September 1900, when he applied to the Dawes Commission for the enrollment of his son William, John Oskison Sr. said that he married a Cherokee woman named Rachel Conner, probably Rachel Crittenden's maiden name, in 1868.

8. Historian Travis wrote: "All full-bloods were quite neighborly and food was divided freely as long as there was any to divide" (20). Good neighborly relationships, especially between Indians and white men, is a recurrent theme in Oskison's fiction (see, e.g., "Tookh Steh's Mistake"). In his essays Oskison often insisted on this aspect to fight white frontier prejudice. He wanted to prove that living with

the Indians was easy. For example, in "Arizona and Forty Thousand Indians" he quotes a white cattleman: "'Shucks! these Indians are the finest people in the world to get along with,' said 'Rimmy Jim' when I asked him if he had ever been troubled. 'They'll look after my stock, when any of it gets over on their range, just like it was their own; of course, they know I'll do the same for them. I ain't never had a bit of trouble—don't ever expect to have any!'"

9. Section 2 of Article 1 of the 1827 Cherokee Constitution read, in part, as follows: "The sovereignty and jurisdiction of this Government shall extend over the country within the boundaries above described, and the land therein is and shall remain the common property of the nation, but the improvements made thereon and in possession of the citizens of the nation, are the exclusive and indefeasible property of the citizens respectively who made or may rightfully be in possession of them." The 1839 Constitution is phrased slightly differently—"the lands of the Cherokee Nation shall remain common property; but the improvements made thereon, and in the possession of the citizens respectively who made, or may rightfully be in possession of them"—but means the same. This provision established a very original property system—somehow blending common property and private property—which allowed Oskison's father, as all other Cherokee citizens, to "own" a farm on land belonging to the Cherokee Nation. The land was free to use by individuals, but all improvements made on it—buildings, clearings, and all other products of individual work—belonged to the individual. See Bloom, "An American Tragedy"; interestingly, Bloom sees in this mixed property system "a fairly pure embodiment of John Locke's natural-right doctrine of private property: 'He hath mixed his labour with it, and joined it to something that is his own, and thereby makes it his property. It being by him removed from the common state that Nature places it in, it hath by this labour something annexed to it that excludes the common right of other men'" (Locke qtd. in Bloom 499).

10. Cabin Creek, also known as Big Cabin Creek, has its source north of Vinita close to the border with Kansas, flows just a few miles west of Vinita, and joins the Neosho River a few miles east of Adair, in present-day Mayes County. In July 1863 a battle took place along this river during the Civil War. Pryor Creek has its source west of Vinita and flows south to Chouteau, Mayes County. This area of Oskison's childhood, mostly located in Coo-Wee-Scoo-Wee District—which covered today's Nowata, Washington, Tulsa, Rogers, and parts of Mayes, Craig, and Wagoner Counties—is the beginning of the prairie just west of the Ozark Mountains.

11. The first neighbor Oskison mentions here is probably Jesse A. Thomas, tribal card number 2978. Fritz cannot be found on the tribal rolls.

12. Pawpaw Creek has its source northwest of Vinita and joins Big Cabin Creek

just a couple of miles west of the town, in the area of Oskison's farm. The Frisco railroad is the St. Louis and San Francisco Railway. Patrick Shanahan was an Irish immigrant of local fame because of the "war" he waged — "Shanahan's war" — against the Frisco in 1882. When the railroad was to link Vinita to Sapulpa, southwest of Tulsa, Shanahan's land was in the way, and he refused the offer made to him. He met the railroad crew armed and resisted during a two-week standoff (O'Dell, "Shanahan").

13. The *St. Louis Globe Democrat*, a daily newspaper, was widely read in Indian Territory at the time. In 1887, it had a circulation of 2,500 copies, which made it the second paper after the *Republican*, with 3,000 copies (1887 *Report Commissioner Indian Affairs* 110).

14. T. DeWitt Talmage (1832–1902) was a very popular Presbyterian preacher whose sermons were published in thousands of national newspapers and magazines weekly.

15. The names Betsy, Liza, and Jennie were recurrently used by Oskison in his fiction. Liza and Jennie are Old Harjo's wives in "The Problem of Old Harjo." Betsy and Jennie are close friends in "The Singing Bird."

16. In an article about his first novel, *Wild Harvest*, Oskison reportedly stated that he "had lived for a time with my full-blood Cherokee Indian relatives . . . in sweet-smelling, wind-swept and bountifully provisioned log cabins on Pawpaw and Big Cabin creeks, and had kept the remembrance of their women's exquisite, courteous and loving kindness to the little boy who couldn't talk their language" (*The Oklahoman* 13 Jan. 1929).

17. Oskison probably refers here to a Baptist missionary whose name appears as Bear Timpson on the Dawes rolls, tribal card number 3210. In chapter 17 of *The Singing Bird*, Paul, the missionary narrator, invites Cherokee preachers to conduct services in the mission chapel. One of his favorite guests is Bear Timson: "One I liked especially came from a remote creekside settlement and described himself as 'a man that plow his fiel' an' make his garden early in mornin' an' Sattidy, teach school eight in mornin' til four o'clock in evenin', preach in little log schoolhouse two times Sunday, an' fin' time also for Sunday school an' temperance society meetin'" (157).

18. Jake Longtail and Jimmy Horsefly are not on the tribal rolls.

19. In Devon Mihesuah's comprehensive study of the Cherokee Female Seminary there is no mention of Fanny Bly, but there is of Fannie Blythe, who graduated on 27 June 1879. In *The Oklahoman*, Oskison told about the sweet memories of his early schooling days: "I had studied my first lessons in a log school-house, under a white schoolma'am who boarded at my home, who drove me to school in the family buggy and implanted in me a fragrant recollection" (13 Jan. 1929). Fannie

Blythe is probably the person to whom Oskison refers. This assumption is reinforced by a clue found in Glenn Shirley's book on Belle Starr, the famous "bandit queen" (see "Fiction" nn. 27, 32 and 66), in which there is a reference to one Fannie Blythe Marks, the widow of Deputy Marshal L. W. Marks, "a deputy marshal for the Vinita District" (152) who chased Belle Starr in 1882. In the next paragraph, Oskison writes that "Fanny Bly" "married a deputy United States marshal." In "The Greater Appeal," first published in 1905 and included in the present volume, one "Jim" Marks is after Belle Starr.

20. According to Travis, "The Cherokees had a system of public schools superior to that of any other Indian tribe, and in many ways compared favorably with those established in the States." He describes the Cherokee school system in detail. Of the seminaries, he writes: "There were two seminaries. The Male Seminary was located about two miles southwest of Tahlequah, while the Female Seminary was a short distance north and east of Park Hill. Both institutions were housed in commodious brick buildings which were identical in architecture. . . . There was an average enrollment of about one hundred twenty-five pupils in each seminary. A charge of five dollars a month was made for each pupil. This paid for board, room, laundry, textbooks, and medical care. In the case of indigent children, employment was provided which made it possible for them to pay their own expenses. No Cherokee boy or girl, who had sufficient ambition to secure an education, was denied that privilege. The course of study included geometry, arithmetic, geography, botany, history, Latin, Greek, psychology, philosophy, and the Bible. The two seminaries provided the majority of the teachers for the primary schools" (23). The Cherokee educational system at the time was largely praised. See also Mooney, among others.

21. At least since the 1850s (see "Introduction" n. 8; "Autobiography" n. 60; "Fiction" nn. 77 and 86), the Indian Affairs authorities had recommended that Congress should take action to deal with the jurisdictional confusion in Indian Territory. As Oskison writes, the tribal courts had no authority to deal with noncitizens, which was indeed very appealing to many white outlaws. What's worse is that when Cherokee citizens were involved in cases also involving U.S. citizens, U.S. justice interfered with Cherokee justice. In a letter dated 9 April 1856, Cherokee Agent George Butler reported examples of such interference to Superintendent of Indian Affairs Charles Dean. A Cherokee citizen named Peak had been arrested by Going Snake district sheriff Eli Sanders and indicted for stealing horses. As his trial in a Cherokee tribunal had to be delayed, and "while the said Peak was a prisoner, under Sanders and guard," Deputy Marshal Russell arrested Peak "from the hands of Sanders on a writ issued by the United States court for stealing a mule from a white man living in the nation" (Butler to Dean, 9 Apr. 1856, 3). Butler added that

Sanders thought, "as the writ issued by the nation was of a prior date to the one issued by the United States, as he had the prisoner in possession, that the marshal should have waited until the Cherokee nation was satisfied." Butler completely concurred. Thus, Butler called his hierarchy's attention on such issues demanding "to learn whether the marshal has the *authority* to take a prisoner from the hands of a regular officer of the nation." He also made clear to his superiors that he thought that "the Cherokee authorities should be treated with respect."

As McLoughlin puts it, this made Butler's position quite awkward since he could not "encourage responsible Cherokee self-government and at the same time allow the U.S. authorities in Arkansas to undermine it" (109). Butler concluded indeed that if the Cherokees "are to be treated as degraded slaves, it is useless for government officers to attempt to give them encouragement." In the 16 April letter that Superintendent Dean sent Commissioner of Indian Affairs George Manypenny along with Butler's letter, we learn that this was not the first time such an issue was brought to the attention of the Interior Department, apparently in vain. Indeed, the conflict of jurisdiction had been made "the subject of a special report from this office [Indian Affairs] of the 7th of October, 1853" (Manypenny to Secretary of the Interior McClelland, 22 May 1856, 2). Dean expressed that this constant interference "of the functionaries of the federal courts with the officials of the Cherokee tribunals, is universally regarded by the Cherokees as an invasion of privileges and rights" guaranteed by treaties signed with the United States. Dean was worried that such practices and such neglect on the part of the department to solve the problem would alienate the members of the Cherokee Nation "whom it is most desirable to attach by sentiments of friendship and cordial good-will to our government and institutions" (Dean to Manypenny, 16 Apr. 1856, 3).

In the 1870s and 1880s the problem had not been solved. In 1884, in his report for the Indian Rights Association, Armstrong wrote of a very practical reason to create a court in Indian Territory: the distance to travel to Fort Smith "has ruined many farmers, through whose long absences crops have spoiled. Farmers and business men cannot afford to be witnesses for the time and money it costs; much petty crime goes unpunished; vagabonds find it profitable to go at Government expense either as witnesses or criminals" (24–25). In his 1887 annual report, the commissioner of Indian Affairs writes about "the urgent necessity for the establishment of a United States court in the Indian Territory," which he had already "discussed at considerable length" in previous reports, apparently to no avail. "I do not know that I can add anything to what I have already said on this subject," he writes, "but I feel it my duty to repeat, with added emphasis, that the necessity for Congressional legislation for the better protection of life and property and the preservation of order among the five civilized tribes increases from year to year, in fact hourly grows in urgency." He says that "the reckless destruction of human life, particularly in the Cherokee and Creek Nations, is appalling to contemplate. Officer and officer has been brutally murdered in attempting to discharge his sworn duty. Murderers escape punishment and even trial" (1887 *Report Commissioner Indian Affairs* liv). The first district court of Indian Territory was established in 1889 in Muskogee.

22. Oskison's father applied to the Dawes Commission for the enrollment of his son Will as a Cherokee citizen in September 1900. When Commissioner Needles asked him about his marital status, John Oskison Sr. answered that he married his second wife, a white woman named Sarah Shanks, in 1878, the year following the death of his first wife, Rachel. When John Milton Oskison applied for enrollment in March 1901, he answered "Sarah" instead of Rachel to the question "What is your mother's name?" Although John and his brothers "resented" their stepmother and the fact that their household was not "harmonious," Sarah had been the motherly figure he had known since he was four. This can explain a Freudian slip. It is also possible that his stepsister Sarah, Rachel's daughter, had become a motherly figure after Rachel's death. Indeed, Oskison wrote that she could, "in a fashion, fill the role of housekeeper" and that "she sulked at giving over housekeeping responsibilities" after Sarah Shanks's arrival in the household.

23. Albert Oskison, also called Bert, will become a relatively well known roper, participating in many contests along with Will Rogers and other famous competitors. An *Indian Chieftain* article dated 2 August 1900, for example, reports his victory at a roping contest taking place on the grounds of Halsell College. This particular contest and others inspired John Oskison to write several stories. In "The Fall of King Chris" (1903), one of the roping contestants at Bluejacket is "JIC-Bert (which was not his name, but a combination of that and his cattle brand), a cool, smooth-cheeked young fellow, with a laugh that exploded like a firecracker." We learn later in this chapter of the autobiography that JIC was the brand chosen by Oskison's father to identify his cattle.

Bert Oskison died on 16 May 1930 in a Vinita hospital under the effects of a general anesthesia administered to him after he injured his finger while cutting wood. His widow, Lizzie Oskison, sued the doctors (see *Oskison v. Bagby*, Supreme Court of Oklahoma). When *Brothers Three* was published, *The Oklahoman* published an article claiming that the book had "revived interest in a celebrated damage suit a few years ago in which the Oskison family figured." According to the article, in spite of rumors that the doctors, defendants in the trial, wanted to sue the author, they were "emphatic in their denials of any plans to sue the author and half-brother of Bert Oskison, whose death occupies so important a part in the book" ("Oskison Book

Causing Talk"). The journalist seems to have given in to sensationalism, though, since the death of Roger, assuming this character was a persona of Bert, which is not likely, has nothing to do with Bert's death, and the novel contains no mention of a trial.

24. The Katy, also known as the MK&T, was the Missouri, Kansas and Texas Railroad. Travis writes: "Railroads were another economic problem facing the Cherokees during this period. The treaty made with the United States government following the Civil War provided for the granting of right of ways to one railroad crossing the Cherokee Nation north and south, and to another crossing from east to west. In the early seventies railroads were constructed over the protest of many citizens. There were a number of objections made to the railroads. In the first place, a portion of their land was taken for rights of ways. Then timber was cut for ties, and coal beds were stripped to supply the engines with fuel. However, the chief complaint was that the railroads would bring a great influx of white settlers who would eventually take the land from the Indians" (21). Seven paragraphs above, Oskison wrote about one of the anti-railroad protesters, Pat Shanahan. Conley writes that in 1871 the Katy "laid tracks from Chetopa, Kansas, through the Cherokee Nation as far as Chouteau, a few miles from the Creek Nation. The Atlantic and Pacific Railroad came in that same year from Seneca, Missouri, and connected with the Katy's line at Vinita" (*The Cherokee Nation* 185). For more on the consequences of railroads through Cherokee country, see "Autobiography" n. 60.

25. Elmira is a small location a couple of miles east of Vacaville and about thirty miles southwest of Sacramento.

26. In *Brothers Three*, Oskison wrote that Henry, the author's persona, "was shivering over 'Jack the Giant Killer'" (23), a popular tale relating the adventures of a young man called Jack who becomes a hero by killing giants.

27. Bird Creek does not exist anymore beyond Temple, about one hundred miles south of Fort Worth, after it was dammed by the Santa Fe Railroad to form Lake Polk in Temple.

28. English novelist Charles Dickens (1812–70) and Scottish novelist Sir Walter Scott (1771–1832) are well-known writers. Charles Reade (1814–84) was a very popular English novelist and dramatist. He published many plays and novels, his most famous being *The Cloister and the Hearth* (1861). If Scott's works might have appealed to young Oskison for their epic and romantic character, Dickens and Reade can be said to have influenced Oskison for their description of lowly, simple people plunged into extraordinary events. *The Old Cap. Collier Library* was a series (first a weekly, then a semi-monthly) featuring detective stories set in either urban centers or the West. It was published by Norman Munro from 1883 to 1899. Old Cap. Collier was also the hero of many of the stories published in the periodical (Cox 198).

In *Brothers Three*, Oskison describes a bookcase in the Odell family's home containing "Shakespeare, Scott, Dickens, Bulwer-Lytton, Charles Reade, a thick 'Garland' of poetry, and a set of the famous speeches that had rung down the ages from the plea of Socrates to the orations of Robert G. Ingersoll" (56). In the same novel, Francis Odell says of his son Henry that he would "rather stick his nose in a book than eat" (44), which can apparently be applied to young Oskison.

29. The practice described here by Oskison was the culmination of Texas cattle owners' intrusion on Cherokee pasturelands. After the Civil War, Texas cattle had started to invade the pasturage of the Five Tribes, where they fattened at no expense for their owners. The Indians immediately started to both resist and benefit from this intrusion by levying per head taxes. The Cherokee government was the first, in December 1867, to levy "a tax of ten cents per head on all animals driven through their Nation" (Graebner 304). However, many cattle owners found a way around paying the taxes, notably by leasing grazing lands from or claiming false sales of cattle to Indian citizens. The Five Tribes passed laws to punish those among their people who would participate in such practices (Graebner 306). Graebner even mentions how some people, like C. M. McClellan, owner of a powerful cattle company, "first claimed Cherokee citizenship, and, when deprived of their cattle by Indian officials, changed their claim to United States citizenship and appealed to the United States Indian agent for protection against Cherokee laws" (307).

30. J. O. Hall, a Cherokee by intermarriage (Dawes Roll No. 30, Census Card No. 3321), was a Vinita Cherokee cattleman and a prominent member of the Cattlemen's Protective Association of the Indian Territory, which gathered several tribal cattlemen's associations. The role of such associations, which were essential to the good management of the cattle industry, was to protect the members from thieves, organize the roundups, advertise brands, etc. (O'Dell, "Cattlemen's").

31. Henry Falling, the "Cherokee cowboy," was born circa 1857 and died in 1906 in Estella—post office established in 1900 (Shirk 200)—about ten miles northwest of Vinita. On 21 September 1900 he applied for enrollment to the commission to the Five Civilized Tribes for himself as a Cherokee by blood, his white wife, Lizzie Falling, as a Cherokee by intermarriage, and his five children. His roll number was 3233. Applications for two more children, born in 1903 and 1905, were sent to the commissioner's office in Muskogee in May 1906. Henry Falling is also a character in Oskison's novel *The Singing Bird* and presumably a model for the recurrent figure of the Indian cowboy in Oskison's fiction at large.

32. John would attend Halsell College at the same time as Ludie Hall. Both their names are listed on the Roll of Honor of Halsell College for December 1892 (Rogers 108).

33. Young Oskison would develop a meaningful relationship with Jack. He would use the mule in a fable told in 1912 in front of the Carlisle students. See "The Enduring Qualities of the Indian" in this volume.

34. Jay-Eye-See was a black gelding who marked the world of horse racing. He was owned by Jerome Increase Case, a wealthy entrepreneur from Racine, Wisconsin, founder of a thresher company, J. I. Case Company. Case named his horse after his initials. On 1 August 1884, at Narragansett Park in Providence, Rhode Island, Jay-Eye-See, driven by Ed Bithers, became "the king of the American turf" when he "surpassed all previous performances, making a mile in 2.10" ("Trotting Record" 3), thus "deposing from her pinnacle of fame William H. Vanderbilt's mare Maud S." ("Jay-Eye-See Trots in 2.10"). "Trotting Record" called the event "the greatest event in the history of the trotting turf," and Jay-Eye-See ran so perfectly that it seemed to the journalist "as if he was but machinery and not a thing of life, so perfect were his actions." After he ruptured a ligament, the trotter was taught to pace and in August 1892 he beat the pacing record, which made him "the world's all-time champion double-gaited racer" (Wendel 10). Jay-Eye-See would live to be thirty-one.

In *Wild Harvest*, Oskison's first novel, in which many episodes are clearly inspired by the author's childhood, the cowboy Tom Winger, during a roundup, "caught a faint-branded JIC steer that had been overlooked as an H G steer" (112).

35. The amount of brand advertising in the papers of Indian Territory is a sign of how flourishing the cattle industry was. Publications such as the *Branding Iron* and the *Indian Chieftain* devoted up to one-fourth of their space to brand advertising. It was the role of the cattlemen's association to publish these brands in order to protect their herds from thieves. In "The Quality of Mercy" (1904), reprinted in this volume, Venita Churchfield complains about the place taken by brand advertisements in her weekly newspaper, *Sachem*. The *Indian Chieftain* was first published as a weekly in Vinita in 1882. W. P. Ross, John Ross's nephew and chief of the Cherokee Nation (1866–67 and 1872–75), and Robert L. Owen, the first U.S. senator of Oklahoma, were counted among its editors. The year 1891 saw the first publication of the *Daily Indian Chieftain*, although sustained publication of the daily did not come before 1898. Oskison would publish several texts in the *Indian Chieftain*, including "Tookh Steh's Mistake" (22 July 1897) and "A Schoolmaster's Dissipation" (23 Dec. 1897), both reprinted in this volume.

36. Gustave Doré (1832–83), a world-famous French illustrator, was primarily known for his illustrations of Dante's *Divine Comedy*, which he completed between 1861 and 1868.

37. John Franklin (1862–1943) was enrolled as a Cherokee by Blood (Dawes Roll No. 16963, Card No. 7127). He was a successful Vinita farmer. He also served as a senator in the Cherokee National Council and as Craig County commissioner

(Rogers 202–3). His brother, Alex Franklin, was a famous roper. He took part in several contests Will Rogers also participated in and Oskison attended. Blake Gore is probably Henry Blake Gore (1869–1931), son of Jonathan Gore, a cattleman from Blue Jacket, enrolled, along with his children, on 20 January 1903 as a Cherokee by Blood (Dawes Roll No. 22251, Card No. 107), and of Sarah Blue Jacket, a Shawnee (*Applications*). Blake's brother, J. Gore Jr., is introduced by Oskison below. He boarded with him during his school years at Willie Halsell College in Vinita and used to tell wonderful tales about his cowboy brother Blake. James (Jim) L. Kell was "a roping-contest buddy of Rogers'" (Rogers 395). His name is alongside Oskison's and Will Rogers's on the Roll of Honor of Willie Halsell College for December 1892 and January 1893 (Rogers 108, 113). The bronco buster Oskison refers to is probably Henry Clasper Woolman (1861–1935), born in Kansas and married to Rose M. Nazworthy, with whom he raised nine children in Vinita. Bill Halsell is William Electious Halsell, one of the most prominent and influential cattlemen in Indian Territory. He was also a banker. His file for application to the commission to the Five Tribes for enrollment as a Cherokee citizen shows that, after he and his wife, part-Cherokee Mary Alice Crutchfield, moved from Texas to the Cherokee Nation, he married her again, this time under Cherokee law. This marriage allowed him to claim lands on which he would build a very prosperous ranching business. Gabe Horner, a successful Texas cattleman in *Wild Harvest* and *Black Jack Davy*, is probably modeled after him. With J. O. Hall, Clem V. Rogers, Nat Skinner, and others, he was a member of the Cattlemen's Protective Association of Indian Territory. Halsell funded the school that would become Willie Halsell College, which young Oskison would attend (see below). Nathaniel Skinner started a successful stock ranch in 1878 in the Vinita area and became a major cattle broker in the Cherokee Nation (Rogers 395). In the early 1890s he was accused, albeit not convicted, of illegally employing white herders (O'Dell, "Skinner"). He was probably related to Heber Skinner, another famous roper, born the same year as Oskison and who attended Halsell with him.

Grover Cleveland was the twenty-second president of the United States. He served between 1885 and 1889 and again between 1893 and 1897. Cleveland was a proponent of small government and the free market. During an economic depression he faced in his second term, he took some very unpopular measures, unsympathetic to poor workers. During a famous strike of the Pullman workers in Chicago in 1894, for example, he sent the troops against the strikers, who were fired upon at the beginning of July 1894. During this crisis he famously declared: "If it takes the entire army and navy of the United States to deliver a post card in Chicago, that card will be delivered." Another measure of the Cleveland administration that may have triggered some "hot debate" in Oskison's community, although it seems surprising that he did not mention it more explicitly, was allotment. In February 1887 Cleveland signed the Dawes Act into law in spite of strong lobbying, notably from the Cherokees (Holm).

38. One Sam Calvert can be found on the Final Rolls: Cherokee by Blood, thirty-seven years old at the time of enrollment, Dawes Roll No. 24340, Census Card no. 4003.

39. The Donnelly family were probably close neighbors of the Oskisons. On present-day maps, Donnelly Hill appears about a mile northwest of Vinita.

40. Spin the plate is a game in which a plate is spun on its edge in the middle of a circle formed by the players. A player is called who must catch the spinning plate before it falls. Going to Jerusalem is another name for musical chairs. A version of the third game mentioned by Oskison is told in *Pioneer Life in Western Pennsylvania*: "Among the young folks the event anticipated most joyously was the 'kissing party,' so called because in all the games, either as a penalty or as part of the play, each girl was kissed by some one of the boys. These games were musical and vocal, usually performed to the strains of a fiddle. When all the guests had gathered and the cabin was swarming with giggling girls . . . and noisy boys . . . the fiddler struck up a tune, a young blade was dragged to the center of the floor, and the play began. The others joined hands and circled about him singing:

King William was King James's son,
And of that royal race he sprung;
He wore a star upon his breast,
To show that he was royal best.
Go choose your east, go choose your west,
Go choose the one that you like best;
If he's not here to take your part,
Go choose another with all your heart.

The boy in the center made a snatch at a buxom girl and pulled her into the center of the circle with him. The singing grew louder:

Down on the carpet you must kneel,
Just as the grass grows in the field;
Salute your bride with kisses sweet,
And then rise up upon your feet.

At this point the girl was kissed soundly by her companion to the accompaniment of giggles and guffaws" (Wright and Corbett 105–6). There were different versions of the song. One with minor differences appears in *Wisconsin Folklore* by James P. Leary. Another one goes:

King William was King James's son;
And from the royal race he sprung.
He wore a star upon his breast,
Pointing to the one that he loved best.
Choose your partner.

After the girl was picked:

Now that you're married, you must be good.
Make your husband split your wood,
Split it fine and carry it in;
Then you may have a kiss again.

41. Robert Louis Stevenson (1850–94) was a popular Scottish writer, best known for his *Strange Case of Dr. Jekyll and Mr. Hyde* (1886) and *Treasure Island*, an adventure story of pirates, published in 1883 as a book after it was serialized between 1881 and 1882. In *Brothers Three*, Roger "took up Henry's often-read copy of 'Treasure Island' to scan briefly a page or two before throwing it down and exclaiming, 'I don't see why Mister wants to read that stuff'" (45). Rudyard Kipling (1865–1936) was a British writer best known for *The Jungle Book* (1894) and *Kim* (1901). *Plain Tales from the Hill* (1888) and *Soldiers Three* (1888) are collections of some of his short stories. The title of the latter obviously inspired Oskison's choice for the title of his third novel. The title of one of his first short stories, "Only the Master Shall Praise," is also from Kipling.

42. Worcester Academy was a Congregational Mission School established at Vinita by Rev. J. W. Scroggs, DD, and named after Rev. Samuel A. Worcester, DD, who had been a missionary among the Cherokees for much of his life. It opened in November 1882 and was supported by the American Home Missionary Society (Garrett). Willie Halsell College was founded in 1887 as Galloway College by Bishop Charles B. Galloway of the Indian Mission Conference of the Methodist Episcopal Church South. When W. E. Halsell donated a large amount of money to erect a new main building, completed in 1891, the school was renamed Willie Halsell College after Halsell's daughter, who had died in 1884 (Rogers 101–4; Attalla). Willie Halsell College graduated its first class in 1894. John M. Oskison was among these first graduates.

43. James G. Mehlin was a white man who married a Cherokee woman in 1868

and who became a prominent farmer (Murchison 323). In 1898 he was co-founder of the Bank of Nowata. His name appears in two court cases, *Mehlin v. Ice* (No. 182, Circuit Court of Appeals, Eighth Circuit, 1 May 1893) and *Superior Oil and Gas Co. v. Mehlin* (No. 436, Supreme Court of Oklahoma, 8 Mar. 1910).

The first case opposed Mehlin and other Cherokee citizens to one Joshua H. Ice, a U.S. citizen, over a land dispute in Alluwe, Cooweescoowee District, present-day New Alluwe, located about ten miles west of Vinita. The sovereignty of the Cherokee Nation's laws and courts was at stake. Mehlin had a writ of ejectment issued against Ice because the latter was occupying lands that Mehlin was entitled to possess. Although the writ of ejectment was in accordance with an act of the Cherokee Council dated 4 December 1877, Ice prosecuted and won on the ground that his ejectment was "too summary to be regarded as due process of law under the constitution of the United States" (*Mehlin v. Ice*). Mehlin then appealed to the Circuit Court of Appeals. Although Ice's attorneys argued that the Cherokee's "title to land is a mere title by occupancy, the title being in the United States," that "in some other respects the Cherokee Nation is very much on the same plane of the Indian tribes generally, and that little or no faith and credit should be accorded to the proceedings of their courts," the Court of Appeals, citing treaties between the Cherokee Nation and the United States, stated that "the tenure by which the Cherokee Nation holds its lands, and its relation to the United States in other respects, are widely different from that of the ordinary Indian tribes." Judge Caldwell further stated that "the right of local self-government has always been claimed and exercised by the Cherokee Nation, and their rights in this regard, so far as relate to their own country and people, have never been questioned by the United States. Nor it is true that the United States has always denied to the Cherokees jurisdiction over white intruders in their country." Caldwell concluded that "the judgment of the court below is reversed, and the cause remanded for a new trial."

In 1910, the second case opposed the Superior Oil and Gas Corporation to Mehlin in the Oklahoma Supreme Court. Mehlin had refused to lease some of his land in spite of a contract he had signed in 1904 stipulating that as soon as his citizenship and his allotment were granted he would lease his land to Superior Oil & Gas Co. The Oklahoma Supreme Court judged the terms of this contract unfair and not "reasonably certain," and ruled in accordance with the doctrine that "oil and gas leases are construed most strongly against the lessee and in favor of the lessor" because of the nature of such exploitation of the land, and of the consequences of any delay of this exploitation, both detrimental to the owner. Oskison might have used the story of Mehlin's conflict with Superior Oil & Gas to write about Roger Odell's mining misfortunes in *Brothers Three*.

Charles Mehlin, Jim's son, was also a close friend of Will Rogers's. His name appears on the Roll of Honor of Willie Halsell College for December 1892 and January 1893.

44. The Annex was actually run by "Aunt Laura" Cooper. As he wrote his autobiography many decades after his years at the Annex, he probably had Mrs. Cooper confused with one of her daughters, Alice. Alice Cooper is on the Roll of Honor of Willie Halsell College for January 1893. Oneida Cooper is on the Roll of Honor for December 1892. Will Rogers also resided at the Annex (Rogers 104, 108, 113).

45. W. P. Bishop was the first principal of Galloway College.

46. Clem Vann Rogers (1839–1911), a prosperous cattleman, was an influential citizen of the Cherokee Nation, a prominent member of the Downing Party, born from a division in the Ross Party in 1867, and named after Lewis Downing, a Keetoowah and a "Pin Indian" — an abolitionist — during the Civil War. Conley describes the Downing Party as "a strange alliance, apparently built on nothing more than hatred of John Ross" (*The Cherokee Nation* 184). Later, Rogers was a delegate for the Democratic Party at the state constitutional convention. Rogers County, county seat Claremore, is located in what was Coo-Wee-Scoo-Wee District and is named after him.

47. In a telegram to a friend before a school reunion, Will Rogers would say of Halsell and Oskison: "Now that I find that they are celebrating the passing out of Willie Halsell Institute well there were guys there that would have put even Harvard or Yale out of business. I believe John Oskison was the only one we really got educated but they taught a lot of 'em to go out and lead fine and useful lives to their communities" (Rogers to Earl Walker, ca. 27 Aug. 1933, in Rogers 109).

48. One Old Cat and Rounders are bat-and-ball games, both at the origin of baseball. Rounders has been practiced in England since the sixteenth century.

49. Son of W. E. Halsell, Ewing Halsell (1877–1965) also became a prominent cattleman in Oklahoma and Texas. He married Lucile Fortner. He and his father created Halsell and Son Oil and Gas Company. He also created his own ranch, the Big Creek Ranch, near Vinita (Rogers 491).

50. William Eugene Rowsey was the second president of Willie Halsell College, from 1892 to 1896. He later became a prominent lawyer and banker in Muskogee (Rogers 106).

51. A yard of roses was a piece of embroidery, quite fashionable at the turn of the century especially as a table-runner, measuring one yard and representing roses.

52. William S. Dugger taught modern languages and oratory. He also served as president of the school from 1902 to 1905 (Rogers 121). According to the *Annual Catalogue of Willie Halsell*, he offered young Oskison the medal for oratory in June

1894. John Barrett is listed on the Roll of Honor for December 1892. An *Indian Chieftain* article dated 29 December 1892 and titled "The College Entertainments" reported that "the oration by John Barrett, 'Shadows on the Mirror,' was good, also the recitation by Miss Cooper, 'Van Bibbler's Rock.'"

53. *Only a Boy* is a novella, published anonymously in 1898 or 1899 but attributed to American humorist and satirist Eugene Field (1850–95). It is also known as *A Summer Amour* and is an erotic letter to a friend written by a middle-aged man remembering the summer of his twelfth year, when he was seduced by an older woman with whom he discovered physical love. The novel popularly known as *Fanny Hill* is in fact *Memoirs of a Woman of Pleasure*, by English writer John Cleland, published in 1748 or 1749. An expurgated version was published in 1750 as *Memoirs of Fanny Hill*. It is said to be the first erotic novel. Peter Sabor, the author of an introduction to the 1985 Penguin edition of this novel, writes that this "underground book . . . has been legally available in America only since 1963 and in England since 1970," which explains why Oskison calls it a "rare item." If Oskison read it, he read only the expurgated edition, since according to Sabor "no accurate text has been published since the first edition of 1748–9" (vii).

54. The Chicago World's Fair, the official name of which was the World's Columbian Exposition to celebrate the four hundredth anniversary of Columbus's arrival, lasted from May to October 1893. About 27 million people are said to have visited it (E. Larson 5). The fair was set in Jackson Park, on the South Side of Chicago, and many of the amusements were on the Midway Plaisance, today the limit of the University of Chicago. Sol Bloom, in charge of selecting the concessions for the Midway Plaisance, saw it as "a great pleasure garden [that] would thrill, titillate, and if all went well perhaps even shock." The Midway "was to be an exotic realm of unusual sights, sounds, and scents. There would be authentic villages from far-off lands inhabited by authentic villagers" (E. Larson 160). The most novel attraction of the Midway was certainly the very first Ferris wheel, designed especially for the Columbian Exposition by George Washington Gale Ferris Jr. Surprisingly enough, Oskison does not mention the most popular attraction of the Midway, located not far from the Ferris wheel, Buffalo Bill's Wild West Show. The "Street in Cairo" amusement featured, for the very first time in the United States, the "hootchy-cootchy," as belly dancing was then known. Little Egypt, stage name of Syrian dancer Farida Mazar (or Mazhar) Spyropoulos, was so popular in this exhibit that in succeeding years, many other dancers would use the same stage name and tour the United States (Carlton). A few pages below, Oskison recalls seeing "pale imitations of Little Egypt" in Vinita. Rembrandt (1606–69) is a well-known Dutch painter. Corot (1796–1875) was a French painter who influenced many impressionist painters. Rosa

Bonheur (1822–99), a painter and sculptor born in Bordeaux, France, painted *The Horse Fair* in 1853. It can be seen in the Metropolitan Museum of Art in New York. Many paintings by Bonheur can be seen in the Musée d'Orsay in Paris.

55. A prairie fire would serve as a backdrop to "When the Grass Grew Long"; "Only the Master Shall Praise" and "Young Henry and the Old Man" would tell of the gathering of a posse; the "fights between marshals and train robbers" can be found in "To 'Youngers' Bend'" and "Working for Fame" as well as "The Greater Appeal."

56. In 1894, they were the first graduates of Willie Halsell College. Regardless of Oskison's father's disappointment, Eva Patton showed outstanding results during her school years at Willie Halsell College. Her name is on the Roll of Honor for December 1892 with the perfect grade of 100, and the *1894 Annual Catalogue* mentions that Patton, "whose average during the entire year including examination was 99.8," received a medal for Scholarship. She married W. E. Rowsey, the president of Willie Halsell College (Rogers 106). The Dawes Roll mentions many Pattons but no Eva. There is one Emma Patton (Dawes Roll No. 22948, Census Card No. 1489), though, whose age at the time of application, twenty-six, could be Eva's age (she graduated the same year as Oskison, who was twenty-six when he applied in 1901).

57. Dr. Benjamin F. Fortner (1847–1917), a graduate of Vanderbilt University's medical school, was established in Vinita but was a very prominent doctor in Indian Territory and the state of Oklahoma. He first worked in Claremore, where he also had a livestock business. He moved to Vinita in 1884. He served on the board of Willie Halsell College and the Worcester Academy. He was one of the pillars of the Indian Territory Medical Association, which he helped organize in 1881 and over which he presided for many years (Clinton). He was also director of the First National Bank of Vinita in 1892 and a surgeon for the Missouri, Kansas and Texas Railway as well as the St. Louis and San Francisco Railway. In 1874 he married Lucy Jennie Gunter, of Cherokee descent, which made him a Cherokee citizen when he applied in 1900 (Dawes Roll No. 23644, Census Card No. 2878). His daughter was Lucile Fortner, one of Oskison's schoolmates, who married Ewing Halsell in 1899.

58. About Hastings, see Introduction and "Essays" n. 129, as well as "In Governing the Indian, Use the Indian!" below. Judge Wade Hampton Kornegay (1865–1939) lived and worked in Vinita for almost fifty years. He was a delegate at the 1907 Constitutional Convention of the state of Oklahoma and a member of Oklahoma Supreme Court in 1931 (Martin). He represented Jim Mehlin in *Superior Oil and Gas Co. v. Mehlin*, decided by the Oklahoma Supreme Court on 8 March 1910. James Sanford Davenport (1864–1940) was born in Cherokee County, Alabama. In 1890 he moved to Muskogee, Indian Territory, where he was admitted to the practice of law before the U.S. Courts of the Indian Territory. In 1893 he established his

practice in Vinita. The year before, he had married Guelielma Ross, John Ross's great-granddaughter. In 1907 he married Byrd Ironside, a descendant of Shawnee leader Tecumseh. From 1901 to 1903 he served as mayor of Vinita. He was also a member of the Cherokee National Council (1897–1901) and speaker of the Cherokee House of Representatives. After statehood he became a member of U.S. Congress (Doyle, "Davenport"). In 1905 he had been a member of the Constitution Committee preparing separate statehood for the state of Sequoyah.

59. In *The Oklahoman*, Oskison said: "I had even spent one summer in a law office in Vinita — the family post office — reading Blackstone and panting with the heat that beat upon the board walls of Mr. Smith's upstairs rooms" (13 Jan. 1929). All students of the law read Blackstone, that is to say, *Commentaries on the Laws of England*, published in 1765 and 1769 by Sir William Blackstone. It is one of the most influential treatises on common law in the United States as well as in Britain. Smith and his partner, McCulloch, were Oskison's attorneys when his enrollment for Cherokee citizenship was suspended. Bill Hastings then represented the Cherokee Nation.

60. The $274 mentioned by Oskison were per capita annuities proceeding from the interests gained by money placed for them in the Treasury after various agreements with the United States and specifically after the sale of the Cherokee Outlet. In *Black Jack Davy*, Jerry Boyd talks with Ned Warrior, an Indian neighbor, about how he could use these: "'With the money you an' Rose an' the boy are goin' to draw at the Payment in August, you could sure fix things up right down there.' Boyd referred to a forthcoming payment for tribal lands sold to the Government, which would amount to nearly three hundred dollars each, almost nine hundred dollars for the three" (62).

In this passage, Oskison is confusing the chronology. In 1894, twenty-four years after his father's arrival, the land had not been allotted to Cherokee citizens yet. Allotment of Cherokee lands was the responsibility of the Dawes Commission, which in 1894 had barely started to get organized. The commission had been created by the act passed on 3 March 1893. Dawes and the two other members of the commission (Meredith Helm Kidd of Indiana and Archibald S. McKennon of Arkansas) were appointed by President Cleveland only on 1 November, and the commissioners did not arrive at Muskogee, Indian Territory, before 10 January 1894. Allotment could not be completed before a roll of citizens had been drawn up, although Congress urged the Dawes Commission to start allotting lands before the roll was final (Carter 125). Still, because of strong resistance from the Cherokees, notably by lobbyists sent to Washington throughout the 1880s and 1890s (see Holm), enrollment was not completed before 1907, and allotment was not completed when a superintendent for the Five Civilized Tribes took over the unfinished work of the Dawes Commission in 1914 (Carter 151). As for the survey of the land, it was far from finished, contrary to what Oskison seems to remember. In fact, in 1894, Agent Dew M. Windom wrote in his report that he thought "a survey of all the lands of this Territory . . . is a condition precedent to allotment" (1894 *Report Commissioner Indian Affairs* 141–42). It would not be achieved before 1897 (Carter 126).

Oskison is right, though, when he writes that there were more whites than Indians in the Cherokee Nation. In 1890, Indian Territory was included for the first time in the decennial United States census, which counted 22,015 Indians and 29,166 whites in the Cherokee Nation. Although the census categorized the inhabitants according to physical appearance without regard to citizenship (Debo, *And Still* 13), we can assume that a large part of these 29,166 whites were non-Cherokee citizens, since we know from the commissioner of Indian Affairs that in 1887 there were 4,815 adopted citizens, only 1,100 of which were white (1887 *Report Commissioner Indian Affairs* 113). Many of these non-citizens were intruders, "that is, people who are living in said nation and occupying its soil contrary to law" (1894 *Report Commissioner Indian Affairs* 145). Immigration, along with intermarriage, increased dramatically when construction of railroads across Indian Territory started (Debo, *And Still* 11). After Congress in the early 1870s authorized railway companies to cross Indian Territory, the "intrusion of whites became not only easy but almost spectacular" (Wardell 262). In January 1880, representatives of the Cherokee, Creek, and Choctaw Indians sent President Rutherford B. Hayes the following communication: "From information received we are advised that white intruders, with their families, in considerable numbers, are beginning to locate on the Cherokee lands in the Indian Territory immediately west of the Arkansas River, and on and contiguous to the Red Fork of that river; also, that the railroad trains of the Missouri, Kansas and Texas Railroad Company, a few days ago, emptied several cars of Texas negroes into our country at a point near Caddo, on the line of the railroad. We respectfully but firmly protest against these infringements of our treaty stipulations, and request your Excellency to immediately inquire into the matter and to put a stop to it, and to have the intruders permanently removed from the Indian country. In this connection we also beg to call your Excellency's attention to the fact that we are advised from sources we deem authentic that the emigration raid which was attempted last Spring on our country, and which your Excellency checked, is in contemplation again by the interested railroad corporations and land pirates who inspired the movement originally, and we respectfully ask that your Excellency take early steps to prevent this unwarranted assault" (*New York Times* 28 Jan. 1880). Between 1870 and 1890 at least six railroads were built across Indian Territory, and Loren Brown points out, "with the coming of each road, many more whites were brought into the region." With the construction crews, "many of whom failed to leave when their work was finished," the personnel to operate the roads, and "the inevitable development of agriculture and commerce that always accompanies railway construction," the Five Tribes were soon "threatened with submersion by the incoming white men" (Brown, "The Establishment" 173). It is interesting to note that the Cherokees had predicted such effects of the railroad intrusion and, in order to limit them, "wish[ed] to build and own, by such company of Cherokee citizens as shall be organized under the authority of the Cherokee National Council, the railroads crossing their own lands, meeting and connecting with such roads as approach their border" (1869 *Report Commissioner Indian Affairs* 99). In a letter included in the 1869 *Annual Report of the Commissioner of Indian Affairs*, Principal Chief Lewis Downing explained indeed that the Cherokees "know that to have the roads contemplated through their country owned by capitalists who are strangers to them, who will look upon their nationality as an encumbrance, and, perhaps, their presence, in any form, as a nuisance, would result in the loss of their lands and destruction of their people" (99). Ely Parker, the first Indian commissioner of Indian Affairs, opposed Indian railroads. According to him, the whites were "qualified by nature and experience" to build the railroads (qtd. in Miner 125).

Because the prosperity of the railway companies depended largely on the business the railroads would generate, they advertised profusely. The intruders seized unoccupied lands, erected improvements, and were very difficult to expel because of the jurisdictional confusion explained earlier (see "Autobiography" n. 21). Not only the Cherokee authorities had no jurisdiction over non-citizens; even the United States Court for the Western District of Arkansas at Fort Smith had only criminal, not civil, jurisdiction over them. In his 1887 annual report, Agent Robert L. Owen of the Indian Territory Union Agency acknowledged that the increase of U.S. citizens in Indian Territory was "not without its embarrassing features . . . for many civil cases arise between themselves" and "there is no court having civil jurisdiction to settle these cases." He also admitted that "the United States district court for the western district of Arkansas has more business than it can possibly attend to" and that consequently many cases "have been passed by because of their minor character when compared to more important criminal matters" (1887 *Report Commissioner Indian Affairs* 115). Even after the establishment of the first Indian Territory federal court at Muskogee by act of 1 March 1889, and the creation of three judicial districts with complete jurisdiction, not much could or would be done to dislodge intruders who had been in the Nation for years. In 1887, Commissioner Atkins had written in his annual report that, in spite of a request from the Cherokee authorities, he refused to remove intruders who had settled in the Nation before 11 August 1886. An act passed by the Cherokee Council in December 1886, based on a decision by the U.S. Supreme Court, vested the Cherokees with the authority to determine all claims to citizenship. However, they had no authority over people who came before 11 August 1886. The commissioner deemed that these intruders had "made valuable improvements in the way of buildings and opening farms, and putting them in a state of cultivation" and thought that "for the Department summarily to eject these persons from the limits of the nation, without just and fair compensation for their improvements, would seem to be an unjust if not a heartless procedure" (1887 *Report Commissioner Indian Affairs* lix). As Cherokee delegates to Washington put it in a report they sent to their principal chief in 1895, "There seems to be a sinister motive for keeping the intruders in our country. It was the contents of the wooden horse emptied inside the walls of Troy, that enabled the Greeks to take that ancient city" (Cherokee Nation Papers Collection). Even if the federal government would later take some action, notably by forming a commission in 1893—of which Clem V. Rogers was a member—to appraise the improvements of intruders with the purpose of removing them, it all seemed to be lip service. When the commissioners had run out of money to accomplish their mission, Congress refused to make any "provision for the payment of the expenses of the removal of the intruders" (1894 *Report Commissioner Indian Affairs* 73). Indeed, statehood was in the minds of many by then, and many white U.S. citizens in Indian Territory would support it.

Oskison used the massive intrusion of white men as a context to Tookh Steh's story (see below). The subject is also tackled in *Wild Harvest*. During a political rally launching the campaign of Vergil Stokes, a white farmer running for a seat in the tribal council, "Sofkey" Horseford, chairman of the meeting, introduces the candidate thus: "Long time ago . . . Eenyan been livin' here in his own country; been livin' easy, gettin' fat like me . . . till white man he come an' say to Eenyan, 'Make some room for me.' Well, all right, but Eenyan say, 'What you goin' to do for me?'" (168–69). The question causes Nan, Oskison's protagonist, to reflect: "First comers were men like Billy Dines, true pioneers who understood the Indian, who were plowmen, ambitious to turn the virgin prairie into productive fields. Then followed her father and Engel, restless drifters in the wake of the first comers. On their heels came Gabe Horner and Winger . . . cattle pioneers. Latest of the invaders were Harvey Stokes and his kind, intent upon turning the luxuriant wild grass into hay and the hay into cash. What had all of these brought to the Indian? Did he agree with Billy Dines that these white men were teachers?" (169). The Indian leader concludes his introductory speech by suggesting that maybe "it be a good thing if some white man come down yonder in the timber an' help make laws so all can live in peace. Me, I think we all got to be good friends, white an' black an' red; live together, like colors of the rainbow in the sky" (169–70). Then Vergil Stokes starts his own speech: "Course us poor intrudin' whites think we've got somethin' to give the Indians. A notion of how white folks live. Maybe it ain't the best way. I don't know. But I know we've got to give an' take in a good many ways. For instance, we've got to have more schools; I don't want my own little old quarter-blood kid growin' up out here on Thunder Creek with no school within ten miles of me" (170).

61. Chapter 12 of *Black Jack Davy* contains descriptions of the "fever of temporary activity" (168) that seized the town during "the Indian Payment." Davy enjoys "watching a multitude of Indians pressing around the pay-tent, taking in the side shows on the magic-sprung Midway Pleasance that would stay for ten days then flit overnight to the site of the next payment fifty miles west" (168). During payment sessions, "store-keepers' clerks stood on the sidewalks as pullers-in, competing with street pedlars; merry-go-rounds, soft-drink booths, chile cooks, friers of chicken and catfish, cheap jewelry vendors had taken spaces in vacant lots and along the sidewalks; horse traders paraded their steeds through the streets; at the edge of Ross Park, the Primrose Comedy Company had pitched a big show tent, and a part of the troupe in a hired carriage drove back and forth and with cornet, trombone and drum called attention to the streamer advertising its repertoire of thrillers. Everywhere was sound, color and smell, loud and coercive" (168–69). Oskison also mentions less reputable characters gathering in the town attracted by the pay-tent: gamblers, bootleggers, outlaws hoping to get their share of the money, and "rouged *nymphs du pave*" (169) — a French phrase that should really be *nymphes du pavé*, literally *nymphs of the cobblestone*, the famous rock that paved the streets of French cities.

62. *East Lynne* was an English sensation novel written by Ellen Wood and published in 1861. It was a best-seller, probably as popular as *Uncle Tom's Cabin*, also mentioned by Oskison, and numerous stage adaptations were produced around the country (Hughes). Henry Irving (1838–1905) was a famous English actor who had a very successful career in London. Among many other leading roles, he played Hamlet, Shylock in *The Merchant of Venice*, MacBeth, and Othello. In the 1890s he toured the United States and encountered success there (Irving). Joseph Jefferson (1829–1905) was an American actor born in Philadelphia into a family of actors. His greatest international success was probably *Rip Van Winkle* by Washington Irving (*Encyclopaedia Britannica*). "Tent shows" refer to the many theater companies, of varying quality, that toured the nation and performed under a tent the popular shows of the time. Harriet Beecher Stowe's *Uncle Tom's Cabin* was probably the most adapted, the most popular and the most performed.

There are many Landrums on the Dawes Roll, but no Mack can be found. One

Mack Landrum from Vinita appears as a member of the Oklahoma Historical Society, at least from 1926 to 1929 ("Meeting of the Board"; "Minutes of the Annual Meeting"). Emory and Henry College, in Virginia, was founded in 1836, is affiliated with the United Methodist Church, and was named after Bishop John Emory and Patrick Henry.

Mack Landrum was probably the son of H. T. Landrum, a prominent attorney of the Cherokee Nation. He was the translator, appointed by Principal Chief Dennis Wolfe Bushyhead, of the laws of the Cherokee Nation to be compiled according to the act of the National Council approved on 19 November 1880 (Cherokee Nation 6). With Clem V. Rogers and Emmett E. Starr, Landrum was also a member of a three-person Cherokee Nation committee, also appointed by Principal Chief Bushyhead in 1883, which ruled that it violated the Cherokee Constitution to deny the Cherokee freedmen their share of the federal per capita payments from which they had been excluded, despite the fact that they had officially been made citizens of the Cherokee Nation by the 1866 treaty signed between the Cherokees and the United States. The Cherokee Senate, however, refused the recommendations of the committee (see "Autobiography" n. 66 and "Essays" n. 129; Rogers 123–24; Carter 108–9).

63. E. D. E. N. Southworth (Emma Dorothy Eliza Nevitte Southworth, 1819–99) was a prolific American writer who published serialized novels mainly in the *National Era* and the *New York Ledger*. Some of her most famous novels were *Retribution* (1846) and *The Hidden Hand* (1859 in its serialized version, 1888 in book form). Long John Silver is the famous character from Stevenson's *Treasure Island*. Mulvaney and Mrs. Hauksbe are characters appearing in several stories by Kipling. Mulvaney appears in 1888 in *The Three Musketeers* along with two other recurrent Kipling characters, Learoyd and Ortheris — whom Oskison refers to in "I Match You: You Match Me" — and reappears in *Soldiers Three*. Mulvaney is an Irishman whose dialect Kipling endeavors to reproduce in his writing. This may have been an influence on Oskison, who also gave local color to his stories by transcribing his characters' dialects and linguistic idiosyncrasies.

64. David Starr Jordan (1851–1931) was president of Indiana University at Bloomington. Thirty-four years old when he took office in 1885, he was the youngest U.S. college president. Then he served as president of Stanford University from 1891 to 1913. He was a world-famous ichthyologist. He also served as the president of the California Academy of Sciences from 1895 to 1898 and from 1901 to 1903 (*Time* 8 June 1931; Stanford, *Sixteenth Annual Register* 9).

65. Leland Stanford Junior University was founded by Leland Stanford and his wife, Jane Lathrop Stanford, in honor of their son, Leland Stanford Jr., who had

died in 1884, at age sixteen, in Florence, Italy. It formally opened to students on 1 October 1891 in Palo Alto, about thirty miles southeast of San Francisco. Leland Stanford was a railroad magnate. In 1861 he co-founded the Central Pacific Railroad. That year he also became governor of California. In 1885 he was elected to the U.S. Senate. The Stanfords used their private fortune for the university and, after Leland Stanford's death in 1893, Jane Lathrop Stanford continued to financially support the university and work for its success (*Time*, 8 June 1931; "Leland Stanford Junior University," *Science* 30 June 1899: 916).

66. Daniel Justice has the following comment about this anecdote: "It was at Stanford that Oskison first encountered integration, expressing racist shock that Whites would heartily welcome and share the dining hall with a Black student" (112). The opinion expressed in this statement seems to exaggerate Oskison's reaction, misrepresents the historical situation within which Oskison operated at the time and ignores Oskison's later stand on the issue. First, Justice sees the presence of the African American student in Stanford as a proof of "integration." The least one can say is that his integration was only relative. After all, "he has a room for himself," Oskison writes. Then, it can hardly be said that Oskison, coming from the Cherokee Nation, "encountered integration" for the first time at Stanford. His social environment had been a mixed one, as evidenced by previous pages of his autobiography, and it included many people of African descent, although he does hardly mention any. In *Wild Harvest*, Oskison mentions freedmen voters interested in Vergil Stokes's campaign for a seat in the tribal council: "Vergil's mid-July meeting was welcomed by farmers and haymen as a brief respite in the busy season's grind of hard work; and it drew the Indian and negro voters (negro 'freedmen' voted by virtue of membership in the tribe granted when they had ceased to be slaves of Indian owners) who were curious to 'size up this white man that wants to help make laws for Indians'" (165–66). According to the United States decennial census, there were 5,127 persons of African descent living in the Cherokee Nation in 1890. The 1866 treaty between the Cherokee Indians and the United States granted the freedmen the same rights as any other Cherokee citizen. By that treaty, the Cherokees "agree[d] that all freedmen who have been liberated by voluntary act of their former owners or by law, as well as free colored persons who were in the country at the commencement of the rebellion, and are now residents therein, or who may return within six months, and their descendants, shall have all rights of native Cherokees" (Article 9). The Cherokee Constitution was amended accordingly in November 1866. Therefore, some form of integration was bound to take place over a few decades within Oskison's community.

Nevertheless, it cannot be denied that the integration of the former slaves met some difficulties. Denial of the rights of African American people had been a long tradition in the Cherokee Nation. The 1839 Constitution stipulated that "no person who is of negro and mulatto parentage, either by the father or mother's side, shall be eligible to hold any office of profit, honor or trust under this Government" (Article 3, Section 5). After the Civil War, as in other southern states, Cherokee schools were segregated. In the 1880s, specifically over the issue of the freedmen, the Cherokee Nation was at odds with the United States, which appeared less reluctant to correct the wrongs African Americans suffered in Indian Territory than the ones suffered by other African Americans in the rest of the nation. In March 1883 the United States bought lands located west of the Arkansas River in the Cherokee Outlet for the relocation of a few Indian tribes. The act of appropriation approved on 3 March 1883 stipulated that the sum of $300,000 "shall be expended as the Acts of the Cherokee legislature direct" (U.S. Laws, 22 Stat., 623). On 19 May 1883 the Cherokee Council, over the veto of Principal Chief Bushyhead, restricted per capita distribution of that money to "citizens of the Cherokee Nation by Cherokee blood," thus excluding Delaware and Shawnee Indians who had been incorporated in the Cherokee Nation by virtue of the 1866 treaty and Cherokee citizens of African descent. The 19 May 1883 act was enforced in spite of the recommendations of a committee appointed by Bushyhead to study the rights of the freedmen, the Delawares, and the Shawnees (see "Autobiography" n. 62 on Landrum). As Tim Gammon remarks, "this attempt to discriminate is unlikely to have been based on monetary considerations alone since the increase *per capita* shares achieved by excluding the freedmen and other Indians was less than two dollars" (359). In what resulted in a weakening of Cherokee sovereignty, the U.S. Congress, on 19 October 1888, passed an "Act to secure to the Cherokee freedmen and others their proportion of certain proceeds of lands, under the act of March third, eighteen hundred and eighty-three" (25 Stat., 608). In response to this act, which "appropriated . . . the sum of seventy-five thousand dollars" to be distributed by the secretary of the interior "among such freedmen and their descendants as are mentioned in the ninth article of the treaty of July nineteenth, eighteen hundred and eighty-three," and stipulated that this amount "shall be charged against the Cherokee Nation, on account of its lands west of the Arkansas River, and shall be a lien on said lands, and which shall be deducted from any payment hereafter made on account of said lands" (25 Stat., 608), the Cherokee Council protested "against the right and power of Congress to make such appropriation, or disposal, or incumbrance of the funds, or upon the lands of the Cherokee Nation without their consent and action." Consequently, the council also resisted any help they could provide in drawing up a roll of freedmen entitled to a share of the proceeds (U.S. Senate, *Letter from the Secretary of the Interior* 3). About a decade later, payment to the freedmen of part of the proceeds from the Cherokee Outlet would encounter other difficulties because the freedmen roll turned out to be inaccurate, with entitled persons not mentioned on the roll and other persons mentioned several times (U.S. Senate, *Payment to Cherokee Freedmen*).

So there was indeed racism in the Cherokee Nation, as there was in the rest of the nation. Still, it seems that Justice's expression of "racist shock" to characterize Oskison's reaction at first sight of the African American student in Stanford is not a complete assessment of his feelings regarding racial relations. If the young southern freshman expressed "racist shock," it was more due to ignorance and a southern background than conviction, as Oskison overtly acknowledges some forty years later via his fiction. In *Brothers Three*, Henry Odell, a fictional version of Oskison, in a conversation with his sister-in-law Ida, reminisces about his years at Stanford, "recalling his first days as a student, the thrill of arrival, his awe of the first group of seniors he saw in animated reunion in the lobby of the great stone-walled dormitory, one of whom was a negro. 'You know, Sis, they don't bar negroes from the California schools, but I didn't know it, and I was horrified. I had carried out there my Southern belief that a black-skinned person must be, biologically, morally, and intellectually, inferior to a white-skinned person. I soon learned that the negro senior whose hand the others were shaking enthusiastically that day was one of the best students in college, and later made a fine reputation as a lawyer.'" To Ida's racist question — "You wouldn't associate with a nigger, Mister?" Odell responds that he was glad to know him and that "if it had been known in California that I was part Indian it would have been worse for me than being part negro. Worse, too, having Japanese blood. Race pride, and prejudice — absurd" (317–18).

67. It is interesting to note here that in 1925, Stanford University president David Starr Jordan was an expert witness for the defense in the Scopes trial, the famous judicial climax in the evolutionism v. creationism debate. John Scopes, a Tennessee teacher, had been charged with teaching evolution. By doing so, he had violated the Butler Act, which, on 13 March 1925, made it unlawful in Tennessee "to teach any theory that denies the story of the Divine Creation of man as taught in the Bible, and to teach instead that man has descended from a lower order of animals" (*Tennessee Evolution Statutes*).

68. Henry Burrowes Lathrop was associate professor of English at Stanford University at the time Oskison was there. He had graduated from Harvard in 1889 (Stanford, *Fourth Annual Register* 12). In 1894–95 he was teaching classes such as "English Composition" and "Forensics" as well as "The English Novel" (*Fourth* 62, 129). He published *The Art of the Novelist* (1919) among other books and articles on early English literature. Alphonso Gerald Newcomer (1864–1913) was a professor

of English. He graduated from Cornell University in 1888, was hired as an assistant professor of English at Stanford in 1891, and became full professor in 1906 (*Fourth* 13; *New York Times* 18 Sept. 1913, 11). He was a specialist of Shakespeare, on whose work he published several articles. During Oskison's time at Stanford, Newcomer gave classes such as "English Prose Writers of the Nineteenth Century," "English Composition," and "Homer" (*Fourth* 62). Later, he taught English poetry (Wordsworth, Shelley, Byron, and Keats), the development of English prose, and Victorian poetry and prose (Stanford, *Sixteenth Annual Register* 101, 102). Melville Best Anderson was also a professor of English. He had graduated from Butler University in 1877. He taught Shakespeare and Milton's *Paradise Lost* (*Fourth* 65–66). William Henry Hudson was a professor of English literature. He taught the history of English drama, the literature of the eighteenth century, and English and American poetry of the nineteenth century (*Fourth* 63–64). By "Pflugel" Oskison means Ewald Flügel (1863–1914), a professor of English philology. Born in Leipzig, Germany, he was hired at Stanford in 1892, where he gave classes on Chaucer, *Beowulf*, and Old and Middle English literature in general (*Fourth* 65, 67; Stanford, *Flügel Memorial Volume* 7).

69. In the *Annual Register* for 1894–95, Oskison is registered as a law student (150). Nathan Abbott (1854–1941) was professor of law at Stanford University from 1895 to 1907. He had graduated from Yale (H. F. Stone). He taught "Criminal Law" and "Real Property," among other subjects (*Fourth* 85).

70. George Kriehn received a PhD from the University of Strasbourg, located then in Germany and now in France. He was a student in history and art in Berlin, Germany, and Florence, among other European cities, but the classes that he appears to have taught in 1894–95 have more to do with the social and economic history of England (*Fourth* 76, 78). In the *Fourth Annual Register* he is listed as an assistant professor of social and economic history (14).

71. Edward Howard Griggs (1868–1951), a graduate from Indiana University (1889) and a professor of ethics, taught "Introduction to Ethics," "The Ethics of Personal Life," "The Ethical Study of Literature," and "The Ethical Study of Autobiography" (*Fourth* 11, 70). He was the author of many books, including *The Soul of Democracy* and *The New Humanism*.

72. Edward A. Ross was an economist and a sociologist with a PhD from Johns Hopkins University (1891). One of the founders of American sociology, he authored about twenty-eight books and two hundred articles (Gillin 281). *Social Control* (1901) was one of his first major books. In 1894–95 he gave classes such as "Economic Problem," "Transportation," "Public Finance," "Money and Credit," and "Sociology" (*Fourth* 10, 80–81).

His dismissal from Stanford University in 1900 was a complex affair. It is mentioned as a reference in any debate about academic freedom. Spellman calls it "a major academic freedom case" (129). At the beginning of the 1890s, Edward Ross was a promising scholar from Indiana University, and he became an influential sociologist. When David Starr Jordan left Indiana University to become president of the new Californian institution, he convinced Ross to come along (Haskell 48). Apparently, Jane Lathrop Stanford had many issues with Ross, and all of them were somehow linked to his "antipathy to big business" (Gillin 282) as embodied by her late husband, Leland Stanford. Spellman mentions Ross's support of Eugene V. Debs in the 1894 Pullman Strike (see "Autobiography" n. 37) as the first of many grievances to come (132). Then, in the very dramatic 1896 presidential campaign, Ross voiced his longtime opposition to the gold standard President Cleveland had adhered to and which, according to Ross, was "automatically increasing the burden of all debts and causing tens of thousands of farmers to lose their homes" (Ross 64). Ross publicly expressed his support of Democrat William Jennings Bryan and authored a campaign pamphlet entitled *Honest Dollars* in favor of bi-metallism and free silver (Ross 66; Haskell 48). Mrs. Stanford, "egged on by the magnates with whom her husband had been associated when he was making his money" (Ross 67), asked President Jordan to fire Ross on account of his partisanship, although, according to Elliott, "there was no pronouncement regarding nonpartisanship in the Founding Grant" of the university, "nor in any of Mr. Stanford's addresses; nor any prohibition of 'partisanship' until Mrs. Stanford herself caused the charter to be amended, subsequent to the 1896 campaign (June 1, 1897)" (337). According to Samuels, there is actually no record of such prohibition even in that 1 June 1897 statement (188–89). In any case, it seems that Mrs. Stanford's opinion, expressed in a 3 October 1902 address, was that "when a professor speaks to a public audience . . . his hearers consider that he appears as a representative of the university of which he is a professor, and therefore voices its views and sentiments" (Samuels 185). Jordan managed to appease Mrs. Stanford by sending Ross on a sabbatical and by "downgrading" his professorship of economics into one of sociology (Spellman 132). However, the last straw, as termed by Mrs. Stanford in a 17 May 1900 letter to President Jordan, was Ross's "third outburst of partisanship" (Samuels 187) in 1900. First, on 7 May, he gave a speech before a labor union gathering in San Francisco in which he criticized "the continued importation of Oriental labor into the United States" (Mohr 40), a labor force that was widely, and at a low cost, used in the construction of railroads, thus contributing to Leland Stanford's fortune. Then, a few weeks later, according to some scholars, he advocated public ownership of municipal utilities and of railroads (Mohr 40; Spellman 132); according to Ross himself, he "touched only incidentally on the matter of public utilities," pointing out "the drift, both here and abroad, toward the municipal ownership of water and gas works" and predicting that, "as regards street railways, American cities would probably pass through a period of municipal ownership and then revert to private ownership under regulation" (Ross 71). In any case, according to Mrs. Stanford, he lent himself to "dangerous socialism" (letter to Jordan, qtd. in Samuels 187). "I think he should now be dismissed," she wrote Jordan on 9 May 1900 (Samuels 186; Mohr 44). Either Oskison and his classmates were "indignant" when they read of the event in the press, since Oskison had left Stanford two years before Ross's dismissal, or they were "indignant" when Ross was sent on a sabbatical a few years earlier. Both events might have been merged in Oskison's memory when he wrote his autobiography more than forty years later.

George Elliott Howard (1849–1928), an 1876 graduate of the University of Nebraska, was a professor of history. At the time Oskison was at Stanford, he was the head of the history department and taught "Constitutional and Political History of the United States since 1775," "History of the English Constitution," and "The French Revolution," among other subjects (Stanford *Fourth* 76). He published numerous books on some of these subjects and others. After Ross issued his statement explaining the reasons for his departure, Howard expressed his support. In his autobiography, Ross reports what Howard allegedly said to his class on the French Revolution: "My conscience will not allow me to speak to you this morning of the evils and bigotry of the French Revolution, when in our own time we can feel the effects among us of the same spirit which prevailed at that time" (77). Howard also declared publicly that "the summary dismissal of Dr. Ross is a blow aimed directly at academic freedom. . . . The blow does not come directly from the founder. It really proceeds from the sinister spirit of social bigotry and commercial intolerance which is just now the deadliest foe of American democracy" (77). In a 10 January 1901 letter, President Jordan asked Howard to apologize for the "breach of courtesy" he demonstrated with his remarks "before your class criticizing the action and the motives of the management of the university." Jordan concluded: "Failing in this it is my request that you at once tender your resignation" (Jordan to Howard, 10 Jan. 1901). Howard concluded the letter he sent as a response on the twelfth: "I have no apology to offer. My conscience is clear. What I have said I have said, as I believe, in the cause of individual justice and academic liberty. Therefore, in response to your demand, I tender you my resignation to take effect at your pleasure" (Howard to Jordan, 12 Jan. 1901). Soon after, other professors resigned in protest, including William Henry Hudson. In May 1901, thirty-seven Stanford professors and associate professors, including Jenkins, Anderson, Flügel, Abbott, and Newcomer, published a statement "to affirm our confidence in the University, its founder and its president." They agreed that "in the dismissal of Professor Ross, no question of academic freedom was involved" and that "President Jordan was justified" (Branner et al.).

73. Oliver Peebles Jenkins (1850–1935) had a PhD from Indiana University (1880). He was a professor of physiology and histology and gave classes such as "Animal Physiology" and "Structure and Functions of the Nervous System and the Sense Organs" (*Fourth* 8, 101–2).

74. In *Brothers Three*, Oskison's semi-autobiographical persona tells the anecdote: "I was taking a course in elementary biology, and the instructor gave me a smear of one-cell microbes on a glass slide to study under a microscope and make notes on. I watched 'em dart about, come together, separate, throw fits — lively as the dickens. I tried to write the usual student observations, then got to imagining them as human, and described their capers and quoted their observations on me and the instructors and professors. I suppose I grew so absorbed that I attracted the department head's attention when he came into the lab. Anyway, before I knew it, Professor Jenkins was standing beside me, and had picked up the pages I'd written. He read 'em, and said, 'Very good, Odell; you ought to send this to the 'Sequoia.' That was our literary paper. I did. It was printed, and of all the joshing, I sure caught it from the other students in that course. But the editor asked me to write more, and after a while I was on the staff of the paper" (327).

75. One Daniel Coolidge, student in English from Riverside, California, is mentioned in the catalog of students of the Stanford *Fourth Annual Register* (136). Dane Coolidge is also mentioned in the *Stanford Quad* as the editor in chief of the *Sequoia* for 1897–98 (*Stanford Quad* 28). Dane Coolidge (1873–1940) would publish a large number of fiction and nonfiction books on the West. He favored Navajo and cowboy subjects: *The Navajo Indians* (with Mary Roberts Coolidge in 1930), *Texas Cowboys* (1937), and *Arizona Cowboys* (1938) are just a few of them.

76. Herbert Hoover would become the thirty-first president of the United States (1929–33). His name appears in the catalog of students of the Stanford *Fourth Annual Register* as a student of geology (144). He had enrolled when Stanford opened, in 1891. Will Irwin, also a Stanford student later mentioned by Oskison (see "Autobiography" n. 81), and a biographer of Hoover, wrote of the links Hoover had with the "barbs." He wrote that "the fraternities combined at birth of the university to control its politics; for though only a minority of the student body, they had no organized opposition." In his second year at the university, Hoover rallied "a prophet of the 'barbs' or non-fraternity men whose appropriate name was Zion" — student in Economics Edwin Ray Zion from Berkeley — and who had earned "the nickname of 'Sosh' — short for Socialist" (Irwin 50). Hoover got elected as treasurer of the student

body. It was the beginning of his political career (53). He graduated as a mining engineer. As U.S. president, Hoover would ask one of his classmates, Ray Lyman Wilbur, to be his secretary of the interior (*Time*, 8 June 1831). Oskison published two texts about Hoover: "Herbert Hoover: Engineer-Economist-Organizer" and "Hoover Message to Export Manufacturers," both in *Industrial Management* in 1921 and 1923, respectively. In another text, "How Can You Help Feed and Clothe the Belgians," published in *World's Work* in January 1915, he wrote: "As active head of . . . the International Commission for Relief in Belgium, an American mining engineer was chosen. Mr. Herbert C. Hoover, with headquarters in London, began to give to the job of relieving Belgium the energy and administrative skill that have made him respected as one of the foremost mining managers in the world" (275). After the 1918 armistice, Lieutenant John M. Oskison, who had served in France with the Seventy-seventh Division, was assigned to the American Relief Administration under Hoover's authority until September 1919. In July he would publish "Back-firing against Bolshevism," in which he would report on the work of that administration. In their introduction to "Herbert Hoover, Engineer-Economist-Organizer," the editors of *Industrial Management* would write of Oskison and his subject that "his estimate of the man is based on a personal contact reaching back to college days, as well as on his intensive study of Mr. Hoover's contributions to the social economic and engineering thought of the times" (2).

77. The catalog of students of the *Fourth Annual Register* mentions Charles Kellogg Field, a student in English, from Alameda. Field entered Stanford in 1891 and graduated in 1895. He was a member of Phi Beta Kappa and Sigma Delta Chi (Millard 251). He would become the editor of *Sunset* magazine, where Oskison would publish "The Singing Bird" in 1925. Irwin calls Field one of the two "university poets" (58). In 1896, under the pen name Carolus Ager, Field published *Four-Leaved Clover: Being Stanford Rhymes*, a collection of short poems dedicated to various people from Stanford. In 1900, with Will H. Irwin, later mentioned by Oskison, he published a collection of short stories titled *Stanford Stories: Tales of a Young University*.

78. Charles Marron Fickert, from Tehachipi, California, appears on page 140 of the catalog of students in the *Fourth Annual Register*. He was a student in history. "*Sp.*" follows the mention of his major, which indicates he was an athlete. Charles Marron Fickert (1874–1937) played for five years for the Stanford football team as left guard and served as captain in 1898. He would graduate from Stanford in 1899. He was admitted to the bar in 1901. In 1904, recommended by David Starr Jordan, he was appointed by President Roosevelt first assistant United States attorney under Marshall Woodsworth. In 1909 he became district attorney of San Francisco, a position he held until 1919 (Millard 151–52). As the San Francisco DA, he helped jail

two Socialist activists, Thomas J. Mooney and Warren K. Billings, in what Kevin Starr calls "the Dreyfus case of mid-twentieth-century California." Starr argues that Fickert, "a politically ambitious district attorney," "collaborated with members of the grand jury to convict Mooney and Billings on the basis of fabricated and altered evidence and perjured testimony" (216).

79. Walter Camp (1859–1925) is considered the father of American football. He played in the first Yale-Harvard game of rugby in 1876 and from then on invented many of the rules that would make American football. He was Yale's first football coach (Powell). In the Stanford *Fourth Annual Register* he is mentioned as an invited lecturer (118). He authored many books on football.

80. Oskison refers here to a case that reached the U.S. Supreme Court in January 1896. It had to do with the subsidy bonds the federal government had granted the Central Pacific Railroad Company, whose shares were mostly owned by Leland Stanford. According to Will Irwin, the very existence of Stanford University was jeopardized (56). The United States sought to establish a claim against the estate of Leland Stanford for more than $15 million under the assumption that the bonds received by the Central Pacific from the United States under the acts of Congress known as "Pacific Railroad Acts" had to be reimbursed. The United States claimed that, under the constitution and laws of California, all stockholders were liable in proportion to the stock owned by them. After Stanford's death, his estate was then assumed to be liable for the huge proportion of the stock he had held. The defendant claimed that the bonds, being issued under acts of the U.S. Congress, do not depend upon the laws of California. Justice Harlan delivered the opinion of the Court regarding the case *United States v. Stanford* and reasserted that "no one of [the Pacific Railroad Acts] contains any clause imposing upon the stockholders of a corporation receiving subsidy bonds personal responsibility for any debt due to the United States from such corporation by reason of its failure to pay those bonds at maturity." The Supreme Court affirmed the dismissal by the lower courts of the bill filed by the United States (*United States v. Stanford*).

81. William Henry Irwin (1873–1948) graduated from Stanford in 1899. He is mentioned on page 144 of the Stanford *Fourth Annual Register* as a student in English from Denver, Colorado. He became a writer and a muckraking journalist. In 1904 he started to work for the *New York Sun* with Samuel Hopkins Adams, another famous muckraker later mentioned by Oskison. In 1906 he became managing editor of *McClure's*. The following year he started writing for *Collier's*, where Oskison would work as well (Applegate 81–82). He coauthored *Stanford Stories* with classmate Charles Field and published, among other books, a biography of classmate Herbert Hoover (*Herbert Hoover: A Reminiscent Biography*, 1928) and *A Reporter in Armageddon* (1918), about his experiences as a World War I correspondent.

Chris Bradley is probably Christopher Mason Bradley of the class of 1901, whose name appears in the *Register for 1899–1900* as a student of English who received a $100 prize offered by the *Cosmopolitan Magazine* for the best essay (145, 173, 210). In 1896, Will Irwin and Chris Bradley authored the "Axe Yell," a chant in support of Stanford athletes (*Stanford Daily* 21 Nov. 2008). With Billy Erb, another Stanford student, Bradley wrote a play titled *Seven Dobbers Down* in which Oskison acted, along with Will Irwin, his brother Wallace, and Charles Kenyon, who would later become a successful playwright. Bradley eventually became a lawyer in Oklahoma (*Washington Post* 3 Nov. 1912).

82. Tom Melbourne was a California farmer, brother of a neighbor of the Oskisons. He is the person mentioned in the first chapter of the autobiography who had recommended the Elmira farm Oskison's father bought in California.

83. This memory inspired Oskison to write several stories. "The Fall of King Chris" features a character named JIC-Bert who takes part in a roping contest organized in Bluejacket on the Fourth of July. In *Brothers Three* a nostalgic Roger tells his sister-in-law from New York: "It was fun to rope when this country was full of Texas cowboys; we used to get up what we called roping contests, first prize five dollars. Ask old-time peelers like Will Rogers where they learned to twirl the twine. I never liked these rodeos they get up just to make money" (181). Bluejacket—post office established in 1882 (Shirk 189)—is located in today's Craig County, approximately seventeen miles north and east of Vinita. The town was born in 1871 as Bluejacket Station on the "Katy"—the Missouri, Kansas and Texas Railway.

84. Hicks is a very common name in the Cherokee Nation. Several Hickses became prominent in one way or another throughout the history of the Nation. Charles R. Hicks had served as principal chief in 1827. Elijah Hicks had been editor of the *Cherokee Phoenix* in New Echota before he arrived in the Claremore area, Indian Territory, in 1839. The one mentioned by Oskison may be Elijah's son, Edward D. Hicks, who was born in 1866 in Fort Gibson and who organized in 1886 a company to finance the construction of a telephone line from Tahlequah to Muskogee and who is remembered as a telephone pioneer in the state of Oklahoma. However, Fullerton writes that E. D. Hicks attended the University of Arkansas, not Princeton ("Notes and Documents" 153–54; Noble 150; Fullerton 252–53). In the Final Rolls, Edward D. Hicks is recorded as No. 13804 and is thirty-seven at the time of enrollment. The only other Hicks on the roll fitting part of Oskison's scant description, "a young Cherokee named Hicks," is Joseph D. Hicks. However, age fourteen at the time of enrollment, he cannot have attended Princeton or any other university at the end of the 1890s when Oskison is playing that tennis game. It is possible, albeit unlikely, that tennis player Hicks was not enrolled. It is likelier that

Oskison's memory is faulty, as he recognizes at some point in his autobiography and as it has already been made obvious in previous notes, when trying to remember the university Hicks attended.

85. Joseph Worcester (1836–1913) was a Harvard graduate, a Swedenborgian pastor, a friend of naturalist John Muir, with whom he had a mutually influential relationship, and the founder of a Swedenborgian congregation in San Francisco in the 1860s.

86. The Barbary Coast was a part of old San Francisco. It was the San Francisco underworld where prostitution and crime were common. It covered part of today's Chinatown, North Beach, Jackson Square, and the financial district. An oft-quoted description of Barbary Coast is from *Lights and Shades of San Francisco* by Benjamin E. Lloyd, published in 1876: "Barbary Coast is the haunt of the low and the vile of every kind. The petty thief, the house burglar, the tramp, the whoremonger, lewd women, cutthroats and murderers, all are found here. Dance-houses and concert-saloons, where blear-eyed men and faded women drink vile liquor, smoke offensive tobacco, engage in vulgar conduct, sing obscene songs, and say and do everything to heap upon themselves more degradation, unrest and misery, are numerous. Low gambling houses, thronged with riot-loving rowdies in all stages of intoxication are there. Opium dens, where heathen Chinese and God-forsaken women and men are sprawled in miscellaneous confusion, disgustingly drowsy, or completely overcome by inhaling the vapors of the nauseous narcotic are there. Licentiousness, debauchery, pollution, loathsome disease, insanity from dissipation, misery, poverty, wealth, profanity, blasphemy, and death, are there. And Hell, yawning to receive the putrid mass, is there also" (79–80).

87. Susan is possibly Susan Brown Bristol, a student in English from Palo Alto (*Fourth* 134).

88. In the aftermath of the Spanish-American War, Spain had ceded the Philippines to the United States in the 1898 Treaty of Paris. However, the Filipino revolutionary forces, which had been fighting for sovereignty for some time, took advantage of the Spanish defeat to declare the independence of the Philippines. The United States refused to recognize it, and the Filipino government declared war on the United States on 2 June 1899. The Philippine-American War took place between 1899 and 1902. In September 1900, John Oskison Sr. applied to the Dawes Commission for the enrollment of his son William, age twenty-eight, away "in the Phillipine [*sic*] Islands." Commissioner Needles concluded: "The name of William M. Oskerson [*sic*] appears upon the authenticated roll of 1880 as Willie Oskerson [*sic*] and also upon the census roll of 1896 as William Oskeson [*sic*]; being duly identified and having made satisfactory proof as to residence, and it being proven satisfactorily that the reason he is not present to enroll himself is from the fact that

he is a United States soldier in the Phillipine Islands and cannot appear, the said William M. Oskerson will be duly listed for enrollment by this Commission as a Cherokee citizen by blood." Yet on 14 March 1903, William M. Oskison applied for enrollment in person. During the examination, the commissioners are trying to establish precisely how long William had been living in and out of the Cherokee Nation. William also tells them he had been in the U.S. Army for eighteen months, that he had enlisted "at Nevada, I couldn't enlist here, I passed the examination here in Vinita," and that he got out of the army on 16 February 1901. To the question "Have you got any property here?" he answers that he has a farm that his father has improved for him. No mention is made of the application his father had filed for him in 1900 or of the fact that Commissioner Needles had declared him a Cherokee citizen by blood then.

89. Leonard Wood was, in the words of biographer Jack McCallum, "a physician, an Indian fighter, a Rough Rider, chief of staff of the army, governor of Cuba and the Philippines, and very nearly president of the United States" (1).

90. Theodore Roosevelt would become the twenty-sixth president of the United States (1901–9). In 1898 he led the U.S. Volunteer Cavalry (Rough Riders) up Kettle Hill at the Battle of San Juan during the Spanish-American War. Richard Oskison would be wounded during this battle. Roosevelt will reappear in some of the following writings by Oskison as well as in several endnotes (see, e.g., "The President and the Indian").

91. Gallina is located at the foot of Redondo Peak and Polvadera Peak, about forty miles straight north of Jemez Pueblo, about fifty miles northwest of Santa Fe, and seventy miles south of Chama, in a quite arid and mountainous area.

92. The Yard is an open area that is the oldest part and the center of the Harvard campus. Memorial Hall, a U.S. National Historic Landmark, was erected in honor of Harvard graduates who fought for the Union in the Civil War. Charles William Eliot (1834–1926) became president of Harvard University in 1869. The *Register of the Alumni of the Leland Stanford Junior University from 1892 to 1899* registers Oskison's address while a Harvard graduate student as 96 Prescott Street, Cambridge, Mass. (Alumni Association 41).

93. Barrett Wendell (1855–1921) was a renowned professor of English. A *New York Times* obituary said of him that "indisputably Barrett Wendell belonged to the great group of Harvard professors which included Norton, Child, Shaler, Royce and William James; but almost as indisputably he stood apart from it—was never really of it.... His mind worked by flashes—flashes of wit, of iconoclastic paradox, of profound intelligence and of almost magical divination; but still, as it seemed to academic Cambridge, it worked uncanonically, irresponsibly" (9 Feb. 1921). He is

the author of numerous books, including one on English composition, a study of Shakespeare among other academic works, as well as a few novels.

Back Bay is the upscale district of Boston. The residents mentioned by Oskison came from families that had been prominent in New England for decades, even centuries. They are called the Boston Brahmin, or Brahman, families. The Brahmins formed a kind of elite that claimed hereditary descent from the original founders of the city of Boston. The "legend" Oskison refers to comes from a doggerel by Harvard student John Collins Bossidy:

And this is good old Boston,
The home of the bean and the cod,
Where the Lowells talk only to Cabots,
And the Cabots talk only to God. (Andrews 53)

One Back Bay resident at the turn of the century was Charles M. Cabot, an investment broker. As a stockholder of the United States Steel Corporation, he advocated for the improvement of working conditions, notably for the end of the seven-day week and the twelve-hour workday (*New York Times* 6 and 16 Apr. 1912). His wife, Bessie Cabot, in May 1911 had convinced Boston strikebreakers not to interfere in a strike against the Kingston Manufacturing Company after a cut of the workers' wages (*New York Times* 30 May 1911).

Godfrey Lowell Cabot (1861–1962) was a cousin and classmate of Abbott Lawrence Lowell (1856–1943), who also had a home in Back Bay, on Marlborough Street where the Cabots also lived, and where Henry Adams (1838–1918) — professor at Harvard, author of *The Education of Henry Adams*, and grandson of John Quincy Adams — had bought a house in the 1870s (F. Russell; Stevenson). Lowell was a lawyer before he became a professor at Harvard, where he taught political science. He succeeded Charles W. Eliot as president of Harvard (1909–33) (Yeomans and Metzger). The Saltonstalls had been involved in New England politics since colonial times, and the family included many governors of the state (Moody). Leverett Saltonstall (1892–1979), who grew up in Back Bay and attended Harvard, served as governor of Massachusetts between 1939 and 1945, when he was elected to the U.S. Senate (Hogarty; *Time* 28 Sept. 1942).

94. Asa Hill was possibly the one taking part, as a young teacher from Rhode Island, in the "Phonetic National Convention" held in New York in August 1852, which aimed at establishing the international phonetic alphabet (*New York Times* 18 Aug. 1852).

95. George Lyman Kittridge taught at Harvard between 1880 and 1936. He was

an authority on folksongs and folklore. He notably published *Witchcraft in Old and New England* (1929). Joseph Addison (1672–1719) was an English essayist and poet. Charles Lamb (1775–1834) was an English critic and essayist. Ralph Waldo Emerson (1803–82) is the well-known American writer.

96. Hugo Münsterberg (1863–1910) was a renowned psychologist. He began teaching at Harvard in 1897. He notably published, among many books, *Psychology and the Teacher.*

97. William James (1842–1910) was a psychologist and a philosopher. He was the brother of novelist Henry James. George Herbert Palmer (1842–1933) graduated from Harvard in 1864 and taught there from 1870 to 1913. Although he served in the departments of English, fine arts, Greek and theology, his main achievement was the development of the department of philosophy. He supported the coming of William James against some opposition, and he secured the coming of Josiah Royce. He also convinced Münsterberg to come to Harvard (Hocking). Josiah Royce (1855–1915), born and raised in California, taught at Harvard from 1885 to 1915. Of international fame, he was one of the most influential philosophers of the beginning of the twentieth century. Hine writes that he "stood among a handful of giants who dominated American philosophy at the turn of the century" (70). His first published book was *The Religious Aspect of Philosophy* (1885). *The Philosophy of Loyalty* (1908) and *The Problem of Christianity* (1913) are two of many other significant works (Randall).

98. Charles Townsend Copeland (1860–1952) was a professor, a poet, and a writer. He lived in Hollis Hall, in the Yard, where students swarmed to what came to be known as Copey's Monday Evenings. Many future celebrated writers—John Dos Passos, T. S. Eliot, John Macy—attended these regular events ("Copey Moves Out"). Copeland had been Helen Keller's instructor. Keller's friend and teacher, Annie Sullivan, said of him that "he helped her to self-expression. And that is what real education means" (Herrmann 141).

99. Edward Sanford Martin (1856–1939) co-founded *Life* in 1883 and was its first editor. According to Christopher Gray, "the original *Life* was sophisticated and satirical." As a Harvard alumnus, he had founded the *Harvard Lampoon* in 1876 (Gray). Charles David Stewart (1868–1960) published *The Fugitive Blacksmith* in 1905.

100. *The Canterbury Tales* is a collection of stories written by Chaucer in the fourteenth century. *Mr. Dooley in Peace and War*, published in book form in 1898, was a collection of syndicated pieces, featuring an Irish immigrant character, written by American author and humorist Finley Peter Dunne (1867–1936).

101. Oskison probably means John Albert Macy. Dorothy Herrmann defines him as "a writer, literary critic, poet, and socialist" (140). He was born in 1877 and was

admitted on a scholarship to Harvard in 1895. While there, he was the editor in chief of the *Harvard Advocate* and editor of the *Lampoon.* Macy was also famous for being the husband of Anne Sullivan, Helen Keller's teacher. Helen Keller, blind and deaf, is well known for overcoming her physical handicaps and less known for being a radical socialist. Macy met Sullivan when he was a Harvard instructor helping Helen to edit her autobiography, *The Story of My Life*. Herrmann, who devotes to Macy a whole chapter titled "John," calls him "a pioneer intellectual in American letters" (150).

102. *Century Magazine*, in which Oskison would publish several texts, was published from 1881 to 1930. Richard Watson Gilder (1844–1909) was a poet and the editor in chief of *Century Magazine* from the beginning of its publication. Robert Underwood Johnson (1853–1937) was associate editor of *Century* from 1881 to 1909, when he succeeded Gilder as editor in chief. He was a writer and, with John Muir, had advocated for the creation of Yosemite National Park in 1890. With Clarence Clough Buell, an authority on the Civil War, he published *Battles and Leaders of the Civil War* in four volumes between 1884 and 1888 (B. Matthews; Strong, "Milestones in California History" and "The Sierra Forest Reserve").

103. Frederic Remington (1861–1909) is probably one of the most famous painters and sculptors of the Old West. He considered his work a recording of a vanishing time. In a note about himself published in an issue of *Collier's Weekly* devoted to his work, he recalled a conversation he had as a young man with an old wagon freighter one night in Montana. "There is no more West," the old man had said. "I knew the railroad was coming — I saw men already swarming into the land. I knew the derby hat, the smoking chimneys, the cord-binder, and the thirty-day note were upon us in a resistless surge. I knew the wild riders and the vacant land were about to vanish forever, and the more I considered the subject the bigger the Forever loomed" (Remington 16).

104. "Only the Master Shall Praise" is a quote from a famous poem written by Kipling in 1892:

> When Earth's last picture is painted, and the tubes are twisted and dried,
> When the oldest colors have faded, and the youngest critic has died,
> We shall rest, and, faith, we shall need it — lie down for an aeon or two,
> Till the Master of All Good Workmen shall put us to work anew.
>
> And those that were good shall be happy: they shall sit in a golden chair;
> They shall splash at a ten-league canvas with brushes of comet's hair;
> They shall find real saints to draw from — Magdalene, Peter and Paul;
> They shall work for an age at a sitting and never be tired at all!

And only the Master shall praise us, and only the Master shall blame;
And no one shall work for money, and no one shall work for fame,
But each for the joy of the working, and each, in his separate star,
Shall draw the Things as he sees It for the God of Things as They are!

(Kipling, *Collected Verse*, 131–32)

In the 1904 *Stanford Quad*, in reference to stories published in *The Sequoia*, Oskison is said to be "a disciple" of Kipling, who is deemed to have had "the strongest" of "all literary influences" in the previous ten years (226).

105. Of what seems to be chapter 5 remains only a lonely page. The rest of the chapter is not with the rest of the autobiography in the Western History Collection at the University of Oklahoma in Norman. The first pages of chapter 6 are also missing, judging by the abrupt beginning of the chapter as presented next. From chapter 6 to the end, the typescript is annotated, corrected in some places where words or bits of sentences are crossed out and replaced by words handwritten, presumably by Oskison himself. There is no such correction found in the previous chapters, which seems to indicate that the first chapters were in a more finished version than the second half of the autobiography.

106. Charles William Eliot was a strong advocate of academic freedom. In an address titled "Academic Freedom" and delivered before the New York Theta chapter of the Phi Beta Kappa society at Cornell University on 29 May 1907, he claimed that, although most boards of trustees govern their institutions of higher education honestly, "there are also numerous boards that have everything to learn with regard to academic freedom." Using strong vocabulary reminiscent of Professor Howard's before his class on the French Revolution, Eliot added that "these barbarous boards exercise an arbitrary power of dismissal. They exclude from the teachings of the university unpopular or dangerous subjects. In some states they even treat professors' positions as common political spoils" (Eliot 3).

107. Charles Eliot Norton (1827–1908) was "arguably the nation's most prominent living intellectual" at the turn of the century (Appel 617). A cousin of Harvard president Charles William Eliot, he was an author and a translator of Dante's *Divine Comedy*. He graduated from Harvard in 1846 and started teaching there in 1875. Between 1864 and 1868 he edited the very influential *North American Review*. He was also a political and social activist who, as early as 1906, supported physician-assisted suicide, or euthanasia (Appel). Ralph Waldo Emerson, James Russell Lowell (1819–91), and Oliver Wendell Holmes (1809–94), all mentioned by Oskison in this paragraph, were friends of Norton's and were all men of letters. Lowell even wrote a poem titled "To Charles Eliot Norton." At Holmes's funeral, Norton said

that the deceased "was the last of that famous group of five men — Emerson, Lowell, Longfellow, Whittier, and Holmes — firm friends, and all of the same stamp" (*New York Times* 9 Oct. 1894).

108. Samuel McChord Crothers (1857–1927) was an influential Unitarian minister. He published numerous essays.

109. In "The Biologist's Quest," a short story published in July 1901 in *Overland Monthly*, Oskison tells of the misadventures of Lake, "a collector of small mammal skins for the Smithsonian authorities in Washington," who "received orders to go down into the Lower California region and make a thorough search" for "a certain species of short tailed rat." Lake is to follow the lead of Aldrich, "who had collected in the Southwest until 1893, when he was killed by a superstitious Mexican." The superstitious Mexican is obviously inspired by the superstitious Italian peasants Coolidge will be warned about.

110. In a letter Oskison sent journalist Frederick Barde in 1911, he wrote that he took his European trip in 1900 and stayed there for about five months.

Marseilles (Marseille) and Genoa (Genova) are two important harbors of the Mediterranean Sea, Marseilles one of the biggest in France, Genoa in northern Italy. Naples (Napoli) is also a large Italian harbor located south of Rome (Roma), on the northern shore of the Gulf or Bay of Naples. Straight south from Naples, on the other side of the bay, is the island of Capri. On the same side of the bay but on the mainland is Sorrento.

111. Wild Bill Newell is someone Oskison probably wrote about in the missing previous chapter of his autobiography.

112. The Blue Grotto, la Grotta Azzurra, is a cave accessible by boat only and well known for the intense blue of its waters. It is one of the main tourist attractions in Capri.

113. Charles Upson Clark (1875–1960) would become a prominent professor of history at Columbia University. When Oskison met him, he was a Fellow in the American School of Classical Studies in Rome, where he worked on the manuscript of Ammianus Marcellinus, whom he considered "the most considerable figure among the later Latin historians" (C. U. Clark 3). In 1904 he published *The Text Tradition of Ammianus Marcellinus*, the PhD dissertation he wrote as he was a tutor in Latin at Yale. In 1919, he was a member of the American Academy at Rome (*New York Times* 16 July 1919). He also published books on Italy and Romania.

114. Betty is also presumably someone Oskison wrote about in the missing chapter of the autobiography.

115. In *Venetian Life* (1867), American author William Dean Howells described the Festa del Redentore, still taking place nowadays, in July, to celebrate the end

of a plague that occurred in 1576: "On the Festa del Redentore (the third Sunday of July) a bridge of boats crosses the great canal of the Giudecca, and vast throngs constantly pass it, day and night. But though the small tradesmen who deal in fried cakes, and in apples, peaches, pears, and other fruits, make intolerable uproar behind their booths on the long quay before the church; though the venders of mulberries (for which the gardens of the Giudecca are famous) fill the air with their sweet jargoning (for their cries are like the shrill notes of so many singing-birds); though thousands of people pace up and down, and come and go upon the bridge, yet the Festa del Redentore has now none of the old-time gayety it wore when the Venetians thronged the gardens, and feasted, sang, danced, and flirted the night away, and at dawn went in their fleets of many-lanterned boats, covering the lagoon with fairy light, to behold the sunrise on the Adriatic Sea" (275). La Giudecca is the island that makes the southern part of the town, separated from the rest by the canal of the Giudecca, to which Oskison refers later by using simply the name of the island.

116. The Dolomites are picturesque mountains of the Italian Alps, in the northern part of the country, about fifty miles north of Venice (Venezia), close to the Austrian border. Innsbruck, in Austria, is about sixty miles north of the Dolomites. When Oskison hiked from Belluno to Toblach (Dobbiaco), he crossed the Dolomites from south to north.

117. The Uffizi Gallery and the Pitti Palace Galleries are prestigious art museums in Florence (Firenze). The Palazzo Pitti dates from the fifteenth century, and the Uffizi was built in 1581. The Ponte Vecchio, literally "Old Bridge," over the Arno River, is one of the most famous bridges in the world. It was built in the fourteenth century. Its particularity is that the street crossing it is bordered with buildings. Giotto's Tower is a bell tower located on the Piazza del Duomo. It is part of the Florence Cathedral. Its Gothic architecture was designed by Giotto (c. 1267–1337), a famous local painter and architect.

118. Fiesole is a small village overlooking Florence from the northeast.

119. From Venice, Oskison wrote "A Letter to His Father," published in the *Indian Chieftain* back home in Vinita, and published again in the present volume after the autobiography.

Venice (Venezia) was built in the middle of a laguna on the Adriatic Sea, on the northeastern coast of Italy. The Lido di Venezia is a peninsula separating the laguna from the sea. The doge was the head of the Republic of Venice when the latter was a powerful and wealthy independent nation whose territory reached far on the other side of the Adriatic. Piazza San Marco is the largest piazza in the town and one of the most famous in the world, notably for its pigeons, well known to tourists. Howells writes about these pigeons: "People who *will* sentimentalize over the pigeons of St. Mark's, may like to know that they have been settled in the city ever since 877. After the religious services on Palm Sunday, it was anciently the custom of the sacristans of St. Mark's to release doves fettered with fragments of paper, and thus partly disabled from flight, for the people to scramble for in the Piazza. The people fatted such of the birds as they caught, and ate them at Easter, but those pigeons which escaped took refuge in the roof of the church, where they gradually assumed a certain sacredness of character, and increased to enormous numbers. They were fed by provision of the Republic, and being neglected at the time of its fall, many of them were starved. But they now flourish on a bequest left by a pious lady for their maintenance, and on the largess of grain and polenta constantly bestowed by strangers" (282).

120. The most famous building in Boston, nicknamed "the Cradle of Liberty," was a gift to the city from Peter Faneuil, a French Huguenot merchant. Originally built as a marketplace in 1742, it served as the venue for Boston town meetings and a forum for resistance during the Revolution.

121. From Titus Livius, *History*, "Prologue."

122. Edward Perkins Clark (1847–1903) became an editorial writer of the *New York Evening Post* in 1885. Before that he had worked for many diverse publications, including *Leslie's Weekly*, where Oskison would publish a few stories (*A Soldier of Conscience*). Catherine Pickens Upson (1851–1935) married Clark in 1874. She was a journalist and a columnist for many publications, including *Atlantic Monthly* and *Harper's*, and an editor for the *New York Evening Post*. She was an activist in the suffrage and temperance movements and founded the Brooklyn Women's Republican Club. She also published several books, notably *That Mary Ann: The Story of a Country Summer* (1893) and *White Butterflies and Other Stories* (1900).

In a letter — reproduced in the present volume after the autobiography — that he sent journalist Frederick Barde in April 1911, Oskison wrote that he had found a job as a reporter at the *New York Evening Post* in 1899, before his trip to Europe in 1900.

123. Mayfield was a small town two miles southeast of downtown Palo Alto until it became part of the latter in 1925. Mayfield was such a rowdy town that it seems to have been a problem for the Stanfords that the town standing so close to their university permitted the sale of alcohol. According to Hoover and Kyle, Stanford asked one of his associates, Timothy Hopkins, to acquire a large tract of land where a new town, University Park, was established and where the sale of alcohol was prohibited until after World War II (Durham; Hoover and Kyle). According to Field and Irwin's *Stanford Stories* — where a character asks another "Are you refining yourself, your fraternity or your favorite side of the student-body by carousing at Mayfield and carrying the viciousness of that town to others where you may represent

the University?" (142) — and to Field's *Four-Leaved Clover*, many Stanford students enjoyed a drinking spree in Mayfield now and then. The Little Vendôme must have been one of Mayfield's bars. Field thus starts a rhyme entitled "Drinking Song":

We'll go down the road to the Little Vendome
When the stars are shining bright,
And we'll fill up our glasses and never go home
Through all the livelong night;
We'll drink, drink, drink, with laughter free,
A toast to our University. (66)

124. Lucerne (Luzern) is located in the center of Switzerland, a bit more than a hundred miles west of Innsbruck. Bertel Thorwaldsen (1770–1844) is a Danish sculptor. In Lucerne can be found one of his famous works, the *Lion* (1819). Representing a dying lion, it commemorates the Swiss Guards who died during the French Revolution. The Kursaal was the casino of the town. Mount Rigi (5,510 feet) and Mount Pilatus (6,888 feet) surround Lucerne and Lake Lucerne, the former on the east and the latter on the west side.

125. Paris's "Bohemia," on the Left Bank of the Seine, is called Le Quartier Latin, the area where the most prestigious universities and high schools of Paris are located. At the center is the Jardin du Luxembourg, created in 1612, where Oskison probably went too early to be able to see the original Statue of Liberty, placed in the garden only in 1906. The Odéon is a theater built at the end of the eighteenth century.

126. The painting described by Oskison is titled *Listening to Beethoven*, by Italian painter Leonello Balestrieri. It was painted in 1900 and won the gold medal at the Paris Exposition the same year. One of the most famous monuments in the world, the Eiffel Tower, was originally intended as a temporary monument built for the Universal Exposition of 1889. It was inaugurated on 31 March 1889. Three years before, Gustave Eiffel had built the internal structure of the Statue of Liberty. If Paris could not be imagined without the Eiffel Tower today, it was very much criticized at the time of its erection, and it was deemed "useless and monstrous" by the most prominent artists of the time (Gounod et al., my translation). However, it was very popular during the exposition, with almost 2 million visitors. During the 1900 exposition more than 1 million visitors, including John M. Oskison and Dane Coolidge, climbed up the Eiffel Tower.

127. Ignacy Paderewski (1860–1941) was a Polish pianist and composer of international fame. Boulevard Saint-Michel is one of the main north-south avenues crossing the Quartier Latin, along the eastern side of the Jardin du Luxembourg.

128. *Au revoir* literally means "to the time I see you again." Oskison will indeed come back to Paris several times, notably during World War I, when he served in the American Relief Administration ("Back-firing").

129. Following the autobiography is a letter, published in the *Indian Chieftain* on 9 August 1900, in which Oskison tells his father about his travels in Europe.

130. If some of Oskison's writings are particularly interesting because they shed light on Indian Territory at a key period of its history, the last chapters of his unfinished autobiography are particularly interesting because they are written by someone who was immersed in what made New York a cultural capital of the world. Kenneth Jackson and David Dunbar call the period between 1898, when the five boroughs become one city, and 1948 — that is to say, a period that almost exactly matches the one Oskison spent in New York — "a kind of golden age" (399). Among other functions of New York as a world capital, it became "the center of the book, magazine, and newspaper world. America's foremost writers and artists made their homes in Greenwich Village" (399), where Oskison lived for a while.

131. Isabel Florence Hapgood (1850–1928) was a renowned commentator of Russian literature and translator of Tolstoy (whom she knew personally), Gogol, and Turgenev, among other Russian authors. She also made regular visits to other well-known Russian personalities. She contributed considerably to the increase of American taste in Russian literature, and she was an advocate for the development of Russian studies (Engerman). She also translated French writer Victor Hugo. According to Sekirin, in 1917 "she was caught in Moscow at the beginning of the Revolution, escaping only through the help of the American consul" (34).

Louis Mouquin owned two restaurants in New York City. One was downtown, on Fulton Street; the other, where Oskison took Isabel Hapgood, was on Twenty-eighth Street and Sixth Avenue, established since 1856. Both places enjoyed a great reputation among the New York artistic and journalistic circles (*New York Times* 11 Feb. 1920). The "Duval chain [of] eating places" refers to a chain of cheap restaurants in Paris created by Pierre-Louis Duval, a butcher, in the 1860s. They were known as "Bouillons Duval" because one of the main dishes served there was *bouillon*, beef broth. Young Coolidge and Oskison, cash-strapped travelers in Europe, must have often frequented these restaurants, which a *New York Times* article called "a godsend to the impecunious" (19 Mar. 1922).

132. The *New York Evening Post* was founded by Alexander Hamilton in 1801, with William Coleman as editor. In founding this publication, Hamilton saw a way for him and his Federalist friends to promote strong central government and strict adherence to the Constitution (Muller 61).

The Samuel Bowles (1851–1915) Oskison mentions by name in this paragraph is the grandson of Samuel Bowles (1797–1851), founder of the *Springfield Republican*, the son of Samuel Bowles II (1826–78), who made the *Springfield Republican* one of the most influential newspapers in the United States and contributed to the establishment of the Republican Party in New England, and the father of Samuel Bowles (1901–86), head of the Connecticut Office of Price Administration (OPA) at the time Oskison was writing his autobiography in the 1940s. Samuel Bowles III had been the editor of the *Springfield Republican*, following in the steps of his father and grandfather, but his father was the one who made it "a potent political weapon" during Reconstruction. Even though the paper kept a political influence under Samuel Bowles III, it is likely Oskison has two of the Samuel Bowles confused ("Samuel Bowles").

Alexander Dana Noyes (1859–1945) was a respected financial editor — first at the *New York Evening Post*, where he started in 1891, then at the *New York Times* from 1920 to his death — and the author of several significant books on the subject of finance, such as *Forty Years of American Finance* (1909), *History of the National-Bank Currency* (1910), *Financial Chapters of the War* (1916), and *The Market Place: Reminiscences of a Financial Editor* (1938). Klein calls him "one of the era's most astute financial writers" and writes that "no journalist knew Wall Street better than Noyes or took a more skeptical view of it. During 1928 and 1929, Noyes had warned *Times* readers repeatedly 'in the strongest and most emphatic language, against the prevalent illusion of perpetually rising prices and perpetually increasing prosperity'" (328–29). In *The Market Place*, Noyes wrote of the panic of 1929 that it brought "a sudden recognition of economic realities. It punctured, almost overnight, the ill-fated Stock Exchange illusions. No more was heard of the new economic era" (351). Oskison, once *Collier's* financial editor, described such illusions in his *Brothers Three*.

Henry Theophilus Finck (1854–1926) and William J. Henderson (1855–1937) were part of the old guard in American criticism (Thompson; Lueders). They were both influential music critics and writers. Finck started his work in 1881 at the *New York Evening Post*, "where his enthusiastic articles on Wagner, Chopin, Liszt, Grieg, MacDowell, and others brought him celebrity and respect" (Lueders 146). He published several books, notably on Wagner — he was called "the most extreme Wagnerite in the United States" by a *New York Times* reviewer of his *Wagner and His Works* — and Paderewski — *Paderewski and His Art* — as well as his reminiscences in *My Adventures in the Golden Age of Music* (1926). William J. Henderson, "the greatest music critic America has produced" according to Thompson, was the *New York Times*'s music critic until 1902 before being the *Sun*'s for thirty-five years. He published influential books such as *Early History of Singing* and *How Music Developed* and "came to be regarded as something of a specialist on the voice" (Thompson

434). Both Finck and Henderson also tackled subjects other than music. A Harvard alumnus, Finck "wrote with equal skill on philosophy, aesthetics, the primitive love impulse, and the neglected sense of smell. W. J. Henderson, besides his authoritative volumes on yachting and naval subjects, published many stories and a volume of poems, *Pipes and Timbrels*" (Lueders 146). J. Rankin Towse (1845–1933) was born in Streatham, England, and studied in Cambridge. He came to the United States in 1869 and worked for the *Evening Sun* from 1870 to 1927, most of this time as dramatic critic. In 1916 he published his reminiscences as *Sixty Years in the Theatre* (*New York Times* Apr. 1933). William Winter (1836–1917), a Harvard graduate, was a drama critic for the *Tribune* from 1865 to 1909 and the author of many books on drama and poetry. In the course of his career he also wrote for *Harper's Weekly*, the *New York Albion*, and the *New York Weekly Review* (Winter).

133. William Lloyd Garrison had been the publisher of *The Liberator*, the abolitionist newspaper of the 1830s. One of his sons, Wendell Phillips Garrison (1840–1907), is probably the "Mr. Garrison" Oskison is writing about. A Harvard graduate in 1861, he helped Edwin L. Godkin found *The Nation* in 1865 and became its literary editor and the editor of the *New York Evening Post* when both publications merged after they were bought by Wendell's brother-in-law, railroad magnate Henry Villard, in 1881. Wendell's nephew, Oswald Garrison Villard, who would own the *Evening Post* at the death of his father, Henry Villard, in 1900, and whom Oskison mentions later, considered Wendell Phillips Garrison "one of the greatest American editors," writing that "no other editor could have worked harder over his proofs and striven more meticulously for absolute accuracy. He had assembled the greatest group of reviewers and writers who had ever contributed to a scholarly American publication" (Villard 129, in Garrison 14).

William Cullen Bryant (1794–1878) was an American poet. He succeeded to William Coleman as the editor in chief of the *Evening Post* and made this paper thrive for many years.

Besides being the founder of *The Nation*, which he meant to make "the best critical journal in literature and in political and social affairs that it was possible to make in America" (*New York Times* 22 May 1902), Edwin Lawrence Godkin (1831–1902) was the editor of the *Post* until 1900. His successor, Rollo Ogden (1856–1937), edited and published *Life and Letters of E. L. Godkin* (1907). Ogden would later become editor of the *New York Times*.

Franklin Clarkin (1869–), after working for the *Providence Journal*, was a reporter and city editor for the *Post* (Providence Journal Company). He had been a war correspondent during the Spanish-American and Russo-Japanese Wars (Washington, Harlan, and Blassingame 129).

134. In the original typescript, "Of course, I said I would." is crossed out here.

135. Oswald Garrison Villard (1872–1949), mentioned in n. 133 above, was William Lloyd Garrison's grandson. Educated at Harvard, he started his career as a newspaperman with the *Philadelphia Press*. As owner and editor of the *New York Evening Post*, he started to voice his liberal ideas and sentiments, which he voiced also as editor of *The Nation* from 1918 to 1932, thus being "a molder and shaker of opinion" (Angoff 234). Some of his liberal ideas he had allegedly expressed in a rather radical way for the time and place: "Roosevelt should nationalize all the public utilities, or most of them — the railroads and the telephones and the telegraph and the water works. What is needed now is boldness," Villard is reported to have claimed at an editorial conference of *The Nation* (Angoff 234). Villard was also a peace advocate. Woodson tells us that although he had been "an admirer of Woodrow Wilson," he took some distance from him when he led the United States in World War I, which Villard opposed. "Villard called the Versailles Treaty a 'peace of vengeance.' He predicted at that time that this treaty would cause the Second World War" (Woodson 105). Oswald Garrison Villard would also be known for his work with the National Association for the Advancement of Colored People and for his lifelong support of equal rights in general.

136. The Ghetto was the name popularly given to the Lower East Side, which is, according to Sanders, "defined in the American consciousness mainly in terms of its Jewish history and character" (Sanders and Gillon 1). "When, at the turn-of-the-century, such fine New York writers as Lincoln Steffens and Hutchins Hapgood wrote of 'the Ghetto,' they were taking in the Lower East Side and its Jews in a single term. For them, the two components were virtually interchangeable: the Jews and the Lower East Side were one" (1). If these journalists spread the word *ghetto* to refer to the Lower East Side, it apparently became prominent when Abraham Cahan published *Yekl: A Tale of the New York Ghetto* in 1896, a title probably inspired by Israel Zangwill's London Ghetto which he had staged in *Children of the Ghetto* in 1892 (Diner, Shandler, and Wenger 17–18).

The University Settlement, which moved to the corner of Eldridge and Rivington Streets in the Lower East Side on 1 January 1899 (Intercollegiate 39), had been inspired by London's Toynbee Hall, "a gathering of a group of educated, socially conscious members of the middle classes within the slums of the East End" (Sanders and Gillon 39). What came to be known as the University Settlement Society was first founded in 1886 by Dr. Stanton Coit as the Neighborhood Guild. In 1891 it changed its name under the presidency of Seth Low, president of Columbia University. Sanders gives a clear description of the University Settlement as he found it in a guidebook of the time: the University Settlement was founded "for the purpose of bringing men of education into closer relations with the laboring classes of the city, for mutual instruction and benefit. It aims to establish 'settlements' in the tenement-house districts, where college men interested in the workers may live, and mingle with their poor neighbors, on terms of perfect equality." It was a way for young men to "carry out, or induce others to carry out, all the reforms, domestic, industrial, educational, provident, or recreative, which the social ideal demands" (39). The University Settlement had a library—"which supplies books to about 100 children daily"—and a kindergarten "with an average daily attendance of 50" (*New York Times* 1 Feb. 1895). It also had a penny provident bank and clubs affording "a place of meeting for over 2,000 persons." Among other activities, it worked for the suppression of sweatshops and "the general welfare of the district" outside the Settlement, and organized "lectures and entertainments" inside (*New York Times* 1 Feb. 1895). Mark Twain gave such a lecture at the 1901 annual meeting (*New York Times* 3 Feb. 1901). It also brought about settlements by arbitration in eviction cases, notably by serving as interpreters between landlords and tenants who "viewed each other with suspicion because they spoke differing languages" (*New York Times* 26 Mar. 1897).

At the 1895 annual meeting, President Seth Low presented "the benefits that may reasonably be expected to arise from such contact [as provided by the Settlement], to society as a whole, and to the individuals concerned" (*New York Times* 1 Feb. 1895). "In the first place, there is the bridging over of the geographical gulf that separates one section of the city from another. This gulf of actual distance is only too typical of the real separation that exists between different elements in our city." Moreover, "the rental of a house where the poor live is larger in proportion to the square feet of air space which the occupants enjoy than it is where the rich dwell. If this be so, it greatly concerns the rich men of the city to know the fact, for it then becomes a matter of good citizenship on their part to work with their fellow-citizens who live among the poor, to see that the poorer parts of the city receive not less from municipal care than the parts where the rich are found." To Low, this was an example of "the sort of knowledge which the dwellers in the University Settlement want to bring home to the minds of the educated men and women of this metropolis. The University Settlement does not so much aim to remedy public and private abuses practiced upon the poor and helpless as it does to supply the knowledge of the need that there is for such help, which the educated and the rich can give." As exemplified by their president, the workers of the University Settlement believed that out of "mutual ignorance is bred mutual suspicion and mutual distrust" and that "these clouds arise constantly under such conditions, tending to exaggerate differences and to obscure points of likeness" (*New York Times* 1 Feb. 1895).

Although not a political organization, the University Settlement got involved in electoral campaigns to inform the citizens of their district and to prevent fraud. In 1895 the *New York Times* attributed to the Settlement's influence "the change of a Tammany majority into a majority in favor of the reform ticket" (*New York Times* 1 Feb. 1895).

As far as Oskison's residence at the Settlement is concerned, there again seems to be some chronological confusion. The year 1900 was the time of his trip to Europe, as testifies his letter to his father, included in the present volume, signed from Venice 16 July 1900 and published in *The Indian Chieftain* on 9 August 1900. In his autobiography, Oskison writes that he lived at the University Settlement after he was back from Europe. Yet Oskison published a text, titled "Public Halls of the East Side," in the 1899 Report of the University Settlement Society. It is possible, though unlikely, that Oskison had actually taken residence at the Settlement before going to Europe and lived there again when he got back. Several times in his autobiography, Oskison expresses he feels trapped in the predicament of the autobiographer who did not keep a diary and who is consequently unsure of his memories. This might be a manifestation of such a predicament. However, in the last chapter of the autobiography he also mentions "my year of residence" at the University Settlement and later "my twelve months at the University Settlement," both phrases making it clear that, as far as he remembered some forty years later, he did not live more than a year there, approximately between the summers of 1899 and 1900.

In *Brothers Three*, Henry meets a social worker from the "Settlement": "Through her, he met others of her kind, more or less wealthy volunteers in the fight for the underprivileged. She put him in friendly contact with the 'Settlement' houses, where her kind lived amid Ghetto and slum stenches and clamor, and attempted to create islands of decent comfort for all who would come, and stimulate ambition among the youngsters. He was surprised by the number of such workers" (373).

137. This insistence on cleanliness seems to have been more than Oskison's own preoccupation. The 1895 *New York Times* article about the annual meeting of the University Settlement reported that "the Settlement has organized a Sanitary Union among the residents of the ward, and has been continuously engaged in efforts toward reforming overcrowded tenement houses, deficient sanitary conditions, and filthy streets" (*New York Times* 1 Feb. 1895).

138. No information on Gail Nichols could be found. James B. Reynolds was an active social reformer. He became head resident of the University Settlement in 1893 (A. F. Davis 181). In his report to the annual meeting in 1895 he said there were six residents in the Settlement where there were two the previous year (*New York Times* 1 Feb. 1895). In 1897, Reynolds appealed for funds for the erection of a new building

on a plot at Eldridge and Rivington acquired by the organization in March 1897 (*New York Times* 26 Mar. 1897). In the first years of the twentieth century there were a dozen resident workers (*New York Times* 28 Nov. 1902). There were about fifty non-resident workers (Intercollegiate 39). The residents received no pay but lived in the house in comfortable, though modest, apartments on the top floor. "Practically their whole time is given up to their various duties, and some of them spend weeks at a time without going outside the district where the institution is situated. In this way, they acquire a knowledge of how 'the other half' lives that residents of Fifth Avenue would not get in a lifetime" (*New York Times* 28 Nov. 1902). In 1900, in a description of the Settlement for the *Bibliography of College, Social, University and Church Settlements*, Reynolds wrote that "since entering the [new] building our work naturally expanded in every direction. The number of residents has doubled . . . , we have immensely increased our usefulness in the neighborhood. We have also been able to express in a practical form our interest in the labor organizations. At present the central labor unions of the city, three unions of men and one of women, meet in our building. All are tenants, and the arrangement is a business one. Our interest in municipal reform has been continued" (Intercollegiate 40).

In 1895, Reynolds had expressed that the purpose of the University Settlement was "to give the people a chance to make their lives more wholesome and their environment more elevating. Because we believe that many of these elevating influences must come from municipal institutions, we have worked to secure the improvement of the public schools, the more efficient service of the Board of Health and Street-Cleaning Departments, and an honest and intelligent Government which will provide for the people all those legitimate contributions to health and right living such as are supplied by the best Governments of Europe" (*New York Times* 1 Feb. 1895). Although the Settlement was not officially affiliated with any political party, James B. Reynolds urged residents in 1896 to "go into politics": "Be earnest, practical, and be active. Political reform is the great moral opportunity of our day" (qtd. in A. F. Davis 180). Besides, the Settlement provided a place for labor unions to meet (Intercollegiate 39). Davis writes that "with Reynolds taking the lead, [Settlement workers] played a significant part in programs for political and social reform in New York City in the last decade of the nineteenth century. Municipal reform in New York became by necessity an anti-Tammany movement. Settlement workers took part in several campaigns against Tammany candidates and got caught up in the spirit of the battle, but they also looked beyond elections to their major goal of humanizing the industrial city" (A. F. Davis 180–81). Reynolds followed Seth Low as his private secretary when the latter became mayor of New York in 1902. In 1906, Reynolds would lead two investigations for President Roosevelt. One on housing conditions in Washington DC, the other on working conditions in the stockyards in Chicago. Mrs. James B. Reynolds was on the Board of Managers of the Women's Auxiliary, a branch of the University Settlement (*New York Times* 17 Feb. 1910).

Owing to the chronological confusion as to when Oskison lived at the Settlement, we cannot be sure that he met in person the many people he mentions or alludes to and who are annotated below. They were well-known people and Oskison might occasionally confuse whom he actually met with whom he read about or heard of.

In a long front-page *New York Times* article dated 28 November 1902, one could read that "it was announced yesterday that J. G. Phelps Stokes, son of Anson Phelps Stokes of this city, had finally removed his belongings from his father's large house at 229 Madison Avenue to the University Settlement, 184 Eldridge Street, and there permanently taken up his abode, with the intention of devoting his life to the settlement work." The Phelps Stokes family was prominent enough for James Graham Phelps Stokes (1872–1960) to be worthy of such attention from the media. His father was a multimillionaire banker and a prominent New York City figure. His brother, Anson Phelps Stokes Jr., was secretary of Yale University, from which J. G. had graduated. Another brother, Isaac Newton Phelps Stokes had been one of the architects of the University Settlement building on Eldridge. In 1905, another front-page article announced J. G. Phelps Stokes's engagement to "Miss Rose Harriet Pastor, a young Jewess, who until two weeks ago was a special writer on *The Jewish Daily News*, and prior to that worked in a Cleveland cigar factory" (*New York Times* 6 Apr. 1905). According to that article, Rose Pastor (1879–1933) had been working at the Settlement for some time previous to the wedding but Phelps Stokes and she had met when she interviewed him for the *Jewish Daily News* in July 1902. She would later become a leader of the Socialist Party and a birth-control advocate.

The Hewitt family was another influential and wealthy family. Abram Stevens Hewitt (1822–1903) joined his name to another prominent one when he married Sarah Cooper, daughter of industrialist Peter Cooper. They fast became successful in the iron-making business. At the beginning of the 1870s, Hewitt contributed in the cleaning of Tammany Hall of the infamous Boss Tweed and his Ring. In 1874 he won a seat in the U.S. House of Representatives. In 1886 he became mayor of New York City by beating Henry George and young Theodore Roosevelt ("Abram Stevens Hewitt"). As mayor of New York, he led a reform program. At the 1898 annual meeting of the University Settlement, a meeting whose main purpose was to raise money for the erection of the new building on Eldridge and Rivington, Hewitt gave an address in which he paid tribute to Arnold Toynbee, the English scholar upon whose ideal Toynbee Hall had been founded in London and by which the University Settlement had been inspired. "Toynbee Hall was built upon his idea," he said, "to re-establish a sense of common brotherhood and common humanity. That also is the basis of the University Settlement—the idea that the rich are to put themselves in contact with the poor, the suffering, the abandoned." He also eloquently pointed at the contrast of the century: "The nineteenth century has done what seemed impossible—it has cheapened the necessaries of life, and increased the wages of those who produced them. And yet in no other period has there been such a contrast of the rich and the poor. That a child can be born in the slums, live all its life in the slums, and die in the slums in our age would be a shock, I think, to the conscience of society. I do not believe that our society can long endure it" (*New York Times* 28 Jan. 1898). Mrs. Edward Ringwood Hewitt was vice-president of the Woman's Auxiliary (*New York Times* 17 Jan. 1900). Edward Ringwood Hewitt (1866–1957), a son of Abram S. Hewitt, was an inventor, a chemist, and the author of several books on fly-fishing. He also published a book on the Bowery, a New York district adjacent to the Lower East Side, in 1897, and an autobiography titled *Those Were the Days: Tales of a Long Life* (1943). Another son of Abram S. Hewitt, Peter Cooper Hewitt (1861–1921), was also an inventor. He notably invented the mercury vapor lamp to simulate daylight in artificial lighting in 1912 ("Century of Science" 332). He also made important contributions to helicopter design and invention ("Man's Efforts" 182).

139. Dr. Edward Livingston Trudeau, a physician and a tuberculosis sufferer, was the founder of the first tuberculosis sanitarium in the United States. The sanitarium started as a house on Saranac Lake, three hundred miles north of New York City, built in 1884 and named the Little Red. There was a laboratory in which Trudeau studied the disease and a hospital where he attempted operations. In 1898, Trudeau claimed he had cured 73 percent of his patients in the first stages of the disease. Trudeau died of tuberculosis in 1915, but his health center continued until 1954 (Epstein; Chalmers).

140. Many of the University Settlement residents in the first decade of the twentieth century were more or less directly involved in three historical events of the time: the growth of the American Socialist Party, the abortive Russian Revolution of 1905, and the panic and depression of 1907. These residents were activist journalists and writers, and they published numerous documents on these subjects. Their names also appear often in the newspapers of the time. Although Oskison evidently knew these people—some of his allusions in this paragraph can be identified as references to some of them—his name does not appear in the documents produced by or about these well-known residents. One reason might be that Oskison was not yet well advanced in his career as a journalist, although he was approximately of the same age. Another reason may simply be that he did not have the same socialist

inclinations as his fellow residents and took some distance from them. In any case, he was not the socialist activist that some of the Settlement residents were. For one thing, as testified by some of his writings, he admired Herbert C. Hoover, a staunch believer in the free market. Then, his experience in Europe as a member of the American Relief Administration under the authority of Hoover during and after World War I brought him close to Bolshevik experiments which he criticized vehemently in "Back-firing against Bolshevism" (1919). In this article for *The Outlook* issue of 30 July 1919, signed by Lieutenant John M. Oskison, he wrote, for example, that "Bolshevism is a cure-all. Its promoters are as shameless in their claims as any street vender of a snakeroot remedy discovered by an old Sioux medicine man and guaranteed to heal tomahawk wounds. . . . To the hungry and hopeless of German Austria and Hungary and Serbia and Rumania and Bulgaria it might very well seem the one way to economic recovery" (510). Never forgetting where he was coming from, he added that "out of Russia the agents of Bolshevism were coming to excite the people to try their remedy. They were like the old outlaw hunters of the West who used to set the prairie afire in a score of places in order to drive the game in front of their guns" (514). To him, his work in the American Relief Administration was contributing to "efforts to stop the spread of an economically insane doctrine" promoted by the Bolsheviks (515). His positions, even if they might not have been so well defined in the first years of the century, could explain why he did not try to remember his fellow Settlement residents more clearly forty years later. A study remains to be done, however, of the influence this reform-minded environment may have had on his work. At the very least, during his stay at the Settlement, Oskison expanded his network.

Apart from Nichols, Oskison, and Phelps Stokes, some of the Settlement residents in 1902, as explicitly testified by a *New York Times* article published that year, were William English Walling, Ernest C. Poole, and Carl Miller, of whom the last "is so interested in the settlement work that he has at his own expense rented a house on the east side, which he is fitting up for a club for boys who run the streets and whom he hopes to reform" (*New York Times* 28 Nov. 1902).

The "official of the Charity Organization Society" was probably Robert Hunter (1874–1942), who published a paper in 1902 in which he studied the "Relation between Social Settlements and Charity Organization." "Having lived in settlements all of the time I have worked in the Charity Organization Society," he wrote, "I have had opportunity to know many workers in both movements" (81). Indeed, before he came to the University Settlement in New York he had been, between 1896 and 1902, the organizing secretary of the Board of Charities in Chicago, where he lived in the Hull House, the Chicago equivalent of the University Settlement

(Bowman). However, Oskison might also refer to Edward T. Devine. In the same paper, Hunter mentions "the present secretary of the New York Charity Organization Society, Mr. Devine" (86), who had been in that position at least since 1901 (American Academy 15). According to A. F. Davis, "Edward T. Devine, of the New York Charity Organization Society," was a "frequent" resident of the University Settlement (22). Devine would become a professor of social economy at Columbia University and publish *Misery and Its Causes* in 1912 (*New York Times* 18 Feb. 1912).

Robert Hunter, however, could also be the resident "who had lived for a time at a London East End settlement." Hunter had indeed been a resident of Toynbee Hall (Boylan 55), where he might have met George Bernard Shaw and the Webbs, of the Fabian Party. In 1902 he replaced James B. Reynolds as head resident of the University Settlement. Hunter asked a friend from Chicago, William English Walling, with the same socialist inclinations, to come to New York: "I wish I might hope to have you come to the Settlement. At present we are overcrowded here but I hope that within a month or so, I shall be able to make arrangements for more room" (in Boylan 55). Hunter then proceeded to make room for some of his reform-minded friends. Oskison is likely to have left then if he had not left earlier (see "Autobiography" n. 136 above). His mention of Phelps Stokes suggests that he stayed long enough to witness the latter's definitive move into the Settlement or that he had been there at the time of one of the millionaire's previous temporary stays. Hunter remained head worker for only one year and was succeeded by James H. Hamilton in 1903 (Kraus 66). He joined the American Socialist Party in 1905. In 1903, he had married J. G. Phelps Stokes's sister, Caroline Stokes (*New York Times* 18 Apr. 1903). In 1904 he published *Poverty*, his best-known book (*New York Times* 7 Jan. 1905).

William English Walling (1877–1936), a Socialist activist born in a southern, proslavery, and wealthy family, was the grandson of William Hayden English, who had run for the Vice-Presidency in 1880 on the ticket with Winfield Scott Hancock. For two years, he lived at the Settlement where he led a "study circle" devoted to "Labor and Social Movements" (*New York Times* 19 Jan. 1906; Nutter 85). Boylan writes that Walling and his Jewish wife, Anna Strunsky, "were among the most glorious of the American left's Beautiful People: 'millionaire Socialists,' rivaled only by the Lincolnesque James Graham Phelps Stokes and his immigrant journalist bride, Rose Pastor" (1). Although he was an American who went by the name of English — nationality and name might have collided in the memory of an Oskison who did not keep a diary and wrote about the events some forty years later — Walling may also have been the "English Fabian Socialist who knew [George] Bernard Shaw" and the Webbs, famous members of the Fabian Party, a reformist movement that Walling actually criticized in his writings. In 1903, Walling helped Mary Kenney

O'Sullivan found the National Women's Trade Union League (Nutter 84). In 1909, he co-founded the National Association for the Advancement of Colored People. In 1905 he visited Russia, where he was arrested for expressing "sympathy for the revolutionists" (*New York Times* 19 Jan. 1906). A few years later he published *Russia's Message to the World.* In 1910 he joined the American Socialist Party. In 1918 he published *Socialism as It Is: A Survey of the World-Wide Revolutionary Movement,* in the preface of which he makes "special mention of the very careful reading of the whole manuscript by Mr. J. G. Phelps Stokes, and of the numerous and vital changes made at his suggestion" (Walling vi). With Phelps Stokes, he also edited *The Socialism of To-Day: A Source-Book of the Present Position and Recent Development of the Socialist and Labor Parties in All Countries* (1916).

Boylan tells us that Hunter also recruited Leroy Scott, "a minor editor at the monthly *Woman's Home Companion,*" where Oskison would publish "Spider and the Fly" in 1911; Howard Brubaker, "a would-be writer just out of Indiana University"; S. G. Lindholm; and Ernest Poole, "a new Princeton graduate from Chicago, who saw himself as a future novelist of the slums" (56–57). Phelps Stokes was also one of Hunter's recruits.

Ernest C. Poole (1880–1950), who graduated in 1902, was a journalist and a novelist. He helped Upton Sinclair gather material for his famous book *The Jungle.* He was a correspondent in Europe during World War I for the *Saturday Evening Post,* and in Russia during the 1917 Revolution for the *New Republic.* His best-known novel is *The Harbor* (1915). In 1918 he received the Pulitzer Prize for his novel titled *His Family* (Hart and Leininger, "Poole"). Poole also had strong socialist sympathies. In 1904, "only twenty-four at the time and crazy to go over there," he wrote later in an autobiographical account of Gorki's visit to New York, he sailed to Russia under contract with *The Outlook,* a widely read magazine of the time — in which Oskison would publish "Back-firing against Bolshevism" in 1919 — and brought money for the revolutionaries. In February 1906, back in New York, Poole helped organize the *A* Club on 3 Fifth Avenue, a small group of writers including Walter Weyl and Howard Brubaker, both from the University Settlement, with visitors such as Jack London, Upton Sinclair, S. S. McClure, and Samuel Clemens (Mark Twain) (Poole 78; McFarland 120–21).

All these University Settlement former residents were familiar with testimonies by their Jewish neighbors of "tyrannical czarist rule and the atrocities committed against Jews" (McFarland). Some — Poole and Walling, but also Brubaker and Arthur Bullard — had taken action the previous year to support the revolutionaries. When Russian novelist and revolutionist Maxim Gorki, notably thanks to the efforts of Walling and Bullard still in Russia, came to New York in April 1906 to raise money for the Bolshevik movement, the *A* Club formed an American committee to help him raise funds with such people as Twain, William Dean Howells, Finley Peter Dunn, Richard Watson Gilder, University Settlement manager Leroy Scott, and Robert Hunter (Poole 78–79; McFarland 123). At the 11 April 1906 dinner that inaugurated this committee, Hunter declared that "the object of the committee is to collect funds to help the movement for Russian freedom. An appeal will be issued to the American public within a couple of days, and there is no doubt that there will be a generous response when we ask Americans to help the oppressed people of Russia to gain the same freedom that our fathers fought for, and which we have enjoyed these hundred years and more" (*New York Times* 12 Apr. 1906).

Walter Weyl, a co-founder of the *New Republic* and an alleged influence on the policies of Theodore Roosevelt and Woodrow Wilson, was also a resident of the Settlement in 1902 (Forcey vii, 66). There he met Poole and Walling and got "caught in a vortex that carried him into real life" (Weyl's diary, qtd. in Forcey 66). He married Poole's sister, Bertha, in 1907 (70). Howard Brubaker, whom Weyl also met at the Settlement, made contributions to Weyl's *New Republic* (207). He also became a contributor to the *New Yorker*. His "Of All Things" column was syndicated nationwide.

Leroy Scott (1875–1929) would become a novelist. In 1910 he published *The Shears of Destiny*, based on his 1905 trip to Russia, and *Counsel for the Defense* in 1912 (J. A. Huston 337). Arthur Bullard (1879–1929), who would become the author of novels and essays, may have been the "talented, self-effacing editorial writer on the *Sun*" Oskison has in mind.

141. English novelist W. Somerset Maugham published *Of Human Bondage* in 1915, telling the life of Philip Carey. As a young adult, Philip falls in love with Mildred, a waitress who does not return his feelings. She gets married, leaving Philip heartbroken. A few years later, Philip meets her again. She had been abandoned and had become a prostitute.

142. Teddy Roosevelt became governor of New York in 1898, after he was back from the Spanish-American War.

143. Richard Harding Davis (1864–1916) was correspondent for the *New York Herald*, the *London Times*, and *Scribner's Magazine* during the Spanish-American War. He also wrote many short stories, novels, and plays, as well as accounts of his numerous travels around the world (R. H. Davis).

144. Lyman Abbott (1835–1922) was a clergyman and the editor of *The Outlook*, formerly the *Christian Union*. In 1888 he succeeded Henry Ward Beecher as pastor of the Plymouth Congregational Church in Brooklyn (Maddox 79). In several books he tried to reconcile the Darwinian theory and Christianity (Hart and Leininger,

"Abbott"). In 1903 he was a member of the Business Committee of the Lake Mohonk Conference of Friends of the Indian (1903 *Proceedings Twenty-first Lake Mohonk Conference*). In 1905 he was elected president of the Lake Mohonk Conference (1905 *Proceedings Twenty-third Lake Mohonk Conference* 10). A supporter of allotment, Abbott "claimed that the Dawes Act had its origins in discussions held in the editorial offices of his journal" (Maddox 80). Maddox wrote interesting pages on Abbott's philosophy and how it relates to the Indian question.

145. "When the Grass Grew Long" was the second of three stories that Oskison would publish in the *Century*. The third would be "The Quality of Mercy."

146. After "Only the Master Shall Praise," Oskison published in the *Century* "When the Grass Grew Long" (1901) and "The Quality of Mercy" (1904). In *McClure's* he published "Young Henry and the Old Man" in 1908.

Cassedy calls the years between 1902 and 1912 "the muckraking decade" (85). *McClure's* indeed took the lead in this kind of journalism. The term was coined by President Theodore Roosevelt, who, in a speech in 1906, referred to investigative journalists by means of a comparison to a character in Bunyan's *Pilgrim's Progress*: "In Bunyan's *Pilgrim's Progress* you may recall the description of the Man with the Muck Rake, the man who could look no way but downward, with the muck rake in his hand; who was offered a celestial crown for his muck rake, but who would neither look up nor regard the crown he was offered, but continued to rake to himself the filth of the floor" (*Man with the Muck Rake*). Two journalists mentioned by Oskison in the next paragraph, Lindsay Denison and Samuel Hopkins Adams, who would work for *McClure's*, as well as some people already mentioned—like Will Irwin, Ernest Poole, Upton Sinclair, and William E. Walling—were famous muckrakers who exposed the abuses of business and the corruption of politics (Filler). One of the most famous muckrakers was Lincoln Steffens, whom Oskison mentions later as managing editor of *McClure's*. At *Collier's*, Oskison himself would do his share of muckraking against the abuses of business and in particular against what he called the "loan sharks" in articles like "John Smith Borrows $20" (1909), "Exploiters of the Needy" (1909), and "Competing with the Sharks" (1910), as well as "The Round-Up of the Financial Swindlers" (1910) and "Separating the Thrifty and Credulous from Their Money" (1913).

147. If Maugham beat him to it, Oskison still wrote a short story, published in *McClure's* in 1927, the inspiration of which might have come to him remembering Ken Stillman's story. Using as a backdrop his experience in France as a member of the American Relief Administration after World War I, and giving it the French local color he could, Oskison wrote, in "Yvonne the Terrible," the story of an American officer, Major Condit, who fell in love with Yvonne, a war-time nurse hired to

"entertain" and "amuse him" (92). When Condit declares his love and proposes to her, she responds with a cruelty similar to Ida's: "'Marry!' she turned startled eyes on him, laughed. 'Now, you make *blague*—you—you—'" She then proceeds to reveal who she is:

> "So you mus' know," she was approaching the end of her story, "that we who are of the theater do not expect to decorate the *foyers* of the bourgeois, the people of respectable tradition. I do not care for them. I make my career, at first in the cabarets of Montmartre, then the Folies Bergères, Casino de Paris, in London, Vienna, Warsaw—everywhere. Before the War, I 'ave earned much money, and I 'ave made economies, so I may live in comfort. In the years of War, I 'ave been nurse, and I 'ave also entertained our soldiers—and yours, as you know. Alors?"
>
> "And kept yourself—unsoiled—Yvonne?" It was an agonized plea.
>
> "Ah, you are stupid!" Her eyes were snapping. "It is difficult to talk with you, but you mus' know. Do you think, my friend, I am *jeune fille*?" she broke off with an ironic smile. (92)

148. Lindsay Denison and Samuel Hopkins Adams (1871–1958) were famous investigative journalists. Both worked at the *New York Sun* at the turn of the century. Adams had been there at least since the beginning of the 1890s (F. M. O'Brien 330). Adams went from the *Sun* to *McClure's* in 1900 (*New York Times* 4 Dec. 1905). In 1905 he worked for *Collier's Weekly*, which Oskison would join a few years later. At *Collier's*, Adams became famous as the author of a series of articles called "The Great American Fraud." *Collier's* announced that these articles, written "after an investigation lasting several months, will not only describe the methods used to humbug the public into buying patent medicines through fake testimonials and lying statements published in the newspapers, but will show that a large number of the so-called 'tonics' are only cocktails in disguise, and that many of these nostrums are directly responsible for the making of drunkards and drug fiends" (Weinberg and Weinberg 177). Adams's articles contributed to the passage of the Pure Food and Drugs Act of 1906 (Cassedy 86). Adams also wrote fiction. Denison worked on the criminal activities of the Black Hand (La Mano Negra) in New York (Nelli 71). He also contributed to *Harper's*.

149. That sea story could not be identified. In 1910 Oskison published a different sea story, in any case a story taking place at sea, titled "Diverse Tongues: A Sketch."

150. Carry A. Nation was called a "saloon-smashing yet fun-loving crusader who fought alcohol, tobacco, and sex with her hatchet" on the cover of Robert Louis Taylor's account of her life and "a hatchet-swinging, God-appointed vigilante with

a really bad public image" by biographer Fran Grace. She became a celebrity in 1900 after several successful saloon-smashing sprees in Kansas.

151. Norman Duncan (1871–1916) was not a Scottish but a Canadian writer. He graduated from Toronto University in 1895. From 1897 to 1901 he worked for the *New York Evening Post*, where he started as a reporter and later became the editor of the Saturday supplement. He published *The Soul of the Street* in 1900. The book is a collection of short stories about the life in the New York Syrian quarter that had been published in the *Atlantic Monthly* and *McClure's* (Duncan 9–11). These are the stories Oskison refers to. An article for the *New York Times Saturday Review of Books*, written by Otis Notman, tells of Duncan's attachment to the Syrian Quarter: "He discovered it when he was a reporter on a paper. He spent all his spare time there for a year. There was a little café he was fond of frequenting, where very strong coffee was to be had, and he used to spend hours there at a little green baize table with an old Syrian, who helped him translate some of the native poetry. Then he made a special study of the Syrian music. . . . After his year among the Syrians he went directly to Newfoundland" (*New York Times* 4 May 1907). In 1900, *McClure's* sent him to that Canadian maritime province. The time he spent there inspired him with *The Cruise of the Shining Light* (1907). In 1907 and 1908, Duncan served as correspondent for *Harper's* in the Middle East.

"Charley Selden" is probably George Charles Selden (1870–?), an 1893 Dartmouth College graduate and author of several books on finance, notably *A Century of Prices* (1919) with Theodore Burton, *Investing for Profit* (1913), *Psychology of the Stock Market* (1912), and *The Machinery of Wall Street: Why It Exists, How It Works and What It Accomplishes* (1917). In the 1910s he was managing editor of *The Magazine of Wall Street*. In 1899 he had been awarded a Schiff Fellowship by Columbia University (Columbia University 419). In the "Introductory Note" to *A Century of Prices*, he is said to be "internationally known for his keen and thorough analyses of the effects of economic factors on business and investments" (Burton and Selden 4). Some of the "thumbnail word sketches" Oskison refers to were published in *Dartmouth Sketches* (1893), coedited by Selden himself. One is "The Old Pine" (93–94), another is "An Unsettled Question" (110–12), in which dry wit is manifest.

"Only a Pansy Blossom" was a popular song written and composed by Eben E. Rexford (words) — "the well-known writer on the subject of flowers" — and Frank Howard (music) between 1883 and 1886 (*New York Times* 14 Mar. 1903).

Tom Jones is the protagonist of *The History of Tom Jones, a Foundling* (1749), and Joseph Andrews is the protagonist of *The History of the Adventures of Joseph Andrews and of His Friend Mr. Abraham Adams* (1742), both by English writer Henry Fielding (1707–54).

152. William Makepeace Thackeray (1811–63) was an English novelist. One of his most famous works is *Vanity Fair* (1848). *Pamela, or, Virtue Rewarded* (1740) and *Clarissa: or, The History of a Young Lady* (1747), whose eponymous character was called Clarissa Harlowe, are epistolary novels, the two most famous works of English novelist Samuel Richardson (1689–1761). Fielding and Richardson are considered the inventors of the modern novel. *The Expedition of Humphrey Clinker* (1771) is also an epistolary novel, by English writer Tobias Smollett (1721–71). Laurence Sterne (1713–68), an English writer of Irish descent, was most famous for his *Life and Opinions of Tristram Shandy, Gentleman* (1759–69 in nine volumes). He also published *A Sentimental Journey through France and Italy* (1768). Anthony Trollope (1815–82) was one of the most prolific English novelists of the Victorian era. Among many others, he published *The Warden* (1855), *Barchester Towers* (1857), and *The Way We Live Now* (1875). Apparently, Selden's roosters inspired Oskison to catch up with the history of the origins of novel writing. James Matthew Barrie (1860–1937) was a Scottish novelist. If he is mostly famous for his play entitled *Peter Pan: The Boy Who Wouldn't Grow Up* (1904), he also wrote some sentimental novels such as *The Little Minister* (1891).

153. *The Virginian: A Horseman of the Plains* was published in 1902 by Owen Wister (1860–1938). Wister graduated from Harvard in 1882. At Harvard he made friends with Theodore Roosevelt, to whom the book is dedicated (Wister v). Wister called his novel a "colonial romance" (vii). It takes place in Wyoming between 1874 and 1890, "a colony as wild as was Virginia one hundred years earlier. As wild, with a scantier population, and the same primitive joys and dangers" (vii). Wister himself, in the preface to his book, gives a definition of the cowboy character that Oskison probably approved: "What is become of the horseman, the cow-puncher, the last romantic figure upon our soil? For he was romantic. Whatever he did, he did with his might. The bread that he earned was earned hard, the wages that he squandered were squandered hard. . . . Well, he will be here among us always, invisible, waiting his chance to live and play as he would like. His wild kind has been among us always, since the beginning: a young man with his temptations, a hero without wings. The cow-puncher's ungoverned hours did not unman him. If he gave his word, he kept it. . . . Nor did he talk lewdly to women. . . . He and his brief epoch make a complete picture, for in themselves they were as complete as the pioneers of the land or the explorers of the sea" (xl). According to Kuenz, the cowboy literary "type" "made his mature literary debut in Owen Wister's 1902 bestseller" (99). Barsness writes that *The Virginian* is the "archetypal western novel" and that Wister "established the cowboy in his definitive form" (609–10).

154. William Dean Howells (1837–1920) was an American realist. He published

The Rise of Silas Lapham in 1885. He also wrote much about the travels he made in Europe (see "Autobiography" n. 115). In 1906 he was a member of the committee formed to help Russian revolutionist Gorki to raise funds (see "Autobiography" n. 140).

Hamlin Garland (b. 1860, West Salem WI; d. 1940, Hollywood CA) was a prolific writer who published a large number of novels and short stories about the midwestern life. *Main-Traveled Roads*, published in 1891, was his first success. He also notably published *The Trail of the Gold Seekers* (1899), inspired by his adventures during the Klondike Gold Rush in Yukon, and *The Captain of the Gray-Horse Troop* (1902), about a young officer being detailed as Indian agent to replace a corrupt predecessor. Oskison mentions this book in "The Outlook for the Indian" (see below). According to Lonnie Underhill, "Garland's treatment of the Indian was sympathetic from the start, and that sympathy caused him to expend much of his energy on works that were as much sociological as literary and essentially reformist rather than aesthetic" (103). According to Owen Reamer, Garland was "the pioneer in this matter of handling of the reservation Indian, and that by his true and sympathetic portraits he made a contribution of lasting importance to American literature" (263).

John Steuart Curry (1897–1946) was born in Kansas and lived many years of his life in Wisconsin. He was famous for the paintings of both states' rural landscapes. When he arrived at the University of Wisconsin at Madison in 1936, he became "the first artist-in-residence at any American university" (Holzbueter 14). He is often considered part of a group of so-called regionalist painters including Tom Benton, Grant Wood, and Charles Burchfield (Czestochowski 70). Besides canvases, he painted a lot of murals, some of which can be seen in the Kansas State Capitol at Topeka.

155. The Authors' Club was created in 1882 in New York (Osborne 3). Osborne writes that "the idea of organizing a club of men of letters here must be credited to Charles de Kay, brother-in-law of the late Richard Watson Gilder, who gave it his hearty concurrence. Pursuant to Mr. de Kay's invitation, there met, on 21 October 1882, at Mr. Gilder's house, 103 East Fifteenth Street, Noah Brooks, Edward Eggleston, Laurence Hutton, Brander Matthews, Edmund Clarence Stedman, Charles de Kay, and Richard Watson Gilder" (3). At a third meeting, in November, a constitution was adopted "prescribing as the standard of eligibility that the candidate must be 'the author of a published book proper to literature or hold a recognized position in other kinds of distinctively literary work.' 'Technical books and journalism as such' were definitely barred, as not being bases of eligibility" (5). According to its own manual, the Authors' Club's "particular business and object . . . shall be literary and library purposes, and the promotion of social intercourse among

authors" (Osborne 8). Illustrious members and honorary members included Samuel Clemens, Carl Schurz, Henry James, Robert Louis Stevenson, Harriet Beecher Stowe, and French author Alphonse Daudet. Henry Holt, mentioned later by Oskison, was also a member (Authors' Club).

156. Edmund Clarence Stedman (1833–1908) was a poet, a critic, and a Wall Street broker. Frank Stockton (1834–1902) was the author of short stories, the most famous of which was "The Lady or the Tiger" (1882). Henry Van Dyke (1852–1933), "minister, diplomat, angler, and popular nature writer" (Burns 29), wrote short stories telling of adventures in the wilderness, like "Au Large" (1895). Thomas Nelson Page (1853–1922) was a Virginian, a diplomat, and a writer. In 1913, Woodrow Wilson appointed him ambassador to Italy. Before that he had been the successful author of novels, stories, and essays about the South (Gaines 328). Flusche calls him "beyond doubt the best-known Southern author during the last years of the nineteenth century" (464).

Silas Wier Mitchell (1829–1914) was a physician, notably Owen Wister's, who became famous worldwide for his so-called rest cure for functional nervous disorders. A specialist of nervous diseases, he notably worked on the effects of peyote upon the system. He published more than two hundred scientific papers. Mitchell was also famous as a writer of short stories and novels such as *Hugh Wynne* and *Circumstance*. In many of his works he used his experience as a neurologist to build his characters. In some novels, such as *Westways: A Village Chronicle*, he used the Civil War, during which he served as acting assisting surgeon of the U.S. Army, as a theme and backdrop (Keen; Carlson; *New York Times* 30 Nov. 1901, 14 Sept. 1913; Kuenz 110; Willard 28; Griffith 247).

Gilbert Parker (1862–1932) was a Canadian author of short stories and novels in which his favorite theme was French Canadian culture. *Pierre and His People* (1892) is probably his most famous work. Some of the short stories it contains were also published in American periodicals. He immigrated to Australia, where he was assistant editor with the *Sydney Morning Herald* before he moved to England, where he had a political career. Married to a New York heiress, he made frequent trips there, notably to advertise his books. A supporter of Arthur Balfour, a Conservative leader who was the British prime minister from 1902 to 1905, he became a Member of Parliament in 1900. He was knighted in 1902. During World War I he was in charge of British propaganda in North America (*New York Times* 5 Dec. 1901, 1 Feb. 1902; G. Parker; Stockdale).

The Players' Club was founded in 1888 by famous Shakespearean actor Edwin Booth (1833–93) at 16 Gramercy Park. According to Parke Godwin, in a commemorative address he gave in 1893, Booth gave the Players' Club "all his available funds;

he gave to it the companions of his long silent life—his books; he gave to it the treasures of his secret heart—his pictures and his relics. His desire was to erect a home where the selected members of his profession might meet with one another, and with the representatives of other professions, in friendly intercourse and on terms of social equality and reciprocal esteem" (The Players, *Memorial Celetration* 41). It had, in the words of one of its first members, "a library which shall contain the dramas of every tongue and the criticism of every time, and where, as the years go on, shall be carefully gathered the history of the stage and the biography of those who belong to it" (The Players, *Excerpts* 13). Clemens, Gilder, Stedman. and Henry Irving were some of the many members. Henry Irving was an English actor who had played with his friend Edwin Booth in many plays. He worked at the Lyceum Theatre, London, managed by Bram Stoker (*New York Times* 11 Nov. 1886).

157. Henry Holt (1840–1926) was a famous publisher, the founder of Henry Holt & Company publishing house. In 1916 he accused periodicals of "sending American literature to the dogs" (Kilmer).

158. Hanner the Runt, the protagonist of "Only the Master Shall Praise."

159. Morgan Robertson (1861–1915) was a popular sea fiction writer. He was found dead in a hotel room of Atlantic City with drugs near him, although overdose was not declared the cause of his death. He had gone to Atlantic City to recover from a nervous breakdown. Going to sea at the age of sixteen for about ten years before the mast, and subsequently living of various jobs from hand to mouth, he was said to be "barely able to keep himself and his wife from starvation." The article reporting his death continues, corroborating what Oskison writes of Robertson: "One day it occurred to him to write a short story of sea life dealing with an incident in his own career. He wrote the story on the bottom of a washtub in the kitchen of his flat on the backs of some circulars which he had been hired to distribute the day before" (*New York Times* 25 Mar. 1915). This first story was "The Derelict Neptune" and was published in *McClure's* (*New York Times* 7 May 1898). According to Bender, Robertson published more than two hundred stories in periodicals including *Collier's* and the *Saturday Evening Post*, and three novels. Probably his most famous work is *Futility; or, The Wreck of the Titan* (1898) because it told, years before the *Titanic* sank, the story of a liner called *The Titan* which sank after hitting an iceberg. Interested in nautical technology, Robertson is also famous for inventing the periscope (Bender 104, 106).

160. Lincoln Steffens (1866–1936) was one of the most famous muckrakers of the beginning of the twentieth century, an "authority on political bosses, Wall Street deals, and the rise of revolutionary sentiment that stretched from California to the upheavals in Mexico and Russia" (Leonard xiii). He was a progressive and a supporter of the 1914 Mexican Revolution and the 1917 Russian Revolution.

161. Here again, Oskison gives us confusing information regarding when, where, and with whom he lived. Although we showed earlier that he probably lived at the University Settlement in 1898, he writes that he lived there after his 1900 trip to Europe. Here he mentions Richard Hovey, introduced to him by his Greenwich Village roommate Emory Pottle, so after his European trip according to his text. Yet Richard Hovey died in 1900. Later in the autobiography, Oskison mentions a story, of which he has "the haziest recollection," for which he won the Black Cat prize as he was still sharing his apartment with Pottle and the others. We know that he won that prize in 1904 and that the story, "The Greater Appeal," was published in 1905. Assuming Oskison does not confuse either roommates or stories, these dates give us a clue of where he lived then. The only certified and precise address we can find for Oskison in the 1900s is 27 West 44th Street, New York, as it is given in the proceedings of the 1907 meeting at Lake Mohonk.

Albert White Vorse (1866–1910), an 1889 Harvard graduate, was a fairly influential editor. In 1892 he had been part of the Peary Relief Expedition, organized to search for the Peary expedition party that had left the previous year to investigate whether Greenland was an island or a continent attached to the North Pole. Explorer Robert Peary would bring to New York six Eskimos whose tragic fate is told by Kenn Harper in the best-seller *Give Me My Father's Body* (1986). Vorse was a member of the American Geographical Society of New York and of the National Geographic Society. He was also a member of the Authors' Club. He was the author of *Laughter of the Sphinx* (1900), a collection of stories inspired by polar explorations and described by a review as "a curious one — arctic romances — the writer depicting the Eskimo through the medium of fiction as he really exists in his frigid home" (*New York Times* 16 June 1910, 28 June 1892; "Transactions of the Society"; *New York Times* 20 Jan. 1900). His wife, Mary Heaton Vorse (1874–1966), was a journalist and a labor activist. She is the author of numerous articles, stories, and books and took part in many labor strikes. She reported from Moscow in 1917 and from Germany in 1933 when Hitler reached power. She supported socialist reform and women's rights (Vorse; Moynihan 289–90).

Richard LeGalliene (1866–1947), Richard Hovey (1864–1900), and Bliss Carman (1861–1929) were all well-known poets at the turn of the century. Carman was a Canadian poet who became successful in 1893 with *Low Tide on Grand Pré*, his first volume of poems (Lynch). Richard Hovey (1864–1900), a Dartmouth graduate, collaborated with Bliss Carman in the writing of several volumes, notably *Songs from Vagabondia*. In 1900 was published his last volume, titled *Taliesin: A Masque*, the fourth part of his *Launcelot and Guinevere: A Poem in Dramas* (Hathaway 476; Dithmar; *New York Times* 27 Mar. 1900; "Mr. Hovey's Last Volume" 246).

162. Emory Pottle, a writer, also served as an ambulance driver during World War I in Verdun, France, the site of one of that war's most terrible battles (*New York Times* 22 June 1917; Hansen 85). In *A Writer or Something*, writer, journalist, and anti-terrorism activist Penelope Tremayne writes about her mother: "my mother had fallen in love with an American of unbelievable good looks called, if you please, Emory Pottle. This paragon was moneyed and serious, his objective was marriage" (66).

The Algonquin Hotel, on 59 West Forty-fourth Street—close to Oskison's address at the end of the 1900s—was the meeting place of artists, writers, and critics who had lunch there on a regular basis in the 1920s and formed the Algonquin Round Table. According to Hassell, the members of the Round Table "did much to establish the hard-boiled, wisecracking, cynical tone of the twenties" (12). One of its most famous members was poet Dorothy Parker (1893–1967), author notably of *Enough Rope* (1926), *Sunset Gun* (1928), and *Death and Taxes* (1931) and of collections of stories such as *Laments for the Living* (1930) and *After These Pleasures* (1933). Critic Edmund Wilson wrote that Parker's "unprecedented feat has been to raise to the dignity of poetry the 'wise-cracking' humor of New York; she has thus almost invented a new kind of epigram; she has made the comic anti-climax tragic" (qtd. in Jackson and Dunbar 548). She worked for *Vanity Fair* and the *New Yorker*. Alexander Woollcott (1887–1943) was "her peer on Broadway and in the lunch room of the Algonquin Hotel" (Van Doren 535). He was mainly known as a journalist and a drama critic. He worked notably for the *New York Times*. Art Samuels (1889–1938) was editor of *Harper's Bazaar*. Edna Ferber (1885–1968) was the author of popular plays and short stories she published in magazines such as *Everybody's* and *The American Magazine* (White). Heywood Broun (1888–1939), a journalist at the *New York World* notably, was a friend of Lincoln Steffens's. During World War I he was a correspondent in France. He was famous for his baseball stories, notably his novel on the game, *The Sun Field* (1923) (Shapiro; Graber). Marjorie (Neysa) McMein (1887–1949), a former student of the Art Institute of Chicago, was famous for her representations of women as chic modern girls in advertisements and on magazine covers, such as the *Saturday Evening Post* ("School of the Art Institute"; Lobo Montalvo et al. 111). F. P. A. was Franklin Pierce Adams (1881–1960), a journalist and columnist born in Chicago who arrived in New York in 1904, where he worked notably for the *New York World* and the *Evening Post* (Kinney 487–88; Seaman 529). Sally James Farnham (1869–1943) was a sculptor who came before the public in 1905. An official ceremony was organized for the unveiling of her statue of Simon Bolivar in Central Park in 1921 (*New York Times* 26 Feb. 1905, 20 Apr. 1921). Actor and *New Yorker* contributor Robert Benchley and *New Yorker* editor Harold Ross were other key members of the Round Table (S. H. Anderson).

163. Henry Harland (1861–1905) was an American author who lived most of his life in London. He started his career writing stories of Jewish life signed with the pseudonym Sidney Luska. Then he became the editor of *The Yellow Book*, a periodical that made its debut in London in April 1894 and in which he wrote critical essays on literature. He also lived in Italy, which inspired him to write some stories, notably *The Cardinal's Snuff-Box* (1900) and *My Friend Prospero* (1904). He died in San Remo. *The Cardinal's Snuff-Box*, a romance, was a very successful novel at the turn of the century (*New York Times* 23 Jan. 1904, 22 Dec. 1905; Gatton; H. O'Brien).

164. Walter Arndt is probably Walter T. Arndt, an active member of the New York Young Republican Club in 1911 who, in 1916, was one of the organizers of Republican presidential candidate Charles E. Hughes's campaign in New York (*New York Times* 23 Nov. 1911, 6 Dec. 1913, 18 June 1916).

165. The story that won the Black Cat prize for Oskison, in 1904, was "The Greater Appeal," included in the present volume.

166. Samuel Sidney McClure (1857–1949), from a family of Irish immigrants in Indiana, was the founder of one of the most popular monthlies and, according to Stinson, the "inventor" of muckrake journalism (203–4). He started publishing *McClure's* in 1893, which he sold for only fifteen cents per issue, a revolution in the world of twenty-five- or thirty-five-cent magazines (Weinberg and Weinberg xiv). Thus, he contributed to the considerable widening of magazine readership. *McClure's* was innovative; "it was illustrated, well edited, and contained both fiction and nonfiction. The first issue included a dialogue between the noted literary figures William Dean Howells and Hjalmar Hjorth Boyesen. . . . It also promised among its future contributors Robert Louis Stevenson, Rudyard Kipling, A. Conan Doyle, Thomas Hardy, John Burroughs, Edward Everett Hale, Hamlin Garland and others of similar caliber" (Weinberg and Weinberg xiv–xv). Willa Cather was one of the authors who reached fame by publishing stories in *McClure's*. Viola Roseboro was also a writer. In 1892 she published a collection of short stories titled *Old Ways and New*. She was a friend of McClure's, worked for his magazine, and published several short stories in it. She is said to have introduced Cather to the publisher (*New York Times* 12 Dec. 1892, 2 June 1906; Skaggs). Oskison's story that Roseboro accepted to publish was "Young Henry and the Old Man," the only one he published in *McClure's*, in 1908.

167. Bob Davis was Robert Hobart Davis (1869–1942), editorial writer of the *New York Sun* and associate editor of *Munsey's*. Born in Nebraska, he went to New York in the mid-1890s after he had started his career as a journalist in San Francisco. He started working for Frank Munsey's magazine in 1903. As an editor for *Munsey's* he published the first story of many writers who would later reach fame (*Time* 16 June 1930).

168. Frank Munsey started to publish his magazine in 1890. In 1893 he followed McClure in widening magazine readership by lowering the price of his from twenty-five cents to ten cents. In Ohmann's terms, Munsey, along with competitors such as McClure, "had 'invented' the general mass circulation magazine." In 1895 the circulation of *Munsey's* was 600,000 (Ohmann 364). A supporter of Theodore Roosevelt when he decided to run for one more term as a Progressive in 1912, Munsey, already the owner of several papers on the eastern seaboard, bought the *New York Press* that year and decided to make it "a Roosevelt organ" (*New York Times* 16 Sept. 1912).

Frank Crowninshield (1872–1947) was a socialite indeed and was called "the man-who-knows-more-celebrities-than-anyone-else-in-New-York" (Watson 176). He was the editor of *Vanity Fair* from 1914 to 1936, when it merged with *Vogue* (Masteller 55). The magazine was published by a friend of Crowninshield's, Condé Nast. According to Endres and Lueck, Crowninshield transformed it from a mere fashion magazine to an arts monthly. In his first editorial, in March 1914, he wrote: "For women, we intend to do something in a noble and missionary spirit, something which, so far as we can observe has never before been done for them by an American magazine. We mean to make frequent appeals to their intellect" (qtd. in Endres and Lueck 398). In the 1920s he was one of the Algonquin Round Table regulars. He was also an art collector and critic (Robb 47) and "acted as one of the seven organizers of the Museum of Modern Art" (Watson 176). The New York Four Hundred referred to the New York social elite. According to Watson, the phrase was coined in 1891 by Ward McAllister "because that number fit into Mrs. John Jacob Astor's ballroom" (174). In 1908 Crowninshield published a "book of etiquette" titled *Manners for the Metropolis* in which could be found "concise rules of deportment for all the more important social ceremonies" of the fast-changing society of the new century (Crowninshield 4). In its review of Crowninshield's guide, the *New York Times* wrote that "those who wish an entrance key to the fantastic life of the New York Four Hundred have it ready to their hands in 'Manners for the Metropolis,' by Francis W. Crowninshield" (6 Dec. 1908).

169. Ossining, where there is the famous Sing Sing prison, is a small town on the Hudson River north of New York City. In a letter reprinted in this volume, written on 13 April 1911 and sent to journalist Frederick S. Barde, Oskison wrote that this job offer came "from a group of village reformers of Ossining, NY, who wanted me to run a new four-page daily newspaper that was established to clean house and stir up a sentiment in favor of good streets and a liberal bond issue for village improvements. The chief owner of the paper also owned a new bank, which wanted to handle the bond issue." This letter is reprinted after the autobiography under the title "An Autobiographical Letter to Journalist Frederick S. Barde." The

title of the newspaper was the *Citizen Sentinel* and later became the *Citizen Register*. In the same letter to Barde, he wrote that he quit the job when he got married in the fall of 1903. His bride was Florence Day Ballard, who divorced him in 1920 "on testimony that the defendant was guilty of misconduct in Paris last August while on duty with the A. E. F." (*New York Times* 12 Feb. 1920).

170. Francis Ellington Leupp (1849–1918) became assistant editor of the *New York Evening Post* soon after he graduated in 1870. In 1889 he became the paper's correspondent in Washington. The *New York Times* article reporting his death called him "a pioneer leader in the movement for civil service reform" and "an advocate of common sense treatment of the Indian" (20 Nov. 1918). In 1895 he was employed by the Indian Rights Association as a lobbyist in Washington (Hoopes 389). As such, he intervened at the Lake Mohonk Conference held that year, where he talked about the Southern Utes (1895 *Proceedings Thirteenth Lake Mohonk Conference* 12–14). The following year he gave a talk about visits he made to several reservations in which he denounced "the fruitlessness of the reservation system" which draws a line between the Indians and "civilization" (1896 *Proceedings Fourteenth Lake Mohonk Conference* 17). He also talked about the "adjustments" that needed to be made to the allotment system and about how the annuities that "the Treasury simply pours . . . into the Indians' laps" (18) discouraged them from working. Leupp also explained that he tried to convince congressmen to pass "legislation to protect the Indians to whom allotments had been made" (20) from the dangers of alcohol (see "Essays" n. 33). In 1897, in a talk titled "Among the Indians of the West" (1897 *Proceedings Fifteenth Lake Mohonk Conference* 12–18), he advocated for the separation of the Indian Office from the Department of the Interior to relieve the secretary from a responsibility he cannot assume efficiently. He also reported on a visit he made to the Fort Sill Apache in Oklahoma Territory (see "An Apache Problem"). In 1904 he was appointed by President Roosevelt commissioner of Indian Affairs, which he remained until 1909. He was a strong advocate of education for the Indians, although, according to Wilbert Ahern, he was wary of nonreservation schools, which, he believed, "undercut self-reliance" ("Indian Education" 96). Leupp said of the issue of Indian education that it "pivot[ed] on the question whether we shall carry civilization to the Indian or carry the Indian to civilization, and the former seems to me infinitely the wiser plan. To plant our schools among the Indians means to bring the older members of the race within the sphere of influence of which every school is a centre. This certainly must be the basis of any practical effort to uplift a whole people" (*The Indian* 135). Leupp was well respected as Indian commissioner. At the 1905 meeting of the Lake Mohonk Conference, a letter was read in which an Indian agent wrote that he was "pleased to inform you that we now have a Commissioner

of Indian Affairs who is wide awake to the best interests of the Indian; I refer to Hon. Francis E. Leupp; . . . I think that in Mr. Leupp we have a man who comes to us better equipped for the position than any man who has ever held the office; he is making many changes which, I am sure, will be for the best interests of the Indian" (1905 *Proceedings Twenty-third Lake Mohonk Conference* 205).

In 1906, while Oskison was on the Press Committee of the conference, Leupp was on the Business Committee (1906 *Proceedings Twenty-fourth Lake Mohonk Conference*). During that meeting, Leupp gave a talk titled "The Indian Policy of Today" in which he talked about the Burke Law, passed in May 1906, "in accordance with my wish," admitted Leupp. The Burke Law, in Leupp's terms, "consists practically of an amendment of [the Dawes Act] so as to adapt it to more modern conditions" (19). According to him, "the most serious defect in the old law" was that it "made an Indian a citizen of the United States and subject to the laws of the State or Territory in which he lived from the moment that his trust patent to his land was issued to him; and then twenty-five years were reserved as a period of tutelage in which he was to be taught how to use his citizenship" (19). With the Burke Law, the Indian received the patent in fee and citizenship after the period of twenty-five years, during which "it is assumed that the government will teach him how to use that privilege which is to be put into his possession" (20). The Burke Law also granted the secretary of the interior the authority "to determine when an Indian is fit to own his land in fee, and then to give it to him" (20). In the same address, Leupp also talked of his efforts to get the Indians out of the reservations: "the big thing we are trying to do now in the way of an improved policy toward the Indian, is to push him out among white people and put him to work there" (23). Oskison and Leupp were of one mind when the latter claimed, "Work, I believe, is the key to the solution of what we call our Indian problem" (24). Leupp discouraged "the practice among Indian tribes of appealing for an opportunity to dig up some old claim under which the Government still owed them an extra pair of cotton socks, or something else of that sort, that had been agreed upon by an ancient treaty" (24), because very often the cost of such procedures made the claims worthless. At the 1907 conference he gave a talk on the "Government's Policy toward the Ute Indians" (21–23) in which he explained the difficulties in dealing with a tribe reluctant to assimilation by means of work. In this speech, Leupp showed that, as sympathetic as he could be to the Indians, he could also be firm. Under applause, he explained that since "going hungry" is a good remedy to "idleness," his office was "cutting down the rations everywhere through the Sioux country, and among the rest these Utes are suffering." He also warned that if the Utes were tempted by revolt, "that revolt will be suppressed, and, if necessary, with an iron hand," concluding that "it was not the government's fault that they took the course they did in order to get into a place where they could live in idleness and eat the bread of charity. If they persist in that course, they will be made to understand what the word 'must' means" (1907 *Proceedings Twenty-fifth Lake Mohonk Conference* 23).

Leupp published several books, notably *The Man Roosevelt: A Portrait Sketch* (1904) and *The Indian and His Problem* (1910).

171. "A Trip to Yosemite Valley" is Oskison's first known published text. It appeared in the *Indian Chieftain* on 8 August 1895. Yosemite Valley became a National Park by act of Congress in 1890, after a campaign organized by naturalist John Muir and Robert Underwood Johnson, whom Oskison would meet as editor of the *Century Magazine*. Tourists had started to come to Yosemite soon after the rush to California.

172. This letter was published in the *Indian Chieftain* on 9 August 1900.

173. This is a reference to Charles Upson Clark, whom Oskison writes about in chapter 6 of his autobiography.

174. This letter, written in 1911, was printed by Littlefield and Parins in the *Native Press Research Journal*, in 1987. Subsequently, Barde and Oskison exchanged several letters, one of which is reprinted below because it gives some hints about what Oskison thought about publishing stories in magazines.

175. *Hidden Water* was one of the first western novels that Coolidge would publish. It was published in October 1910 by A. C. McClurg and Co.

176. This first novel is not identified. As Littlefield and Parins suggested in their annotations to this letter when they published it in the *Native Press Research Journal*, it might have been used as a basis for one of Oskison's later novels,

177. Littlefield and Parins note that the fire mentioned by Oskison "occurred on March 26, 1911, destroyed the Triangle Shirtwaist Company, killing 141 workers who were trapped on the upper floors" ("Autobiographical Letter" 7). Frank Howard Dodd (1844–1916) started to work in the publishing business with his father, Moses W. Dodd, who had founded a publishing firm in 1839. In 1870, with Edward S. Mead, he founded the Dodd, Mead & Co. firm. As head of the firm, in 1902, he published the *New International Encyclopedia*, to which Oskison probably refers to here (*New York Times* 11 Jan. 1916).

178. Boss Brayton of Rhode Island is Charles Ray Brayton (1840–1910). He was a member of the Executive Committee of the Republican Party State Central Committee, from which he resigned in 1907 (*New York Times* 5 July 1907). In his autobiography, Lincoln Steffens wrote of "the Rhode Island system" he uncovered after "two eastern newspapers came out with exposures of Rhode Island" and "showed that the people there were bought with cash at the polls, first by the old aristocracy, then by the modern business leaders who were selling their stealing to

Wall Street and sending the head of the Rhode Island system, Nelson W. Aldrich, to the U.S. Senate" (464). One of the articles Steffens refers to might be the one Oskison wrote. However, it could not be identified precisely. Steffens continued by describing the system in which Brayton was involved: "There was an elected governor, for example; at that time, he was Dr. Lucius F. C. Garvin, a fine old New England gentleman. . . . Governor Garvin sat helpless, neglected, alone in his office, with plenty of time to tell me all about the conditions which distressed him and to confess his utter lack of power. He was not the actual governor. A blind man, General Charles R. Brayton, the political boss, was the actual, permanent governor or dictator of Rhode Island. . . . General Brayton received in the sheriff's office the lines of visitors who had business with the State, openly. And openly he did that business. He ran the Legislature across the hall. He said so; everybody knew it; and he ran it for business men. He said that he used to represent (and make the Legislature and the State government represent) the New York, New Haven and Hartford Railroad" (465).

179. In 1908, *Collier's* published a series titled "Senate Undesirables" in which senators were accused of "bribing legislators to secure their election" in the pre–Seventeenth Amendment days when senators were not elected directly by voters, and of having too close ties to business (Harrison 32–33). Oskison's contribution, "Long of Kansas," was published in the 18 July 1908 issue. After serving in the House of Representatives in the 1890s, Chester Isaiah Long (1860–1934) served in the Senate from 1903 to 1909. In 1903 some Republicans pushed to have him on the 1904 presidential ticket with Roosevelt, to no avail (*New York Times* 3 Feb. 1903). He failed to be reelected to the Senate in 1908 (*New York Times* 6 Aug. 1908). Oskison's article might have contributed to his failure. Oskison started a typical muckraking piece by stating in his first sentence that "Chester I. Long, senior United States Senator from Kansas, doesn't 'belong' in his State." He called him "a 'railroad Senator'" — that is to say, a senator who consistently voted in the interests of the railroad companies — "and a conservative force" in a "progressive Kansas" which "has suffered too many injustices from the railroads, has fought too hard to release her Legislature from their grip." He characterized him as "a spendthrift and libertine with offices and promises" (8). Assessing Long's career, Oskison wrote that "consistently, on legislation in which the State has a vital interest, Long has lined up with the 'interest' and against the people" and referred to a list "showing Long's votes on thirty-five different measures for some form of relief from railroad or corporation oppression" (9). In the same article, Oskison encouraged Kansas voters to choose Long's opponent, Joseph L. Bristow — "tireless corrector of graft in the postal department, hard-working investigator of affairs at Panama, and a

logical, clear-headed critic of railroad domination in Kansas" (8) — in the upcoming primary due to take place two weeks after publication. On 5 August, Senator Long would concede Bristow's nomination (*New York Times* 6 Aug. 1908).

The "loan sharks" series is made up of "John Smith Borrows $20" (Sept. 1909), "Exploiters of the Needy" (Oct. 1909) and "Competing with the Sharks" (Feb. 1910). Littlefield and Parins noted that Russell Sage (1816–1906) had been a congressman from New York and a financier "well known as a money lender in his later life." They also note that he had been a "business associate of Jay Gould, the latter of whom was a relative of Florence Day Oskison" ("Autobiographical Letter" 7). The Russell Sage Foundation was founded in 1907 and is dedicated to "the improvement of social and living conditions in America" (www.russellsage.org). Oskison "fired bird shot" at the "get-rich-quick tribe" in "The Round-Up of the Financial Swindlers" (Dec. 1910) just a few months before he wrote this letter.

2. FICTION

1. Oskison wrote "I Match You: You Match Me" when he was at Stanford. It was first published in the *Sequoia*, Stanford's magazine. On 27 May 1897 the Vinita *Indian Chieftain* published it with the proud heading "Novelette by a Vinita Boy" and the following introduction: "Under the above caption John M. Oskison, now a student at Leland Stanford university, writes a story for the Sequoia, the university magazine, which we reproduce, that his friends may get an insight into the bent of the young man's mind."

2. At Stanford, such were called the students who graduated in 1895 because they had entered the university in 1891, the year it opened. One of those pioneers, Charles Kellogg Field, in his collection of "Stanford Rhymes" (see "Autobiography" n. 77), dedicates the first text, "The Days of '91," to "the Pioneer Class."

3. "Tookh Steh's Mistake" was first published in the *Indian Chieftain* on 22 July 1897. It was reprinted in Littlefield and Parins, *Native American Writing in the Southeast.*

4. There are several places called White Oak in Indian Territory, but this one is probably the hamlet located about four miles west of Vinita, today along Route 66. It was part of Oskison's childhood geography.

5. "The commission" is the Dawes Commission, whose mission in Indian Territory was to put an end to tribal government and bring allotment to the Five Civilized Tribes.

6. Federal officials' interference with the business of the Cherokee courts was very common and made law and order difficult to enforce in the Cherokee Nation (see "Autobiography" nn. 21 and 60).

7. "A Schoolmaster's Dissipation" was first published in the 25 December 1897 issue of the *Indian Chieftain*.

8. *Enoch Arden* is an epic poem written by English poet Alfred Lord Tennyson and published in the United States in 1866. Enoch Arden is a sailor who disappears for many years after a shipwreck. When he gets back home, his wife is married again.

9. Reverend Scott might be a reference to missionary J. A. Scott, who would start at Oklahoma Station the Oklahoma Baptist Orphan's Home at the turn of the century (Drake 403).

10. Cherryvale is located in Kansas, about fifteen miles north of the Cherokee Nation.

11. Cabin Creek is a tributary of the Grand River, which, according to Grant Foreman, is the name given the upper reaches of the Neosho River (see "Autobiography" n. 10). The Neosho (Grand) River comes south from Kansas and flows through Miami, in the northeastern corner of the state of Oklahoma, and then converges with the Arkansas River and the Verdigris River near Fort Gibson. Grand River served as a boundary between the Delaware District in the Cherokee Nation and the territory reserved for several other tribes (the Quapaws, Peorias, Ottawas, Shawnees, Modocs, Wyandottes, and Senecas).

12. "Only the Master Shall Praise" was first published in *Century Illustrated Magazine* (1881–1906) in January 1900 and was illustrated by renowned artist of the West Frederic Remington. It was the prize story in the *Century*'s competition for college graduates of 1898. When Oskison wrote it, he was completing his BA at Leland Stanford Junior University. In his 1911 letter to Barde, Oskison humbly explains his choice for a title and his success in winning the prize: "To the competition I sent one of my Indian Territory stories, artfully disguised in a title quoted from Kipling—'Only the Master Shall Praise.' Maybe the Kipling title did it—it's hard to imagine now how popular Kipling was in the spring of 1899—or maybe the chance to put Frederick Remington on to a new job of illustrating tempted the editors" ("An Autobiographical Letter"). For more on Kipling's quote, see "Autobiography" n. 104. Three drawings illustrated the short story: the first one, with the caption "Going to the Celebration," shows two riders on a path coming leisurely toward the viewer, one man with a floppy hat at the back. The second, a one-page illustration evocative of some of Remington's famous sculptures, captioned "These are the motions that make a bronco-buster's life shorter," shows a rider holding firm on a bucking mule, his hat flying behind him. The third shows a group of horse-mounted men stopped in a prairie; five of them face two others; the caption says "I reckon ye got the man all right." The story was reprinted in Littlefield and Parins, *Native American Writing in the Southeast* 65–75.

13. Big Creek is located about twenty miles northwest of Vinita, five miles northeast of Nowata. Ewing Halsell, William Halsell's son, had a cattle ranch on seventeen thousand acres there (O'Dell, "Halsell").

14. Coffeyville is a small town in the south of Kansas, just a few miles north of Nowata County, Oklahoma. In 1892, Coffeyville was the site of a Dalton gang robbery, a relation of which Oskison gives in "Working for Fame" (1903).

15. Jesse and Frank James, as well as four Younger brothers (Cole, Jim, John, and Bob), were infamous outlaws. Cole and Jim, and the James brothers, rode with Quantrill's Raiders during the American Civil War. William Clark Quantrill (1837–65) and his raiders were famous for their guerrilla warfare against Union soldiers and civilians. After the war, both gangs robbed numerous banks and trains, sometimes working together. Cole consorted with Belle Starr, Sam Starr's wife. All these outlaws appear in several stories by Oskison such as "To 'Youngers' Bend,'" "Working for Fame," and "The Greater Appeal."

16. The Verdigris River flows from north to south, in Kansas through Coffeyville and in Oklahoma just east of Nowata, a few miles west of Vinita. It is part of Oskison's childhood map. It continues south and flows through Oologah, Will Rogers's hometown, and just west of Claremore. In his autobiography, Oskison writes that Clem Rogers's ranch was located near the Verdigris River. It converges with the Arkansas River and the Neosho (Grand) River in the Three Forks Area, between Muskogee and Fort Gibson, in today's Muskogee County.

17. "When The Grass Grew Long" was first published in *Century Illustrated Magazine* in June 1901. It was reprinted in Littlefield and Parins, *Native American Writing in the Southeast* 76–79.

18. In his autobiography, Oskison spells Paw Paw Creek *Pawpaw* Creek (see "Autobiography" n. 12).

19. "The Biologist's Quest" was first published in July 1901 in the *Overland Monthly*.

20. This poem was published notably in the *San Francisco Chronicle* on 1 March 1903, with the indication "John M. Oskison in *Leslie's Weekly*." Although the date of its first publication in *Leslie's Weekly* is not known, January or February 1903 would be a safe guess. Many of Oskison's writings were syndicated and published in diverse local newspapers.

21. "To 'Youngers' Bend'" was first published in June 1903 in *Frank Leslie's Popular Monthly*. The editors published the following original footnote: "The material for the stories of Western train robbers, of which this is the first, was collected for *Leslie's Monthly* by Mr. Oskison, who traveled extensively through the wilder West, interviewing the survivors and witnesses of the actual events he describes. — The editors."

The same footnote accompanied "Working for Fame," published in the same magazine two months later and reprinted in this volume. No such footnote was printed for "A Border Judge and His Court," also in *Frank Leslie's*, although it is obviously based on true events and a true character, Judge Isaac C. Parker. The placement of these three stories in the "Fiction" section of the present volume may be subject to argument. They are obviously fictionalized renditions of real events that journalist-Oskison researched. Because the voice of the journalist, however, disappears behind a narrator that is sometimes omniscient, because the tone and the mode of narration is so different from explicitly journalistic writings, and because the reader cannot be sure, without researching, that the events described actually happened, I chose to consider them as fiction writing. Ronnow calls them "journalistic fiction" (*John Milton Oskison* 37).

22. Gad's Hill was a little station town in southeastern Missouri, in present-day Wayne County. The St. Louis Iron Mountain and Southern Railway, also called the Iron Mountain Railroad, was originally established to convey iron ore from Iron Mountain, south of St. Louis, to St. Louis. Later it linked St. Louis to Texarkana, Arkansas, via Little Rock. The railroad was robbed by the Younger Gang on 31 January 1874 at Gad's Hill and by the Dalton Gang on 3 November 1893 at Olyphant, Arkansas.

23. Buell lists the prisoners as "the railroad agent, a saloon-keeper, blacksmith, two wood-choppers, and the son of Dr. John M. Rock" (66). A comparison of Oskison's and Buell's accounts, as they are quoted in the following notes, suggests that Oskison read Buell or that both used the same sources.

24. Buell relates the events in a similar way and adds names: "No one was seen when the train stopped, but in a moment thereafter Cole Younger mounted the cab and, with drawn pistol, compelled the engineer and fireman to leave the engine and walk out into the woods. Mr. Alford, the conductor, was arrested by Jesse James as he stepped from the train to ascertain the cause of the display of the red flag. He was forced to give up his watch and $75.00 in money, after which he was placed in the station house" (67).

25. Cole Younger (1844–1902) and Bob Younger (1853–89), two of four criminal Younger brothers, were raised in Missouri, near Kansas City. Cole, as well as Miller, McCoy, and Reed, rode with Quantrill's Raiders during the Civil War. Jim Reed was married to Myra Maybelle Shirley before she married Sam Starr and became famous as Belle Starr, the "bandit queen," protagonist of Oskison's "The Greater Appeal." Clell Miller grew up in Missouri. He was shot dead on 7 September 1876 during the infamous bank robbery in Northfield, Minnesota, mentioned later by Oskison (Beights 162). The Younger brothers were often in league with the James brothers, Frank and Jesse (Beights; O'Neal; R. B. Smith; J. L. Huston).

Oskison is very assertive in naming the culprits. However, according to Beights, several other bandits were suspected, including the James brothers and former Quantrill lieutenant William Greenwood (159–60). Buell named Frank James as the leader of the five. According to him, the others were Cole and Jim Younger, Clell Miller, and Jesse James (66–67). Many sources cite the James brothers as taking part, and even leading, the Gad's Hill robbery. According to Dyer and Settle, that robbery is actually the one that contributed to the legend of the Jameses robbing only from rich men. The outlaws were reported to have examined the hands of each male passenger "to determine if he was a workingman, the robbers stating . . . that they 'did not want to rob workingmen or ladies, but the money and valuables of the plug-hat gentlemen were what they sought'" (Settle 49; Dyer 56).

26. Two weeks before the robbery at Gad's Hill, a stagecoach had been robbed between Hot Springs and Malvern, Arkansas, presumably by the same outlaws (Settle 49). Buell writes that Frank James, Cole and Jim Younger, Arthur McCoy, and Clell Miller committed the crime (166).

27. Buell also reported the event: "On the 7th of April, 1874, . . . the stage running between Austin and San Antonio, Texas, was robbed under the following circumstances: On the day in question, the regular mail stage, carrying eleven passengers, was stopped by five masked bandits, at seven o'clock in the evening, twenty-three miles from Austin. . . . Among the passengers was Mr. Breckenridge, president of the First National Bank of San Antonio, who had one thousand dollars on his person. Bishop Gregg, of the same city was also in the party, and three ladies, whose fright at seeing such display of fire-arms, produced a panic inside the stage. The robbers were very courteous, but exacting, forcing an immediate compliance with their every request. All the passengers were made to get out and form in line, in the rear of the stage, where they were examined for money and valuables by two of the bandits, while the other three stood guard over their victims. The ladies, aside from the respectful language used toward them, were not partially treated by the outlaws, but, like their male companions, they were persuaded, by the peculiar means of the robbers, to give up all their money and watches. The total amount secured, including that gathered from the mail-bags, was about $3,000. Having appropriated all the valuables the passengers possessed, the bandits cut out the lead span of horses and taking these with them, they rode away rapidly toward the north" (176–77). Although the perpetrators of this robbery are not known with absolute certainty either, Buell writes that "there are hundreds who maintain that the robbers were Jesse and Frank James, Clell Miller, Cole Younger and Arthur McCoy" (178).

28. Buell continues in a phrasing very close to Oskison's: "The loss of two horses so delayed the stage that it was not until four o'clock on the following morning

that it reached Austin; this prevented an early report of the robbery, so that fully eighteen hours had elapsed after the perpetration of the outrage, before the sheriff, with ten men, went in pursuit. The search for the robbers was fruitless for more than two weeks, the trail, seemingly, being thoroughly covered. After the sheriff returned home, a reward of $500 was offered for the capture of the bandits" (177).

29. Tom Starr was a famous Cherokee outlaw. Conley writes of Tom Starr and his son Sam that they "had been set in opposition to the Cherokee Nation government at least since the killing of James Starr. Having taken to violence and lawlessness initially because of their hatred of John Ross, they simply stayed on that road" (*The Cherokee Nation* 186). James Starr, Tom's father, had been a signer of the Treaty of New Echota and had moved west in 1836. He escaped assassination on the day Major Ridge and Elias Boudinot were killed, 22 June 1839 (Shirley, *Belle Starr* 79–80), but he was assassinated in 1845. Conley writes that "Tom Starr vowed revenge": "In later years, he claimed to have killed all the men in the party that had killed his father and young brother except for a few who had died before he could get to them" (*Cherokee Encyclopedia* 227). Glenn Shirley relates an anecdote about Tom Starr that gives an idea of the violence he seems to have been capable of. Starr was reported admitting that while the house of Benjamin Vore (a Ross man) was burning after Tom and his brothers had set it afire, "a little boy about five years old came running out and begged him not to kill him, and Tom . . . just picked him up and threw him in the fire. He said he didn't think God would ever forgive him for that" (*Belle Starr* 81).

The Starrs' home at Youngers' Bend is known to have been a hideout for outlaws at least since immediately after the Civil War. In a few anecdotes recorded by Carolyn Thomas Foreman in 1956, William H. Ballentine, a notable Cherokee citizen, tells us that "right after the Civil War, Jesse and Frank James came in this country and after a while Cole Younger and his brothers joined them and they stayed around the Starr's home in the Younger's Bend [*sic*]. When they planned to rob the bank at Northfield, Minnesota, they came to get Jim Reed to go with them. He was married to Belle then, before she married [Sam] Starr" (C. T. Foreman 426).

Some fifteen miles separate Briartown—post office established in 1882 (Shirk 190)—at the very southern tip of the Cherokee Nation, and Eufaula—post office established in 1874 (Shirk 201)—in the Creek Nation, close to the eastern border separating the Creek from the Cherokee Nation. Briartown is located just north of the Canadian River before it separates into two branches. Eufaula is in the fork formed by the North Canadian River (the northern branch of the Canadian River) and the Canadian River (the southern branch).

30. John T. Morris was a deputy sheriff. He killed Jim Reed near Paris, Texas

(Shirley, "When the Outlaw" 22). In *Belle Starr*, Shirley reproduces Morris's statement at the coroner's in Paris published in the *Dallas Commercial* of 10 August 1874: "My name is John T. Morris. I came up with the deceased yesterday about 10 o'clock at Henry Russell's about 20 miles northwest of Paris in this county—was well acquainted with the deceased. . . . This morning we started for Arkansas together, travelled on until dinner time, when I proposed to stop and get dinner, to which he agreed. We stopped at Mr. S. M. Harvey's house for dinner. . . . I got done eating before Reed and went back into the main room, and explained to Harvey, Reed's character, and asked him to assist in his arrest, which he agreed to do. Mr. Harvey and I went out to the horses . . . took the pistols off of Reed's and my horse. We went to the dining room where Reed was still eating. I said to Reed, "Jim, throw up your hands," he said he would do so, but ran under the table, and raised up with the table and ran towards the door with the table in advance. I shot two holes through the table. After he dropped the table I shot him in the right side. He ran his hand in his pocket to draw a cylinder as I thought. I shot at him four times, and hit him twice, once a scalping shot in the head and once in the right side. . . . After he got out of the house, he ran up to me and grabbed me—my pistol refusing to fire—and as he rushed against me, I fell and he fell too. I then called upon Mr. Harvey to assist me in his arrest, which he did and we thus secured him" (119–20).

31. According to Buell, Cole Younger and Frank James, in September 1875, organized a bank robbery in Huntington, Virginia, with Tom McDaniels, a brother of Bud McDaniels's, one former henchman (186). Two weeks after that robbery, Tom McDaniels was killed at Pine Hill, Kentucky by two brothers named Dillon who had taken part in the chase (188–90).

After the Missouri Pacific Railroad robbery of 7 July 1876, the suspected criminals were pursued for several weeks. On 1 August, Hobbs Kerry and Bruce Younger were arrested at Joplin and Granby, both located in southwestern Missouri, close to the Cherokee Nation border. However, Buell writes that Younger was discharged. Kerry made a confession to the crime and explained that Cole and Bob Younger, the James brothers, Clell Miller, Charley Pitts and Bill Chadwell took part in it (200–201). Charley Pitts was caught on Spring River, in the southeastern corner of Kansas, but escaped (201).

Buell gives a detailed account of the Northfield, Minnesota, robbery (202–25). It occurred on 7 September 1876. Among the outlaws participating were three Younger brothers (Cole, Bob and Jim), Charley Pitts, Clell Miller, Bill Chadwell, and Frank and Jesse James. Miller and Chadwell were killed during the firing that took place in the street outside the bank. Charley Pitts was killed several weeks later during the pursuit of the outlaws. The three Younger brothers were wounded and captured.

From Balentine we learn that "Tom Starr refused to go because it was too far from home and they didn't know the people or the country" (C. T. Foreman 426).

32. "A Border Judge and His Court" was first published in July 1903 in *Frank Leslie's Popular Monthly*.

33. Fred Harvey Harrington wrote that Parker "sentenced more than a hundred fifty persons to be hanged. Some of these died before they could be claimed by the gallows. Some were pardoned by the President. Others won their freedom after appealing their cases to the Supreme Court of the United States. Even so, four score paid the final penalty—enough to give nation-wide notoriety to the Fort Smith court" (60). John Miller gave slightly different numbers: "During his tenure he tried more than three-hundred men and women on charges of murder. One-hundred sixty-four were found guilty of murder by juries" (63–64). However, if the legend of the "Hanging Judge"—as Parker was nicknamed—was based on the cases the mass media was fond of reporting—and the ones Oskison related in this text—Harrington recalled that "most of his time was given to less dramatic work," having to do with "revenue laws, protection of the mails, and liquor traffic problems" (61). Mary Stolberg wrote that eighty-three men were "hanged on his gallows" (3).

Oskison might have used Judge Parker as a model for "Judge Pease—the hangin' judge" (*Black Jack Davy* 16) in *Black Jack Davy*, his second novel, published in 1926 (see n. 44 below).

34. Born in Ohio in 1838, Parker moved to St. Joseph, Missouri, in 1859 where he practiced law for fourteen years, notably as a city attorney and judge of the Ninth Judicial Circuit. Until the Civil War he was a Democrat. During the war, however, he became a Republican and was an elector for Lincoln in 1864. From 1870 he served two terms as a representative in the U.S. Congress. In 1874 he was defeated for a seat in the Senate. The following year, President Grant appointed him chief justice for Utah Territory, but Parker requested to be appointed federal judge in Fort Smith, Arkansas (F. H. Harrington 59; Miller 58; Stolberg 4–5).

35. What is known as the Brooks-Baxter War was a conflict internal to the Republican Party that engulfed Arkansas politics between 1871 and 1875. This conflict sometimes "resulted in widespread violence and chaos," in the terms of Stolberg (8), who argues that Parker's appointment at Fort Smith rather than in Utah was at the request of the Arkansas senators who asked "for an out-of-state judicial appointee because bitter politics made it impossible to find a satisfactory applicant from the state" (9). At the November 1872 elections, Joseph Brooks was the gubernatorial nominee representing a dissenting group of the Republican Party, the Liberal Republican, with the support of the Arkansas Democrats. Elisha Baxter was the regular Republicans' nominee. After an election ridden with strong suspicions of voting

frauds on both sides, Baxter was sworn in as governor, although the Brooksites had not conceded defeat. In 1873 Brooks filed a complaint "charging that Baxter had usurped the governor's office" (Woodward 323). In 1874 Brooks was declared the legal governor of Arkansas by Circuit Judge John Whytock. Woodward calls what followed "an armed *coup d'état*": "Brooks led a band of his armed followers to the State House in Little Rock, had the sheriff deliver the writ of ouster to Baxter, and stationed guards in and around the building. Baxter was told that he was no longer the state's governor" (326). Both Brooks and Baxter gathered militias. Armed skirmishes ensued in Little Rock. In May 1874, President Grant "ruled that Elisha Baxter was the rightful governor of Arkansas. . . . The Brooks and Baxter War thus ended and the militias dispersed" (334). For more details see also Atkinson, "The Brooks-Baxter Contest."

According to John Miller, in such a political context, "President Grant thought it best to appoint a man from without the state that was not identified with either wing of the Republican party" (59). All historians of Judge Parker agree that he had a lot to do to build anew the people's confidence in the court. As a Republican appointee in a state where the Democrats had control, he was considered a carpetbagger. Miller wrote that his predecessor, William Story, had been "a weak and vacillating judge, if not a corrupt one. The business of the court had been neglected and the bar was in almost open rebellion against the manner in which the court had been conducted. The people had no respect for it" (59). According to Stolberg, Story "resigned to avoid impeachment for mishandling court funds" (10).

36. Although Parker, as a congressman, had "introduced a bill to create the Oklahoma Territory—a measure bitterly opposed by members of the Five Civilized Tribes who correctly saw it as an attempt to undermine their self-government," Stolberg argued that by the end of his service as a judge, "Parker had become one of the Indians' main supporters" (4). Harrington noted that Parker had "definite sympathy for the Indian. This feeling, too, developed with the years. Parker sent several red men to the gallows, and many more to jail and to the penitentiary. But at least as often he gave sentences to white men who had injured Indians. He tried to stop encroachments on Indian timber areas, he pronounced judgment against 'boomers' who wanted Indian land, he did what he could to make the Indian country a fit region for the red men" (F. H. Harrington 62). Miller and Stolberg quoted Parker saying that "the territory was set apart for the Indians in 1828. The government at that time promised them protection. That promise has always been ignored. The only protection that has ever been afforded them is through the courts. To us who have been located on this borderland has fallen the task of acting as protectors" (Miller 64; Stolberg 20). Although his court had jurisdiction over all crimes committed

in the Indian Territory involving a Euro-American citizen, Parker expressed in his first charge to the grand jury, on 10 May 1875, that he was willing to cooperate with Indian authorities: the statute defining the court's jurisdiction over Indian Territory "throws upon you and upon me, and upon every officer of the court the responsibility of seeing to it, that the laws for the protection of that country and its people are so enforced, that the good shall be protected from the bad and that with the aid of Indians through their local laws and by their co-operation with and assistance of the officers of this court, life, liberty and property shall be as safe as it is possible to make them under the circumstances surrounding them" (Parker in F. H. Harrington 66). Moreover, in the same speech, Parker made clear to the jurors that it was their "sworn duty to so far check and restrain this demoralizing influence [the illegal sale of alcohol] upon the Indians as it is possible for you to do" (67). In an 1896 interview, Parker said of the Indians: "Twenty-one years' experience with them has taught me that they are a religiously-inclined, law-abiding, authority-respecting people. The Indian race is not one of criminals. There have been sporadic cases of crime among them, it is true, but as a people they are good citizens" (in Stolberg 21).

37. F. H. Harrington's numbers are somewhat different than Oskison's: "In Isaac Parker's first term on the federal bench (spring term, 1875), eight murder cases ended in conviction in the Fort Smith court" (71). However, Miller's numbers concur with Oskison's: "During the first term, eighteen murder trials were held with fifteen convictions for murder or manslaughter" (63).

38. Cherokee Bill's real name was Crawford Goldsby. He was born at Fort Gibson, Indian Territory, in 1876 and "became an outlaw at the age of fourteen. He shot a man with whom he had quarreled, and from that time until his arrest he was on the scout" (*New York Times* 18 Mar. 1896). Miller wrote that Cherokee Bill "claimed to be one-half Indian, one-half white and one-half Negro" (66). According to Miller, "the only conviction for murder committed in Arkansas was that of 'Cherokee Bill,' who had been convicted of a murder committed in the Indian Territory and, while his case was on appeal, he killed a guard in the jail, a Mr. Larry Keating who had refused to surrender the keys to the prisoner" (66).

According to a 19 September 1895 *New York Times* article, with "Cherokee Bill" as the appellant, the U.S. Supreme Court had, "for the first time in its history . . . pending before it two appeals by one person from judgments sentencing him to be hanged for murder, the two crimes having been committed on different days and at places separated by many miles." On 27 February 1895, "Cherokee Bill" had been convicted "of the murder of Ernest Melton, in the Cherokee Nation . . . , Nov. 18, 1894, and sentenced to be hanged June 25, 1895." This murder, continued the article, "from the record, was committed out of pure wantonness. 'Cherokee' and a companion, in broad daylight, rode up to the store of John Shufeldt, in Lenepah, and robbed the cash drawer and safe. As they were leaving the building 'Cherokee' saw Melton watching them from a window in an adjoining house and shot him through the head, instantly killing him." From the judgment for this case, Cherokee Bill's attorney filed an appeal that reached the Supreme Court on 20 May 1895. "In the meantime he was confined in the jail at Fort Smith pending action upon the appeal. July 26 he shot and killed Lawrence Keating, a guard in the jail, two revolvers having been smuggled into the building by the prisoners. Saturday, Aug. 10, he was convicted of this second murder; two days later Judge Parker sentenced him to be hanged Sept. 10. The execution of this sentence was stayed by the filing of the appeal, and 'Cherokee Bill' is still in jail."

After "Cherokee Bill" was sentenced to death for the second time, Parker was reported saying to him: "Cherokee Bill . . . you revel in the destruction of human life. The many murders you have committed, and your reckless and wanton character, show you to be a human monster" (qtd. in Miller 66). On 18 March 1896 the *New York Times* published an article titled "Cherokee Bill Dies Smiling." The journalist wrote: "At 2:15 p.m. to-day Crawford Goldsby, alias Cherokee Bill, was hanged. He was declared dead in ten minutes. The desperado showed no fear, and went to the trap the coolest man in the party." According to the article, when he was asked whether he had any last words he answered "'No, I came here to die, not to talk.' Turning he kissed his mother good bye, and with a smile on his face walked to his place on the trap."

39. Tom Root was notably famous for the robbery of a train loaded with lawmen at Blackstone, north of Muskogee (A. Shoemaker 8). Among the outlaws he robbed trains with was Jim Reed, a member of the Younger Gang (*New York Times* 24 Dec. 1894).

40. Although F. H. Harrington wrote that the first man Parker sentenced to death was John Whittington, Lamar Riggs and Mary Stolberg confirm that Daniel Evans, "who was convicted of killing his nineteen-year-old friend a year earlier in order to get the victim's boots" (Stolberg 12), was the first man sentenced to death by Parker, "eight days after he arrived" (Riggs 86). Riggs wrote that "after sentencing him to death, Parker was choked with emotion and finally wept" (86). Riggs then cited James Moore ("who had killed a deputy"), John Wittington, Sam Fooy, Smoker Mankiller, and Edmund Campbell as five convicts to be hanged along with Evans on 3 September 1875 (87). According to Stolberg, with this mass execution, "Parker launched his reputation as the 'Hanging Judge.' . . . The unusual event of a mass hanging received enthusiastic national as well as local coverage" (12–13). Harrington reprinted the statement made against Whittington on 26 June 1875. Although this

statement does not make clear whether Parker actually wept, it does suggest that giving such a sentence was "not an easy thing to do," as Oskison put it. Parker told Whittington that "the feelings and emotions with which I enter upon the discharge of the solemn and important duty which devolves upon the court and which I am now about to perform are too powerful to be expressed." He added that "to pronounce the dreadful sentence of the law which is . . . to deprive him of existence and to send him to the bar of his Creator and his God where his destiny must be fixed for eternity, is at all times and under any circumstances a most painful duty to a court. But to be compelled in the discharge of my duty to consign to the gallows a young man who but for his crime might have been a useful member of society, who has but just entered upon a vigorous manhood standing as you do to others in the delicate relationship of husband and father, pressed upon my feelings with a weight which I can neither resist nor express" (Parker in F. H. Harrington 72–73).

41. Miller wrote that "to those who accept the fictionalized portrayal of the bad man of those days as a Rob Roy or Robin Hood and see them as protectors of the weak and refuse to accept the actual facts, Judge Parker appears to have been a tyrant and another bloody Jeffreys" (73).

42. F. H. Harrington implicitly concurred that Parker was not influenced by politics: "Parker was appointed as a Republican, and, as manuscript records show, continued to be actively associated with Republican politicians until he died. Arkansas was Democratic; but the state appreciated Parker's honesty and zeal" (61). Miller wrote that "politics helped him in making his court effective, although he never engaged therein for political purposes. But he did not hesitate to use his influence to obtain appointments of honest and competent officials" (64). Stolberg wrote that Parker's actions, at least as far as the effectiveness of the court was concerned, were "tinged by politics" (14).

43. Pale death stalks with impartial step through the cottages of the poor and the palaces of kings. — *Od.* I., 4, 12 [original footnote].

44. In *Black Jack Davy*, Judge Pease, whom Davy calls "the hangin' judge" (16) and whose court is located in the fictional town of Tarko, tells the story of a gang of outlaws that his officers chased in No Man's Land: "Well, these wild boys came to a signpost where two trails fork that read, 'Five Hundred Miles to Tarko,' and one of them rode up to it and scratched out the word Tarko and wrote, underneath, the word 'Hell.' Then they riddled the board with bullets before riding out of the court's jurisdiction" (17–18).

45. "Working for Fame" was first published in 1903 in *Frank Leslie's Monthly*, with illustrations by N. C. Wyeth. Original footnote: "The material for this story was collected for *Leslie's Monthly* by Mr. Oskison, who traveled extensively through

the wilder West, interviewing the survivors and witnesses of the actual events he describes."

46. Robin Hood is the famous legendary hero of Nottingham, England, in the Middle Ages. Legend has it that he robbed only the rich and gave his gains to the poor. Dick Turpin was an eighteenth-century English robber whose life became legend when author W. H. Ainsworth published a romance about him titled *Rockwood* (1834).

47. Adeline Lee Younger and James Lewis Dalton were the parents of the Dalton Gang (Ohnick 31). Ohnick writes that James Lewis Dalton was born in Kentucky.

48. Kingfisher — whose post office was established in July 1889 (Shirk 241) — is located in what was Oklahoma Territory, about twenty miles northwest of today's Oklahoma City. Shirley explains how the family got their quarter sections: "When the Oklahoma District was opened in 1889, sections 16 and 36 of each township were set aside for the support of common schools. These lands were not entrusted to the territory but were administered by the Department of the Interior until statehood. Since no provision had been made for their immediate use, Governor Steele granted permission to settlers who had failed to secure homesteads to move onto the school lands, each reserving one hundred sixty acres. After her husband's death, Adeline Dalton and her teen-aged daughters Eva, Leona, and Nannie made their way to Oklahoma Territory in a covered wagon. The tract Adeline chose was in a school section six miles northeast of Kingfisher" (*West of Hell's Fringe* 43–44).

Ohnick writes about the family wanderings: "the family was near Denver, Colorado, in 1860, and then near Lawrence, Kansas, in 1861. Later they moved to Liberty, Missouri, to get out of the fighting zone. Census records show they were in Cass Co. Missouri in 1870, and in Bates Co. Missouri in 1880. All of these western Missouri counties suffered greatly during the Civil War and it is almost certain that some of the moves the family made were the result of the war" (32).

49. Miller confirms that "Four of the Dalton brothers were at one time deputy marshals. Frank was killed in line of duty, but Bob, Grat and Emmett resigned their positions to become outlaws" (65).

50. Ohnick confirms this passage from one side of the law to the other: "Robert [Bob], Gratton [*sic*] and an older brother, Frank, had all served as U.S. deputy marshals out of Fort Smith, Arkansas, before the younger brothers turned to crime. Emmett had also served as a posseman with his brothers. Frank Dalton was killed while trying to arrest whiskey runners in the Indian Territory. After his death the other three brothers were accused of stealing horses. The ex-police Daltons then left the Oklahoma Territory and joined the older brothers in California and shortly after turned to robbing trains" (30).

As possemen, the Daltons worked in Cherokee territory and nearby: "Deputy Marshall Floyd Wilson, one of the most active officers in the Cherokee Nation, had work for them. For instance, near Vinita in February, 1890, Grat assisted in arresting a Missouri Pacific Railroad foreman who was charged with beating an employee almost to death with a shovel; the accused was delivered to the Muskogee court for trial. Near Claremore in April, Bob and Emmett acquitted themselves admirably as members of a Wilson posse which captured Carroll Collier and Bud Maxfield, two dangerous convicts who had escaped from the penitentiary in Arkansas" (Shirley, *West of Hell's Fringe* 44).

51. Shirley gives a more violent account of the event since he writes that "the express manager resisted, and in the exchange of gunfire, fireman George W. Radcliff was wounded in the abdomen and died the following day" (*West of Hell's Fringe* 46–47).

52. Shirley reproduces a San Francisco circular dated 26 March 1891, which partly said: "The Grand Jury of Tulare county have indicted Bob and Emmett Dalton as principals in said crime, and William Marion Dalton and Gratton Dalton as accessories; the two latter named being now in jail at Tulare county awaiting trial. The Southern Pacific Company hereby withdraws said general reward in regard to Bob and Emmett Dalton, and in lieu thereof offers to pay $1,500 each for the arrest of Bob and Emmett Dalton, *upon their delivery to any duly authorized agent or representative of the State of California, or at any jail in any of the States or Territories of the United States*" (*West of Hell's Fringe* 46).

53. Eva, a daughter of Adeline Dalton's, married John W. Whipple, "who operated a meat market in Kingfisher and sold farm implements to area settlers" (Shirley, *West of Hell's Fringe* 44). Ohnick gives him different initials — J. N. Whipple — but informs us that he and Eva got married on 15 October 1887 in Meade, Kansas.

54. While Shirley tells this story, he also claims that it "is mostly fiction" and explains that "no Dalton threat to the city was ever written. Whipple was not charged with receiving stolen property . . . when Payne came to seize the horse, Whipple resisted. He was jailed at Wichita for 'obstructing an officer' and was discharged without prosecution on May 18, 1891, by order of Marshal Grimes" (*West of Hell' Fringe* 61).

Shirley gives a description of Deputy Marshal Ransom Payne: "Payne was a tall, strongly built man of forty with clean-cut features and a straggly blond moustache. A native of Iowa educated in Kentucky, he had been on the southwestern frontier about eight years and was a successful real estate agent in Wichita before accepting a commission under Marshal Jones of Kansas to police the Oklahoma District before and after the opening. Since the district's organization into a territory, he had served under Marshal Grimes in the same capacity. He was well known as 'a fearless enemy of evil-doers and a shrewd discoverer of apparently lost trails' with 'enough deeds of extraordinary bravery to fill a volume'" (*West of Hell's Fringe* 48).

In an autobiographical book titled *Beyond the Law*, Emmett Dalton gives a different description of Ransom Payne, "the joke of the United States Marshal's office, who never attempted to use his gun and later on was fired by United States Marshal Grimes for allowing the usage of his name as a hero in a 'fake book' purporting to give lives of the Dalton boys" (72). Sparing no kind words for the deputy marshal, Dalton continues: "There were sporadic activities of different amateur sleuths who sought the limelight for the instant by rushing to the fore, riding about in a haphazard manner supposedly on a 'warm trail.' These self-styled 'trackers of the Daltons' were seeking cheap fame rather than us. Also they were careful not to get too far away from the money chest of the company. As long as supposed 'clews' could be furnished the company, it was willing to 'grub stake' some of these 'trailers,' and Ransom Payne made a profitable living out of us for a year or more, although he never was within miles of us only at Whorton" (72–73). He then goes on to tell an anecdote making a coward of Payne.

55. According to Shirley, Wharton Station was located in today's southern part of Perry, about thirty miles north of Guthrie (*West of Hell's Fringe* 55). Attacking Ransom Payne might not have been the actual reason behind the attack of the Texas Express at Wharton. Shirley even questions the very presence of Payne in the train, claiming that at the time of the robbery, the U.S. deputy marshal "was far from the scene, trying to 'strike the Dalton trail' on the Sac and Fox Reservation" (56). Emmett Dalton, after relating the story of the robbery, writes that "the boys learned later that on the train at Whorton [*sic*] was United States Marshal Ransom Payne" (72). He also writes that "after the Whorton robbery there was no sense of wrong-doing to act as a canker in our souls. We had not raised our hands against society as a whole, but against the express company which had made up probable as bitter as any of its thousands of enemies." He goes on to correct false impressions about the Daltons: "Right here and now let me correct an impression that has gone broadcast: the Dalton boys were not swashbuckling freebooters, devil-may-care bandits, riding into this or that small settlement, shooting and looting as they went. Our spleen was directed against the company, and it alone" (73–74).

Although legend has it that Bob Dalton made a prisoner of the agent, Shirley simply claims "it didn't happen" (55). Emmett Dalton does not say anything about this episode either. He writes that "the plan of action was simple as we saw it. Bob and Newcomb were to walk down to Whorton and wait for the ten-thirty train to arrive. As the conductor gave the signal to go ahead they were to jump into the engine cab, overpower the fireman and engineer and force them to run the train to the stockyards, where Bryant was waiting. Then they would force the crew to get on the ground, uncouple the engine, force open the express car, take what they could get and rejoin Bryant at the fence, where he was waiting with the horses. Everything worked to perfection as they had planned" (67).

56. Arkansas City, Kansas, is located about four miles north of the Cherokee Outlet. About eighty miles to the south is Guthrie, Oklahoma Territory, about twenty miles north of today's Oklahoma City. Between the two places, the Santa Fe line goes through Red Rock and Wharton (Perry), both places where the Daltons robbed a train.

57. According to Emmett Dalton, "about nine thousand dollars was the haul" (71). However, Shirley tells us that "a report from the Topeka headquarters of the Santa Fe gave the amount as $1,500, while Wells Fargo tallied the loss at $1,745" (*West of Hell's Fringe* 58).

58. Emmett Dalton dedicates a chapter to the "death of Charles Bryant" (79–84), also known as Black-Faced Charley (Shirley, *West of Hell's Fringe* 63). Bryant took part in several Dalton crimes. According to both Dalton and Shirley, Bryant was not arrested at his sister's home, contrary to Payne's supposed testimony. After the Wharton train robbery, he was captured in his hotel room in Hennessey—northwest of Oklahoma City, about fifteen miles just north of Kingfisher—where he lay sick, by the town's marshal, Ed Short (Shirley, *West of Hell's Fringe* 63–64; Dalton 79). Shirley and Dalton tell different versions of the capture. For Shirley, Bryant was surprised by Short and tried to resist arrest. For Dalton, he surrendered, too sick to resist. Both Bryant and Short died in a gunfight that Shirley tells in much more detail and which he calls "the most spectacular gun duel between two men of iron nerve in the history of the West" (66). According to Shirley, the event actually took place at the little station of Waukomis, about five miles south of Enid, itself located about thirty-five miles north of Kingfisher.

59. Adair—post office established in 1883 (Shirk 185)—is located less than fifteen miles south of Vinita. Red Rock is located in what used to be the Cherokee Outlet, about twenty-five miles northeast of Wharton, where the Daltons had already robbed a train, and about fifty miles north of today's Oklahoma City. According to Shirley, the Daltons "had word . . . that seventy thousand dollars in Indian annuity money was to be expressed on the Santa Fe to the Sac and Fox Agency" (*West of Hell's Fringe* 77). They attacked the train on 1 June 1892. Emmett Dalton, however, admits that "the proceeds were not as much as we expected" but recalls it was "about seven thousand eight hundred dollars" (120).

60. Dalton writes that as soon as Bob and Doolin "mounted the engine cab in the old way, it was easy to see that something was wrong. Shots began to come

from the train and the engineer and fireman proved stubborn. Then it began to rain shots from the train, each shooting this way and that. The boys were surprised and almost dumbfounded. This opposition was something new to them. Here is what happened: Some one, they never did know just who, warned the company that they were likely to hold up the train, and a posse in charge of Detective L. L. Kinney, United States Marshal Sid Johnson and Charley La Flore, chief of the Indian police, with eleven other deputies, were on the train waiting for the attack" (126–27). According to Dalton, "this their last train robbery was really the only time they met with a pretense of resistance" (128).

61. Richard L. Broadwell and William St. Power, alias Bill Powers, were Dalton confederates in many of their crimes, including those already mentioned by Oskison. Bill Powers had been Emmett's saddle companion when the latter worked on the X Bar X Ranch, located in the Triangle Country—the fork formed by the Arkansas River in the north and the Cimarron River in the south, west of Tulsa. On that ranch, Emmett also met Dick Broadwell (Shirley, *West of Hell's Fringe* 40).

Coffeyville is located just above the border between Indian Territory and Kansas, on a line straight north from Nowata. According to Emmett Dalton, the three brothers—Bob, Grat, and Emmett—expected the proceeds from these robberies to take them to South America.

62. "The Fall of King Chris" was first published in 1903 in *Frank Leslie's Popular Monthly*.

63. In his autobiography Oskison mentions Bluejacket, where he goes to attend a roping contest with his brother Bert. See "Autobiography" nn. 23 and 83.

64. Jim Hopkins (1875–1966), of Pryor Creek, was a world-record roper who took part in some of the same contests as Will Rogers and Bert Oskison. He was born in Texas but as a young man moved to Indian Territory, where he worked on the ranches of Charles McClellan and Clem V. Rogers, Will Rogers's father. He was considered one of "the best ropers of his time" and he "toured with many Wild West and rodeo shows," including Buffalo Bill's Wild West and the 101 Ranch show (Rogers 494). No information could be found on Tom Cochran, but it is very likely that he was also a real local roping fame. Chelsea—post office established in November 1882—is located in the Cherokee Nation about fifteen miles southwest of Vinita.

65. "The Fall of King Chris" echoes many autobiographical facts. It is likely, for example, that Will Rogers inspired this description of Chris Farrell's character. Roper and humorist Will Rogers, who attended Willie Halsell College at the same time Oskison did, was a lifelong friend of his.

66. Galahad and Launcelot (or Lancelot) were knights of King Arthur's Round Table. Sam Bass (1851–78) was an outlaw who robbed trains and banks mostly in Texas. Wayne Gard, his biographer, called him the "Texas Robin Hood" (236).

67. Thompson Creek is located northwest of Vinita, between Estella and Centralia. JIC was the cattle brand used by Oskison's father. Bert was the name of his younger half brother (see "Autobiography"). Albert James "Bert" Oskison made a name for himself as a prize-winning roper. He and Will Rogers participated in the same roping contests. Another autobiographical element in this story is the character of the New York newspaperman "taking a close-to look at the West," a self-deprecating representation of the author. Lightning Creek is in the vicinity of Nowata, northwest of Vinita. The other ropers mentioned here could not be formally identified.

68. Springfield is located in southwestern Missouri, about fifty miles away from the Cherokee Nation.

69. Bill Seymour is also one of the two protagonists in "Only the Master Shall Praise," in which he also has a drinking problem.

70. "The Quality of Mercy" was first published in June 1904, in the *Century Magazine*. It was subtitled "A Story of the Indian Territory."

71. No Black Oak could be located in Indian Territory. However, four miles west of Vinita is White Oak, not far from where Oskison lived (see "Fiction" n. 4). Oskison could be playing with names here, as with the name of the protagonist, which is very close to the name of his hometown. By incorporating all these real-life references, Black Oak might be a fictional representation of Vinita itself, and the *Sachem* might be the *Indian Chieftain*, one of the Vinita papers in which the branding section could take up to one-fourth of the space (see "Autobiography" n. 35).

72. Fourteen Mile Creek is located about eight miles north of Tahlequah. Locust Creek flows from east to west about two miles southeast of Vinita.

73. Southwest City is a small town in the extreme southwestern corner of Missouri, on the border with Indian Territory, less than a mile from the Arkansas border.

74. Portia is the character in Shakespeare's *The Merchant of Venice* who gives the speech that inspired the title of the story. Disguised as a judge, she attempts to convince Shylock not to take the pound of flesh that he claims Antonio owes him:

The quality of mercy is not strained,
It droppeth as the gentle rain from heaven
Upon the place beneath. It is twice blest,
It blesseth him that gives and him that takes.
'Tis mightiest in the mightiest, it becomes
The thronèd monarch better than his crown.
His sceptre shows the force of temporal power,
The attribute to awe and majesty,
Wherein doth sit the dread and fear of kings;

But mercy is above this sceptred sway,
It is enthronèd in the hearts of kings,
It is an attribute to God himself,
And earthly power doth then show likest God's
When mercy seasons justice. Therefore, Jew,
Though justice be thy plea, consider this:
That in the course of justice none of us
Should see salvation. We do pray for mercy,
And that same prayer doth teach us all to render
The deeds of mercy. I have spoke thus much
To mitigate the justice of thy plea,
Which if thou follow, this strict court of Venice
Must needs give sentence 'gainst the merchant there. (4.1)

75. Denison, Texas, is located two miles south of the Oklahoma border, on the Katy line, southeast of today's Lake Texoma.

76. In 1904 Oskison won a prize in the Black Cat story contest with "The Greater Appeal." It was published in *Black Cat* magazine in 1905.

77. Muscogee — post office established in January 1872 (Shirk 217) — is in the Creek Nation. Its name was changed to Muskogee in July 1900 (Shirk 217). For a possible inspiration for Deputy Marshal "Jim" Marks, see "Autobiography" n. 19.

78. Belle Starr married Jim Reed first, then Sam Starr. See "Fiction" nn. 15, 25, and 29.

79. Sam Starr's farm, Youngers' Bend, was located near Briartown, about fifty miles south of Muskogee (see "Fiction" n. 29).

80. Pleasant Porter (1840–1907) was a rancher, a businessman, and the principal chief of the Creek Nation. He was elected for the first time in 1899 and remained the principal chief until the end of tribal governments in 1906. For more on Pleasant Porter see "Essays" n. 30.

81. François Delsarte was a French musician, opera singer, and acting teacher who developed an acting style that became very popular in the United States and that was made of a set of gestures and attitudes corresponding to human emotions.

82. "The Problem of Old Harjo" was first published in April 1907 in *Southern Workman*. It was reprinted in Bernd Peyer, ed., *The Singing Spirit* (1989), 128–35; in Paula Gunn Allen, ed., *Voice of the Turtle* (1994), 136–44; and in Littlefield and Parins, *Native American Writing in the Southeast* 80–86.

83. The "certain statesman" Oskison refers to here is very certainly Reed Smoot, and the "wagonload of protests" are some of the "memorials, petitions, personal

applications" that "the public has deluged the Senate with" in what is known as the Reed Smoot case (Cullom 572). Utah was admitted as a state in 1896, "one condition being that polygamous or plural marriages should be forever prohibited" (Smoot 117). The practice had been forbidden by a Mormon manifesto in 1890. In 1903, Reed Smoot was elected senator. Immediately, many protests were filed against Smoot, who was an apostle of the Mormon Church and accused of being a polygamist. The Senate Committee on Privileges and Elections urged the Senate to investigate these protests against the senator. According to a 13 December 1903 article in the *New York Times*, many petitions were filed for the expulsion of Smoot from his Senate seat. After a long battle taking place during a period contemporary to Oskison's writing of "The Problem of Old Harjo," Senators Foraker, Beveridge, Dillingham, Hopkins, and Knox submitted their report to the Senate. Smoot himself writes that the report "was endorsed by the affirmative vote of seven out of the thirteen members of the Committee on Privileges and Elections which heard the testimony, and by almost two-thirds of the United States Senate" (120). The report said notably that "the conditions existing in Utah since Reed Smoot became an official of the Mormon Church in 1900 have been such that non-Mormons and Mormons alike have acquiesced in polygamous cohabitation on the part of those who married before the manifesto of 1890, as an evil that could best be gotten rid of by simply tolerating it until in the natural course of events it shall have passed out of existence" (Smoot 120). The report concluded that "with this disposition prevailing everywhere in the State of Utah among all classes — the Gentile or non-Mormon population as well as among the Mormons — the undersigned are of the opinion that there is no just ground for expelling Senator Smoot or for finding him disqualified to hold the seat he occupies because of the fact that he, in common with all the people of his State, has not made war upon, but has acquiesced in, a condition for which he had no original responsibility" (120–21). So Smoot retained his seat even with the approval of senators such as Shelby M. Cullom of Illinois, who wrote in a text about the decision that his "record has been one of persistent, unqualified opposition to Mormonism as it has been in the past, and as it is to-day if the same evils still exist or just so far as they exist" (573). According to Cullom, "the charges themselves were weak, being from their inception aimed more at Mormonism than at Reed Smoot" (575). This is indeed what is suggested by a *New York Times* article reporting the charges read at the beginning of the hearing: "The Mormon priesthood, according to the doctrine of the Church and the belief and practice of its membership, is vested with, and assumes to exercise, supreme authority in all things temporal and spiritual, civil and political. The head of the Church claims to receive divine revelations, and these Reed Smoot, by his covenants and obligations, is bound to accept and obey" (17 Jan. 1904). Judging by this charge and others, the separation of church and state seemed also to be at stake.

In a 1939 interview, Reed Smoot acknowledged that President Theodore Roosevelt "had stood like a Gibraltar against the expulsion or exclusion of Smoot. His influence had been decisive in persuading certain Republican members of the Committee on Privileges and Elections, which heard the case for and against the fledgling Senator, to speak and vote for his retention" (Merrill 440–41).

84. "Young Henry and the Old Man" was first published in *McClure's* in June 1908.

85. Kep Queen was a notorious outlaw who robbed a bank at Cisco, Texas in 1887. He then tried to find refuge in the Cherokee Nation. He was killed there, near Claremore, in November 1888 by a posse led by Sheriff Bud Sanders.

86. For Cabin Creek, see "Autobiography" n. 10. Brunner might be inspired by Heck Bruner who, with Paden Tolbert (see n. 88 below) and others, was one of the U.S. deputy marshals who called themselves "the Men Who Rode for Parker" (Shirley, "When the Outlaw" 22). Judge Isaac Charles Parker, also known as "the Hanging Judge," presided over the Fort Smith court, which had jurisdiction over Indian Territory, from 1875 to 1896. He is the subject of "A Border Judge and His Court," reprinted in this volume.

87. For "the Katy and 'Frisco road," see "Autobiography" n. 24.

88. For Pryor Creek, see "Autobiography" n. 10. Red Oak—post office established in March 1868 (Shirk 224)—in the Choctaw Nation, is located about fifty miles south of Muskogee, forty miles southwest of Fort Smith and thirty miles east of McAlester. Paden Tolbert was a U.S. deputy marshal. In November 1892 he led a posse against Ned Christie, a Cherokee citizen famously and wrongly accused of murdering U.S. Marshal Dan Maples. The posse killed Christie on 3 November (Burton). The town of Paden, in Okfuskee County, east of Oklahoma City and southwest of Tulsa, is named after him (Funchess).

89. "Koenig's Discovery" was first published in *Collier's Weekly* on 28 May 1910. It was illustrated by an unknown author. Under the title, the editors printed "It is the Law in the Primitive Man's Country That to Have is to Hold."

90. "Out of the Night That Covers" was first published in *Delineator* in August 1911.

91. Jim Freeman, editor of the *Circletown Weekly Round-Up*, will also be at the center of "The Man Who Interfered," published four years later. In a letter written on 21 July 1911 and addressed to *Kansas City Star* journalist Frederick S. Barde, along with the August issue of the *Delineator* containing "Out of the Night That Covers," Oskison wrote: "In it is an Oklahoma story of mine which you may be interested to read. The town in mind in that story is Centralia, which the newspaper directory

credits with a population of 450. It is entirely primitive and twenty miles from the railroad. The editor, however, in my story is, I believe a pretty good portrait of T. F. McKane who started the Centralia *Weekly Standard* in 1903, and who has worked it up to a circulation of 240. Mac is a mighty good fellow, representative of the sort of man who have done most for Oklahoma." Centralia — post office established in 1899 (Shirk 193) — is located about fifteen miles northwest of Vinita.

92. For the Verdigris River, see "Fiction" n. 16.

93. *Pagliacci*, an opera by Ruggero Leoncavallo, premiered in Milan in 1892. The characters are actors in a commedia del'arte company. One of them, Canio, is a jealous husband whose wife, Nedda, cheats on him with Silvio. The affair is brought to light on stage during a performance of the troupe, thus showing that actors can be overcome by real feelings while pretending to be characters.

94. "Walla Tenaka — Creek" is the fictionalized version of a true story and was first published in *Collier's Weekly*, in July 1913. The true Walla Tenaka was not Creek but Choctaw (*L'Abeille* 13 Feb. 1906; *Hopkinsville Kentuckian* 3 Mar. 1906). The lines following the title were introducing the story in *Collier's* but were probably not Oskison's. Editors would often precede stories they published with their own comments.

95. The real Walla Tenaka, from the sources that could be found, never even violated his parole. In this piece of fiction, Oskison apparently blended at least two events, one occurring in 1906 and involving a man called Robert L. Folsom, the other involving Walla Tenaka and taking place "a few years" before 1906 (*L'Abeille de la Nouvelle Orléans*)

According to articles published in *L'Abeille de La Nouvelle Orléans* on 31 February 1906 and in the *Hopkinsville Kentuckian* on 6 March 1906, Walla Tenaka, "a full-blood Choctaw, by profession a ball player" (*L'Abeille*) was released after he was sentenced to death for murder "upon his promise to appear on the date set for execution. He played ball all summer and came back in the fall and was shot" (*Kentuckian*). *L'Abeille* explained that "between the day of sentence and the day of execution intervened the baseball season" and that "the doomed prisoner was turned loose without any formality of bail, instructed when to return and be executed. He played ball as if no unusual condition existed and upon the arrival of the fatal day was on hand and faced the rifles without flinching." *L'Abeille* concluded that according to the Choctaws, "no other outcome was possible." Indeed, "in the lofty character of their code and the rigid adherence to its unwritten provisions," the paper explained, the Choctaws "rise above any body of white men in the world. The Choctaw gives his spoken pledge and no bond is asked. If charged with crime or under conviction, he goes his way until the appointed time, and then he comes unsought and unattended to face trial or death. That such should be his conduct is accepted by his fellows as mere matter of course." The *Kentuckian* article explained that "Choctaw Indians sentenced to death are frequently allowed to go free until they can harvest their crops or do some other necessary work, and never until now has one defaulted." Until then indeed, since Walla Tenaka was given as an illustration of a Choctaw practice in articles that dealt with the very first parole violation in Choctaw history. One Robert L. Folsom "is the first man of that tribe to violate the tradition of his race by breaking his parole. In 1903 he killed Alfred Strickland, another Choctaw, and was arrested. On the theory that a Choctaw Indian never 'jumps' his bond, he was released on his own recognizance" (*Kentuckian*). *L'Abeille* did not give the name of "the Choctaw whose faithlessness has hurt the pride of his people," but it expressed clearly how serious his fault had been. Under its title "Honor of the Choctaws," the New Orleans paper printed "Whole Nation Is Shocked by a Breach of Faith on the Part of One."

The first parole violation by a Choctaw confounded the New Orleans journalist, whose dubious conclusion is worth quoting. He wondered, "Is it possible that the Choctaw is becoming too civilized? If he is to be regarded in the future as no more honest than the paleface, the change must be deplored. When a white man is charged with serious offense he must remain in prison or give substantial bail. For him to give this and then vanish, not to show himself again, is no uncommon procedure. To trust a white murderer at large on the theory that he would voluntarily walk to execution would be a piece of folly. The Indian, stoical, untaught in any academic school of conduct, lacking the advantage of generations trained in morals, yet can give a lesson to those who should be his superiors."

In a 1956 issue of *Oklahoma Today*, George Phinney reported on his meeting with Frank "Pistol Pete" Easton, "a one-time cowboy, scout, Indian fighter, trail rider, and Deputy U.S. marshal" under Judge Isaac "Hanging Judge" Parker. This man told the reporter a story that echoes Walla Tenaka's: "Of his years as Deputy U.S. Marshal under . . . Parker of Ft. Smith, Pistol Pete likes to recall one time an Indian condemned for murder, was to be hanged on a certain day. The date was several weeks in the future. Friends and relatives of the Indian asked that he be released to play ball as he was one of their star players. Judge Parker demurred. Deputy Easton knew Indian nature. He told Judge Parker if the Indian failed to show up for execution he'd let them slip the noose around his own neck. That cinched it. The Indian was released. Pete says one of the deputies asked him, 'Frank, hain't yuh worried?' It was a few days before execution day. 'Naw, I says, Ifen I was scairt, I'd be humpin' it out o' here. That Injun'll be aroun' on time.' Sure enough on the morning he was to be hanged, the Indian showed up, walked to the gallows, and went to the Happy Hunting Ground without a murmur" (5).

96. Okmulgee — formerly called Okmulkee, post office established in November 1883 (Shirk 219) — capital of the Creek Nation, is located approximately thirty miles south of Tulsa.

97. Oskison writes in his autobiography that one of these officials struggling with white outlaws was married to his teacher Fanny Bly (very probably Fannie Blythe), "a deputy United States marshal who had much to do with curbing the depredations of white outlaws when Indian Territory, where the tribal courts lacked jurisdiction over them, became a favorite refuge" ("Old I.T."). Just like the problem of jurisdictional conflict discussed in "Autobiography" nn. 21 and 60, the problem of lack of jurisdiction over white outlaws and the plague of illegally sold whiskey were old ones. In an April 1856 letter, Cherokee Agent George Butler called the attention of Superintendent Charles Dean to the fact that some white men who lived in the Cherokee Nation "are a great disadvantage to the Indian by selling whiskey indirectly, and otherwise keeping a disorderly house" (Butler to Dean, 12 Apr. 1856, 5). When such men were expelled from the territory, they kept coming back with complete impunity. According to Butler, the Intercourse Act of 1834 "says they must be put out, but makes no penalty for their return." Dean, in his letter to his superior, bluntly criticized this flaw of the law: "What then? Is the power of government to be brought into contempt? Is it unable to enforce its own decrees? Such a state of things is as demoralizing as it is absurd" (Dean to Manypenny, 16 Apr. 1856, 4). When Commissioner of Indian Affairs George Manypenny recommended amending the 1834 law, he added that "the evils incident to its defects are the cause of complaint, not only among the Cherokees, but throughout the Indian Territory" (Manypenny to McClelland, 22 May 1856, 2).

98. "The Apples of Hesperides, Kansas" was first published in *Forum* in March 1914.

99. "The Man Who Interfered" was first published in *Southern Workman* 44 (Oct. 1915): 557–67.

100. Jim Freeman is also the protagonist of "Out of the Night That Covers." The setting is also the same in both stories.

101. The Spavinaw Hills are located in the Delaware District between Vinita and Tahlequah, east of the Neosho River, thirty-five miles southeast of Centralia — the town Circletown is modeled on.

102. "The Other Partner" was first published in *Collier's Weekly* in December 1924. It was illustrated by Harold Brett.

103. Alva, Woods County, is located in the western part of the former Cherokee Outlet, about one hundred miles northwest of Oklahoma City.

104. Ardmore is located about one hundred miles south of Oklahoma City, about

twenty miles north of the Texas border on the way to Dallas on Interstate 35. Lawton, next to Fort Sill, is about sixty miles southwest of Oklahoma City, on Interstate 44.

105. The Mann Act of 1910 is also known as the White Slave Traffic Act and deals with prostitution. It made it a felony to transport a woman to another state for prostitution, but it was also used to prosecute men who transported women across state boundaries for consensual sex.

106. The *Mona Lisa*, the famous painting by Leonardo da Vinci, was stolen from the Louvre in 1911.

107. "The Singing Bird" was first published in *Sunset Magazine* March 1925: 5–8. It was reprinted in Bernd Peyer, ed., *The Singing Spirit* (1989); and Paula Gunn Allen, ed., *Voice of the Turtle* (1994). In *Sunset* the story was illustrated by Ralph Jenners. Apart from the title, itself indicating some thematic similarity, this short story has little in common with the posthumously published novel.

108. According to Conley "the Keetoowah Society is an ancient full-blood society" (*Cherokee Encyclopedia* 136). However, it is under the influence of a Welsh missionary, Rev. Evan Jones (1788–1872), that "fullblood, traditional Cherokees, known as Keetoowahs, devoted to the preservation of Cherokee culture and politically opposed to mixed-bloods in the tribal government, became active abolitionists. They were also called 'Pin Indians' because of identifying crossed pins that they wore under the lapels of their coats" (*The Cherokee Nation* 174). Conley also states that all Keetoowahs were opposed to the Dawes allotment policy (*Cherokee Encyclopedia* 136). The Nighthawk Keetoowahs were under the leadership of Redbird Smith and defended the rights of the Cherokees to self-determination.

3. ESSAYS

1. "Cherokee Migration" was published in the *Tahlequah Arrow* on 31 May 1902. It might have been published previously in the *New York Post*, since the text is presented in the *Arrow* as being "by John M. Oskison in the New York Post."

2. Oskison's phrasing can appear ambiguous. The removal of the tribe was actually decided by the Treaty of New Echota in 1835. That treaty followed the 1830 Removal Act, which gave concrete expression to a policy that had been in the minds of federal officials for years. Thomas Jefferson, at the beginning of the nineteenth century, was already thinking of removing the tribes to western lands. The forced removal of the Cherokees who had not accepted the Treaty of New Echota began in 1838.

3. The Treaty of 1817 was negotiated by General Andrew Jackson, who would later, as president of the United States, sign the Removal Act. By the Treaty of 1817, the Cherokees were forced to cede lands in the east in exchange for the lands the Western Cherokee had been occupying in western Arkansas, on the Arkansas and

White Rivers, since 1811. These Cherokees had decided to leave their ancestral lands in the East to satisfy, in the words of the treaty, a "desire to continue the hunter life" (Kappler 141). It is also probable that they saw leaving as the only way to escape harassment by white settlers. In any case, after they arrived on the Arkansas and White Rivers in 1811 they were not welcomed by the Osages, who were occupying the lands already. As a consequence, agent William L. Lovely secured territories in what would be the Cherokee Nation in eastern Oklahoma (Conley, *The Cherokee Nation* 100).

4. One Captain Stephenson, or J. R. Stephenson, disbursing agent, appears on several documents listing the "payments made by J. R. Stephenson Under Treaty of 1835, Cherokee Claims for Commutation of Transportation and Subsistence" (Stricklin). Probably the same person, as Lieutenant James R. Stephenson, appears as "Disbursing Agent Choctaw removal," located at "Fort Towson, A.T." (Arkansas Territory) in 1833, in the official "Correspondence on the Subject of the Emigration of Indians." Captain Page also had a long experience in removing Indians. In 1831, John Page, "Captain 4th U.S. Infantry," was stationed at Fort Mitchell, Creek Nation, Alabama. Learning that "it appears to be the object of the Government, when Indians are to be removed, to detail an officer of the United States' army to perform that duty, instead of giving it to citizens, as has been the custom heretofore," Page, in November 1831, applied for "the appointment of assistant quartermaster." He wrote in his application letter that "it has been my lot to be stationed among the Choctaw, Creek, and Seminole nations of Indians for the most part of twelve years. I am tolerably well versed in some of their languages, and well acquainted with the Indian character, which is a very important point when business is to be transacted with them" (Page to Jesup). In the same letter, Page shows he is also well versed in the cynicism underlying federal removal policies. Although he is writing about the Creeks specifically, a long quote can be useful to understand a process that was similar to all removed tribes: "It appears to be the object of the President of the United States to remove all the Indians to the west of the Mississippi. There were a number of the Creeks, say fifteen hundred or two thousand, that consented to go last year; but the President did not see fit to remove them unless the whole consented to go. His object might have been to save expense in removing them at two different times; but the difference of expense in making two expeditions ought not to be but very trifling with the proper arrangements. If fifteen hundred or two thousand consented to go, there would only be transportation and rations required for that number; if six thousand went, every thing in proportion would be required. I do not think the Creeks can be got off in one body; but, if a certain number should consent to go, it will separate friends and families; and the balance, I

have no doubt, would consent to go, as the laws of Georgia are extended over them, and the white inhabitants getting more numerous among them. They feel themselves more oppressed every day, and will be convinced it is to their interest to remove. Should the Creeks go, it will be the first step in getting the Seminoles to remove" (Page to Jesup). In a 26 July 1832 letter to Brigadier General George Gibson, Page would accept a position "as disbursing officer in removing the Choctaw Indians" (Page to Gibson).

5. "The President and the Old Man: Rich Opportunity for the Red Man" was first published in the *Vinita Weekly Chieftain*, on 25 December 1902.

6. Oskison refers to the Second Annual Message that Roosevelt delivered to the Senate and House of Representatives in Congress on 2 December 1902. In this very long address, the president tackled Indian policy among many other diverse topics. Before the passage quoted by Oskison, Roosevelt introduced the subject by claiming that "in dealing with the Indians our aim should be their ultimate absorption into the body of our people," although he specified why "in many cases this absorption must and should be very slow." Indeed, besides the tribes of the Indian Territory he talks about in the terms quoted by Oskison, "there are other tribes which have yet made no perceptible advance toward such equality" between mixed-bloods and whites. "To force such tribes too fast is to prevent their going forward at all. Moreover, the tribes live under widely different conditions. Where a tribe has made considerable advance and lives on fertile farming soil it is possible to allot the members lands in severalty much as is the case with white settlers. There are other tribes where such a course is not desirable. On the arid prairie lands the effort should be to induce the Indians to lead pastoral rather than agricultural lives, and to permit them to settle in villages rather than to force them into isolation." Oskison no doubt agreed with the rest of the five paragraphs the president dedicated to the Indians. After praising the "large Indian schools situated remote from any Indian reservation," Roosevelt recognized that much more work needed to be done on the reservations, notably to give the Indians the means to become self-reliant not only by making them "either tillers of the soil or stock raisers" but also by diversifying their activities, including "industrial or even commercial pursuits." Each should be given the opportunity to follow "his own bent," an idea that Oskison would advocate repeatedly in other essays, notably in "Making the Indian an Individual." Finally, Roosevelt, who would put an end to the spoils system in Indian Affairs appointments, recommended demanding standards for the government officials dealing with the tribes, "and where misconduct can be proved the punishment should be exemplary."

7. In spite of a very controversial speech in which he famously declared that he did not "go so far as to think that the only good Indians are dead Indians, but I believe

nine out of ten are, and I shouldn't like to inquire too closely into the case of the tenth" (qtd. in Hagedorn 1921), Roosevelt advocated assimilation of the Indians by means of missionary work, allotment in severalty, education, and citizenship. William Hagan shows well how this made him a valuable ally of Herbert Welsh and his Indian Rights Association when he was Civil Service commissioner between 1889 and 1895 ("Civil"). In the words of Hauptman, this collaboration shows "his affinity to the prototype of Eastern reformer of Indian policy in this period" (1). Roosevelt also wanted "some peculiar modifications of the law" to make it "possible to arrange to have most of the positions at the Indian agencies filled by civilized Indians" (Roosevelt to Welsh, 13 Feb. 1891, qtd. in Hagan, "Civil" 192). Although he believed that assimilation was the only chance that the Indians had to survive, he also believed in social Darwinism and was convinced that not all Indians would be able to adapt: "We must protect and guard them up to a certain point: but all the while we must be fitting them as best we can for rough contact with the world, and, finally, when all, humanly speaking, is done that can be done, we must turn them loose, hardening our hearts to the fact that many will sink, exactly as many will swim" (*Report of Hon. Theodore Roosevelt Made to the United States Civil Service Commission*, 8–9, qtd. in "Civil" 195). Finally, Hagan explains that Roosevelt defended the mixed-bloods and those who were pejoratively called "squaw men," whom he saw "as providing a way out of camp life for the women who had become their wives" ("Civil" 196). For an exhaustive and meticulous study of the relationship between Roosevelt and the Eastern reformers, see Hagan, *Theodore Roosevelt*, 1997.

8. See "Autobiography" nn. 21 and 60. The first district court of the Indian Territory was established at Muskogee by act of Congress on 1 March 1889. Grant Foreman writes about what the *Muskogee Phoenix* called "one of the most eventful days in its history": "For days past a constant stream of strangers had been pouring into the little town. While many of them were lawyers who intended to make Muskogee their future home, not a few came only to be present at the opening of the first white man's court ever held in the Indian Territory" ("Oklahoma's First Court" 457).

9. This is a reference to the Nighthawk Keetoowah Society. Following the lead of Redbird Smith, they resisted allotment and enrollment as long as they could. Conley confirms that "there were rumors of an Indian uprising, and Redbird Smith and other Keetoowah leaders were again arrested and thrown in jail" (*The Cherokee Nation* 198).

10. A Single Statehood Convention was held in Claremore on 3 December 1902. The principles and resolutions that resulted from this convention were in favor of the union of the Twin Territories into a single state (Campbell 265; Doyle, "Single versus Double" 268).

11. "The Outlook for the Indian" was first published in 1903 in *Southern Workman.*

12. Standing Rock was a Sioux reservation where the Sioux raised cattle on unfenced grazing lands. In 1901, Commissioner of Indian Affairs William A. Jones authorized white ranchers to let their cattle graze on reservation lands and forced the Sioux to accept the leasing of about 1 million acres. Jones argued that millions of acres were unoccupied on this reservation. His opinion was also that "where the Indians . . . are receiving gratuitous rations they have no right to object to the Government developing the resources of the reservation for grazing purposes, because the grass goes to waste annually unless it is used as it grows" (Jones to C. W. Crouse, qtd. in Hagan, *Theodore Roosevelt* 91). However, Jones had a hidden agenda. According to Hagan, "the Chicago, Milwaukee & St. Paul Railroad was behind his efforts to open Standing Rock to non-Indian cattle" (91–92). Several groups of reformers, notably the Indian Rights Association and the Women's National Indian Association, were informed of the affair by the Sioux delegation sent to Washington. All opposed the leasing and weighed on President Roosevelt to act. In 1902 the latter sent George Bird Grinnell (see n. 13 below) as an investigator. Grinnell's report was very critical of Indian policies as led by Commissioner Jones and led to the discharge of Standing Rock agent George H. Bingenheimer. A detailed account of the Standing Rock leases crisis can be found in chapter 5, "Land Problems," of Hagan's *Theodore Roosevelt*, 1997.

Hamlin Garland's novel *The Captain of the Gray-Horse Troop* (1902) is the story of Captain Curtis, "considered a crank on trees and Indians by his fellow-officers" (Garland 9), of his struggle for the welfare of Indians and his "campaign against invading stockmen" (Garland 133). He is detailed to Fort Smith as the Tetong reservation Indian agent. His mission is to discharge the former agent, Senett. Senett and Senator Brisbane have let white cattle raisers encroach on Tetong grazing lands. Brisbane, an Indian-hater who proposes to remove the Tetong, "having leagued himself with even less masterly than himself but quite as unscrupulous, had set to work to grasp and hold the natural resources of the Great Territory — he laid strong fists upon the mines and forests and grass of the wild land. Once grasped, nothing was ever surrendered" (Garland 50)

13. Hamlin Garland, in 1903, described his friend George Bird Grinnell (1849–1938) as "a singular mixture of the old Manhattan and the old borderman. No one would suspect . . . but he is honorary chief of several tribes of red people, that he was on the war path with the Pawnee in the Sixties, and that he is one of the best informed writers on these subjects in America" (qtd. in Hagan, *Theodore Roosevelt* 139). Although Hagan finds this description exaggerated, Grinnell was indeed knowledgeable in Indian cultures, in particular the Pawnee, Cheyenne, and Blackfoot ones.

Originally a naturalist, he accompanied General Custer in his expedition to the Black Hills in 1874. Throughout several other expeditions, notably to Yellowstone, the naturalist, sportsman, and lover of nature became a conservationist (Fisher 5). In 1886 he founded the Audubon Society, a society for the protection of birds that grew to become an organization using its influence for the protection of wildlife. He was also at the origin of the creation of Glacier National Park in Montana by an act of Congress in 1910, and he became president of the National Park Association in 1925 (Fisher 9–10).

According to Fisher, Grinnell's interest in Indian cultures began in 1870, "when he was associated with Pawnee scouts in a hostile Indian country" (6). Just like many other Friends of the Indian, Grinnell's concern for the Native Americans was ambiguous. During his first trips west, Sherry Smith suggests, "Grinnell saw Indians as simply another feature of the endlessly fascinating Great Plains fauna" (20). He believed in the superiority of "civilization" over the Indian ways and the naturalist and paleontologist in him saw the Native Americans as "living fossils, doomed to extinction but capable of speaking, telling stories, and explaining themselves" (22). His interest and concern for the welfare of the Indians grew every time he went west, and he published numerous volumes about different aspects of their customs and practices. According to Smith, "while he felt no compulsion to halt progress, he did want to preserve remnants of America's frontier past," be they natural beauties or Native American traditional cultures. Smith adds that, "assuming that traditional Plains Indian life could not survive in the modern world but believing its elimination would diminish that world, Grinnell spent nearly half his life recording histories, traditions, and cultural practices that, he concluded, inexorably evaporated with the death of each 'old-time Indian'" (19). He was a reformer, but, Hagan tells us, unlike other Friends of the Indian, he strongly opposed allotment in severalty. Like Oskison, he believed the Indians should be taught to be self-reliant and self-sufficient. Hagan writes: "When in 1902 a contact on the reservation reported to him that the discontinuance of rations for most Indians . . . would be disastrous for the Blackfeet, Grinnell disagreed. 'I do not think things will be as bad as you foretell,' he wrote, 'and I do not see how the Indians are ever to learn to do any work if they are supported by the government.' And he added, 'I feel sure that if I were guaranteed clothes and grub I should never do a lick of work'" (*Theodore Roosevelt* 140–41). Hagan also tells us that President Theodore Roosevelt consulted Grinnell on the passages of his State of the Union messages concerning the Indians. For more on Grinnell and his ambivalent stances regarding the Indians, see Smith as well as Grinnell's voluminous work, some of which is still in print today; for example, *The Fighting Cheyennes*, *Blackfeet Indian Stories*, or *The Cheyenne Indians*.

14. The Sherman Institute was an off-reservation vocational school located in Riverside, southern California, a few miles east of Los Angeles. It opened in 1902, a year before Oskison wrote this essay. If the institute indeed had a farm in Arlington where Indians learned to be farmers specialized in vegetable growing notably, the school was also an industrial vocational school where boys learned carpentry or blacksmithing and girls were taught sewing, housekeeping, and nursing. A personal account of the Sherman Institute can be found in Polingaysi Qoyawayma, *No Turning Back* (1964). Qoyawayma (1892–1990), who went to the Sherman Institute voluntarily as a teenager, captured the ambivalent feelings she had on arrival there: "Riverside. Land of oranges. Land of perfume. Time of torture" (59). Qoyawayma talks of the work the students had to do at the institute, "which included scrubbing floors, doing dishes, making beds, and helping in various other departments" (63), but also of many fond memories and of her pride in the education she received. For more on Sherman Institute and other schools, see Keller, *Empty Beds*, and Adams, *Education for Extinction*.

15. "Friends of the Indian" was first published in *The Nation* in October 1905. This text and the two following it, "Lake Mohonk Conference" and "The Need of Publicity in Indian Affairs," have the Lake Mohonk Conference as a common denominator.

The Lake Mohonk Conference of Friends of the Indian, according to Hagan, was "instituted by the Quaker educator Albert K. Smiley, a member of the Board of Indian Commissioners. From 1883 to 1912, he sponsored annually a conference at his resort which attracted government officials, congressmen, and reformers. Out of their sessions came programs which subsequently inspired much criticism, but which then represented majority thinking of friends of the Indian. The policies they recommended were those that guided administration of Indian affairs during the next quarter-century" (*American Indians* 136). The Lake Mohonk Conference of Friends of the Indian and the Indian Rights Association, mentioned by Oskison in the first paragraph of "Friends of the Indian," were two of several reform groups that, at the turn of the century, advocated the assimilation of the Indians. Other groups of what are called Eastern reformers included the Women's National Indian Association and the United States Board of Indian Commissioners. According to Hauptman, "behind both the Eastern reformers' and Roosevelt's attitudes was the seldom challenged assumption that it was possible to kill the Indian but save the man" (2). The purpose of the Friends of the Indian was to transform the Indians into American citizens, notably by means of education in Indian schools such as the one at Carlisle, Pennsylvania.

In October 1904 the conference, by resolution, approved changing its name to the "Lake Mohonk Conference of Friends of the Indian and Other Dependent Peoples." Indeed, the preface to the 1904 *Proceedings* stated, "in view of the fact that some reforms in the Indian service which had absorbed much attention at past conferences were on a fair way to realization, it was deemed an auspicious time to effect a proposed extension of the scope of the Conference to include discussion of questions, except those having a purely political bearing, affecting the welfare of the peoples of the Philippines, Porto Rico, and Hawaii" (1904 *Proceedings Twenty-second Lake Mohonk Conference*).

Oskison became a member of the conference in 1904. In 1905, he was elected member of the Press Committee (1905 *Proceedings Twenty-third Lake Mohonk Conference* 10). That year he published a review of its proceedings, titled "Lake Mohonk Conference," in *The Native American*. At the 1906 annual meeting he gave a talk on "the Need of Publicity in Indian Affairs," the third text of the trilogy. He remained a member of the conference at least until 1909, but had any official responsibility in it only until 1907, the last year he was on the Press Committee. In 1915 Oskison was invited to give an address again, also published in this volume, titled "A Bigger Load for Educated Indians."

16. Charles J. Bonaparte (1851–1921), great-nephew of Napoléon, was the founder of the National Civil Service Reform League. From 1902 to 1904 he was a member of the Board of Indian Commissioners. In 1904 he was president of the Lake Mohonk Conference to which Oskison is referring to here. In 1908 Bonaparte would be appointed attorney general of the United States by President Theodore Roosevelt. As such he would create a special investigative force, the Bureau of Investigation, under the authority of the Department of Justice. In 1935 this small unit would be renamed the Federal Bureau of Investigation.

A more extensive quote from Bonaparte's opening address than the one given in this essay sheds light on a point Oskison makes in this text and others: "It is the duty of this Conference, Ladies and Gentlemen, to enlighten, arouse and guide public opinion, first, as to the existence and gravity of the dangers to be met; secondly, in the search for a remedy. I venture to offer it two words of caution. The first is suggested to my mind by the remark of a naval officer who said 'the Service would never be worth a ——' (I fear he used here a bad word) 'until all the well-meaning people in it had been hanged.' There is no field in which zeal needs more urgently to be coupled with knowledge and tempered with discretion than in criticism of Indian affairs. Dependent and helpless people are, by a law of nature, at once credulous and suspicious: talk on the part of those stronger than themselves, which might otherwise be merely untimely or injudicious, when overheard by them, may readily become harmful and even dangerous" (Bonaparte 15).

17. The Indian Rights Association is another one of the many associations of reformers. It was founded in Philadelphia in 1882 by Herbert Welsh and Henry Spackman Pancoast, with Charles. C. Painter as a lobbyist in Washington. The association was very influential and was notably consulted by the presidents before the appointment of Indian commissioners. In particular, it influenced Theodore Roosevelt's Indian policy, as governor of New York and as president of the United States. For more on the subject see Hagan, *The Indian Rights Association* (1985). Hagan also explores the links between the IRA and Roosevelt in "Civil Service Commissioner."

18. The Pimas call themselves Akimel O'odham, which means River People. They have lived on the banks of the Gila River since long before the arrival of European settlers. When the Euro-Americans reached the area they diverted the waters of the Gila River in order to irrigate their fields. Consequently, the once flourishing agricultural economy of the Pima and the Pee-Posh (Maricopa) started to suffer in the 1880s. According to Pritzker's encyclopedia, "by 1870, Pima wheat production had reached 3 million pounds" (62). In an appeal to Congress in 1911, Chief of the Pimas Antonito Azul quoted an 1888 official report by the Pima Reservation agent, who had written that the Pima Indians "can be termed substantially a self-supporting people," but had added that "the lands near their reservations are being rapidly taken up and constant encroachment upon their water rights will occur unless the agent is vigilant and energetic in the discharge of his duties" (Azul 4). In 1901 the agent reported that "after putting forth every possible effort (such as white men would never make) to raise a crop and make themselves self-sustaining, these worthy Indians are again stranded on the desert with scant provisions sufficient for only a few weeks' subsistence" (Azul 4).

The 1904 report of the commissioner of Indian Affairs mentions a report dated 1 March 1886, that is to say, approximately eighteen years before Oskison wrote this essay, which "invited the attention of the department to a letter from Agent Wheeler, stating that there was a project on foot to take the water from the Gila River, at a point 12 miles above the town of Florence, by means of an irrigation canal, in such quantities as would practically destroy the farms of the Indians." The 1904 report adds that "the investigation . . . made by the Geological Survey . . . established the fact that the construction of the proposed dam would result disastrously to the Indians. The report of the Geological Survey was communicated to the department with the recommendation that the subject be again referred to the Attorney General, with request that the United States attorney be directed to take the necessary steps to enjoin the canal company from any diversion of the waters of the Gila River to the injury of the Indians" (qtd. in United States. Cong. House 29).

As a result of the Geological Survey report, "some offers of compromise were made by the canal company and legal steps were held in abeyance until the canal was constructed, and no successful attempt was ever made to prevent the diversion of the river by the Florence Canal or to compel such diverters to supply the Indians with water for irrigation; and the matter was finally allowed to drop by the Department of Justice" (Lippincott 68).

After it received a petition dated 31 July 1911 from the chiefs of the Pima Tribe of Indians, the Indian Rights Association, in the person of S. M. Brosius, would try to influence Congress into securing the rights of the Pima Indians to water supply. Brosius argued that the Indians were "entitled, as a matter of right through prior appropriation, to the natural flow of the water of the Gila River" (Brosius 9).

19. A more substantial quote from the district attorney can be found in the report of the commissioner of Indian Affairs for 1904: "June 10, 1904, Supt. Alexander reported that all data relative to the recovering of water to the Pima Indians by judicial proceedings had been furnished the district attorney, and that in consultation with him the attorney had said that 'there are 960 persons using water from the Gila River above the point where the Pima Indians divert the water of the Gila for their lands; that there is no doubt but that the case could be taken up and prosecuted to a favorable ending, but the interests are so varied and the water is diverted by the whites as far as 300 miles above the Indians' point of diversion that should a favorable decree be given by the court it would be impossible for the court to enforce its decree, and that the expense of prosecuting such a suit would cost between twenty and thirty thousand dollars" (United States. Cong. House, *Conserving the Rights of Pima Indians* 29).

20. Bishop Henry Benjamin Whipple (1822–1901), a longtime missionary and defender of Indian rights, was a regular speaker at the Lake Mohonk Conference and an admirer of the work done by Senator Dawes and Captain Pratt. From the number of times his name is mentioned in the proceedings of the conference year after year, it appears that he was quite an influential figure on the Friends of the Indian. When he could not attend the conference, he usually sent letters in which he raised important — and controversial — questions to guide the discussions of the Friends of the Indian. In one such letter, read at the 1895 conference, he bluntly asked: "1. Is it right or just for us to attempt to relieve our consciences of the guilt of past neglect by thrushing the Indian into citizenship, and say, 'Sink or swim'? 2. Is there any possible way to protect these poor brown brothers from the curse of the fire-water, which is worse than ever before? 3. Ought not Congress to provide for administration of law or reserve by making the agent or some one a stipendiary magistrate? 4. Is there any remedy for the leasing of Indian land to perpetuate the

old curse of heathen pauperism? 5. Is it not a solemn duty we owe to them to prevent the alienation of their land?" (1895 *Proceedings Thirteenth Lake Mohonk Conference* 59). In 1896 Whipple gave an address in reaction to one given by his "friend Captain Pratt, that he concluded by emphasizing the following points: "first, the folly of teaching Indian children in their own language; after learning they have no books to read; second, the impossibility of the Indian becoming civilized without government. And, let me say, we have not reached that point yet. Many of the difficulties of which Captain Pratt speaks can be solved the moment we give him exactly the same protection as we give to the white man. Third, individual rights of property. These, with the religion of Jesus Christ, will give to the Indian, as it has given to man all through the ages, manhood and freedom" (1896 *Proceedings Fourteenth Lake Mohonk Conference* 41). In 1897 he told the conference of his long experience among "The Indians of Minnesota" (1897 *Proceedings Fifteenth Lake Mohonk Conference* 43–48).

The Nineteenth Annual Meeting of the Lake Mohonk Conference of Friends of the Indian took place in October 1901, only a few weeks after Bishop Whipple's death. Before a tribute from Rev. J. J. Enmegahbowh, an Anishinaabe (Chippewa) priest ordained by Whipple, James Grant Wilson said: "Two men in this broad land of ours have won the noble title of the Apostle to the Indians. It was first worn by Rev. John Elliott in the seventeenth century. The other was well known to this Conference and well loved, Henry B. Whipple" (1901 *Proceedings Nineteenth Lake Mohonk Conference* 24). Whipple spent many years among the Sioux and the Anishinaabeg in Minnesota. He wrote of his experience notably in a text published in the *North American Review* in which he showed uncommon open-mindedness to Indian cultures and vehement criticism of federal policies regarding the Indians. Of the past "Indian system," he wrote that "its emoluments were rewards for political service, and most of its solemn treaties were framed to use the Indian as a key to unlock the public treasury. At best it established heathen almshouses to graduate savage paupers" (433). In the same text he also wrote that some of the "unwritten Indian tongues are marvelous for their beauty and power, and are capable of conveying as nice shades of meaning as classic Greek" (432). He added that he "believed that these wandering redmen were children of one God and Father, and that he loved them as he loved us" (433). In a letter sent to the conference, Mrs. Whipple wrote that "two hundred Chippewa Indians came to attend [his funeral], some coming more than a hundred miles to look once more on the beautiful face of their ever-faithful friend, to whom they gave the appropriate title of 'Straight Tongue" (1901 *Proceedings Nineteenth Lake Mohonk Conference* 25). In the memorial that was held in his honor by the conference members on 18 October, it was said that "his forty years' missionary labors for the Indians; his quick grasp of their wretched condition; his sagacious practical work for their relief, — fitted him to speak with authority upon Indian affairs; and such was his courage that no opposition or threat of violence could thwart or daunt him" (118). It was also acknowledged that he had "gained a thorough knowledge of the Indian condition and needs, and he had the wisdom to forecast some of the most important measures of reform which have since been adopted. He opposed, like Monroe, treating with Indians as sovereign nations; he condemned appointment of agents as a reward for political services. Before the Lake Mohonk Conference discussed land in severalty, he demanded for the Indian an individual right to the soil. His memorial in 1862, and his report in 1866, are said to have led to the organization of the Board of Indian Commissioners" (118).

21. Before removal, the Poncas were located at the confluence of the Niobrara and Missouri Rivers, in the Territory of Dakota. The Ponca removal was one more proof, if any was needed, that adjustment to the white man's ways did not protect a Native American tribe from being removed. In a report to the Senate dated 31 May 1880, Senator Dawes wrote that the Ponca Indians "had made considerable advances in civilization, and at the time of their removal were living in very comfortable houses built by themselves. . . . Upon their reservation there was also a school-house and school in operation, a church where the missionaries of the Episcopal Church were doing a good work for their improvement. They cultivated the land, and many of them had farms of considerable size occupied in severalty, and altogether they presented one of the most encouraging and hopeful of all the fields for Indian improvement and self-support" (*Report: Removal of the Ponca Indians* ii). Besides, Dawes acknowledged that "in all accounts of the character of these Indians, and in all mention of them in official reports, they are described as among the most peaceful and quiet of all the Indians in the United States. Their disposition toward the United States has been uniformly friendly; they had never been known to cause trouble or disturbance, to make war upon the Indians or upon settlers; they were always ready to interfere between hostile Indians and the whites, and to ward off incursions of the Sioux and other wild Indians. They were deemed by the settlers on the Nebraska frontier as in some sense a defense to them against hostile acts of the wild Indians farther north and west, and were considered at all times by them as a protection in the many wars which the United States have heretofore had with the Sioux and other wild Indians of the Northwest. They were always ready, and on many occasions did render very valuable assistance to us" (ii).

After a five-page statement of the good character of the Ponca Indians, quoting the treaties between the tribe and the United States, as well as all kinds of reports by agents and missionaries asserting that the Poncas were the friendliest, the most peaceful and even the most "submissive," Dawes reasserted "their title to their reservation and their right to remain there undisturbed under a grant of the fee to them by the United States, with a covenant on their part to defend these Indians in their peaceable possession of the same" (v). Yet, in 1868, the United States provided a reservation for different bands of Sioux Indians in a territory in northwest Nebraska including within its limits the Ponca reservation. In his report for 1878, Commissioner of Indian Affairs Hayt called this treaty with the Sioux "a blunder" by which "the 96,000 acres belonging to the Poncas were ceded to the Sioux." He added that "the negotiators had no right whatever to make the cession, and the bad feeling between the Sioux and the Poncas, which had existed for a long time, compelled the removal of the latter to the Indian Territory" (xxxvi). The commissioner claimed that "in this removal, I am sorry to be compelled to say, the Poncas were wronged, and restitution should be made as far as it is in the power of the government to do so. For the violation of their treaty no adequate return has yet been made. They gave up lands, houses, and agricultural implements. The houses and implements will be returned to them; their lands should be immediately paid for, and the title to their present location should be made secure. But the removal inflicted a far greater injury upon the Poncas, for which no reparation can be made — the loss by death of many of their number, caused by change of climate" (xxxvi–xxxvii).

As an appendix to his report, Dawes included "complaints by settlers in Nebraska, near the Ponca Reservation in Dakota, of depredations committed by the Indians belonging on that reservation" (381). Such complaints in the 1870s may have helped convince the federal government to remove the Poncas to Indian Territory.

22. The National Audubon Society was incorporated in New York State in 1905. It was — and still is today — a conservationist organization, especially dedicated to birds. It was named after John James Audubon (1785–1851), a prominent naturalist who published seminal works on ornithology. Naturalist and *Forest and Stream* editor George Bird Grinnell, whom Oskison mentioned in "The Outlook for the Indian," founded the first Audubon Society in 1886 (see n. 13 above). Grinnell spent his boyhood in Audubon Park, the family's estate located in today's Washington Heights, Manhattan, and attended Lucy Audubon's school. See www.audubon.org and Grinnell, "Recollections of Audubon Park," 1920.

23. In the *Lone Wolf v. Hitchcock* decision (1903), the Supreme Court ruled that Congress had plenary authority over Indian nations. The case was an attempt at hindering allotment. At the end of the nineteenth century, a Kiowa chief, Lone Wolf, was forced to take an allotment, like many of his fellow tribespeople. He went to court to stop the selection of his own allotment. Blue Clark explains that the allotment of the whole Kiowa, Comanche, and Plains Apache Reservation in

southwestern Oklahoma was at stake, as well as the opening of the so-called surplus to white homesteaders putting more and more pressure on Congress, not to mention the consequences on the allotment of many other reservations that would have ensued had Lone Wolf won his case (B. Clark 2). Often called "the Indian's Dred Scott" to emphasize how shameful and retrograde that decision was, *Lone Wolf v. Hitchcock* was a departure from the Cherokee cases doctrine (phrased by Chief Justice Marshall in *Cherokee Nation v. Georgia* in 1831 and *Worcester v. Georgia* in 1832) defining the Native American nations as "domestic dependent nations" and emphasizing inherent tribal sovereignty. According to Jill Norgren, "*Lone Wolf* has permitted the United States to appropriate tribal lands and resources under the guise of fulfilling federal trust responsibilities" (592).

24. Before Roosevelt appointed him secretary of war in 1904, William Howard Taft had been sent to the Philippines by President McKinley as governor-general. In 1909 he took office as president of the United States. He was appointed chief justice of the Supreme Court by President Harding in 1921.

25. This review of the twenty-third annual meeting of the Lake Mohonk Conference was published on 4 November 1905 in *The Native American*.

26. Oskison mentions the Lacey Bill again in "Remaining Causes of Indian Discontent," reprinted below. The Lacey Bill was signed into law on 2 March 1907 by President Roosevelt. John F. Lacey, Republican of Iowa, had been a member of the House Committee on Indian Affairs since 1901. The 1907 Lacey Act is not to be confused with a 1900 Lacey Act about wildlife protection. Lacey also authored the 1906 Antiquities Act for the preservation of archaeological sites.

27. This is an address that Oskison delivered at the twenty-fourth annual meeting of the Lake Mohonk Conference of Friends of the Indian and Other Dependent Peoples, on the first day of the meeting, 17 October 1906. It was published in the proceedings of the meeting in 1906.

28. Quanah Parker was a leader of the Kwahadi Comanches whose mother was a white woman raised among the Comanches. In 1874 he led a group of Kwahadis, as well as some Cheyennes and Arapahos, on "a war to save the buffalo," an attack against white buffalo hunters at Adobe Walls on the Canadian River in today's Hutchinson County, in the Texas panhandle. Quanah Parker surrendered soon after this battle and chose to adjust to the new way of life, although he had too many wives to suit the white men's moral standards. His response, when he was asked to get rid of a few of them and keep one only, was not unlike Old Harjo's in Oskison's story above: "A long time ago I lived free among the buffalo on the Staked Plains and had as many wives as I wanted, according to the laws of my people. I used to go to war in Texas and Mexico. You wanted me to stop fighting and sent messages

all the time: 'You stop, Quanah. You come here. You sit down, Quanah.' You did not say anything then, 'How many wives you got, Quanah.' Now I come and sit down as you want. You talk about wives; which one I throw away? You pick him? You little girl, you go 'way; you got no papa—you pick him? You little fellow, you go 'way; you got no papa—you pick him?" (qtd. in Debo, *A History* 287).

29. Mrs. Jackson is Helen Hunt Jackson (1830–85). She was an activist for Indian rights and published *A Century of Dishonor* in 1881, an essay, and *Ramona*, a novel, in 1884. She was made into an activist by a talk she heard Ponca chief Standing Bear give in Boston to raise sympathy for his tribe, badly treated and unfairly removed by the United States (see n. 21 above). According to Valerie Sherer Mathes, Jackson was profoundly changed by Standing Bear's story: "Never before interested in humanitarian causes, she would dedicate the rest of her life to Indian reform. When she saw the dignified and courteous sixty-year-old Ponca chief whose gentle face was 'stamped with unutterable sadness,' something reached deep into her being. 'I shall be found with 'Indians' engraved on my brain when I am dead,' she wrote to a friend. 'A fire had been kindled within me which will never go out'" (43).

30. Debo says of Pleasant Porter that he was "the great and wise Chief of the Creeks" (*And Still* 13). According to Porter, when the Dawes Commission came to treat with the Five Tribes, there were only three ways to resist: "by fighting, which would have meant destruction; by emigration, by which they would have lost their country and would have found no place to go; and by passive resistance, which would have been futile" (*And Still* 33). So he accepted to treat but later declared: "I will tell you what I have felt and I ought not to have felt that way. I have said that I was conscious that I was compelled under the advance of civilization to sign the paper now that I know took the lifeblood of my people" (qtd. in *And Still* 33–34).

W. C. Rogers was the principal chief of the Cherokees at the time the federal government put an end to tribal governments in March 1906. Rogers and Porter were two of the Five Nations principal chiefs who, in 1905, called for a constitutional convention in order to create a state named Sequoyah separate from the future state of Oklahoma (Debo, *And Still* 162).

31. "Remaining Causes of Indian Discontent" was first published in *North American Review* in March 1907. It was published again in the *North American Review* in 1973. An introductory sentence followed Oskison's name before the article in 1973: "The first NAR writer to concern himself almost exclusively with money matters, Oskison sees the cash distribution of Trust and Treaty funds as solving (?) the remaining Indian problems."

32. Oskison refers to what O'Neill called the "anguished odyssey" of the Utes from the Uintah and Ouray Reservation in Utah between 1906 and 1908. In 1903 a

minority of Utes signed the allotment article. In the summer of 1906, a few months before Oskison wrote this essay, a few hundreds — two hundred according to the commissioner of Indian Affairs, four hundred according to Lewis — of White River Utes, who passed for traditionalists, or "nonprogressive" (1907 *Report Commissioner Indian Affairs* 125), left their reservation and went to the Pine Ridge Reservation, South Dakota, "there to enjoy an unrestricted communal life" (Lewis 125). This is how Francis Leupp, commissioner of Indian Affairs at the time, later characterized the incident in *The Indian and His Problem*: "During the autumn of 1906 some two hundred men, women and children of the Ute tribe deserted their fertile reservation in Utah because they did not like the prospect of having to work for their living, and started to march in a body across the country to South Dakota, where they had been misled into believing that the Sioux Indians occupied all the land and would welcome them as guests and settlers" (170). In the 1907 annual report of the commissioner of Indian Affairs, these resisting Utes were referred to as "the Absentee Utes" (125). The Indian agent of the Uintah and Ouray Agency reported that "their dissatisfaction with the Government was the result of the changes which had recently been brought about through allotments having been made to them and their surplus lands thrown open to public settlement; that since the opening of the reservation they had been able to secure all the intoxicating liquor they wanted; and that as a result several Indians had been killed and the lives of settlers threatened by drunken Indians, all of which aggravated the situation" (125).

Lewis writes that the "White River Utes did return to the allotted reservation in 1908, under military guard, physically defeated, and with little means of support. Many had no idea where their allotments were, had nothing to work their land with if they wanted to, and were reluctant to work for wages on the ongoing Uintah Irrigation Project. Many ultimately leased their lands to white settlers, hoping to earn some money and protect their water rights against usufruct Utah water laws" (128–29).

33. Oskison refers to the Supreme Court decision 197 U.S. 488 "In the Matter of the Application of Albert Heff for a Writ of Habeas Corpus," argued on 10 January 1905 and decided on 10 April 1905. In October 1904, Albert Heff was convicted in Kansas for selling alcohol to John Butler, a member of the Kickapoo tribe and as such "a ward of the government." The law on which Heff's conviction was founded was an act of Congress dated 30 January 1897, providing "that any person who shall sell . . . any ardent or other intoxicating liquor of any kind whatsoever . . . to any Indian to whom allotment of land has been made while the title to the same shall be held in trust by the government, or to any Indian a ward of the government under charge of any Indian superintendent or agent . . . shall be punished." The petitioner

contended that this act was unconstitutional because the act of 8 February 1887 (the Dawes Act) provided that, in the words of Justice Brewer, "each and every Indian to whom allotments have been made shall be subject to the laws, both civil and criminal, of the state in which they may reside, and further, that John Butler, having . . . received an allotment of land in severalty . . . is no longer a ward of the government, but a citizen of the United States and of the State of Kansas, and subject to the laws . . . of said state." Brewer strengthened the decision of the Court, which would be favorable to Heff, by demonstrating that "a new policy [had] found expression in the legislation of Congress — a policy which looks to the breaking up of tribal relations, the establishing of the separate Indians in individual homes, free from national guardianship and charged with all the rights and obligations of citizens of the United States." As a consequence, the act of 30 January 1897 was declared unconstitutional.

Commissioner Francis E. Leupp (see "Autobiography" n. 170), in 1906, declared that "under the decision of the Supreme Court in the Heff Case we have no assurance that we can absolutely prevent an Indian allottee from drinking himself to death any time he wishes, or anybody from giving him as much liquor as he asks for, but we propose to throw all possible obstacles in the way" ("The Indian Policy" 22). One such obstacle was the Burke Act, supported by Leupp and passed in May 1906, which amended the Dawes Act so as to grant citizenship only after a period of tutelage which, in the terms of the commissioner, "gives us an opportunity to try, at any rate, to strengthen his character against the approaches of the adversary" (22). Leupp had advocated for such protection against the dangers of alcohol for many years. At the 1896 Lake Mohonk Conference, as a Washington agent for the Indian Rights Association, he had explained that he was trying to convince congressmen to pass a law to protect the Indians to whom allotments had been made. Senator Pettigrew had answered that they "cannot do anything of that kind. It would be unconstitutional. Those Indians are citizens; and there is no way of preventing them, by United States law, from buying liquor if they want to." Yet Leupp did not give up and asked a prominent member of the House Committee on Indian Affairs how come they had "reported a liquor bill favorably" when they knew very well it was unconstitutional. This unnamed member replied: "Oh, that whole constitutional question was argued in our committee till I grew tired and exclaimed, 'Gentlemen, we can talk over this thing till doomsday and get no nearer a conclusion. The only thing for us to do is to pass the bill and let the Constitution go to Ballyhack!'" That they did indeed and passed the 30 January 1897 law mentioned above, which the Supreme Court subsequently declared unconstitutional (Leupp, "Visits" 20).

34. "Making an Individual of the Indian" was first published in June 1907 in

Everybody's Magazine. Several captioned photographs of Indians at work illustrated the text: "An Indian car-tender in a construction camp" (724), "'Bird-in-the-morning,' a Crow Indian scraper driver" (725), "The sewing-room in a school at Pine Ridge, South Dakota" (726), "Printing office in a school, at Pine Ridge, South Dakota" (727), "Apaches mixing concrete at a construction camp near Livingston, Arizona" (728), "Apaches working on the Salt River power canal in Arizona" (729), "A Navajo Indiana at work with a steam drill" (733). One picture was captioned "Apache squaws supplement the earnings of their men by making baskets" (732). There was also a profile portrait of "Charles Doxon, an Onondagan, Director of Manual Training Work at Hampton Institute" (725), wearing a suit, and two full-length portraits: one in traditional regalia of "Captain John Long Day, a Sioux Indian scout, of Pine Ridge, South Dakota" (730), and one in western clothes of "The Rev. Wah-Ku-Te-Mo-Me, a full-blooded Sioux who is the congregational minister at Standing Rock, SD" (731).

35. James Fenimore Cooper (1789–1851), American novelist, is most famous for his novel *The Last of the Mohicans* (1826). George Catlin (1796–1872) was one of the first major artists to travel west to paint the Indians and their customs. In the 1830s, from St. Louis, he visited many tribes and painted portraits, landscapes, and buffalo-hunting scenes. When he realized that the cultures he was painting were threatened by western expansion, he became an activist. In 1841 he published *Letters and Notes on the Manners, Customs, and Condition of the North American Indians.*

36. Arthur P. Davis, chief engineer of the United States Reclamation Service, wrote that the Huntley irrigation project provided "for the diversion of water from the Yellowstone River at a point three miles above Huntley, Montana" (A. P. Davis 209). The Huntley Project was one of twenty-six irrigation projects approved by the secretary of the interior in the first years of the Reclamation Service (later called the Bureau of Reclamation), created on 17 June 1902 by the Reclamation Act in order to lead a new "policy of internal improvement" (203). John H. Beacom explains that the Reclamation Act "provided that all moneys received from the sale and disposal of public lands in Arizona, California, Colorado, Idaho, Kansas, Montana, Nebraska, Nevada, New Mexico, North Dakota, Oklahoma, Oregon, South Dakota, Utah, Washington, and Wyoming, on and after July 1, 1900, should be set aside as a special fund in the Treasury, to be known as the 'Reclamation Fund,' to be used in the examination and survey for, and the construction and maintenance of, irrigation works for the storage, diversion, and development of waters for the reclamation of arid and semi-arid lands in the above states and territories. The Secretary of the Interior was made the administrator of this fund" (403–4). The Huntley project, authorized by Congress in April 1905, was located on lands that the Crow Indians

had ceded to the United States by a treaty approved by Congress in April 1904. The water of the Huntley Project, diverted near Billings, would irrigate some thirty thousand acres of land (Blanchard 215). These lands were opened to settlement in June 1907 (A. P. Davis 210).

The construction of the Zuni dam, or Blackrock dam, started in 1903. John Harper, the superintendent of irrigation for the Pueblos and Jicarillas, who recommended the dam in 1902, wrote in one of his reports that "the Indians are industrious and will utilize the water as soon as it is provided them, and their entire status will be quickly and permanently bettered. Many times this amount has been expended on equal numbers of Indians of other tribes, for subsistence alone, leaving them no better prepared to earn a living than thirty years ago. This work will be an investment, not an expense" (in Wessel 6). The dam was supposed to be completed in 1905, but much unexpected difficulty extended its construction to 1909. Christian W. McMillen calls the Zuni dam project "the Indian Service's $300,000 silt-clogged white elephant" (437). According to McMillen, the strength of Zuni religious practices and rituals explain the failure of the Blackrock dam. When the dam was originally "designed to replace religious and agricultural ritual . . . with a rational, market-oriented life-style" (444). While Oskison praises the work of the Hopi night foreman, McMillen's explanation for the failure of the dam sounds different: "When Harper commenced work in the summer of 1904, he expected a sizable labor force, but by midseason summer solstice ceremonies had begun, and the Zuni labor force evaporated. In August, Zuni and Navajo laborers left to harvest corn. And when harvest season was over, the Navajo went deer hunting and the Zuni began to prepare for Shalako — several weeks of ceremony that precede the winter solstice ceremony, teshkwi. Once Shalako began, the Zuni again abandoned work on the dam" (445).

37. Bishop William Hobart Hare (1838–1909) spent many years among Native American communities in the Dakota Territory. Notably, he was in charge of the instruction of the Ponca Indians before their removal (see n. 29 above). With Bishop Whipple, he was one of the main leaders of the Episcopal Church in the frontier.

In his essay "The Establishment of Christianity among the Sioux," Vine V. Deloria Sr. relates the story of his uncle Amos Ross: "At the time of the Sioux uprising in Minnesota, he and his family, who belonged to one of the Santee bands, were living near the Canadian line. They were unaware of the fighting raging in the southern part of Minnesota. Nevertheless, they woke one morning to find themselves completely surrounded by soldiers. The commander ordered them to line up, wearing only the clothes they had on. They had to leave everything, including their tipis and horses, and they were marched south" (106). They were taken to Fort Snelling. "Missionaries came to them, taught them about the Bible, and taught them to read and write.

They also taught them about baptism. One missionary lined the Indians up and baptized them one by one, using a Bible to keep himself supplied with names. He must have been at the book of Amos when Uncle Ross knelt down. The missionary said to the interpreter, 'Tell him that his name is going to be Amos. Tell him to say it.' And so he said it, and then he was baptized" (107). One of the missionaries present at Fort Snelling was Bishop Whipple. When Bishop Hare took charge of Amos Ross's band in 1873 on their reservation, he trained Ross as a deacon "and finally ordained him as a priest in 1892. Then he was sent out to missionize among the Rosebud Sioux at Yankton" (107). Finally he served on the Pine Ridge Reservation. According to Deloria, at the time Ross retired "he had eleven churches, eleven ministers, and a total membership of 1,776 people. He certainly did an admirable job as a priest for his Master" (107).

38. In 1908, Reuben Quick Bear was one of the plaintiffs in a U.S. Supreme Court case — *Reuben Quick Bear v. Leupp* — initiated by the Indian Rights Association to challenge the use of tribal funds and treaty funds to finance a sectarian school in the Rosebud Reservation. In a decision written by Chief Justice Fuller, the Court ruled in favor of the commissioner of Indian Affairs, who had signed a contract with the Bureau of Catholic Indian Missions to open a school, thus deciding that tribal funds and treaty payments were not public appropriations since they were monies belonging to the Indians and could be used by them — actually "administered for them by the government," in Fuller's terms, or "dealt with by the government as if it belonged to them, as morally it does" — to educate their children "in the schools of their choice." In that case, the plaintiffs contended that the contract between the commissioner of Indian Affairs and the Bureau of Catholic Missions went against the spirit of the First Amendment of the Constitution, which states that "Congress shall make no law respecting an establishment of religion, or prohibiting the free exercise thereof." Chief Justice Fuller agreed with the Court of Appeals, which stated that because "the 'treaty' and 'trust' moneys are the only moneys that the Indians can lay claim to as matter of right; the only sums on which they are entitled to rely as theirs for education . . . it seems inconceivable that Congress shall have intended to prohibit them from receiving religious education at their own cost if they desire it; such an intent would be one to prohibit the free exercise of religion amongst the Indians, and such would be the effect of the construction for which the complainants contend."

39. Zander Big Crow attended Blackpipe Creek Day School. Willard Standing Bear was a half brother of Luther Standing Bear, author of *My Indian Boyhood* (1931) and *Land of the Spotted Eagle* (1933), both sons of Chief Standing Bear and of different mothers (Sprague 87). Like Reuben Quick Bear, Willard Standing Bear attended Carlisle.

40. "Returned" students were Indian students who came back to the reservation after attending nonreservation schools. After they were back, some used the experience they acquired in the "white man's school" to protect tribal interests and rights; others felt utterly disconnected and alienated from the community and its traditions and culture; and still others went back "to the blanket," that is to say, turned their back on the "white" education they received and stuck to the old ways. For studies of the "returned Indians" see Ahern, "The 'Returned Indians'" and "An Experiment Aborted"; Adams, *Education for Extinction*.

41. Sibyl Carter was an Episcopal deaconess who taught Anishinaabeg and Dakota women lace making at the White Earth Reservation (Densmore, "Minnesota Missionary" 310). She founded the Sibyl Carter Indian Lace Association (Blatti 6).

42. Oskison refers to the Roes, not the Rowes. Rev. Walter C. Roe was a pastor of a Presbyterian church in Dallas before he moved to the Colony Mission at the invitation of Frank Hall Wright (Harper 255). Colony, where the agency of the Cheyennes and Arapahoes was, is located about sixty miles west of Oklahoma City, about ten miles south of Weatherford, Oklahoma. In 1896 the Roes established the Mohonk Lodge "as a philanthropic institution at Colony" (M. H. Wright 396). It was "planned to provide the Indians an opportunity for self-support; to uphold the returned students from the Indian schools; and to supply a substitute for the old-time tribal social life" (396). Although Roe was a missionary of the Dutch Reformed Church, the lodge was operated along "strictly undenominational lines, with funds contributed from people of all classes and shades of belief" (396–97). Fort Sill Apache Jason Betzinez mentions Dr. Roe in his autobiography *I Fought with Geronimo*. When Congress started to talk about removing the Fort Sill Apaches to the Mescalero Reservation in New Mexico (see "An Apache Problem"), two missionaries, Legters and Roe, helped them resist: "The aid which these two churchmen could give was not inconsiderable. Through their connections they were able to exert influence on religious groups and other well-minded citizens throughout the United States. Public opinion in our behalf was aroused. Furthermore Dr. Roe counted several influential congressmen among his friends. Altogether, through the powerful efforts of Dr. Roe, the tide turned in favor of the Apaches. Dr. Roe was a frail man but possessed of a brilliant intellect and a strong spirit" (192–93).

The "Industrial Department" of the Mohonk Lodge was directed by Reese Kincaide, a former Fort Worth businessman, and by his wife, Walter Roe's sister, for more than fifty years. In an obituary in the *Chronicles of Oklahoma*, M. H. Wright pays tribute to Kincaide by saying that "his friendship for the Indians in Christian fellowship, his deep insight into Indian ways and characters, and his efficient management of the industrial work at Mohonk Lodge have made a significant and unique contribution to Indian community life in Western Oklahoma" (396). Kincaide arrived at Colony in 1902, called by his brother-in-law. Under his direction, the Mohonk Lodge provided "an outlet for the sale of the native Indian arts, especially the beadwork in which the Cheyenne and Arapaho people were noted" (397).

43. Charles Alexander Eastman tells of this work in his second autobiography, *From the Deep Woods to Civilization* (1916). He is also the author of *Indian Boyhood* (1902), his first autobiography, and *The Soul of the Indian* (1911), among other books and articles, many of which were published in the *Quarterly Journal of the Society of American Indians*. Eastman, also known as Ohiyesa, was raised to become a Sioux warrior, with the mission of avenging the supposed death of his father, until the age of sixteen. Then his father, Jacob Eastman, came back and convinced his son to go to the white man's school and follow the white man's ways. Eastman became a medical doctor and worked at Pine Ridge Reservation, where he was at the time of the Wounded Knee massacre (for a study of Eastman's autobiographies, see Larré, *Autobiographie amérindienne*).

Francis La Flesche (1857–1932) was a famous ethnologist who published numerous books and articles on the Omaha and Osage Indians, some in collaboration with anthropologist Alice Fletcher and others by himself. He was the son of Joseph La Flesche, a principal chief of the Omaha and of French descent. Joseph sent his son Francis to the Presbyterian School at Bellevue, Nebraska, an experience that Francis recorded in *The Middle Five: Indian Schoolboys of the Omaha Tribe*, published in 1900. He worked in the Office of Indian Affairs and then for the Bureau of American Ethnology in 1910. He started his career in "salvage anthropology" — the most common form of anthropology at the turn of the century, consisting of recording vanishing customs and practices — by working with Fletcher when she came to the Omaha tribe in 1881. Both worked on several projects, notably on recording Omaha songs and publishing *A Study of Omaha Indian Music* in 1893 (La Flesche; Alexander; Mark; Densmore, "Survival").

Angel de Cora (1869–1919), of Winnebago and French ancestry, taught art at Carlisle for nine years, starting in 1906. Ewers called her "not only one of the best-educated Indians of either sex in this country, but the most successful Indian artist of the time" (4). She was a graduate of Hampton Institute. She also studied with "America's leading illustrator of the 1890s, Howard Pyle" (5). Jacqueline Fear-Segal writes that when De Cora was invited by Commissioner of Indian Affairs Leupp to teach at Carlisle, "she made a condition of her appointment that she would not 'be expected to teach in the white man's way, but shall be given complete liberty to develop the art of my own race.' For decades, Carlisle pupils had been taught the formal rules of western painting and drawing. De Cora confessed that 'when I first introduced the subject — Indian art — to the Carlisle students, I experienced the discouraging sensation that I was addressing members of an alien race'" (337). In a paper titled "Indian Art — Its Present and Future," which she read at a meeting of the Anthropological Society of Washington in May 1908, Angel de Cora declared that "my work at Carlisle has been to encourage the school Indian to keep up his native art. It was uphill work at first, for my pupils are all young people, most of whom have spent their days at school and have had little or no home influence. I ask my pupils to make a design for a frieze or wall decoration, also borders for printing, and designs for embroidery for rugs. The ones who respond to my request are the full-bloods, and they lead the rest on in the work" ("Proceedings of the Anthropological Society of Washington" 293–94). She married one of her Carlisle students, William (Lone Star) Dietz (Ewers 5). De Cora believed that art could be a way to achieve the kind of integration to American society that Oskison called for. Through their art, Indians could compete with white men and be part of society as Indian artists: "We Indians think we can contribute something to American art, and in time I hope to train my artists sufficiently well that their work will find a commercial value in manufacturing concerns where good designs are needed. . . . In the field of decorative art, if not in realistic art, let the Indian contribute his gift" (294). Oskison and De Cora met at least once, on 13 October 1911, at the First Annual Conference of the Society of American Indians, where she gave a talk titled "The Preservation of Native Indian Art" just before Oskison talked about "The Indian in the Professions" (*Report of the Executive Council*). For a study of De Cora's work, see Hutchinson.

Charles Doxon was a student at Hampton Institute before he worked there as a manual training teacher (Spack 65). He was also a member of the Society of American Indians and attended their first conference, where he chaired the afternoon session when Oskison spoke of professional Indians (*Report of the Executive Council*).

44. Charles E. Dagenett headed the Indian Employment Bureau at the invitation of Francis Leupp. He was a Carlisle graduate. Leupp, who had created the Employment Bureau, instructed Dagenett to "gather up all the able bodied Indians who . . . have been moved to think that they would like to earn some money, and plant them upon ranches, upon railroads, in mines — wherever in the outer world, in short, there is an opening for a dollar to be got for a day's work" (Hoxie 15). According to Hoxie "in its first year (1906–1907), the employment bureau placed 5,000 tribesmen in Colorado beet fields and on Southwestern sheep ranches and construction projects. By 1909, the bureau had extended its operations to Montana, the Dakotas, California, and Wisconsin" (15). Dagenett was one of the founders of the Society of American Indians in 1911.

45. This is a reference to the Lacey Act (see "Remaining Causes for Indian Discontent" and n. 26 above).

46. Oskison refers here to Roosevelt's putting an end to the spoils system in Indian affairs. Vice-President Roosevelt's becoming president after the assassination of President McKinley in September 1901 revived great hopes among Indian reformers. The spoils system had been a target of the Friends of the Indian for many years. One of them, E. H. Clement, at the Tenth Annual Meeting of the Lake Mohonk Conference, had depicted the Indian agent as "a survival on our age of the absolute power of the old feudal lord in his inaccessible crag or desert. No man outside Russia, I suppose, in modern society, holds in his hands today the fate of so many men, women, and children, without check and without law that is effective. And yet this man, this person charged with such enormous and such difficult and delicate work for humanity, is any politician who is out of a job! It is something monstrous to think of. It is something so outrageous that it seems to me as if . . . this must hasten on the extinction of that odious system of political spoils. The most impressive failure of the late administration was the clean sweep in the Indian agents" (1892 *Proceedings Lake Mohonk Conference* 86). At the Seventeenth Annual Meeting, in 1899, Rev. H. B. Frissell had characterized one of the evils of the spoils system and called for its end: "In every agency there are difficulties with the white men near it, especially where there is good land. Sometimes it is the cattle men who make the trouble, and under the spoils system the agent himself becomes a worker with the cattle men and with the land men against the Indians, and farther up the river in Wisconsin, with the timber men. He becomes, not the agent of the Indian, but of the white men outside of the reservation. Certainly nothing could emphasize more than that fact the necessity of putting the agencies entirely out of reach of the spoils system" (1899 *Proceedings Lake Mohonk Conference* 37).

In October 1901, in his opening address, titled "The Next Step to Be Taken," Merrill Gates expressed his satisfaction that "there is no longer a 'clean sweep' for partisan reasons after each general election" but deemed that the Indian Service "still suffers terribly from the appointment of incapable and worthless agents by local and political influence, and purely from partisan considerations" (1901 *Proceedings Lake Mohonk Conference* 3). Gates also remembered that in 1892 Theodore Roosevelt, "then Civil Service Commissioner, . . . said that the President of the United States . . . could, if he chose, put an end to many of the evils attaching to the present system of appointing agents, by declaring that he would not nominate as Indian agent any man whose fitness for the service had not been tested and approved by examination, or by some competent commission; and we have confidence that Theodore Roosevelt, as President of the United States, knowing the actual condition of affairs upon our Western Indian reservations by personal observation as no other President has ever known them . . . will carry into effect the reforms which, as Commissioner, he saw were so much needed in order to secure well qualified and effective men as Indian agents, and to keep in positions where their experience will be of service to the nation and the Indians, the agents who show themselves capable" (3–4). At the same meeting, just about a month after Roosevelt was sworn in, William Dudley Foulke — to whom Roosevelt had only a few days before announced his pending appointment to the Civil Service Commission (Hagan, *Theodore Roosevelt* 71) — gave a talk titled "Indian Agents and the Spoils System." He started very enthusiastically: "I cannot conceive of any time more favorable for effective work than the present. There is now . . . at the head of our Government — the Chief Executive of the United States — a man who has appeared at previous Conferences, and shown his interest in the Indians; a man whose name stands as the synonym for civic righteousness. So this is the time for work" (1901 *Proceedings Lake Mohonk Conference* 68). Foulke, after enumerating the clean sweeps that had occurred under Cleveland, Harrison, and McKinley in the previous fifteen years, accused Congress of being "the bulwark of the spoils system," a system in which the only thing considered, instead of "the fitness of the man for the place," is "the number of votes his influence can secure for the Senator or member of Congress who secures his appointment" (68). Foulke then proceeded to explain how this could be changed within the frame of the Constitution, which imposed that appointments should be made by the president and confirmed by the Senate: "the President has the right, in conjunction with the Civil Service Commission, to provide rules for his own guidance, and to say that he will nominate no man unless that man has proved his qualifications for the office by prescribed tests. If the President will adopt rules of this description, it will practically eliminate patronage appointments" (69). Such competence, Foulke suggested, should be shown by "long experience in the service," such experience as acquired by superintendents of schools or by military personnel. Foulke finally gave his audience hope: "I have reason to think this may be accomplished. I had a conversation last week with the President regarding the importance of applying civil service reform principles to the appointment of Indian agents. I am not authorized to speak for him, but I am sure his mind is not inhospitable to a plan something like that suggested" (69).

47. "A Carlisle Commencement" was published in *Collier's Weekly* in June 1910 and reprinted in the Carlisle publication, *The Red Man*, under the title "Carlisle Commencement as Seen by *Collier's Weekly*." In *Collier's Weekly* the title was followed by "Putting Exhibits A, B, C and D of the 'Show Me' Graduation Program at the Government's Biggest Non-Reservation Indian School."

48. Brown University, in Providence, Rhode Island, was founded in 1764 as the first Baptist College. William Herbert Perry Faunce (1859–1930) was a pastor and

the president of Brown University from 1899 to 1929. He published *The Educational Ideal in the Ministry* (1908), *What Does Christianity Mean?* (1912), and *Facing Life* (1932). In many of his books he endeavored to show the educational role of the minister (*New York Times* 27 Feb. 1909).

49. The "outing system" was a practice in use in nonreservation Indian schools such as Carlisle by which the students, mainly during summer breaks, were sent as laborers to local Euro-American homes and farms. It allowed them to put their training into practice and provided cheap labor for their employers. Originally, it was an idea of Carlisle's founder, Richard Henry Pratt, who saw the system as the "supreme Americanizer" (qtd. in Trennert 267), an essential tool in the context of assimilation policies of the end of the nineteenth century. According to Trennert, as the "outing system" became generalized, however, "local citizens gave scant thought to the educational benefits a school would bring and tended to view the institution as a reservoir of cheap labor" (278). The local housewives "expected school authorities to provide them with 'properly instructed and trained' girls" (278).

50. Moses Friedman was superintendent of Carlisle at the time.

51. The commissioner of Indian Affairs at the time this article was published was Robert G. Valentine (1909–13). The governor of Pennsylvania was Republican Edwin Sydney Stuart (1907–11).

52. *Nabucodonosor*, better known as *Nabucco*, is an opera composed by Italian composer Giuseppe Verdi. It was first performed in 1842.

53. *The Captain of Plymouth* is a comic opera in three acts written by Seymour Tibbals and composed by Harry Eldridge, first published in 1904. It was performed at several Carlisle commencement ceremonies (at least in 1909 and 1910).

54. Geraldine Farrar (1882–1967) was a well-known film actress and soprano opera singer. In 1916 she published an autobiography, *The Story of an American Singer*, in which she told of the beginning of her career onstage. After studying several years in European capitals, she made her New York debut in 1906 as Juliette in Gounod's opera *Romeo and Juliette*. On the silver screen she notably performed as Carmen in Cecil B. DeMille's silent movie adaptation and as Joan of Arc.

Mary Garden (1874–1967), a soprano, was born in Aberdeen, Scotland. She started a successful career in Paris at the beginning of the twentieth century and arrived in New York in 1907. Later, she would work for the Chicago Civic Opera. She performed in major operas of her days, by Debussy and Massenet among others. She also appeared in silent movies by Samuel Goldwyn.

55. Glenn S. "Pop" Warner was Cornell's football coach before Pratt hired him in 1899 as Carlisle's football and baseball coach and director of the athletics department. Powers-Beck gives an explanation of the end of the Carlisle baseball program: "When

Carlisle ended its college baseball program in 1910, it was partly because the program could not succeed against top-flight competition while many of its best athletes were away playing semipro ball or competing on the track squad. Furthermore, Warner did not wish for professional baseball to taint the victories of the college football team, and Carlisle Superintendent Moses Friedman did not want professional sports to jeopardize the integrity of the school's academic programs" (514).

One of the two students playing for professional baseball teams Oskison refers to might well be Jim Thorpe, the famous and incredibly versatile Sac and Fox athlete of Carlisle who was once known as "the greatest athlete in the world" and "one of America's most wonderful football players." Although Thorpe won the Pentathlon and the Decathlon at the Stockholm, Sweden, Olympics of 1912, he had to relinquish his prizes and titles after admitting he had played professional baseball in the summer of 1909 and 1910. Moses Friedman, in a letter to James Sullivan, secretary of the Amateur Athletic Union, claimed that "the Faculty of the school and the athletic director, Mr. Glenn Warner, were without any knowledge of this fact" and said that he felt "it is a most unpleasant affair, and has brought gloom on the entire institution" (*New York Times* 28 Jan. 1913).

In 1914, two investigations, one conducted by the Department of the Interior, the other by a congressional commission, concluded that the Carlisle athletic program "was accorded too high a status and was being grossly mismanaged under Superintendent Moses Friedman and Coach Glenn Warner" (Adams, "More Than a Game" 44). As a consequence, both Friedman and Warner were removed.

56. Lewis Tewanima (1888–1969) was a Hopi Carlisle graduate. He won the silver medal at the 1912 Olympics for the 10,000-meter run. He ran the marathon at the Olympics in 1908 and 1912.

57. This number is 144 in the version of this article reprinted in *The Red Man.*

58. "The Indian in the Professions" was first a paper Oskison gave at the First Annual Conference of the Society of American Indians, held from 12 to 16 October 1911 at Columbus, Ohio. This text can be found in *Report of the Executive Council on the Proceedings of the Annual Conference*, 94–98. A slightly different version was published in *The Red Man*, a publication by the press of the Carlisle Indian School, in January 1912. The text printed in this volume is the one from *The Red Man*, but I included between brackets — besides a few variations — a whole passage that was in the SAI *Proceedings* version and deleted from the *Red Man* version.

59. Charles D. Carter, a Chickasaw, was a representative for the state of Oklahoma. He was a member of the Society of American Indians and an advocate of citizenship for Indians (Hertzberg 118, 187). At the SAI conference where Oskison read this paper, Carter read one titled "Citizenship for the Indian." As a congressman he

was famous for a piece of legislation called the Carter Code Bill, meant to define Indian status. The bill, presented in 1919, provided that "every person of the Indian blood shall be called a citizen of the United States and be subject to all civil and criminal laws, without in any way interfering with his tribal rights, and that he shall, upon his competency being established, receive a patent in fee for his lands" (J. W. Harrington). A contemporary description of Carter presented him as "a valuable member of the Committee on Indian Affairs in Congress, having an intimate knowledge of the red man and the conditions which surround him. He is in favor of the removal of the restrictions on the sale of all Indian lands except the homesteads of full bloods, and believes that there is no reason why an Indian should not work and take care of himself. He maintains that the present paternal system, by which most of the Indians hold their lands and are not subject to taxation, has a tendency toward degeneration and is a policy that has outlived its usefulness" (Chapple 80).

Charles Curtis, of Kaw ancestry, was first elected senator for Kansas in 1907. In 1929 he would be elected vice-president of the United States, in the Hoover administration.

60. This is a reference to the maladministration the Pueblo Indians suffered at the hands of Superintendent Crandall. Oskison contributed to the publicizing of that scandal, which is the subject of "The Little Mother of the Pueblos," reprinted in this volume. The Council of Santa Clara Indians also sent an appeal to the Society of American Indians dated 11 October 1911: "Espanola, NM, Oct. 11, 1911. To Tom L. Sloan, Care American Indian Association in Session, Columbus, Ohio. For seven years many hundreds of cattle belonging to white and Mexican politicians have overrun our reservation and fee simple lands destroying our crops, breaking down our fences, devastating our fields and depriving us of our livelihood. The Indian Office knows all about this, but compels us to endure these outrages. This is but one of the many wrongs inflicted upon the Pueblo Indians by the Indian administration for political advantages. We have protested repeatedly for years, but get nothing but lies and insults in return. We beg of you to help us if it is in your power to do so. (Signed) Santiago Naranjo, Governor of Santa Clara, Victoriano Sisneros, Lieutenant Governor, Leander Tafoya, Chief Principale [*sic*], Francisco Naranjo, ex-Governor, Pedro Baca, ex-Lieutenant Governor, Pedro Cajete, ex-Governor" (qtd. in Johnson 27).

61. Caleb Sickles was an active member of the Society of American Indians. At Carlisle he had been a baseball player. In Tiffin, Ohio, he became a baseball coach at Heidelberg University (Powers-Beck 37). Josiah Powlas graduated from Carlisle in 1891. He was the agency physician at Oneida. Thomas Mani graduated from the University of Minnesota Law School. Edward Rogers, an Anishinaabe,

graduated from Carlisle in 1897 and coached the Carlisle football team in 1904. Oscar Davis might be Dr. O. DeForest Davis, who also gave a paper on the Indian in the Professions just after Oskison at the SAI Conference. Anishinaabe Charles Albert Bender (1883–1954), also known as "Chief" Bender, was a pitcher in Major League Baseball. He pitched for the Philadelphia Athletics between 1903 and 1914 and for the Phillies in 1916 and 1917 (*Encyclopaedia Britannica*).

62. Jacob Morgan, in 1937, would chair the Navajo Tribal Constitutional Committee.

63. Jeffe could not be identified. Hughes is very probably George Hughes, from Tahlequah, I.T., registered as a law student in the Stanford *Fourth Annual Register* (144).

64. Dennis Wolfe Bushyhead (1826–98), of an influential Cherokee family, was principal chief of the Cherokees from 1879 to 1887, that is, at a time when he had to deal with increasing numbers of white intruders, the building of railroads, and the leasing of the Cherokee Outlet (see "Autobiography" n. 60). He had four sons, Jesse C., Dennis W. Jr., James Butler and Francis Taylor. The one Oskison refers to could not be identified with assurance. Jesse C. was a doctor at Claremore in the 1930s (Meserve 357); James Butler was identified as a member of the surveying crew that worked for the Dawes Commission in the Choctaw Nation in 1902 and as a retired St. Louis attorney in 1962 (Oklahoma Historical Society, "Land Surveyors").

65. Little Bison was the son of Chief Big Foot, who was killed in the battle of Little Big Horn. He was educated at the University of Texas. In a speech he gave at a meeting of the League of Political Education in April 1910, he advocated for a more practical education for the Indians, "by means of which they could earn a living" (*New York Times* 7 Apr. 1910). "The Indian has no capital," he said, "and little land, and what there is of that is arid. You have taken from the Indian the buffalo and the deer, by which he was able to live." Little Bison then proceeded to ask financial support to help him take his people to South America, where he had sixteen thousand acres of land, and "where they can take care of themselves." The previous summer he had gone to Nicaragua to arrange for the concession of land with President Zelaya. Several papers reported his arriving at New Orleans from this trip on 24 July, and his announcement that he would "immediately take 100 Indian families to Nicaragua and that this colony will soon be increased by the addition of several hundred other families of North American Indians" (*L'Abeille* 25 Aug. 1909; *St. Paul Dispatch* 24 July 1909; *New York Daily Tribune* 25 July 1909). In January 1910, Little Bison had tried to go to Nicaragua to prepare the coming of eight thousand Sioux Indians. However, he arrived there at a critical moment in the Nicaraguan revolution and was prevented from entering the country by President

Madriz, who had just succeeded Zelaya, and who suspected these newcomers would be recruited in the insurgent army under General Estrada (*New York Times* 7 Feb. 1910). General Estrada, whom Little Bison had managed to meet, agreed to the coming of the Sioux. Estrada would control the government in August 1910. In May 1910, an article published in *L'Abeille de la Nouvelle Orléans* reported that the "colony of red men is doing well, and the future is one of great promise." Back to the United States for a few weeks, Little Bison was planning to go back to his settlement on the headwaters of the Coco River in the interior of Nicaragua, "and to take back with him other Indians to develop the land, to work at rubber plantations, coffee, sheep, cattle and horses." The article added that "two streams of rapid current furnish power for the industrial and dynamic needs of the colony. The waters abound in fish and the country is full of game — wild hog, mountain cow, jaguars." At the time of the article, only five Indians were established in the new territory but Little Bison intended to place about sixty persons in the following year. According to *L'Abeille*, "Little Bison's scheme for redeeming his people from ill health and loss of ambition has the backing of such persons as George Bird Grinnell" among other influential figures (11 May 1910).

66. "The Enduring Qualities of the Indian" was a commencement address Oskison gave at Carlisle on 3 April 1912. The address was titled thus in the table of contents of the issue of *The Red Man*, "a magazine issued in the interest of the Native American by Carlisle," where it was published in May 1912.

67. "The Little Mother of the Pueblos" was first published in *The Delineator* in March 1913.

68. Before serving as day school teacher at Santa Clara from September 1901 to December 1907, Clara D. True, a member of the Woman's Christian Temperance Union, had worked for six years as principal of the BIA boarding school at the Lower Brule Agency on the Sioux Reservation (M. D. Jacobs 197). According to a pamphlet published in 1912 by William Eugene Johnson (1862–1945) — a Friend of the Indian, a Prohibitionist, and a government agent who worked several years in Indian Territory at suppressing the liquor traffic and whom Oskison mentions a few paragraphs below — she arrived at Santa Clara Pueblo with her mother, Mrs. Francis D. True, who had been sent as "government housekeeper" (7). The numerous letters she wrote during this period and sent to the Superintendent of the Santa Fe Indian School are a useful source of information about the conditions of her job there. Johnson was told of their devotion to Clara True by several members of the Santa Clara Pueblo. "Miss True is the only sister that I have," Francisco Naranjo said. "As long as I live, Senora True will be my mother," said Leandro Tafoya. While working at Santa Clara, True, an uplifter in the arts and crafts movement,

encouraged Superintendent Crandall to send Santa Clara potters to the World's Fair in St. Louis in 1904 (201).

Just like William E. Johnson, True occasionally participated in the Lake Mohonk Conference. In 1908 she gave a talk titled "Co-operation with the Government in Indian Affairs." To introduce her, Commissioner Leupp praised her work as he had had the opportunity to witness it during a visit at Santa Clara. He told his audience that while there, the governor and a few of his chief counselors had told him "they were afraid my coming meant that Miss True was to be taken away from them, and they wanted her to stay there as long as she lived! I answered that I could not promise just that, but she should stay until needed somewhere else — until some Indians had a more crying demand for her services than their own." According to him, the Morongo Indians in California had such a crying demand some time later. "Here was a place which had been sadly neglected," he said. "The agency had run down; the liquor evil had become a scourge; the Indians were described to me in the neighborhood as 'good for nothing.' There were a few people among them, who, like the righteous handful in Lot's day might be regarded as redeeming the rest, but they were so very few that it looked like a hopeless case. I needed a good strong man to step in there, take the liquor business by the throat, and carry the boot-leggers and the conscientious dramsellers off to the penitentiary; to teach the Indians to care for their farms and insist upon their being men and not mere government dependents." He concluded that "after studying my field staff over thoroughly, I decided that the very man to do that was Miss Clara True" (1908 *Proceedings Twenty-sixth Lake Mohonk Conference* 25). True thus became superintendent at the Morongo Reservation for two years.

Corroborating Oskison, Jacobs writes that in 1910, True returned to New Mexico "to settle in the Espanola Valley, close to Santa Clara Pueblo, where she remained active in Indian reform in an unofficial capacity" (197). Johnson's pamphlet explains how True struggled against corruption in the BIA. According to Jacobs, in the 1920s "she turned toward condemning what she believed to be the immoral dances of the Pueblos." Jacobs writes that she "believed Indian women to be victimized by supposedly nefarious Indian men, and she sought to rescue them from their degraded condition" (197).

69. This is a reference to the kiva, where the Pueblo Indians hold their ceremonies.

70. William Eugene Johnson wrote in his pamphlet *The Story of Juan Cruz* — which Oskison probably read — that the first winter after her arrival, "a dreadful epidemic of diphtheria of the most malignant type" broke out. "Fourteen children out of the Indian school were buried." Clara D. True and her mother were left alone to help the community. Alone, they "renovated and fumigated sixty Indian homes — every

house in the village. They burned the old bedding and blankets. They pacified and comforted the Indians. They purchased on their own credit new bedding, new blankets, disinfectants, groceries and supplies. They stamped out the epidemic" (7–8).

71. Johnson writes that during the epidemic "Superintendent Crandall, who displayed great energy in keeping away from the danger zone, finally wired Miss True to do the best she could" (7). After the epidemic, Clara True "sought Superintendent Crandall's aid in inducing the Government to re-imburse her for the bedding, blankets and supplies purchased during the epidemic. He flatly refused. 'You had no authority to make those purchases,' he angerly declared, 'and I will just make an example of you for exceeding your authority in this way; you will have to pay for those things yourself" (8).

72. Johnson writes in more detail of a land robbery under Crandall's administration much larger in proportion than what Oskison's figures suggest. The Santa Clara Valley was "judicially determined to mean the 'cañon' of Santa Clara River, and the ninety thousand acres of land [supposed to belong to Santa Clara Pueblo] dwindled to about *nine hundred* acres, which were patented to the Indians" (5). Although this robbery was partly corrected by an "Executive Order" thirty-thousand-acre Indian reservation granted by President Roosevelt after Commissioner Leupp was alerted, Crandall managed to swindle the Indians out of this Executive Order land. He allowed American and Mexican cattleman to have their cattle graze on Indian land so that "American and Mexican politicians . . . took possession of the Indian thirty-thousand-acre reservation and also of their fee simple lands, and held possession for seven years without compensation to the Indians" (5). Johnson also writes of Crandall being accused by Indians of "selling whiskey illegally at his drug store in Santa Fe. They worked up evidence in three good cases against the store and tried to get indictments from the grand jury. The forearm of the grand jury was a partner with Crandall in the drug store. . . . This, together with complaints about their being plundered of their lands, enraged Superintendent Crandall and he started a campaign of revenge" (7).

73. In 1910, Johnson "began operating among these Pueblos in divers ways, all looking to the rooting out of the liquor traffic which was playing havoc among them" (8). Juan Cruz, whom Johnson calls "a young Indian Sir Galahad from Pueblo San Juan" (8), was one of the deputies Johnson hired to help him in his fight against the liquor traffic. Clara True was another one. Johnson tells of "the tragedy of Chamita": "Supt. Crandall advised the rough, drunken Indians that my deputies had no 'authority' and that no attention should be paid to them. Under the inspiration of that advice, four rough Indians of bad character, attacked Juan Cruz, while he was in the act of taking a bottle of whiskey which the leader, Dolores Garcia had

just purchased. The Indians beat Juan with stones and clubs, mashing in his mouth and loosening two of his teeth. Juan drew his revolver and, in defense of his life, fired into the darkness, the bullet hitting Garcia who died an hour later" (10–11).

74. Assistant Commissioner Abbott sent Johnson the following telegram: "Washington, DC, Feb. 9, 1911. Johnson, Special Officer, Care Supt. Perry, Albuquerque, NM. Your telegram seventh, Cruz shooting. Since Cruz not authorized Government employee your service, *take no steps regarding his defense*. Consult Supt. Crandall and give him all information in your possession" (Johnson 11).

75. The Juan Cruz Defense Committee consisted of Mrs. H. M. Byrd of Santa Fe, Mrs. Katherine B. Patterson of Santa Fe, Mary T. Bryan of Espanola, and Clara D. True of Espanola (all from New Mexico). Johnson reproduces the telegram sent him by Commissioner Valentine urging him to "help in his fullest possible protection every way in your power" (12).

76. Johnson claimed he resigned (16–17). His pamphlet suggests that the inspector that Oskison mentions was Shelby M. Singleton. His report is likely to be a damning one for Crandall. In a long letter Johnson wrote to Assistant Secretary of the Interior Samuel Adams, who had accused him of preferring to resign "rather than meet certain definite charges," Johnson wrote that "for the details of this booze peddling superintendent, you only have to refer to the voluminous report of Inspector Shelby M. Singleton, which report has been in your possession for seven months, and which apparently is also 'difficult for you to see'" (20). Johnson corroborates Oskison's reference to secrecy. A few pages further in his letter, Johnson accuses Adams of "concealing the report of Inspector Shelby M. Singleton, detailing the appalling rottenness of your own administration in New Mexico" (23). In a footnote, Johnson tells the reader of his pamphlet that "Inspector Singleton recommended that [Crandall] be dismissed, and since the first edition of this pamphlet was printed, it is announced that he has been 'transferred,' thus fully justifying the accusations of the Indians against him" (23). Singleton also recommended "that the Santa Clara Pueblo Indians be paid $2,000 damages for this seven years of looting" (27). As a conclusion to his letter, Johnson urged Adams to "let everything come out. Suppose that you now give out copies of the big report of Inspector Singleton on the rotten condition of your administration in New Mexico. People are clamoring for it and you are standing them off with letters saying that the 'report is still under discussion,' etc. You have had it 'under discussion' for seven months. Why not turn it loose and let the people 'discuss' it for a while" (25).

77. "An Apache Problem" was first published in the *Quarterly Journal of the Society of American Indians* in April 1913.

78. Geronimo actually died on 17 February 1909. He was about eighty years old.

His grave, marked by a stone pyramid, can be seen within the Fort Sill military complex.

79. Angie Debo and other scholars do not give exactly the same subdivisions of the Apache people. Debo writes that "it is impossible to untangle completely the tribal divisions of the Apaches" (*Geronimo* 9).

80. For firsthand accounts of the events mentioned by Oskison in this essay and of Apache resistance in general, see Geronimo's laconic and Betzinez's detailed autobiographies as well as Eve Ball's *Indeh: An Apache Odyssey*.

81. "They went peacefully" does not reflect Betzinez's version of the episode, according to which the leaders went in shackles while the rest "were formed into a column" before they "started off toward the west" to an unknown destination. Oskison seems to be more accurate in describing the "rocky, desolate waste" that was San Carlos. Betzinez wrote that, nearing their destination, they saw "no horses, cattle, or sheep, for the land would scarcely support any living creature. The land looked parched, barren, and unproductive — quite different from our beautiful Warm Springs reservation." He added that they "were completely downcast over the prospect of having to live in this hot, desolate country" (46).

82. According to Benedict Jozhe, a tribal chairman of the Fort Sill Apaches, "after the dominant leaders of the Chiricahua and Nednai Apaches died or were killed, Geronimo influenced the leaders of these tribes," but "Geronimo was never considered a chief by the Apaches" (430). Taza, Cochise's son, succeeded his father as leader of the Chiricahuas. About Cochise, Jozhe writes that "much has been written about Cochise and his story has had wide coverage on television and in the movies that his story is well known" (430) Suffice it to say that he was a great leader of the Chiricahua Apaches, and that he was one of the leaders in an uprising that began in 1861.

83. Debo calls General George Crook (1828–90) "the greatest Indian fighter ever produced by the United States Army" (*Geronimo* 81). After fighting Indians in the Pacific Northwest, he was placed in charge of Arizona Territory, where he arrived in June 1871. He famously relied on Apache scouts to pursue the rebels. General Nelson Appleton Miles (1839–1925) relieved Crook in 1886. Another Indian fighter, he had participated in several successful campaigns in the 1870s. Captain Henry W. Lawton (1843–99) pursued and brought back Geronimo's band in 1886. The town of Lawton, Oklahoma, which grew next to Fort Sill, is named after him.

84. About Mt. Vernon Barracks, Betzinez writes that while they were there "the Apache prisoners of war had suffered an increasingly high death rate. Finally it was decided to move them to a higher altitude and a drier climate. General Miles suggested that they go to Camp Supply, an old frontier post in Oklahoma which was

scheduled for abandonment. But Captain Hugh L. Scott, who had become known for his good work with the Indians, persuaded Miles that Fort Sill was a better location" (Betzinez 165). Geronimo said that they "were not healthy in this place, for the climate disagreed with us. So many of our people died that I consented to let one of my wives go to the Mescalero agency in New Mexico to live" (Geronimo 157).

85. Captain Witherspoon is probably Edward Taylor Witherspoon. Captain Scott is Hugh Lenox Scott. In 1897, at the Fifteenth Annual Meeting of the Lake Mohonk Conference of Friends of the Indian, Francis E. Leupp (see "Autobiography" n. 170) called Captain Hugh L. Scott, who was in charge of the prisoners of war, "a thorough-going businessman as well as an officer" and "a hearty friend of the Indian" (Leupp, "Among the Indians" 14). The paternalistic figure typical of the federal authority, "in matters of discipline Captain Scott is judge, jury, and executioner" (14). He also made sure to assimilate the Chiricahua Apaches by means of working, making them the main providers of hay for the military and good borers of wells for the neighboring settlements (15).

86. Betzinez, who got an education at Carlisle, expressed in his autobiography a quite positive view of their life at Fort Sill, where the settlement of the Apaches "demonstrated that under proper instruction even wild Indians can be made self-supporting and kept contented" (170). He praises the War Department for this success and adds one more critique of the Department of the Interior and its personnel: "This all happened while the Indians were under the control of the War Department. I have always been convinced that our people did much better under this agency than under the Department of the Interior. Under the latter we were repeatedly deprived of our land and other rights. . . . We had been forcibly taken from our assigned reservation, which had been granted to us in perpetuity, and exiled to a barren land of hostile surroundings and unfriendly Indians and whites. Not until we were made 'prisoners' and supervised by Army officers did we get fair treatment and an opportunity to make something of ourselves" (Betzinez 170). Interestingly, in 1897 an agent for the Indian Rights Association was hinting at the same kind of wariness of the Department of the Interior in dealing with the Chiricahua Apaches of Fort Sill. At the Fifteenth Annual Meeting of the Lake Mohonk Conference of Friends of the Indian held that year, Francis Leupp declared that Captain Hugh L. Scott "could not have done one half what he has done had he been an agent under the Interior Department. He is under the War Department, and that Department is willing to let him alone and allow him to do his duty without political or other interference" ("Among the Indians" 15).

Leupp told the Friends of the Indian about his visit to the Fort Sill Apaches. He explained that the Indian Rights Association had tried to have these Indians settled in North Carolina mountains, "where they could be taught agriculture" (14) but that the governor of that state opposed such settlement on the ground that his state was "a model commonwealth, and that to settle these 'red-handed assassins' there would deal a terrible blow to its peace and good order" (14). When Leupp visited Fort Sill in the summer of 1897, Scott had just "had the Indians build houses for themselves, they cutting the wood and drawing it to the spots where the houses were to be erected. He counseled with them as to the choice of sites, and divided them into villages. The sites were all selected from a sanitary point of view as well as for the landscape, and he has yielded, as far as possible, to the prepossessions of the Indians, so that they would have as little ground for discontent as possible" (14).

Leupp also mentioned Geronimo in his talk at Lake Mohonk: "Geronimo, the big medicine man who was the chief agitator in the time of the last Apache trouble, now does his honest eight hours a day of farm work, and tries to act as if he rather liked it. Moreover, he is wearing the uniform of a United States scout, and taking his place regularly in the inspections and other exercises. Captain Scott has never done anything to degrade Geronimo in the eyes of his former followers, but has simply set him down where he belonged, in the ranks. Geronimo does not wear a chevron on his arm. The men who do have shown special aptitude for their work and a disposition to help their people" (15).

87. The congressmen Oskison refers to are Senator Thomas P. Gore, who was with Robert L. Owen one of the first two senators of Oklahoma, and Charles D. Carter (see n. 59 above), who was elected representative in the Fourth District, where Fort Sill is located, when Oklahoma became a state in 1907. The Fort Sill School of Fire for the Field Artillery, later renamed the U.S. Army Field Artillery School, was created in June 1911.

88. Betzinez tells us that he was one of the six Apaches — "five of them representing the group who wished to move to New Mexico, while I went on behalf of those who preferred to stay in Oklahoma" (193) — to visit the western reservations with Scott.

89. According to Betzinez, he was the only one with a negative report of his visit to the Mescalero Reservation. The other delegates "decided to return to Fort Sill with a favorable report to the tribe" (193). They had been convinced by the "excellent hunting" and by the "three million dollars worth of timber" that the reservation contained according to what the Mescaleros had told them (193). Back from their trip, "a tribal council was called to listen to our reports and recommendations. On the basis of what the other five had to say, the leaders decided that the Apaches would request that they be assigned to the Mescalero reservation" (195).

90. The appropriation bill Oskison mentions was passed on 24 August 1912. Debo explains that this appropriation was indeed "for their settlement on lands to

be selected for them by the secretaries of war and the interior" (*Geronimo* 447). The number of Apaches who stayed vary slightly from one source to another. Betzinez writes that 127 decided to leave and 87 decided to stay. The annual report of the commissioner of Indian Affairs for 1913 makes the following statement: "The survivors of Geronimo's band of Apaches and their descendants, who for many years have been living at Fort Sill, Oklahoma, as prisoners of war, have been released, some going to the Mescalero Apache Reservation in New Mexico, and others remaining in Oklahoma. On 2 April 1913, 183 of these Indians in charge of Major Geo. W. Goode, United States Army, went to Mescalero, where they are now living with this branch of their kindred, under the supervision of the superintendent of the Mescalero Reservation. The transfer of these Indians was made with their consent and under the terms of the act of Congress passed at the last session making the necessary appropriations for the purpose. There were 78 of the band who elected to remain in Oklahoma, where they will be permanently located on allotments provided for them" (34). The following year, the commissioner's report states that "all adult Indians among those who elected to remain in Oklahoma, instead of going to the Mescalero Reservation in New Mexico, as 187 members of the band elected to do during the fiscal year 1913, have been allotted suitable tracts of land which were purchased for them" (56). It goes on to say that "all reports concerning the part of the band remaining in Oklahoma are to the effect that they are now reasonably comfortably situated and bid fair to become industrious, self-supporting Indians." On the other hand, "the part of the band who removed to the Mescalero Reservation in New Mexico have possibly not made so much advancement, but these Indians have been placed in a position to commence farming, and have been reported as fairly comfortable and satisfied during the year" (57). In 1915, the annual report contains a short statement about the allotment of Fort Sill Apaches: "Of the survivors and descendants of Geronimo's Band of Apaches, formerly held as prisoners of war at Fort Sill, Okla., 187 removed to the Mescalero Reservation, N. Mex., and 84 stayed in Oklahoma, where suitable tracts of from 80 to 160 acres have been purchased for 69 of them. This leaves 15 yet to be provided for when additional funds have been procured for this purpose" (29). On top of the $200,000 appropriated in August 1912, $100,000 more were appropriated by act of Congress on 30 June 1913 (104).

91. Oskison deals with the Fort Sill Apache's lot again in "The New Indian Leadership" below.

92. "Acquiring a Standard of Value" was an address delivered before the Third Annual Conference of the Society of American Indians at Denver, Colorado. It was published in the *Quarterly Journal of the Society of American Indians* in 1914.

93. The Harveyizing process is a metallurgical process invented by H. A. Harvey

in which "carbon is absorbed by iron at temperatures well below the point of fusion" (Aston 570). It was mostly used in the naval industry. The purpose of the process was to strengthen armor plates used in the building of ships. In Oskison's mind, the process is to be likened to amalgamation, a word he used to refer to the Indians' integration to American society.

94. At the time, Arizona had only one representative, Democrat Carl Hayden, who would be known for his career-long support for reclamation projects. The 1914 annual report of the commissioner of Indian Affairs states that the Indian Office received "the report of the Board of Engineer Officers upon the proposed San Carlos Dam and irrigation project" and that "upon the suggestion of this office an item was included in the Indian appropriation act for sufficient funds for completing the investigation shown in the report as necessary before proceeding with actual construction of the project" (38). In table 32 of this report, titled "Buildings, etc., under construction during fiscal year ended June 30, 1914," the construction of "2 steel highway bridges over Gila and San Carlos Rivers, White Mountain Reservation" is noted, for a cost of $53,600 (174). Two years later, the commissioner would report that "construction and maintenance of roads on the several reservations by the use of tribal funds and general appropriations have been developed as rapidly as practicable. A good road has been built on the San Carlos Reservation between bridges across the San Carlos and Gila Rivers by the use of $20,000 appropriated by the State of Arizona" (1916 *Report Commissioner Indian Affairs* 51–52).

95. The original footnote read as follows: "Mr. Vincent Natalish, an Apache and a civil engineer, has studied this situation carefully for the Indian Bureau and has reported his findings."

Vincent Natalish was a grandson of Apache leader Victorio. He was educated at Carlisle, from which he graduated in 1899 and where he was trained to be a civil engineer. He also studied at Yale. He became a supervisor of Indian instruction and helped establish many schools among the Apaches, notably in Arizona (*New York Times* 15 Dec. 1912, 6 Oct. 1922). Oskison mentions him in "The New Indian Leadership."

96. Rev. Sherman Coolidge (1862–1932), an Arapaho Indian, was a founding member of the Society of American Indians and its president for a few years (Iverson 108). As a child, Runs-on-top was taken captive by the Bannocks and later adopted by Captain Charles A. Coolidge and his wife, who renamed him Sherman Coolidge. His foster parents sent him to Shattuck Military School in Faribault, Minnesota. He later attended Seabury Divinity School near Chicago. In 1884, Henry Whipple ordained him a deacon in the Episcopal Church (Peyer, *American Indian Nonfiction* 349).

97. "Arizona and Forty Thousand Indians" was first published in *Southern Workman* in March 1914. The text was illustrated with five photographs: the first, untitled, showed an Indian wearing a headband and sitting on the ground of an arid landscape (148); another one showed "Chief Yuma Frank of the Fort McDowell Apaches" (151); a third showed "an Apache papoose" in a cradle carried on a woman's back (153); a fourth showed "Apache basket-makers" (154); the fifth showed "Indian hunters in the hills east of the Verde" (155).

98. Strangely enough, the annual reports of the commissioner of Indian Affairs do not mention this incident. A 19 November 1913 *New York Times* article says that "recalcitrant Navajos . . . have been defying the law for the last two months" and that "in the hope that the excited Navajo Indians, who are now defying the Government authorities at Beautiful Mountain, NM, may be induced to yield peaceably and surrender the eight renegades sought to be arrested, the War Department today ordered Gen. Hugh L. Scott, commanding the Second Cavalry Brigade at Fort Bliss, Texas, who has great influence with them, to proceed to confer with the Indian chiefs." "To back Gen. Scott's mission with a show of force," it was also decided to dispatch a squadron of the Twelfth Cavalry. Berger tells us that the whole incident started with the story of Bi-joshi, a Navajo who wanted to marry a woman from Ship Rock but who was unwilling to leave her family to go live with him at Beautiful Mountain, New Mexico. "So it was arranged that he would marry her two sisters as well. In 1913, however, the Indian agent William T. Shelton ordered two of the sisters to go away. Bi-joshi refused to comply, and the three sisters were arrested while the father and the son were away. When they came with several others to free the women, Shelton claimed it was a rebellion, and General Hugh Scott and Twelfth Cavalry came to his aid. Bi-joshi ultimately surrendered to prevent bloodshed, and the Navajo men who participated were jailed for twenty days for unlawful assembly" (37).

99. Democrat Carl Hayden was the representative for the state of Arizona; Henry F. Ashurst and Marcus A. Smith, both Democrats, were the senators.

100. Senator Albert B. Fall, a Republican, was senator of New Mexico from 1912 to 1921.

101. Dr. Montezuma (c. 1866–1923) was born Wassaja. His biographer, Peter Iverson, calls him "one of the most famous Indians of his day" (3). He was born among the Yavapai Indians (also known as the Mohave-Apaches) in Arizona. At the age of four or five he was taken captive by the Pima Indians. Later he was adopted by an Italian American named Carlo Gentile, who baptized Wassaja Carlos Montezuma. He attended schools in Chicago and in New York, enrolled at the University of Illinois, and later became a physician. He served in the Bureau of Indian Affairs, later

became a member of the Society of American Indians, within which he advocated the end of the Indian Service and of governmental paternalism, and is remembered as one of the most prominent activists of Indian rights. For more on Montezuma's work for the Arizona Indians, see in particular chapter 6, "Indian Rights and Water Rights in Southern Arizona," of Iverson's biography.

102. For the Gila River issue, see n. 19 above; for the San Carlos dam issue, see n. 94 above.

103. The commissioner of Indian Affairs reported in 1914 that "approximately 42,700 head of cattle belonging to cattlemen are being cared for" on the San Carlos Reservation and "about 21,375 cattle and 52,000 sheep" on the Fort Apache Reservation (1914 *Report Commissioner Indian Affairs* 29).

104. See "Acquiring a Standard of Value."

105. The issue of water rights appears in several of Oskison's texts. In fact, the issue was of paramount importance and the source of many conflicts and sufferings in the last decade of the nineteenth century and at least the first two decades of the twentieth. In 1913, as well as in subsequent reports, Commissioner of Indian Affairs Cato Sells calls the attention of the authorities on the problem. "The Indian water-right situation on a large number of reservations is such as to demand most serious consideration," he writes. He explains that "unfortunately, legislation has been enacted by Congress which makes beneficial use of water on Indian lands within certain reservations necessary, if the water rights are to be held by the Indians. Congress has provided appropriations for constructing expensive irrigation projects on several reservations, reimbursable out of Indian funds, and the Indians are required to make beneficial use of the water on said reservations within a limited time. If this is not done they will be in danger of losing their water rights and forfeiting the same to subsequent appropriators of the water. On a large number of the reservations agricultural lands are practically valueless without water" (4–5). Then, Commissioner Sells recommends a principle similar to the one underlying the allotment system: "The Government holds the allotment lands in trust for the benefit of Indians for a period of 25 years, because of the fact that they are deemed incompetent to protect their property rights. It seems equally important to conserve the water rights of the Indians, at the same time encouraging them to make beneficial use of the water by farming their allotments" (5). Furthermore, the commissioner remarks that "Indian tribal funds have been used in construction and maintenance of irrigation projects, and that only a certain portion of the Indians have received any benefit from the irrigation systems" (5).

106. "The Closing Chapter: Passing of the Old Indian" was first published in *Munsey's* magazine in 1914 and reprinted that May in *The Indian Leader*.

107. Numbers of pre-contact Native American population, obviously, are only estimates. These estimates have varied along with the evolution of twentieth-century research. Today, most researchers agree that the Indian population in North America was closer to 4 million individuals (Denevan).

108. The death rate found in the 1913 annual report of the commissioner of Indian Affairs is "32.24 per thousand, while the Census Bureau gives 16 per thousand in the registration area of the United States" (3–4). Tuberculosis is reported to be responsible for 32 percent of the whole number of deaths reported from the various Indian reservations (3).

109. The numbers of the annual report for the fiscal year ending in June 1914 are corroborating Oskison's numbers except for the evaluation of Indian land and property. The Indian Office estimate is even higher, at $900 million.

110. Oskison probably got some of his numbers from the annual report for the fiscal year ended on 30 June 1913, although some variations can be found. Notably, the report's number of Indian employees in the Indian Service is 5,693. The school numbers found in the report, however, corroborate Oskison's: the report counts 223 day schools; 76 boarding schools located on the reservations, and 35 boarding schools located off the reservations, a total of 111 boarding schools; 58,721 children in all kinds of schools, including 25,000 in boarding schools and 22,500 in mission and public schools. The commissioner also reports that 82,470 children are of school age, taking note of a lack of schools "leaving 17,500 normal and defective Indian children unprovided for." The report states that the government has spent $80,000,000 for Indian schools since 1876 (3, 154–59).

As far as allotment is concerned, the 1913 report numbers vary slightly from Oskison's. Commissioner Cato Sells writes that "it is estimated that there have been allotted to 180,000 Indians about 34,000,000 acres and there remain to be allotted about 39,000,000 acres. There are nearly 120,000 unallotted Indians. There has been expended for allotment work heretofore completed about $4,500,000, and it is believed that it will require at least $3,000,000 to complete the allotment work." Besides, the commissioner thought that "the earliest possible completion of the allotment work is desirable, as it is the main chance of perhaps 70 per cent of the Indians to become self-supporting, and this work is also preliminary to the opening of reservations. The settlement of white people in the Indian country will result in very materially increasing the value of the lands retained by the Indians as their allotments, for it will be the means of locating therein free schools, churches, good roads, and other agencies of a modern and progressive community" (2).

111. The theory has actually existed for much longer. Some early missionaries saw in the Indians' physical features, traditions, and languages signs that reminded them

of the traditions and languages of the Hebrews. In 1634, Roger Williams—English missionary, friend of the Narragansett Indians, and founder of Rhode Island—wrote in *A Key into the Language of America* that he and others "have conceived some of their words to hold affinity with the Hebrew. Secondly, they constantly anoint their heads as the Jews did. Thirdly, they give dowries for their wives, as the Jews did. Fourthly (and which I have not so observed amongst other nations as amongst the Jews, and these:) they constantly separate their women (during the time of their monthly sickness) in a little house alone by themselves four or five days, and hold it an irreligious thing for either father or husband or any male to come near them" (229). In an attempt at being scientifically balanced, Williams also mentions other theories of the origin of the Indians, one tracing it to Iceland, another to Mongolia. He also mentions "a greater affinity of their language with the Greek tongue" (229). In 1683, William Penn wrote that as far as the origin of the Indians is concerned, "I am ready to believe them of the Jewish race, I mean of the stock of the ten tribes, and that for the following reasons: first, they were to go to a land not planted nor known, which to be sure Asia and Africa were, if not Europe; and he who intended that extraordinary judgment upon them might make the passage not uneasy for them, as it is *not impossible in itself from the easternmost parts of Asia to the westernmost of America*" (150; emphasis in original). He then gives other reasons that have to do with similar physical features and similar customs and rituals.

In the eighteenth and nineteenth centuries, though it was debated, the theory was quite popular among leading missionaries and intellectuals. In 1775, James Adair, defined on the title page of his book as "a trader with the Indians, and Resident in their Country for Forty Years," published *The History of the American Indians.* He introduces a chapter entitled "Observations, and Arguments, in Proof of the American Indians Being Descended from the Jews" by saying that "a number of particulars present themselves in favour of a Jewish descent" (15). His first argument is that the Indians live in tribes: "As the Israelites were divided into Tribes, and had chiefs over them, so the Indians divide themselves" (15). Then he argues that, like the Hebrews, who "were ordered to worship at Jerusalem, *Jehovah* the true and living God," and unlike the "ancient heathens," who "worshipped a plurality of gods," the Indians "pay their religious devoir to *Loak-Ishtohoollo-Aba*, 'the great, beneficent, supreme, holy spirit of fire,' who resides (as they think) above the clouds, and on earth also with unpolluted people. He is with them the sole author of warmth, light, and of all animal and vegetable life. They do not pay the least perceivable adoration to any images, or to dead persons; neither to the celestial luminaries, nor evil spirits, nor any created being whatsoever. They are utter strangers to all the gestures practised by the pagans in their religious rites" (18–19). Other arguments, which

Adair develops at length, were that "the Indian *language*, and *dialects*, appear to have the very idiom and genius of the *Hebrew*" (37; emphasis in original); that the Indians "count Time after the manner of the Hebrews" (74); that "in conformity to, or after the manner of the Jews, the Indian Americans have their Prophets, High-Priests, and others of a religious order" (80); that "their Festivals, Fasts, and Religious Rites, have also a great resemblance to those of the Hebrews" (94); that "the Indians have customs consonant to the Mosaic Laws of Uncleanness. They oblige their women in their *lunar retreats*, to build small huts, at as considerable a distance from their dwelling-houses, as they imagine may be out of the enemies reach, where, during the space of that period, they are obliged to stay at the risque of their lives" (123); etc.

In 1819 an English traveler to the United States, Emanuel Howitt, wrote that "from what I have seen and read of [the Indians] since my arrival in this country, I am perfectly convinced of the justice of Wm. Penn's bold conjecture, at his first acquaintance with them, 'that they are descendants of the *Lost ten tribes of Israel*'" (161–62). Although Howitt admits that he might be seen as too credulous and confesses "our propensity to enlist our imaginations in the cause of our inclinations to the marvelous, and to warp every little coincidence in those we contemplate with those whom we seek, till they appear striking marks and conclusive evidences," he continues by stating that he has been convinced "before the vast body of evidence now collected, and collected too from a great variety of most authentic and respectable sources" (162). Hoping that this theory "will prove a means of causing us to regard these 'children of the Great Spirit' with a more favorable and brotherly eye," Howitt asserts that he "cannot entertain a doubt, but that he whose eye surveys the universe, conducted these tribes from the midst of nations with whom it was impossible they could ever amalgamate, into this great western wilderness, and has here fulfilled upon them many of his predicted judgments" (162–63). Although Penn's idea of the origin of the Indians, as well as "that of a passage from Asia, was extremely ridiculed," according to Howitt, "subsequent discoveries have however proved the latter, and it is remarkable that almost all travelers and missionaries have added their corroborative testimony to the former" (166). This "evidence" was collected in what Howitt seems to consider the authoritative work on the subject, a volume by one "Dr. Boudinot of Philadelphia," of whom he proceeds to quote long passages for his readers in England.

In 1816, Elias Boudinot (1740–1821), president of the Continental Congress from 1782 to 1783, had published *A Star in the West: A Humble Attempt to Discover the Long Lost Ten Tribes of Israel Preparatory to their Return to their Beloved City, Jerusalem*, a substantial book corroborating former proponents of the theory and in which Boudinot also founded his conclusions on similarities observed, notably by the first Spanish visitors, between the Indian and Hebrew languages, customs, and practices.

Pequot author William Apess subscribed to the theory. In the appendix to his autobiography, *A Son of the Forest*, the purpose of which is to provide the reader with "some general observations on the origin and character of the Indians" (52), he writes that "when I take into consideration the many ancient usages and customs observed religiously by them, and which have so near and close resemblance to the manners, etc., of the ancient Israelites, I am led to believe that they are none other than the descendants of Jacob and the long lost tribes of Israel" (53). He then quotes Boudinot's *A Star in the West* at length. Of particular interest to the Pequot writer is a remark by Boudinot about Apess's very tribe: "This nation of Pequods were a principal nation of the east, and very naturally reminds one of the similarity of the same name in Jeremiah 50:21, where the inhabitants of Pekod are particularly mentioned; and also in Ezekiel 23:23. The difference in spelling one with a *k*, and the other with a *q*, is no uncommon thing. The Indian languages being very guttural, the *k* is generally used where an Englishman would use the *q*" (Boudinot 141, qtd. in Apess 56). Apart from Boudinot, his main source, Apess cites quite a few writers who subscribe to the theory, "as some of the best writers of the age," according to him, such as John West, who lived among Indians in the 1820s. West, described on the title page of his journal as "late chaplain to the Hon. The Hudson's Bay Company," writes of the Anishinaabeg that "they have customs, such as separation for forty days at the birth of a child, setting apart the female in a separate lodge at peculiar seasons, and forbidding her to touch any articles in common use, which bear a strong resemblance to the laws of uncleanness, and separation commanded to be observed towards Jewish females. These strongly corroborate the idea, that they are of Asiatic origin; descended from some of the scattered tribes of the children of Israel: and through some ancient transmigration, came over by Kamtchatka into these wild and extensive territories" (55). In 1831 Apess published an essay titled *The Indians: The Ten Lost Tribes* in which he very assertively writes: "That the Indians are indeed no other than the descendants of the ten lost tribes, the subscriber has no doubt" (114).

What makes this theory interesting is obviously not its scientific value but how its proponents used it. As Apess put it, if indeed the Indians were the descendants of Israel, it would prove that, "though cast off for their heinous transgressions, they have not been altogether forsaken and will hereafter appear to have been, in all their dispersions and wanderings, the subjects of God's divine protection and gracious care" (*A Son* 53). In a context where the Indians were most of the time dehumanized, presenting them as the descendants of a people protected by God was a welcome change for many missionaries and Indian intellectuals.

112. The Prince Madoc legend is another extraordinary one. According to historian Gwyn A. Williams, "the Madoc story first appeared in print in the 1580s." The story asserted that "America had first been discovered by a Welshman, Madoc, son of Owain Gwynedd . . . in 1170. He had returned to Wales in the grip of a civil war and carried away settlers on a second journey." Gwyn Williams published a letter that Sir Walter Raleigh wrote in 1595 from the "Island of Trinadada [*sic*]," an island he had just conquered from the Spaniards. To justify this action, he calls the Spaniards usurpers of lands first conquered by a British prince. As Raleigh explains, "the great and valiant Prince Madock ap Owen Guyneth . . . being provided with a powerfull fleete and Men of War, . . . takeing with him Many Noble Brittons both of Wales and of the Northern race besides Valliant Men from Irland and other adventurers for new and great discoverys, did first come into these Seas in the year of Salvation . . . 1164 and the second time in 1170 and did Make notable discovery conquest and settlements of all the Parts of the said great Continent of America and of all the Islands round that Mighty tract of Land and in all the seas, from the Latitude of 36 degrees North all along and round the saide Continente Unto this said Island of Trinadada passing unto Guyeneth, Guyneth or Guyannah, to which Vast Space of Country he, the said prince Madock ap Owen Guyneth gave his own Name . . . now corrupted and Calld Guyannah" (Williams 138). Thus Madock, or Modoc, had preceded Columbus by more than three centuries. If Raleigh is to be believed, not only was Columbus late, but Hernán Cortés, conqueror of the Aztecs, unwittingly conquered a people descendant of the Welsh and Britons. Indeed, the lands claimed by Raleigh included the "great, wealthy and vast Empire of Mexico (otherwise The Empire of Madock) which he, the said Madock ap Owen Guyneth did first conquer and People with his Welshmen and his Brittons and his tribes of brave adventurers, from whence he did carry into Wales three Several times Mighty store of massey silver and gold, precious stones, diamonds and emeralds etc etc. And his race thereafter reigned Emperors of Mexico until Montazuma." Raleigh further argued that, according to several testimonies, "the Mexican Tongue, their habits, manners and various British Customs still remain amongst the Descendants of the first Welsh Settlers in Mexico at this day, 431 since the Royal Race of Prince Owen Gwyneth possessed the Mexican Empire" (Williams 138).

In the seveenteenth century, the story claimed that "Welsh-speaking Indians, clearly descendants of Madoc's men, were said to have been encountered on the American mainland" (Williams 140). The legend would live on, told and told again in many explorers' relations. Williams counted that by 1900 at least fifteen Indian languages had been identified as Welsh.

One of these accounts can be found in the journal of a British missionary. In 1764, missionary Charles Beatty published his journal of a tour among the Indians in Pennsylvania. In a footnote, he relates the story of one Benjamin Sutton he met in the Allegheny Mountains: Sutton "had been taken captive by the Indians, had been in different nations, and lived many years among them. He informed us, when he was with the Choctaw Nation, or Tribe of Indians, at the Mississippi river, he went to an Indian town, a very considerable distance from New-orleans, whose inhabitants were of different complexions, not so tawny as those of the other Indians, and who spoke Welch. He said he saw a book among them, which he supposed was a Welch [*sic*] bible, which they carefully kept wrapped up in a skin, but that they could not read it; and that he heard some of those Indians afterwards in the Lower Shawanaugh town, speak Welch with one Lewis, a Welchman, captive there. This Welch tribe now live on the west side of the Mississippi river, a great way above New-orleans" (24–25). Beatty then adds elements corroborating the existence of a Welsh tribe: "Levi Hicks, before mentioned, as being among the Indians from his youth, told us he had been, when attending an embassy, in a town of Indians, on the west of Mississippi river, who talked Welch (as he was told, for he did not understand them); and our interpreter, Joseph, saw some Indians, whom he supposed to be of the same tribe, who talked Welch, for he told us some of the words they said, which he knew to be Welch, as he had been acquainted with some Welch people" (25). Beatty proceeds by relating a story he heard of an unnamed clergyman, maybe the Welsh preacher Oskison refers to, who, "many years ago, . . . went from Britain to Virginia, and having lived some time there, went from thence to South Carolina; but, either because the climate did not agree with him, or for some other reason, resolved to return to Virginia, and accordingly set out by land, accompanied with some other persons; but travelling through the back parts of the country, which was then very thinly inhabited, . . . he fell in with a party of Indian warriors, going to attack the inhabitants of Virginia, against whom they had declared war. The Indians, upon examining the clergyman, and finding that he was going to Virginia, looked upon him and his companions as belonging to Virginia, and therefore took them all prisoners, and let them know they must die. The clergyman, in preparation for another world, went to prayer, and, being a Welchman, prayed in the Welch language. . . . One or more of the party of the Indians was much surprised to hear him pray in their language. — Upon this they spake [*sic*] to him, and finding that he could understand their speech, they got the sentence of death reversed — and thus this happy circumstance was the means of saving his life. They took him back with them into their country, where he found a tribe, whose native language was Welch, though the dialect was a little different from his own, which he soon came to understand. They shewed . . . him a book, which he found to be a bible, but which they could not read, and, if I mistake not, his ability to read it tended to raise their regard for him" (25–26).

Welsh ancestry of Native Americans was still asserted in the nineteenth century, notably in the writings of artist George Catlin, after eighteenth- and nineteenth-century explorers reported their encounters with blond Mandan Indians. Blondism, as well as "other non-Indian physical traits, an unusual language and mythology, fortified villages and a developed horticulture provided the evidence" for the theory (Newman 255).

113. Scientific truth about legendary figures Dekanawida and Hiawatha has not been easy to determine, in spite of the work of two early ethnologists who attempted to separate history from legend, Seneca Arthur C. Parker and Tuscarora J. N. B. Hewitt. According to Emily Davis, who wrote about Hewitt's work, it seems clear at least that the Hiawatha of the famous poem by Longfellow had little to do with the real Hiawatha, an Iroquois who, in the mid-sixteenth century, served as a mouthpiece for Dekanawida. Together, they told of the latter's "dream of brotherhood, to band together the Iroquois tribes and eventually all the world" (123). At the end of three decades of campaigning, the Iroquois Confederacy gathered five — the Mohawk, Oneida, Onondaga, Cayuga, and Seneca — then six — with the Tuscarora — Indian nations from the northeastern region of present-day United States and southeastern region of present-day Canada. According to legend, Dekanawida was a messenger from the Creator, born of a virgin mother. Davis and others argue that this first confederacy inspired the founding fathers to form the United States. According to Renée Jacobs, the Great Law of Peace — commonly called Iroquois Constitution — "provided for federalism, separation of powers, equitable distribution of wealth, accountability of elected officials, freedom of assembly, speech, and religion, and a system of natural rights that influenced thinkers like Benjamin Franklin, Jean-Jacques Rousseau, and Frederick Engels" (497). Another remarkable feature of the Great Law was the place accorded women in the political process. The U.S. Congress acknowledged the influence of the Great Law on the U.S. Constitution in 1988.

Dee Brown calls Red Cloud (Mahpiua-luta) the "outstanding leader" of the Oglala Tetons (10). In the 1860s, with other leaders such as Crazy Horse and Spotted Tail, he had taken up arms against the opening of the Bozeman Trail across Sioux territories. This would be remembered as "Red Cloud's War," or the "Powder River War" (1866–68). In 1868 he negotiated the terms of the Treaty of Fort Laramie. The 1871 report of the commissioner of Indian Affairs stated that Red Cloud's Indians had "abandoned the war-path in the spring of 1870" (1871 *Report Commissioner Indian Affairs* 13). However, the commissioner wrote, "the Sioux are extremely sensitive in regard to the slightest encroachment upon their reservation, or the hunting grounds allotted to them in the treaty of 1868. . . . They are impressed with the conviction that where one white man is allowed to enter their territory many will inevitably follow" (13). It was conceded that "in view of their experience, we cannot think them unreasonable in this" (13). The same report includes one of a council held at Fort Laramie on 12 June 1871 during a visit to the Oglala by Special Commissioner Felix R. Brunot. Red Cloud started the council in the following way: "I am Red Cloud. The Great Spirit raised both the white man and the Indian. I think he raised the Indian first. He raised me in this land and it belongs to me. The white man was raised over the great waters, and his land is over there. Since they crossed the sea, I have given them room. There are now white people all about me. I have but a small spot of land left. The Great Spirit told me to keep it" (23). During this council, Red Cloud resisted the establishment of an agency: "I have consulted the Great Spirit, and do not want a strange man for agent. There are plenty of men who can read and write, who are married to my people, and they can take care of me and my agency, and I can put my own young men to work" (24). At the end of the 1880s and the beginning of the 1890s, during the Ghost Dance movement, which the whites interpreted as a hostile movement, Red Cloud acted as a peacemaker. According to Robert Larson, although Red Cloud was sympathetic to the hopes his people had in the Ghost Dance, he was never involved in it and actually "grew uncomfortable with the increasingly frenzied movement" (22). In December 1890, just before the Wounded Knee Massacre, he met with other Sioux leaders "to discuss ways of diffusing the crisis" (23).

During the Revolutionary War, Joseph Brant (a Mohawk leader), Red Jacket, and Cornplanter (two Seneca leaders), sided with the British.

Cornplanter (Ga-yan-ta-wan-ka or Kayenthoghke) was chief warrior of the Senecas and half brother to Handsome Lake, the Seneca prophet. One of his biographers, Thomas Abler, writes that "Cornplanter and his generation experienced the turmoil and destruction of war and the need to alter their entire way of life in response to the extensive settlement of their former territories by non-Indians after the American Revolution. They had to decide whether they should adopt the teachings of Christian missionaries, and whether Seneca children should attend formal schools to acquire the language and literacy of their new neighbors. They had to learn new skills to survive within the transformed economic landscape these new neighbors had brought with them" (4). In 1784, a year after the British defeat stated by the 1783 Treaty of Paris, he signed the rather harsh peace treaty of Fort Stanwix with the Americans, by which the Indians ceded huge territories in the Ohio Valley and in New York. Cornplanter returned to meet angry crowds. During further negotiations with the

United States in the 1790s, Cornplanter became wary and more vigilant, declaring, e.g., to a U.S. envoy that the Senecas considered the proceedings of previous treaties "as unjust" (qtd. in Campisi and Starna 478). In 1794 he refused to sign the Treaty of Canandaigua because he thought that the Six Nations had been deceived by the Treaty of Fort Stanwix (483).

During the Revolutionary War, Joseph Brant led a band of Mohawks to Canada. Brant was a respected statesman who had attended Dartmouth, the famous school directed by Eleazar Wheelock and partly funded by Samson Occom's fund-raising tour in Britain. He also remained wary of U.S. intentions regarding the Iroquois.

114. Red Jacket (c. 1750–1830), or Sagoyewatha, was a Seneca leader. William Stone, his first biographer, wrote: "That he was an orator, in the most exalted sense of the term, of great and commanding power, is the universal testimony of all who enjoyed opportunities of forming a just opinion on the subject" (2). Jadviga da Costa Nunes calls him "a brilliant Seneca orator who attempted to diminish the encroaching tide of white civilization upon the Indian's land and way of life after the Revolutionary War" (5). After Cornplanter ceded land by the Treaty of Fort Stanwix, Red Jacket "began to assume a role of leadership among his people by capitalizing on Cornplanter's misfortune" (5). Jack Campisi and William Starna explain that when, at the beginning of the 1790s, the United States endeavored to secure Iroquois neutrality regarding the conflicts with western tribes such as the Miami, Red Jacket was one of the leaders who remained cautious of U.S. intentions (473).

115. Metacom is also known as Metacomet and as King Philip. He was a leader of the Wampanoag tribe. In June 1675 what is known as King Philip's War started. It ended the following year. In this war, Metacom had federated several New England tribes and spread the fight across Massachusetts and the Connecticut Valley. The Indians had many victories and came close to eradicating the English presence on their territories. Thousands of people, English and Indians from several tribes, were killed. Entire English villages were destroyed.

Massasoit, Metacom's father, was the tribe's leader when the Pilgrim fathers settled at Plymouth. In March 1621 he sent Samoset and Squanto as ambassadors to the newcomers to welcome them and start diplomacy. He signed a treaty of peace with John Carver, first governor of Plymouth Colony. Massasoit allowed the English to stay and entertained with them a friendly relationship until his death in 1660.

116. Osceola opposed removal of the Seminoles from Florida and fought during what is known as the Second Seminole War (1835–42). He was captured under a white flag during a meeting he had asked for with the American military in order to discuss peace terms (Boyd 295–97). He died at Fort Moultrie in 1838, as George Catlin was painting his portrait (303–4). An editorial from the *Charleston Courier*

dated 6 January 1838, a few days after Osceola's arrival at Fort Moultrie, shows how sympathetic the public had been to his cause: "In our humble opinion, he has been to the full, as much sinned against as sinning. Treacherous he may have been, but we cannot forget that he was provoked by treachery, and captured by treachery. We are fairly even with him. We now owe him the respect which the brave ever feel toward the brave; which the victorious cannot violate without brutality towards the vanquished, which the commonest laws of humanity and civilization enforce towards prisoners of war. We sincerely trust that no citizen of Charleston will so far forget the character of a Carolinian, as to offer indignity to a fallen man. A tear of forgiveness and generous sympathy is much better due to the once terrible, now stricken warrior of the Seminoles" ("Osceola and the Charlestonians" 247–48).

117. Tecumseh (1768–1813) was a Shawnee leader who, with his brother Tenskwatawa, attempted to unite Indian tribes against U.S. expansionism. In 1938 Oskison published a biography of Tecumseh titled *Tecumseh and His Times*. He wrote in its foreword that Tecumseh "was the dreamer of a hopeless dream which other Indian leaders, from Dekanawida to Pontiac, had fought to turn into reality. Though he lived to see its frustration, he followed it straightforwardly and courageously to the inevitable end — his death while battling for the right of his red brothers to live in freedom according to their own conception" (vii). Tecumseh died during the Battle of the Thames in 1813.

118. Black Hawk (1767–1838), a leader of the Sacs and Foxes, resisted white encroachment and removal west of the Mississippi in what history remembers as the "Black Hawk War" (1832). In 1833, Black Hawk decided to resist white definitions of himself and his war and related his version in an autobiography written with the help of interpreter Antoine LeClair. In a note before Black Hawk's pages, the editor wrote about the motivations of the author: "Several accounts of the late war having been published, in which he thinks justice is not done to himself or nation, he determined to make known to the world, the injuries his people have received from the whites — the causes which brought on the war on the part of his nation, and a general history of it throughout the campaign. In his opinion, this is the only method now left him, to rescue his little Band — the remnant of those who fought bravely with him — from the effects of the statements that have already gone forth" (Black Hawk 38).

According to Black Hawk, Keokuk was the "war-chief" at the time resistance started. Black Hawk said that when Keokuk consented to leave their village on the eastern side of the Mississippi, he "raised the standard of opposition to Ke-o-kuk, with a full determination not to leave my village" (99). Keokuk failed to convince Black Hawk to comply with the U.S. demands.

119. Sitting Bull (Tatanka Yotanka) was a great leader of the Hunkpapa Sioux. He resisted white encroachments all his life, participating in several wars against the white man, such as the Powder River War along with Red Cloud, and the War for the Black Hills in 1876. He was among the victors of General Custer at the Little Bighorn. Sitting Bull was killed outside his tent during his arrest by the Indian police on 15 December 1890, at the height of the Ghost Dance and less than two weeks before the Wounded Knee massacre.

Dee Brown writes of Spotted Tail, spokesman for the Brulé Tetons, that "he enjoyed his way of life and the land he lived upon, but was willing to compromise to avoid war" (10). With Red Cloud and Sitting Bull, Spotted Tail resisted the opening of the Bozeman Trail and the invasion of the Black Hills as long as he could, although he was lured into signing treaties (Debo, *A History* 233; D. Brown 142, 279). Spotted Tail was assassinated by another Brulé, Crow Dog, in 1881.

The best and most objective source of information about Little Crow is probably Gary Clayton Anderson's biography of this Mdewakanton Sioux leader, chosen by his people to be their spokesman to the white men. After doing what he could to avoid the war — "Little Crow realistically saw accommodation as a viable and necessary alternative to resistance" (Anderson 4) — Little Crow finally led his band into the 1862 Sioux uprising in Minnesota. He was shot by a settler in July 1863.

120. Dr. William Torrey Harris (1835–1909), who served as commissioner of education from 1889 to 1906, called the Indians "Homeric children." In *The Indian and His Problem*, Francis E. Leupp comments on this phrase. According to him, it was a way for Harris to answer the characterization of the Indians as treacherous by nature. Leupp explains how he understands Harris's phrase: the Indians "have an oriental code of ethics which holds hospitality so sacred that if an Indian takes you into his home as a guest you are absolutely under his protection during your stay. But the same code which rigidly recognizes the rights and privileges of friendship, and even one's duty toward the stranger who is temporarily sharing one's camp, ignores every consideration in the treatment of an enemy except the desire to inflict upon him any injury possible. The maxim, 'all's fair in war,' often current among whites who carry honor to the extreme of generosity in dealing with a foe, to an Indian means what it says. His mind is of the simple type which in a hostile atmosphere knows no sentimental restraints, but despises all forms except such as may be needed to mislead an intended victim. Remove the alluring gloss which poesy has spread over the conduct of the worthies who figured in the siege of Troy, and do we find any larger element of virtuous motive there than in the standards respected by our aboriginal race? Yet Homer's people we do not denounce as innately vicious because the stage which human development had reached in their era failed to foreshadow some of the best features of our modern civilization" (6–7).

121. About the Apache leaders, see "An Apache Problem."

122. Chief Joseph was a leader of the Nez Percés. When in the mid-1870s, contrary to treaty terms, white encroachment increased on lands reserved for the Nez Percés in northeastern Oregon, violence occurred, although Joseph advised against it. In July 1877, in order to escape war and find freedom, he decided to take his people to Canada through Montana. This three-month flight with the U.S. Army in pursuit made a hero of Chief Joseph. In the introduction to his 1952 relation of Joseph's flight, Verne Dusenberry writes that "to follow Joseph's trail today with all the assistance this mechanized age provides would be an impossibility because of the still uncharted wilderness country he covered. To realize that seventy-five years ago Joseph led his men, women, and children — numbering nearly seven hundred — and all their earthly belongings plus a pony herd of approximately 1,500 horses across Idaho and Montana makes his march almost unbelievable" (43). At the end of September, Chief Joseph was arrested by General Miles. In the 1878 annual report of the commissioner of Indian Affairs can be found the number of prisoners at Fort Leavenworth as reported by the War Department on 4 December 1877: "79 men, 178 women, and 174 children, making a total of 431." The small number of men compared to women and children is proof that no violence was intended by the fugitives. Under the responsibility of the Fort Leavenworth authorities, Commissioner Hayt writes, Chief Joseph and his band were camped at "the worst possible place that could have been selected; and the sanitary condition of the Indians proved it." A doctor in charge said that "one-half could be said to be sick, and all were affected by the poisonous malaria of the camp." Hayt adds that "within a few months they have lost by death more than one-quarter of the entire number" (xxxiii). The rest were taken to Indian Territory. Hayt wrote that Chief Joseph was "one of the most gentlemanly and well-behaved Indians that I ever met. He is bright and intelligent, and is anxious for the welfare of his people" (xxxiv).

123. About Massasoit, see n. 115 above. Mingo chief Logan (Tah-Ga-Jute) became famous for a message he sent Governor of Virginia Lord Dunmore in 1774 that was almost immediately written down and printed in several papers, in the American colonies as well as in Europe (Seeber). However, Thomas Jefferson widely contributed to Logan's worldwide fame when he used his speech to prove to European philosophers that nature had not granted the American man with "genius and mental powers" inferior to those of the "Homo sapiens Europaeus" (*Notes* 187). Before quoting at length what would become one of the most famous speeches by an Indian orator, Jefferson tells the story of the murder of Logan's family: "In the spring of the year 1774, a robbery and murder were committed on an inhabitant of the frontiers of Virginia, by two Indians of the Shawanee tribe. The neighbouring

whites, according to their custom, undertook to punish this outrage in a summary way. Col. Cresap, a man infamous for the many murders he had committed on those much-injured people, collected a party, and proceeded down the Kanhaway in quest of vengeance. Unfortunately a canoe of women and children, with one man only, was seen coming from the opposite shore, unarmed and unsuspecting an hostile attack from the whites. Cresap and his party . . . , the moment the canoe reached the shore, singled out their objects, and, at one fire, killed every person in it. This happened to be the family of Logan, who had long been distinguished as a friend of the whites" (188). Historian Jack Sosin, however, has a different version of the event. He argues that "a party of border ruffians led by Michael Greathouse lured a small band of Mingo across the river at Yellow Creek, plied them with liquor, and murdered all but one infant — men, women, and children were indiscriminately slaughtered. The entire family of the Mingo chief, Logan, was wiped out" (44). In any case, a war ensued that opposed Shawnee, Mingo, and Delaware Indians to the Virginia militia. After a scalping raid against Virginians for revenge, Logan, according to Sosin, "declared himself satisfied for the loss of his family" (45). But the whites pushed the Indians to continue the war until the fall of 1774. After defeat, Logan sent his message to Governor Dunmore: "I appeal to any white man to say, if ever he entered Logan's cabin hungry, and he gave him not meat; if ever he came cold and naked, and he clothed him not. During the course of the last long and bloody war, Logan remained idle in his cabin an advocate for peace. Such was my love for the whites, that my countrymen pointed as they passed, and said, 'Logan is the friend of the white men.' I had even thought to have lived with you, but for the injuries of one man, Col. Cresap, the last spring, in cold blood, and unprovoked, murdered all the relations of Logan, not sparing even my women and children. There runs not a drop of my blood in the veins of any living creature. This called on me for revenge. I have sought it: I have killed many: I have fully glutted my vengeance. For my country, I rejoice at the beams of peace. But do not harbor a thought that mine is the joy of fear. Logan never felt fear. He will not turn on his heel to save his life. Who is there to mourn for Logan? — Not one" (in Jefferson 188–89). Jefferson challenged "the whole orations of Demosthenes and Cicero, and of any more eminent orator, if Europe has furnished more eminent, to produce a single passage, superior to the speech of Logan" (188).

Tedysking is Oskison's spelling of Teedyusking (Heckewelder and Du Ponceau give Tedeuskung and Tadeuskund as alternative spellings), a noted Delaware chief who had made peace with the British of Pennsylvania in 1761 (Heckewelder 58). According to John Heckewelder, liquor might have something to do with his death. He writes that "in the month of April, 1763, a melancholy event took place at

Wyoming, on Susquehannah, where the principal chief of the Delawares, east of the mountains, named Tadeuskund, was burnt to death in his own house. Various were the conjectures as to the cause of his house taking fire; but the general belief was, that it had been a premeditated act, done with the knowledge or consent of some of the men of the village. It appeared probable, that to carry the resolution into effect, liquor had been brought into the village, it being known that this chief was fond of it, who after having drank to excess, had retired to his house to sleep; but no sooner was this known, than the house was discovered in flames; and, to prevent a disclosure of the persons who had committed the act, every house in the village was fired and burnt down to the ground, to make it appear as if a general conflagration had by accident taken place. Tadeuskund had been a useful man in his place, and to the nation he belonged; but in the opinion of the Six Nations, he assumed more authority than belonged to him as a Delaware chief, and fearing that he might not fall into their measures of joining in a new war against the English, they perhaps concerted the plan of destroying him" (66–67).

124. The story of Sacagawea (or Sacajawea) is well known. Lewis and Clark met her and her French husband, Toussaint Charbonneau, among the Mandans. They accompanied and guided the expedition up the Missouri. Sacagawea's presence was particularly fortunate on 17 August 1805 when the expedition started to negotiate with the Shoshones to be allowed on their territory. The Shoshones were the young woman's tribe, away from whom she had been taken prisoner by a Minnetaree raid party several years before. As the explorers sat with Shoshone chief Cameahwait, Sacagawea recognized her brother. Expedition member Nicholas Biddle wrote that as "the conference was to be opened, and glad of an opportunity of being able to converse more intelligibly, Sacajawea was sent for; she came into the tent, sat down, and was beginning to interpret, when in the person of Cameahwait she recognized her brother: She instantly jummped [*sic*] up, and ran and embraced him, throwing over him her blanket and weeping profusely" (DeVoto 203).

Chief Washakie (c. 1798–1900), of Shoshoni and Flathead descent, a peaceful leader of the Shoshoni Indians, saw his territories crossed by the constant stream of white settlers on their way first to Oregon, then to the Mormons' Utah, then to California. According to Debo, Washakie saw "the futility of resistance [and] sought the best terms he could" (*A History* 162). He fought with General Crook in the battle of the Rosebud against the Sioux in 1876. Liquor traffic was one of the plagues he endeavored to fight among the Shoshones, especially after his son was killed in a drunken row (1886 *Report Commissioner Indian Affairs* 259). After the Powder River War in the 1860s, Washakie was forced to accommodate the rebellious Arapaho Indians, traditional enemies of the Shoshonis, on his reservation (Debo, *A History* 241).

Carl Schurz, secretary of the interior between 1876 and 1881 under President Hayes, wrote that the Ute leader Chief Ouray "was probably the only man among them who had a clear conception of the whole extent of" the inevitable change in their condition in a Euro-American world (21). Schurz considered Ouray "a man of a comprehensive mind, of large views, appreciating with great clearness not only the present situation of his race, but also its future destiny and the measures necessary to save the Indians from destruction and to assimilate them with the white people with whom they have to live" (19). Ouray (1833–80) was a peacemaker. Peggy Benjamin wrote that "no man tried more valiantly to bring peace between the Indians and the intruding whites than the remarkable Ute Chief, Ouray. Frustrated by self-seeking white officials and his own Utes who split into hostile bands under subchiefs, Ouray spent more than 20 years trying to bring compromise and peace. His own people accused him of duplicity when he and his attractive wife, Chipeta, accepted the white man's ways of life and tried to act as a bridge between the free and easy tribal ways and the imposed will of men like Nathan Meeker and their 'civilization'" (31). In 1879 his efforts toward peace were shattered by a rebellion, led by Captain Jack, that ended in what is known as the Meeker Massacre. Nathan Meeker was an Indian agent who tried to transform the Utes into farmers. A *New York Times* article relating the events at the time stated that "two hundred Arapahoes had joined Jack and many others from the neighboring tribes, and, had it not been for the timely arrival of Chief Ouray's order to cease fighting, the name of Merritt and his command would have passed into history by the side of Custer, with the same epitaph—annihilated by Indians" (29 Oct. 1879). This rebellion, combined with pressure from the people of Colorado, resulted in significant cessions of lands.

For the tragic story of the Poncas—the inclusion of their lands in the Great Sioux Reservation, their subsequent removal to Indian Territory, and the heavy toll it took on the tribe—see n. 21 above. With the help of reformer Thomas Tibbles, Standing Bear, who opposed the removal and had been arrested for leaving the reservation, toured the East to tell of the bad treatment suffered by the Poncas and to raise sympathy for their cause. His talks convinced such people as Senator Dawes and Helen Hunt Jackson. According to Stanley Clark, during removal one of Standing Bear's daughters died. After they arrived to Indian Territory, he lost another child as well as his wife's mother and grandmother.

125. Francisco Naranjo, a governor of Santa Clara Pueblo and a dear friend of Clara D. True, was one of the Pueblo leaders who denounced the maladministration of their people by BIA officials (see "The Little Mother of the Pueblos" and endnotes). He reportedly said, "God gave us the land, but the United States surveyed us out of it" (Johnson 5). He was the president of the Pueblo Indians Temperance Society

and the leader of a federation of Pueblos whose purpose, according to Johnson, was "to cut out the liquor traffic and to endeavor to protect themselves from the land and pasturage robberies that were being indicted upon them" (10).

126. This address was given at the thirty-third annual Lake Mohonk Conference on the Indian and Other Dependent Peoples, held on 20, 21, and 22 October 1915. Oskison spoke on the last day.

127. At the end of his address, the chairman said, "Mr. Oskison has certainly brought us some interesting and practical suggestions. I am going to ask him how far the papers, periodicals and magazines are publishing the news of the reservations? I think a great deal of information could be thus published and would be extremely interesting." Oskison answered: "I believe there is not sufficient information published, Mr. Chairman. The Carlisle magazine is publishing a number of good things but I would suggest that we have a regular publication dealing with Indian problems" (177).

128. "In Governing the Indian, Use the Indian!" was published in February 1917 in the law review *Case and Comment*. It was almost simultaneously published in the *American Indian Magazine*. One noticeable difference between the two publications is that the exclamation mark disappeared from the title in the latter publication. In *Case and Comment*, a photograph — inscribed "Copyright Rodman Wanamaker 1915" and captioned "Chief Plenty Coups (Crow) addressing the last great Indian council, Valley of the Little Big Horn, Montana" — as well as a head-and-shoulders portrait of Oskison accompanied the text.

129. Oskison might refer here to a case that opposed the Cherokee Nation, represented by Bill Hastings, to Moses Whitmire, trustee for freedmen of the Cherokee Nation. At the core of the problem was what is called the Kern-Clifton Roll, the roll of Cherokee freedmen entitled to Cherokee citizenship and to a share of Cherokee property. Hastings became the attorney for the Cherokee Nation in 1896, at the time the Dawes Commission started to work with the Cherokees. On behalf of the Cherokee Nation, Hastings notably "protest[ed] against the listing for enrollment of the said John Oskison as a Cherokee citizen by blood, because of the fact of non-residence, and the further fact that his father was not readmitted to citizenship after an absence" (*Applications*).

In 1895 the U.S. Court of Claims issued decrees in *Moses Whitmire, trustee v. The Cherokee Nation*, which held that freedmen were entitled to participate in the distribution of tribal land (Carter 112). These decrees were based on Article 9 of the 1866 treaty, which stipulated that "all freedmen who have been liberated by voluntary act of their former owners or by law, as well as all free colored persons who were in the country at the commencement of the rebellion, and are now residents therein, or who may return within six months, and their descendants, shall have all the rights of native Cherokees." The Court of Claims also affirmed the Wallace Roll, registering the Delawares, Shawnees, and freedmen who had claimed they had been excluded from Cherokee Outlet payments. Since the Cherokee Nation objected to the Wallace Roll, a commission was created to establish a new roll. The result was what is known as the Kern-Clifton Roll. It was "approved by the Secretary [of the Interior] on the eighteenth of January, 1897, and in the succeeding months the moneys available for distribution were paid to the persons whose names were on the roll" (*Cherokee Nation v. Whitmire*). But controversy was aroused again. Corruption was suspected. Principal Chief Mayes called the roll "a disgraceful farce" (qtd. in Carter 113). As a consequence, the National Council asked Hastings and two other officials to take a census (Carter 113). The Dawes Commission used this census to establish its final rolls, "which were finally approved by the Secretary on March 4, 1907, [and] from which were excluded a large number of freedmen whose names were on the Kern-Clifton roll, with the consequence that such persons so excluded will receive no allotments of lands or share in the moneys which stand to the credit of the Cherokee Nation in the Treasury of the United States" (*Cherokee Nation v. Whitmire*). In May 1908 the excluded freedmen "asserted a right under the decrees [of 1895] and acts of Congress to be upon the rolls, to be allotted lands and to share in the distribution of funds, and prayed that the action of the Dawes Commission and of the Secretary of the Interior be declared unlawful, and that the Cherokee Nation and the United States be enjoined from discriminating between such freedmen and other citizens of the Cherokee Nation . . . and that it and the United States be further enjoined from further disturbing such freedmen in the possession and occupation of their homes and improvements, and to reinstate such of them as have been ousted from such possession" (*Cherokee Nation v. Whitmire*). In February 1911 the U.S. Court of Claims ruled that more than seventeen hundred persons listed on the Kern-Clifton Roll were entitled to an allotment, although they were not on the Dawes Roll. The Cherokee Nation, represented by Hastings, appealed to the Supreme Court, which reversed the lower court's decision in *Cherokee Nation v. Whitmire, trustee for Freedmen of the Cherokee Nation* on 29 January 1912. To explain the decision, Justice McKenna argued that "the Congress had power to alter the decree and to adopt other means or ways for the disposition of the property than there provided." The other means adopted by Congress was the Dawes Commission. Besides, although Congress "accepted the decree as a correct interpretation of Art. IX of the treaty as to the rights of freedmen," it "did not accept the Kern-Clifton roll as an authentic identification of the individual freedmen. It had been challenged. It had been made up with haste and under circumstances which caused question to its correctness. It had not received judicial approval." McKenna concluded that the Supreme Court was "not required to consider the reasons which induced Congress to direct that a roll be made by the Dawes Commission. Congress had the power, and, as we have decided, exercised it" (*Cherokee Nation v. Whitmire*).

For more biographical information on Hastings, see "Introduction" n. 14.

130. Oskison gives examples of such young Indians — "subjects of the white man" — in "The New Indian Leadership."

131. Merrill E. Gates (1848–1922), secretary of the Board of Indian Commissioners for many years, was a longtime and very influential Friend of the Indian. As early as 1885, when he was president of Rutgers College, he attended the Third Lake Mohonk Conference of the Friends of the Indian, during which he spoke to pay tribute to Helen Hunt Jackson and other people who, like her, lived among the Indians, people who have "this earnest zeal, this warm giving up of the life" (1885 *Proceedings Third Lake Mohonk Conference* 70). He was elected president of the Lake Mohonk Conference in 1895 and for several subsequent years. At the time he was president of Amherst College and chairman of the Board of Indian Commissioners (1895 *Proceedings Thirteenth Lake Mohonk Conference* 119). In the address he gave to open the fourteenth conference, in 1896, he expressed his satisfaction that he and his fellow Friends of the Indian could "put the reservation in the past tense! The reservation, from which every influence of the virtues of civilization was carefully shut out, while all the damning vices that are the bane of civilized communities found constant access, has been from the beginning a curse to Indians and whites" (1896 *Proceedings Fourteenth Lake Mohonk Conference* 8–9). He also called his fellow members' attention to the dangers of "the transition period from barbarous reservation life, with its savage communism, to homes upon land held in severalty." Holding land in severalty was necessary, but not without citizenship (9). Exhorting the Friends of the Indian to patience, he also made a comparison between children, Indians, and mankind which can be seen as a good illustration of the reformers' mind-set of the time: "Childhood properly studied recalls not only 'trailing clouds of glory,' whence it came, but also something of the history of the earlier stages of development through which the race has passed. Traces of the feelings of the savage are to be found in early boyhood in all healthy children; and the converse of this record of the race, written in the childish organism and experience of the individual, we find ourselves face to face with when we attempt to do for the Indian race in one or two generations what unaided Nature by her slower methods takes hundreds of years to do. To transform savages into civilized and enlightened citizens is a process requiring time. Education, Christian training, and the helpful hand of Christian friends may greatly shorten the time which is

required for this transformation. But no educational processes, and not even the transforming power of the Christian life can entirely annihilate or completely and immediately overcome the impulses and tendencies which are directly inherited from ages of savage descent" (10). In the same address Gates called for the end of the Indian Territory as such, this "un-American and unstatesmanlike experiment of the *imperium in imperio*" (13). In his opening address in 1900 he praised the General Allotment Act for being "a mighty pulverizing engine for breaking up the tribal mass," (1900 *Proceedings Eighteenth Lake Mohonk Conference* 16), an expression that President Roosevelt would use in his State of the Union Address on 3 December 1901: "In my judgment the time has arrived when we should definitely make up our minds to recognize the Indian as an individual and not as a member of a tribe. The General Allotment Act is a mighty pulverizing engine to break up the tribal mass. It acts directly upon the family and the individual." In subsequent years Gates gave different talks at the conference, notably one titled "The Next Great Step to Break Up Tribal Funds into Individual Holdings" at the twentieth meeting (1902 *Proceedings Twentieth Lake Mohonk Conference* 118–27), and others about visits to reservations he had made (e.g., "A Visit to the Northern Reservations in Oregon and Montana" at the Seventeenth Meeting in 1899).

132. The passages between quotation marks are from Dr. Gates. The first passage here and others below are also quoted in "The New Indian Leadership."

Shorty White-Grass was a South Piegan warrior, born in 1827. According to Lloyd J. Dempsey, his war exploits, along with Wolf Tail's, were painted on a robe in 1892 (71).

133. "The New Indian Leadership" was first published in *The American Indian Magazine* in the spring 1917. It was more recently published in Bernd Peyer's anthology *American Indian Nonfiction*.

134. Oskison might refer here to a visit he made with Carlos Montezuma which he relates in "Arizona and Forty Thousand Indians." During such a visit, "Dr. Montezuma was charged with being a trouble-maker and a contract-seeker, and we were ordered not to hold any meetings with the Indians."

135. See "Acquiring a Standard of Value" above and n. 94 above. Also "Arizona and Forty Thousand Indians."

136. The Indian police was created by act of Congress of 27 May 1878. According to the annual report of the commissioner of Indian Affairs that year, "the aggregate force [was] not to exceed 50 officers and 430 privates" (xlii). The commissioner also writes that although "too short a time has elapsed to perfect or thoroughly test the workings of the system . . . the results of the experiment at the thirty agencies in which it has been tried are entirely satisfactory, and commend it as an effective instrument

of civilization." Furthermore, he recommends that the "police organization should be followed up by the adoption of a code of laws for Indians, and peace and good order among them will result." In the same report, several agents express their satisfaction, and the Indians', with the new force. One, however, Agent Critchlow of Uintah Valley Agency in Utah, wrote that "it took our Indians some time to make up their minds relative to this matter, and I desired that they should understand it as fully as possible, and go into it with their own consent. I gave them ample time after its presentation to them to make up their minds on the subject. They finally concluded it was a good thing and adopted it. Some difficulty was met in the selection of those most suitable for the service, some of those best qualified not being willing to give up their farming operations for the service" (127). James Patten, agent of the Shoshone and Bannock Agency in Wyoming Territory, wrote that although he endeavored to organize the Indian police, "composed of the Shoshones and Arapahoes," he succeeded "only with the latter tribe. The Shoshones complain of the smallness of the wages" (152). The appropriation act of 27 May 1878, reproduced in the same report, gave $30,000 "for the services of not exceeding four hundred and thirty privates at five dollars per month each, and not exceeding fifty officers at eight dollars per month each, of Indian police to be employed in maintaining order and prohibiting illegal traffic in liquor on the several Indian reservations" (188).

137. According to what Oskison writes in "In Governing the Indian," the "man in the Indian service" is Dr. Merrill Gates, also mentioned later in "The New Indian Leadership."

138. See "In Governing the Indian, Use the Indian!" above and n. 131 above.

139. Vincent Natalish; see n. 95 above.

140. See "An Apache Problem."

141. Henry Roe Cloud, or Wa-Na-Xi-Lay, (c. 1884–1950), a Winnebago Indian, was a Yale-educated member of the Society of American Indians. In 1913 he was ordained a Presbyterian minister. In 1926 he worked with Lewis Meriam on his famous report. In 1933, President Franklin Delano Roosevelt appointed him superintendent of Haskell Institute, an Indian school in Lawrence, Kansas (Satz 208). He and Oskison seem to have agreed on how the Indian should adjust to the modern world. In an essay he published in 1924 titled "The Future of the Red Men in America," Cloud wrote that "the task of conserving what is distinctive in aboriginal American life is one which should engage the interest of every thinking citizen. The America of tomorrow will not have this inheritance of the first American if the boys and girls of this race are not adequately educated and trained in those qualities of character which stand the test of life's vigorous demands" (384).

142. Fort Sumner personnel were in charge of the internment of the Navajos at nearby Bosque Redondo during the period Oskison refers to.

In his annual report for 1862, Commissioner of Indian Affairs William P. Dole wrote that "during the past four years [the Navajos] have been a continual scourge to the people of New Mexico, and have committed innumerable depredations upon their settlements. There is absolutely no security, except armed force, in any part of the large region of country through which they roam; and the last has proved even more disastrous than former years." According to him, "the government has so long delayed the adoption of some efficient policy, that they have become insolent and defiant, construing our forbearance as an evidence of weakness" (1862 *Report Commissioner Indian Affairs* 35). In 1865 Superintendent Felipe Delgado wrote in his report that the Navajos, "this formidable tribe, . . . have been for the last century a scourge to the Territory, constantly preying upon the flocks and herds of the inhabitants, and every year murdering more or less of the citizens" (1865 *Report Commissioner Indian Affairs* 161). In October 1862 the New Mexico superintendent, J. L. Collins, wrote that "whilst the Navajoes remain in this hostile condition it is not necessary to make recommendations in regard to their future management by the Indian department. For the present, the best and only thing that can be advantageously done with them is to let them be well punished by the military arm of the government. To enable him to properly discharge his duties in this respect, and at the same time guard the other interests of the Territory, General Carleton has asked for permission to raise another regiment of volunteers. In this he should meet with the favor and assistance of the Indian department, for we may rest assured that no civil authority can be exercised over these hostile tribes and bands until they are thoroughly convinced of the power of the government to enforce its will amongst them" (241).

In 1863 General J. H. Carleton was authorized, Delgado writes, to "conceiv[e] and carr[y] into effect the policy of locating them on a reservation. To this end he instituted a campaign against them, under the command of Colonel Kit Carson, and from the energy and promptness with which it was prosecuted during the months of winter in a cold and rigorous climate, this hardy mountaineer overcame all obstructions and brought it to a happy issue in subduing the Indians to a great extent, and removing them to the reservation at the Bosque Redondo" (1865 *Report Commissioner Indian Affairs* 161). The Navajos' removal to Bosque Redondo is known as the Long Walk. The Navajos would remain prisoners of war until 1868.

"The reservation at Bosque Redondo was (by recommendation from this office of January 14, 1864, laid before the President of the United States, and approved by him, as appears from department letter of January 16, 1864) set apart for the Apaches, it being intended to colonize all of the various bands of that tribe upon it; and as it was estimated to contain about 6,000 or 7,000 acres of arable land, it was deemed sufficient for the purposes" (1865 *Report Commissioner Indian Affairs* 20). In his report for 1865, Commissioner of Indian Affairs D. N. Cooley stated that although the Apaches and the Navajos were enemy tribes, the latter had been "taken prisoners by the military forces, and removed to the reservation at Bosque Redondo on the Pecos River, in the eastern part of the [New Mexico] Territory in 1863–64, and numbering, at latest accounts, a little over 7,000; their original home being in what is now Arizona, though ranging into northwestern New Mexico" (20). This situation illustrated perfectly how the Indians could sometimes be trapped in the administrative friction between the Indian Service and the War Department. Commissioner Cooley admits his confusion: "In regard to the Navajos, now established at the Bosque Redondo reservation, the accumulated testimony is so conflicting, derived from sources equally entitled to credit, and from persons who should have, and, so far as appears, have had but one object in view — the best interest of the government and of the Indians, that I am reluctant at present to express a decided opinion in regard to the permanent policy to be adopted" (21). On the one hand, Superintendent Steck expressed his conviction that "the Bosque Redondo reservation was barely sufficient for the Apaches, for whom it was set apart," "that the Navajos and Apaches could not live together upon it," and "that the Navajos could best support themselves upon a reservation in their own country, where they had always been an agricultural and pastoral people, raising large crops, and making their own garments from the produce of their own flocks." He added a very pragmatic reason not to keep them at Bosque Redondo: feeding them would cost a lot of money when they could provide for their own needs. On the other hand, General Carleton insisted that, "for the sake of permanent peace, the Navajos must be taken entirely away from their own country, and that when once settled upon a reservation they could provide for their own support" (21). In his report to his superior, Superintendent Delgado, Steck's successor, claims that a large majority of the Navajos "profess to be entirely satisfied," although he concedes that some of them, "who have never had any restraint upon their licentiousness, and who are unwilling to be forced to relinquish their former roving life and settle down to quiet agricultural pursuits, have attempted to escape. . . . It requires time to subjugate this class. It cannot be expected that all of them will at once consent to give up their nomadic life and become civilized" (1865 *Report Commissioner Indian Affairs* 161). As for his recommendations, they seem to differ from his predecessor's. He thought the Navajos, as well as the Apaches, should remain under military authority at least for a while longer and suggested the purchase of sheep and goats that would allow the Navajos to manufacture blankets and clothing, which would "greatly lessen the expense of those articles. . . . In this way as their farms and flocks increased they would become more and more interested, until finally they would be but little or no trouble or expense to the government" (162).

The Navajos were finally released in 1868. By treaty they were given "a reservation of 3,328,000 acres in the northwestern part of New Mexico and northeastern part of Arizona" (1872 *Report Commissioner Indian Affairs* 52). The report of the commissioner of Indian Affairs for 1869 states that the Navajos, "now in their old home, number between eight and ten thousand, the former number being on the reservation, and about two thousand living with other tribes or roaming at large." Ely S. Parker added that there were many complaints against the Navajos "on account of depredations committed upon citizens, which induced Governor Mitchell to issue a proclamation declaring the whole people to be outlaws," a measure that Parker thought completely unjustified "as the main body of the tribe were on their own lands or near thereto, peaceable and endeavoring to fulfill their treaty obligations" (1869 *Report Commissioner Indian Affairs* 22). The 1872 report states that after they have been removed, the Navajos "remained quiet and peaceable, many of them being engaged in agriculture and in raising sheep and goats. Of these they have large flocks, numbering 130,000 head, which supply them not only with subsistence but also with material from which they manufacture the celebrated, and, for warmth and durability, unequaled, Navajo blanket. They also have a stock of 10,000 horses" (1872 *Report Commissioner Indian Affairs* 53). Commissioner Francis A. Walker added that the Navajos "are industrious, attend faithfully to their crops, and even put in a second crop when the first, as frequently happens, is destroyed by drought or frost" (53).

Bibliography

OSKISON'S WORKS

I list below, in chronological order, the texts by Oskison that are published or mentioned in this volume. It is not an exhaustive list of his writings, but the reader will find other bibliographies of Oskison's work in Daniel F. Littlefield Jr. and James W. Parins, *A Biobibliography of Native American Writers, 1772–1924*, and in John Milton Oskison, *The Singing Bird*. However, some texts appear here that are not mentioned in those previous bibliographies. Therefore, the three are complementary and should lay the groundwork for researchers who would undertake an exhaustive bibliography of Oskison, whose texts are very probably not all known yet. With that in mind, I also include texts that are not reprinted in this volume but which are not included in the two bibliographies cited above.

Autobiographical Accounts

"A Trip to Yosemite Valley." *Indian Chieftain* 8 Aug. 1895: 2.

"A Letter to His Father: John Oskison Writes of His Visit in Europe." *Indian Chieftain* 9 Aug. 1900.

"An Autobiographical Letter to Journalist Frederick S. Barde." Published as "A Letter by John Milton Oskison (1874–1947), Cherokee Journalist." *Native Press Research Journal* 6 (Fall 1987): 1–7.

Correspondence with Frederick S. Barde. Frederick S. Barde Collection, Oklahoma History Center.

Fiction and Biographies

"I Match You: You Match Me." *Indian Chieftain* 27 May 1897.

"Tookh Steh's Mistake." *Indian Chieftain* 22 July 1897.

"A Schoolmaster's Dissipation." *Indian Chieftain* 25 Dec. 1897.

"'Only the Master Shall Praise.'" *Century Illustrated Magazine* Jan. 1900: 327–35.

"When the Grass Grew Long." *Century Illustrated Magazine* June 1901: 247–50.

"The Biologist's Quest." *Overland Monthly* July–Dec. 1901: 52–57.

"I Saw an Eagle Strike." *San Francisco Chronicle* 1 Mar. 1903: 7.

"To 'Youngers' Bend.'" *Frank Leslie's Popular Monthly* June 1903: 182–88.
"A Border Judge and His Court." *Frank Leslie's Popular Monthly* July 1903: 18–23.
"Working for Fame." *Frank Leslie's Popular Monthly* Oct. 1903: 372–82.
"The Fall of King Chris." *Frank Leslie's Popular Monthly* Oct. 1903: 586–93.
"'The Quality of Mercy.'" *Century Magazine* June 1904: 178–81.
"The Greater Appeal." *The Black Cat* 11. Boston: Shortstory, 1905. 28–35.
"The Problem of Old Harjo." *Southern Workman* Apr. 1907: 235–41.
"Young Henry and the Old Man." *McClure's* June 1908: 237.
"Koenig's Discovery." *Collier's Weekly* 28 May 1910: 20–21.
"Diverse Tongues: A Sketch." *Current Literature* 49 (Sept. 1910): 343–44.
"Out of the Night That Covers." *Delineator* 78 (Aug. 1911): 80, 125.
"Walla Tenaka—Creek." *Collier's Weekly* 12 July 1913: 16–17, 32–33.
"The Apples of Hesperides, Kansas." *Forum* Mar. 1914: 391–408.
"Grady's Squad: A Plattsburg Yarn." *New York Tribune* 13 Aug. 1916: 2.
"The Man Who Interfered." *Southern Workman* Oct. 1915: 557–67.
"The Other Partner." *Collier's Weekly* 6 Dec. 1924: 14–15, 30–32.
"The Singing Bird." *Sunset Magazine* Mar. 1925: 5–8, 87–89.
Wild Harvest: A Novel of Transition Days in Oklahoma. New York: D. Appleton, 1925.
Black Jack Davy. New York: D. Appleton, 1926.
"Yvonne the Terrible." *McClure's* Oct. 1927: 45–47, 88–92.
"The Seventh Age." *Rotarian* Feb. 1928: 12–13, 39–43.
Brothers Three. New York: Macmillan, 1935.
"Unconquerable: The Story of John Ross, Chief of the Cherokees, 1828–1866." Unpublished (1936). McFarlin Library. Department of Special Collections and University Archives. University of Tulsa.
Tecumseh and His Times: The Story of a Great Indian. New York: Putnam, 1938.
The Singing Bird. Norman: Oklahoma University Press, 2007.

Nonfiction on Indian Subjects

"Cherokee Migration." *Tahlequah Arrow* 31 May 1902.
"The President and the Indian: Rich Opportunity for the Red Man." *Vinita Weekly Chieftain* 25 Dec. 1902.
"The Outlook for the Indian." *Southern Workman* June 1903: 270–73.
"Friends of the Indian." *The Nation; A Weekly Journal* Oct. 1905: 332–33.
"Lake Mohonk Conference." *Native American* 4 Nov. 1905: 391–93.
"The Need of Publicity in Indian Affairs." *Proceedings of the Twenty-fourth Annual Meeting of the Lake Mohonk Conference of Friends of the Indian and Other Dependent Peoples*. Lake Mohonk Conference, 1906. 38–40.
"Remaining Causes of Indian Discontent." *North American Review* 1 Mar. 1907: 486–93.

"Making an Individual of the Indian." *Everybody's Magazine* June 1907: 723–33.
"A Carlisle Commencement." *Collier's Weekly* 4 June 1910: 21–22. Reprinted as "Carlisle Commencement as Seen by *Collier's Weekly.*" *The Red Man* Sept. 1910: 18–22.
"The Indian in the Professions." *Report of the Executive Council on the Proceedings of the First Annual Conference of the Society of American Indians.* Washington DC: Society of American Indians, 1912. 94–98.
"The Indian in the Professions." *The Red Man* Jan. 1912: 201–4. Published by The Carlisle Indian Press, Carlisle, Pennsylvania.
"The Enduring Qualities of the Indian." *The Red Man* May 1912: 396–98. Published by The Carlisle Indian Press, Carlisle, Pennsylvania.
"The Little Mother of the Pueblos." *Delineator* 81 (Mar. 1913): 170.
"An Apache Problem." *Quarterly Journal of the Society of American Indians* 1 (Apr. 1913): 25–29.
"Acquiring a Standard of Value." *Quarterly Journal of the Society of American Indians* 2 (Jan.–Mar. 1914): 47–50.
"Arizona and Forty Thousand Indians." *Southern Workman* Mar. 1914: 148–56.
"The Closing Chapter: Passing of the Old Indian." *The Indian Leader* 17 (May 1914): 6–11.
"A Bigger Load for Educated Indians." *Report of the Thirty-Third Annual Lake Mohonk Conference on the Indian and Other Dependent Peoples.* Lake Mohonk Conference, 1915. 174–77.
"In Governing the Indian, Use the Indian!" *Case and Comment* 23.9 (1917): 722–26.
"In Governing the Indian, Use the Indian." *American Indian Magazine* 5.1 (1917): 36–41.
"The New Indian Leadership." *American Indian Magazine* 5.2 (1917): 93–100.
Oklahoma: A Guide to the Sooner State. Ed. Angie Debo and John M. Oskison. Comp. Workers of the Writers' Program of the Work Projects Administration in the State of Oklahoma. Norman: University of Oklahoma Press, 1941.

Nonfiction on Non-Indian Subjects

"Public Halls of the East Side." *University Settlement of New York Report.* New York, 1899. 38–40.
"Long of Kansas." *Collier's Weekly* 18 July 1908: 8–9, 22.
"John Smith Borrows $20." *Collier's Weekly* 4 Sept. 1909: 14.
"Exploiters of the Needy." *Collier's Weekly* 2 Oct. 1909: 17–18.
"Competing with the Sharks." *Collier's Weekly* 5 Feb. 5 1910: 19–20.
"Round-up of the Financial Swindlers." *Collier's Weekly* 31 Dec. 1910: 19–20.
"The Spider and the Fly: A Warning to Women against Financial Snares." *Woman's Home Companion* Oct. 1911: 9.

"Separating the Thrifty and Credulous from their Money." *Chicago Tribune* 9 Mar. 1913.
"Boosting the Thrift Idea." *Collier's Weekly* 4 Apr. 1914: 22.
"A Less Known Edison." *World's Work* June 1914: 180–85.
"A Chemist Who Became King of an Industry." *World's Work* July 1914: 310–15.
"The American Creator of the Aluminum Age." *World's Work* Aug. 1914: 438–45.
"Why Am I an American?" *World's Work* Dec. 1914: 209–13.
"How Can You Help Feed and Clothe the Belgians." *World's Work* Jan. 1915: 275–77.
"Back-firing against Bolshevism." *Outlook* 30 July 1919: 510–15.
"Herbert Hoover: Engineer-Economist-Organizer." *Industrial Management* 1 Jan. 1921: 2–6.
"Hoover Message to Export Manufacturers." *Industrial Management* 65 (Mar. 1923): 131–35.

ABOUT OSKISON

In the following references the reader will find information about Oskison's life or work. Their contents are entirely or only partially dedicated to Oskison. A few of these references include some of Oskison's texts, while others mention his name only in passing.

Allen, Paula Gunn. *The Sacred Hoop: Recovering the Feminine in American Indian Traditions*. Boston: Beacon Press, 1992.
———, ed. *Voice of the Turtle: American Indian Literature, 1900–1970*. New York: Ballantine Books, 1994.
Anderson, LaVere. "John Oskison." *Tulsa Daily World* Feb. 1947. John Milton Oskison Collection, box O-8, folder 1, Western History Collections, Norman, University of Oklahoma.
———. "John Oskison Comes Back Home to Write Novel about a Little Known Phase of Oklahoma's Past." *Tulsa Daily World* 29 Jan. 1939.
Applegate, Edd. *Muckrakers: A Biographical Dictionary of Writers and Editors*. Lanham MD: Scarecrow Press, 2008.
"Authors Here Change East's Idea of State." *The Oklahoman* 10 Dec. 1930: 10.
Barde, Frederick. "An Oklahoma Indian's Long Road to Literary Success." *Oklahoma City Times-Journal* 2 July 1911.
Bataille, Gretchen M. "American Indian Novels." *Rocky Mountain Review of Language and Literature* 47½ (1993): 61–66.
Brandt, Joseph A. "The Story of John Oskison." *Daily Oklahoman* 1 Mar. 1936.
"City Club Hears Talk by Writer." *The Oklahoman* 20 Dec. 1930: 5.
Conley, Robert J. *Cherokee Thoughts, Honest and Uncensored*. Norman: University of Oklahoma Press, 2008.

"Death Stills Pen of Noted Writer." *Tulsa Daily World* 27 Feb. 1947.
"Did He Heed Call of Wild?" *San Francisco Chronicle* 5 Sept. 1906: 3.
"Elegant History of Political Parties Is Funny History." *The Oklahoman* 13 Jan. 1929: 63.
"Good Course in Behavior Sought for Biographies." *The Oklahoman* 28 Dec. 1930: 46.
Hill, Randall T. G. "Methodological Approaches to Native American Narrative and the Role of Performance." *American Indian Quarterly* 21.1 (1997): 111–47.
"Indian Conference Will Not Be Held." *The Oklahoman* 3 Oct. 1917: 2.
Jacobson, Angeline. *Contemporary Native American Literature: A Selected and Partially Annotated Bibliography*. Metuchen NJ: Scarecrow Press, 1977.
"John Oskison, 72, Wrote of Indians." *New York Times* 27 Feb. 1947.
"John Oskison, Writer, Divorced." *New York Times* 12 Feb. 1920: 28.
Justice, Daniel. *Our Fire Survives the Storm: A Cherokee Literary History*. Minneapolis: University of Minnesota Press, 2006.
Kaufman, Kenneth C. "The Way I See It." *The Oklahoman* 1 Sept. 1935: 47.
Larré, Lionel. "John Milton Oskison, an Indian Cowboy." *A Usable Past: Tradition in North American Arts and Literatures*. Ed. Simone Pellerin. Pessac: Presses Universitaires de Bordeaux, 2010. 99–109.
Larson, Charles. *American Indian Fiction*. Albuquerque: University of New Mexico Press, 1978.
Littlefield, Daniel F., Jr., and James W. Parins. *A Biobibliography of Native American Writers, 1772–1924*. Metuchen NJ: Scarecrow Press, 1981.
———. *Native American Writing in the Southeast: An Anthology, 1875–1935*. Jackson: University Press of Mississippi, 1995.
———. "Short Fiction Writers of the Indian Territory." *American Studies* (Lawrence KS) 23.1 (1982): 23–38.
Maddox, Lucy. *Citizen Indians: Native American Intellectuals, Race and Reform*. Ithaca NY: Cornell University Press, 2005.
"Noted Author to Return to Vinita—If He Can Find Room." *Tulsa Tribune* 25 Mar. 1946: 4.
Oaks, Priscilla. "The First Generation of Native American Novelists." *MELUS* 5.1 (1978): 57–65.
"Oklahoma Writers." *The Oklahoman* 26 Sept. 1926: 62.
"Oklahoma Biographs." *The Oklahoman* 7 July 1935: 49.
"Oskison Book Causing Talk in Home City." *The Oklahoman* 29 Oct. 1935: 4.
"Outlines Policy Toward Indians." *Poughkeepsie Eagle News* 21 Oct. 1915: 6.
Peyer, Bernd, ed. *American Indian Nonfiction: An Anthology of Writings, 1760s–1930s*. Norman: University of Oklahoma Press, 2007.

———, ed. *The Singing Spirit: Early Short Stories by North American Indians.* Tucson: University of Arizona Press, 1989.

Powell, Timothy B., and Melinda Smith Mullikin. Introduction. *The Singing Bird: A Cherokee Novel.* Norman: University of Oklahoma Press, 2007. xix–xlvii.

Ronnow, Gretchen. "John Milton Oskison." *Handbook of Native American Literature.* Ed. Andrew Wiget. New York: Garland, 1996. 271–75.

———. "John Milton Oskison, Cherokee Journalist: A Singer of the Semiotics of Power." *Native Press Research Journal* 4 (Spring 1987): 1–14.

———. *John Milton Oskison: Native American Modernist.* PhD diss., University of Arizona, 1993.

Ruoff, A. LaVonne Brown. *American Indian Literatures.* New York: Modern Language Association of America, 1990.

Stensland, Anna Lee. *Literature by and about the American Indian: An Annotated Bibliography for Junior and Senior High School Students.* Urbana IL: National Council of Teachers of English, 1973.

Strickland, Arnie. "John Milton Oskison: A Writer of the Transitional Period of the Oklahoma Territory." *Southwestern American Literature* 2.2 (1972): 125–34.

"The Author! Author! Page." *McClure's* Oct. 1927: 6.

"The Making and Saving of 'Kindling.'" *Washington Post* 3 Nov. 1912: 3.

Vizenor, Gerald. "Native American Indian Literature: Critical Metaphors of the Ghost Dance." *World Literature Today* 66.2 (1992): 223–28.

Weaver, Jace. Foreword. *The Singing Bird.* Norman: University of Oklahoma Press, 2007. ix–xv.

Weinberg, Lila, and Arthur Weinberg, eds. *The Muckrakers: The Era in Journalism That Moved America to Reform — The Most Significant Magazine Articles of 1902–1912.* New York: Capricorn Book, 1964.

Wiget, Andrew. *Native American Literature.* Boston: Twayne, 1985.

Womack, Craig S. "A Single Decade: Book-Length Native Literary Criticism between 1986 and 1997." *Reasoning Together: The Native Critics Collective.* Ed. Janice Acoose et al. Norman: University of Oklahoma Press, 2008. 3–104.

OTHER WORKS CITED

Unpublished Sources

Alumni Association. *Register of the Alumni of the Leland Stanford Junior University from 1892 to 1899.* Stanford University, 1899.

Applications for Enrollment of the Commission to the Five Civilized Tribes, 1898–1914. The National Archives. Record Group 75.

Armstrong, Samuel C. *Report of a Trip Made in Behalf of the Indian Rights Association to Some Indian Reservations of the Southwest.* Philadelphia, 1884.

Azul, Antonito. "The Pima Indians Relate the Story of Their Wrongs." 1911. United States. Cong. House. *Conserving the Rights of Pima Indians, Arizona*. Presented by John H. Stephens. U.S. 62nd Cong., 2nd sess. Doc. 521. Washington, 1912. 4–9.

Beatty, Charles. *The Journal of a Two Months Tour; With a View of Promoting Religion among the Frontier Inhabitants of Pensylvania, and of Introducing Christianity among the Indians to the Westward of the Alegh-geny Mountains. To which are added, Remarks on the Language and Customs of some particular Tribes among the Indians, with a Brief Account of the Various Attempts that have been Made to Civilize and Convert Them, for the First Settlement of New England to this Day*. London, 1768.

Brosius, S. M., to John H. Stephens. United States. Cong. House. *Conserving the Rights of Pima Indians, Arizona*. Presented by John Hall Stephens. U.S. 62nd Cong., 2nd sess. Doc. 521. Washington, 1912. 9–10.

Bushyhead, Dennis Wolf. "Proclamation of D. W. Bushyhead, July 30, 1885." Dennis Wolf Bushyhead Collection, Western History Collection, Manuscript Division, Box III, Folder 169.

Butler, George, to Charles W. Dean, 9 Apr. 1856 and 12 Apr. 1856. United States. Cong. House. *Federal and Cherokee Courts*. U.S. 34th Cong., 1st sess. Ex. Doc. 113. Washington, 1856. 3–4, 5.

Cherokee Nation Papers Collection. University of Oklahoma, Western History Collections, Manuscript Division.

Cherokee Nation v. Whitmire, trustee for Freedmen of the Cherokee Nation. No. 223 U.S. 108. Supreme Ct. of the U.S. 29 Jan. 1912.

Constitution of the Cherokee Nation, 1869. http://www.cherokeeobserver.org/Issues/1839constitution.html.

Dean, Charles W., to George W. Manypenny, 16 Apr. 1856 (1st letter). United States. Cong. House. *Federal and Cherokee Courts*. U.S. 34th Cong., 1st sess. Ex. Doc. 113. Washington, 1856. 2–3.

Dean, Charles W., to George W. Manypenny, 16 Apr. 1856 (2nd letter). United States. Cong. House. *Federal and Cherokee Courts*. U.S. 34th Cong., 1st sess. Ex. Doc. 113. Washington, 1856. 4–5.

Final Rolls of Citizens and Freedmen of the Five Civilized Tribes in Indian Territory. The National Archives. Record Group 75: Records of the Bureau of Indian Affairs, 1793–1989. 1907.

Godwin, Parke. "Commemorative Address." The Players. *Memorial Celebration of the Sixtieth Anniversary of the Birth of Edwin Booth*. New York, 1893. 20–44.

Intercollegiate Community Service Association. *Bibliography of College, Social, University and Church Settlements*. Compiled by Caroline Williamson Montgomery. New York, 1900.

In the Matter of the Application of Albert Heff for a Writ of Habeas Corpus. No. 197 U.S. 488. Supreme Ct. of the U.S. 10 Apr. 1905.

Jones, William A. Personal Letterbook, Record Group 75, National Archives.

Leland Stanford Junior University. *Fourth Annual Register, 1894–1895*. Palo Alto CA: Stanford University, 1895.

———. *Register for 1899–1900*. Stanford University, 1900.

———. *Sixteenth Annual Register, 1906–1907*. Stanford University, 1907.

———. *Flügel Memorial Volume*. Palo Alto CA: Stanford University, 1916.

Lippincott, Joseph Barlow. "Storage of Water on Gila River, Arizona." United States. Cong. House. *Conserving the Rights of Pima Indians, Arizona*. Presented by John H. Stephens. U.S. 62nd Cong., 2nd sess. Doc. 521. Washington, 1912. 66–77.

Lone Wolf v. Ethan A. Hitchcock. No. 187 U.S. 553. Supreme Ct. of the U.S. 5 Jan. 1903.

Manypenny, George, to Robert McClelland, May 22, 1856. United States. Cong. House. *Federal and Cherokee Courts*. U.S. 34th Cong., 1st sess. Ex. Doc. 113. Washington, 1856. 2.

Mehlin et al. v. Ice. No. 182. Circuit Court of Appeals, Eighth Circuit. 1 May 1893.

Oskison v. Bagby. No. 1935 OK 670. Supreme Court of Oklahoma. 11 June 1935.

Page, John, to Brigadier General George Gibson, July 26, 1832. United States. *Correspondence on the Subject of the Emigration of Indians between the 30th November, 1831, and 27th December, 1833, with abstracts of Expenditures by Disbursing Agents*. Washington DC: Government Printing Office, 1834.

Page, John, to Major General Thomas S. Jesup, Quartermaster General U.S.A., 14 Nov. 1831. United States. *Correspondence on the Subject of the Emigration of Indians between the 30th November, 1831, and 27th December, 1833, with abstracts of Expenditures by Disbursing Agents*. Washington: Government Printing Office, 1834.

The Players. *Excerpts from the Many Good Words Uttered in Honor of Edwin Booth*. New York, 1889.

———. *Memorial Celebration of the Sixtieth Anniversary of the Birth of Edwin Booth*. New York, 1893.

Reuben Quick Bear v. Leupp. No. 210 U.S. 50. Supreme Ct. of the U.S.18 May 1908.

Roosevelt, Theodore, to Herbert Welsh, 13 Feb. 1891, Indian Rights Association Papers, Historical Society of Pennsylvania.

Roosevelt, Theodore. *The Man with the Muck Rake*. 15 Apr. 1906.

———. *Second Annual Message to Congress*. 2 Dec. 1902.

———. *State of the Union Message*. 3 Dec. 1901.

Society of American Indians. *Report of the Executive Council on the Proceedings of the First Annual Conference of the Society of American Indians*. Washington DC, 1912.

Stanford University. *The Stanford Quad: Being the Year Book of the Junior Class of Stanford 1901*. Associated Students of Stanford University, 1900.

———. *The Quad 1904: Being the Year Book of the Junior Class of Leland Stanford Junior University*. Associated Students of Stanford University, 1903.

Superior Oil & Gas Co. v. Mehlin. No. 436. Supreme Court of Oklahoma. 8 Mar. 1910.

Tennessee Evolution Statutes. http://www.law.umkc.edu/faculty/projects/scopes/tennstat.htm.

Treaty with the Cherokee Nation, 19 July 1866. Washington DC: Government Printing Office, 1866.

United States. *Correspondence on the Subject of the Emigration of Indians between the 30th November, 1831, and 27th December, 1833, with abstracts of Expenditures by Disbursing Agents*. Washington DC: Government Printing Office, 1834.

United States. Bureau of the Census. *Extra Census Bulletin: The Five Civilized Tribes in Indian Territory: The Cherokee, Chickasaw, Choctaw, Creek and Seminole nations*. Washington DC: Government Printing Office, 1894.

United States. Cong. House. *Conserving the Rights of Pima Indians, Arizona. Letters and Petitions with Reference to Conserving the Rights of the Pima Indians of Arizona to the Lands of their Reservation and the Necessary Water Supply for Irrigation*. Presented by John Hall Stephens. U.S. 62nd Cong., 2nd sess. Doc. 521. Washington, 1912.

———. *Federal and Cherokee Courts. Message from the President of the United States, Communicating Papers Relative to a Conflict of Jurisdiction between the Federal and Cherokee Courts*. U.S. 34th Cong., 1st sess. Ex. Doc. 113. Washington, 1856.

———. *Relief of Apache Indians Confined at Fort Sill Military Reservation, Oklahoma*. 62nd Cong., 3rd sess., 1913. Doc. 1249, Vol. 6503.

United States. Cong. Senate. *Report: Removal of the Ponca Indians*. 46th Cong., 2nd sess. Report No. 670. Washington, 1880.

———. *Letter from the Secretary of the Interior Transmitting Papers Relative to an Appropriation for the Benefit of the Cherokee Freedmen*. U.S. 50th Cong., 2nd sess. Ex. Doc. 83. Washington, 1889.

———. *Payment to Cherokee Freedmen*. U.S. 55th Cong., 1st sess. Doc. No. 136. Washington, 1897.

United States. Department of the Interior. *Annual Report of the Commissioner of Indian Affairs, 1859*. Washington DC: Government Printing Office, 1859.

———. *Report of the Commissioner of Indian Affairs for the Year 1862*. Washington DC: Government Printing Office, 1863.

———. *Report of the Commissioner of Indian Affairs for the Year 1865*. Washington DC: Government Printing Office, 1865.

———. *Report of the Commissioner of Indian Affairs, Made to the Secretary of the Interior for the Year 1869*. Washington DC: Government Printing Office, 1870.

———. *Annual Report of the Commissioner of Indian Affairs to the Secretary of the Interior for the Year 1872*. Washington DC: Government Printing Office, 1872.

———. *Annual Report of the Commissioner of Indian Affairs to the Secretary of the Interior for the Year 1878*. Washington DC: Government Printing Office, 1878.

———. *Annual Report of the Commissioner of Indian Affairs, 1884*. Washington DC: Government Printing Office, 1884.

———. *Annual Report of the Commissioner of Indian Affairs to the Secretary of the Interior for the Year 1886*. Washington DC: Government Printing Office, 1886.

———. *Annual Report of the Commissioner of Indian Affairs 1887*. Washington DC: Government Printing Office, 1887.

———. *Annual Report of the Commissioner of Indian Affairs 1894*. Washington DC: Government Printing Office, 1895.

———. *Report of the Commissioner of Indian Affairs to the Secretary of the Interior 1907*. Washington DC: Government Printing Office, 1907.

———. *Report of the Commissioner of Indian Affairs to the Secretary of the Interior for the Fiscal Year Ended June 30 1913*. Washington DC: Government Printing Office, 1913.

———. *Report of the Commissioner of Indian Affairs to the Secretary of the Interior for the Fiscal Year Ended June 30 1914*. Washington DC: Government Printing Office, 1914.

———. *Report of the Commissioner of Indian Affairs to the Secretary of the Interior for the Fiscal Year Ended June 30 1915*. Washington DC: Government Printing Office, 1915.

———. *Report of the Commissioner of Indian Affairs to the Secretary of the Interior for the Fiscal Year Ended June 30 1916*. Washington DC: Government Printing Office, 1916.

United States. Department of the Interior. Bureau of Indian Affairs. *Letters Received from Day School Teacher Clara D. True*. Record Group 75.

United States Laws, 22 Statutes at Large 623. Washington DC: Government Printing Office, 1883.

United States Laws, 25 Statutes at Large 608. Washington DC: Government Printing Office, 1888.

United States v. Stanford. No. 161 U.S. 412. Supreme Ct. of the U.S. 2 Mar. 1896.

Willie Halsell School. *1894 Annual Catalogue of Willie Halsell School*. Vinita, I.T., 1894.

Published Sources

Abbott, Devon. "'Commendable Progress': Acculturation at the Cherokee Female Seminary." *American Indian Quarterly* 11.3 (1987): 187–201.

Abler, Thomas Struthers. *Cornplanter: Chief Warrior of the Allegany Senecas*. New York: Syracuse University Press, 2007.

"About Authors." *New York Times* 14 Mar. 1903: Section Saturday Review of Books and Art, BR16.

"Abram Stevens Hewitt." *Encyclopaedia Britannica*. 2009. Encyclopaedia Britannica Online.

Adair, James. *The History of the American Indians, Particularly those Nations Adjoining to the Mississippi, East and West Florida, Georgia, South and North Carolina, and Virginia*. London, 1775.

Adams, David Wallace. *Education for Extinction: American Indians and the Boarding School Experience, 1875–1928*. Lawrence: University Press of Kansas, 1995.

———. "More Than a Game: The Carlisle Indians Take to the Gridiron, 1893–1917." *Western Historical Quarterly* 32.1 (2001): 25–53.

"After the Bill Doolin Gang." *New York Times* 24 Dec. 1894: 1.

Ahern, Wilbert H. "An Experiment Aborted: Returned Indian Students in the Indian School Service, 1881–1908." *Ethnohistory* 44.2 (1997): 263–304.

———. "Indian Education and Bureaucracy: The School of Morris, 1887–1909." *Minnesota History* 49.3 (1984): 82–98.

———. "The 'Returned Indians': Hampton Institute and Its Indian Alumni, 1879–1893." *Journal of Ethnic Studies* 10 (Winter 1983): 101–24.

"Albert White Vorse." *New York Times* 16 June 1910: 9.

Alexander, Hartley B. "Francis La Flesche." *American Anthropologist* ns 35.2 (1933): 328–31.

American Academy of Political and Social Science. *Handbook of the American Academy of Political and Social Science*. Philadelphia: American Academy of Political and Social Science, 1901.

Anderson, Gary Clayton. *Little Crow: Spokesman for the Sioux*. St. Paul: Minnesota Historical Society Press, 1986.

Anderson, Susan Heller. "City Makes It Official: Algonquin Is Landmark." *New York Times* 20 Sept. 1987.

"And Mr. Little Bison Spoke." *New York Times* 7 Apr. 1910: 8.

Andrews, Robert, ed. *Famous Lines: A Columbia Dictionary of Familiar Quotations*. New York: Columbia University Press, 1996.

Angoff, Charles. "Oswald Garrison Villard and *The Nation*: A Memoir." *Antioch Review* 23.2 (1963): 232–40.

Apess, William. *The Indians: The Ten Lost Tribes*. 1831. *On Our Own Ground: The Complete Writings of William Apess, A Pequot*. Ed. Barry O'Connell. Amherst: University of Massachusetts Press, 1992.

———. *A Son of the Forest*. 1829 and 1831. *On Our Own Ground: The Complete Writings of William Apess, A Pequot*. Ed. Barry O'Connell. Amherst: University of Massachusetts Press, 1992.

Appel, Jacob M. "A Duty to Kill? A Duty to Die? Rethinking the Euthanasia Controversy of 1906." *Bulletin of the History of Medicine* 78.3 (2004): 610–34.

Archuleta, Margaret L., Brenda J. Child, and Tsianina Lomawaima, eds. *Away from Home: American Indian Boarding School Experiences, 1879–2000*. Phoenix: Heard Museum, 2000.

Aston, James. "The Solidification of Alloys and Magmas." *Journal of Geology* 17.6 (1909): 569–85.

Atkinson, James H. "The Brooks-Baxter Contest." *Arkansas Historical Quarterly* 4.2 (1945): 124–49.

Attalla, Meghan I. "Galloway College." *Encyclopedia of Oklahoma History and Culture*. Oklahoma City: Oklahoma Historical Society, http://digital.library.okstate.edu/encyclopedia

Authors' Club. *The Authors' Club*. New York, 1902.

Baird, W. David. "Are the Five Tribes of Oklahoma 'Real' Indians?" *Western Historical Quarterly* 21.1 (1990): 5–18.

Ball, Eve. *Indeh: An Apache Odyssey*. Provo: Brigham Young University Press, 1980.

"Barrett Wendell." *New York Times* 9 Feb. 1921: 7.

Barsness, John A. "Theodore Roosevelt as Cowboy: The Virginian as Jacksonian Man." *American Quarterly* 21.3 (1969): 609–19.

"Bazaar for Settlement." *New York Times* 17 Feb. 1910: 9.

Beacom, John H. "Irrigation in the United States: Its Geographical and Economical Results." *Geographical Journal* 29.4 (1907): 400–423.

Beights, Ronald H. *Jesse James and the First Missouri Train Robbery*. Gretna LA: Pelican Publishing Company, 2002.

Bender, Bert. *Sea-Brothers: The Tradition of American Sea Fiction from "Moby-Dick" to the Present*. Philadelphia: University of Pennsylvania Press, 1988.

Benjamin, Peggy H. "The Last of Captain Jack." *Magazine of Western History* 10.2 (1960): 22–31.

Bensen, Robert, ed. *Children of the Dragonfly: Native American Voices on Child Custody and Education*. Tucson: University of Arizona Press, 2001.

Berger, Bethany Ruth. "After Pocahontas: Indian Women and the Law, 1830–1934." *American Indian Law Review* 21.1 (1997): 1–62.

Betzinez, Jason, with Wilbur Sturtevant Nye. *I Fought with Geronimo.* Harrisburg PA: Stackpole, 1959. Reprint, Lincoln: University of Nebraska Press, 1987.

Black Hawk. *An Autobiography.* 1833. Ed. Donald Jackson. Urbana: University of Illinois Press, 1990.

Blanchard, C. J. "National Reclamation of Arid Lands." *Bulletin of the American Geographical Society* 38.4 (1906): 209–23.

Blatti, Jo. *Women's History in Minnesota: A Survey of Published Sources and Dissertations.* St. Paul: Minnesota Historical Society Press, 1993.

Bloom, Khaled J. "An American Tragedy of the Commons: Land and Labor in the Cherokee Nation, 1870–1900." *Agricultural History* 76.3 (2002): 497–523.

Bonaparte, Charles J. "Opening Address." *Proceedings of the Twenty-second Annual Meeting of the Lake Mohonk Conference of Friends of the Indian and Other Dependent Peoples.* Lake Mohonk Conference, 1904. 10–16.

"Books and Authors." *New York Times* 18 Feb. 1912: Section Review of Books, BR84.

Boudinot, Elias. *A Star in the West: A Humble Attempt to Discover the Long Lost Ten Tribes of Israel Preparatory to their Return to their Beloved City, Jerusalem.* Trenton NJ: D. Fenton, S. Hutchinson, & J. Dunham, 1816.

Bowman, John S. "Hunter, (Wiles) Robert." *The Cambridge Dictionary of American Biography.* Cambridge University Press, 1995.

Boyd, Mark F. "Asi-Yaholo or Osceola." *Florida Historical Quarterly* 33.3–4 (1955): 249–305.

Boylan, James. *Revolutionary Lives: Anna Strunsky and William English Walling.* Amherst: University of Massachusetts Press, 1998.

Branner, J. C., O. P. Jenkins, et al. "To the Friends of Stanford University." *Science* 10 May 1901: 751.

"Brayton Resigns." *New York Times* 5 July 1907: 4.

"Bristow's Nomination Sure." *New York Times* 6 Aug. 1908: 2.

Brown, Dee. *Bury My Heart at Wounded Knee: An Indian History of the American West.* New York: Henry Holt, 1970.

Brown, Loren N. "The Dawes Commission." *Chronicles of Oklahoma* 9.1 (1931): 71–105.

———. "The Establishment of the Dawes Commission for Indian Territory." *Chronicles of Oklahoma* 18.2 (1940): 171–81.

Buell, J. W. *The Border Bandits: An Authentic and Thrilling History of the Most Noted Bandits of Ancient or Modern Times, the Younger Brothers, Jesse and Frank James and their Comrades in Crime.* St. Louis: Historical Publishing Co., 1881.

Burns, Sarah. "Revitalizing the 'Painted-Out' North: Winslow Homer, Manly Health, and New England Regionalism in Turn-of-the-Century America." *American Art* 9.2 (1995): 21–37.

Burton, Art T. "Christie, Ned (1852–1892)." *Encyclopedia of Oklahoma History and Culture*. Oklahoma City: Oklahoma Historical Society, http://digital.library.okstate.edu/encyclopedia.

Burton, Theodore E., and George Charles Selden. *A Century of Prices: An Examination of Economic and Financial Conditions as Reflected in Prices, Money Rates, etc., during the Past 100 Years, with a View to Establishing General Principles Which May Aid in Interpreting the Present and Future*. New York: The Magazine of Wall Street, 1919.

Byers, Ann. *The Trail of Tears: A Primary Source History of the Forced Relocation of the Cherokee Nation*. New York: Rosen Publishing Group, 2004.

Campbell, William P. "The Oklahoma Historical Society: A Review in 1905." *Chronicles of Oklahoma* 39.3 (1961): 214–301.

Campisi, Jack, and William A. Starna. "On the Road to Canandaigua: The Treaty of 1794." *American Indian Quarterly* 19.4 (1995): 467–90.

Carlson, A. J. "Silas Weir Mitchell, 1829–1914." *Science* 27 May 1938: 474–78.

Carlton, Donna. *Looking for Little Egypt*. Bloomington IN: International Dance Discovery Books, 1994.

Carr, Aaron A. *Eye Killers*. Norman: University of Oklahoma Press, 1995.

Carter, Kent. *The Dawes Commission and the Allotment of the Five Civilized Tribes, 1893–1914*. Orem UT: Ancestry.com, 1999.

"Carter Sweat Blood." *McAlester Daily News* 31 July 1908: 2.

Cassedy, James H. "Muckraking and Medicine: Samuel Hopkins Adams." *American Quarterly* 16.1 (1964): 85–99.

"Century of Science Progress Reviewed for Celebration." *Science News-Letter* 21 Nov. 1936: 331–32.

Chalmers, Stephen. *The Beloved Physician, Edward Livingston Trudeau*. New York: Houghton Mifflin, 1916.

Chapple, Joseph Mitchell. "At the Turn of the Furrow: The Story of Oklahoma." *National Magazine: An Illustrated American Monthly* Apr. 1908: 65–80.

"Cherokee Bill Dies Smiling." *New York Times* 18 Mar. 1896: 3.

Cherokee Nation. *Constitution and Laws of the Cherokee Nation*. Oklahoma City: Oklahoma Publishing Co., 1969.

Child, Brenda J. *Boarding School Seasons: American Indian Families, 1900–1940*. Lincoln: University of Nebraska Press, 1998.

"Civil War in Fiction." *New York Times* 14 Sept. 1913: Section Review of Books, BR465.

Clark, Blue. *"Lone Wolf v. Hitchcock": Treaty Rights and Indian Law at the End of the Nineteenth Century*. Lincoln: University of Nebraska Press, 1999.

Clark, Charles Upson. *The Text Tradition of Ammianus Marcellinus.* New Haven CT, 1904.
Clark, Stanley. "Ponca Publicity." *Mississippi Valley Historical Review* 29.4 (1943): 495–516.
"Clergymen in a Libel Suit." *New York Times* 8 June 1880: 3.
Clinton, Fred S. "The Indian Territory Medical Association." *Chronicles of Oklahoma* 26.1 (1948): 23–55.
Cloud, Henry Roe. "The Future of the Red Men in America." *Missionary Review of the World* 47 (July 1924): 529–32. Reprinted in *American Indian Nonfiction: An Anthology of Writings, 1760s–1930s.* Ed. Bernd C. Peyer. Norman: University of Oklahoma Press, 2007. 384–87.
"The College Entertainments." *Indian Chieftain* 29 Dec. 1892.
Columbia University. *Columbia University Quarterly* 4 (1899).
"Commends Italy's Regime in Albania." *New York Times* 16 July 1919: 24.
Confer, Clarissa W. *The Cherokee Nation in the Civil War.* Norman: University of Oklahoma Press, 2007.
Conley, Robert J. *A Cherokee Encyclopedia.* Albuquerque: University of New Mexico, 2007.
———. *The Cherokee Nation: A History.* Albuquerque: University of New Mexico Press, 2005.
"Constitution and Laws of the Society of American Indians." *Quarterly Journal of the Society of American Indians* 2.4 (1914): 324–28.
"Copey Moves Out." *Time* 12 Sept. 1932.
"The Cowboys' Show." *Memphis Commercial Appeal* 31 May 1901.
Cox, Randolph J. *The Dime Novel Companion: A Source Book.* Santa Barbara CA: Greenwood Publishing Group, 2000.
Crowninshield, Frank. *Manners for the Metropolis: An Entrance Key to the Fantastic Life of the 400.* New York: Appleton, 1909.
Cullom, Shelby M. "The Reed Smoot Decision." *North American Review* 15 Mar. 1907: 572–76.
Czestochowski, Joseph S. "John Steuart Curry's Lithographs: A Portrait of a Rural America." *American Art Journal* 9.2 (1977): 68–82.
Da Costa Nunes, Jadviga. "Red Jacket: The Man and His Portraits." *American Art Journal* 12.3 (1980): 5–20.
Dale, Edward Everett. "The Cherokee Strip Live Stock Association." *Chronicles of Oklahoma* 5.1 (1927): 58–78.
———. "The Spirit of Oklahoma." *Oklahoma: A Guide to the Sooner State.* Ed. Angie Debo and John M. Oskison. Norman: University of Oklahoma Press, 1941. 3–6.

Dalton, Emmett. *Beyond the Law*. 1918. Gretna LA: Pelican Pouch Edition, 2002.

Davis, Allen Freeman. *Spearheads for Reform: The Social Settlements and the Progressive Movement 1890–1914*. New Brunswick NJ: Rutgers University Press, 1967.

Davis, Arthur P. "Reclamation of Arid West by Federal Government." *Annals of the American Academy of Political and Social Science* 31 (Jan. 1908): 203–18.

Davis, Emily C. "What Hiawatha Was Made Of." *Science News-Letter* 25 Aug. 1934: 122–24.

Davis, John Benjamin. "Public Education among the Cherokee Indians." *Peabody Journal of Education* 7.3 (1929): 168–73.

Davis, Richard Harding. *Adventures and Letters of Richard Harding Davis*. New York: Scribner, 1917.

Dawes, Henry L. "Senator Dawes' Address." *Proceedings of the Third Annual Meeting of the Lake Mohonk Conference of Friends of the Indian*. Philadelphia, 1886. 34–45.

Debo, Angie. *And Still the Waters Run: The Betrayal of the Five Civilized Tribes*. Princeton: Princeton University Press, 1940.

———. "Cherokee Paper Is Old Timer." *Oklahoma City Times* 24 Feb. 1954. Angie Debo Collection, box D-33, folder 7, Western History Collections, Norman, University of Oklahoma.

———. *Geronimo: The Man, His Time, His Place*. Norman: University of Oklahoma Press, 1976.

———. *A History of the Indians of the United States*. Norman: University of Oklahoma Press, 1970.

———. "Sequoyah Honors Recalled." *Oklahoma City Times* 11 Dec. 1953. Angie Debo Collection, box D-33, folder 7, Western History Collections, Norman, University of Oklahoma.

Deloria, Vine, Jr. *Custer Died for Your Sins: An Indian Manifesto*. 1969. Norman: University of Oklahoma Press, 1988.

Deloria, Vine V., Sr. "The Establishment of Christianity among the Sioux." *Sioux Indian Religion*. Ed. Raymond J. DeMallie and Douglas R. Parks. Norman: University Press of Oklahoma, 1987. 91–111.

Dempsey, Lloyd James. *Blackfoot War Art: Pictographs of the Reservation Period, 1880–2000*. Norman: University of Oklahoma Press, 2007.

Denevan, William M., ed. *The Native Population of the Americas in 1492*. 2nd ed. Madison: University of Wisconsin Press, 1992.

Densmore, Frances. "A Minnesota Missionary Journey of 1893." *Minnesota History* 20.3 (1939): 310–13.

———. "The Survival of Omaha Songs." *American Anthropologist* ns 46.3 (1944): 418–20.

DeVoto, Bernard, ed. *The Journals of Lewis and Clark*. Boston: Houghton Mifflin, 1953.

Diner, Hasia R., Jeffrey Shandler, and Beth S. Wenger. *Remembering the Lower East Side: American Jewish Reflections*. Bloomington: Indiana University Press, 2001.

Dithmar, Edward A. "Unpublished Work of Richard Hovey." *New York Times* 23 May 1908: Section Saturday Review of Books, BR287.

Doran, Michael F. "Antebellum Cattle Herding in the Indian Territory." *Geographical Review* 66.1 (1976): 48–58.

Doyle, Thomas H. "James Sanford Davenport: Lawyer, Statesman and Judge, 1864–1940." *Chronicles of Oklahoma* 22.4 (1944): 405–9.

———. "Single versus Double Statehood." *Chronicles of Oklahoma* 5.3 (1927): 266–86.

Dozier, Edward P. *The Pueblo Indians of North America*. New York: Holt, Rinehart & Winston, 1970.

"Dr. Holmes's Peaceful End." *New York Times* 9 Oct. 1894: 3.

"Dr. S. Wier Mitchell. The Home and Personality of the Author of 'Hugh Wynne' and 'Circumstance.'" *New York Times* 30 Nov. 1901: Section Saturday Review of Books and Art, BR4.

Drake, Florence. "Tecumseh at the Turn of the Century." *Chronicles of Oklahoma* 38.4 (1960): 397–408.

Duncan, Norman. *Harbor Tales Down North*. New York: Fleming H. Revell, 1918.

Durham, David L. *California's Geographic Names: A Gazetteer of Historic and Modern Names of the State*. Fresno CA: Quill Driver Books, 1998.

Dusenberry, Verne. "Chief Joseph's Flight through Montana: 1877." *Montana Magazine of History* 2.4 (1952): 43–51.

Dyer, Robert L. *Jesse James and the Civil War in Missouri*. Columbia: University of Missouri Press, 1994.

Eastman, Charles Alexander. *From the Deep Woods to Civilization*. 1916. Lincoln: University of Nebraska Press, 1977.

———. *Indian Boyhood*. 1902. New York: Dover, 1971.

"The East Side's Morals." *New York Times* 17 Jan. 1900: 10.

"Edwin L. Godkin." *New York Times* 22 May 1902: 8.

Eliot, Charles William. "Academic Freedom." *Science* 5 July 1907: 1–12.

Elliott, Orin Leslie. *Stanford University: The First Twenty-five Years*. Palo Alto CA: Stanford University Press, 1937.

Endres, Kathleen L., and Therese L. Lueck. *Women's Periodicals in the United States: Consumer Magazines*. Westport CT: Greenwood Press, 1995.

Engerman, David C. *Modernization from the Other Shore: American Intellectuals and the Romance of Russian Development*. Cambridge: Harvard University Press, 2003.

Epstein, Randi Hutter. "A Magic Mountain of Fresh Air, Sexual Frolicking and, Oh, Yes, Recovery." *New York Times* 27 May 2003.

Ewers, John C. "Five Strings to His Bow: The Remarkable Career of William (Lone Star) Dietz Artist—Athlete—Actor—Teacher—Football Coach." *Montana: The Magazine of Western History* 27.1 (1977): 2–13.

Fear-Segal, Jacqueline. "Nineteenth-Century Indian Education: Universalism versus Evolutionism." *Journal of American Studies* 33.2 (1999): 323–41.

Field, Charles Kellogg (as Carolus Ager). *Four-Leaved Clover: Stanford Rhymes.* San Francisco: William Doxey, 1896.

Field, Charles Kellog, and Will Irwin. *Stanford Stories: Tales of a Young University.* New York: Doubleday, Page, 1900.

Filler, Louis. *The Muckrakers.* Palo Alto: Stanford University Press, 1993.

Fishback, William M. "The Failure of Government in the Indian Territory." *American Magazine of Civics* 6 (Jan. 1895): 96–98.

Fisher, Albert Kenrick. "In Memoriam: George Bird Grinnell Born September 20, 1849–Died April 11, 1938." *The Auk* 56.1 (1939): 1–12.

Flusche, Michael. "Thomas Nelson Page: The Quandary of a Literary Gentleman." *Virginia Magazine of History and Biography* 84.4 (1976): 464–85.

Forcey, Charles. *The Crossroads of Liberalism: Croly, Weyl, Lippman, and the Progressive Era, 1900–1925.* New York: Oxford University Press, 1961.

Foreman, Carolyn Thomas. "The Balentines, Father and Son, in the Indian Territory." *Chronicles of Oklahoma* 34.4 (1956): 417–28.

Foreman, Grant. "Early Trails through Oklahoma." *Chronicles of Oklahoma* 3.2 (1925): 99–119.

———. "Historical Phases of the Grand River Valley." *Chronicles of Oklahoma* 25.2 (1947): 141–52.

———. "Oklahoma's First Court." *Chronicles of Oklahoma* 13.4 (1935): 457–69.

Foulke, William Dudley. "Indian Agents and the Spoils System." *Proceedings of the Nineteenth Annual Meeting of the Lake Mohonk Conference of Friends of the Indian 1901.* Lake Mohonk Conference, 1902.

"Francis E. Leupp Dies." *New York Times* 20 Nov. 1918: 15.

"Frank H. Dodd Dies after Grip Attack." *New York Times* 11 Jan. 1916: 11.

"Frank Munsey Buys the New York Press." *New York Times* 16 Sept. 1912: 22.

Frisbie, Charlotte J., and David P. McAllester, eds. *Navajo Blessingway Singer: the Autobiography of Frank Mitchell, 1881–1967.* Albuquerque: University of New Mexico Press, 2003.

Fritz, Henry E. *The Movement for Indian Assimilation, 1860–1890.* Philadelphia: University of Pennsylvania Press, 1963.

Fullerton, Eula E. "The Story of the Telephone in Oklahoma." *Chronicles of Oklahoma* 12.3 (1934): 251–57.

Funchess, Joe Spencer. "Paden." *Encyclopedia of Oklahoma History and Culture.* Oklahoma City: Oklahoma Historical Society, http://digital.library.okstate.edu/encyclopedia.

Gaines, Anne-Rosewell J. "Political Reward and Recognition: Woodrow Wilson Appoints Thomas Nelson Page Ambassador to Italy." *Virginia Magazine of History and Biography* 89.3 (1981): 328–40.

Gammon, Tim. "Black Freedmen and the Cherokee Nation." *Journal of American Studies* 11.3 (1977): 357–64.

Gannett, Henry. "Indian Territory." *Journal of the American Geographical Review of New York* 27.3 (1895): 272–76.

Gard, Wayne. *Sam Bass.* 1936. Lincoln: University of Nebraska Press, 1969.

Garland, Hamlin. *The Captain of the Gray-Horse Troop.* New York: Harper & Brothers, 1902.

Garrett, Kathleen. "Worcester, the Pride of the West." *Chronicles of Oklahoma* 30.4 (1952): 386–86.

Garrison, William Lloyd. *The Letters of William Lloyd Garrison.* Vol. 6. Cambridge: Harvard University Press, 1981.

Gates, Merrill E. "Address of President Merrill E. Gates." *Proceedings of the Fourteenth Annual Meeting of the Lake Mohonk Conference of Friends of the Indian 1896.* Lake Mohonk Conference, 1897.

———. "The Next Steps to Be Taken." *Proceedings of the Nineteenth Annual Meeting of the Lake Mohonk Conference of Friends of the Indian 1901.* Lake Mohonk Conference, 1902.

Gatton, John Spalding. "'Much Talk of the Y. B.': Henry Harland and the Debut of *The Yellow Book.*" *Victorian Periodicals Review* 13.4 (1980): 132–34.

Geronimo. *Geronimo: His Own Story.* Ed. S. M. Barrett. New York: Ballantine Books, 1971.

"Gets Labor Plea to Steel Stockholders." *New York Times* 6 Apr. 1912: 14.

"Gilbert Parker: His Home in London and His Visit to This Country." *New York Times* 1 Feb. 1902: Section Saturday Review of Books and Art, BR11.

Gillin, John L. "In Memoriam, Edward Alsworth Ross, 1866–1951." *American Journal of Sociology* 57.3 (1951): 281–82.

Gittinger, Roy. *The Formation of the State of Oklahoma, 1803–1906.* Norman: University of Oklahoma Press, 1939.

"Give 'em the Axe!" *Stanford Daily* 21 Nov. 2008.

"Gorki and Twain Plead for Revolution." *New York Times* 12 Apr. 1906.

Gounod, Charles, et al. "Protestation contre la Tour de M. Eiffel." *Le Temps* 14 Feb. 1887.

Graber, Ralph S. "Baseball in American Fiction." *English Journal* 56.8 (1967): 1107–14.

Grace, Fran. *Carry A. Nation: Retelling the Life*. Bloomington: Indiana University Press, 2001.

Graebner, Norman Arthur. "History of Cattle Ranching in Eastern Oklahoma." *Chronicles of Oklahoma* 21.3 (1943): 300–311.

Gray, Christopher. "Streetscapes: The Herald Square Hotel; Old Life Building Getting a New Look." *New York Times* 5 Nov. 1995.

Griffith, Kelley, Jr. "Weir Mitchell and the Genteel Romance." *American Literature* 44.2 (1972): 247–61.

Grinnell, George Bird. "Recollections of Audubon Park." *The Auk* 37.3 (1920): 372–80.

"Guide Posts for Getting On in Society." *New York Times* 6 Dec. 1908: Part Five Magazine Section, SM5.

Hagan, William T. *American Indians*. 3rd ed. Chicago: University of Chicago Press, 1993.

———. "Civil Service Commissioner Theodore Roosevelt and the Indian Rights Association." *Pacific Historical Review* 44.2 (1975): 187–200.

———. *The Indian Rights Association*. Tucson: University of Arizona Press, 1985.

———. *Taking Indian Lands: The Cherokee (Jerome) Commission 1889–1893*. Norman: University of Oklahoma Press, 2003.

———. *Theodore Roosevelt and Six Friends of the Indian*. Norman: University of Oklahoma Press, 1997.

Hagedorn, Hermann. *Roosevelt in the Bad Lands*. Boston: Houghton Mifflin Company, 1921.

Hansen, Arlen J. *Gentlemen Volunteers: The Story of the American Ambulance Drivers in the Great War, August 1914–September 1918*. New York: Arcade Publishing, 1996.

Harper, Richard H. "The Missionary Work of the Reformed (Dutch) Church in America in Oklahoma." *Chronicles of Oklahoma* 18.3 (1940): 252–65.

Harrington, Fred Harvey, ed. "Hanging Judge Parker: The Man and Not the Legend." *Arkansas Historical Quarterly* 5.1 (1946): 58–77.

Harrington, John Walker. "Self-Determination for the American Red Man." *New York Times* 10 Aug. 1919: Magazine Section, SM3; 15.

Harrison, Robert. *Congress, Progressive Reform, and the New American State*. Cambridge: Cambridge University, 2004.

Hart, James D., and Phillip W. Leininger. "Abbott, Lyman." *The Oxford Companion to American Literature*. Oxford: Oxford University Press, 1995.

———. "Poole, Ernest." *The Oxford Companion to American Literature*. Oxford: Oxford University Press, 1995.

Haskell, Thomas L. "Justifying the Rights of Academic Freedom in the Era of 'Power/Knowledge.'" *The Future of Academic Freedom*. Ed. Louis Menand. Chicago: University of Chicago Press, 1996. 43–90.

Hassell, James E. "Russian Refugees in France and the United States between the World Wars." *Transactions of the American Philosophical Society* ns 81.7 (1991): i–vii, 1–96.

Hathaway, R. H. "The Poetry of Bliss Carman." *Sewanee Review* 33.4 (1925): 469–83.

Hauptman, Laurence M. "Governor Theodore Roosevelt and the Indians of New York State." *Proceedings of the American Philosophical Society* 21 Feb. 1975: 1–7.

Heckewelder, John. *A Narrative of the Mission of the United Brethren among the Delaware and Mohegan Indians, from its Commencement, in the Year 1740, to the Close of the Year 1808*. Philadelphia: McCarty & Davis, 1820.

Heckewelder, John, and Peter S. Du Ponceau. "Names Which the Lenni Lenape or Delaware Indians, Who Once Inhabited this Country, Had Given to Rivers, Streams, Places, etc. etc. Within the Now States of Pennsylvania, New Jersey, Maryland and Virginia: And Also Names of Chieftains and Distinguished Men of That Nation; with the Significations of Those Names, and Biographical Sketches of Some of Those Men. By the Late Rev. John Heckewelder, of Bethlehem, Pennsylvania. Communicated to the American Philosophical Society April 5, 1822, and Now Published by Their Order; Revised and Prepared for the Press by Peter S. Du Ponceau." *Transactions of the American Philosophical Society* ns 4 (1834): 351–96.

"Henry Harland Dead." *New York Times* 22 Dec. 1905: 9.

"Henry Irving's Tour." *New York Times* 11 Nov. 1886: 8.

Herrmann, Dorothy. *Helen Keller*. Chicago: University of Chicago Press, 1998.

Hertzberg, Hazel W. *The Search for an American Indian Identity: Modern Pan-Indian Movements*. Syracuse NY: Syracuse University Press, 1971.

"Higher Standards in the Ministry." *New York Times* 27 Feb. 1909: Section Review of Books, BR116.

Hine, Robert V. "The Western Intellectual Josiah Royce." *Magazine of Western History* 41.3 (1991): 70–72.

Hine, Robert V., and John Mack Faragher. *The American West: A New Interpretive History*. New Haven: Yale University Press, 2000.

Hocking, William Ernest. "George Herbert Palmer (1842–1933)." *Proceedings of the American Academy of Arts and Sciences* 69.13 (1935): 533–35.

Hogarty, Richard A. *Massachusetts Politics and Public Policy: Studies in Power and Leadership*. Amherst: University of Massachusetts Press, 2002.

Holm, Tom. "Indian Lobbyists: Cherokee Opposition to the Allotment of Tribal Lands." *American Indian Quarterly* 5.2 (1979): 115–34.

Holzbueter, John O. "John Steuart Curry: A Populist Artist from Kansas Embraces Progressivism." *Wisconsin Magazine of History* 84.1 (2000): 14–19.

"Honor of the Choctaws." *L'Abeille de la Nouvelle Orléans* 13 Feb. 1906.

Hoopes, Alban W. "Preliminary Report upon the Correspondence of the Indian Rights Association in the Welsh Collection." *Pennsylvania Magazine of History and Biography* 67.4 (1943): 382–89.

Hoover, Mildred B., and Douglas E. Kyle. *Historic Spots in California*. 5th ed. Palo Alto CA: Stanford University Press, 2002.

"Hostile and Friendly Indians." *New York Times* 28 Jan. 1880: 2.

Howard, George E., to David S. Jordan, 12 Jan. 1901. "Leland Stanford Junior University." *Science* 25 Jan. 1901: 142.

Howells, William Dean. *Venetian Life*. New York: Hurd and Houghton, 1867.

Howitt, Emanuel. *Selections from Letters written during a tour through the United States, in the Summer and Autumn of 1819; illustrative of the Character of the Native Indians, and of their Descent from the Lost Ten Tribes of Israel; as well as descriptive of the Present Situation and Sufferings of Emigrants and of the Soil and State of Agriculture*. Nottingham, 1820.

Hoxie, Frederick E. "Redefining Indian Education: Thomas J. Morgan's Program in Disarray." *Arizona and the West* 24.1 (1982): 5–18.

Hughes, Winifred. *The Maniac in the Cellar: Sensation Novels of the 1860s*. Princeton NJ: Princeton University Press, 1980.

Hunter, Robert. "The Relation between Social Settlements and Charity Organization." *Journal of Political Economy* 11.1 (1902): 75–88.

———. "Those Underfed Children." *New York Times* 5 Feb. 1905: 8.

Huston, James Alvin. *A Hoosier Sampler: An Anthology of Indiana Writers*. Lanham MD: University Press of America, 2000.

Huston, James L. "Quantrill's Raiders." *Encyclopedia of Oklahoma History and Culture*. Oklahoma City: Oklahoma Historical Society, http://digital.library.okstate.edu/encyclopedia.

Hutchinson, Elizabeth. "Modern Native American Art: Angel DeCora's Transcultural Aesthetics." *Art Bulletin* 83.4 (2001): 740–56.

"Indian Athletes Honored." *New York Times* 22 Mar. 1909: 8.

"Indians Do Well in Cities." *New York Times* 15 Dec. 1912: Section Society Drama Music Fashions Automobiles, page X8.

"Indians Go to Nicaragua." *L'Abeille de la Nouvelle Orléans* 11 May 1910: 6.

Irving, Laurence. *Henry Irving: The Actor and His World*. New York: Macmillan, 1952.

Irwin, Will. *Herbert Hoover: A Reminiscent Biography*. New York: The Century Co., 1928.

"Is a Dishonored Choctaw." *Hopkinsville Kentuckian* 3 Mar. 1906.
"Its Work for the Poor: What the University Settlement Society Has Accomplished." *New York Times* 1 Feb. 1895: 15.
Iverson, Peter. *Carlos Montezuma and the Changing World of American Indians*. Albuquerque: University of New Mexico Press, 1982.
"J. G. Phelps Stokes on Lower East Side." *New York Times* 28 Nov. 1902: 1.
"J. G. Phelps Stokes to Wed Young Jewess." *New York Times* 6 Apr. 1905: 1.
Jackson, Kenneth T., and David S. Dunbar, eds. *Empire City: New York through the Centuries*. New York: Columbia University Press, 2002.
Jacobs, Margaret D. "Shaping a New Way: White Women and the Movement to Promote Pueblo Indian Arts and Crafts, 1900–1935." *Journal of the Southwest* 40.2 (1998): 187–215.
Jacobs, Renée. "Iroquois Great Law of Peace and the United States Constitution: How the Founding Fathers Ignored the Clan Mothers." *American Indian Law Review* 16.2 (1991): 497–531.
"Jay-Eye-See Trots in 2.10." *New York Times* 2 Aug. 1884.
Jefferson, Thomas. *Notes on the State of Virginia*. 1782. *Thomas Jefferson: Writings*. Ed. Merrill D. Peterson. New York: Literary Classics of the United States, 1984.
Johnson, William Eugene. *The Story of Juan Cruz*. Washington DC, 1912.
Jordan, David Starr, to George E. Howard, 10 Jan. 1901. "Leland Stanford Junior University." *Science* 25 Jan. 1901: 142.
Jozhe, Benedict. "A Brief History of the Fort Sill Apache Tribe." *Chronicles of Oklahoma* 39.4 (1961): 427–32.
Kappler, Charles J., ed. *Indian Affairs: Laws and Treaties*. Vol. 2. Washington DC: Government Printing Office, 1904.
Keen, W. W. "Silas Weir Mitchell (1829–1914)." *Proceedings of the American Academy of Arts and Sciences* 59.17 (1925): 644–49.
Keller, Jean A. *Empty Beds: Indian Student Health at Sherman Institute, 1902–1922*. East Lansing: Michigan State University Press, 2002.
Kelly, Lawrence C. *The Assault on Assimilation: John Collier and the Origins of Indian Policy Reform*. Albuquerque: University of New Mexico Press, 1983.
Kidwell, Clara Sue, and Alan Velie. *Native American Studies*. Lincoln: University of Nebraska Press, 2005.
Kilmer, Joyce. "American Literature Is Going to the Dogs." *New York Times* 9 Jan. 1916: Section Magazine, SM14.
King, Duane H., ed., *The Cherokee Indian Nation: A Troubled History*; Knoxville: University of Tennessee Press, 1979.
King, J. Berry. "Judge William Pressley Thompson." *Chronicles of Oklahoma* 19.1 (1941): 3–9.

King, Tom, and N. Scott Momaday. "A MELUS Interview: N. Scott Momaday. Literature and the Native Writer." *MELUS* 10.4 (1983): 66–72.

Kinney, Arthur F. "Dorothy Parker's Letters to Alexander Woollcott." *Massachusetts Review* 30.3 (1989): 487–515.

Kipling, Rudyard. *Collected Verse of Rudyard Kipling*. New York: Doubleday, Page, 1907.

Klein, Maury. "The Stock Market Crash of 1929: A Review Article." *Business History Review* 75.2 (2001): 325–51.

Kraus, Harry P. *The Settlement House Movement in New York City, 1886–1914*. New York: Arno Press, 1980.

Kuenz, Jane. "The Cowboy Businessman and 'The Course of Empire': Owen Wister's *The Virginian*." *Cultural Critique* 48 (Spring 2001): 98–128.

Kymlicka, Will. *Multicultural Citizenship: A Liberal Theory of Minority Rights.* Oxford: Oxford University Press, 1995.

La Flesche, Francis. *The Middle Five: Indian Schoolboys of the Omaha Tribe.* Lincoln: University of Nebraska Press, 1963.

Lake Mohonk Conference. *Proceedings of the Third Annual Meeting of the Lake Mohonk Conference of Friends of the Indian, Held October 7 to 9, 1885*. Philadelphia, 1886.

———. *Proceedings of the Tenth Annual Meeting of the Lake Mohonk Conference of Friends of the Indian 1892*. Ed. Martha D. Adams. Lake Mohonk Conference, 1893.

———. *Proceedings of the Thirteenth Annual Meeting of the Lake Mohonk Conference of Friends of the Indian 1895*. Reported and ed. Isabel C. Barrows. Lake Mohonk Conference, 1896.

———. *Proceedings of the Fourteenth Annual Meeting of the Lake Mohonk Conference of Friends of the Indian 1896*. Reported and ed. Isabel C. Barrows. Lake Mohonk Conference, 1897.

———. *Proceedings of the Fifteenth Annual Meeting of the Lake Mohonk Conference of Friends of the Indian 1897*. Reported by Isabel C. Barrows. Lake Mohonk Conference, 1897.

———. *Proceedings of the Seventeenth Annual Meeting of the Lake Mohonk Conference of Friends of the Indian 1899*. Reported and ed. Isabel C. Barrows. Lake Mohonk Conference, 1900.

———. *Proceedings of the Eighteenth Annual Meeting of the Lake Mohonk Conference of Friends of the Indian 1900.* Reported and ed. Isabel C. Barrows. Lake Mohonk Conference, 1901.

———. *Proceedings of the Nineteenth Annual Meeting of the Lake Mohonk Conference of Friends of the Indian 1901*. Reported and ed. Isabel C. Barrows. Lake Mohonk Conference, 1902.

———. *Proceedings of the Twentieth Annual Meeting of the Lake Mohonk Conference of Friends of the Indian 1902*. Reported and ed. Isabel C. Barrows. Lake Mohonk Conference, 1903.

———. *Proceedings of the Twenty-first Annual Meeting of the Lake Mohonk Conference of Friends of the Indian 1903*. Reported by Wm. J. Rose. Lake Mohonk Conference, 1904.

———. *Proceedings of the Twenty-second Annual Meeting of the Lake Mohonk Conference of Friends of the Indian and Other Dependent Peoples 1904*. Reported by Wm. J. Rose. Lake Mohonk Conference, 1904.

———. *Proceedings of the Twenty-third Annual Meeting of the Lake Mohonk Conference of Friends of the Indian and Other Dependent Peoples 1905*. Reported by Miss. Lilian D. Powers. Lake Mohonk Conference, 1905.

———. *Proceedings of the Twenty-fourth Annual Meeting of the Lake Mohonk Conference of Friends of the Indian and Other Dependent Peoples 1906*. Reported by Miss Lilian D. Powers. Lake Mohonk Conference, 1906.

———. *Proceedings of the Twenty-fifth Annual Meeting of the Lake Mohonk Conference of Friends of the Indian and Other Dependent Peoples 1907*. Reported by Miss Lilian D. Powers. Lake Mohonk Conference, 1907.

———. *Report of the Twenty-sixth Annual Meeting of the Lake Mohonk Conference of Friends of the Indian and Other Dependent Peoples 1908*. Reported by Miss Lilian D. Powers. Lake Mohonk Conference, 1908.

———. *Report of the Twenty-seventh Annual Meeting of the Lake Mohonk Conference of Friends of the Indian and Other Dependent Peoples 1909*. Reported by Miss Lilian D. Powers. Lake Mohonk Conference, 1909.

———. *Report of the Thirty-Third Annual Lake Mohonk Conference on the Indian and Other Dependent Peoples*. Lake Mohonk Conference, 1915.

Larré, Lionel. *Autobiographie amérindienne: Pouvoir et résistance de l'écriture de soi*. Pessac: Presses universitaires de Bordeaux, 2009.

———. "De la résistance armée à la résistance politique: L'autobiographie de Black Hawk." *Le travail de la résistance dans les sociétés, les littératures et les arts en Amérique du Nord*. Ed. Yves-Charles Grandjeat. Pessac: MSHA, 2008. 99–108.

———. "N. Scott Momaday's West." *Exploring the American Literary West: International Perspectives*. Ed. David Rio. Bilbao: Universidad del Pais Vasco, 2006. 141–49.

Larson, Erik. *The Devil in the White City*. New York: Random House, 2003.

Larson, Robert W. "Part II: Red Cloud: The Reservation Years." *Montana: The Magazine of Western History* 47.2 (1997): 14–25.

LaVelle, John P. "The General Allotment Act 'Eligibility' Hoax: Distortions of

Law, Policy, and History in Derogation of Indian Tribes." *Wicazo Sa Review* 14.1 (1999): 251–302.

Leary, James P. *Wisconsin Folklore*. Madison: University of Wisconsin Press, 1999.

"Leland Stanford Junior University." *Science* 30 June 1899: 916.

"Leland Stanford Junior University." *Science* 25 Jan. 1901: 142–43.

Leonard, Thomas C. Foreword. *The Autobiography of Lincoln Steffens*. Berkeley CA: Heyday Books, 2005. xiii–xviii.

Leupp, Francis E. "Among the Indians of the West." *Proceedings of the Fifteenth Annual Meeting of the Lake Mohonk Conference of Friends of the Indian 1897*. Lake Mohonk Conference, 1897. 12–18.

———. "The Government's Policy toward the Ute Indians." *Proceedings of the Twenty-fifth Annual Meeting of the Lake Mohonk Conference of Friends of the Indian and Other Dependent Peoples 1907*. Lake Mohonk Conference, 1907. 21–23.

———. *The Indian and His Problem*. New York: Charles Scribner's Sons, 1910.

———. "The Indian Policy of Today." *Proceedings of the Twenty-fourth Annual Meeting of the Lake Mohonk Conference of Friends of the Indian and Other Dependent Peoples*. Lake Mohonk Conference, 1906. 19–33.

———. "The Southern Utes." *Proceedings of the Thirteenth Annual Meeting of the Lake Mohonk Conference of Friends of the Indian 1895*. Lake Mohonk Conference, 1896. 12–14.

———. "Visits to Reservations." *Proceedings of the Fourteenth Annual Meeting of the Lake Mohonk Conference of Friends of the Indian 1896*. Lake Mohonk Conference, 1897. 17–20.

Lévi-Strauss, Claude. *Race et histoire: Race et culture*. 1952 and 1971. Paris: Albin Michel/Editions UNESCO, coll. Bibliothèque AM Idées, 2001.

Lewis, David Rich. "Reservation Leadership and the Progressive-Traditional Dichotomy: William Wash and the Northern Utes, 1865–1928." *Ethnohistory* 38.2 (1991): 124–48.

"Life on the East Side." *New York Times* 29 Apr. 1900: 30.

"Literary Paris." *New York Times* 19 Mar. 1922.

Lloyd, Benjamin E. *Lights and Shades of San Francisco*. San Francisco, 1876.

Lobo Montalvo, Maria Luisa, Zoila Lapique Becali, Narciso G. Menocal, and Edward Shaw. "The Years of *Social*." *Journal of Decorative and Propaganda Arts* 22 (1996): 105–31.

Locke, John. *Concerning Civil Government. Second Essay.* Chicago: Encyclopedia Britannica, 1952.

Lomawaima, Tsianina K. *They Called It Prairie Light: The Story of Chilocco Indian School.* Lincoln: University of Nebraska Press, 1994.

Lueders, Edward G. "Music Criticism in America." *American Quarterly* 3.2 (1951): 142–51.

Lynch, Gerald. Introduction. *Bliss Carman: A Reappraisal.* Ottawa: University of Ottawa Press, 1990. 1–5.

"Madriz Bars Sioux Chief." *New York Times* 7 Feb. 1910: 3.

Mankiller, Wilma, and Michael Wallis. *Mankiller: A Chief and Her People.* New York: St. Martin's Griffin, 1993.

"Man's Efforts to Fly Straight Up." *Science News-Letter* 20 Sept. 1930: 182–83, 190.

"Many Noted Persons on Steamship Oceanic." *New York Times* 5 Dec. 1901: 14.

Mark, Joan. "Francis La Flesche: The American Indian as Anthropologist." *Isis* 73.4 (1982): 497–510.

"Mark Twain Tells about Pawnbrokers." *New York Times* 3 Feb. 1901.

Markham, Edwin. "A Book on Poverty." *New York Times* 7 Jan. 1905: Section Review of Books, BR1.

Martin, Benjamin. "Necrology: Judge Wade Hampton Kornegay, 1865–1939." *Chronicles of Oklahoma* 18.1 (1940): 92–93.

Masteller, Richard N. "Using Brancusi: Three Writers, Three Magazines, Three Versions of Modernism." *American Art* 11.1 (1997): 47–67.

Mathes, Valerie Sherer. "Helen Hunt Jackson and the Ponca Controversy." *Montana: The Magazine of Western History* 39.1 (1989): 42–53.

Mathews, John Joseph. *Sundown.* 1934. Norman: University of Oklahoma Press, 1988.

———. *Talking to the Moon.* 1945. Norman: University of Oklahoma Press, 1981.

Matthews, Brander. "Richard Watson Gilder." *North American Review* Jan. 1910: 39–48.

Maxwell, Amos D. *The Sequoyah Constitutional Convention.* Boston: Meador, 1953.

McCallum, Jack. *Leonard Wood: Rough Rider, Surgeon, Architect of American Imperialism.* New York: New York University Press, 2006.

McFarland, Gerald W. *Inside Greenwich Village: A New York City Neighborhood, 1898–1918.* Amherst: University of Massachusetts Press, 2001.

McLoughlin, William Gerald. *After the Trail of Tears: The Cherokees' Struggle for Sovereignty, 1839–1880.* Chapel Hill: University of North Carolina Press, 1993.

McMillen, Christian W. "Rain, Ritual, and Reclamation: The Failure of Irrigation on the Zuni and Navajo Reservations, 1883–1914." *Western Historical Quarterly* 31.4 (2000): 435–56.

McNickle, D'Arcy. *The Surrounded.* 1936. Albuquerque: University of New Mexico Press, 1978.

"Meeting of the Board of Directors, October 14, 1926." *Chronicles of Oklahoma* 4.4 (1926): 370–73.

Merrill, M. R. "Theodore Roosevelt and Reed Smoot." *Western Political Quarterly* 4.3 (1951): 440–53.

Meserve, John Bartlett. "Chief Dennis Wolfe Bushyhead." *Chronicles of Oklahoma* 14.3 (1936): 349–59.

Mihesuah, Devon A. *Cultivating the Rosebuds: The Education of Women at the Cherokee Female Seminary, 1851–1909*. Urbana: University of Illinois Press, 1993.

———. "Out of the 'Graves of the Polluted Debauches': The Boys of the Cherokee Male Seminary." *American Indian Quarterly* 15.4 (1991): 503–21.

Milam, Joe B. "The Opening of the Cherokee Outlet." *Chronicles of Oklahoma* 9.3 (1931): 268–86.

Millard, Bailey. *The San Francisco Bay Region*. Vol. 3. Washington DC: The American Historical Society, 1924.

Miller, John E. "Isaac Charles Parker." *Arkansas Historical Quarterly* 31.1 (1972): 57–74.

Miner, H. Craig. "Cherokee Sovereignty in the Gilded Age: The Outlet Question." *Chronicles of Oklahoma* 71.2 (1993): 118–37.

"Minutes of the Annual Meeting." *Chronicles of Oklahoma* 7.1 (1929): 133–36.

Mohr, James C. "Academic Turmoil and Public Opinion: The Ross Case at Stanford." *Pacific Historical Review* 39 (Feb. 1970): 39–61.

Momaday, N. Scott. *House Made of Dawn*. New York: Harper & Row, 1968.

———. *The Names: A Memoir*. Tucson: University of Arizona Press, 1976.

———. *The Way to Rainy Mountain*. Albuquerque: University of New Mexico Press, 1969.

Moody, Robert E., ed. *The Saltonstall Papers, 1607–1815. Selected and Edited and with Biographies of Ten Members of the Saltonstall Family in Six Generations*. Boston: Massachusetts Historical Society, 1972.

Mooney, James. *History, Myths, and Sacred Formulas of the Cherokees*. Asheville NC: Bright Mountain Books, 1992.

"More Trouble For 'Cherokee Bill.'" *New York Times* 24 Nov. 1895: 17.

"Morgan Robertson." *New York Times* 7 May 1898: Section Saturday Review of Books and Art, RBA307.

"Morgan Robertson Dies Standing Up." *New York Times* 25 Mar. 1915: 1.

Moynihan, Ruth B. "Suffrage Biographies: A Review Essay." *NWSA Journal* 3.2 (1991): 289–97.

"Mr. Hovey's Last Volume." *Sewanee Review* 8.2 (1900): 246–47.

Murchison, A. H. "Intermarried-Whites in the Cherokee Nation between the Years 1865 and 1887." *Chronicles of Oklahoma* 6.3 (1928): 299–327.

Muller, Gilbert H. *William Cullen Bryant: Author of America*. New York: SUNY Press, 2008.

Nelli, Humbert S. *The Business of Crime: Italians and Syndicate Crime in the United States*. Chicago: University of Chicago Press, 1981.

Newman, Marshall T. "The Blond Mandan: A Critical Review of an Old Problem." *Southwestern Journal of Anthropology* 6.3 (1950): 255–72.

Noble, John M. "Early Telephone History of Oklahoma." *Chronicles of Oklahoma* 5.2 (1927): 149–65.

Norgren, Jill. "*Lone Wolf v. Hitchcock*." *Oxford Guide to the Supreme Court of the United States*. Ed. Kermit L. Hall. 2nd ed. Oxford: Oxford University Press, 2005. 592.

"Notes and Documents." *Chronicles of Oklahoma* 25.2 (1947): 153–58.

"Notes from Philadelphia." *New York Times* 20 Jan. 1900: Section Saturday Review of Books and Art, BR13.

Notman, Otis. "Talks with Popular Authors." *New York Times Saturday Review of Books* 4 May 1907: Section Review of Books, BR286.

Nutter, Kathleen Banks. *The Necessity of Organization: Mary Kenney O'Sullivan and Trade Unionism for Women, 1892–1912*. New York: Routledge, 1999.

O'Brien, Frank Michael. *The Story of the "Sun."* New York: George H. Doran, 1918.

O'Brien, Justin. "Henry Harland, an American Forerunner of Proust." *Modern Language Notes* 54.6 (1939): 420–28.

O'Dell, Larry. "Cattlemen's Protective Association of Indian Territory." *Encyclopedia of Oklahoma History and Culture*. Oklahoma City: Oklahoma Historical Society, http://digital.library.okstate.edu/encyclopedia

———. "Halsell, William Electious (1850–1934) and Ewing (1877–1965)." *Encyclopedia of Oklahoma History and Culture*. Oklahoma City: Oklahoma Historical Society, http://digital.library.okstate.edu/encyclopedia.

———. "Shanahan, Patrick (1834–1906)." *Encyclopedia of Oklahoma History and Culture*. Oklahoma City: Oklahoma Historical Society, http://digital.library.okstate.edu/encyclopedia.

———. "Skinner, Nat (1851–?)." *Encyclopedia of Oklahoma History and Culture*. Oklahoma City: Oklahoma Historical Society, http://digital.library.okstate.edu/encyclopedia.

O'Neal, Bill. "Younger Gang." *Encyclopedia of Oklahoma History and Culture*. Oklahoma City: Oklahoma Historical Society, http://digital.library.okstate.edu/encyclopedia.

O'Neill, Floyd A. "An Anguished Odyssey: The Flight of the Utes, 1906–1908." *Utah Historical Quarterly* 36 (Fall 1968): 315–27.

Ohmann, Richard. "History and Literary History: The Case of Mass Culture." *Poetics Today* 9.2 (1988): 357–75.

Ohnick, Nancy. *The Dalton Gang and Their Family Ties*. 3rd ed. Meade KS: Prairie Books, 2005.

Oklahoma Historical Society. "Land Surveyors with the Dawes Commission in the Indian Territory." *Chronicles of Oklahoma* 40.3 (1962): 302–6.

"Olympic Prizes Lost; Thorpe No Amateur." *New York Times* 28 Jan. 1913: 1.

"On the Farm." *Time* 8 June 1931.

Ortiz, Simon J. "Towards a National Indian Literature: Cultural Authenticity in Nationalism." *MELUS* 8.2 (1981): 7–12.

Osborne, Duffield. *The Authors Club: An Historical Sketch*. New York: Knickerbocker Press, 1913.

"Osceola and the Charlestonians." *Florida Historical Quarterly* 33.3–4 (1955): 247–48.

"Out of School Days into Republicanism." *New York Times* 23 Nov. 1911: 2.

Parker, Gilbert. "Mr. Balfour and His Opportunities." *North American Review* Oct. 1902: 433–48.

Parker, Isaac C. "The charge to the grand jury of Isaac C. Parker, judge of the United States court for the Western District of Arkansas, at Fort Smith, Arkansas, May 10, 1875, as reported in the Fort Smith (Arkansas) *New Era*, May 12, 1875." In "Hanging Judge Parker: The Man and Not the Legend," ed. Fred Harvey Harrington. Special issue. *Arkansas Historical Quarterly* 5.1 (1946): 62–71.

———. "Judge Parker first pronounces the death sentence in the Fort Smith Court: statement made June 26, 1875, as reported in Fort Smith (Arkansas) *New Era*, June 30, 1875." In "Hanging Judge Parker: The Man and Not the Legend," ed. Fred Harvey Harrington. Special issue. *Arkansas Historical Quarterly* 5.1 (1946): 72–76.

"Peary Relief Expedition." *New York Times* 28 June 1892: 8.

Penn, William. *Letter to the Committee of the Free Society of Traders*. 1683. *Memoirs of the Private and Public Life of William Penn; who Settled the State of Pennsylvania, and Founded the City of Philadelphia*. Ed. Thomas Clarkson. Dover NH: Samuel C. Stevens, 1827.

Perdue, Theda. *"Mixed Blood" Indians: Racial Construction in the Early South*. Athens: University of Georgia Press, 2003.

Perdue, Theda, and Michael D. Green. *The Cherokee Nation and the Trail of Tears*. New York: Viking, 2007.

———, eds. *The Cherokee Removal: A Brief History with Documents*. Boston: Bedford Books of St. Martin's Press, 1995.

Philp, Kenneth R. *John Collier's Crusade for Indian Reform, 1920–1954*. Tucson: University of Arizona Press, 1977.

Phinney, George. "Pistol Pete of Perkins." *Oklahoma Today* 6.8 (1956): 4–5.

Phipps, Larry. "Fred S. Barde." *Oklahoma Today* 15.2 (1965): 1–34.

"The Phonetic National Convention." *New York Times* 18 Aug. 1852.
Poole, Ernest. "Maxim Gorki in New York." *Slavonic and East European Review. American Series* 3.1 (1944): 77–83.
Powell, Harford. *Walter Camp: The Father of American Football.* Boston: Little, Brown, 1926.
Powers-Beck, Jeffrey. *The American Integration of Baseball.* Lincoln: University of Nebraska Press, 2004.
———. "'Chief': The American Integration of Baseball, 1897–1945." *American Indian Quarterly* 25.4 (2001): 508–38.
Pritzker, Barry. *A Native American Encyclopedia: History, Culture, and Peoples.* Oxford: Oxford University Press, 2000.
"Proceedings of the Anthropological Society of Washington." *American Anthropologist* ns 10.2 (1908): 286–95.
Providence Journal Company. *Half a Century with the Providence Journal; being a Record of the Events and Associates Connected with the Past Fifty Years of Life of Henry R. Davis, Secretary of the Company.* Providence: The Journal Company, 1904.
Prucha, Francis Paul. Foreword. *John Collier's Crusade for Indian Reform, 1920–1954.* Ed. Kenneth R. Philp. Tucson: University of Arizona Press, 1977. ix–xii.
"The Publishers." *New York Times* 2 June 1906: Review of Books, BR363.
Qoyawayma, Polingaysi (Elizabeth Q. White), with Vada F. Carlson. *No Turning Back: A Hopi Indian Woman's Struggle to Live in Two Worlds.* Albuquerque: University of New Mexico Press, 1964.
Randall, John Herman, Jr. "Josiah Royce and American Idealism." *Journal of Philosophy* 63.3 (1966): 57–83.
"Ready to Fight For Monroe Doctrine, Plans to Invite World Disarmament, Says Harding at Bolivar Unveiling." *New York Times* 20 Apr. 1921: 1.
Reamer, Owen J. "Garland and the Indian." *New Mexico Quarterly* 34 (Autumn 1964): 257–80.
"Recalling Bob Davis." *Time* 16 June 1930.
"Red Cross Total Now $62,000,000." *New York Times* 22 June 1917: 1.
Reed, Gerard. "Postremoval Factionalism in the Cherokee Nation." *The Cherokee Indian Nation.* Ed. Duane H. King. Knoxville: University of Tennessee Press, 1979. 148–63.
Remington, Frederic. "A Few Words from Mr. Remington." *Collier's Weekly* 18 Mar. 1905: 16.
"Republicans United on Advanced Creed." *New York Times* 6 Dec. 1913: 1.
Ridge, John. "Letter to Albert Gallatin, February 27, 1826." *The Cherokee Removal:*

A Brief History with Documents. Ed. Theda Perdue and Michael D. Green. 2nd ed. Boston: Bedford/St. Martin's, 2005. 35–44.

Riggs, Lamar. "Judge Isaac C. Parker." *Arkansas Historical Quarterly* 14.1 (1955): 85–89.

Robb, Matthew H. "Only Collect." *Record of the Art Museum, Princeton University* 64 (2005): 42–51.

Rogers, Will. *The Papers of Will Rogers*. Ed. Arthur Frank Wertheim and Barbara Bair. Norman: University of Oklahoma Press, 1995.

Roll of Honor, Willie Halsell College, Dec. 1892, Vinita, I.T. In Will Rogers, *The Papers of Will Rogers*. Norman: University of Oklahoma Press, 1995. 108.

"Roosevelt and Long." *New York Times* 3 Feb. 1903: 1.

"Roping Contest. Bert Oskinson [*sic*] Captures First Prize in 50 Seconds." *Indian Chieftain* 2 Aug. 1900.

"Roping Contest." *Indian Chieftain* 13 Sept. 1900.

Ross, Edward A. *Seventy Years of It*. New York: Appleton-Century Company, 1936.

Ruppel, Kristin T. *Unearthing Indian Land: Living with the Legacies of Allotment*. Tucson: University of Arizona Press, 2008.

Russell, Francis. *A City in Terror: Calvin Coolidge and the 1919 Boston Police Strike*. Boston: Beacon Press, 2005.

Russell, Steve. *Sequoyah Rising: Problems in Post-Colonial Tribal Governance*. Durham NC: Carolina Academic Press, 2010.

"Russian Police Arrest William E. Walling." *New York Times* 19 Jan. 1906: 7.

Sabor, Peter. Introduction. *Memoirs of a Woman of Pleasure*. By John Cleland. Oxford: Oxford University Press, 1985. vii–xxxi.

"Sally James Farnham, Sculptor." *New York Times* 26 Feb. 1905: Second Magazine Section, X7.

"Samuel Bowles." *The Columbia Encyclopedia*. 6th ed. 2008.

Samuels, Warren J. "The Firing of E. A. Ross from Stanford University: Injustice Compounded by Deception?" *Journal of Economic Education* 22.2 (1991): 183–90.

Sanders, Ronald, and Edmund Vincent Gillon. *The Lower East Side: A Guide to Its Jewish Past with 99 New Photographs*. New York: Dover, 1979.

Satz, Ronald N. "'Tell Those Gray Haired Men What They Should Know': The Hayward Indian Congress of 1934." *Wisconsin Magazine of History* 77.3 (1994): 196–224.

"Says Hamon Wanted Gore's Bill Killed." *New York Times* 10 Aug. 1910: 3.

"The School of the Art Institute." *Bulletin of the Art Institute of Chicago (1907–1951)* 32.2 Part I (1938): 13–24.

Schurz, Carl. "Present Aspects of the Indian Problem." *North American Review* July 1881: 1–24.

Seaman, William M. "Horace and Newspaper Columnists." *Classical Journal* 38.9 (1943): 526–33.

Seeber, Edward D. "Chief Logan's Speech in France." *Modern Language Notes* 61.6 (1946): 412–16.

Sekirin, Peter, ed. *Americans in Conversation with Tolstoy: Selected Accounts, 1887–1923*. Jefferson NC: McFarland, 2006.

Selden, George Charles, and Arthur George Bugbee. *Dartmouth Sketches*. Dartmouth College, 1893.

Settle, William A. *Jesse James Was His Name*. Columbia: University Press of Missouri, 1966.

Shakespeare, William. *The Oxford Shakespeare: The Complete Works*. Oxford: Oxford University Press, 1994.

Shapiro, Herbert. "Lincoln Steffens: Light and Shadow on His Historical Image." *American Journal of Economics and Sociology* 31.3 (1972): 319–26.

Shirk, George H. "First Post Offices within the Boundaries of Oklahoma." *Chronicles of Oklahoma* 26.2 (1948): 179–244.

Shirley, Glenn. *Belle Starr and Her Times: The Literature, the Facts, and the Legends*. Norman: University of Oklahoma Press, 1982.

———. *Law West of Fort Smith: A History of Frontier Justice in the Indian Territory, 1834–1896*. New York: Holt, 1957.

———. *West of Hell's Fringe: Crime, Criminals, and the Federal Peace Officer in Oklahoma Territory, 1889–1907*. Norman: University of Oklahoma Press, 1978.

———. "When the Outlaw Rode in Oklahoma." *Oklahoma Today* 37.1 (1987): 18–24.

Shoemaker, Arthur. "Robbery on the Rails." *Oklahoma Today* 20.4 (1970): 6–9.

Shoemaker, Nancy, ed. *American Indians*. Malden MA: Blackwell, 2001.

Silko, Leslie Marmon. *Ceremony*. New York: Viking Press, 1977.

"Sioux Colony in Nicaragua." *New York Daily Tribune* 25 July 1909: 3.

"Sioux Indians to Nicaragua." *St. Paul Dispatch* 25 July 1909.

"Sioux to Quit Dakotas." *L'Abeille de la Nouvelle Orléans* 25 Aug. 1909: 8.

Skaggs, Merrill M. "Viola Roseboro': A Prototype for Cather's *My Mortal Enemy*." *Mississippi Quarterly* 54.1 (2000): 5–21.

Smith, Robert Barr. "James Gang." *Encyclopedia of Oklahoma History and Culture*. Oklahoma City: Oklahoma Historical Society, http://digital.library.okstate.edu/encyclopedia

Smith, Sherry L. "George Bird Grinnell and the 'Vanishing' Plains Indians." *Montana: The Magazine of Western History* 50.3 (2000): 18–31.

Smoot, Reed. "The Passing of Polygamy." *North American Review* Jan. 1908: 117–23.

"Smoot Hearing Begun by Senate Committee." *New York Times* 17 Jan. 1904: 5.

"Smoot to Have Hearing." *New York Times* 13 Dec. 1903: 13.
A Soldier of Conscience: Edward Perkins Clark: Born October 21, 1847, Died February 16, 1903. Brooklyn: Eagle Press, 1903.
"Some New Publications." *New York Times* 12 Dec. 1892: 3.
Sosin, Jack M. "The British Indian Department and Dunmore's War." *Virginia Magazine of History and Biography* 74.1 (1966): 34–50.
"Speaker Appoints House Committees." *New York Times* 11 Dec. 1901: 3.
Spellman, William E. "The Economics of Edward Alsworth Ross." *American Journal of Economics and Sociology* 38.2 (1979): 129–40.
Sprague, Donovin Arleigh. *Rosebud Sioux*. Charleston SC: Arcadia, 2005.
Starr, Emmet. *History of the Cherokee Indians and Their Legends and Folk Lore*. 1921. Reprint, Millwood NY: Klaus Reprint, 1977.
Starr, Kevin. *Endangered Dreams: The Great Depression in California*. Oxford: Oxford University Press, 1996.
"Steel Committee Condemns Long Day." *New York Times* 16 Apr. 1912: 18.
Steffens, Lincoln. *The Autobiography of Lincoln Steffens*. 1931. Berkeley CA: Heyday Books, 2005.
Stevenson, Elizabeth. *Henry Adams: A Biography*. Piscataway NJ: Transaction, 1997.
Stinson, Robert. "S. S. McClure's *My Autobiography*: The Progressive as Self-Made Man." *American Quarterly* 22.2 Part 1 (1970): 203–12.
Stockdale, John C. "The French Canadian According to Gilbert Parker." *Modern Language Studies* 3.2 (1973): 97–105.
Stolberg, Mary M. "Politician, Populist, Reformer: A Reexamination of 'Hanging Judge' Isaac C. Parker." *Arkansas Historical Quarterly* 47.1 (1988): 3–28.
Stone, Harlan Fiske. "Nathan Abbott." *Columbia Law Review* 41.4 (1941): 577–78.
Stone, William. *Life and Times of Sa-go-ye-wat-ha or Red Jacket*. New York, 1841.
Strickland, Rennard. *The Indian in Oklahoma*. Norman: University of Oklahoma Press, 1980.
Stricklin, Dawn C., comp. *Cherokee Claims for Transportation and Subsistence, Special File 154*. Vol. 1. Westminster MD: Heritage Books, 2007.
"Strike Closes Mouquin's." *New York Times* 11 Feb. 1920.
Strong, Douglas H. "Milestones in California History: The Birth of the Sierra Club." *California History* 71.2 (1992).
———. "The Sierra Forest Reserve: The Movement to Preserve the San Joaquin Valley Watershed." *California Historical Society Quarterly* 46.1 (1967): 3–17.
Sturm, Circe. *Blood Politics: Race, Culture, and Identity in the Cherokee Nation of Oklahoma*. Berkeley: University of California Press, 2002.
"Sun Men, New and Old, Honor Chester S. Lord." *New York Times* 4 Dec. 1905: 7.

"Surviving the Ute Massacre." *New York Times* 29 Oct. 1879: 1.

Tatum, Lawrie. *Our Red Brothers and the Peace Policy of President Ulysses S. Grant.* Philadelphia, 1899. Reprint, Lincoln: University of Nebraska Press, 1970.

Taylor, Robert Louis. *Vessel of Wrath: The Life and Times of Carry Nation.* New York: The New American Library, 1966.

"Territory Boys Ground Steers in Stirring Style at Springfield Thursday." *Daily Chieftain* 6 Sept. 1901.

Teuton, Sean. "A Question of Relationship: Internationalism and Assimilation in Recent American Indian Studies." *American Literary History* 18.1 (2006): 152–74.

"'They're Off!' at the Hughes Headquarters." *New York Times* 18 June 1916: Magazine, SM7.

Thompson, Oscar. "An American School of Criticism: The Legacy Left by W. J. Henderson, Richard Aldrich, and Their Colleagues of the Old Guard." *Musical Quarterly* 23.4 (1937): 428–39.

Tinnin, Ida Wetzel. "Educational and Cultural Influences of the Cherokee Seminaries." *Chronicles of Oklahoma* 37.1 (1959): 59–67.

"Transactions of the Society." *Journal of the American Geographical Society of New York* 31.5 (1899): 515–16.

Travis, V. A. "Life in the Cherokee Nation a Decade after the Civil War." *Chronicles of Oklahoma* 4.1 (1926): 16–30.

Tremayne, Penelope. *A Writer or Something.* New York: HarperCollins, 1988.

Trennert, Robert A. "From Carlisle to Phoenix: The Rise and Fall of the Indian Outing System, 1878–1930." *Pacific Historical Review* 52.3 (1983): 267–91.

"The Trotting Record Broken by Jay-Eye-See." *Deseret News* 2 Aug. 1884.

Underhill, Lonnie E. "Hamlin Garland and the Indian." *American Indian Quarterly* 1.2 (1974): 103–13.

"Under Two Sentences to Death." *New York Times* 19 Sept. 1895: 1.

"The University Settlement." *New York Times* 26 Mar. 1897: 12.

"University Settlement: The Society, at Its Annual Meeting, Starts a Fund for a New Home." *New York Times* 28 Jan. 1898: 14.

"U.S. at War: Blue Bloods v. Blue." *Time* 28 Sept. 1942.

Utley, Robert M. "The Celebrated Peace Policy of General Grant." *North Dakota History* 20 (July 1953): 121–42.

Van Doren, Mark. "Dorothy Parker." *English Journal* 23.7 (1934): 535–43.

"Verse by the Late Richard Hovey." *New York Times* 17 Mar. 1900: Section Saturday Review of Books and Art, BR13.

Villard, Oswald Garrison. *Fighting Years: Memoirs of a Liberal Editor.* New York: Harcourt, Brace, 1939.

"Vincent Natalish, Indian Educator." *New York Times* 6 Oct. 1922: 19.

Vorse, Mary Heaton. "And the Workers Say . . ." *Public Opinion Quarterly* 7.3 (1943): 443–56.

"A Wagnerite on Wagner." *New York Times* 14 May 1893: 19.

Walling, William English. *Socialism as It Is: A Survey of the World-Wide Revolutionary Movement*. New York: Macmillan, 1918.

Wardell, Morris L. *A Political History of the Cherokee Nation 1838–1907*. Norman: University of Oklahoma Press, 1938.

Warrior, Robert Allen. *Tribal Secrets: Recovering American Indian Intellectual Traditions*. Minneapolis: University of Minnesota Press, 1995.

Washington, Booker T., Louis R. Harlan, and John W. Blassingame. *The Booker T. Washington Papers*. Vol. 9, *1906–1908*. Urbana: University of Illinois Press, 1972.

Washington Post 25 Feb. 1889: 4.

Watson, Steven. *Prepare for Saints: Gertrude Stein, Virgil Thompson, and the Mainstreaming of American Modernism*. Berkeley: University of California Press, 2000.

"Wealthy Woman as Picket." *New York Times* 30 May 1911: 2.

Weaver, Jace. *That the People Might Live: Native American Literatures and Native American Community*. New York: Oxford University Press, 1997.

Wendel, C. H. *150 Years of J. I. Case*. Iola WI: Krause, 2005.

Wessel, Thomas R. "Phantom Experiment Station: Government Agriculture on the Zuni Reservation." *Agricultural History* 61.4 (1987): 1–12.

West, John. *The Substance of a Journal during a Residence at the Red River Colony, British North America; and Frequent Excursions among the North-West American Indians, in the Years 1820, 1821, 1822, 1823*. London: Seeley and Son, 1824.

"What Is Doing in Society." *New York Times* 18 Apr. 1903: 9.

Whipple, Henry B. "My Life among the Indians." *North American Review* Apr. 1890: 432–39.

White, William Allen. "A Friend's Story of Edna Ferber." *English Journal* 19.2 (1930): 101–6.

Whitney, Robert L. "Grant's Indian Peace Policy on the Yakima Reservation, 1870–82." *The Western American Indian: Case Studies in Tribal History*. Ed. Richard N. Ellis. Lincoln: University of Nebraska Press, 1972. 50–60.

Willard, William. "The First Amendment, Anglo-Conformity and American Indian Religious Freedom." *Wicazo Sa Review* 7.1 (1991): 25–41.

Williams, Gwyn A. "Welsh Indians: The Madoc Legend and the First Welsh Radicalism." *History Workshop* 1 (Spring 1976): 136–54.

Williams, Roger. *A Key into the Language of America*. 1634. *The Norton Anthology of American Literature*. Gen. ed. Nina Baym. 6th ed. Vol. A. New York: Norton, 2003.

Winter, William. *The Wallet of Time: Containing Personal, Biographical, and Critical Reminiscences of the American Theatre*. New York: Moffat, Yard, 1913.

Wister, Owen. *The Virginian: A Horseman of the Plains*. New York: Macmillan, 1902.

"With Henry Harland in Italy." *New York Times* 23 Jan. 1904: Saturday Review of Books, BR59.

Woodson, C. G. "Oswald Garrison Villard." *Journal of Negro History* 35.1 (1950): 105–6.

Woodward, Earl F. "The Brooks and Baxter War in Arkansas, 1872–1874." *Arkansas Historical Quarterly* 30.4 (1971): 315–36.

Wright, J. E., and Doris S. Corbett. *Pioneer Life in Western Pennsylvania*. Pittsburgh: University of Pittsburgh Press, 1968.

Wright, Muriel H. "The Passing of Mr. Reese Kincaide, Director of the Historic Mohonk Lodge in Oklahoma." *Chronicles of Oklahoma* 33.3 (1955): 396–97.

Yeomans, Henry Aaron, and Walter P. Metzger. *Abbott Lawrence Lowell, 1856–1943*. Cambridge: Harvard University Press, 1948.

IN THE AMERICAN INDIAN LIVES SERIES

I Stand in the Center of the Good: Interviews with Contemporary Native American Artists
Edited by Lawrence Abbott

Authentic Alaska: Voices of Its Native Writers
Edited by Susan B. Andrews and John Creed

Searching for My Destiny
By George Blue Spruce Jr.
As told to Deanne Durrett

Dreaming the Dawn: Conversations with Native Artists and Activists
By E. K. Caldwell
Introduction by Elizabeth Woody

Chief: The Life History of Eugene Delorme, Imprisoned Santee Sioux
Edited by Inéz Cardozo-Freeman

Chevato: The Story of the Apache Warrior Who Captured Herman Lehmann
By William Chebahtah
and Nancy McGown Minor

Winged Words: American Indian Writers Speak
Edited by Laura Coltelli

Life, Letters and Speeches
By George Copway (Kahgegagahbowh)
Edited by A. LaVonne Brown Ruoff and Donald B. Smith

Life Lived Like a Story: Life Stories of Three Yukon Native Elders
By Julie Cruikshank in collaboration with Angela Sidney, Kitty Smith, and Annie Ned

LaDonna Harris: A Comanche Life
By LaDonna Harris
Edited by H. Henrietta Stockel

Rock, Ghost, Willow, Deer: A Story of Survival
By Allison Adelle Hedge Coke

Essie's Story: The Life and Legacy of a Shoshone Teacher
By Esther Burnett Horne and Sally McBeth

Song of Rita Joe: Autobiography of a Mi'kmaq Poet
By Rita Joe

Viet Cong at Wounded Knee: The Trail of a Blackfeet Activist
By Woody Kipp

Catch Colt
By Sidner J. Larson

Alanis Obomsawin: The Vision of a Native Filmmaker
By Randolph Lewis

Alex Posey: Creek Poet, Journalist, and Humorist
By Daniel F. Littlefield Jr.

First to Fight
By Henry Mihesuah
Edited by Devon Abbott Mihesuah

Mourning Dove: A Salishan Autobiography
Edited by Jay Miller

I'll Go and Do More: Annie Dodge Wauneka, Navajo Leader and Activist
By Carolyn Niethammer

Tales of the Old Indian Territory and Essays on the Indian Condition
By John Milton Oskison
Edited by Lionel Larré

Elias Cornelius Boudinot: A Life on the Cherokee Border
By James W. Parins

John Rollin Ridge: His Life and Works
By James W. Parins

Singing an Indian Song: A Biography of D'Arcy McNickle
By Dorothy R. Parker

Crashing Thunder: The Autobiography of an American Indian
Edited by Paul Radin

Turtle Lung Woman's Granddaughter
By Delphine Red Shirt and Lone Woman

Telling a Good One: The Process of a Native American Collaborative Biography
By Theodore Rios and Kathleen Mullen Sands

William W. Warren: The Life, Letters, and Times of an Ojibwe Leader
By Theresa M. Schenck

Sacred Feathers: The Reverend Peter Jones (Kahkewaquonaby) and the Mississauga Indians
By Donald B. Smith

Grandmother's Grandchild: My Crow Indian Life
By Alma Hogan Snell
Edited by Becky Matthews
Foreword by Peter Nabokov

No One Ever Asked Me: The World War II Memoirs of an Omaha Indian Soldier
By Hollis D. Stabler
Edited by Victoria Smith

Blue Jacket: Warrior of the Shawnees
By John Sugden

Muscogee Daughter: My Sojourn to the Miss America Pageant
By Susan Supernaw
Foreword by Geary Hobson

I Tell You Now: Autobiographical Essays by Native American Writers
Edited by Brian Swann and Arnold Krupat

Postindian Conversations
By Gerald Vizenor and A. Robert Lee

Chainbreaker: The Revolutionary War Memoirs of Governor Blacksnake
As told to Benjamin Williams
Edited by Thomas S. Abler

Standing in the Light: A Lakota Way of Seeing
By Severt Young Bear and R. D. Theisz

Sarah Winnemucca
By Sally Zanjani

To order or obtain more information on these or other University of Nebraska Press titles, visit www.nebraskapress.unl.edu.

www.ingramcontent.com/pod-product-compliance
Lightning Source LLC
Chambersburg PA
CBHW050502110726
47899CB00003B/1045

* 9 7 8 0 8 0 3 2 3 7 9 2 6 *